Upper Saddle River, New Jersey

Library of Congress Cataloging-in-Publication Data

The musician's business & legal guide/compiled and edited by Mark Halloran ; a presentation of the Beverly Hills Bar Association, Committee for the Arts.—3rd ed.

p. cm.

Rev. ed of: The musician's business and legal guide. Rev. 2nd ed. c1996.

Includes index.

ISBN 0-13-031681-4 (paperback)

1. Music trade—Law and legislation—United States. 2. Musicians—Legal status, laws, etc.—United States. 3. Music—Economic aspects—United States. 4. Copyright—Music—United States. I. Title: Musician's business and legal guide. II. Halloran, Mark E. III. Beverly Hills Bar Association. Committee for the Arts. IV. Musician's business and legal guide.

ML3790 .M84 2001
780'.23'73—dc21

2001024939

A Division of Pearson Education
Upper Saddle River, NJ 07458

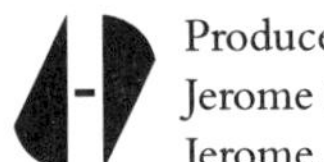

Produced by
Jerome Headlands Press, Inc.
Jerome, Arizona 86331

Cover and book design—Sullivan Santamaria Design, Inc.
Still-life photography—Michael Thompson
Copyeditor—George Glassman
Index—Rebecca R. Plunkett Indexing Services

Manufactured in the United States of America

10 9 8 7 6 5 4 3 2

ISBN 0-13-031681-4

Prentice Hall International (UK) Limited, *London*
Prentice-Hall of Australia Pty. Limited, *Sydney*
Prentice-Hall Canada Inc., *Toronto*
Prentice-Hall Hispanoamericana, S.A., *Mexico*
Prentice-Hall of India Private Limited, *New Delhi*
Prentice-Hall of Japan, Inc., *Tokyo*
Pearson Education Asia Pte. Ltd., *Singapore*
Editora Prentice-Hall do Brasil, Ltda., *Rio de Janeiro*

Contents

Preface

Welcome to the third edition of this book. (There were also three prior editions published under the title *The Musician's Manual,* the first in 1979.) As the music business changes, we strive to keep each new edition current. We have updated all the chapters and have added five new ones: Digital Downloads and Streaming: Copyright and Distribution Issues; International Copyright, Getting Started as an Internet Artist, Royalty Statements: Audits and Lawsuits; and The Internet and Music. However, the basic messages from the first edition remain constant. At some point in your professional music career, you will learn that there are legal questions implicit in almost everything you do. Whether you write, perform or sell a song, your actions give rise to rights and obligations that you should consider. The time to learn is now.

The purpose of this book is to demystify the music business and the seemingly indecipherable body of law that shapes it. And to help you "make it" by explaining the industry and the laws that govern it.

This book is a collection of chapters written by people that work in the music industry. Many are lawyers; some are musicians. We have tried to make our information comprehensible to everyone, and have avoided presupposing a lot of knowledge on your part.

At this point, we must present a few warnings. First, there is no substitute for obtaining competent help as you build your career. Talent agents, personal managers, lawyers and business managers are trained to guide you. Their expertise costs money, but you must think of these expenses as an investment in your career. Also, the chapters written by lawyers are designed to identify problems, not to give specific solutions. If you have a legal problem, do not rely on the information contained in this book; see an attorney. The chapters in this book are not the law, but merely describe legal applications, in general terms, for the music industry. Additionally, before you photocopy our forms for submittal, check with the organizations to which you are submitting-they may require you to fill out their original forms. In many cases, these forms may be downloaded and submitted via the Internet.

There has been a radical change in the way musicians can access information since our last edition—the Internet. The U.S. Copyright Office and virtually all other major organizations involved in the music business now have Web sites that make their information instantly available and up-to-date.

The Internet is also a new source of distribution of both songs and sound recordings, and as acts as an advertising and promotional tool for musicians. There has been a flurry of lawsuits against those that have given away the music you create. Thankfully, the music copyright owners have either prevailed in court or have negotiated settlements-but regulating the Internet in a way to protect your works and have their use paid for, remains the greatest challenge.

One final note-although this book is a useful tool, musicians should write music, not contracts. Unless you devote your time and energy to developing and exploiting your talent, this book doesn't matter. Make it matter.

Mark Halloran, Esq.
Coauthor and Editor

Acknowledgments

This book was originally compiled from materials prepared for a Beverly Hills Bar Association Committee for the Arts Symposium for Musicians held in 1979. Since then, the book has been updated many times and now has a life of its own.

Initially, my thanks to Jordan Kerner (cofounder and cochair, along with Evanne Levin, of the Committee for the Arts) and Norman Beil (Committee for the Arts member), who invited my participation.

I also wish to thank Gunnar Erickson and Ned Hearn with whom I cowrote *The Musician's Guide to Copyright* for Bay Area Lawyers for the Arts in 1978. Gunnar and Ned have been terrific mentors in my career as a lawyer and as a writer, and I am honored to be Gunnar's law partner.

Although I have contributed chapters and edited, this book is the sum total of the contributions of many authors. With this in mind, I thank the following authors that made contributions to prior editions: John Braheny, Wayne Coleman, William Dobishinski, Richard Flohil, Marshall Gelfand, Todd Gelfand and Diane Rapaport

It often takes more energy and effort to update a chapter than to write one from scratch. Thus, I offer kudos to the following authors that spent their precious time in revising their chapters for this edition: Stephen Bigger, Bartley Day, Robert Dudnik, Steven Gardner, Brad Gelfond, Ronald Gertz, Ned Hearn, Neville Johnson, Christopher Knab, Evanne Levin, Linda Newmark, Peter Paterno, Jack Phillips, Margaret Robley, Alfred Schlesinger, James Sedivy, Madeleine Seltzer, Gregory Victoroff and Thomas White.

The vitality of this book has been augmented by the following authors that contributed new chapters to this edition: Steven Ames Brown, Ned Hearn, E. Scott Johnson, Neville Johnson and Peter Spellman. Thank you to Lawrence Blake and Dan Stuart who chose to analyze a new contract for their chapter, Analysis of a Recording Contract.

For their assistance with compiling and updating the Resource Directory, I would like to thank the following individuals: Pat Bradley, Association For Independent Music (AFIM), and Diane Rapaport; and for their help on earlier versions, Committee for the Arts volunteer, William Vu Tam Anh; Marianne Borselle, Debra Graff, Peter Spellman, Harris Tulchin, Sue Tillman and Gregory Victoroff.

Thanks to my assistant, Susan Hart, for her research on my chapters.

Combining the styles of so many authors into one cohesive unit is always a challenge. I would like to thank our copyeditor George Glassman for his help in creating a clear and comprehensible book.

Thanks also to Sullivan Santamaria Design for designing the *Guide's* new, updated look, and to Rebecca Plunkett for providing an excellent index.

Special thanks are due to the following people that provided assistance with sample agreements used in the book: Lawrence Blake, Vincent Castellucci of the Harry Fox Agency, Inc., Ron McGowan, Dan Stuart and Suzy Vaughan.

This book would not exist in its current form without the help of Diane Rapaport and Sue Tillman of Jerome Headlands Press. Their contribution in coordinating the revisions and design is incalculable.

Lastly, Prentice Hall has done a terrific job in distributing the book and my thanks to them.

Mark Halloran, Esq.

Introduction

Music. It is impossible to imagine human history and culture without it. Whether it is the Israelites singing God's praises after crossing the Red Sea, monks chanting their hymns during the Middle Ages, or fife and drum players leading soldiers into battle during the American Revolution, our culture and past are framed by music.

As we stand at the beginning of a new millennium, it is indisputable that we have greater access to more diverse types of music than at any time during our history. From a legal standpoint, it is also indisputable that the rights of musicians have never been in a greater state of flux.

For these reasons, the people that have donated their time and talent to writing the chapters of this *Musician's Business and Legal Guide* deserve special thanks. But these authors are also deserving of acknowledgment for reasons that go far beyond their professional talents.

In their own way, these authors are honoring a tradition that, though not as old as music itself, is nonetheless one of the most distinct and treasured characteristics of the legal and business professions—pro bono services. Through their volunteer efforts, for which they received absolutely no compensation, the authors of this book committed themselves to give back to the artistic community they serve.

This *Guide* began as a project of the Committee for the Arts of the Beverly Hills Bar Association Barristers. The Barristers are the young lawyers division of the bar, and Committee for the Arts was started by Barristers Evanne Levin and Jordan Kerner more than two decades ago with the goal of creating low-cost programs and materials for struggling artists. Thus was born the first edition of the *Musician's Business and Legal Guide* (originally published as *The Musician's Manual).*

Many of the authors of this *Guide* were part of that original core. Although none of them are Barristers anymore, they have uncomplainingly worked to revise and update their materials for this edition. All of them deserve our appreciation, but original CFTA members Stephen Bigger, Lawrence J. Blake, Steven H. Gardner, Brad Gelfond, Ronald H. Gertz, Mark Halloran (who acted as the editor for this revised *Guide*, as well as the very well-received Second Edition), Edward R. Hearn, Neville L. Johnson, Evanne L. Levin (founding Cochair and Cofounder of the Committee for the Arts), Peter T. Paterno, James A. Sedivy, and Gregory T. Victoroff deserve special recognition.

Even though its founders have long since moved on to other endeavors, Committee for the Arts continues the mission. CFTA is now working on a major revision and update to its *Writer's Guide,* and continues to offer programs aimed at assisting artists in this rapidly changing technological and legal climate.

None of it would have been possible without the volunteer efforts of those that created and now revised this *Guide.* Whether you are a musician or a lawyer, I am sure that you will find the product of those efforts to be invaluable.

Stephen L. Raucher
President, Beverly Hills Bar Association Barristers, 1999-2000

Getting Started: Music as a Business

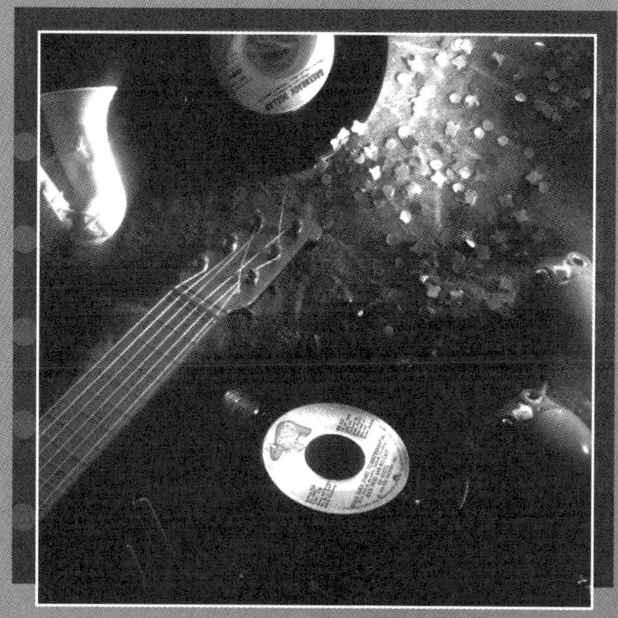

GROUP BREAKUPS

ENTERTAINMENT GROUP NAMES: SELECTION AND PROTECTION

BUSINESS ENTITIES

HOW TO SET UP A MONEY DEAL

MUSIC ATTORNEYS

MEDIATION FOR MUSICIANS

Group Breakups

BY PETER T. PATERNO

The best time to plan for a group breakup is at the outset of the relationship. This chapter will discuss the problems that arise at the time of a breakup (or, more commonly, at the time a member of the group chooses to leave), and will describe some planning devices that can help avoid these problems.

MEET THE RUMMIES

The Rummies are a successful recording group on the White Noise label. The Rummies consist of the following four individuals:

Richie, the drummer, a former butcher who does not know one chord from another, but is tough on the backbeat.

John, the bass player, a former session player with the creativity and stage presence of a cadaver.

David, the flashy lead guitarist who writes about half of the group's material.

Fred, the lead singer and occasional rhythm guitar player who writes the rest of the group's material.

THE INITIAL BREAKUP

John, the bass player decides to leave the group to become a Moonie (the religious organization, not the rock group). At this point, the group is required to notify White Noise that John has decided to leave the group (Section 2.01.2(a)(i) of Exhibit 1, Group Artist Rider).

The remaining members of the group decide to find a new bass player. After a quick search, they settle upon Floydine, a bass player for a local punk rock group. White Noise, quite concerned that this new bass player will affect the Rummies' bubblegum sound, refuses to allow Floydine to join the group. The group is outraged, and wants to know what right White Noise has to keep them from letting whomever they choose join their group. Unfortunately, the Rummies have not read their contract. The contract essentially provides that White Noise has a right to veto any replacement members selected by the group (Section 2.01.2(a)(i) of Exhibit 1, Group Artist Rider). While White Noise may have been willing to give up this right in initial negotiations, the Rummies' lawyer never raised the point, and the Rummies are now paying the price.

In fact, under the provisions of the Group Artist Rider, the record company retains the right to split up the group in the event of a leaving member situation and may thereafter treat each member of the group as a leaving member (Section 2.01.2(a)(ii) of Exhibit 1, Group Artist Rider). Provisions such as these give the record company considerable leverage in a leaving member situation. They permit the record company to threaten to break up the group and keep certain members. (It should be pointed out that it is unlikely that a record company would actually try to assert this right.) In any event, some foresight by the group's lawyers would probably have resulted in the tempering of much of this language.

White Noise and the Rummies eventually agree on a replacement bass player named Craig. Craig will become bound to the terms of the Rummies' recording contract with White Noise (Section 2.01.2(a)(i) of Exhibit 1, Group Artist Rider). Although White Noise has the right to retain John's services as a solo recording artist (Section 2.01.2(b) of Exhibit 1, Group Artist Rider), it is quite satisfied, given John's distinct lack of creative talents, to let John sign with the Moonies.

CRAIG SIGNS ON

With the departure of John and the addition of Craig, the Rummies have some fairly complicated financial problems to think about. John is entitled to receive his share of the group's royalties on all albums on which he participated. In general, however, a record company will keep all royalties earned by a recording artist until such time as the artist has "paid back" all advances made to him, including any recording costs incurred by the artist in making records. Until those advances are paid back, the artist is "unrecouped." The advances are not actually returnable—i.e., the artist has no general obligation to pay them back—but the record company has the right to recoup them from any royalties earned by the artist. As a result, an artist can have significant record sales and still not receive any royalties from those sales. It might be that advances to the group and recording costs, both incurred after John's departure, will place the group in an unrecouped position with White Noise. If subsequent earnings are not ample enough to recoup these advances, the group may not have sufficient funds to pay John his share of royalties for the records on which he participated.

Craig faces the opposite side of this problem. It may be that when Craig joins the group, the Rummies' royalty account is in a seriously unrecouped position. Craig may prove to be the catalyst the band needs to obtain massive commercial success, which will lead to large royalties. Craig may feel, however, that his share of the royalties should not be used to recoup advances and recording costs in which he did not share.

The best way to handle the problems outlined above is for the group to enter into a formal partnership agreement or to incorporate. This should be done as early in the group's career as is financially possible. The partnership agreement, or, in the case of an incorporation, the bylaws or shareholders' agreement, should contain buy out and buy in provisions that provide an adequate vehicle for dealing with the legal and financial ramifications of a leaving member situation. These are sophisticated agreements, which require considerable legal expertise to prepare, and a discussion of their specific terms is beyond the scope of this article. References below to a partnership agreement will apply with equal force to a shareholders' agreement; the choice of entity (i.e., partnership or corporation) will not affect the basic terms that should be in these agreements. Consult your attorney to determine which will work best for your group.

TREATMENT OF THE LEAVING MEMBER

After receiving a large advance, the Rummies spend six months in the studio recording their next album. The album is an incredible stiff. Fred believes the group is not a proper forum for exhibiting his talent and decides to leave. Once again, the group notifies White Noise of the leaving member situation (Section 2.01.2(a)(i) of Exhibit 1, Group Artist Rider).

White Noise is interested in keeping Fred as a solo recording artist. It therefore exercises the leaving member option to which it is entitled under its recording contract with the Rummies (Section 2.01.2(b) of Exhibit 1, Group Artist Rider). By exercising its rights under the leaving member clause of its contract with the Rummies, White Noise will now have the exclusive right to Fred's services as a solo recording artist. Unfortunately, the terms of Fred's contract with White Noise are not very favorable to Fred. Generally, the terms of a leaving member contract will be the standard terms contained in the record company's form contract (Section 2.01.2(b) of Exhibit 1, Group Artist Rider). The number of renewal terms of that contract will usually be the number of renewal terms remaining at the time the member becomes a leaving member (Section 2.01.2(b)(1) of Exhibit 1, Group Artist Rider), no advances will be provided, the royalty rate will be significantly lower than the group's royalty rate (Section 2.01.2(b)(3) of Exhibit 1, Group Artist Rider), the recording commitment may be lower (Section 2.01.2(b)(2) of Exhibit 1, Group Artist Rider), and most deal points negotiated in the group's contract will be deleted from the leaving member's contract. Fred, who considers himself a major talent and a superstar but for White Noise's lack of support, is not pleased with this state of affairs. There are, however, several reasons for having leaving member provisions that are worse than the provisions of the group's recording contract.

Initially, the record company does not want to provide an incentive for a member to leave the group. For instance, if, instead of splitting advances and royalties three or four ways, a member could receive the same advances or royalties as the group does and keep them entirely for himself, he might be more inclined to leave the group. In addition, when a record company retains a leaving member, it often has no idea how that member will fare as a solo artist. Accordingly, it will not wish to risk as much money on or commit to record as many records with the leaving member. At the time a member leaves the group, the record company will want as few obstacles as possible standing in the way of its decision as to whether or not to retain that person, since it is taking a risk on whether the leaving member will be able to generate the same quality and chemistry with a new band as he did with the old.

Knowing these justifications does not make Fred feel any better, however. Having just left the group, he is staring at a contract that he does not feel is fit for an artist of his stature. Often, if the record company is interested enough in an artist to exercise its leaving member option, it will be interested enough to renegotiate the contract. Just incidentally, this willingness to renegotiate will arise to some extent from the record company's lack of certainty as to its rights under the leaving member clause. The effectiveness of a leaving member clause has never been tested in the courts. Also, because the clause operates by reference to a contract that was drafted to deal with a group, it typically suffers from ambiguities and lacunae. Moreover, the record company is desirous of coercing additional product out of the artist. Leaving members generally leave when there are less than the customary seven or eight option albums left for the record company to exercise. By exercising its option to retain Fred, White Noise is committing itself to Fred's new career. If White Noise is going to spend the time and money necessary to develop Fred as a solo artist, it wants to be assured of receiving the maximum amount of product in return for its commitment. In any event, White Noise will probably elect to renegotiate. However, since the terms of the leaving member contract are so onerous, Fred will be renegotiating from a position of weakness, unless the amount of product he owes White Noise is quite small (e.g., if there are only one or two albums left in the Rummies' contract).

Another problem Fred faces arises from the fact that because of the group's disastrous last album, the Rummies are in a seriously unrecouped position. White Noise may try to recoup the Rummies' deficit position from Fred's earnings as a solo artist. Thus, if Fred is quite successful, and the Rummies fade, Fred's initial platinum album may go entirely towards paying off the Rummies' unrecouped royalty account.

If White Noise retains the right to recoup the Rummies' deficit from Fred's royalties as a solo artist (cross-collateralization), Fred would be much better off if White Noise dropped him and let him sign with another record company. White Noise would then have no right of recoupment against Fred's subsequent royalties (since they would have been earned with another record company) and would have been left solely with the Rummies' earnings to recoup the Rummies' deficit balance. At best, Fred should be treated by White Noise as a new artist who has signed a new contract and should be given a fresh start and a zero-balance royalty account. At worst, Fred should be responsible for no more than his pro rata share of any deficit incurred by the Rummies. To the extent that Fred's earnings are used to pay the Rummies' deficit balance, Fred should later be credited with any royalties the Rummies do manage to

SUMMARY OF CRITICAL LEAVING MEMBER ISSUES TO BE SETTLED BY AGREEMENT

- The method of orderly withdrawal of old members from and addition of new members to a group should be spelled out.
- The equitable division of advances and royalties among old and new members, with an eye towards the recoupment problems discussed above, must be delineated.
- Who owns the group name?
- What happens at the complete breakup and dissolution of the group with regard to the assets and liabilities of the group and its members?
- Language that provides the record company with an absolute veto power in the selection of replacement members should be avoided.
- Provisions that may provide the record company the unfettered right, in a leaving member situation, to break up the group and treat all the members as leaving members should be avoided, if possible.
- Provisions that allow the record company to cross-collateralize advances and charges under the particular recording contract against charges and advances under other agreements between the record company and the group or its members can (hopefully) be written more favorably for the group.
- Unfavorable provisions (e.g., lower royalty rates, smaller advances, and commitment by the record company to a fewer number of "firm" LPs) in the leaving member's contract must be discussed.

accumulate. It should be noted, however, that the group has an interest in whether or not Fred's earnings can be used to recoup their deficit. Since Fred received his share of the group's advances and recording costs, the group might be justified in requesting some recoupment out of Fred's earnings.

There is a familiar solution to the problems a leaving member will face in his contractual relations with the record company that retains his services as a recording artist—proper planning by the group and its lawyer. In many record contract negotiations, the leaving member provisions of the contract are given short shrift. More attention should be paid to these provisions, and to the extent that the group is able, it should attempt to make the leaving member provisions as favorable to the group as possible. Not only will this provide a leaving member with better contract terms if he is forced to perform under the leaving member clause, but it will also provide the leaving member with a stronger bargaining position in the event of a renegotiation.

The financial problems of a leaving member situation can be minimized through preplanning. The cross-collateralization problem discussed above can probably be satisfactorily resolved in initial negotiations for the group's record contract. Intragroup problems of recoupment should be dealt with in the group's partnership agreement.

UP FROM THE ASHES

The Rummies, sans Fred, decide to continue on as a power trio. A little later, Richie is reading the trades when he notices that a group called "John and the Rummies" is playing revival meetings throughout the Midwest. After a little research, the group discovers that John has gone back to playing music and is actively seeking a recording contract. The group is disturbed by this development since John is doing a lot of their old hits and the public believes that John and the Rummies is the same group as the Rummies. White Noise is also quite concerned, since it does not want a group on a competing label using the Rummies' name and possibly hurting the Rummies' sales. Many record companies have provisions in their contracts preventing leaving members from using the group name as long as any members of the group are still under contract to the record company. Unfortunately, the same lawyer who negotiated the Rummies' contract with White Noise originally drafted the White Noise recording agreement form, and did not cover this point.

White Noise and the Rummies file suit against John to keep him from using the Rummies' name, but, given the absence of any clearly defined rights regarding the group name, the lawsuit will be over at about the same time the Electric Prunes have their next hit. The entire problem could have been avoided if the group had included provisions dealing with the ownership of the group name in their partnership agreement.

DOWN FOR THE COUNT

David discovers that his dog loves Richie more than it loves him. He cannot stand the competition and decides to leave the group. White Noise Records exercises its leaving member option and keeps David as a recording artist (Section 2.01.2(b) of Exhibit 1, Group Artist Rider). However, White Noise decides that its mailroom staff has more talent than the remaining members of the Rummies, and it decides to drop the group (Section 2.01.2(a)(ii) of Exhibit 1, Group Artist Rider). Richie and Craig realize they have no future as rock and roll stars and decide to join the A&R department at White Noise Records. However, the group has pending litigation against John, payments to make on the group bus, a lawsuit from a Bakersfield promoter on a concert for which they did not show, and a large quantity of equipment, which Richie, David and Craig all think they own. David consults his lawyer at Pig, Pork, Swine & Razorback regarding the impending lawsuit over these items and asks how he can avoid some of these problems in his new group. After discussing David's situation, the lawyer sits down and prepares a draft of a partnership agreement, which resolves the critical issues. Now, with all his bases covered, David lies in bed, safe and secure. He reads his partnership agreement and the leaving member clause of his contract with White Noise, and dreams of the day when his new group can break up.

GROUP ARTIST RIDER

Author's note: This rider is commonly appended to recording contracts or incorporated into the contract. See contract provision 20 in the chapter, Analysis of a Recording Contract.

GROUP ARTIST RIDER annexed to and made part of the agreement dated _______________ between _______________ (name of record company) and the _______________ (name of Artist or group).

The provisions of this Rider shall be deemed to be part of the aforesaid (recording) agreement. To the extent that anything in said agreement is inconsistent with any provisions of this Rider, the latter shall govern. Numerical designations in this rider refer to the related provisions of the aforesaid agreement.

2.01.1 (a) The Artist's obligations under this agreement are joint and several and all references herein to the "Artist" shall include all members of the group inclusively and each member of the group individually, unless otherwise specified.
(b) Notwithstanding any change in the membership of the group, ___________ (name of record company) shall continue to have the right to remit all payments under this agreement in the name of the ___________ (name of Artist/group).

2.01.2 (a) If any member of the Artist shall cease to perform as a member of the group:
(i) You shall promptly notify _____________ (name of record company) thereof and such leaving member shall be replaced by a new member, if you and _______________ (name of record company) so agree. Such new member shall thereafter be deemed substituted as a party to this agreement in the place of such leaving member and, by performing hereunder, shall automatically be bound by all the terms and conditions of this agreement. Upon _____________ (name of record company)'s request, you will cause any such new member to execute and deliver to ______________ (name of record company) such documents as _____________ (name of record company), in its judgment, may deem necessary or advisable to effectuate the foregoing sentence. Thereafter, you shall have no further obligation to furnish the services of the leaving member for performances hereunder, but you (and such leaving member individually) shall continue to be bound by the other provisions of this agreement, including, without limitation, subparagraph 2.01.2(b) below.
(ii) Notwithstanding anything to the contrary contained herein, _______________ (name of record company) shall have the right to terminate the term of this agreement with respect to the remaining members of the Artist by written notice given to you at any time prior to the expiration of ninety (90) days after _____________ (name of record company)'s receipt of your said notice to _____________ (name of record company). In the event of such termination, all members of the Artist shall be deemed leaving members as of the date of such termination notice, and paragraph 2.01.2(b) hereof shall be applicable to all of them, collectively or individually, as _____________ (name of record company) shall elect.

(b) ______________ (name of record company) shall have, and you and the Artist hereby grant to _____________ (name of record company), an option to engage the exclusive services of such leaving member as a recording artist ("Leaving Member Option"). Such Leaving Member Option may be exercised by _____________ (name of record company) by notice to such leaving member at any time prior to the expiration of ninety (90) days after the date of: (1) _____________ (name of record company)'s receipt of your notice provided for in section 2.01.2(a)(i), or (2) ________________ (name of record company)'s termination notice pursuant to section 2.01.2(a)(ii), as the case may be. If ______________ (name of record company) exercises such Option, the leaving member concerned shall be deemed to have executed ______________ (name of record company)'s then current standard form of term recording agreement for the services of an individual artist containing the following provisions:

(i) A term consisting of an initial period of one year commencing on the date of _____________ (name of record company)'s exercise of such Leaving Member Option, which term may be extended by _____________ (name of record company), at its election exercisable in the manner provided in paragraph 1.01, for the same number of additional periods as the number of option periods, if any, remaining pursuant to paragraph 1.02 at the time of ______________ (name of record company)'s exercise of the Leaving Member Option;

(ii) A Minimum Recording Commitment, for each Contract Period of such term, of two (2) satisfactory Sides, or their equivalent; and

(iii) A basic royalty at the rate of five percent (5%) in respect of phonograph records embodying performances recorded during such term.

____

(NAME OF RECORD COMPANY), A DIVISION OF

____

(NAME OF RECORD COMPANY), INC.

____

BY

____

(NAME OF ARTIST OR GROUP)

____

BY

Entertainment Group Names: Selection and Protection

BY STEPHEN BIGGER

The first rule in selecting a name for an entertainment group is a simple one: *Be original.* It can, however, be quite difficult to put this rule into practice, since the field is very crowded. A brief check of a trade reference such as the *Billboard International Talent & Touring Directory* shows, for example, two different performers named Johnny O, and different groups called The Dixie Cups and The Dixie Kups, as well as two groups named Joyful Noise and The Joyful Noyze.

One reason why it is important to create an entirely original name is to avoid being sued for infringing someone else's name. Rights in a group name or a trademark usually derive from priority of use. This means that a prior group, even a small one, can successfully stop a new and more successful group from using the same name, at least in the area of the prior group's reputation. Another good reason for being original is that it will be easier to protect the name if you are the first one to use it. If you know that there is already a group called The Sledgehammers, it would be a poor choice to call your group The Sledgehammer Band.

SERVICE MARKS

A group name used for entertainment services is legally known as a service mark. What is the difference between a service mark and a trademark? A trademark is a brand name used for a product. A trademark can be a word, a logo design, or both together. A service mark is also a brand name, but is used for services rather than for physical goods. Can a service mark also be used as a trademark? Yes. For example, a group name can be used as a trademark for such things as T-shirts, toys, games or other merchandising items. However, use of a group name as a service mark for entertainment services will not necessarily entitle you to use the same mark as a trademark for goods. Again, in the United States, trademark and service mark rights are usually created by use and therefore, in order to create rights in a trademark for a product, it is usually necessary to use the mark by actually selling the product bearing the trademark to the public.

Although the owner of a trademark for a particular product or service generally cannot stop someone else from using the same or similar name on a completely different type of product or service, there is an exception for famous names and trademarks. It would not be a good idea to call your new group something like Pepsi-Cola, since to do so would be inviting a lawsuit from the owners of this famous name. No one would confuse a bottle of rum with a diamond ring, but the owners of the famous Bacardi name were able to stop someone else from using that name on jewelry. Yes, there are exceptions. For example, a group called The Cadillacs is listed in the *Billboard Directory.* Still, it is not a good idea to court lawsuits by trading on someone else's famous name.

A trademark for a record label can usually coexist with the same or similar name for an entertainment group, publishing company, talent agency and so forth without problems. There is a Genesis record label and also a group by that name. It would be best, however, for a group to find a completely original name so that no confusion could exist with a record or publishing company of the same name. And, there is that famous trademark exception: if someone were to adopt the name BMG or EMI for the name of their group, you can be sure that they would quickly find themselves on the wrong end of a lawsuit brought by the owner of the famous trademark.

Likewise, the title of a song or record album can usually coexist with the same or similar name of an entertainment group, especially if the words are commonplace and the group name is not famous. Not long ago, for the first time, a federal court ruled on just such an issue in a case where a little-known rock band named Pump, composed of a group of singing body-builders, sued the famous Aerosmith entertainment group, trying to stop their sale of an album of the same name. At the time the lawsuit was filed, Aerosmith had already sold over one million copies of their *Pump* album in the U.S. and 600,000 copies abroad. Although the band had a federal registration for the word Pump combined with a barbell design covering entertainment services, and had played at a few local high school concerts in the New England area, the court held that the *Bigfoot* case (see below) did not apply, since no likelihood of confusion had been established between the group and the Aerosmith record album title. The attorneys for the Aerosmith group presented a number of examples where group names had peacefully coexisted, without confusion, with similar album or song titles. A song and album named *The Kiss* coexisted with the Kiss group name and the album *Rumors* (by Fleetwood Mac) coexisted with The Rumors group name. Does this mean that the little-known group named Pump could, by the same token, issue a record album titled *Aerosmith* and get away with it? Absolutely not! The extensive fame and reputation of the Aerosmith group name precludes it. In cases of this kind, where it is *not* a question of group name versus group name, but rather group name versus something else, the relative fame of the group name is an important and probably crucial factor.

Special problems may arise when a group name is going to be used with the name of a star performer. Some thought should be given as to whether the star should have any rights in the group name or should that name belong separately to the group, whether or not it continues to perform with the star. (See also the chapter, Group Breakups.)

Previously, it was not possible to obtain a federal service mark registration (granted by the U.S. Patent and Trademark Office) for the name of an individual performer. That was changed some years ago when Johnny Carson was able to convince the Patent Office that he was entitled to register his name, but only upon proving that the name was used together with the words "in concert" in connection with entertainment services.

A common question is whether anyone can use his or her own name as a performer, even if it may conflict with the name of someone famous. The answer is, not necessarily. If your name happens to be Neil Diamond, you would have a difficult time convincing a court that you were entitled to use that name, as a singer, in view of the likelihood of confusion with the famous Neil Diamond.

RESEARCHING THE NAME

As soon as you have selected a name for the group, and before it is used, a search should be conducted to see whether the proposed name conflicts with any prior name. As mentioned above, rights in a group name or trademark usually derive from priority of use. Therefore, if a prior group has used the same or a similar name, it is entitled to object to your use of that name, at least in the area of its reputation.

Trade references that are easily checked include the *Billboard International Talent and Touring Directory* (performing artists section), and Muze's *PhonoLog*, a comprehensive guide to recorded music (available at many record stores), which is updated biweekly and currently lists over 40,000 artists' names. The *Billboard International Talent and Touring Directory* lists active performing groups, but it includes only those that request to be listed (by responding to an annual questionnaire). Record stores generally have databases that can be searched for current recordings by artist or by group name.

You can also check a number of sources on the Internet that could prove helpful in clearing your group name. You can use search engines such as AltaVista *(www.altavista.com)* or Yahoo! *(www.yahoo.com)* to see what similar group names pop up. Check music Web sites such as CDnow *(www.cdnow.com),* All Music Guide *(www.allmusic.com),* and Ultimate Band List *(http://ubl.artistdirect.com).* It is important to note that the absence of a band name on the Internet does *not* mean that the name is available for you to use. It is still important to conduct a regular trademark search of the kind mentioned below.

A search should be conducted through a professional searching bureau to see whether the name has been registered as a trademark or service mark with either the U.S. Patent and Trademark Office in Washington, D.C. (federal registration) or with the Secretary of State in any of the 50 states (state registration). A comprehensive search by a professional searching bureau will cover the federal trademark register, all of the state trademark registers, and common law rights (that is, trademarks and names in use but not necessarily registered) reflected in trade directories, as well as Internet references including domain names etc. It is advisable to have the results of such a search reviewed by an attorney who is experienced in trademark law to give you some sense of the relative importance of the various references turned up in the search.

CREATING RIGHTS IN THE NAME

In the United States, rights in a group name, trademark or service mark are usually created by use and *not* by registration or any other kind of filing or claim. So, can you "reserve" a name before you use it? Yes, by filing a federal "intent to use" trademark or service mark application (see the section titled U.S. Trademark Registration).

Reserving a name for incorporation with the Secretary of State of your particular state, or filing a fictitious business name statement will not create any rights in the name that you can enforce against the first commercial user of the same or a similar name. Likewise, the mere fact of registering a domain name on the Internet will not create any protectable rights in the name. (For further details, see the comments below under Rights in Cyberspace).

The United States is a common law jurisdiction where you acquire trademark rights by using the mark, quite apart from any statutory registration procedure. In several European and Latin American countries, however, trademark rights are created solely by registration. The U.S. system is designed to protect the person who has created some reputation in a name by using it even if he or she cannot afford to register the name. This positive aspect, whereby prior users cannot lose their rights as long as they continue to use the name, despite any subsequent user who may be bigger or more famous, also includes an element of uncertainty. Even if you conduct an extensive search, you cannot be absolutely certain that you are not infringing on the rights of some prior group that may be performing in some backwater. There is nothing you can do to dislodge the rights of such a group, provided that they continue to use the name and maintain some kind of public reputation.

If you search the name you wish to use and find another group with the same or a similar name you have two choices: (1) use a different name or (2) try to buy the rights to the name from the prior group. Do not ignore the rights of the prior group, even if you are about to sign a big recording contract and they have never recorded their music. To try to "roll over" a prior, relatively unknown, group because you are bigger, more famous, or better financed, could be a fatal mistake.

What if you discover that there was a prior group of the same or similar name, but they are no longer performing? Do they still have any rights in the name? That depends on the circumstances. If the prior group still has some kind of residual reputation, even though they are not currently performing, it could be very dangerous to use the name without coming to terms with them, either by obtaining their permission to use the name or (preferably) an assignment of their rights. Rights in a group name, like other property rights, can be sold or transferred to someone else, even though such rights are not physical property.

In one case involving the group name The Buckinghams, the court protected the residual reputation of a group that had been disbanded for five years. Although the group had not performed for that period of time, the members had no intention to abandon the name, and they continued to collect royalties from their records that were currently being sold. The Buckinghams were, therefore, entitled to stop another group from using the name, even though they had stopped performing and making records.

Territoriality

Another basic concept in trademark and service mark law is that of "territoriality." In the entertainment area, this means that it is possible for two groups to operate under the same name in different parts of the country and for each of them to own the name in its own territory. Of course, everyone wants to own their own group name for the entire country, if not the entire world. However, if two groups, each without knowledge of the other, independently adopt the same name, then both are entitled to use it in their respective territories. It is even possible for each of the parties to obtain a separate federal registration, with an appropriate limitation as to the area of the group's reputation. If, however, you are aware of a group in another part of the country that has the name you wish to use, then you cannot, without risking a lawsuit, use the name in the other group's territory, either by performing there, distributing records, or engaging in advertising or promotional activities for your group. Since every group hopes to be successful nationwide, and to perform and distribute records on a national basis, it makes no sense to pick a name used by another group even if it is purely local, unrecorded, and in a different part of the country. Further, if it can be shown that you were aware of the other group's name before you began use of that name, your adoption of the name was not "innocent," and a court may rule against your right to use the name even in your own territory.

Ownership of the Name

After selecting the name and searching it, the next important step in protecting the name is to decide who is going to own it and to put this decision in writing. Even if you cannot afford a lawyer, confirm your agreement in writing. This can be as simple as a signed and dated statement that says that if Tom, Dick, or Harry leaves the group, then the departing member will have no right to use the group name, which shall continue to be owned by the remaining members of the group. A simple agreement along these lines can help avoid complicated hassles and problems in the future.

Doesn't the person who thought up the name own it? No. Remember, the group name is like a brand name for a product. It identifies to the public the services provided by the group. Rights in the name are only created when it is used to create a public reputation. (With the single exception of a federal "intent to use" trademark or service mark application that must be validated by actual commercial use of the name before registration is granted.) If one member of the group thinks up the group name, that person does not, individually, own the name. Ordinarily, the entity that actually uses the name owns it, subject to some agreement to the contrary. It would be possible, although not usual, for some other party to own the group name, such as the manager of the group, the record company, or the financial backer. However, any such unusual ownership arrangement should be confirmed by a written agreement. If there is nothing in writing to the contrary, the general assumption is that the members of the group, as a whole, own the group name and any member or members leaving the group would have no further rights in the use of the name.

There are some interesting decisions in this area. In the *Rare Earth* case, a federal district court held that in the event of a group breakup, where the group was organized as a corporation, the faction having working corporate control would prevail in a dispute over the right to use the name. In a Michigan state court decision involving The Dramatics name, the court held that upon dissolution, where a partnership made no advanced disposition of the group name, the group name became "the property of the partners in common and belongs to each of them with a right to use it in common, but not the exclusion of the other partners." In other words, after the breakup of the group, you could have three or four different individuals calling themselves The Dramatics. Such a result seems in the interests of no one and underlines the advisability of having a written agreement, at the outset, as to the ownership of the group name.

Typically, a group starts out as a partnership and the members own the group name in common. In other words, they have the right to use the group name together, but not separately. The question of ownership can be simplified to some degree by having the members of the group form a corporation that will own the name. Then, if a federal registration is obtained in the name of the corporation, the departure of one or more members will not affect the title to the registration.

A situation that can become complicated is when a solo performer works with a group and the performer and the group use separate names. The solo performer may believe, if there is no agreement to the contrary, that he or she has some rights to the ownership of the group name. Imagine that a solo performer named Lucky Starr and a backup group called The Sledgehammers perform together. They sign their first contract with a record company, and the record company designs a composite logo for the entire performing unit including the words Lucky Starr & the Sledgehammers. Together, the solo performer and the group obtain a federal registration for the composite mark (including both names and the logo design). If the parties have a falling-out, you can imagine how difficult it will be to answer the question of who owns what. (See the chapter, Group Breakups.)

On the question of ownership of the copyright in a logo design prepared, for example, by an artist hired by the record company, it would be advisable to have an agreement with the artist and the record company confirming that the ownership in the copyright for the logo design belongs to the group, or at least that the record company makes no claim to the words that are included in the logo design. Otherwise, if there is a disagreement between the record company and the group, the record company may claim that it owns the logo design. Generally though, the fact that the record company's artist designed the logo would not give it any ownership rights in the name, since the group owns the name in whatever form it is depicted.

Rights in Cyberspace

Registering a domain name on the Internet does not automatically give you any rights in the name. A domain name registration will, however, block someone else from registering exactly the same domain name—but not some minor variation thereof. If, for example, your group name is The Sledgehammers, and someone else has registered the domain name "sledgehammers.com," that would not prevent you from registering a domain name like "sledgehammersband.com." Accordingly, unless someone else is actually trying to "steal" your group name, it may be best to simply avoid the problem entirely by selecting a slightly different domain name. Usually, no one would want to intentionally copy your name unless your group is already famous. The trick is to register your group's domain name before you become famous in order to avoid problems later on. If however your group has become famous overnight, and someone else beats you to the punch with a domain name registration, you can still possibly "recapture" the name through various legal procedures that are now available to protect well-known names against "cyberpiracy." Recent successful recapture cases include the "mariahcarey.com" and "juliaroberts.com" domain names. In the latter case, the famous actress recaptured her domain name under a new procedure called the Uniform Dispute Resolution Policy (UDRP), which involves a special tribunal designed to settle domain name disputes of this kind. The arbitration panel in that case found that the actress Julia Roberts has a common law trademark right in her name, i.e., she has rights in the name even though it was not registered as a trademark, and they also found that the person who had registered her name was acting in bad faith with the intent of profiting from the unauthorized registration. Generally, if someone tries to hijack your group name in cyberspace, you will need a lawyer to sue them to recapture the name or to utilize the special UDRP procedure mentioned above (generally much less expensive than filing a lawsuit).

There is also a federal law that protects against "cybersquatting" or the hijacking of domain names, entitled the Anticybersquatting Consumer Protection Act (ACPA), effective in 1999. Both the ACPA and UDRP procedures apply essentially the same standards for achieving similar results. Generally, however, the UDRP procedure is faster and less costly. Under the ACPA procedure, a court action would be required—but this may also provide broader relief in the form of an award of monetary damages or a court injunction that would go beyond the simple recapture of the domain name and prevent the use of any unauthorized content on the objectionable Web site.

U.S. TRADEMARK REGISTRATION

Although U.S. trademark rights are usually created and must be maintained by use rather than by registration, it is advisable to register a trademark. State trademark registrations are obtained from the local Secretary of State and a federal registration may be obtained at the U.S. Patent and Trademark Office in Washington, D.C. The rights conferred by federal registration are so much wider than those afforded by a state registration that normally a federal registration, which covers the entire country, would be the only registration of the group name that you would want and need.

Since the amendment of the U.S. Federal Trademark Law in 1989, it is possible to reserve a name in advance of any actual commercial use by filing an intent to use trademark or service mark application for federal registration—so long as there is a bona fide intention to use the mark on the specific goods or services covered by the application. The simple filing of such an application will create superior rights in the name, even if some other party begins later use of the same or a similar name before the applicant begins commercial use. For this reason, it is now *very* important to *search* a group name to see whether a federal application for registration has been filed for the same or a similar name (even in the absence of any public use by the applicant), which may bar the use of a new group name. The intent to use trademark or service mark application must be validated by filing evidence of actual commercial use of the name before the registration is granted. If such evidence is not filed within four years, the application will be declared invalid.

A federal trademark or service mark registration provides very important rights in court, including the right to sue for trademark infringement in federal district court. It provides an arsenal of procedural weapons that can be used against an infringer, including extensive discovery procedures that allow you to discover the evidence and information available to the other side. Significantly, a federal registration also provides "constructive notice," so that any subsequent user of the same or a similar name is deemed to have knowledge of your rights. Someone with constructive notice cannot claim that he or she innocently adopted the name and is entitled to use it notwithstanding your prior registration. Only a federal registration entitles the owner to use the ® symbol denoting a federally registered mark.

The ™ symbol is unofficial and without any legal meaning or definition under federal or state statutes. It has been used on an optional basis to indicate a claim to trademark ownership for an unregistered trademark. Sometimes the ™ symbol is used to indicate a service mark. It is not essential to use either symbol and, in fact, their use is not especially popular in the entertainment world, except on merchandising items. However, it is advisable to use the ® symbol if you have a federally registered mark since it puts other parties on actual notice of your federal registration and may affect the question of damages (i.e., whether the damages should be counted from the beginning of the infringement or from when the infringer was notified in writing by you or your lawyer).

Registration Procedure

The procedure for obtaining a federal trademark or service mark registration begins with the filing of an application for registration with the U.S. Patent and Trademark Office in Washington, D.C. Before that application can be filed, it is necessary to have used the mark in interstate commerce (that is, commerce across state lines)—or to base the application on a bona fide intent to use the mark on the goods or services specified in the application. This requirement of use in interstate commerce for a federal application is met if there is a public performance by the group under the group name in a place that attracts an interstate clientele or where the group performance is advertised in a newspaper or publication that crosses state lines. When based on preapplication use, a federal application requires the submission of specimens showing the use of the name. Usually, this would be in the form of advertisements or promotional materials for the public performance of the group. The Patent Office *does not* accept album covers bearing the group name as specimens of use for entertainment services. This narrow view is established practice at the Patent Office. Hopefully, someday someone will challenge this practice by an appeal to the Trademark Trial and Appeal Board or to the courts, and win.

If no problems are encountered, it takes about one year to obtain a federal registration after filing the application. The application procedure has two stages. The first involves an official examination by the Patent Office for both registrability of the mark and any prior registrations for similar marks, which may be cited against the new application as barring registration. The second stage is the opposition period, during which the application is published in the *U.S. Official Gazette* (Trademark Section) and may be opposed by any party wishing to do so within 30 days following the publication date. The *U.S. Official Gazette* is issued weekly and may be ordered by writing to the Superintendent of Documents, Government Printing Office, Washington, D.C. 20402.

The cost of obtaining a federal registration (excluding special problems) is several hundred dollars, which includes official filing fees and legal fees. If a determined adversary opposes an application, the defense of the application is tantamount to fighting a lawsuit in federal court. This could cost thousands of dollars. The applicant, of course, has the option of defending against the opposition or withdrawing the application without incurring any additional expense.

After a federal registration is obtained, it is necessary to continue use of the name in order to preserve the validity of the registration. A federal registration may be canceled for abandonment of the name. The statute provides (effective 1996) that three years' nonuse constitutes prima facie (a legally sufficient case on its face) abandonment. Further, after the fifth anniversary of the registration, it is necessary to file (within one year) an affidavit that confirms that the use of the name has been continued. An affidavit of incontestability should be filed at the same time, provided that the name has been used continuously for the past five years. This will make the registration incontestable (it cannot be canceled by someone else based on a prior registration or on a claim of prior use). Renewal of the registration is required every ten years.

Foreign Registration

Generally, you will want foreign registration for only those countries where you have, or believe you will have, some real commercial interest. Frequently, new groups will search their chosen name in the United States and Canada at the same time, and if the name is clear, file in both countries. A more expansive plan of initial protection might also include a trademark application in the European Community which would cover, in just one application, all 15 member countries of the European Union as follows: Austria, Belgium, Denmark, Finland, France, Germany, Great Britain, Greece, Ireland, Italy, Luxembourg, Netherlands, Portugal, Spain and Sweden.

The United States is a member country of the Paris Convention, the Magna Carta of the international patent and trademark field. It is possible, under this convention, to file foreign applications within a six-month term following the filing of a U.S. application, claiming the priority date of the U.S. application. This can be very helpful for a group that becomes famous overnight, and is faced with infringements in countries where others try to register the name before the group has had the opportunity to get applications on file. There are approximately 175 trademark jurisdictions in the world. The cost of registering a name as a trademark or service mark in all of these jurisdictions, without any special problems, is about $250,000. If there are Patent Office or third-party objections, the cost could escalate to over $500,000. Approximately 125 countries provide for the registration of service marks, which is what you really want, rather than a trademark registration. Some jurisdictions have no provisions for the registration of service marks, although the trend is towards the adoption of registered service mark protection.

The Latin American countries and a number of countries in Europe (France, Germany, Italy and Spain) are "first to file" countries, where trademark and service mark rights derive from registration rather than from use. In other words, the first to register the name is the one who owns it. There are exceptions for famous names (if they can be proven by evidence of local reputation), which are, under the Paris Convention, entitled to special protection even in the absence of registration.

If someone has filed for your group name, prior to you, in a first-to-file country such as France, and you try to perform or sell records in that country, the owner of the registration would be entitled to stop you from performing in France under that name *and* stop you from selling records bearing that group name.

Prior use is not required for filing trademark or service mark applications in most foreign countries. In Australia, Canada, and the United States, an application can be filed based on either prior use or proposed use. You may reserve a name in foreign countries by filing a trademark or service mark application, even before you use the name. However, many of these countries have user requirements after registration, so that if you do not use the name within a certain period of time, your registration will be canceled for nonuse.

MINIMUM PROTECTION: DOING IT YOURSELF

Even if your group is starting out on a shoestring budget and you cannot afford a lawyer, you can still take some of the most important steps in selecting and protecting the group name.

First, you can engage in some minimal searching, which will entail little or no expense, including checking the pop artists section in Muze's *PhonoLog*. You can also check the *Billboard International Talent and Touring Directory* to see if there are names listed that are the same or similar to yours. Further, you can check *The Trademark Register,* which lists all federal registrations, by class, that are currently in force. You should check International Class 41, which covers entertainment services. *The Trademark Register* may be ordered by writing to that publication at the National Press Building, Suite 1297, Washington, D.C. 20045. Some libraries carry it as a reference work. You can also check this resource online at *www.trademarkregister.com* at minimal expense (i.e., currently $19.95 per day for a 12-hour day of searching!). This is an official publication of the U.S. Patent and Trademark Office in Washington, D.C.

You can make an informal survey of people you know in entertainment to see whether they have heard of any name that is the same or similar to the one you propose to use. You could order a search report from a professional searching bureau at a cost of approximately $400 for a comprehensive search covering federal and state registrations and common law rights. It is advisable to have a trademark lawyer review such a search. Professional searching bureaus are listed in the telephone yellow pages under "Trademark Agents" or "Trademark Consultants."

After you have satisfied yourself as best you can that the use of the proposed name will not infringe on the rights of some other group, the most important thing you can do is to go ahead and use the name publicly so that you create rights in the name. Keep a careful record of the performance places, dates and publicity, so that you can, if necessary, prove that you used the name, in what territory and for how long. It is also helpful in protecting the name to use it consistently and with some continuity. If the name is unused for a period of time and you no longer have a public reputation in the name, you have lost your rights in that name.

Finally, you can stand up for your rights once you have used the name, notwithstanding any big group that comes along later and tries to bluff you into discontinuing the name because they are famous and you are not. Remember the *Bigfoot* case and the *Flash* decision mentioned earlier. Do not let your group be pushed around if, in fact,

THE LITTLE GUY PREVAILS

- In the landmark *Bigfoot* case, a large tire company knew of a smaller company on the West Coast that had been using the trademark Bigfoot. They very effectively wiped out the reputation of the smaller company by blitzing the media on a nationwide basis, so that by the time they were through, Bigfoot meant only one thing to the public and that was the tire sold by the larger company. When the case came before the court, it resulted in the largest award ever given in a U.S. trademark case: over $19,000,000 in damages, in view of the deliberate infringement, by the larger company, of the smaller company's trademark rights. (In the trial court, there was a punitive damage award by the jury of $16,800,000 and an actual damage award of $2,800,000, both of which were upheld on posttrial motions. However, on appeal, the higher court reduced the awards to something over $4,000,000 for punitive damages and $600,000 for actual damages.)

- In a more recent decision, which cited the *Bigfoot* case, a court awarded $250,000 in damages to a little-known group called The Rubberband, which had prior use and a federal registration and had objected to a later use of the name by the well-known group, Bootsy's Rubber Band. The court noted that the later group's fame had effectively wiped out any reputation that the earlier group had, and held that the little-known group was entitled to receive all of the profits earned by the willful infringement of their name, although the newcomer was allowed to keep its name.

- Another pertinent case concerned the right to use the group name Flash. A California group by that name had performed in the San Francisco Bay Area but had never recorded an album. There was also an English group called Flash, which had recorded with a major company. When the records bearing their group name were distributed in the San Francisco area, the unrecorded Bay Area group was able to stop distribution of them based on their prior use and reputation for that territory.

you are the prior user. As the prior user, you have superior rights, at least for the area of your reputation, and you can enforce them against any subsequent user no matter how big or famous.

MAXIMUM PROTECTION

If you have just become famous and have signed a big recording contract, you will want to decide how extensively you should protect the group name by way of registration. You should focus on those foreign jurisdictions where service marks can be registered for entertainment services. The most important are Australia, the Benelux area, Brazil, Canada, Denmark, Finland, France, Germany, Great Britain, Italy, Japan, Mexico, Norway, South Africa, Spain, Sweden and Switzerland. Also remember that you can file a single trademark application in the European Community, which will cover most of the latter European jurisdictions as well as the other member countries of the European Union.

You can obtain trademark registrations in jurisdictions (such as India, the Bahamas and Jamaica), where service mark registrations are not available, to cover merchandising items like T-shirts, toys, games or whatever. Generally, however, it is not worthwhile to spend the money on trademark registrations for merchandising items unless you have a real commercial interest in merchandising the name in those jurisdictions. Many of these countries have user requirements, so that a registration is subject to cancellation after five years of nonuse (or some lesser period).

If you do intend to actively merchandise the group name, it is highly advisable to obtain trademark registrations for the merchandising items, especially in those jurisdictions where trademark rights derive from registration rather than from use. Without a trademark registration for the goods concerned, you have nothing to license to another party for manufacturing the goods and selling them in the local jurisdiction. The chapter, Merchandising Agreements, discusses this issue more fully.

You may also want to consider defensive merchandising, registering the mark for merchandising items, simply to prevent someone else from doing so. For example, a famous performer may not wish to merchandise his or her name in order to sell T-shirts, but may be plagued by unscrupulous persons that capitalize on the name by emblazoning it on T-shirts anyway. The famous performer has two choices in these cases, ignore the infringements or try to stop them.

The most effective way of stopping infringements of this kind is to register the name for merchandising items and then license the name on a selective basis to create trademark rights in the area of most active infringements. A case in point is that of the unauthorized sale, in Great Britain, of T-shirts bearing the group name Abba. In that case, the merchandising company representing the famous Swedish group was not able to stop the sale of the T-shirts, since they were being sold by the first user, despite the fact that there was no connection with or authorization from the famous group. The English court indicated (in 1976) that the fame of the Abba name for entertainment services in Great Britain (where service marks were not yet registrable) was not enough to entitle the group or its merchandising company to prevent use of the name on T-shirts by the unauthorized party, who was the first user of the name on the goods in the jurisdiction.

Since the amendment of the U.K. Trademark Law in 1994, the registration of an entertainment group name provides a basis for stopping the unauthorized use of the name on the same kind of goods or services covered by the registration. There is also a provision in the new law that protects registered marks, which are well-known in the U.K., against use of the same name on dissimilar goods or services if such use would take unfair advantage of, or be detrimental to, the character of the well-known mark. In order to take advantage of this expanded protection, however, it is crucial to obtain a U.K. registration of the name for the goods or services for which the name has become well known. If, however, you obtain a European Community trademark registration, you would not need a separate national U.K. registration.

There is some question about whether the use of a group name on only the front (or back) of a T-shirt is, in fact, trademark use. It is better, from the standpoint of trademark protection, if the group name also appears on the neck label, indicating that it is the brand name for the shirt itself. Otherwise, an infringer may be able to claim that the use of the group name on only the front of the shirt is an ornamental use (open to anyone) and not a trademark, which only the trademark owner is entitled to use or authorize. Also, adding the ™ symbol to the name on the front of the shirt (or the ® symbol if the name is federally registered as a trademark for shirts) helps to show that trademark rights are being claimed.

Finally, a maximum approach to protection of a group name should include a system to watch for infringements. There are trademark surveillance services that survey trademark journals, where applications are published for opposition purposes, which are available in something like 150 countries. Costs average $400 per year for surveillance on an international basis. In this way, you will be informed if someone in Peru or France or Sweden files to appropriate your group's name for entertainment services, merchandising items or whatever and you will have the opportunity to oppose the applications or obtain cancellation of the resulting registration before it can be used to damage or block your rights in the name in that country.

Business Entities

BY EDWARD (NED) R. HEARN

There are mainly four forms of business that can be used to organize your music business affairs. These are (1) sole proprietorship (a single self-employed individual running the business); (2) partnership (two or more self-employed people running the business); (3) corporation (which can be owned by one or more individuals and is organized under specific state laws); or (4) a limited liability company, which has elements of a partnership and a corporation. Each of these forms has special features that should be examined when making a decision about how to organize your business. These features include, among others, expenses, personal liability, and taxes. You should seek professional advice to determine the best form for your particular situation before investing too much time and money in your enterprise. The cost of planning to minimize problems is *much less* than the cost of trying to cure those problems after they have materialized.

SOLE PROPRIETORSHIP

A sole proprietorship is a business conducted by one individual who is the sole owner. If you have your own business for the purpose of making money, whether by making or selling records, writing and publishing songs, operating a recording studio or performing solo, you have a proprietorship business, and this material applies to you.

A proprietorship is the simplest form of business to start because it generally requires no contracts (contracts require at least two people) and only a few special papers have to be prepared. These papers include a fictitious business name statement, commonly called a DBA ("doing business as"), which identifies you as the owner by your name and address and the name under which you are doing business. Note, however, that a DBA generally needs to be filed only if you use a name other than your own to do business. That statement must be filed with the county recorder located in your local county courthouse. After filing with the county recorder, you must publish a legal notice statement of your doing business. You can inquire at your county recorder's office to find out which local newspapers publish the notices and have the least expensive legal notice rates. Certain local governments may require the proprietor to obtain a separate business license or that license may be covered by the fictitious business name filing. Your county recorder's office can fill you in on this.

If you sell goods at retail, you will need a permit issued by the appropriate tax authority. This is discussed later in this chapter in the section titled, General Business Obligations.

You, as the sole proprietor, are the only one who makes decisions on how the business should operate and what its focus should be. With a proprietorship, you enjoy all the profits, but must absorb all the losses. Employees do not participate in the ownership. A proprietor who has employees must withhold income and social security taxes, unemployment, and other insurances required by state and federal law and must submit the withheld sums to the appropriate government agencies. While a proprietorship usually has fewer regulatory and record-keeping requirements than a partnership or corporation, you *must* focus on the reports to be filed with the local, state, and federal taxing authorities. If you are going to hire employees, be certain to contact each of those authorities to obtain the required forms and instructional booklets that tell you what to do. A good bookkeeper or accountant will be able to assist you with that part of your business. These requirements are discussed in more detail later in this chapter.

As a proprietorship, you are responsible for your acts and, in general, the acts of your employees. If, for example, you or one of your employees should injure someone in a car accident while promoting your record to radio stations, you would be responsible for compensating the injured party. A judgment against you would enable the judgment creditor (the person who won the suit and to whom you owe the money) to look to all your assets, both business and personal, to recover on the judgment. You should obtain insurance to provide coverage from the liabilities that can occur in running a business.

The entire income of a proprietor is taxable income, but business expenses and losses are deductible from income. Proprietors, as self-employed, must file quarterly estimated income tax returns and make prepayment of anticipated taxes with the Internal Revenue Service and the state tax authorities. The estimated tax is based on a projection of expected income during your first year of business and thereafter on your prior years taxes. You should consult an accountant who has a tax orientation to assist you in these matters.

PARTNERSHIPS

If your band of one, or your one-person record or publishing company has grown to two or more people that share the profits and losses, and you plan to stay in business for a while, you have a partnership. A partnership is defined as an association of two or more persons conducting a business on a continuing basis as co-owners for profit. Usually, the relationship among the partners is governed by a written partnership agreement that details the rights and responsibilities of each partner. Although you do not need a written contract to be considered a partnership, obtaining a written partnership agreement is recommended. If there is no written partnership agreement, state statutes control the relations of the partners with each other. The partners can be individuals, other partnerships, corporations, limited liability companies, or any combination of these. Each partner contributes property, services, or money to the business of the partnership. Partners also may loan property, money, or services to the partnership.

General Partnership

In a partnership, each of the partners has an undivided equal interest in all of the partnership property, unless, by contract, they provide for their interests to be unequal. Essentially, each partner owns the assets in common with the other partners and has a duty to each of the other partners to take care of that property and not to dispose of it without the consent of the other partners.

WHEN THERE ARE NO WRITTEN PARTNERSHIP AGREEMENTS

A frequently raised issue is how to structure the business arrangements among the members of a band. Whenever two or more musicians form a band, they have formed a general partnership. While it is important to have a written agreement at some point, most struggling bands cannot afford to hire a lawyer to prepare one for them. If this is the case, it is important for the members of the band to work out answers among themselves. Communicate with each other. Seek professional help. Follow your instincts on what seems fair and reasonable to you. A good issue on which to focus is to determine at what point your band should make an effort to have a written agreement. It is far less expensive to plan your business properly in the beginning than it is to resolve problems after the fact, especially if the resolution takes the form of expensive litigation. If you cannot reach an agreement, maybe that is a sign you should not be in business together.

Legal Presumptions

If the members of a band have formed a partnership by working together but do not have a written agreement, state statutes presume that certain conditions apply to the band's arrangements. These conditions are that each partner; (a) has an equal vote in the affairs of the partnership and a majority vote determines the decision of the partners; (b) owns an equal share in the assets of the partnership, which include equipment purchased by the band, the name of the band, and income; (c) shares equally in the profits and losses of the partnership; and (d) is responsible for the acts of all of the other partners performed in pursuing the partnership business. If a partner, for example, delivers the band's independently produced recording to record stores for sale and in the course of making a delivery has a car accident, then all of the partners are liable for any damages.

Leaving Members

When there is no written agreement and a partner leaves the partnership, whether willingly or at the demand of the other partners, then the band's partnership terminates automatically. The band has a responsibility to pay all of the debts of the partnership and, if necessary, sell the partnership's assets to do so. If thereafter, the remaining members of the partnership wish to continue performing as a band they may, but in effect, they form a new partnership and start over again. If the band's creditors cooperate, you may be able to avoid having to liquidate the band's assets so long as the remaining band members continue paying the creditors. You need to work out with the departing members their continuing responsibility to make payments owed or to receive payments due. If you do not want to deal with a dissolution and liquidation under these circumstances you need a written partnership agreement.

Taxes

The partnership does not pay taxes on income earned by the band. Instead, the band files an informational tax return on Federal Partnership Return of Income Form 1065, wherein each partner states their distributive share of income or loss. Then each partner lists and adds or subtracts that share of income or loss on their individual tax return.

PARTNERSHIPS: CRITICAL WRITTEN AGREEMENT DECISIONS

Acquired Property

When a band acquires property, such as a sound or lighting system, each of its members assumes a share of that system's cost. The partners should be aware of their payment responsibilities and what happens if somebody leaves the band. For example, will the departing member have to continue to make payment? Do the remaining members of the band have any obligation to pay the departing member for the equipment based on its market value or the money paid by the departing member, if the band is going to keep that equipment?

Name

If the band becomes well known and its name is recognizable to a large audience, who will have the rights in the name if the band breaks up, or individual members leave the band? Partnership agreements generally state that the group, as a whole, owns the name. A provision should be included in the agreement stating that if any member leaves the group, whether voluntarily or otherwise, that member surrenders the right to use the band name, which will stay with the remaining members of the group. Any incoming member would have to acknowledge in writing that the name of the band does belong to the partnership and the new member does not own any rights in the band's name greater than the partnership interests allocated to that new member.

The partnership agreement could provide that none of the band members may use the name if the group should completely disband, or that any one of the members could buy from the others the right to use the name at a value to be established by binding arbitration with expert testimony concerning the valuation of the band's name, if the members cannot agree among themselves.

Leaving Members

Prior to signing long-term contracts such as recording or publishing agreements, the band should determine how to resolve the issues regarding the rights of departing and new band members concerning services already performed or commitments that have to be met under those agreements and the sharing of recoupable costs for projects predating and postdating the leaving and new band members.

Song Rights

Can the departing member take his or her songs when they leave the group? If the songs were cowritten with remaining band members, the band can continue to use the songs and record them, as can the departing member, but each will have to report to the other their respective shares of income earned from such usages. When the departing member is the sole author of certain compositions, the band could be prevented from recording them, if they had not already been released on commercially distributed phonorecords, and from performing them if they had not yet been licensed to a performing rights society like BMI or ASCAP. Sometimes bands form a publishing company as part of the assets of the partnership, which will control what happens when a writer member leaves the band. Usually the band will continue to be able to use the songs as will the departing member.

Each person who is a partner may act on behalf of the partnership and that act binds all of the partners in the partnership. Each person in the partnership is liable for the business obligations of the partnership incurred by any of the partners. In other words, if your partner signs a business commitment to pay for advertising for the business, you as a partner are responsible with the other partners for making payment. On contract actions, the creditor can sue all of the partners, but cannot single out any one partner to sue exclusive of the others. A tort claim (inflicting harm on another person or property) for injuries is different. If, for example, a partner runs a car through a record store display window while delivering records in the normal course of partnership business, each partner is severally (individually) liable and the store owner could sue any individual partner or all the partners in the partnership.

The personal assets of the partners can be taken by the creditors of the business, but only after all of the partnership assets have been taken and the personal creditors of the individual partners have satisfied their claims out of the partners' personal assets. For example, the business creditors must exhaust all of the property and money of the partnership before they can look to your car, stereo, or instrument, and the person you still owe for the car, stereo, or instrument has to be paid before the business creditor can claim any of these prized items. Some states' laws will allow certain "necessary" property of the debtor to be exempt from creditors' claims, such as food and clothing.

Death or withdrawal of a partner (or some other specified event set out in a partnership agreement) will dissolve the partnership. By written agreement, however, the partners can provide that the partnership will continue despite a partner's death or withdrawal. In that case, the agreement establishes distribution rules to determine how the departing partner is to be compensated (this is called a buy out) and how the partnership is to continue without the deceased or withdrawn partner.

As with a proprietorship, a partnership must file a fictitious business name statement (if all the partners' surnames are not in the partnership name) and publish a doing-business statement in a local county newspaper. You also must file a form SS-4 with the Internal Revenue Service to obtain an employer identification tax number *even if you do not employ anybody.* These forms can be obtained by calling, faxing, writing or emailing to your regional Internal Revenue Service center. The performing rights organizations, ASCAP, BMI and SESAC, ask publisher members to include their employer identification tax numbers on their membership applications. You must also secure any required local licenses and permits.

In a general partnership, all of the partners participate in the control of the business. Partners may agree among themselves to assign specific duties according to ability. Voting on business decisions may be equal, or may be weighted according to capital contribution (money and property contributed to making the partnership work), or on some other basis.

The profits, losses, and risks are shared equally among the partners unless they agree, in writing, to a different division.

At income tax time, the partnership files an informational tax return, describing losses or profits, but the partnership itself pays no taxes. Rather, the losses or profits are passed through to the individual partners for reporting on their individual tax returns (thus, a partnership is often described as a tax conduit) and again, unless the agreement provides otherwise, losses or profits are shared equally. As with a proprietorship, the partners must file quarterly returns and personal income tax prepayments.

On dissolution of the partnership, the assets of the partnership are liquidated (turned into cash) and the creditors of the partnership are paid first. The balance of the liquidated assets, if any, is distributed to the partners, first to repay loans by any of the partners to the partnership, secondly to return any money or assets contributed by the partners, and finally to the partners according to how they share profits.

Joint Venture

A joint venture is a form of business relationship consisting of an association of two or more persons, partnerships, corporations, limited liability companies or some combination thereof, for the purpose of accomplishing a single or limited series of business transactions for profit rather than carrying on a continuous business. A joint venture is a partnership with respect to all the applicable rules discussed above and the terms of the relationship should be governed by a written agreement. Examples of a musical joint venture include recording a single album, producing one video, or promoting a concert.

Limited Partnership

A limited partnership functions as a financing vehicle to raise capital to fund identified business goals. It consists of a least two people, corporations, partnerships, or some combination thereof. A limited partnership requires at least one general partner, whether a person, another partnership, or a corporation, and one or more limited partners as investors. The limited partners contribute capital but take no part in the management of the business and have no liability beyond the amount of money that each contributed to the partnership and any profits owed to them under the limited partnership. Should a limited partner become involved in the management of the business then he or she would lose this limited liability status. Generally, a limited partnership is for an established duration and must be set out in a written limited partnership agreement. State and federal securities laws that regulate investments apply to limited partnerships and a discussion of these laws is found in the chapter, How to Set Up a Money Deal.

CORPORATIONS

At some point in your career, you may decide that it is time to incorporate, either because you have reached a high income level, or because you wish to protect your personal assets from the claims of your business creditors. Frequently, successful entertainers form what in the business is known as a "loan-out" corporation. In other words, you have yourself incorporated and that corporation agrees to make your services available to other parties (for example, record companies) in any particular deal.

What does it mean to be a corporation? Corporations differ substantially from proprietorships and partnerships. A corporation is an artificial, separate, legal entity recognized by state law, the formation of which is regulated by procedures established by state law. Ownership of a corporation is obtained by buying shares of stock for value. A corporation can be owned by one or more persons (including a partnership) or other corporations. A corporation can be owned privately (the stock is not traded on the stock market) or publicly (the corporation's stock is sold on the stock market and is held by the public at large).

The corporation is a separate legal entity with a life apart from the persons that own and operate it. Corporations raise capital by selling shares. The issuance of shares in the corporation is a security subject to state and, under some circumstance, federal securities laws. Like an individual or a partnership, a corporation can own, buy, or sell property in its own name, enter into contracts, borrow money, raise capital, and do the various kinds of activities that a proprietorship and partnership can do.

The corporation is governed by a board of directors elected by the shareholders. In turn, the corporation is managed by officers (such as a president and treasurer) that are employees of the corporation hired by the board of directors. In loan-out corporations, the officers and directors usually are the individuals that form the corporation and are the shareholders. If the corporation was formed by one person, then that person usually holds all of the officer positions and is the sole director.

Risks of the business are borne by the corporation. The shareholders' liabilities are limited to the amounts invested in the corporation and their share of the profits. The investments are usually evidenced by issued shares (stock).

The corporation must file annual tax returns and pay taxes on profits. After taxes, profits can be retained for operating capital or distributed to shareholders as dividends, which are taxable as income. Profits are shared among shareholders in proportion to their ownership participation. Unlike partnerships, there is no passing of profits and losses from a corporation to the individual owners of shares except in a Chapter S corporation.

With a Chapter S corporation, the shareholders get the benefits of a partnership by having profits and losses passed through to them for tax purposes, while they retain the benefit of the corporation's limited liability status. Losses passed through to the shareholders cannot exceed the amounts invested by the shareholders.

A corporation is brought into existence by filing a document known as the articles of incorporation (or charter or articles of association in some states), the filing of which, for example costs $100 in California, plus a prepayment of an annual minimum franchise tax payment, currently $800. Forming a corporation, however, will cost more than this because of attorneys' fees to organize the corporation and prepare shareholder and buy/sell agreements concerning the stock issued to the shareholders. In addition, there may be local fees for permits and business licenses.

Shares of publicly held companies are generally transferable from one owner to a subsequent owner on the open market. With nonpublic corporations, there is no ready market for the shares and the shareholders have to seek out specific buyers. Also, the law often restricts the sale of shares, and requires that certain procedures, established by state and federal statutes, be followed before they can be sold. Also, the shareholders may have agreements among themselves, or the corporation may have provisions in its bylaws that put limitations on a shareholder's transfer of stock. This is a complex area that

THE CASE OF DEEP PURPLE

An example of the issues involved when a group disbands but its product still sells involved the group Deep Purple, which had not been performing as a band for many years. Its records, however, still sold. One of the original members of that band formed a new group. None of the other members of that new group had been members of the original Deep Purple.

This new group began to perform under the name Deep Purple. The corporation, owned by the original members of Deep Purple and their management, still owned the rights to the name Deep Purple. They sued the new Deep Purple to stop them from performing under that name and were awarded damages of $672,000; compensatory damages (actual damages suffered by the corporation) were $168,000 and $504,000 was for punitive damages.

Since then, the authorized Deep Purple has reformed and resumed performing and recording.

requires professional counsel on securities, tax, and accounting issues and is too involved a topic to examine in this chapter. You should be aware that these are considerations that require some attention and you will need professional advice when it comes time to focus on them.

The rules that govern the operation of the corporation are known as the bylaws and these are adopted at the beginning of the life of the corporation. Generally, the officers of the corporation are empowered to operate the daily affairs of the corporation, subject to approval or disapproval by the board of directors, which in turn answers to the shareholders. The board of directors will hold periodic meetings to review the acts of the officers. The shareholders will hold periodic meetings to review the board of directors.

Voting among shareholders is based on the number of shares owned—generally one vote per share. Shareholders are sometimes divided into different classes. Some classes of shares may be nonvoting. Some corporations' bylaws provide for "cumulative" voting for the directors of the board. In other words, a shareholder can multiply the number of his or her shares (e.g., 100 out of 500) by the number of board positions (e.g., three) and apply all of the total (300) to one candidate on the board, and thereby increase that shareholder's assurance of placing a representative on the board.

The corporation's existence is perpetual unless the shareholders vote to terminate the corporation or the corporation cannot continue financially. On dissolution, creditors, such as banks, trade creditors, employees and taxing bodies are paid first. Then shareholders receive a return of capital (that is, they get back what they paid for their shares if the dissolved corporation has sufficient funds), and finally, a distribution of assets and profits, if any.

LIMITED LIABILITY COMPANIES (LLCS)

Over the past 20 years, a new form of business has been evolving, which has come into its own in only the past number of years. It is called a "limited liability company" (LLC) and has elements of both a partnership and a corporation. This chapter provides a brief summary of LLCs, which can be advantageous for entertainers that work in a group, such as a performing and recording band. Discuss with your attorney the pros and cons of structuring your business as an LLC, instead of as a partnership or regular corporation (usually a Chapter S).

An LLC is an organization in which the owners (members) have an interest in the LLC and are parties to a contract, known as the operating agreement, which details the rights and duties of the members and acts as the guiding rules for the LLC. Some state statutes require that the operating agreement be in writing, but this can vary from state to state. Generally, a written agreement better serves the interests and needs of the members regardless of statutes.

There are two types of LLCs, member-managed, in which members, by statute, have the agency and authority to make management decisions; and manager-managed, in which the members are not the agents of the LLC and have the authority to make only major decisions, leaving the authority to exercise day-to-day management decisions to the managers. For the most part, bands that organize as an LLC should be member-managed.

LLCs provide limited liability (as do corporations) and the freedom to establish ownership and management relationships, as in partnerships, based on the contract of the members. LLCs may elect to be treated as partnerships for tax purposes. While there are still some issues concerning the application of partnership tax considerations to LLCs, the overriding trend among the state and federal taxing authorities supports that approach. These elements may cause LLCs to be increasingly preferred for performing and recording groups.

The members of the LLC are not individually liable for the obligations and liabilities of the organization. This also extends to the relationships among members. While general partners, in a partnership, have an obligation to contribute to the partnership and indemnify other partners for losses and obligations incurred in carrying on the business, no such individual obligations exist for members in an LLC. Generally, the LLC will be required to indemnify a member for obligations incurred by the members in carrying on the business of the LLC. But, if the LLC does not have sufficient assets to fully indemnify the member, the member may not look to the individual assets of other members for contribution, as may a partner in a general partnership.

Under most LLC statutes, members have the right to withdraw at any time and demand payment for their interest. This right to return an interest to a member of the LLC is similar to the rule that applies to partnerships. Some state statutes limit members' rights to withdraw or to demand that the LLC purchase their interests, unless the members have agreed otherwise. Consequently, like a partnership (or like shareholder agreements with a corporation), the operating agreement among the members of the LLC should specify the conditions under which the LLC is obligated to purchase the interests of a leaving member. The disassociation from the LLC by a member, due to death, bankruptcy, dissolution, or some other event will cause the dissolution of the LLC unless the remaining members consent to continue the business. Structuring the operating agreement so that an LLC does not dissolve upon the disassociation by a member is especially helpful when the organization holds title to property, like copyrights, or rights to income, like advances and royalty payments under a recording agreement, which might be adversely affected by the dissolution and reformation of the business that technically accompanies the withdrawal of a member.

The need to get professional counsel when you begin your own business cannot be stressed too strongly. Your lawyer or accountant will help you determine which form will be best for your situation and, thereafter, will monitor the operation of your business to decide whether you should switch to another form as your needs change.

LEGAL OBLIGATIONS OF EMPLOYERS AND BUSINESS

As an individual involved in the music business, you may find it necessary to hire others to work for you. If you hire employees, you must satisfy certain obligations imposed on employers by state and federal laws. This section briefly identifies those obligations and others of which you should be aware. If you start your own business and hire employees, consult with an attorney or accountant, or at least with the appropriate government officials to make certain that the federal and state laws regarding wages, benefits, hours, compensation, insurance, taxes, licenses, and other matters are satisfied.

Employers' Tax Obligations

Becoming an employer imposes a host of form-filing obligations. One of the first things an employer must do is obtain an employer identification number from the Internal Revenue Service. This number must be shown on all federal tax returns, statements, and other documents. Application for this number is made on form SS-4, which may be obtained from and filed with your local IRS office.

Generally, employers must withhold federal income and social security taxes as well as state income taxes and other state taxes from the wages they pay to their employees. Contact your nearest IRS office and the local office of your state taxing bureau to obtain the necessary information on the procedures for withholding such taxes.

The employer must have all employees complete the employee withholding allowance certificate (form W-4). If the employee had no federal income tax liability for the preceding year and anticipates no liability for the current year, the employee withholding exemption certificate form W-4E should be completed. These forms should be returned to your local IRS office. Based on the information contained in the W-4 forms and in tax tables (which should be included in the information you receive from the federal and state taxing authorities) you will be able to determine the amount of income and social security taxes to be withheld from each wage payment and the amount of the employer's matching contributions for social security taxes.

The withheld income and social security taxes are deposited along with federal tax deposit form 8109 at an authorized commercial bank depository or the Federal Reserve bank in your area. The deposits are required on a monthly, semimonthly, or quarterly basis, depending on the amount of the tax involved. Form 941, which describes the amounts withheld, must be filed on a quarterly basis.

The employer must furnish to each employee two copies of the annual wage and tax statement form W-2 for the calendar year no later than January 31 following the end of the calendar tax year, including a federal copy, state copy, city copy (for certain jurisdictions that impose a city income tax, like New York and California), and employee record copy. If the service of the employee is terminated before the end of the year, the W-2 form must be submitted to the employee not later than 30 days after the last payment of wages to that employee. This W-2 form is an informational one for the purpose of advising the employee how much tax money was withheld and it may be combined with state and city withholding statements. It must be used by the employee in filing annual income tax returns.

It is important to remember that if you are the person responsible for withholding taxes on behalf of employees (yourself or others), you may become personally liable for a 100% penalty on the amount that should have been withheld if you fail to comply with these obligations.

Note also that the employer may be subject to federal and state unemployment taxes and to withholding on state disability insurance taxes. You should consult your accountant or the local office of the IRS, the state unemployment compensation bureau, and the state disability insurance office to find out the details on unemployment taxes and disability insurance. Generally, the procedures for withholding money for these programs are similar to those for withholding federal and state income taxes and social security taxes.

If you hire independent contractors that will be responsible for making their own tax payments, it should be clear that they are operating their own businesses, have been retained by you to perform services, are not under your control or direction, and will be performing the same or similar services for others. Also, you should file a 1099 form with the IRS by February 28th of each year identifying the independent contractors and the amounts paid for the services. Examples of independent contractors include; someone to set up and engineer the sound for a showcase concert; a producer to oversee and produce a recording of the masters for your albums; an arranger to arrange your original compositions for your album. The IRS is particularly interested in independent contractors you retain, that perhaps should have been treated as employees, so be sure to review with your accountant the current rules and regulations that distinguish employees from independent contractors.

Other Employer Obligations

Most employers are subject to state workers' compensation laws. These laws impose liability on the employer for industrial accidents sustained by employees regardless of the employer's negligence. They provide a schedule of benefits to be paid to the employees for injuries or to their heirs if the employees are killed in an accident. It is important that you obtain sufficient workers' compensation liability insurance from an authorized insurer or a certificate of consent from your state's director of industrial relations if you are going to self-insure. Generally, insurance coverage can be obtained through the local office of your state's compensation insurance fund or through a private licensed workers' compensation carrier.

Both state and federal laws impose minimum obligations on the employer concerning wages, hours, and working conditions. You can obtain detailed information by contacting the Department of Labor, Department of Industrial Welfare or Department of Industrial Relations in your state as well as the U.S. Department of Labor. Both state and federal laws impose obligations on the employer to refrain from discrimination in hiring and in the conditions of employment. You must be careful to comply with these laws.

GENERAL BUSINESS OBLIGATIONS

As a business, you have certain additional obligations. We will not go into detail here, but will simply identify problem areas with the advice that you become aware of them either by consulting with your local, state, and federal authorities or with an attorney.

If you engage in retail sales to consumers, you must comply with state sales and use taxes. Generally, this tax is imposed on the consumer but the seller is obligated to collect the tax. On the seller's failure to collect, he or she will be obligated to pay the sums to the state that should have been collected from the consumer. Also, as a seller of retail goods, you must obtain a seller's permit from the local office of your state taxing authority. If you sell your product to a distributor who will in turn sell to retailers or if you sell directly to a retailer, then you need to obtain a resale tax exemption certificate from the state.

Note that businesses in most states must pay personal property tax on certain items of personal property that the business owns or possesses at a certain time in each calendar year. You must file a property statement with the county assessor within the period of time required by state law. You should check with your accountant or state's business property tax department to obtain the necessary information to enable you to comply with the state's laws on such taxes.

It is advisable to obtain casualty and public liability insurance and you should consult with local insurance agents to give you advice on this matter.

Many trades, occupations, and businesses are required to obtain state and sometimes local business licenses. Again, consult with your local and state authorities to determine what your obligations are.

It should be clear from the items discussed here that starting a business involves numerous filings and much record keeping. These requirements are unquestionably a burden, particularly for a small business. While it may be possible to ignore them and "fly below radar" for awhile, the odds are against doing it for long. The more successful the enterprise, the sooner it will become visible.

The recommended approach is to comply from the outset. If the requirements seem confusing or you do not have sufficient business experience to feel confident that you have undertaken all the proper steps, have an accountant, businessperson or lawyer look over what you have done and advise you. Once your bookkeeping and reporting systems are established, they are not difficult to maintain.

How to Set Up a Money Deal

BY EDWARD (NED) R. HEARN

This chapter explores some of the forms of financing that are available and shows how to analyze and structure a financial package to obtain the money for your project. The examples used will draw on the music industry, but the concepts and ways of structuring deals apply whether you are a musician, writer, actor, or, for that matter, if you want to establish your own instrument manufacturing company.

DEVELOPING THE BUSINESS PLAN

A business plan tells potential investors who you are. It describes your professional goals, what you plan to do to achieve those goals, and how that achievement can generate income to pay back the investor and further finance your career. An outline of the general headings of a business plan is at the end of this article.

Identifying Your Goals

The first and most important thing to be done is to identify the reasons you need to raise money. To establish a clear focus, you must determine your career goals, your immediate project goals, and your strengths and weaknesses. Identifying your goals, such as securing a recording contract or getting a name artist to record your songs, will assist you in determining a feasible project to undertake to achieve that end. The project might be producing an independent record so you can market it and demonstrate that there is an audience for your product or it could be preparing a publishing demo to shop your songs.

You need to analyze your strengths and weaknesses. What is your best selling point? Pinpointing your strongest talents will assist in determining the project that would be most appropriate to achieve your goals. If your best skill is songwriting, perhaps you should raise funds to do a publishing demo of some of your songs to send to publishers and to performers that record material written by others. If your best talent is performance skill, perhaps you should develop a video package that will show the style you use to slay your audience. Money can be raised for other projects as well, such as producing a master sound recording, backing a tour for promotional or showcase purposes, buying equipment to enhance your stage show, or hiring a publicist to orchestrate a media blitz before you storm into Los Angeles.

Reaching a final decision on your goals and the projects designed to achieve them is a precondition to figuring out how much money you must raise and what kind of information to include in the business plan you will present to prospective investors.

Preparing the Budget

Once you have decided on the project, your next step is to determine its costs. You must develop a budget that shows the amount of money you need and how it will be spent. To do this, you must research the cost of each of the various elements of your project. If you plan to produce your own recording, you must budget the cost of studio time, tape, musicians, arrangers, producer and engineer, mixing, mastering, manufacturing, cover art, design, packaging, distribution, advertising and marketing. Each project has its own cost items. It is your responsibility to develop a clear and accurate picture of what those costs will be. The section in this chapter entitled, Identifying and Evaluating Sources of Income, discusses analyzing future sources of income to be used in scheduling payback arrangements with investors.

Preparing the Proposal

Once you have established your goals, the project, and the amount of money you will need, you must reduce all that information to a proposal or business plan to submit to individuals that may have an interest in funding your project. The proposal should itemize the elements we have just explored, explain what the end product will be, how your business operates, how marketing the product or implementing the service will assist you in developing your career, and how money will be earned to repay the investors. The proposal should also contain information on your background and the current status of your career, and a clear statement of your goals. There is no better way to force yourself to develop a clear focus than having to articulate it to others, especially if you are asking them for money.

RAISING CAPITAL

Your project, most likely, will be financed by one of three methods: self-financing, borrowing or profit sharing. This section will discuss these methods and the advantages and drawbacks inherent in each.

Self-Financing

The best way to retain full control of your project is to use your own money. It is the only technique that allows you to be free of financial obligations to lenders and gives you maximum artistic and financial control. Although it means that you must bear all the risk of the project, it also means that you will enjoy all the benefits.

Self-financing also minimizes the paperwork, record keeping, and other business complications involved in other ways of raising money.

Borrowing

If you are not in a position to self-finance, borrowing is the second basic technique for raising funds. Borrowing means accepting a loan for a fixed sum and agreeing to repay that sum plus a specified percentage of interest by a certain time. Arrangements where the return to the lender depends on the success of the project will be discussed under the section on investments and profit sharing.

Loans are, usually, absolute obligations that must be repaid whether or not the project is successful. If the rate of interest is high, you will have to earn a substantial amount of money from the project before you make any profit. For example, on a loan of $10,000 at 18% annual simple interest payable in two years, your interest obligation would be more than $3,600. To pay back the principal and interest on a self-produced recording that sells for $7.25 (average wholesale price), you would have to sell about 1,875 recordings, plus an additional number to cover your cost of sales. Only then would you be able to sell for a profit. As costs climb, of course, the number of recordings you must sell to break even also rises.

Loan Sources

There are several possible sources of loans. The first are commercial sources. They include banks, finance companies, savings and loan associations, and credit cards with cash advance provisions.

Interest on commercial loans, secured by such collateral as a home, auto, recording or performing equipment or even the cosignature of a person in whom the bank has confidence will usually be lower than interest on unsecured loans. The reason is obvious: the risk is lower. Loans backed with collateral or the cosignature of a creditworthy individual are also easier to secure.

In deciding whether or not to give you a personal loan, a bank will look at your credit rating and at whether you own property that can be used as collateral for the loan. Unfortunately, musicians' credit ratings are not always good, because of the fluctuating conditions of their employment. But if you have a credit card or two and have lived in the same place for a couple of years without having trouble paying the rent, you may be able to convince a bank to loan you a modest amount of money (e.g., $5,000). Some banks will loan more than this amount if the borrower's credit rating is good. Banks may want to see your income tax returns for the last couple of years.

Some banks refuse to make a personal loan of more than $5,000 unless it is secured by collateral, such as a house in which you have equity. If you are looking for a loan to buy new keyboard equipment, you will find that banks generally will not consider securing the equipment itself as collateral. Some banks will let you use an automobile as collateral, however, provided you have title to it.

In the event you do not qualify for a personal loan yourself, you can ask a relative or a friend to act as a cosigner, which means they promise to make the payments if you are unable to. The bank will be more concerned with their credit rating than with yours, but will still want to make sure that you actually have the ability to make the payments.

In addition to personal loans, banks regularly make commercial loans to businesses. You may feel that since music is your business, you belong in this category, but you will find that commercial loans have their own rules and regulations. If you have a solidly established band with ongoing income, a commercial loan might be your best option. But if what you have in mind is borrowing money to start a project, you will probably have to go with a personal loan. When you become more established, some banks, especially those with operating offices in Los Angeles or New York, may lend money secured by the copyrights in your songs, master recordings, and other intellectual property.

A commercial loan package usually contains your business plan, the profit and loss statements of your business, tax returns for the last two or three years, and a personal financial statement. Banks will check your credit history. They need to know you have a sound financial plan and that you are financially responsible. They will generally insist that you put up as much as 50% of the money for improving the business out of your own pocket, with the loan supplying the balance.

Since commercial lenders make money lending money, you should shop for the best deal. This should also apply to loans from individuals that lend money to you for your project as a business venture, even if they are personal friends.

A second source for loans is family and friends. Usually, they will lend money at a rate lower than that of a commercial lender. The important thing to consider when borrowing from friends is that strong pressure for timely repayment may result, which often is more burdensome (because of the personal nature of the debt) than the legal obligation to repay.

When you borrow from friends, the usury laws of most states come into play. These statutes limit the amount of interest a private lender can charge a borrower. Banks and other commercial lenders are generally exempt from the usury limits and can charge higher rates.

Whether you borrow from friends or from commercial lenders, you will want to structure a written repayment plan that states the amount of money that was borrowed, the rate of interest, and the method of repayment.

This can be a simple written promissory note: "On or before June 15, 2003, John Debtor promises to pay Sally Lender the sum of $2,500 plus 9% interest per annum from January 1, 2000, (signed) John Debtor."

The note from a commercial lender is more complex, but it will contain similar elements. Sometimes commercial loans are structured so that you pay a smaller monthly amount the first two years and a larger one the next two to three years. Once again, you should shop for the most favorable terms, interest and monthly pay back amounts.

INVESTMENTS/PROFIT SHARING

If self-financing is not an option and you have not been able to obtain a loan, the third option is to find candidates to fund your project, such as investors, and offer them a profit share. The arrangement can take several forms, depending on whether the investor is "active" or "passive." The different alternatives are discussed below.

Active Investors

Active investors are individuals that put up money to finance a project for another person and become involved in the project (or fail to take adequate action to insulate themselves from responsibility). They assume all of the risks of the business, including financial liability for all losses, even if the losses go beyond the amount invested. Generally, such persons are responsible for the obligations of the business even if they have not given their approval or have not been involved in incurring business debts.

The forms of businesses in which the financing participants are active include general partnerships, joint ventures, corporations and limited liability companies. The profits or losses of such businesses are shared among the participants according to the nature of their agreement. These business structures are discussed more fully in the chapter, Business Entities.

A general partnership is co-ownership of an ongoing enterprise in which the partners share both control and profits. A joint venture is a general partnership that either has a very short term or a limited purpose. For example, the production of a single recording by a group of people could be structured as a joint venture.

The general partners and the joint venturers are each personally liable for all the debts of the enterprise. The liability is not limited to the amount that they invested or to the debts that were incurred with their approval. All of the personal assets of each of the general partners or joint venturers are liable for repayment of the debts incurred by the enterprise.

If a corporation or a limited liability company is formed, then even if the project is a total failure, only the assets of the corporation or the limited liability company are vulnerable to the business creditors. A corporation is a separate entity formed under state laws. This also is the case for a limited liability company. The ownership of a corporation is divided among its shareholders, and the ownership of a limited liability company is divided among its members. A corporate structure provides limited liability to the shareholders. This also is the case for a limited liability company. If you are thinking about setting up a corporation or a limited liability company, you will need some sound legal advice.

Passive Investors

A more complex category of investments is that in which backers provide money for the project but take no role in the management and affairs of the project. Such backers are passive investors whose return is based on the success of the project.

The primary advantage of profit sharing arrangements, from the point of view of the person getting the money, is that the downside risks are shared. If a project fails to recoup the money invested, you are not obligated to repay the investors. Offsetting this advantage are several problems that make profit sharing the most complicated form of financing a project.

The foremost problem is security law requirements. Any time one enters into an agreement in which people give money for a project with the understanding that part of the profits are to be shared with them and the investors do not actively participate in the management of the funds or the operation of the business, a "security" has been sold. A security can be a promissory note, stock, points or any other form of participation in a profit sharing arrangement, either written or oral, where the investor's role in the business is passive. The investments of a general partner or joint venturer may be treated as a security, but they are a different class of security because those investors are actively involved in the business. The level of protection required for active investors is less stringent than for passive investors. Active investors are liable for the debts of the business beyond just the amount of their investment, while passive investors are only responsible for the debts of a business up to the amount of their investment.

Limited partnerships, promissory notes structured with profit sharing, corporate stock, limited liability company membership and contracts providing for points participation, where the persons that put up the money are not active in your business, are all securities, and state and federal securities statutes must be satisfied when these types of funding are used. Failure to comply may have serious civil and, in extreme circumstances, in situations involving fraud, even criminal consequences.

What does this legal talk mean to you? Why should you have to worry about it if all you want to do is raise some money to record some music or finance a performance tour? The securities laws were enacted to protect investors from being harmed by the fraud of others or by their own lack of sophistication or even their inability to afford to lose the money they invest in the project. The legal burden falls on the one seeking to raise the money to make certain the investors are getting a fair deal and fully understand the risks involved. "Let the seller beware," is the rule that operates.

If you want people to invest money without allowing them a hand in controlling the project, then you should be willing to accept some responsibility to them. Willing or not, state and federal statutes place responsibility on you.

Investment Loans Conditional on the Success of the Venture

In these types of loans, the debt is evidenced by a promissory note and repayment is conditional on the success of the funded project. The note should set out the terms of repayment, including interest rates and payment schedules.

A common form of this kind of loan is a "point" arrangement in which a percentage (points) of sales from the funded project are shared with an investor who puts in only time or with some other investor who puts in only money. Another form is a percent interest in the income (or losses) generated by the business. This arrangement can be provided in a written contract rather than in the form of a conditional promissory note.

Limited Partnerships

Like a general partnership, a limited partnership has co-ownership and shared profits, but only some of the participants are entitled to control or manage the enterprise. Those persons are termed the general partners. The other investors are called limited partners and their only involvement is the passive one of putting funds into the project.

A partner receives that percentage of the business profits or losses set out in the agreement between the partners, for example, 20% of the net profits up to $10,000 and 10% of the net profits after the first $10,000. The term of the limited partnership is often limited to a specified period. If the project has not earned the hoped for return by the end of the term, the investor has to absorb the loss.

There are rules in the federal law and in several states that apply to limited partnerships and other security investments that are structured as private offerings (i.e., to only a small number of people), which are easier to qualify under than the laws regarding public offerings (i.e., to the general public).

Corporate Shares and Limited Liability Company Memberships

Another way to raise investment capital is through the sale of shares in a corporation or memberships in a limited liability company. Corporate shares and limited liability company memberships are securities that usually are sold for a stated number of dollars per share or membership. That money is used to operate the business or pay for a specific project. Shareholders or members own whatever percentage of the corporation or limited liability company their shares represent in relation to the total number of shares sold.

Shareholders or members participate in the profits of the corporation or limited liability company when they are distributed as dividends and vote on shareholder or member issues according to their percentage of ownership.

Whatever method of financing you use, it is wise to check with your lawyer and set up a good financial record keeping system with your bookkeeper.

COMPLYING WITH LEGAL STATUTES

After deciding on the legal structure to use in raising the money for your project, you must make certain that your efforts comply with state and federal law. California statutes require that (unless an exemption applies), the party raising and accepting investment capital must file documents with the Commissioner of Corporations explaining, in part, the proposed investment project, how the money will be used, all of the risks in the venture, the financial ability of the investors, and the background of the persons seeking the funding. The commissioner must conclude that the proposed offer and sale is "fair, just and equitable." On an affirmative finding, the commissioner will issue a permit authorizing the sale. A negative conclusion will bar the sale. Most states have statutes imposing similar requirements.

Fundamental in any offering of a security (whether public or nonpublic), is the disclosure, to potential investors, of all the risks involved in the project, including the risk that the project may fail, that no profit may be made, and that the investors may never have their investment returned. In seeking investment money, you must disclose, in writing, the risks, the background of the principals (the people starting and running the business), the nature of the proposed business, the manner in which the money will be used, and the way that the investor will share in any profits (or losses). Also, the offer and sale of securities that involves an interstate transaction may require registration of those securities with the Securities and Exchange Commission (SEC) in Washington, D.C. Knowledgeable legal counsel should be obtained before seeking to offer any securities.

State Law Exemptions

Under the securities statutes and regulations of most states, there are certain exemptions from the requirement to obtain a permit. These exemptions occur only in very specific situations. Three common exemptions are the nonpublic partnership interest, the limited number of shareholder exemptions for corporations, and the nonpublic debt security (note for a loan). In California, a limited partnership interest or other security will be presumed to be a nonpublic offering not requiring a permit from the commissioner provided that (1) there is no advertising of the investment; (2) there are no more than 35 investors contributing to the project; (3) the investor represents that he or she is purchasing the interest for his or her own account and not with the intent to distribute the interest to others; and (4) either the persons investing the money have a preexisting business or personal relationship with you, or their professional financial advisor can reasonably be presumed to have the ability to protect their interests because of the advisor's business experience. Also, a notice detailing information about the investment must be filed with the Commissioner's Office, which office establishes the kind of information that must be presented.

If the financing arrangement is to be in the form of a debt that is secured by a note with payment to the investor to come from the proceeds, if any, of the venture, then the requirements just described must be met to qualify the arrangement as an exempt nonpublic debt offering under California law. However, the investments may not be taken from more than 10 persons. This description is overly simplified and is not intended to be a full explanation of all the nuances and requirements of the security statutes and regulations. Its purpose is merely to give you a sense of how the laws operate.

IDENTIFYING AND EVALUATING SOURCES OF INCOME

If you lack your own money for your project, and do not have the credit necessary to borrow money, then you must face the reality of raising investment capital and complying with the appropriate securities statutes discussed above. Probably the most frustrating aspect of this will be your quest to identify the angel who will give you the money you need. Frequently, investors are attracted by the idea of putting money into entertainment projects because of the mistaken impression that it is a glamorous business and they desire to be associated with the glamour, or they have read that the entertainment industry can generate a substantial amount of money and wish to gamble that they will earn a great return if your project is successful.

For the most part, the money usually comes from family, friends, or interested persons that have seen your talents and wish to be involved in developing your potential. If the money does come from family and friends, however, it is critical that you act in a businesslike manner to help preserve your personal relationships.

Unfortunately, there is no magic source of money. It will be up to you to identify who has enough faith in your talents and future to make their money available. Other possible sources of money are investment counselors and accountants that are searching for reasonable business opportunities for their clients. In reviewing proposals for investments, financial advisors analyze the possibilities of eventual return on the investment and the tax benefits, if any, that may be made available to the investors.

Educating Investors About Risk

Once you have identified individuals that are willing to put money into your project, it is very important that you examine their expectations and compare them with your own perspective. It is crucial for you to educate your investors about the risks, the rewards, and all the problems and variables that can arise over which you may have little or no control. Investors need to know how much money is required for your project in order to evaluate whether they can afford it. If they have any reservations, you should uncover them. If the reservations cannot be resolved, you should not accept money from them. Spend time talking with them and make certain that you really understand each other and that they are people to whom you want to be committed.

Fair Return/Profit Sharing

In discussing payback, essentially as profit sharing, with the investor, you need to identify and explore three specific areas. What will be the share of the investor's participation? For how long will the investor participate? And from what sources of income will the investor be repaid? The argument that the investor can make, and it is a good one, is that he or she is taking a substantial risk in putting money into your project that could be invested in other ways for a more certain return. As a consequence, the investor will insist on a very healthy return. This is not unreasonable, provided it leaves you with enough to continue your life and career.

Measuring a fair return or profit sharing with the investor is a function of how badly you need the money and how eager the investor is to put money into your project. This will frequently determine how much each side is willing to offer. Investors generally have alternative places to put their money for a good return, and if you have no other source of income for a project, you may not be in a position to do a lot of arguing. If you have to give up an amount that you feel will hurt your business or your ability to fund your career, then you should not accept the money; go look for another investor.

A more constructive way of measuring a reasonable return is to look at the amount of risk assumed by the investor in relation to the amount of money invested; the smaller the number of dollars and the smaller the risk of failure, the smaller the return. For example, if your project cost $2,000 it would be hard to justify returning 10% of your income for life to an investor. A more fair return would be the return of the money plus an additional percentage, e.g., 50%. If however, the investor put $200,000 into your project, it is easy to justify committing a reasonable percentage of your income (e.g., 10% to 15%) to the investor (after out-of-pocket deductions for payments to certain third parties, such as managers and business creditors) for a substantial period of time (e.g., five years to seven years) or until a return of a multiple of the amount of the investment (e.g., two to four times), whichever happens first, at which time the participation stops. If the investment is for a specific project, e.g., a full CD of your recorded musical performances, first dollars in could be used to reimburse the investor, with additional money being split evenly until the investor has gotten two to three times the investment, and thereafter a reduced percentage, e.g., 20% to 25%, to the investor for so long as that recorded project is generating income, without any restrictions in time.

You can determine the proper percentage to offer to an investor by looking at how much you can afford to give up. Remember, there are only so many slices in the money pie, and if you give up too many slices there will be little for you to eat. Consequently, you should identify all of your existing commitments, such as those to managers, attorneys, other investors, partners, and the like. After you pay those people, you will still need money to run your business and support your personal needs. You must carefully analyze your income potential and anticipated expenses.

It is important to specify the sources of income from which the investor will be repaid. Will the money be coming from the revenue generated by the project itself or will it be coming from other sources such as record sales, live performances, music publishing, or merchandising? These points must be clearly and carefully thought out before you commit to a participation with an investor.

CONCLUSION

There are no simple answers. Deals can be structured in many ways. Your decisions depend on a business analysis of your funding sources, the urgency of your needs, the risks the investors are taking, their alternative investment possibilities, and your other money commitments. Do your homework and be very careful about the commitments you make. When in doubt, seek advice. If the deal does not make sense or does not feel good to you, trust your instincts and walk away. Do not be pressured into a commitment that may later hinder your career. In any event, be honest with yourself; figure out your goals, your value system and what you are willing and not willing to give up. Only by taking all these factors into account can you arrive at a financial package that will work for you. Once you set up such a package, however, you may be able to accomplish career objectives otherwise beyond your reach.

BUSINESS PLAN OUTLINE

Here are the topics usually covered in business plans. Even if you are not using a business plan to find financing for your project, it will help identify your goals, outline the strengths and weaknesses of your project, and help determine when your project will make a profit. In short, a business plan is the map that shows how to get from an idea stage to project completion and profit.

When you want to obtain investment money, the business plan is a vital sales tool that can impress prospective investors with your planning ability and general competence as a manager.

1. Summary of your project, including the money you need to successfully launch it and reach your market.
2. Company description (history, background and management).
3. Description of your background.
4. Description of industry you are operating in.
5. Project description and planning schedule.
6. Description of the market for your project.
   A. Market size
   B. Market trends
   C. Competition
7. Marketing plan.
   A. Estimated sales and market share
   B. Strategy
   C. Pricing
   D. Sales and distribution
   E. Publicity and advertising
8. Operations (If project is a product [i.e., a compact disc or new software], describe how it will be produced, manufactured, marketed and distributed).
9. Project timeline.
10. Critical risks and problems.
11. Financial information.
    A. Financing required
    B. Current financial statements
    C. Financial projection (three-year profit and loss, cash flow and balance sheet projections).

Music Attorneys

BY MARK HALLORAN

Musicians face myriad legal problems throughout their careers. Only a competent attorney, knowledgeable of the music business, can help a musician effectively solve these problems. The following will discuss music attorneys—who they are, what they do, what they cost, and what their obligations are to you.

An attorney (lawyer) is a professional with legal training who is licensed to practice law in a particular state or states. Typically, an attorney must be a college and law school graduate. Full-time law schools have broad-based curriculums that last three years—there are no "majors" in law school. After graduation, the student must pass a state's bar exam. The bar is a state sponsored monopoly—only attorneys can practice law. The traditional professional activities of lawyers fall into roughly four categories: consulting with clients; drafting and negotiating legal documents; representing clients before the courts; and insuring compliance, by clients, with local, state and national laws and contracts (such as union agreements), which govern the client's business activities. For musicians, the most important of these four functions is the lawyer's drafting and negotiating legal agreements.

SPECIALIZATION

Most attorneys specialize. The primary reason for specialization is the complexity of the problems that confront the professional and the sophistication and training necessary to apply the correct problem-solving tools. The law is far too complex and fast changing for a lawyer to have adequate competence in all areas. Specialists can do a better job for their clients because of their acquired experience in particular areas.

Due to the growth and complexity of the entertainment field, a legal specialty, called entertainment law, has arisen. Music lawyers are entertainment lawyers that specialize in the legal and business aspects of the music business.

A recent trend is the certification of lawyers that practice a specialty. In California, for example, there are five certified specialties: criminal law, workers' compensation, taxation, patent law, and family law. Entertainment law is not one of the certified specialties. Thus, at this time, there are no state certified music lawyers in California (or elsewhere). This does not mean lawyers cannot specialize in representing music industry clients. They can and do. What distinguishes a music attorney, then, is not certification, but that he or she has experience in solving the problems musicians encounter. It is not necessary for an attorney to specialize exclusively in music to have enough expertise to help you. In fact, only a handful of lawyers (mostly in Los Angeles, New York and Nashville) are exclusively music attorneys.

MUSIC ATTORNEY FUNCTIONS

Recording and publishing agreements can be incredibly complex, and proper negotiating and drafting require superior legal skills and a thorough knowledge of music business practice. This is especially true since recording and publishing agreements can last for many years, and the typical artist's career, at least at the top, is short.

In addition to negotiating and drafting a wide variety of agreements for songwriters, recording artists, record companies, music publishers, record producers, personal managers and music investors, some music attorneys solicit deals for their clients by "shopping" (distributing) demo tapes. Over time they develop relationships with people and companies in the industry, and their recommendation of a music client is sometimes influential in obtaining a contract. Most music attorneys, however, do not find deals for their clients. That task is left to the musicians and their managers. The attorney's foremost functions are structuring, negotiating and documenting deals to maximize benefits to their client.

Another important function of the music attorney is to act as a business hub, coordinating the activities of your agent, personal manager and business manager. Because music attorneys deal with these representatives, they develop a working knowledge of their functions in the music industry and help to insure that they act in your best interests.

Music attorneys are sometimes empowered to be attorneys-in-fact for their clients with respect to collecting money. In this regard, they collect and receive all monies due you or your companies from all sources, based on your agreements with them. They deposit, into a client trust account, all checks and monies payable to you and your companies and deduct any fees for attorney compensation before remitting the remainder.

A music attorney may also provide general career advice, such as you would expect from a personal manager. This can be crucial in the early stages of your career, as it is often difficult to attract competent, experienced personal managers until you are signed to a major label. Some music attorneys also act officially as managers, although this is unusual.

FINDING A MUSIC ATTORNEY

Music attorneys may work alone (sole practitioners), or as part of a law firm. Entertainment divisions of large firms are often divided into two departments: TV/film and music. Generally, the more experienced lawyers (often partners, which are owners of the firm), negotiate the big deals, while the nonpartners (associates) negotiate the small ones. Associates also usually do the lion's share of drafting agreements.

In recent years, the large firms have lost many of their clients to smaller "boutique" entertainment law firms, which typically have 10 to 20 lawyers. Many boutique entertainment firms charge either a flat amount or 5% of the dollar value of the deal negotiated, rather than bill on an hourly basis. Although percentage arrangements may be advantageous when you are unable to afford hourly rates, you may end up paying more than the hourly rate. Remember that your income is also diminished by your personal manager (10% to 25%), agent (10%) and your business manager (5%), and then by federal and state taxes.

Few music lawyers will take clients "on the come" (work free until the client is successful). Attorneys must cover their overhead and the music industry is overcrowded and fiercely competitive. The odds are a music lawyer will never collect delayed fees from an aspiring client.

You should interview a number of lawyers before retaining one. It is important to retain an attorney who specializes in entertainment law and knows how the industry works. A working knowledge of the standard (and nonstandard) contracts is mandatory—attorneys that do not have this knowledge will spend a lot of your money researching or buying time from another entertainment attorney, or even steering you wrong. Do not be afraid to interview a lawyer, but be sure to make your intention clear when making the appointment, and confirm you will not be charged for the time. Be prepared to ask pointed (but not confrontational) questions about the lawyer's music business experience. Do not try to use the interview as a ruse for getting free legal help—that is not fair and will put off the attorney. Talk to successful musicians and managers that can recommend lawyers. The fact that you know someone who has an ongoing relationship with the attorney should help you get in the door.

There are various ways to find a music attorney. Some well-known practitioners, such as John Branca (Aerosmith), Don Passman (Janet Jackson), Lee Phillips (Barbra Streisand) and Alan Grubman (Madonna), command coverage in the music industry press—but they are inundated by potential clients.

Another way to meet music lawyers is to attend music conferences. Prominent music attorneys are often invited to appear at music symposia, and some business relationships are started as a result of meetings at such functions. However, it may not be advisable to retain an attorney who is far beyond your status in the industry, because high-powered music lawyers will first serve their successful clients—if it's your telephone call or Michael Jackson's, their choice is clear!

Lawyer Referral Services

Many lawyer referral services have been established that will discuss problems and refer the caller to an attorney on the service's referral panel. This attorney will interview the referred client for a moderate fee. After the first interview, fee arrangements and the legal services to be rendered are left up to the lawyer and client. Sometimes, fees are split between the referral panel and the lawyer. In California the best-known referral service is California Lawyers for the Arts (CLA). This nonprofit organization, based in San Francisco, is devoted exclusively to the arts. CLA has been authorized by the California State Bar Association to refer clients statewide.

In Los Angeles, you can call the Lawyer Referral Service of the Los Angeles County Bar Association for recommendations. The Beverly Hills Bar Association Committee for the Arts Lawyer Referral and Information Service offers lawyer referrals to those with entertainment-related legal problems. These referral panels only provide you with the name of an attorney, registered with them, who claims to have some experience in your area of concern. The panels do not rate lawyers or guarantee that the attorney will have the skills and experience you need. It should also be noted that the "heavyweights," usually, are not on these panels.

If you live outside California, check with your state or local bar association for lawyer referral services.

WHEN TO SEE A MUSIC ATTORNEY

The cardinal rule is—see a lawyer before you sign anything except autographs. In essence, when you sign a contract, you are setting up law with the other party that will govern your relationship. Even though in some instances a lawyer may not be able to negotiate more favorable contract terms for you, at the very least he or she can explain the agreement so you know what you are getting into. Most likely, however, your lawyer can help by negotiating terms more favorable to you. These terms might include higher advances and royalty rates in recording contracts, partial ownership of your copyright and a participation in the publisher's share of revenue in publishing contracts, and perhaps a way to get you released from a contract if it does not work out. You should consult with an attorney when establishing contracts with your other advisors, such as your talent agent, your business manager and especially your personal manager. Do not sign a contract and assume you can get out of it.

Be wary of people that give you form or standard contracts to sign, saying that "everybody accepts these terms." Although standard contracts exist, they are drafted by attorneys that are out to protect their clients' interests, not yours. Odds are that your attorney also has a standard contract—but it's much more favorable to you. The negotiating process consists of each side making specific demands and seeing if the other side will agree. If you retain a lawyer, the other side may give in to at least some of your demands. Together, the opposing lawyers can identify issues and potential problems. The result is a contract that is different from the form contract and more favorable to you.

First Meeting

Your first meeting with an attorney will probably be arranged over the phone. You should be prepared to talk about two things at that meeting: your specific legal needs and your fee arrangement with the attorney.

Fees

Lawyers cost money. Many lawyers cost a lot. Fees can exceed $400 an hour. Non-superstar music attorneys normally charge $150 to $300 per hour. The legal fee for negotiating an agreement with a major record company, even by a relatively low-priced attorney, will be $3,000 to $10,000.

Lawyers sell services. They must cover their overhead, which often exceeds 50% of the billing rate, and make a decent profit.

You should realize that in retaining a lawyer you are making a contract, even if your agreement is not written. In return for a fee, your lawyer promises to render legal services on your behalf and both parties should do their best to fulfill their obligations.

It is preferable for the fee agreement to be written. In California, if the bill will likely exceed $1,000, or is based on a percentage, the fee arrangement must be written.

Not all lawyers charge on a per hour basis. Some will charge a set fee, such as $5,000, to negotiate or draft a contract. Others will charge a percentage of the money you receive under contracts they negotiate. This fee generally runs 5% of the deal, although the percentages and structures of these types of arrangements vary greatly. You should check around to see if the fee arrangement proposed by the lawyer is competitive, although price (whether low or high) is not necessarily an accurate indication of the value or quality of the attorney's work. Cautious lawyers will remind you that you have the right to seek the advice of another lawyer as to the propriety of the fee arrangement. Many lawyers will represent you on a percentage basis for negotiating only a specific contract. Additional services, such as tax advice, formation of corporations, etc., will have separate and additional charges.

Lawyers generally ask reimbursement for their out-of-pocket costs, which may include long-distance telephone calls, photocopies, word processing, postage, messenger service, fax, etc. These expenses typically are not considered part of the hourly fee, which only covers the lawyer's services.

Fee Payment

The quickest way to sour your attorney-client relationship is to not pay your bill. Lawyers that bill on an hourly basis will render a monthly statement that sets out the services rendered, date of services, costs, and the total bill. If you cannot pay the bill, at least call to say so and arrange some payment schedule. Some music attorneys will accept partial payment and continue to work for you.

In the good old days lawyers rarely sued their clients for nonpayment. Now they are doing so with increasing regularity. In California, you have the right to a fee arbitration if the lawyer's claim exceeds $5,000 (the small claims court limit). The lawyer will send a notice to you, advising you of your right to arbitrate. You must respond within 30 days or lose your arbitration right.

Retainers

Many lawyers require a retainer (initial payment). Most retainers are credited against your bill, but make sure that is your agreement. Thus, if you retain an attorney with $2,500 it is usual for that $2,500 to be credited to your account. These funds are held "in trust" for you until your lawyer renders sufficient legal services to earn them. For example, in the first month your attorney negotiates a publishing contract and spends ten hours at $300 an hour doing it. You will get a bill showing $2,500 received and $3,000 for services rendered. Thus, you owe $500 at that point. Some attorneys require that you keep replenishing the retainer. In the foregoing example, you would be billed $3,000 so the retainer would be brought back up to $2,500. Keep a record of all legal bills so you can try to deduct them as business expenses. You should also keep copies of all documents and correspondence.

Conflicts of Interest

In return for the monopoly on practicing law, lawyers are constrained by very special ethical obligations. Like all agents, lawyers have a "fiduciary" obligation to their "principal"—you. The heart of this obligation is that they must act with your best interests as the goal in all situations.

As part of this obligation lawyers have an ethical duty to avoid so-called conflicts of interest. If you think your attorney may be representing conflicting interests you should seriously contemplate retaining a different lawyer. Closely scrutinize the conflict, especially in recording contract situations. The most prevalent conflict of interest occurs when a lawyer concurrently represents multiple clients with potentially adverse interests. For example, assume your attorney represents XYZ Records and XYZ Records wants to sign you to a recording contract. XYZ wants to give you as little as they can; you want as much as you can get. This is a conflict of interest, as your interest and XYZ's interest are opposed to one another, or "adverse."

Under the California Rules of Professional Conduct (3-310), if this type of conflict arises, the lawyer must disclose his or her relationship with the adverse party and obtain both clients' written consent to dual representation. A lawyer cannot represent both parties except with the written consent of all parties concerned. Lawyers violating this rule are subject to discipline by the state bar, as well as malpractice claims by clients whose interests are damaged by the lawyer with the conflict. Similar legal controls are in effect in other states.

A lawyer may represent multiple clients with adverse interests if (1) it is obvious that he or she can adequately represent the interests of each; and (2) each client consents to the representation after full disclosure of the possible effect of such representation on the exercise of the lawyer's independent professional judgment on behalf of each. The conflict of interest situation extends to all members of a law firm. Under the American Bar Association's Code of Professional Responsibility, a lawyer cannot avoid a conflict by referring you to someone else in the firm.

In our previous hypothetical situation, it may be that the attorney for XYZ Records can adequately represent you in your negotiations with XYZ. After discussing the conflict, he or she may present you with what is known as a "conflict" letter. This letter will say: (1) the lawyer informed you of the conflict; (2) it is suggested you seek independent counsel; (3) the agreement is fair to you; (4) you consent to your lawyer's representation of the other party; and (5) you will not claim in the future that your lawyer breached his or her fiduciary duty (trust) to you in regard to the conflict. This letter, at least in theory, protects the attorney from your future claim that you were not fairly represented. The ethical lawyer will act in accordance with the terms of the conflict letter, which you will be asked to sign. You should feel free to have another lawyer look at it.

TIPS FOR DEVELOPING A GOOD WORKING RELATIONSHIP WITH YOUR LAWYER

- Remember, your lawyer's time is money. If you are organized in your legal and business affairs, it makes your lawyer's job easier and less expensive for you.
- Keep accurate records and communicate in *writing*. People read faster than they talk and written communications provide records.
- Always be honest with your lawyer. They operate more efficiently on facts than on lies.
- Pay your bills on time.
- Keep your lawyer informed. An ounce of prevention is worth a pound of cure in music business legal affairs.
- Prepare for meetings with your lawyer. Bring all documents that might be useful, such as letters and your calendar.
- Do not sign anything until your lawyer has reviewed it.

If the conflict cannot be overcome, you have to get another lawyer. The lawyer with the conflict may suggest specific counsel, or, preferably, provide you with a list of competent lawyers and leave the choice to you. The fact you are referred to another lawyer does not mean the lawyer with the conflict cannot subsequently represent you. He or she just cannot represent you with regard to the conflict situation.

Confidentiality

Your lawyer is under a duty to keep your communications confidential. Frequently, negotiations are secret and it is in your best interest to keep them that way. News can get out, though, as when the trades note that a particular record company is negotiating with a specific act. Conceivably, this can help you if more than one company is interested in you. Your lawyer can play them one against the other. However, your lawyer needs your consent to leak information.

Changing Lawyers

Although many attorney-client relationships are long lasting, you may find that you want to change attorneys. If you do, you should inform your new attorney of your previous relationship. Your new lawyer cannot simultaneously represent you in a matter that is being handled by another lawyer.

The technical description used by the bar is that you "discharge" your lawyer. By law, a client has an absolute right to discharge an attorney at any time, regardless of the reason. This does not mean that you do not have to pay the discharged lawyer for the services already provided. As an initial step, your new lawyer will want to obtain your previous files. The fact you owe your old lawyer money is irrelevant as far as turning over the files is concerned. Your previous lawyer still has a duty to represent your best interests, which includes turning over the files and cooperating with your new lawyer.

You should note that your attorney can also sever this relationship (except in litigation where court permission is sometimes required), but must avoid prejudicing your rights by giving you notice and time to hire another lawyer. And all your papers and any unearned retainer must be delivered to you.

CONCLUSION

Developing an effective lawyer/musician relationship can be a valuable step in your career. Your decision in selecting an attorney is crucial—it should be an informed decision and should be done as early in your career as possible.

ATTORNEY/CLIENT FEE LETTER AGREEMENT
HOURLY ARRANGEMENT

Dear Client:

It is a pleasure to undertake your representation in connection with the above referenced matter.

We are writing this letter to set forth the basis under which our firm will represent you, your related entities and any other persons or entities that you request us to represent with respect to this matter.

Our fees on all matters will be based on the guidelines set forth in the Rules of Professional Conduct of the State Bar of California. Our hourly rates range between $80 and $350 per hour, depending on which attorney or paralegal performed the work. Fees for services will be charged on a minimum quarter-hourly basis and, when services are rendered outside our office, you will be charged on a portal-to-portal basis. We will be sending you itemized monthly statements, which will be due upon receipt and will include our costs advanced in connection with your representation. Such cost charges include, but are not limited to, messenger service, shipping, postage, copying expenses and telephone charges.

An initial retainer fee in the sum of $________ is due at the commencement of our representation. * The retainer will be applied to fees and costs as they are incurred. You will not receive any interest on the retainer, and upon completion of our work, any remaining balance will be either refunded to you or applied toward future legal services rendered by our firm on your behalf. At this time, the services contemplated will encompass representing you in connection with:

(Specific contract or project is outlined here.)

It is the policy of our firm to look to clients jointly and severally regarding any fees incurred either on their behalf or at their direction on behalf of any person, firm or entity for which our clients request we render services. This firm reserves the right to withdraw from this matter at any time should fees and costs not be paid as agreed. In the event it becomes necessary for this firm to take legal action for the collection of fees and costs due, the prevailing party in such action shall be entitled to collect attorneys' fees from the other party.

If the foregoing agrees with your understanding, please execute the enclosed copy of this letter and return it in the envelope provided, together with your check in the sum of $___________ as our retainer, as explained above.

If you have any questions concerning this agreement, please do not hesitate to contact me. Additionally, if at any time you have questions regarding anything relating to our services or fees charged, we encourage you to bring such matters to our attention so that we may discuss and resolve them at once.

We look forward to the opportunity of working with you on this matter.

Yours truly,

* *(Optional—We acknowledge receipt of the sum of $__________ and will proceed on your behalf at once.)*

PERCENTAGE FEE LETTER AGREEMENT

Dear Client:

This letter will confirm our agreement with you whereby we agree to render our services as your attorneys in connection with your professional career.

You engage us during the period of this agreement as your attorneys and will cause any companies connected with your professional career in which you have any controlling interest to engage us as their attorneys in connection with all legal matters pertaining to your professional career in the entertainment industry. The term of this agreement shall commence on the date hereof, and shall continue until terminated by either of us by written notice, which shall be personally delivered, sent by facsimile, or mailed by certified or registered mail, postage prepaid, to the respective address set forth on this page (or to such other address as either of us may notify the other of). No termination shall affect our right to be paid our percentage fee described below.

For our services to be rendered during the term of this agreement you and each of your companies (but not both regarding the same gross consideration) will pay us as and when received by you or such companies, respectively, beginning as of the date hereof, five percent (5%) of all gross consideration (including salaries, bonuses, percentages, commissions, royalties, profit shares, stock interests, and all other forms of compensation of any nature and from any source), prior to any withholding or deductions, earned, accrued, paid or payable (directly or indirectly) to you or your companies from and after the date hereof, for your services or the services of such companies in connection with any facet of your professional career in the entertainment industry rendered during the term hereof, or for such services rendered by you or such companies pursuant to any agreement (oral or written) (and any extensions, renewals, substitutions, or resumptions thereof) substantially negotiated or entered into during the term hereof (irrespective of when such services under such agreement were or are to be rendered), whether such gross consideration is received by you or your companies (or any third party on your or their behalf) during or after the term hereof.

Notwithstanding anything in the preceding paragraph to the contrary, the aforesaid percentage shall be ten percent (10%) (not five percent [5%]) with respect to gross consideration as defined above that is not subject to being commissioned by a licensed artist's manager (commonly referred to as an "agent"). Our additional compensation with respect to such uncommissioned gross consideration arises out of situations where no licensed artist's manager is involved, resulting in greater responsibility on our part in connection with the negotiations in connection therewith. There shall be no inference from this increase that we in any way agree to seek personal employment for you.

The services that we shall be expected to render in return for the above compensation shall include reviewing, drafting, modifying, negotiating and otherwise assisting you in connection with all agreements, contracts or other legal matters in connection with your professional career in the entertainment industry, and consulting with you and advising you regarding all other legal aspects of your professional career in the entertainment industry; but the services we shall be expected to render in return for the above compensation shall not include matters that involve litigation, arbitration or other contested proceedings, planning or the preparation of tax returns, preparation or administration of pension or profit sharing plans, or matters pertaining to your personal life or other businesses as opposed to your professional career.

You understand, of course, if we represent you in any such matter involving litigation, arbitration or other contested proceedings, the preparation or administration of profit sharing plans, or matters pertaining to your personal life or other businesses, as opposed to your professional career, we shall be paid an additional reasonable fee for such services, to be agreed upon between us, and costs reasonably incurred in connection therewith.

You are hereby authorizing us and empower us, and appoint us as your attorneys-in-fact and as attorneys-in-fact for your companies to collect and receive all monies due you or your companies from all sources relating to this agreement, to negotiate and endorse your (or your companies') name(s) upon and deposit into our clients' trust account all checks and other monies payable to you or your companies, to deduct therefrom our compensation as set forth above, together with any costs advanced by us and to remit the remainder to you or your companies as the case may be.

The terms "you" and "your," as used herein, shall refer to you or any firm, partnership, corporation or other entity owned or controlled by you.

If the foregoing meets with your approval, please sign and return the original and one copy of this letter; the other copy is for your files.

Inasmuch as this letter constitutes an agreement between us, we cannot, of course, advise you concerning it, and we suggest that you retain outside counsel to advise you concerning this agreement.

Yours truly,

ATTORNEY CONFLICT OF INTEREST WAIVER LETTER

Dear Attorney:

We understand that you have been representing and continue to represent each of us in connection with a variety of matters. We also understand that you have and may in the future represent one of us in matters involving the other and in which the other has been or will be represented by his own counsel.

We would like your firm to represent us in connection with the following matters:

(Description of project/contract, etc.)

In connection with the above, you have advised us of the following terms of the provisions of Section 3-310 of the California State Rules of Professional Conduct: *

"(A) If a member has or had a relationship with another party interested in the representation, or has an interest in its subject matter, the member shall not accept or continue such representation without all affected clients' informed written consent."

"(B) A member shall not concurrently represent clients whose interests conflict, except with their informed written consent."

You have also advised us of the following provisions of California Evidence Code Section 962 relating to the attorney-client privilege:

"Where two or more clients have retained or consulted a lawyer upon a matter of common interest, none of them, nor the successor in interest of any of them, may claim a privilege under this article as to a communication made in the course of that relationship when such communication is offered in a civil proceeding between one of such clients (or his successor in interest) and another of such clients (or his successor in interest)."

Notwithstanding such joint representation and any actual or potential conflict of interest, we hereby request that you represent both of us in connection with the aforesaid matters and consent to such representation. Furthermore, we acknowledge and agree that at no time will your representation of us be construed, claimed or deemed to be a breach of a fiduciary relationship, a conflict of interest or a violation of any other obligation to either of us. We each agree that at no time shall we claim or contend that you should be or are disqualified from representing either of us in connection with said matter or any other matter, related or unrelated.

Yours truly,

*(*These are similar to other states' rules of professional conduct.*)

Mediation for Musicians

BY MADELEINE E. SELTZER

Inherent in any agreement is the possibility of disagreement. When the relationship between a musician or composer and his or her manager, agent, record company, producer, etc., breaks down, or a dispute arises, it may be advisable to consider mediation as a means of resolving the problem. Mediation is usually superior to the traditional manner of settling disputes in our society—litigation in the courts—for a variety of reasons. It is particularly well-suited for resolving disputes involving musicians and composers because of its unique characteristics and should be considered before other options are pursued.

GENERAL PRINCIPLES

Mediation is a form of alternative dispute resolution (resolving disagreements outside of the court system). It differs from other alternative dispute resolution methods in that the parties themselves craft their own settlement. Ideally, mediation removes the adversary structure of the conflict in which only one party comes out the winner. Instead of a judge or arbitrator imposing a decision, a neutral third party, the mediator, assists them in the process of determining solutions. Because the parties deal directly with each other, set their own agenda, and work out their own resolution, mediation allows them to explore their relationship and the difficulties that led to their conflicts and helps them to reach creative solutions.

Mediation has other attractive features. First, it is low risk because it is voluntary and nonbinding. If it does not result in a mutually agreeable settlement of the dispute, the parties are free to pursue other courses of action, including litigation. Second, it is flexible, adaptable and applicable to almost any kind of dispute; it can be utilized at any stage of a conflict; and the parties can choose any available mediator. Third, it is informal—there are few structural or substantive rules such as rules of evidence or procedure, or legal precedents that must be followed. Finally, it is cost-effective—legal fees are minimized, and mediation takes much less time to conclude than other methods of dispute resolution. Also, the nonadversarial and cooperative nature of mediation helps avoid the costs associated with the damage or destruction of the business relationship, enabling it to continue profitably. In addition, the emotional costs of litigation are avoided; agreements arrived at through mediation are usually quite durable, thereby minimizing the possibility of future disputes.

HOW MEDIATION WORKS

Mediation may involve two individuals, several individuals, or even groups, and one mediator or two comediators. Mediators try to facilitate discussion among the parties and create an environment that allows them to communicate effectively, express their grievances and discover their own road to settlement of their conflict. The mediator may also help by articulating a potential agreement that the parties are close to reaching: that is, the mediator may help to draft an agreement that fairly, fully and specifically incorporates the parties' intentions.

The mediation process is quite simple. It usually begins with each party giving his or her account of the situation that led to the mediation. Then, with the help of the mediator, the parties set an agenda as to how they want the mediation to proceed. Issues are narrowed, and with the use of various devices employed by the mediator, such as private meetings with the individual parties (caucusing), the resolution process begins. The goal is to reach a written agreement as to some, if not all, of the matters in dispute. Such agreements are usually enforceable as contracts in courts of law.

In order to encourage free and uninhibited dialogue among the parties, it is imperative that all oral and written information presented in a mediation be treated as confidential. Therefore, the parties are encouraged to enter into a confidentiality agreement before the commencement of the mediation to ensure that the information provided will not be used in a subsequent legal proceeding. Some states, such as California, Colorado and Virginia have enacted legislation ensuring confidentiality. For example, according to California Code, "...evidence of anything said or of any admission made in the course of the mediation is not admissible in evidence or subject to discovery, and disclosure of this evidence shall not be compelled, in any action or proceeding in which, pursuant to law, testimony can be compelled to be given." This rule also applies to documents. In addition, the statute pronounces that, "When persons agree to conduct or participate in mediation for the sole purpose of compromising, settling, or resolving a dispute...all communications, negotiations, or settlement discussions by and between participants or mediators in the mediation shall remain confidential."

ARTS ARBITRATION AND MEDIATION SERVICES: A MODEL PROGRAM

The California Lawyers for the Arts (CLA), a nonprofit organization that has served and promoted the interests of artists, including musicians and composers, in California for many years, established Arts Arbitration and Mediation Services (AAMS) in 1980. It was the first program in the country to offer alternative dispute resolution services to artists and it has served as a model for similar services in other states. These programs are now part of Arts Resolution Services, a national mediation program for the arts. The national hotline number is 1-800-526-TALA (8252).

Since its inception, AAMS has resolved over 1100 cases with the help of a panel of specially trained volunteer mediators and arbitrators whose backgrounds include the arts, the music industry, law, and business. According to a spokesperson for the Southern California office of CLA, many of the disputes involve musicians and composers and include such issues as copyright, royalties, personality conflicts, negotiating collaborations, contracts and payment for work. The majority of these matters are resolved to the satisfaction of all the parties.

Because of all of the advantages of mediation described here, it is advisable that mediation clauses be included in standard agreements. By so doing, the parties will be required to employ mediation before other methods of dispute resolution are used.

MEDIATION: A PROCESS OF BEST RESORT

There is often an emotional undercurrent in disputes that involve musicians and composers, particularly when their work is at issue. These issues may include the content of the work; credit for work performed; and the factors that contributed to the production of the work. Mediation allows for the airing of feelings and enables the intangible and even irrational elements of a situation to be given as much weight as the tangible and rational. Rules of law and other external standards such as the market value of the services or work produced need not control the result in a mediation. The parties create their own rules to fashion their own particular resolution. The musician or composer retains the power that he or she may have historically relinquished to other representatives or lawyers. This gives them dignity and a sense of control that they may not otherwise have. Unlike judges and arbitrators whose function is to impose their will and decide the matter, the mediator is there to facilitate the process. If the parties have not entered into a written contract it makes the enforcement of their rights and obligations very difficult using traditional means and the relatively inexpensive cost of mediation makes it an extremely attractive alternative to litigation. Finally, since mediation tends to preserve rather than destroy relationships, it is preferable to other forms of dispute resolution.

Protecting Your Compositions

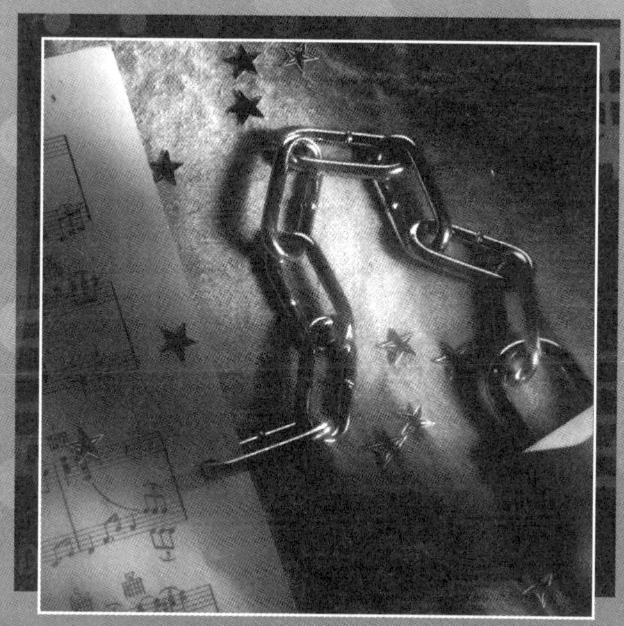

COPYRIGHTS: THE LAW AND YOU

COPYRIGHT INFRINGEMENT

SAMPLING

COLLABORATOR/SONGWRITER AGREEMENTS

DIGITAL DOWNLOADS AND STREAMING: COPYRIGHT AND DISTRIBUTION ISSUES

INTERNATIONAL COPYRIGHT

Copyrights: The Law and You

BY MARK HALLORAN

A copyright is a property right, comprised of a set of legally enforceable privileges, granted by law to creators of artistic works such as songs and recordings. These privileges ("exclusive rights") vary depending on the type of creation. The most important are the exclusive right to make and sell copies of the creation, and (especially in the case of music), the exclusive right to publicly perform it. Copyright owners make money by selling or licensing these rights to others, or by exploiting the rights themselves.

Although the copyright law recognizes that artistic creations ("works") other than music are copyrightable, the most important artistic creation for a musician is what the law terms a "musical work," that is, a musical composition such as a song or instrumental piece. For simplicity's sake, we will refer to a musical work as a "song."

Two prerequisites must be met before a song can be protected by copyright. The song must be original to the author, and fixed in a tangible medium of expression. "Original" means that you yourself created the work (rather than copied it). "Fixed in a tangible medium of expression" means you put your song on paper, tape or any other medium from which it can be perceived either directly or with the aid of a machine or device (such as a CD player) for more than a very short period of time. Singing a song in a club does not fix that song for you to have a copyright in it. Once you have recorded a demo or written a lead sheet, the song is fixed. Copyright law terms you the "author" of the song, and you are the initial owner.

The recording of a song is called a "sound recording." Sound recordings have separate copyrights from songs, as discussed below.

THE BUNDLE OF COPYRIGHTS

The U.S. Copyright Act gives copyright owners the right to control the use of their compositions in the following ways:

- Reproduction of the work in copies or phonorecords
- Distribution of the work for sale to the public
- Public performance of the work
- The creation of derivative works based upon the copyrighted work
- Display of the work in printed form, such as sheet music

Arrangements of copyrighted material may be copyrighted only when made by the owner(s) of the copyright or with their consent.

If you cowrite a song with the intention of making an inseparable whole, you have created a "joint work." Unless you agree otherwise, the writers own the song prorata (e.g., if two writers, the split is fifty-fifty; three writers, one-third each). The issues peculiar to joint works are discussed in the chapter, Collaborator/Songwriter Agreements.

Ideas are not copyrightable. The originators of rap could not copyright one rap song and then say that everyone is forbidden to write rap songs. Only the expression of the idea, that is, what has been put on paper, disc or tape, is protected. Thus, you are free to write a rap song even if you did not originate the rap mode. You cannot, however, steal a previous rap song note for note and word for word.

Song titles are not copyrightable, as they do not possess sufficient expressive content. However, this does not mean you could write a new song and entitle it "Like a Rolling Stone" with total impunity. The owners of "Like a Rolling Stone" may have legal recourse, but this recourse is under laws other than copyright law.

PUBLIC DOMAIN SONGS

Not all songs are protected by copyright. Songs whose copyright terms have lapsed fall into the "public domain"; the public owns them. You are free to use a song in the public domain in any way you choose. Many new songs take material liberally from the public domain.

New material added to public domain songs makes these compositions eligible for copyright to the extent new material is added—the public domain portion is not resurrected to copyright status. New material includes new lyrics, changes in melodies, arrangements, and compilations of versions of the same song. In the copyright form PA, line 5, "Previous Registration" and line 6, "Derivative Work or Compilation" ask you to furnish pertinent information regarding public domain work.

New copyrights based on public domain material make it possible for writers and publishers to receive performance monies, and mechanical license fees from record companies.

If you are unsure as to whether a song is public domain, you can have the Copyright Office or a private search service check the copyright status. The Copyright Office charges $65 per hour and normally takes six weeks to do a search. Private services may charge on a sliding scale, but are quicker than the Copyright Office.

For information on copyright searches, you can call the Reference and Bibliography Section of the Copyright Office or search the Copyright Office Web site.

You should be aware that even if a song or recording is in the public domain in the United States, it may still be protected by copyright overseas. To be used worldwide without permission, a public domain song must be cleared worldwide.

You can call ASCAP or BMI to determine the publisher of a song, or search their Web sites. CD labels typically list songwriters and publishers, as well as the record company that owns the recording.

COPYRIGHTS, PATENTS AND TRADEMARKS

Copyright protects works that are artistic in nature, such as songs and sound recordings. Patents protect new and useful inventions, such as new processes and machines. Trademarks are words or symbols used in association with products or services, which distinguish those goods or services in the marketplace. A registered trademark's notice is ®. Do not confuse it with the copyright notices, which include the symbols © and ℗.

Copyrights, patents and trademarks make up the bulk of what is known as "intellectual property law." This body of law recognizes that the products of people's minds that are in tangible form have a value that should be protected.

Generally, in the music field, you can get a copyright for two types of creations: musical works and sound recordings. Although dramatic works (such as a musical play, e.g., *Phantom of the Opera*) may include accompanying music, they are beyond the scope of this discussion.

Interestingly, the copyright law does not define "musical works." However, what most people consider a song is a musical work. Both the music and the lyrics (or each of them separately) can constitute a musical work.

A sound recording is a work comprised of a series of recorded sounds. Thus, the sounds recorded on a compact disc constitute a sound recording. You must distinguish between the musical work and the sound recording. Linda Ronstadt's version of Roy Orbison's song "Blue Bayou," which you hear when her album is played, is a sound recording. However, "Blue Bayou" the musical work, is distinct from Ronstadt's performance as embodied in the sound recording.

Sound recordings are comprised of the efforts of many people—the instrumentalists, vocalists, engineers and producers—all of whom may be considered to have constituted copyrightable elements of a sound recording. The Copyright Act does not legislate how the authorship and ownership in sound recordings is to be divided. It is clear the featured vocalist is initially an "author," but unclear whether the instrumentalists, back-up vocalists, and the producer are "authors," which is determined on a case-by-case basis.

The distinction between musical works and sound recordings is important when it comes to public performance income (i.e., fees paid for the public performance of copyrighted material by users such as television broadcasters and radio stations). In the United States, there is no exclusive right to publicly perform a sound recording (except for digital audio recordings, discussed below), even if you own it, but there is as to a musical work. Accordingly, public performance royalties (distributed by ASCAP, BMI and SESAC) are paid to the writer and publisher of the musical work, not the performer or owner of the sound recording. Thus, the public performance income generated by Ronstadt's version of "Blue Bayou" is paid to the writer and publisher of the song, not to Ronstadt or her record company.

Congress has considered, but not passed, bills that would create a general public performance right in sound recordings. Systems similar to those of ASCAP and BMI could be used to compute frequency of performances, and the money would be distributed by the licensing agency among record companies, producers and performers. It should be noted that public performance income from the exploitation of sound recordings is currently paid in some countries outside the United States but it is not yet a significant source of revenue to U.S. record companies and recording artists.

Many provisions of the Copyright Act refer to "phonorecords." A phonorecord is the physical object (tape, cassette, record, compact disc or other device) that embodies the sounds of a sound recording. When you buy a compact disc, you have purchased a phonorecord that embodies a sound recording. However, although you own the compact disc, you do not own the sound recording or the musical work—the copyright owner has only parted with the physical embodiment of the copyrighted works, not ownership in the sound recording or the musical work.

COPYRIGHT REGISTRATION

Some people are under the misapprehension that you send to Washington, D.C. to get a copyright. What you send for is not a "copyright"—which you get as soon as you fix the work in a tangible medium of expression—but a copyright registration, a very valuable piece of paper that is not only evidence of your claim to copyright, but also makes it easier for you to sue if someone infringes your copyright. In general, failure to register does not invalidate the copyright, and as of March 1, 1989, you are no longer legally required to put a copyright notice on published copies.

The fastest way to get copyright registration forms is to download them from the Copyright Office Web site *(www.loc.gov/copyright)*. You can also get free copyright registration forms by writing to the Library of Congress, Washington, DC 20559, or calling the Copyright Office at (202) 707-3000 (if you are not sure which form you need), or (202) 707-9100 (if you know the specific form you want). Allow at least two to four weeks for delivery. This time does vary, however, so ask the person at the Copyright Office how long you will have to wait. The Copyright Office is very helpful with questions regarding registration. Sample forms are duplicated at the end of this chapter. You should keep at least one original form on file so you can photocopy it. You may also order Copyright Office circulars, which are written in plain English and are very helpful, either by Internet, letter or phone.

REGISTERING COLLECTIONS

A group of unpublished songs may be registered as a collection under the following conditions:

- The elements of the collection are assembled in an orderly form.
- The combined elements bear a single title identifying the collection as a whole.
- The copyright claimant in all the elements and in the collection as a whole is the same.
- All of the elements are by the same author, or, if they are by different authors, at least one of the authors has contributed copyrightable authorship to each element.

(From Circular 1 "Copyright Basics," available at no charge from the U.S. Copyright Office.)

What to Submit

To register a copyright in a song, you submit the appropriate form plus one lead sheet, CD or cassette if the work is not published (i.e., copies have not been distributed to the public). The CD or cassette need only contain words, basic melody and rhythm; it does not have to be a fully arranged and beautifully produced demo. You must submit two lead sheets, or two CDs or cassettes if the work is published. The appropriate forms for registering a song are form PA (performing arts) or SR (sound recording). When you are the copyright owner of all the songs on the sound recording, form SR covers both the copyright of the songs and the copyright in the sound recording. Please note that the Copyright Office keeps the materials you submit, and stores them as a national artistic treasure of the Library of Congress.

Registering Collections

You may register many songs for a single fee by putting them on a CD or tape and registering them as a collection by using form PA. The biggest drawback to this method is that since the songs are clumped together as one work under one title it is difficult to identify just one of the songs. If you want to pull out one of the songs, you can do so by filing form CA (correction and amplification) or by registering a separate form PA for the song.

Alternative Registration

At the outset, it must be emphasized that no alternative means of registration will protect your songs to the extent that formal registration with the Copyright Office does. Because of the high cost of copyright registration (currently $30 per song), and the technical requirements of the Copyright Office, alternative forms of registration have arisen. The primary reason for using an alternative registration method is to provide proof of the date of creation (fixation) of a song, which is crucial in determining who first created copyright in the song.

So-called poor man's copyright consists of enclosing a copy of your song in an envelope, sending it by registered mail to yourself, and not opening the envelope. The postmark serves as proof as to the date of creation of the song. Some variations of the poor man's copyright theme include having a notary public notarize a lead sheet with their signature and date, placing lead sheets or tapes of the song in a safe deposit box, and having people listen to a song so that they can testify that the song had been created as of a certain date.

PROPER COPYRIGHT NOTICE

Proper notice of a claim to copyright in a song or sound recording is an important step in protecting your rights, since it puts people on notice that you claim the copyright. Failure to attach proper notice to published copies, however, no longer invalidates your copyright. There are separate symbols for notice of copyright in songs (sheet music, written lyrics) © and in sound recordings (CDs, cassettes, etc.) ℗. The copyright notices for songs and sound recordings must include three elements: the symbol © or ℗, the year of publication, and the name of the copyright owner. The word "Copyright," or the abbreviation "Copr.," may be used instead of the symbol ©. Proper notices are illustrated below.

A copyright notice for a song fixed on sheet music should look something like this:

© 2001 Sally Songwriter.

All Rights Reserved.

Notices that vary from this form are common. A popular one is "Copyright © 2001 Sally Songwriter," or "© Copr. Sally Songwriter 2001." All the law requires is that these three symbols "give reasonable notice of the claim of copyright."

U.S. copyright law does not suggest the words "All Rights Reserved," but they are recommended because they provide additional copyright protection in certain South American countries.

The copyright notice for sound recordings fixed in tapes, records or CDs looks something like this:

℗ 2001 XYZ Records.

All Rights Reserved.

This notice may be put on the surface, label or container of the phonorecord.

Omission of Notice

Under the pre-1978 U.S. Copyright Law, omission of a copyright notice on published copies was fatal to a claim of copyright. This is not true under the present law.

Copyright Notice on Demos

Legally you do not have to put any copyright notice on unpublished lead sheets, or demonstration tapes or CDs. However, the prudent thing to do is to put the appropriate notice on every one of your songs, CDs and tapes.

Put a © notice on every lead sheet or lyric sheet as soon as you write it down. Put a ℗ notice on every tape or record you submit or loan. This puts people on notice that you are claiming copyright in your songs and recordings and that you take your craft seriously.

PUBLICATION

A song is published when it is distributed to the public by sale or by some other means. The most common way songs are first published is through the distribution of records containing them. Be sure the appropriate copyright notice is affixed to the record, tape, sheet music or other physical embodiment of the work.

RECORDING A COPYRIGHTED SONG

The copyright law gives the owner of a copyrighted song the exclusive right to make the first sound recording of the song. However, once the song has been recorded and distributed to the public, others are entitled to make their own recordings of that work and distribute them in phonorecords.

If you want to record a song, you have two alternatives: you may negotiate a "mechanical license" from the copyright owner; or you may use the "compulsory mechanical license" provision of the copyright law, which does not require that you gain permission of the copyright holder, but does require you to account to the copyright holder and to pay fixed rates per song for each record manufactured and sold. In practice, however, the vast majority of mechanical licenses are negotiated through The Harry Fox Agency in New York. Mechanical license fees are paid to that agency, which deducts its administration fee, and remits the balance to the copyright holder (usually a publisher) on a quarterly basis.

DURATION OF COPYRIGHTS

Copyright protection begins on the date of creation (i.e., fixation in a tangible medium of expression) and as of 1998, in most cases, lasts for the lifetime of the author plus 70 years. Thus, if you write a song in 2001, and die in the year 2020, the copyright lasts until 2090. If there is a coauthor or authors, then the 70 years are measured from the last surviving author's death.

"Works made for hire" (discussed below) are protected for 95 years from the date of publication, or for 120 years from the date of creation (fixation), whichever is shorter.

TRANSFER AND LICENSING OF COPYRIGHTS

Copyrights, like other property, can be divided, bought and sold. When you license ASCAP to collect public performance royalties you have, in effect, transferred part of your copyright to ASCAP. You still own the rest of the copyright, however. Also, in typical music publishing and record deals, you transfer your copyright to the label or publisher, in return for their promise to pay you royalties.

You can also give permission to someone to exploit your copyright without transferring ownership. This is called a "license." For example, someone may record and distribute your song under a mechanical license—but you still own the song. Another common license is a "synchronization license," whereby you or your publisher gives permission for your song to be included in a film or television program.

If you transfer your copyright, or any exclusive right under copyright, the transfer of ownership must be in writing and be signed by the copyright owner (you). The transfer should be recorded in the Copyright Office, but it is not legally required. Recording of the transfer document is important to the person to whom the copyright is transferred, as it is a prerequisite for bringing a copyright infringement suit. Also, conflicts may emerge between persons that claim the same copyright. In such cases, the first to record the transfer will prevail in a lawsuit arising from a dispute over copyright ownership. Failure to register the transfer, however, does not invalidate the transfer.

Reacquiring Copyright

The present law provides that an author or author's heirs may reacquire a copyright between the 35th and 40th year after transfer by serving a written notice on the person who, at that time, holds the copyright. They then regain ownership of the copyright for the rest of its duration. This does not apply to works made for hire as your employer or the person commissioning the song is deemed the author and owner of the song.

Obviously, for you or your heir to take advantage of this provision you must keep good records and a prospective calendar.

WORKS MADE FOR HIRE

Songwriters are frequently hired to write songs. In such cases, they are described as "employees for hire" or "writers for hire," in songwriting contracts. The significance of this is that the employer (person who hired the writer) is deemed to be the author of the song, and owns the song unless the contract states otherwise. If a song is not produced by an employee in the course of his or her employment, it will be considered a work made for hire only if there is a written agreement to consider it such and the song falls into the specific list of "specially ordered or commissioned works" found in the Copyright Act. Remember, in the work-made-for-hire situation, you do not have copyright in the song as your employer or commissioner is the author of the song. The Copyright Act lists the following uses as specially ordered or commissioned works—a contribution to a collective work; a part of a motion picture or other audiovisual work; a translation; a supplementary work; a compilation; an instructional text; a test; answer material for a test; or an atlas. The same analysis applies when you create sound recordings for record labels.

In 1998, at the behest of the record labels, the Copyright Act was amended to include sound recordings as specially ordered or commissioned works. However, after a battle between the record companies and recording artists, sound recordings were deleted from the list of specifically ordered or commissioned works in late 2000. Notwithstanding this deletion, record companies still take the position in their contracts that the sound recordings are works made for hire as a contribution to a collective work. The significance to recording artists is that they or their heirs may have the ability to terminate the transfer of their sound recordings to record companies in the window from 35 to 40 years after assignment if the transfer was indeed an assignment and not a work made for hire. There is no termination right for works made for hire. The issue of whether sound recordings under recording contracts are subject to termination has not been adjudicated yet, but it surely will, starting no later than 2013 (35 years after January 1, 1978, when the 1976 Copyright Act came into effect).

COPYRIGHT INFRINGEMENT

A work is infringed when any of the exclusive rights in a copyright are violated. Persons that infringe copyrights are subject to both civil and criminal penalties. Here are some examples:

You write a song, and the sheet music is sold in a store. An infringer purchases the sheet music, duplicates it and sells it. This is an infringement of your right to reproduce the work and of your exclusive right to distribute copies of the work to the public.

You record an album containing your songs, and an infringer reproduces hundreds of CDs and sells them. This violates your exclusive reproduction and distribution rights and infringes your rights in both the songs and the sound recordings fixed in the album. Consequently, you and your record company can sue for infringement.

George Harrison was found to have infringed the Chiffons' 1962 classic "He's So Fine" with his 1970 hit "My Sweet Lord." The court found the music of the two songs to be identical. Even though the lyrics and concepts of his song were different, and Harrison only subconsciously took from "He's So Fine," it was still an infringement.

Statute of Limitations

The copyright law has a statute of limitations. In cases of infringement, you have three years from the initial date of infringement to bring suit. Any delay, however, can harm you. See a lawyer as soon as you learn of an unauthorized use of your song or recording.

Imitating a Performer

As long as you have permission to rerecord a song (whether from the copyright owner or by filing the compulsory mechanical license), you can try to make it sound like the original. As discussed above, you get permission to record the song by getting a compulsory license through complying with copyright law formalities, or by obtaining a negotiated license from the owner of the copyright in the song. You do not have to have the permission of the original performer unless that performer happens to have the rights to the song. If you record "Born in the U.S.A." you can try to sound like Bruce Springsteen, but you must have permission to record the song.

You should be careful, however, if an advertising agency hires you to imitate the sound of a well-known performer. Recent cases involving Bette Midler and Tom Waits have led to substantial judgments against advertising agencies that deliberately had singers imitate their voices.

Infringement Remedies

The remedies provided by law in an infringement suit include both injunctions, impounding infringing articles, and money damages. If you prove infringement at a preliminary stage of the suit, the court will make the infringer stop.

This is a form of injunction—that is, a court order against the infringer. The court can also order the impoundment of the allegedly infringing copies or phonorecords as well as the machinery that produced them.

Since proving money damages is difficult the law sets "statutory damages," which generally run from $750 to $30,000 for a single act of copyright infringement, and up to $150,000 if the infringement is willful.

If you win your infringement suit you may elect to receive either the actual damages you suffered plus the profits the infringer earned from the infringement, or statutory damages. In certain instances, the court will also award court costs and attorneys' fees. Remember, statutory damages and attorneys' fees will be awarded only if you make timely registration of your copyright with the Copyright Office.

The copyright law also provides for criminal penalties.

FAIR USE

Generally, a person who wishes to use copyrighted material must seek permission of the copyright holder. However, the law recognizes certain limited uses of copyrighted material without permission as "fair use." In broad terms, the doctrine of fair use means that in some circumstances, where the use is reasonable and not harmful to the copyright owner's rights, copyrighted material may be used, to a limited extent, without permission of the copyright owner. Under this doctrine, critics have been held to be free to publish short extracts or quotations for purposes of illustration or comment, and record reviewers may quote from songs. Also, in a recent high-profile case, Two Live Crew was found not to have infringed a song by doing a parody of it.

The line between fair use and infringement is unclear and not easily defined. There is no specific number of words, lines or notes that can be safely taken without permission. Acknowledging the source of the copyrighted material does not avoid infringement. The safe course is to get permission before using copyrighted material. The Copyright Office cannot give this permission. It will supply information regarding copyright ownership as disclosed by a search of its records.

Use of copyrighted material without permission (even in a parody), should be avoided unless it is clear that the doctrine of fair use would apply to the situation. If there is any doubt, consult an attorney.

We all know that new songs frequently incorporate parts of old ones. A pervasive myth is that you can graft four bars from a copyrighted song without subjecting yourself to a lawsuit by the copyright owner, as taking four bars is a fair use. In fact, there is no such provision in the law. The test is whether the amount taken from the old song was substantial. A judge or jury applies this rather loose standard when they listen to your song. Remember, there is no standard measure of how much music, or how many lyrics can be incorporated in a new song without infringing the old.

DIGITAL AUDIO RECORDING TECHNOLOGY (DART) ACT

On October 7, 1992, the U.S. Congress passed the Digital Audio Recording Technology (DART) Act. The act requires manufacturers and importers of digital audio recording devices and media that distribute the products in the United States to pay a set percentage royalty of the transfer price to the Licensing Division of the Copyright Office which invests the fees in U.S. Treasury securities until royalties are distributed. The Copyright Arbitration Royalty Panel (CARP), administered by the Librarian of Congress, adjusts copyright royalty rates and distributes royalties to eligible claimants that file proper and timely claims.

The law also requires manufacturers of digital audio equipment to install serial copy-prevention systems that permit copies to be made from original recordings, but not from copies, thereby preventing unauthorized mass duplication.

DART is an attempt to balance the concerns of copyright owners and music publishers about unlawful infringement (unauthorized tape duplication and distribution) with the public's demand for DAT technology. The act includes a special provision that protects the consumer against an infringement action when the consumer uses the technology to create a digital copy for private noncommercial use.

The royalty fees are deposited into two funds, a Sound Recordings Fund and a Musical Works Fund. The money in the Sound Recordings Fund is allocated to copyright owners of sound recordings (not copyright owners of the musical compositions), featured artists, nonfeatured musicians and nonfeatured artists. The Musical Works Fund is distributed to music publishers and songwriters.

The total royalty pool is allocated by the following percentages:

Record companies	38.41%
Featured artists	25.60%
Songwriters	16.66%
Music publishers	16.66%
Musicians	1.75%
Background vocalists	0.92%

Under DART, the copyright owners of the sound recording and the American Federation of Musicians jointly appoint an independent administrator for the Nonfeatured Musicians Subfund; and the copyright owners of the sound recording and the American Federation of Television and Radio Artists jointly appoint an independent administrator for the Nonfeatured Vocalists Subfund. Although there could be two independent administrators, a single person has administered both funds to date.

The rest of the royalty pool is distributed among copyright owners that have filed claims and whose musical works or sound recordings have been embodied in a digital or analog musical recording lawfully made; and distributed in the form of digital or analog musical recordings or disseminated to the public by video or audio transmissions.

Claimants should send CARP an original and two copies of a letter stating the basis for the claim during January or February following the year for which royalties are sought. The Copyright Office does not provide special claim forms. In their letter, the claimant must provide (1) the full legal name of the person or entity claiming royalty payments; (2) the telephone number, facsimile number, if any, and the full address, including a specific street name and number or rural route, of the place of business of the person or entity; (3) a statement as to how the claimant fits the definition of interested copyright party; (4) a statement indicating the fund (and fund segment, e.g., nonfeatured vocalist) the claim is for; and (5) identification of at least one musical work or sound recording establishing the basis for the claim. All claims must be signed by the claimant or the claimant's representative. Claims filed for more than one subfund must be filed separately. Joint claims must include a statement of authorization and the name of each claimant to the joint claim.

In March, CARP writes to the claimants and tells them what other claimants have filed. It is then up to the claimants to negotiate in good faith with each other to reach a settlement on how to distribute the funds for which they are applying. Once this is done, the Librarian of Congress places a notice in the Federal Register that asks whether there are any controversies among the claimants as to the distribution of royalties. If there are no controversies, the Copyright Office distributes the royalties.

If the claimants cannot reach an agreement, the Librarian designates the CARP panel to arbitrate a distribution settlement among claimants. In this case, the claimants will bear the entire cost of the arbitration proceeding in proportion to their share of the distribution.

Claims and statements should be sent by certified mail, return receipt requested, to: Copyright Arbitration Royalty Panel, P.O. Box 70977, Southwest Station, Washington, DC 20024.

For more information, call CARP, (202) 707-8380.

CONCLUSION

Musician and songwriters should have a basic understanding of copyright law. When you write or record a song, you have certain valuable rights in that song that you can exploit. By knowing your rights you can protect them; when you have a specific problem, you should consult an attorney for guidance.

SUMMARY OF NOTICES THAT APPEAR ON RECORDINGS

Item	Location	Purpose
℗ year, owner	Typically on label and packaging	Gives notices of owner of sound recording.
© year, owner	Label, packaging	Provides notice of ownership of the art and text on the label and packaging when the owner of the sound recording is the same.
© year, owner	Beside specific text or art on packaging	Identifies ownership of specific text or art when they are owned by another.
© year, owner	At end of written lyric	Provides notice of ownership of songs.
All Rights Reserved	After each © notice	Provides notice required for copyright protection in certain foreign countries.
Used by permission	After certain © notices	Typically used when permission to use another's copyrighted work has been granted.
Unauthorized reproduction prohibited, etc.	Packaging	Optional warning designed to deter infringement; can take various forms*
Songwriters' names	Adjacent to song titles	Not required by copyright law, but customarily added as a matter of courtesy or as required by contract to facilitate payment of songwriter royalties.
BMI/ASCAP/SESAC	Next to song title	Not part of the copyright notice, but identifies the performing rights society that licenses the song for public performances and collects royalties on behalf of the songwriter and publisher.
Playing time	Next to song title	Not part of the copyright notice but convenient for disc jockeys.

*(*i.e., "WARNING: Unauthorized reproduction of this recording is prohibited by federal law and is subject to criminal prosecution" or "Unauthorized duplication is a violation of applicable laws".*)

Fees are effective through June 30, 2002. After that date, check the Copyright Office Website at www.loc.gov/copyright or call (202) 707-3000 for current fee information.

FORM PA

For a Work of the Performing Arts
UNITED STATES COPYRIGHT OFFICE

REGISTRATION NUMBER

PA PAU

EFFECTIVE DATE OF REGISTRATION

Month Day Year

DO NOT WRITE ABOVE THIS LINE. IF YOU NEED MORE SPACE, USE A SEPARATE CONTINUATION SHEET.

1

TITLE OF THIS WORK ▼

PREVIOUS OR ALTERNATIVE TITLES ▼

NATURE OF THIS WORK ▼ See instructions

2

a

NAME OF AUTHOR ▼

DATES OF BIRTH AND DEATH
Year Born ▼ Year Died ▼

Was this contribution to the work a "work made for hire"?
☐ Yes
☐ No

AUTHOR'S NATIONALITY OR DOMICILE
Name of Country
OR { Citizen of ▶ ______ / Domiciled in ▶ ______

WAS THIS AUTHOR'S CONTRIBUTION TO THE WORK
Anonymous? ☐ Yes ☐ No
Pseudonymous? ☐ Yes ☐ No
If the answer to either of these questions is "Yes," see detailed instructions.

NATURE OF AUTHORSHIP Briefly describe nature of material created by this author in which copyright is claimed. ▼

NOTE

Under the law, the "author" of a "work made for hire" is generally the employer, not the employee (see instructions). For any part of this work that was "made for hire" check "Yes" in the space provided, give the employer (or other person for whom the work was prepared) as "Author" of that part, and leave the space for dates of birth and death blank.

b

NAME OF AUTHOR ▼

DATES OF BIRTH AND DEATH
Year Born ▼ Year Died ▼

Was this contribution to the work a "work made for hire"?
☐ Yes
☐ No

AUTHOR'S NATIONALITY OR DOMICILE
Name of Country
OR { Citizen of ▶ ______ / Domiciled in ▶ ______

WAS THIS AUTHOR'S CONTRIBUTION TO THE WORK
Anonymous? ☐ Yes ☐ No
Pseudonymous? ☐ Yes ☐ No
If the answer to either of these questions is "Yes," see detailed instructions.

NATURE OF AUTHORSHIP Briefly describe nature of material created by this author in which copyright is claimed. ▼

c

NAME OF AUTHOR ▼

DATES OF BIRTH AND DEATH
Year Born ▼ Year Died ▼

Was this contribution to the work a "work made for hire"?
☐ Yes
☐ No

AUTHOR'S NATIONALITY OR DOMICILE
Name of Country
OR { Citizen of ▶ ______ / Domiciled in ▶ ______

WAS THIS AUTHOR'S CONTRIBUTION TO THE WORK
Anonymous? ☐ Yes ☐ No
Pseudonymous? ☐ Yes ☐ No
If the answer to either of these questions is "Yes," see detailed instructions.

NATURE OF AUTHORSHIP Briefly describe nature of material created by this author in which copyright is claimed. ▼

3

a YEAR IN WHICH CREATION OF THIS WORK WAS COMPLETED **This information must be given in all cases.**
______ ◀ Year

b DATE AND NATION OF FIRST PUBLICATION OF THIS PARTICULAR WORK
Complete this information ONLY if this work has been published.
Month ▶ ______ Day ▶ ______ Year ▶ ______
______ ◀ Nation

4

See instructions before completing this space.

COPYRIGHT CLAIMANT(S) Name and address must be given even if the claimant is the same as the author given in space 2. ▼

TRANSFER If the claimant(s) named here in space 4 is (are) different from the author(s) named in space 2, give a brief statement of how the claimant(s) obtained ownership of the copyright. ▼

DO NOT WRITE HERE
OFFICE USE ONLY

APPLICATION RECEIVED

ONE DEPOSIT RECEIVED

TWO DEPOSITS RECEIVED

FUNDS RECEIVED

MORE ON BACK ▶
• Complete all applicable spaces (numbers 5-9) on the reverse side of this page.
• See detailed instructions.
• Sign the form at line 8.

DO NOT WRITE HERE

Page 1 of ______ pages

EXAMINED BY

FORM PA

CHECKED BY

☐ CORRESPONDENCE Yes

FOR COPYRIGHT OFFICE USE ONLY

DO NOT WRITE ABOVE THIS LINE. IF YOU NEED MORE SPACE, USE A SEPARATE CONTINUATION SHEET.

5

PREVIOUS REGISTRATION Has registration for this work, or for an earlier version of this work, already been made in the Copyright Office?
☐ **Yes** ☐ **No** If your answer is "Yes," why is another registration being sought? (Check appropriate box.) ▼ If your answer is "no," go to space 7.
a. ☐ This is the first published edition of a work previously registered in unpublished form.
b. ☐ This is the first application submitted by this author as copyright claimant.
c. ☐ This is a changed version of the work, as shown by space 6 on this application.
If your answer is "Yes," give: **Previous Registration Number** ▼ **Year of Registration** ▼

6

DERIVATIVE WORK OR COMPILATION Complete both space 6a and 6b for a derivative work; complete only 6b for a compilation.

a **Preexisting Material** Identify any preexisting work or works that this work is based on or incorporates. ▼

See instructions before completing this space.

b **Material Added to This Work** Give a brief, general statement of the material that has been added to this work and in which copyright is claimed. ▼

7

a **DEPOSIT ACCOUNT** If the registration fee is to be charged to a Deposit Account established in the Copyright Office, give name and number of Account.
Name ▼ **Account Number** ▼

b **CORRESPONDENCE** Give name and address to which correspondence about this application should be sent. Name/Address/Apt/City/State/ZIP ▼

Area code and daytime telephone number ▶ ( ) Fax number ▶ ( )
Email ▶

8

CERTIFICATION* I, the undersigned, hereby certify that I am the

Check only one ▶
- ☐ author
- ☐ other copyright claimant
- ☐ owner of exclusive right(s)
- ☐ authorized agent of ______

Name of author or other copyright claimant, or owner of exclusive right(s) ▲

of the work identified in this application and that the statements made by me in this application are correct to the best of my knowledge.

Typed or printed name and date ▼ If this application gives a date of publication in space 3, do not sign and submit it before that date.

Date ▶

Handwritten signature (X) ▼

x ______

9

Certificate will be mailed in window envelope to this address:

Name ▼
Number/Street/Apt ▼
City/State/ZIP ▼

YOU MUST:
- Complete all necessary spaces
- Sign your application in space 8

SEND ALL 3 ELEMENTS IN THE SAME PACKAGE:
1. Application form
2. Nonrefundable filing fee in check or money order payable to *Register of Copyrights*
3. Deposit material

MAIL TO:
Library of Congress
Copyright Office
101 Independence Avenue, S.E.
Washington, D.C. 20559-6000

As of July 1, 1999, the filing fee for Form PA is $30.

*17 U.S.C. § 506(e): Any person who knowingly makes a false representation of a material fact in the application for copyright registration provided for by section 409, or in any written statement filed in connection with the application, shall be fined not more than $2,500.

June 1999—200,000
WEB REV: June 1999
PRINTED ON RECYCLED PAPER
☆U.S. GOVERNMENT PRINTING OFFICE: 1999-454-879/68

Fees are effective through June 30, 2002. After that date, check the Copyright Office Website at www.loc.gov/copyright or call (202) 707-3000 for current fee information.

FORM SR

For a Sound Recording
UNITED STATES COPYRIGHT OFFICE

REGISTRATION NUMBER

SR SRU

EFFECTIVE DATE OF REGISTRATION

Month Day Year

DO NOT WRITE ABOVE THIS LINE. IF YOU NEED MORE SPACE, USE A SEPARATE CONTINUATION SHEET.

1

TITLE OF THIS WORK ▼

PREVIOUS, ALTERNATIVE, OR CONTENTS TITLES (CIRCLE ONE) ▼

2

a NAME OF AUTHOR ▼

DATES OF BIRTH AND DEATH
Year Born ▼ Year Died ▼

Was this contribution to the work a "work made for hire"?
❑ Yes
❑ No

AUTHOR'S NATIONALITY OR DOMICILE
Name of Country
OR { Citizen of ▶ ______
Domiciled in ▶ ______

WAS THIS AUTHOR'S CONTRIBUTION TO THE WORK
Anonymous? ❑ Yes ❑ No
Pseudonymous? ❑ Yes ❑ No
If the answer to either of these questions is "Yes," see detailed instructions.

NATURE OF AUTHORSHIP Briefly describe nature of material created by this author in which copyright is claimed. ▼

NOTE

Under the law, the "author" of a "work made for hire" is generally the employer, not the employee (see instructions). For any part of this work that was "made for hire," check "Yes" in the space provided, give the employer (or other person for whom the work was prepared) as "Author" of that part, and leave the space for dates of birth and death blank.

b NAME OF AUTHOR ▼

DATES OF BIRTH AND DEATH
Year Born ▼ Year Died ▼

Was this contribution to the work a "work made for hire"?
❑ Yes
❑ No

AUTHOR'S NATIONALITY OR DOMICILE
Name of Country
OR { Citizen of ▶ ______
Domiciled in ▶ ______

WAS THIS AUTHOR'S CONTRIBUTION TO THE WORK
Anonymous? ❑ Yes ❑ No
Pseudonymous? ❑ Yes ❑ No
If the answer to either of these questions is "Yes," see detailed instructions.

NATURE OF AUTHORSHIP Briefly describe nature of material created by this author in which copyright is claimed. ▼

c NAME OF AUTHOR ▼

DATES OF BIRTH AND DEATH
Year Born ▼ Year Died ▼

Was this contribution to the work a "work made for hire"?
❑ Yes
❑ No

AUTHOR'S NATIONALITY OR DOMICILE
Name of Country
OR { Citizen of ▶ ______
Domiciled in ▶ ______

WAS THIS AUTHOR'S CONTRIBUTION TO THE WORK
Anonymous? ❑ Yes ❑ No
Pseudonymous? ❑ Yes ❑ No
If the answer to either of these questions is "Yes," see detailed instructions.

NATURE OF AUTHORSHIP Briefly describe nature of material created by this author in which copyright is claimed. ▼

3

a YEAR IN WHICH CREATION OF THIS WORK WAS COMPLETED
______ ◀ Year
This information must be given in all cases.

b DATE AND NATION OF FIRST PUBLICATION OF THIS PARTICULAR WORK
Complete this information ONLY if this work has been published.
Month ▶ ______ Day ▶ ______ Year ▶ ______
______ ◀ Nation

4

See instructions before completing this space.

a COPYRIGHT CLAIMANT(S) Name and address must be given even if the claimant is the same as the author given in space 2. ▼

b TRANSFER If the claimant(s) named here in space 4 is (are) different from the author(s) named in space 2, give a brief statement of how the claimant(s) obtained ownership of the copyright. ▼

DO NOT WRITE HERE
OFFICE USE ONLY

APPLICATION RECEIVED

ONE DEPOSIT RECEIVED

TWO DEPOSITS RECEIVED

FUNDS RECEIVED

MORE ON BACK ▶ • Complete all applicable spaces (numbers 5-9) on the reverse side of this page.
• See detailed instructions. • Sign the form at line 8.

DO NOT WRITE HERE

Page 1 of ______ pages

EXAMINED BY

FORM SR

CHECKED BY

CORRESPONDENCE
❑ Yes

FOR COPYRIGHT OFFICE USE ONLY

DO NOT WRITE ABOVE THIS LINE. IF YOU NEED MORE SPACE, USE A SEPARATE CONTINUATION SHEET.

5

PREVIOUS REGISTRATION Has registration for this work, or for an earlier version of this work, already been made in the Copyright Office?
❑ **Yes** ❑ **No** If your answer is "Yes," why is another registration being sought? (Check appropriate box) ▼

a. ❑ This work was previously registered in unpublished form and now has been published for the first time.

b. ❑ This is the first application submitted by this author as copyright claimant.

c. ❑ This is a changed version of the work, as shown by space 6 on this application.

If your answer is "Yes," give: **Previous Registration Number** ▼ **Year of Registration** ▼

6

See instructions before completing this space.

DERIVATIVE WORK OR COMPILATION

a **Preexisting Material** Identify any preexisting work or works that this work is based on or incorporates. ▼

b **Material Added to This Work** Give a brief, general statement of the material that has been added to this work and in which copyright is claimed. ▼

7

DEPOSIT ACCOUNT If the registration fee is to be charged to a Deposit Account established in the Copyright Office, give name and number of Account.

a **Name** ▼ **Account Number** ▼

b **CORRESPONDENCE** Give name and address to which correspondence about this application should be sent. Name/Address/Apt/City/State/ZIP ▼

Area code and daytime telephone number ▶ Fax number ▶

Email ▶

8

CERTIFICATION* I, the undersigned, hereby certify that I am the

Check only one ▼

❑ author ❑ owner of exclusive right(s)

❑ other copyright claimant ❑ authorized agent of ____________________

Name of author or other copyright claimant, or owner of exclusive right(s) ▲

of the work identified in this application and that the statements made by me in this application are correct to the best of my knowledge.

Typed or printed name and date ▼ If this application gives a date of publication in space 3, do not sign and submit it before that date.

Date▶

Handwritten signature (x) ▼

X ________________________________

9

Certificate will be mailed in window envelope to this address

Name ▼

Number/Street/Apt ▼

City/State/ZIP ▼

YOU MUST:
- Complete all necessary spaces
- Sign your application in space 8

SEND ALL 3 ELEMENTS IN THE SAME PACKAGE:
1. Application form
2. Nonrefundable filing fee in check or money order payable to *Register of Copyrights*
3. Deposit material

MAIL TO:
Library of Congress
Copyright Office
101 Independence Avenue, S.E.
Washington, D.C. 20559-6000

As of July 1, 1999, the filing fee for Form SR is $30.

*17 U.S.C. § 506(e): Any person who knowingly makes a false representation of a material fact in the application for copyright registration provided for by section 409, or in any written statement filed in connection with the application, shall be fined not more than $2,500.

June 1999—50,000
WEB REV: June 1999

PRINTED ON RECYCLED PAPER

☆U.S. GOVERNMENT PRINTING OFFICE: 1999-454-879/48

Copyright Infringement

BY ROBERT M. DUDNIK

To establish a claim of copyright infringement, the plaintiff (person who files the lawsuit) must first demonstrate either ownership of the copyright of the song that was supposedly copied, or ownership of a copyright interest in that song, such as an exclusive license. The plaintiff must then demonstrate that the composer of defendant's song in fact copied from plaintiff's song and that the material that was copied results in a finding of copyright infringement. Once infringement is established, then the question becomes what remedies are available to the plaintiff.

ESTABLISHING OWNERSHIP

Copyright of a song is established when the work is first fixed in a tangible form—for example, notated on paper or recorded on tape. Registration of the song with the Copyright Office is not a prerequisite to the song being protected by copyright. However, before an infringement case may be filed in court, the owner of the copyright must, as a general rule, register the song with the Copyright Office. (Prompt registration will be beneficial in terms of remedies in the event the song is infringed.)

Typically, the copyright owner will be either the composer of the song, the employer of the composer (if the composer wrote the song during the course and scope of employment as a work for hire) or a person or company to whom the composer of the song transferred a copyright interest in the song.

Proof of ownership may become complicated where the plaintiff is not the composer of the song but, instead, claims ownership either as the employer of the composer or by virtue of a transfer in ownership. Further, the fact that the plaintiff has registered the song with the Copyright Office and has claimed ownership of the song on the registration certificate does not conclusively establish that the plaintiff is, in fact, the true owner of the copyright in the song.

ESTABLISHING COPYING

A composer who is charged with copyright infringement rarely admits copying from the plaintiff's song. And it is very unusual for there to be what the law calls "direct" evidence of copying, such as testimony by a witness who observed the composer listening to the plaintiff's song while writing the defendant's.

Since admissions of plagiarism as well as other forms of direct evidence of copying are hard to come by, the law permits a copyright plaintiff to prove copying through "circumstantial" evidence—by showing that the composer of defendant's song had "access" to plaintiff's song and that the two songs in issue are "substantially similar."

Access

Access means that there is a "reasonable possibility" that the composer of defendant's song heard plaintiff's song or saw a print version of it before writing defendant's song. If the plaintiff can establish only that there is a "bare possibility" that the composer of defendant's song heard or viewed a printed version of the song before defendant's song was written, then plaintiff has not established access and, with one exception discussed below, plaintiff's case will be dismissed from court.

A plaintiff can establish access under this reasonable possibility test by showing that the composer of defendant's song, as a member of the general public, had a reasonable opportunity to have been exposed to plaintiff's song. For example, where plaintiff's song was a major hit before defendant's song was written, access would ordinarily be established. This is true even if the composer of defendant's song denies having heard plaintiff's song since, in the eyes of the law, there was a reasonable possibility that the defendant would have heard plaintiff's song on the radio or on television. If, on the other hand, plaintiff's song received only limited airplay in one region of the country and little other exposure, and the composer of defendant's song could show that he never visited that region while plaintiff's song was being played, access would, ordinarily, not be established. As another example, if plaintiff's song was played during only a few club dates, access would ordinarily not be established unless it could be shown that the composer of defendant's song frequented one or more of the clubs where plaintiff's song was performed.

There is a second way of establishing access. If the plaintiff can establish that plaintiff's song was auditioned for or submitted to the composer of defendant's song before defendant's song was written, then access would be established. Access might also be established where plaintiff's song was auditioned for or submitted to a business associate or close friend of the composer of defendant's song. More difficult questions arise where plaintiff's song was auditioned for or submitted to a large company, such as a major record label, with which the composer of defendant's song has a business relationship.

In the end, the question of whether access is established is usually one of degree, which raises interesting and difficult issues for lawyers and judges. However, it is clear that the stronger the showing of access, the greater the chance plaintiff will have of proving copying by circumstantial evidence.

Substantial Similarity

As mentioned above, to prove copying by circumstantial evidence, the plaintiff must, ordinarily, show not only access, but also that there are elements in the two songs in issue that are substantially similar.

There is no precise definition of substantially similar. Clearly, it means something less than identical and something more than a little bit alike. Probably the best way of defining substantially similar is "so similar that an ordinary listener to music would believe that there was a strong possibility that one song, or at least an important part of it, was copied from the other."

As discussed above, even where the two songs in issue are substantially similar, the plaintiff's case will ordinarily be dismissed from court if the plaintiff cannot also present evidence of access. There is, however, one very narrow exception to the general rule that both access and substantial similarity must be proved to establish copying by circumstantial evidence. Where an expert witness will testify that the similarity between plaintiff's song and defendant's song is so overwhelming that there is no explanation for the similarity between them other than that one was copied from the other, access will be "inferred" from the similarity and the plaintiff will not be required to present any other evidence showing access, so long as there is some evidence that plaintiff's song was written before defendant's. It should, however, be pointed out that it is a rare case where this exception—known as the "striking similarity doctrine"—to the general rule would be applicable.

ESTABLISHING INDEPENDENT CREATION

It is important to keep in mind that the plaintiff does not conclusively establish copying just by presenting evidence showing both access and substantial similarity. Presentation of this evidence merely means that the issue of copying will be presented to the jury. Even if the plaintiff proves both access and substantial similarity, the defendant can win by convincing the jury that defendant's song was created independently of plaintiff's song. Regardless of how similar the songs in issue are, if the defendant did not in fact copy from the plaintiff's song, there can be no finding of copyright infringement. This is true even if the songs are identical—without copying there cannot be infringement. This is the law's way of recognizing that two composers could conceivably compose the very same song without either having heard the other's composition.

To establish independent creation (lack of copying), defendant will attempt to show a number of things. First, defendant will try to prove that the composer of defendant's song had solid musical training and a substantial background in music. This supports the conclusion that there was no need to copy from anything to write a good song.

Second, defendant will attempt to show that the composer of defendant's song wrote several hit songs before writing defendant's song. This supports the conclusion that the composer is skilled and successful and had no motivation or need to copy.

Third, and of great importance in persuading a jury that the similarity between the songs in issue did not result from copying, defendant will try to present music researchers and expert witnesses that can testify, using examples, that several songs or other musical works, written prior to plaintiff's and defendant's songs, are similar to both of them. This evidence is used to show that the musical elements causing the aural similarity between the two songs are elements commonly used by composers of popular music. This increases the likelihood that the similarities between the songs are coincidental and, thus, decreases the likelihood that defendant's song was copied from plaintiff's.

The law has long recognized that there are limits on the abilities of songwriters to combine notes, chords and rhythms so as to make music that will be relatively easy for most musicians to play, as well as both pleasing and accessible to the musically untrained. Because of these limits, courts recognize that simple musical phrases are likely to recur in popular songs spontaneously—not as the result of one composer copying from another. Consequently, defendant will attempt to prove (using expert witnesses), that the musical elements of defendant's song, upon which the plaintiff's claim of copying is based, are simple musical elements that are pleasing to the musically-unsophisticated audience for contemporary popular music and are relatively easy for most musicians to perform.

Finally, defendant will attempt to show that the composer of defendant's song previously wrote one or more songs that also contained the musical elements supposedly copied from plaintiff's song. If defendant had used these same elements in songs written before there was a possibility of hearing plaintiff's song, it would be unlikely that defendant's song was copied from plaintiff's. It is, after all, ordinarily permissible to use material from one's own compositions, and composers of contemporary music often write songs that, in terms of the music, are very much like their earlier songs. If, however, a composer uses material from one of his or her songs that is now owned by someone else, a problem may arise.

In the final analysis, assuming that plaintiff puts on evidence sufficient to make a showing of access and substantial similarity, and defendant then puts on evidence of independent creation, it will be for the jury to determine whether the composer of defendant's song in fact copied from plaintiff's.

ESTABLISHING INFRINGEMENT

Even if the plaintiff establishes ownership of plaintiff's song and that the composer of defendant's song copied from it, still more must be shown to establish infringement.

The plaintiff must show that more than a minimal amount of material contained in defendant's song was copied from plaintiff's. However, contrary to what many musicians believe, there is no legal rule stating that a composer may freely borrow four bars, or six notes, or any other set amount of material from a copyrighted work without being found liable for infringement. Indeed, the copying of a very brief musical passage from plaintiff's song may result in a finding of infringement if that passage is qualitatively important to both songs in issue. For example, the copying of a brief melodic "hook" might well result in infringement if that hook is the centerpiece of plaintiff's song and is important in defendant's.

Defendant will not avoid liability for infringement by showing that there is much material in defendant's song that is not in any way similar to, and thus not copied from, plaintiff's song. For example, if the basis of plaintiff's claim is a strong musical similarity between the choruses of the two songs, defendant cannot avoid a finding of infringement by showing that the verses and bridges of the songs are totally dissimilar and there is no similarity in lyrics.

Copyright law does not protect ideas, only their expression. Accordingly, to establish infringement, plaintiff must demonstrate that the composer of defendant's song copied both the musical ideas and the manner in which the composer of plaintiff's song expressed those ideas. The distinction between a musical idea and the manner in which it is expressed is quite puzzling to musicians, lawyers and judges. Nevertheless, it is a distinction that is central to United States copyright law.

The material that was copied from the plaintiff's song must have been "original" to its composer for there to be infringement. That is so because the copyright in a song protects only those musical elements, and combinations of musical elements, that are original to its composer. If certain elements of a copyrighted song were original and others were copied from an earlier song, the copyright in the song is valid, but protection in the song extends only to those elements that were original to its composer. It must, however, be understood that original does not mean novel or unique. For example, if a composer writes a theme that is similar (or identical) to an earlier one without copying from it, then, under copyright law, that composer's theme is considered his original theme.

The fair use doctrine may provide a defense even where the composer of defendant's song is found to have copied from plaintiff's song. However, this defense—which involves the weighing of several factors—is rarely useful in music infringement cases except where the defendant's song is a musical parody.

Finally, plaintiff is not required to show that the composer of defendant's song deliberately infringed the copyright in plaintiff's song. In fact, plaintiff need not even establish that the copying was a conscious act. Subconscious copying will result in a finding of infringement.

Significantly, if defendant's song is found by the jury to be an infringing copy of plaintiff's song, everyone who commercially exploits defendant's song will be liable for infringement, regardless of whether they had any reason to suspect that defendant's song infringed plaintiff's. Thus, a record company that innocently puts out a record containing a performance of defendant's song is liable for copyright infringement even if it has no possible way of knowing that the song is infringing, and even if the person or company supplying the recording represented and warranted that the song did not infringe any other musical work. The same is true with respect to a motion picture company that innocently includes defendant's song in the soundtrack of one of its films, and a manufacturer that innocently employs defendant's song in a television commercial.

The fact that companies in this position are treated as infringers, despite their lack of knowledge, is of great consequence, since the remedies available to a winning plaintiff apply to these companies.

REMEDIES

It is important to note that, after being charged with infringement, a losing defendant cannot avoid the remedies discussed below by expressing a willingness either to negotiate a "fair" license to use plaintiff's song or to pay plaintiff the prevailing "statutory rate" for a compulsory mechanical license, assuming the defendant could have avoided liability in the first place by paying plaintiff the statutory rate.

The four most important remedies available to a winning plaintiff are (1) injunctive relief, (2) statutory damages, (3) actual damages, and (4) the profits of each of the infringing defendants that is attributable to their use of infringing musical material (often perceived as the pot of gold at the end of the rainbow).

Injunctive Relief

Injunctive relief is a court order enjoining (i.e., prohibiting) each of the defendants from further distributing and selling works, such as recordings, which contain material that infringes plaintiff's song. For example, if one of the defendants is a record company that has released a recording containing a song that is found to infringe plaintiff's song, the record company may be enjoined from further distributing and selling the recording until the infringing song is removed. Similarly, if one of the defendants is a motion picture company that has released a film containing infringing music, the company may be ordered to discontinue distribution and exhibition of the film unless the infringing music is removed from the soundtrack. If, however, the amount of infringing material in a work is insignificant when compared to that which is contained in the rest of the work, it is unlikely that the court would issue an injunction order unless it would be relatively easy to delete the infringing material.

Where a plaintiff is able to obtain an order enjoining a defendant from commercially exploiting a work—such as a successful recording or film—which is producing substantial revenues for that defendant, plaintiff will have enormous economic leverage, permitting plaintiff to dictate the terms of a monetary settlement with that defendant.

Statutory Damages

Statutory damages are a form of damages provided for in the Copyright Act. They are calculated by multiplying a set amount of money, which varies depending on certain factors, times the number of infringements. This calculation can, however, become very complicated. Ordinarily, statutory damages are not nearly as meaningful to a plaintiff as any of the other remedies. Nevertheless, if an infringement action is contemplated or pursued, the option of statutory damages should be examined carefully, especially where it would be difficult to prove actual damages and the defendants' profits were minimal or nonexistent.

Actual Damage

Actual damages are those damages actually suffered by the plaintiff as the result of the infringement of plaintiff's song. For example, if defendant's song was comprised of music copied from plaintiff's song, coupled with obscene or distasteful lyrics, plaintiff might find it difficult to thereafter commercially exploit the song. Or if a song that infringed plaintiff's song was included on the soundtrack of a successful film, plaintiff might well find it difficult to license the song to a motion picture company. In sum, any use of an infringing song that tends either to make plaintiff's song "old news" or to tarnish it is damaging to the plaintiff, and the plaintiff (generally through the use of expert witnesses) will attempt to prove the monetary extent of those damages.

Award of Profits

Often the most significant remedy available to a prevailing plaintiff is an award of the profits of each of the defendants that are attributable to the use of the infringing material. Profits, simply put, means revenues minus properly deductible costs and expenses, including, in some cases, income taxes. The issues that relate to the calculation of an award of profits are among the most challenging faced by lawyers involved in copyright cases.

In establishing the profits of an infringing defendant, the plaintiff is only required to present proof of the gross revenues realized by the defendant from its exploitation of the infringing song or, where the infringing song is embodied in a larger work, such as a motion picture or an album containing a number of other songs, from defendant's exploitation of that larger work. Defendant is then required to prove its properly deductible costs and expenses, which gives rise to a series of complicated accounting questions that are too complex to be treated in this chapter.

Since a prevailing plaintiff is entitled only to the profits attributable to the use of infringing material, two separate issues frequently arise. First, a determination must be made as to what extent the commercial success of the infringing song is attributable to its inclusion of infringing material, as distinguished from other factors, for example, its use of noninfringing material or the talent of the performer who sings it. This question will often be the subject of expert testimony, with the plaintiff trying to prove that the infringing material was crucial to the popularity of the infringing song, and the defendant trying to prove that the infringing material played an insignificant role in the infringing song's success.

Second, where the infringing song is embodied in a work (such as a CD or a motion picture) that includes other material that has no connection with plaintiff's song, another question becomes how much of the profits realized from the exploitation of that work is attributable to the infringing song and how much to the other material? For example, where the infringing song is one of 10 cuts on a recording, more than 10% of the profits realized by the record company from its sales of that recording would be attributable to the infringing song if it was the hit, or one of the hits, which drove up sales, and less than 10% if it was not one of the hits and therefore received little airplay.

Where an infringing song is used on the soundtrack of a motion picture, how much of the motion picture studio's profits from its distribution of the film were attributable to the song's presence on the soundtrack? If the infringing song's inclusion on the soundtrack constituted an incidental or minor use, only a minuscule percentage of the film's profits would be attributable to its inclusion. If, on the other hand, the song was the film's title song, which was released on a recording that was successfully used to promote the film and keep the radio-listening public reminded that the film was in theaters, the plaintiff's case for profits would be much better.

A very difficult question arises where an infringing song is used in a commercial for a product, such as a beer. The question then becomes how much of the company's profits from beer sales were attributable to the use of the song in the commercial?

In dealing with the difficult questions regarding attribution of profits discussed above, both plaintiff and defendant will rely upon statistics, sales figures and expert testimony in their attempts to maximize (in the case of the plaintiff) or minimize (in the defendant's case) the significance of the song in "selling" the recording, the film or the beer.

Punitive Damages/Attorneys' Fees

Finally, there is the question of whether punitive damages and attorneys' fees are available as remedies. The Copyright Act does not provide for punitive damages and the prevailing view is that punitive damages are not a remedy available to a successful plaintiff. Unlike most cases filed in U.S. courts, the prevailing (winning) party in an infringement case may be entitled to an award of his, her or its attorneys' fees. A number of factors are considered in determining whether the prevailing party will be awarded fees and the courts are presently grappling on a case-by-case basis with the issue of whether the prevailing party will receive such an award.

Sampling

BY GREGORY T. VICTOROFF, ESQ.

At its best, sampling benefits society by creating valuable new contributions to modern music literature. At its worst, sampling is vandalism and stealing; chopping up and ripping off songs and recordings by other artists without permission or payment and fraudulently passing off the joint work as the work of a single artist, without giving credit to the sampled work or the unwilling collaborators. The practice is not new. In the 19th century, Rachmaninoff, Brahams, and Liszt "borrowed" material from contemporary Niccolo Paganini's Caprice for use in their own compositions.

With the advent of digital technology, MP3, Napster, more refined MIDI programs, affordable off-the-shelf samplers and widespread use of personal computers, sampling sounds and manipulating them has become relatively easy. As a result, sampling has opened a Pandora's box of old and new sound combinations, and with that, the necessity for new interpretations of the issues of copyright infringement, privacy rights, and unfair competition.

COPYRIGHT INFRINGEMENT

One of the many rights included in copyright is the right to copy a copyrighted work. Unauthorized sampling violates this right by copying a portion of a copyrighted work for a new recording.

The music publisher, by itself or together with the songwriter, usually owns the copyright in the song. The recording company usually owns the copyright in the sound recording. In December 1999, Congress amended section 101 of the Copyright Act to include *sound recordings* among the nine (now ten) categories of works that may be owned by an employer or commission party as works made for hire. These copyright owners are most directly affected by sampling and have the right to sue unauthorized samplers in federal court for copyright infringement. (See also the chapter, Copyrights: The Law and You.)

BREACHES OF CONTRACT

Warranties

Copyright infringement from illegal sampling may breach warranty provisions in recording contracts. Provisions called "Warranties," "Representations" and "Indemnifications" are almost always found in contracts between musicians and record companies; musicians and producers; producers and record companies; music publishers and record companies; songwriters and music publishers; record companies and distributors; and between distributors and record stores. According to these clauses, the person who provides the product (e.g., the songs, recordings, publishing rights, records, tapes, CDs) promises the person buying or licensing the product (the record company, Web site or record store) that the recordings do not infringe anyone's copyrights or other rights.

If a lawsuit for illegal sampling is filed, it could result in lawsuits for "breach of warranty" between each person that sells the illegally sampled product. Claims apply from person to person along the record-making and marketing chain, creating a duty to indemnify each other person along the chain. Unless expressly disclaimed, the same chain of written and implied indemnities apply to transmissions of digital sound recordings using the Internet. Final legal responsibility may lie with the recording artist. The indemnification rights that exist between each person or company in the process trigger one another like a chain reaction. This can result in hundreds of thousands of dollars in liability to the sampling artist.

Indemnification provisions require the record distributor to pay the retailer's damages and attorneys' fees, the record company is required to pay the distributor's fees and damages, the producer pays the record company's fees and damages and the artist may be technically liable for everyone's attorneys' fees and damages.

Unsatisfactory Masters

Another potential problem for musicians that sample is that most recording contracts give the record company the right to reject unsatisfactory masters. Masters that infringe copyrights of other sound recordings or musical compositions can be so rejected.

Artists are required to obtain copyright licenses ("clearances") from the owners of sampled material or deliver substitute masters, which do not contain samples, to satisfy contract obligations to record companies.

Failure to comply with a record company's master delivery requirements could result in the artist having to repay recording fund advances and possibly defending legal claims for breach of contract.

Fair Use Defense

The defense of fair use permits reasonable unauthorized copying from a copyrighted work, when the copying does not substantially impair present or potential value of the original work, and in some way advances the public benefit.

One rationale for the so-called fair use defense to copyright infringement is that only a small portion of the copyright work is copied. For many years there was a popular myth among musicians and producers that up to eight bars of a song was fair use and could be copied without constituting copyright infringement. This is not true. The rules determining which uses are fair uses, and not copyright infringement are not clear or simple. Many different economic and artistic factors go into determining whether or not a given use will be a productive and fair use. All of the circumstances of each case must be considered. The fair use standard for sound recordings is, however, generally stricter than for fair uses of musical compositions.

The reason for this difference is that U.S. copyright law only protects the expression of ideas, not the idea itself. Since there are a limited number of musical notes, copyright law treats single notes like ideas, and does not protect them. For this reason, it is safe to say that borrowing one note from a song will usually be a fair use of the copyright in the song, and not an actionable infringement. Borrowing more than one note, however, could be trouble. Lawsuits have involved copying as few as four notes from "I Love New York" and three words from "I Got Rhythm."

By selecting and arranging several notes in a particular sequence, composers create copyrightable musical compositions, or songs. Songs are the expression of the composer's creativity and are protected by copyright.

But different fair use standards apply to sound recordings. Since there is virtually an unlimited number of sounds that can be recorded, sound recordings are, by definition, comprised of pure, copyrightable expression.

For musicians, engineers and producers, the practical effect of the two different fair use standards is that sampling a small portion of a musical composition may sometimes be fair use because copying a small portion may borrow uncopyrightable single notes like uncopyrightable ideas. But sampling even a fraction of a second of a sound recording is copying of pure, copyrightable expression and is more likely to be an unfair use, constituting copyright infringement.

One way some producers and engineers that sample attempt to reduce the chances of a successful copyright infringement lawsuit is by electronically processing ("camouflaging") portions of the sampled sounds beyond the point of their being easily recognizable. Filtering, synthesizing, or distorting recorded sounds can help conceal the sampled material while still retaining the essence of an instrumental lick or vocal phrase embodied in a few seconds of sound. Adding newly created sounds to the underlying sampling further dilutes the material. This is an attempt to change the sampled materials so that even though material was illegally *copied*, there is no substantial similarity, thus avoiding a suit for copyright infringement.

UNFAIR COMPETITION

State and federal unfair competition laws apply when the record buying public is misled as to the source or true origin of recordings that contain sampled material.

The Lanham Act is a federal law that punishes deceptive trade practices that mislead consumers about what they are buying or who made the product.

If a consumer is confused by hearing sampled vocal tracks of James Brown, or sampled guitar licks by Eddie Van Halen, and mistakenly buys a record only to discover that he or she has bought a recording by a different artist, the consumer has been deceived by the sampling. Such confusion and deception is a form of unfair competition, which can give rise to legal claims for Lanham Act violations that can be brought in state or federal court, or unfair competition claims that may be brought in state court. All of the previous warnings about the costs of litigation apply here as well.

RIGHTS OF PRIVACY VIOLATIONS

When sampled material incorporates a person's voice, statutory, and common-law rights of privacy ("rights of publicity") may be violated. In California, Civil Code section 3344 establishes civil liability for the unauthorized commercial use of any living person's voice. Such a use would include sampling.

Although current federal moral rights legislation does not protect sound recordings or voices, such protection may be available in the future. Meanwhile, many state laws make unauthorized sampling of voices a violation of state right-of-publicity laws. Further, if the sampled voice was originally recorded without the vocalist's permission, sampling such an unauthorized recording may violate other state privacy laws as well.

FEDERAL ANTIBOOTLEGGING STATUTES

Effective December 8, 1994 the adoption of the Uruguay Round Agreements Act by the U.S. Congress amended U.S. law by adding both civil and criminal penalties for the unauthorized recording or videotaping of live musical performances.

Any person who recorded or sampled in the past, or records or samples in the future, any part of any live musical performance without the performer's consent, can now be sued under the new federal law for the same statutory damages, actual damages and attorneys' fees that are available in a traditional copyright infringement suit.

Previously, unauthorized recording of live performances was prohibited only under certain state laws.

Federal copyright law (17 U.S.C. §1101 *et seq.*) can now be used to prosecute so-called bootleggers that secretly record or sample live musical performances, or copy such illegal recordings by including sampled portions in new recordings. This strict new law also prohibits selling or even transporting bootlegged recordings.

Remarkably, the law is retroactive, protecting even pre-1994 recordings if they are currently being sold or distributed, and has no statute of limitations, so that arguably suit can be brought against bootleggers and sellers of bootlegged recordings 10, 20, even 100 years after the unauthorized recording was made, if the unauthorized recordings are sold or distributed after the effective date of the Act. Unlike copyrights, which usually only last for the life of the author plus 50 years, the new federal musical performance rights are perpetual, lasting forever. Moreover, the defense of fair use may not apply to such unauthorized recordings because the fair use defense in section 107 of the Copyright Act was not incorporated into the statute.

Of even greater concern are newly enacted criminal penalties (18 U.S.C. §2319A) of forfeiture, seizure, destruction, and up to ten years imprisonment for knowingly, for profit, making or distributing copies of illegally recorded performances, transmitting an illegally recorded performance, or distributing, selling, renting, or even transporting illegally recorded performances, even if the performance occurred outside the United States!

The serious implications of this new law for outlaw samplers are obvious. Sampling any part of a live performance, or any part of an unauthorized recording of a live musical performance triggers a minefield of federal civil and criminal penalties. Great care should be taken to avoid using such bootlegged recordings in any way.

NO ELECTRONIC THEFT ACT

Both civil and criminal liability may result from sampling preexisting recordings or compositions acquired from unauthorized MP3-type files in electronic or digital form using the global computer network, commonly referred to as the Internet. In late 1999, Jeffrey Gerard Levy, a 22-year-old University of Oregon student was sentenced to two years probation after pleading guilty to illegally distributing copyrighted materials including MP3 files, movie clips, and software. As the first person convicted under the No Electronic Theft (NET) Act, Levy could have been sentenced to three years in prison and fined up to $250,000.

PENALTIES

Attorneys are always expensive. Entertainment attorneys usually charge $100 to $400 per hour. Those that are experienced in federal court copyright litigation often charge even more. Court costs and one side's attorneys' fees in a copyright trial average about $350,000. If you lose the trial you will have to pay the judgment against you, which

LANDMARK LAWSUITS

In one of the most publicized sampling cases, the publisher of songwriter Gilbert O'Sullivan's song "Alone Again (Naturally)" successfully sued rap artist Biz Markie, Warner Brothers Records, and others for sampling three words and a small portion of music from O'Sullivan's song without permission for Markie's rap tune "Alone Again."

A lawsuit involving the unauthorized use of drumbeats sought strict enforcement of copyright laws against sampling. Tuff City Records sued Sony Music and Def Jam Records claiming that two singles by rap artist L. L. Cool J ("Around the Way Girl" and "Six Minutes of Pleasure") contained drum track samples from "Impeach the Presidents," a 1973 song by the Honeydrippers and that another Def Jam Record, "Give the People" included vocal samples from the same Honeydrippers song.

The case is important because the common practice of sampling drumbeats is often overlooked as a minor use, too insignificant to bother clearing. This lawsuit reinforces the rule that any sampling of a sound recording may lead to a lawsuit for copyright infringement. Courts have also found a particular harmony or the repetition of the word "uh-oh" in a distinctive rhythm sufficiently original to be protectable by copyright.

A lawsuit testing the limits of the fair use defense was brought by the Ireland-based rock group U2. The band, its recording company, Island Records, and music publisher Warner-Chappell Music sued the group Negativland for sampling a part of the U2 song, "I Still Haven't Found What I'm Looking For" without the group's permission. While attorneys for U2 claimed that the sampling was consumer fraud, Negativland maintained that the use was parody, satire, and cultural criticism, and was therefore protected under the fair use doctrine. The case was settled out of court. Negativland agreed to recall the single and return copies to Island Records for destruction.

Jarvis v. A&M Records was a lawsuit over the taking of eight words ("Ooh ooh ooh ooh...move...free your body") and a keyboard line. The sampling party argued that the amount of material taken was too insignificant to constitute copyright infringement. The federal district court in New Jersey disagreed and refused to dismiss the suit, ruling that even similarity of fragmented portions of the song could constitute infringement if the portions taken were qualitatively important.

could be as high as $100,000 for a single willful infringement (higher if there are substantial profits involved). An appeal of a judgment against you involves still more attorneys' fees and sometimes requires the posting of a bond.

In some cases a copyright infringer may have to pay the winning party's attorneys' fees. Copyright law also authorizes injunctions against the sale of CDs, tapes, and records containing illegally sampled material, seizure and destruction of infringing matter, and other criminal penalties.

In short, defending a copyright infringement lawsuit is a substantial expense and a risky proposition, exposing one to the possibility of hundreds of thousands of dollars in legal fees and costs.

Even if a particular sampling does not constitute copyright infringement, and is a fair use, it must still avoid violation of state and federal unfair competition laws.

COPYRIGHT CLEARANCES

Obtaining advance "permission," "copyright licenses" or "clearances" from owners of both the musical composition and the sound recording you want to sample is the best way to avoid the problems and expenses that can result from illegal sampling.

Many factors affect whether and when musicians should request and pay for clearances for samples. Although copyright laws and general music industry practices do not give rise to a lawsuit in every sampling situation, the enormous expenses of any sampling dispute should be avoided whenever possible.

In many cases, it is wise to clear samples early in the recording process even if, eventually, they are not used, because when the record is finished and the sample must be cleared, the artist will have little leverage in negotiating clearance fees.

In some cities, special music clearance firms routinely request, negotiate, prepare, and process clearances for sampled materials for a fee. They know reasonable rates for clearances and will prepare valid copyright licenses for less cost to the requesting party than will most music attorneys.

Clearance Costs: Royalties

The cost of clearances is a major consideration in deciding whether to sample. Generally, record companies will not pay an artist more than the full statutory mechanical license fee for permission to sell recordings of the artist's composition. In 2000, the statutory rate was 7.55¢ per unit, for up to five minutes of a recording. However, most record companies and others typically negotiate mechanical license fees of only 50% to 75% of the statutory rate to record an entire composition. Out of that mechanical license fee, the sampling artist must pay the owners of any sampled material. If the clearance fees for the sampled material are too high, none of the mechanical license fee will be left for the sampling artist, and the sampled cut may end up costing the artist more than is earned by the entire composition.

Sampling royalty rates for musical compositions can range from 10% to 25% of the statutory rate. Sampling royalty rates for sound recordings range from .5¢ to 3¢ per unit sold.

Clearance costs double or triple when more than one sampled track is included in a recording. Imagine, for example, a composition containing Phil Collins' snare drum sound, Jimi Hendrix's guitar sound, Phil Lesh's bass, and Little Richard's voice. In this case, combined sampling clearance fees would make the multitrack recording impossibly expensive.

Sampling clearance practices vary widely throughout the music industry. Fees are affected by both the quantity of material being sampled (a second or less is a "minor use," five seconds is a "major use") and the quality of the sampled material (i.e., a highly recognizable lyric sung by a famous artist would be more expensive than an anonymous bass drum track). Certain artists demand exorbitant fees to discourage sampling. On the other hand, some music publishers offer compositions in their catalogs and actively encourage sampling. Prices are affected by the popularity and prestige of the sampling artist and the uniqueness and value of the sampled sounds.

Clearance Costs: Buyouts and Co-Ownership

A percentage of the mechanical license fee (royalty) is one type of clearance fee. Another, is a one-time flat-fee payment (buyout) for the use of sampled material. Buyout fees range from $250 to $10,000, depending on the demands of the copyright owners. Up to $50,000 may be charged for a major use of a famous artist's performance or song. An upper limit on the number of units embodying the sampled material that may be sold may be imposed by some licensors, requiring additional payment at a higher royalty rate or an entirely new license if the maximum is exceeded.

More frequently, music publishers and record companies demand to be co-owners of the new composition as a condition of granting permission to sample. The option of assigning a share of the publishing (i.e., the copyright) in the song containing the sampled material to a publisher or record company may be helpful to the sampling artist, particularly when a buyout of all rights is not possible. Assigning a portion of the copyright in lieu of a cash advance may be less of a financial burden on an artist, enabling a song to be released where the cost or unavailability of a license would otherwise preclude the record from being distributed legally. If you license the sample for a percentage of the statutory rate, and you later want to license your song with the sample in it for a film, the film producer must obtain separate permission from the publisher who has granted the license. That publisher must always be consulted in new licensing situations. On the other hand, if you negotiate a buyout, you are free from any continuing obligation to the publisher. Similarly, if you negotiate income participation, which is to sell a percentage of your song in return for permission to sample, the publisher becomes a part owner of your song, and may or may not have approval rights in future licensing of the new work depending on the administration terms in the sampling license. Percentage of income participation ranges from 5% for a minimal use within the song to as much as 75% if the sample has been utilized throughout the song and is an integral part of the work.

AMERICAN FEDERATION OF MUSICIANS PAYMENTS

Under certain circumstances, the American Federation of Musicians (AFM) collects fees for its member musicians when a record company uses a sample of a preexisting recording in a new recording. When a portion of a recording containing the performance of an AFM member, who is a "nonroyalty artist," (i.e., a musician who plays on the recording but does not receive record royalties), not a self-contained royalty group or symphonic musician, is sampled under the following AFM definition, the company owning the recording that is being sampled makes a one time lump sum payment of $400 for the first sample (regardless of how many times it is used in the new recording) and a one-time lump sum payment of $250 for each additional sample from the same recording, plus 2% of the gross revenue received by the company in excess of $25,000, less the lump sum payments that have already been made. These payments are made to the Phonograph Record Manufacturers' Special Payments Fund, which are then distributed to the musician members. The AFM's definition of sampling is "a recording encoded into a digital sampler, computer, digital hard drive storage unit or other device for subsequent playback on a digital synthesizer or other play-back device for use in another song (but not a remix or reedit of the new song)." Note that the definition includes not only samples embodied in traditional tapes and CDs, but also includes samples embodied on synthesizers, samplers, and other playback devices.

SOUNDTRACK SAMPLING

Occasionally, artists sample things other than music, such as audio bytes from feature films, television shows, or news footage. In these cases, permission must be obtained from the owner of the footage. Fees range from $1000 to $8000 per minute for buyouts, which must be negotiated directly with the representative for the actor who's voice is being sampled. The minimum fee for such use is the Screen Actors Guild's full day rate, which is currently $617. Private licensing agents such as CMG in Indianapolis, Indiana may charge far more for permission to sample the voice of someone of the caliber of Elvis or Marilyn Monroe. If a film or television program is used, payments may also be due to the writers' and directors' guilds and to the American Federation of Musicians.

CONCLUSION

Throughout history, every new development in music has been greeted with suspicion by the music establishment of the day. Polyphony (playing harmonies) was considered demonic in medieval times, and was punishable by burning at the stake. As modern musicians explore innovative chord progressions, syncopated rhythms, and new electronic instruments, we all learn more about the musical landscape around us. Only time will tell whether samplers will be viewed as musical innovators or plagiarists.

SAMPLE USE AGREEMENTS

The Master Sample Use License Agreement and Mechanical License are short-form examples of licenses to incorporate or sample portions of a recording of a musical composition. Permission to sample the musical composition is granted by the music publisher(s) in the Mechanical License; permission to sample the recording of the musical composition is granted by the record company in the Master Sample Use License Agreement.

Fees for using the master and the musical composition are expressed as a one-time flat fee or buyout, and perpetual, worldwide rights are granted. As discussed above, such extensive rights may not always be granted. Limits on the term, territory or number of units that may be sold, co-ownership and coadministration of the recording and co-ownership of the musical composition embodying the sampled material, or statutory compulsory license fees on every copy sold, may be required by certain record companies and music publishers.

MASTER SAMPLE USE LICENSE AGREEMENT

In consideration of either (the sum of $ ______ which covers ____ % of the copyright) or (granting ____ % of the copyright and publishing right [and coadministration rights]) for the rights and license herein granted thereto, _________ (Record Company), hereinafter referred to as "Licensor," hereby grants to _________ (sampling Artist and/or recording company), hereinafter referred to as "Licensee," the nonexclusive, limited right, license, privilege and authority, but not the obligation, to use a portion of the Master Recording, defined below (hereinafter referred to as the "Master"), as embodied in the tape approved by Licensor, with no greater usage of the Master than is contained in the approved tape (the "Usage"), in the manufacture, distribution, and sale of any phonorecord (as that term is defined in Section 101 of the Copyright Act) entitled "__________ " ("Album"), performed by __________ ("Artist") embodying the recording __________ ("Master") as performed by __________ "Sample Artist"), and produced by __________ ("Producer"). Licensor additionally grants to Licensee the right to exploit, advertise, publicize, and promote such Master, as embodied in the phonorecord, in all media, markets, and formats now known or hereafter devised.

1. The term of this agreement ("Term") will begin on the date hereof and shall continue in perpetuity.

2. The territory covered by this agreement is ___________________________.

3. It is expressly understood and agreed that any compensation to be paid herein to Licensor is wholly contingent upon the embodiment of the Master within the phonorecord and that nothing herein shall obligate or require Licensee to commit to such usage. However, such compensation shall in no way be reduced by a lesser use of the Recording than the Usage provided for herein.

4. Licensor warrants only that it has the legal right to grant the aforesaid master recording use rights subject to the terms, conditions, limitations, restrictions, and reservations herein contained, and that this license is given and accepted without any other warranty or recourse. In the event said warranty is breached, Licensor's total liability

shall not exceed the lesser of the actual damages incurred by Licensee or the total consideration paid hereunder to Licensor.

5. Licensor reserves unto itself all rights and uses of every kind and nature whatsoever in and to the Master other than the limited rights specifically licensed hereunder, including the sole right to exercise and to authorize others to exercise such rights at any and all times and places without limitation.

6. This license is binding upon and shall inure to the benefit of the respective successors and assigns of the parties hereto.

7. This contract is entered into in the State of California and its validity, construction, interpretation, and legal effect shall be governed by the laws of the State of California applicable to contracts entered into and performed entirely therein.

8. This agreement contains the entire understanding of the parties relating to the subject matter herein contained.

IN WITNESS WHEREOF, the parties have caused the foregoing to be executed as of this ______ day of ________, 200___.

AGREED TO AND ACCEPTED:

______________________________	______________________________
LICENSOR (COMPANY NAME)	LICENSEE (COMPANY NAME)
______________________________	______________________________
BY (SIGNATURE)	BY (SIGNATURE)
______________________________	______________________________
NAME AND TITLE (AN AUTHORIZED SIGNATORY)	NAME AND TITLE (AN AUTHORIZED SIGNATORY)
______________________________	______________________________
FEDERAL I.D./SS#	FEDERAL I.D./SS#

MECHANICAL LICENSE

In consideration of the sum of $ ________ which covers _____ % of the copyright and full payment for the rights and license herein granted thereto, __________ ("Licensor") hereby grants to __________ ("Licensee") the nonexclusive right, license, privilege, and authority to use, in whole or in part, the copyrighted musical composition known as __________ written by __________ and __________ (hereinafter referred to as the "Composition"):

1. In the recording, making, and distribution of phonorecords (as that term is defined in Section 101 of the Copyright Act) to be made and distributed throughout the world in accordance with the provisions of Section 115 of the Copyright Act of the United States of America of October 19, 1976, as amended (the "Act"), except it is agreed that: (1) Licensee need not serve or file the notices required under the Act; (2)

consideration for such license shall be in the form of a one-time flat-fee buyout; (3) Licensee shall have the unlimited right to utilize the Composition, or any portion thereof, as embodied in the phonorecord, in any and all media now known or hereafter devised for the purpose of promoting the sale of the phonorecord which is the subject of this agreement; and (4) this license shall be worldwide.

2. This license permits the use of the Composition or any portion thereof, in the particular recordings made in connection with the sound recording __________ ("Album") by __________ ("Artist"), and permits the use of such recording in any phonorecord in which the recording may be embodied in whatever form now known or hereafter devised. This license includes the privilege of making a musical arrangement of the Composition to the extent necessary to conform it to the style or manner of interpretation of the performance involved.

3. Licensor warrants and represents that it has the right to enter into this agreement and to grant to Licensee all of the rights granted herein, and that the exercise by Licensee of any and all of the rights granted to Licensee in this agreement will not violate or infringe upon any common-law or statutory rights of any person, firm, or corporation including, without limitation, contractual rights, copyrights, and rights of privacy.

4. This license is binding upon and shall inure to the benefit of the respective successors, assigns, and sublicensees of the parties hereto.

5. This agreement sets forth the entire understanding of the parties with respect to the subject matter hereof, and may not be modified or amended except by written agreement executed by the parties.

6. This license may not be terminated for any reason, is entered into in the State of California, and its validity, construction, interpretation, and legal effect shall be governed by the laws of the State of California applicable to contracts entered into and performed entirely therein.

IN WITNESS WHEREOF, the parties have entered into this license agreement as of this _________ day of ___________, 200__.

AGREED TO AND ACCEPTED:

______________________________	______________________________
LICENSOR (COMPANY NAME)	LICENSEE (COMPANY NAME)
______________________________	______________________________
BY (SIGNATURE)	BY (SIGNATURE)
______________________________	______________________________
NAME AND TITLE (AN AUTHORIZED SIGNATORY)	NAME AND TITLE (AN AUTHORIZED SIGNATORY)
______________________________	______________________________
FEDERAL I.D./SS#	FEDERAL I.D./SS#

Special thanks to Suzy Vaughan, Esq. and Ron McGowan for their generous assistance in the preparation of these agreements.

Collaborator/Songwriter Agreements

BY MARK HALLORAN AND EDWARD (NED) R. HEARN

If you cowrite a song with someone, both of you own the song as "joint owners" in what the copyright law calls a "joint work." This is irrespective of whether one of you writes the music and the other the lyrics, or you both write music and lyrics. Both of you have an "undivided" ownership in the song (i.e., you each own 50% of the whole song). There is not a separate copyright in the music and lyrics. There is one copyright in both.

The essence of cowriting is writing together to create a single song, regardless of who contributes what. This does not mean that you have to work together, or that your creative contribution be equal in quality or quantity. You also do not need to have an express "collaboration agreement," although it is a good idea, given the myriad issues that can arise.

One of the most famous cowriting teams is Bernie Taupin and Elton John. Bernie, on his own, first writes the lyrics. John, on his own, then writes the music. Since both Bernie and Elton intend that their work be a united whole, the result is a joint work, which they co-own fifty-fifty.

PERCENTAGE OWNERSHIP

As joint owners you and your cowriter can divide your song ownership in whatever proportion you want. In the absence of an agreement you share equally, even if it is clear that your contributions are not equal. Thus, if there are two songwriters, you own the song fifty-fifty; three songwriters, one-third each; etc. Dividing the ownership ratably is also the most common way to divide ownership in a written collaboration agreement.

One common benchmark in dividing ownership is that the lyrics are worth 50% and the music 50%. For example, if two people write the music and one person writes the lyrics, they may agree to divide the ownership 25% each for the two music writers, with the lyricist retaining the remaining 50%. However, if there is no such agreement, each would own 33.3% of the song.

GRANT OF RIGHTS

Now that we have determined who owns the song, who controls it? It is crucial to the exploitation of the song that there be a central place to license the work and collect money.

Coadministration of Licenses

It is usually more convenient for one music publisher to collect and divide all the income. Licensing can become complicated when a licensee has to seek the approval of, and document permission from, multiple publishers. However, many cowriters prefer that there be separate administration among the various publishing companies. This has its advantages. You have control over to whom licenses are granted, how much is charged, how the money is collected, and what costs are incurred.

As joint owner (in the United States), you may exploit the song yourself and also grant nonexclusive licenses. Still, you must account to your cowriters for the money that is generated from the nonexclusive licenses.

A license is permission to use a work. It is not a transfer of copyright ownership, which requires the permission of all songwriters (although you could transfer just your share to another without affecting the ownership interests of the other cowriters/co-owners). (See discussion below.)

- Public Performances. Public performances agreements must be entered into with ASCAP, BMI or SESAC. Typically, they are done in the name of the songwriter's publishing company. If cowriters want to use one company, they may use that company and divide the publisher's share of the income. Or, each of the separate publishing companies may enter into a performance agreement for its share with ASCAP, BMI or SESAC with each collecting its respective percentage of the publisher's share of the public performance income. Writers should join ASCAP, BMI or SESAC, to collect their portion of the songwriters' shares of the public performance income.

- Mechanical Licenses. Mechanical licenses are nonexclusive, any cowriter can grant them, but must account to and pay the other cowriters, or instruct the licensed party that the cowriter's shares be paid directly to them.

- Print Rights. These agreements are usually exclusive, and all cowriters must agree in writing.

- Subpublishing Rights. Foreign subpublishing deals are usually exclusive, and all cowriters must agree in writing. Additionally, most foreign jurisdictions require that all co-owners agree to licensing, so the subpublishers are going to want to have all cowriters sign. If agreement cannot be reached on a shared subpublisher, you can, however, still make arrangements with one to represent just your interest share in the songs' copyrights.

DIVISION OF INCOME

Just as a contributing author is entitled to a ratable share of ownership, the coauthor is also entitled to the same ratable share of income, absent an agreement to the contrary.

PURSUIT OF INFRINGEMENT

One obligation that cowriters have together is to protect the copyright. This includes pursuing infringers. Can you sue even if a co-owner does not want to sue? The answer appears to be yes, at least with respect to your interest in the copyright. However, the court may require that you bring in the cowriter(s) as a coplaintiff, so it is best that you decide to sue together.

What if you have to sue a co-owner, for example, for failure to account to and pay you? You may, but you do not have to, bring in all the other co-owners in order to sue.

COPYRIGHT DURATION

The basic rule is that the copyright of a song written after January 1, 1976 lasts for the life of the author plus 70 years. In the case of a joint work, the copyright lasts for the life of the last surviving author plus 70 years.

COPYRIGHT TRANSFERS

Each collaborator, independently of the other collaborators, has the right to transfer his or her copyright ownership to another party. That transfer may be for the full copyright share of the collaborator to a publisher, or a partial copyright transfer to a copublisher. A collaborator may also grant all administration and supervision rights of that collaborator's share to a third party as the publishing administrator, while still retaining ownership of the copyright.

If one collaborator transfers his or her copyright interests to a third party, but the second collaborator does not do the same, then the third party would co-own the copyright with the other collaborator. At the same time, the second collaborator has the option to transfer his or her copyright interest, in the whole or in part, or just the administration rights, to the same new owner as did the first collaborator, or to a different party.

Unless either collaborator has granted to the other collaborator the administration rights in the copyright for the song, the new co-owner will have to share decision-making and the publisher's income share with the collaborator that did not transfer his or her interests. The accounting can become cumbersome if income sharing and accounting procedures are not coordinated.

DIFFERENT PERFORMING RIGHTS SOCIETY AFFILIATIONS

It is also possible for each coauthor to belong to a different performing rights society, namely ASCAP, BMI or SESAC. If that is the case, then a share of the performance income collection would be allocated to each collaborator's affiliated performing rights society. For example, if the song is performed as a part of a soundtrack to a television program, then, with the performance rights for that song being divided between two different performing rights groups, the performance fee also would be so divided. Each performing rights group would receive its allocated share and distribute it to the collaborator affiliated with it. It is quite possible that one collaborator, being paid by a different performing rights society, would not receive the same amount of writer and publisher performance income as the other, since each of the performing rights societies uses a different reporting mechanism.

SONGWRITERS AS MEMBERS OF DIFFERENT BANDS

In the event one of the collaborating songwriters is a member of a band and the other is not, the collaborator who is a member of the band will have the authority to allow the band to rehearse and perform the collaborated song in live concerts and to record the song for release on phonorecords. While, technically, it is best to have both writers approve and issue a combined use license, i.e., a mechanical license to reproduce the song on phonorecords, each has the authority to do so, but must account to the collaborator who is not a band member for their share of writer and publisher income. Most record labels will want to get both coauthors and copublishers to provide written authorization for the initial reproduction of that song on phonorecords. After the first release of the phonorecords, a compulsory mechanical license procedure may apply to any future recordings of that song, whether by that same or any other band.

CONTROLLED COMPOSITION CLAUSE

Of particular significance is the situation where one of the coauthors is a band member (while the other is not) and has a recording agreement with a record label that requires the writer/band member to agree to a controlled composition clause in the recording agreement. This clause authorizes the record company to pay a reduced mechanical royalty, usually 75% of the prevailing statutory mechanical rate, as the royalty fee for the right to reproduce the song on phonorecords that are sold to the public.

Generally, the recording artist/collaborating writer will be required by the record company to represent that he or she has obtained permission from the collaborating writer who is not the band member and not a signatory to the recording agreement to issue a mechanical license for the reduced rate. But often, the recording artist/collaborating writer cannot guarantee that, and most likely will not be able to provide the record label with written authorization from the collaborator accepting a reduced mechanical royalty rate. In those situations, the record company will have to pay the collaborating writer who is not a member of the band nor a signatory to the recording agreement that cowriter's share of mechanicals, both as writer and copublisher, at full statutory rate, while paying the collaborator, who is a signatory, the reduced rate. It is also possible that the rate for the recording artist/collaborating writer will be reduced even further, given the need to pay the unsigned collaborator the higher amount, which will reduce the amount available to pay the recording artist/collaborating writer.

By way of illustration, assume that the maximum pool of mechanical royalties for all of the songs on the recording artist's album is 56.625¢ (75% of 75.5¢), as distinct from the current statutory rate of 7.55¢ per song, which would earn 75.5¢ if ten songs are on the album. (Note that the statutory rate will change to 8¢ per song on January 1, 2002.) The payout to the collaborating coauthor who is not a signatory to the recording agreement will reduce the overall pool available for mechanical royalties, causing the amount payable to the collaborator/band member to be even less than the 75% fractional statutory rate. For example, if that nonsignatory collaborating coauthor has contributed half of the material on four different songs, he/she will get full statutory for his/her share of those songs, .5 x 7.55¢ x 4 = 15.1¢, which will be deducted from the maximum pool of 56.625¢, leaving 41.525¢ to be allocated to the signatory collaborating songwriters for the other six songs that were fully written by them and for the other four coauthored by them with the nonsignatory collaborator. This is effectively 5.19¢ for each full song and 2.595¢ for each of the four collaborated songs.

COACCOUNTING

Any income that either collaborating writer receives from the commercial exploitation of the song, whether it is from their own use or from use by an authorized third party, must be accounted for and apportioned to the other collaborating songwriter. Such payments should be made in a timely manner, for example, no less than 30 days after receipt. Also, statements that accompany the payments to the first collaborator should be copied and forwarded with the payment to the other collaborator.

FUTURE GENERATIONS

The rights of each deceased coauthor will pass on to the benefit of the heir(s) and descendant(s) of that coauthor, either by way of a will (testate) or without a will (intestate). If there is no will, the distribution will be governed by state statutes, usually to surviving spouses and children, on a first priority basis, before other relatives. It then would be the heir or the executor of the estate of the deceased who will have the authority to grant and make decisions with respect to the use of a collaborated composition. By the same token, the surviving collaborator will have the authority to continue to exploit the song while having a reporting and payment sharing obligation to the deceased's descendants or executor. The estate of the deceased collaborator can exploit the song too, and must account to the surviving coauthor.

Digital Downloads and Streaming: Copyright and Distribution Issues

BY EDWARD (NED) R. HEARN

Now is probably the most exciting and dynamic time for musicians and composers since Thomas Edison designed and patented the phonograph in 1877. The development of digital compression technology (i.e., MP3), concurrent with the development of Internet technology, has created an environment that has shaken many of the old rules of the music industry and seriously challenged the traditional music business to adapt to changes in consumer preferences. MP3 and similar technologies, and free peer-to-peer file sharing services such as Napster, Gnutella and FreeNet, coupled with high-speed T1, cable and DSL lines, have created a whole new paradigm on how to provide consumers with recorded music.

Laws that address digital delivery continue to evolve, as do new contractual agreements and economic models by which music publishers and record companies attempt to control the economic returns due them and the creators of music and sound recordings. This chapter discusses the rights of recording artists and composers. It will explain how the recent changes to the Copyright Act attempt to create a mechanism to provide an economic return for composing and recording in the digital media world.

The chapter also provides examples of new models that are being developed to convince consumers they should be willing to pay to enjoy the convenience and breadth of choice these new services offer.

DIGITAL PERFORMANCE OF SOUND RECORDINGS

When you compose and record music, you essentially create two properties, both of which are protected by the copyright laws—the music you write and the musical performances you record.

As the copyright owner of the music and the sound recording, you have the exclusive right to reproduce, distribute, display, perform and create derivative works with those properties, with the sole exception that, in the United States you have no exclusive rights to perform the sound recording (as distinct from the performance of the music on the sound recording), namely anyone can perform the sound recording without having to make any payment to you for it. Examples of performing the sound recording include playing, broadcasting, or transmitting those sound recordings over radio or television. This situation is the result of effective lobbying by the broadcast industry when sound recordings first became subject to federal copyright protection in 1972. The broadcast industry was able to get Congress to exclude from the exclusive rights of the owner of sound recordings the right to perform those works, since the broadcast industry already was paying the music publishers royalties for the performance of the music contained on the recordings (namely, the payments collected by BMI, ASCAP and SESAC). These royalties are distinct from synchronization fees paid for the right to fix and reproduce the music and the sound recording on the soundtrack of an audiovisual production.

The record companies were determined not to let their experience with the performance of sound recordings on radio be repeated in the digital world. Consequently, amendments to the Copyright Act were enacted in 1995, namely the Digital Performance Right in Sound Recordings Act (DPRSRA) and in 1998, the Digital Millennium Copyright Act (DMCA). The DPRSRA vests, in the owner of the sound recording, the exclusive right to control the *digital* performance of the sound recordings over cable and satellite. The DMCA applies the same exclusive right to the owner of the sound recording with respect to webcasting over the Internet. Under each of these Acts, fees must be paid for the performance of the sound recording in the digital medium. The companies that wish to perform the sound recording digitally must get either a voluntary or a compulsory license if they are to avoid copyright infringement claims. The provisions of both acts are very complex, and at the end of this chapter there is a description of the requirements that must be satisfied for cable, satellite companies, and webcasters to qualify for a compulsory license; i.e., getting permission from the record companies and owners of the sound recordings to digitally perform them is not necessary so long as the intent to rely on the compulsory license procedure is filed with the Copyright Office and the rules that regulate the scope of performances under the compulsory parameters are satisfied.

If the cable, satellite industries and webcasters do not satisfy the compulsory license provisions that concern the digitally transmitted performance of the sound recordings, then they must get permission from the owners of the sound recordings. The granting of such permission is voluntary and the owners can set their own rates.

With regard to the compulsory licensing under the DPRSRA, the record, cable, and satellite industries tried to negotiate and establish the rates that would be used to compute the fees to be paid. They could not reach agreement and an arbitration panel, under the auspices of the Copyright Office, reviewed the matter and set the rates. The record companies were arguing for a royalty of 15% to 20% of the receipts of the cable and satellite companies, and the latter were offering 1% to 2% of their revenues. The final license fees imposed on the cable and satellite industries were 6.5% of the gross revenues. The fees paid, based on those percentages, are allocated 50% to the record company (i.e., the owner of the sound recording), 45% to the featured artist, 2.5% to nonfeatured musicians, and 2.5% to nonfeatured vocalists. There have been millions of dollars collected to date under the DPRSRA, which have been paid to the Recording Industry Association of America (RIAA) as the representative of the sound recording copyright owners. The RIAA has disbursed that money to its label members. Most of the money has gone to the major labels, and there is much controversy over the appropriateness of using the RIAA as the distributing agency, since it does not represent the interests of all of the smaller independent labels, although a number of the independent labels have authorized the RIAA to act as their collection agency. There also is the issue of whether and when the labels will pass on to the artists their share of such fees, which for the most part has not yet happened.

A similar situation occurred under the DMCA with respect to webcasters. As the representatives of the record and webcasting industries were not able to settle on fees, the matter has been submitted to arbitration under the auspices of the Copyright Office, and that process is scheduled to commence in the summer of 2001. The disparity in fees sought by the labels and offered by the webcasters parallels the same positions experienced between the record companies and the satellite and cable companies. There is still some distance to travel before fees are identified, paid and allocated. Estimates of projected income have been as high as $400 million a year. Battle lines also have been drawn on who will be appointed by the Copyright Office to collect and distribute these fees. The RIAA, through its SoundExchange, Music Reports Inc., and the performing rights societies, have expressed an interest or intent in taking on that task.

There also is the issue of the record companies' responsibility to pay artists their share of those sound recording performance fees, and whether those fees will be paid if artists have unrecouped recording accounts or whether those fees would be applied to those accounts. Different labels apply different approaches, and the contracts between the artists and the labels will determine the results. For the present, the record labels have indicated that these webcasting sound recording performance royalties should be paid to the artists directly by the authorized collection agency.

A real-life example of the revenue that webcasting or streaming over the Internet generates can be found in the litigation and settlements between MP3.com and the major record companies. Four of them, BMG, EMI, Sony and Warner Music, have settled for about $20 million each. Universal Music, which is the only company to go to trial and win, has settled for $53.4 million. The basis of this suit was that the My.MP3.com storage and streaming service resulted in copyright infringement because MP3.com loaded (i.e., copied) compact discs of major labels and independent labels into its servers without permission. No permissions were obtained and no fees were established or paid by MP3.com prior to launching its My.MP3.com services. The performances of the sound recordings, by way of their being streamed to the consumer, were copyright infringements, since streaming selections on demand does not qualify as a use that falls within the compulsory license provisions of webcasting uses (see box at end of chapter).

Universal Music announced that $25 million of the $53.4 million settlement would be allocated to its artists. None of the other labels have done the same, although, a few have expressed that it is their intent to share the settlement fees and future licensing fees with their artists. A portion of the MP3.com settlement is for past infringing acts and some is to be applied as an advance for future loading and streaming. Part of the negotiation by the labels with MP3.com also provided for approximately 1.5¢ to be paid for a sound recording each time it is loaded into a consumer's digital locker, and .33¢ paid each time the sound recording is streamed to a customer. Licensing deals with comparable fees have been made voluntarily by the labels and the RIAA with other digital storage and streaming companies, such as Musicbank, and portals such as Yahoo!, through which music travels digitally to consumers.

DIGITAL PERFORMANCE OF MUSIC

In addition to fees for the streaming of sound recordings by satellite, cable or webcasting, the streaming companies must sign license agreements with the music performing rights societies, BMI, ASCAP and SESAC, for the performance of the music embodied on the sound recordings. The performing rights societies will allocate those fees to the publishers and writers. There has been no dispute about the right of the performing rights societies to collect such sums and the obligation of the satellite, cable and webcasting companies to obtain licenses and pay. The issue has been how much to pay. The Web sites of the performing rights societies provide details on how they compute the fees for the performance of music over the Internet. Fees have been negotiated on a case-by-case basis. Most cable and satellite companies, and webcasters and streaming media companies, such as MyPlay and Musicbank, as well as some Internet service providers, such as Yahoo!, have obtained licenses from the performing rights societies.

Publishers, through the National Music Publishers Association (NMPA), also sued MP3.com for the unauthorized mechanical reproduction of the music on the MP3.com servers and the streaming or performance of that music to My.MP3.com customers. A $30 million settlement has been negotiated on that suit, with 50% of that money applied to the past infringement and 50% treated as an advance against future royalties, which are computed at 10¢ the first time a song is loaded into the server, and .25¢ each time a song is streamed to a customer. The NMPA has made similar licensing deals with other digital Internet streaming companies, such as Musicbank. The NMPA also has sued Universal for failing to get permission and pay fees (the amount of which still has not yet been set) for performing music over the Internet through Universal's Farmclub.com subscription service.

The NMPA and RIAA also have asked the Copyright Office for an arbitration hearing on what Internet streaming subscription services should pay to music publishers for the performance of the music through their services.

In addition, the NMPA takes the position that a digital delivery or download of a phonorecord containing music requires payment of a performance fee as well as a mechanical royalty (see paragraph below on mechanical royalties for digital phonorecord deliveries).

DIGITAL PHONORECORD DELIVERIES OF SOUND RECORDINGS

Since the right to reproduce and distribute copies of sound recordings is recognized as an exclusive right of the copyright owner, the DPRSRA and the DMCA did not have to address the rules that would apply to digital phonorecord deliveries as they relate to sound recordings. Rather, the economics of digital phonorecord delivery is evolving based on marketplace experiments and contractual arrangements between recording companies and other owners of sound recordings, and artists and the third parties that license those sound recordings to distribute them digitally to consumers. Sound recordings can be digitally delivered directly to consumers over the Web, and through kiosks at retail outlets that have connections to the Internet. At the kiosks, consumers can download masters and have them burned into compact discs or loaded into portable MP3 players.

Record companies have been including provisions in their contracts that treat digital phonorecord deliveries essentially the same as the physical sale of phonorecords, but at reduced royalty rates. A typical provision reads as follows:

> *Notwithstanding anything to the contrary contained herein, the royalty rate for any phonorecord in a New Technology Configuration shall be two-thirds (2/3) of the otherwise applicable royalty rate set forth in this Agreement for traditional configurations (i.e., if the royalty on a master is fifteen percent (15%), the company will*

instead use ten percent (10%) to compute the royalty). New Technology Configurations shall mean phonorecords in the following configurations: minidiscs, laserdiscs, enhanced CDs, CD-ROMs, DVDs, digitally delivered or distributed copies of Master Recordings over the Internet or other networked systems, and other phonorecords embodying, employing, or otherwise utilizing nonanalog technology (including now known and hereafter developed), exclusive, however, of audio compact discs, which shall not be treated as a New Technology Configuration.

Sometimes, the agreements provide for an increase in the royalty percentage from 66.67% (or whatever the starting rate is) to a higher rate, which is based on the penetration level of the New Technology Configuration in the market. For example, "The royalty for phonorecords in a New Technology Configuration will be increased from 66.67% to 75% when the New Technology Configuration's share of the market is equal to or exceeds 30%."

In lieu of a "packaging deduction" for digitally distributed phonorecords of the master recording, the labels will take a "digitization fee" of 25%. This will therefore reduce the measuring royalty base sales price by 25%. Digitization fees include such costs as encryption, compression/decompression technologies (codecs), digital rights management, hosting, servicing, and financial clearinghouse fees.

Record company agreements often attempt to incorporate, into New Technology Configuration royalties, the reductions that apply to the "old media" with respect to reduced royalties. This includes singles, 12-inch singles, EPs, videos, budget records and midprice records, as well as the ubiquitous free good deductions, when any of those categories are relevant in a New Technology Configuration.

As always, the bottom line on the resulting royalty rate depends on the bargaining leverage of the label, producer and artist.

Labels try to make distinctions between tangible records for which they may agree to certain marketing and use restrictions, such as limitations on coupling, and intangible records where they try to avoid restrictions on such things as coupling, since part of the attraction for digitally distributing individual tracks is that consumers can create their own compilations.

The major labels usually price digital download programs at retail store prices for physical copies. They often require the downloading of complicated digital media protocols that take a long time to download, and which usually results in the consumer being too discouraged to pursue that approach to buying the music. Although the consumer can access these digital delivery methods directly, the major labels prefer that consumers go through the Web site versions of retail stores, such as Tower and Virgin, and Web-based retailers, like Amazon.com and Getmusic.com. Some major labels, like BMG, Sony and Universal, use these retail sites as "agents," and let them keep a percentage of the transaction, for example, 15% to 20%, with the rest going to the labels. Others, like Warner Music and EMI, use a wholesale approach, and charge the reseller a stated amount and the reseller keeps the difference from what it charges the consumer.

With regard to licenses to third parties to digitally deliver phonorecords, the economics of those deals vary. Examples include the following:

- EMusic: digital distribution to consumers with a fifty-fifty split of net after defined expenses (approximately 20¢) shared by EMusic and the licensing label, which, in turn, shares its 50% with artists, usually on a fifty-fifty basis. Deductions include credit card transaction fees, sales tax, credits, returns, mechanicals, public performance fees, union payments, Internet advertising and promotion costs, and referral fees.

- Liquid Audio: provides digital downloads through Liquid Network Affiliates and takes 30% of the wholesale price to the retailer as a distribution fee. The balance (70%) goes to the licensor, who is responsible for all third-party costs, which include artist and producer royalties, mechanicals, and union fees. The retail Web site that handles the sale to the consumer keeps the difference between what it charges and the wholesale price it pays to Liquid Audio.

These models have changed and will change many times again. The marketplace in the world of digital phonorecord deliveries is evolving quickly. Some of the referenced companies may go out of business or be acquired by other companies. It is your responsibility to stay abreast of new models as they evolve. Work with record industry professionals that are conversant with the economic changes in the digital music world in your efforts to stay abreast.

DIGITAL PHONORECORD DELIVERIES OF MUSIC

When a record is manufactured and sold, the record company must pay a mechanical royalty to the publisher for the reproduction of the music on the phonorecords. Likewise, the DPRSRA provided that a mechanical royalty must be paid for music that is digitally downloaded just as the mechanical royalty is paid for music on phonorecords sold in hard medium. Most record contracts try to limit the statutory rate that has to be paid for the reproduction of music on phonorecords written by the recording artist (i.e., a controlled composition) to 75% of the statutory rate, often with a cap of 10 to 12 songs per album as opposed to the actual number of compositions on an album if there are more than that. Under the directives of the DPRSRA the RIAA and the NMPA agreed that, until December 31, 2000, the same mechanical royalty rate would apply to both physical phonorecords and digital phonorecord deliveries (DPDs). A new mechanical rate was to be negotiated for music on digital phonorecord deliveries made after December 31, 2000, but as of the writing of this chapter no new rate has been established, and it is likely that the determination of a new rate will require yet another arbitration proceeding supervised by the Copyright Office. The various industry players also have asked the Copyright Office to determine mechanical royalty rates for "incidental" DPDs, e.g., digital phonorecord deliveries that time out or that are "streamed" on demand and temporarily buffered or cached in that process.

Under the DPRSRA, contractual efforts to impose a fractional limit on mechanical royalties for music on digitally delivered phonorecords that is written or controlled by an artist is not permitted, except for agreements that predate June 22, 1995 or agreements made after the date when the songs in question were recorded with the artist/songwriter thereafter agreeing, in writing, to a reduced rate. Absent these qualifications, the full statutory mechanical royalty rate must be paid for music on digital phonorecord deliveries. The current rate (in effect for the two-year period beginning January 1, 2000) is 7.55¢ per song or 1.45¢ per minute of playing time, whichever is greater. The per minute rate applies when the recorded song is longer than five minutes. For physical phonorecords, this rate is scheduled to increase to 8¢ per song or 1.55¢ per minute of playing time, commencing January 1, 2002; and 8.5¢ per song or

1.65¢ per minute of playing time, commencing January 1, 2004; and 9.1¢ per song or 1.75¢ per minute of playing time, commencing January 1, 2006. The representatives of the record and music publishing industries will meet, determine, and submit to the Copyright Office for approval mutually agreed to schedules for rates commencing January 1, 2008. In addition, the NMPA has taken the position that a digital phonorecord delivery, in addition to requiring a mechanical royalty, requires a music performance fee (such as digital performance of music) since the digital delivery includes a performance.

EVOLVING BUSINESS MODELS

The new statutes have attempted to blend the old and new approaches, with the old being to extend the mechanical royalty rate to digital phonorecord deliveries of music, and to require a royalty for the digital delivery of the sound recording. The new approach is the requirement for the payment of fees for the digital performances of the sound recordings.

Various business models will be studied and implemented to determine how to monetize the commercial use of music through the new technologies. There have been efforts to create encrypted environments to secure control over the digital distribution of music and sound recordings, such as the music industry's efforts at developing SDMI (Secure Digital Music Initiative) protocols. But the reality is, there is still no such thing as a foolproof encryption system that prevents unauthorized distribution of music files. If music can be obtained easily and for free through Napster, FreeNet or Gnutella, why pay for it? Consequently, music publishers and record companies will have to implement new music and sound recording access models that make consumers willing to pay for music they could get for free. This is important for the future of the record and music publishing businesses and the artists that need the new technology to be monetized.

A sampling of some models includes per unit and subscription downloading, subscription streaming, including on demand, and super distribution. Under a subscription model for customized streaming audio services, upon the payment of a monthly fee, consumers get access to specific kinds of music by genre, artist or album cut. All of the majors are now developing and implementing streaming services. You can choose what you want to hear, or accept the selection process of the streaming entity, and the music can be streamed to your computer, portable player, and car by way of satellite or wireless technology. The storage lockers/streaming services of MyPlay, My.MP3.com, and Musicbank fall into this category, but generally require that you already own a copy of the physical record. The fee paid is for the convenience of "anywhere/anytime" access, for the use of the storage space, and to cover some of the costs of streaming on demand as a performance of the sound recording and music, which, as described earlier, are subject to the performance fee rights of the copyright owners.

Some digital phonorecord delivery companies have per title charges, such as EMusic at 99¢ per track or $8.99 per album, or an all-you-can-download subscription service. EMusic currently offers two subscription models: a $14.99 per month plan, which requires a minimum sign-up period of three months, and a $9.99 per month plan, with a minimum sign-up period of 12 months. Another example is Bertelsmann (BMG Music), which is investigating a subscription approach with respect to its involvement with Napster, which has been a free service. The record labels also are exploring digital downloads through retailers, so they do not alienate the brick and mortar stores still needed to deliver physical goods to consumers.

Independents that cannot afford to establish their own digital delivery systems have the option of using third parties to provide distribution. Navarre Corporation *(www.navarre.com)* and RedDotNet *(www.reddotnet.com)*, an Alliance Entertainment Corp. company, can digitally deliver for their distributed labels. They provide digital rights management, codec, and watermarking systems and generally deliver the digital phonorecord through a retailer's Web site or an in-store kiosk of a retailer.

The super distribution method encodes music files so that the initial acquirer is able to pass them on to others. There is a payment collection mechanism that flows back to the labels and the artists, with perhaps the person who first paid for the download of the digital phonorecord and song passing on the file to another (or series of others) and getting a share of the payment in the nature of an agency fee.

Technology needs to evolve so that the titles chosen by consumers are tracked for the purpose of royalty accounting to the record companies, artists, publishers and writers.

The challenge is to figure out how to collect the money and disburse it to the creators of music in a world where free has become the norm. Each participant in the distribution chain will thus pay for access and use.

As of the final editing of this chapter, the Ninth Circuit Federal Court of Appeals in the Napster case concluded, at least with respect to the current phase of that case, that the record companies and music publishers demonstrated a likelihood that they would prevail at a trial in proving that Napster committed both contributory and vicarious copyright infringement by providing the system for its millions of registered members to file share (P2P, or peer-to-peer) the copyrighted, recorded musical masters of others. The trial court, on remand, in turn instructed Napster to take down or block access to unauthorized files within three business days of receiving written notice from copyright holders that also must identify the names of the recordings to which they hold the copyrights, and provide evidence that those masters are being traded on Napster and the identifying name of the sending party. Napster in turn is developing and licensing third-party systems to assist in filtering out and blocking access to the unauthorized files.

By the time this book is published, many more chapters on the status of Napster and its progeny will have been written, including the status of the arrangements between Napster and Bertelsmann (the owner of BMG Music, RCA Records, and Arista Records, among others) to convert Napster to an authorized and monetized file sharing business.

QUALIFICATIONS FOR COMPULSORY LICENSE UNDER THE DIGITAL PERFORMANCE RIGHT IN SOUND RECORDINGS ACT OF 1995 (DPRSRA)

In 1995, the DPRSRA provided a public performance right in a sound recording for the copyright owner, for the first time in the United States (amending Section 106 and Section 114 of the Copyright Act). This grant applied, however, only in certain limited circumstances, as detailed below.

- Public performance by means of digital audio interactive and on-demand transmissions for which a voluntary license is required; therefore, it is the exclusive right of the sound recording owner (i.e., the record company) to decide whether to issue a license permitting interactive transmissions.

- Public performance by means of subscription noninteractive transmission—for which a compulsory blanket license applies; i.e., a voluntary license is not required from the sound recording owner. (This legislation fostered a debate on whether the DPRSRA applied to Internet webcasters and resulted in a provision being included in the Digital Millennium Copyright Act of 1998.)

- DPRSRA does not apply to digital broadcasters (i.e., transmissions by FCC licensed terrestrial broadcast stations), which are exempt from needing a public performance license (whether voluntary or compulsory) for sound recordings. There is an open issue on whether the DMCA applies to the simulcast of such stations' programs over the Internet.

The following are the conditions that must be met for a Web broadcaster to qualify for compulsory license, without which transmission would be an infringement of copyright:

- Must not exceed "sound recording performance complement;" i.e., over a three-hour period, cannot transmit more than two consecutive or three total selections from one sound recording; or more than four songs, or three in a row, from the same artist.

- Must transmit owner encoded copyright information with recordings; i.e., must identify sound recordings, the album and featured artist.

- Prior announcements are not permitted, cannot publish a program guide.

- Looped or continuous programs may not be less than three hours in duration; and programs of less than one hour and performed at scheduled times may be performed only three times in a two-week period, or four times in a two-week period if one hour or more in duration.

- Archived programs (i.e., previously performed programs or series of programs) may not be less than five hours in duration and may reside on the Web site for no more than a total of two weeks.

1998 DIGITAL MILLENNIUM COPYRIGHT ACT (DMCA-SECTION 405)

The DMCA further amends Section 114 of the Copyright Act by granting a public performance license for digital transmission or streaming of sound recordings by webcasters, i.e. playing or performing (as distinct from a digital download) of audio musical sound recordings over the Internet. This activity does not fall directly within the categories addressed by the DPRSRA, and Section 405 of the DMCA amended the DPRSRA to expand the statutory (compulsory) license for nonsubscription transmission to include webcasting as a new category of eligible transmission, and therefore subject to a compulsory license. As such, the sound recording's copyright owner cannot prevent the webcasting provided that all of the criteria required by the statute (see below) are satisfied by the webcaster and it has timely filed for a compulsory license.

Webcasters took the position that the DPRSRA did not apply to them as their conduct was a "nonsubscription transmission" and "noninteractive," and therefore exempt from requiring the permission of sound recording copyright owners.

RIAA's position was that webcasters were required to get licenses from the sound recording copyright owners (i.e., the DPRSRA's exemptions were only available to FCC terrestrial licensed broadcasters).

The DMCA confirmed that a license, either compulsory or voluntary, was required, by providing that the sound recording copyright owners have the exclusive right to control online or Internet delivery of their sound recordings.

The statutory license applies, however, only to certain noninteractive subscription and nonsubscription transmissions. Interactive service is defined in the DMCA to exclude transmission of songs specifically requested by and for a particular user, and programming that is specifically designed for a particular user.

To be eligible for the statutory license, a webcaster's service and programming must meet several criteria. Services that do not meet the criteria need to obtain (i.e., negotiate) voluntary licenses directly from the recording companies or through the RIAA clearinghouse.

The eligibility criteria for the compulsory license includes the following:

1. Programming must comply with limitations designed to assure the sound recording copyright owner that webcasting (which generally occurs as uninterrupted programming) does not displace sales of records. As a condition for eligibility—
   a) programming should comply with the "sound recording performance complement," which is defined under current law (as provided in the DPRSRA), to provide that over a

CONTINUED ON NEXT PAGE

three-hour period, a service should not intentionally program more than three songs or more than two in a row from the same recording, or four songs or more than three in a row from the same recording artist or anthology;

b) archived programs that, when accessed, always start in the same place and play in the same order should be at least five hours long, and should not be available for more than two weeks at a time;

c) continuous looped programs that always perform in the same order, but are accessed in a continuous play stream should be at least three hours long; and,

d) rebroadcasts of programs can occur at scheduled times three times in a two-week period for programs of less than an hour and four times for programs of an hour or more.

2. The webcaster is not permitted to publish advance program guides or use other means to announce when particular sound recordings will be played.

3. The webcaster must use only sound recordings that are authorized for performance in the United States (e.g., not play bootleg recordings).

4. Within one year of enactment (i.e., by October 28, 1999), webcasters must provide some means for end users to identify the song, artist and album title of the recording as it is being played.

5. Any identification or technological protection information included in the sound recording must be passed through, as long as it does not impose substantial costs or burdens on the webcaster, or create any audible or visible effects for the end user.

6. The webcaster must not deploy or support technological means to evade these requirements.

7. To the extent it is technologically available, the webcaster must set transmissions so that receiving software will inhibit the end user from doing any direct digital copying of the transmitted data, and must not explicitly encourage home taping.

International Copyright

BY E. SCOTT JOHNSON, ESQ

The first thing to know about international copyright is that there is no such thing. Copyright protection exists only under the laws of individual countries, and those laws vary as to categories of works protected, rights protected, duration of protection, and remedies for infringement. Even though you cannot register an "international copyright" as such, your music is automatically protected under the copyright laws of foreign countries with which your home country has copyright treaty or convention relations. That includes almost every country in the world for U.S. nationals, and every country with a significant music market has agreed to extend the same copyright protection to U.S. works that it accords to its own citizens. This is known as "national treatment."

Copyright law typically protects the right to reproduce, distribute, publicly perform and prepare "derivative works," including arrangements. These are "economic rights," and do not always include "authorization rights." For example, in the United States, once a song has been released on records, tapes or CDs, another recording artist may release a cover version of that song without first securing authorization from the copyright owner, under the compulsory licensing provisions of the U.S. Copyright Act. The song's owner may not refuse to grant a mechanical license, so long as the song is not significantly altered (stylistic interpretations are okay), payment required under the statute is made (i.e., the copyright owner's economic right is satisfied) and the other requirements of the compulsory licensing provisions of the U.S. Copyright Act are met. Despite the lack of an authorization right for cover recordings, the copyright owner could refuse to authorize synchronization of the song in a television commercial. In that case, there is no compulsory license under U.S. copyright law, so the copyright owner enjoys both an economic right *and* an authorization right. Countries vary in scope of the authorization rights granted to copyright owners, as reflected in differing approaches to legal principles such as "fair use," "compulsory license" and "moral rights."

Some countries provide strong moral rights or "droit morale" laws, according creators (generally referred to as "authors"—whether of music, literature, artwork or any other copyrightable work) special rights above and beyond the economic and authorization rights incident to copyright ownership. Moral rights generally belong to the author irrespective of who owns the copyright, and may include a number of special rights, including the right to require name credit on copies ("paternity"), and to prevent unauthorized changes to a work ("integrity"). Following its accession to the Berne Convention in 1989, the United States added limited moral rights provisions to the U.S. Copyright Act, applicable only to certain works of visual art. The United States does not accord moral rights to composers or performers of musical compositions. In fact, U.S. recording artists are often asked to waive moral rights by contract, through special provisions in recording contracts, intended to divest the artist of moral rights that may apply in foreign countries. It is beyond the scope of this chapter to assess whether a contractual waiver of moral rights in a U.S. contract would be effective under the domestic laws of any particular foreign country to actually waive an author's moral rights.

NATIONAL TREATMENT

The common feature of the important copyright conventions and treaties, and of the GATT Accord on Trade-Related Aspects of Intellectual Property Rights (TRIPS) is the requirement that each signatory country accord works from other signatory countries national treatment under the domestic copyright law of the country in which protection is sought. This means, for example, that a U.S. songwriter's music will be protected automatically under Italian copyright law on the same basis as if the songwriter was an Italian citizen, or first published the music in Italy. Likewise, Italian songwriters are entitled to protection under U.S. copyright law, because both countries are members of the Berne Convention, which requires national treatment as a condition of membership. This is good news for U.S. copyright owners, because copyright protection in foreign countries is automatic, and often more favorable to authors than U.S. copyright law.

Domestic copyright law generally does not protect you abroad. If your copyright is infringed in a foreign country, you usually cannot bring your infringement case in a U.S. court, or seek remedies under U.S. copyright law in a foreign court. In most instances, you will need to bring your copyright infringement claim in a court in the foreign country where the infringement occurred, under that country's laws. If the infringing product is distributed worldwide, you may have separate infringement claims in each country where the product is distributed. But even for a product released only abroad, a basis may exist for a U.S. claim. If, for example, a videotape distributed in Germany was produced in the United States, where your music was recorded onto the video master without your permission, that act of unauthorized copying within the United States would infringe at least one of your exclusive rights under U.S. copyright law, and you could bring an infringement claim in a U.S. federal court against the U.S. producer, in addition to any claim you may have in Germany under German law. Moreover, you might be able to recover the U.S. defendant's *German* profits in a U.S. court, as a remedy for its infringing activities in the United States.

Unlike patent law, which requires formal filings within strict time frames, and the timely payment of fees to secure patent protection in each country, protection under the copyright laws of foreign countries is generally automatic. The Berne Convention, of which the United States is a member, prohibits such formal barriers to protection and requires national treatment and minimum standards of protection as a condition of adherence. Where a U.S. patent owner would have to make timely filings and pay governmental fees to secure and maintain patent protection in France, for example, a U.S. copyright owner need merely assert copyright ownership and establish the work's status as a "Berne work" in order to secure copyright protection in France.

National treatment does not guarantee that the copyright laws in every foreign country will provide protection equivalent to United States copyright law. For example, in some countries, the term of protection for sound recordings, photographs and certain other works may be shorter than in the United States. Sound recordings in the United States are often treated as works made for hire for record companies, and the term of protection for a U.S. work-made-for-hire sound recording is the shorter of 95 years from date of publication or 120 years from date of creation, just like other works protected under copyright. If owned by individual producer or artist, the term of protection for U.S. sound recordings is the life of the last surviving author plus 70 years. But in many countries, sound recordings are protected for only 50 years. Not every country protects sound recordings under copyright law; many countries treat them as a separate category of property right—called in international copyright parlance a "neighboring right" or "related right" law. The Rome Convention, among others, contemplates reciprocal protection for sound recordings under related rights laws of its signatories.

There are permitted exceptions to the national treatment principle. A common exception concerns duration of copyright protection. Many countries follow the "rule of the shorter term," which provides that copyright protection will last for the shorter of (i) the term of protection available for the work under the national laws of the foreign country where protection is sought, or (ii) the term of protection afforded to the work in the home country. The rule of the shorter term is part of the copyright law of many (but not all) countries, on the theory that a country ought not be required to protect foreign works longer than the foreign author's home country protects such works. The rule of the shorter term may operate to deny protection for pre-1978 United States works, which are protected under U.S. copyright law for a term of years following the registration or first publication date, rather than a term of years after the death of the author. Pre-1978 U.S. copyrights may lapse in the United States prior to expiration of the term of protection that would apply to the same work in foreign countries, which generally provide copyright terms measured by the "life of the author" plus fifty, sixty, seventy or more years. So, for example, if a songwriter's U.S. copyrights expired in 1995, but the songwriter died in 1960, in foreign countries that do *not* apply the rule or the shorter term, the songs would remain in copyright until 2010 or later (2030 in many cases, because the term now is life plus 70 years throughout most of Europe and elsewhere). If the songwriter had been an Italian citizen, though, the song would ordinarily be protected under the national laws of Italy for the life-plus-70-years term, but under the rule of the shorter term followed in Italian copyright law, a pre-1978 U.S. song for which the U.S. copyright had expired, generally would not be protected under Italian copyright law, even if the composer is still alive. That seems simple enough, but this can be a complex area, not easily susceptible to hard-and-fast rules. For example, if a pre-1989 (year of U.S. Berne accession) U.S. song qualified for protection in a non-Universal Copyright Convention Berne country (in UCC countries, the United States would be the home country for purposes of applying the rule of the shorter term) by the back-door-to-Berne procedure discussed below, the song would be treated as originating from the Berne country in which it was "simultaneously" (or first) published, which would have provided a copyright term of at least life plus 50 years, potentially longer than the U.S. term of protection.

While there are few examples of U.S. songwriters that outlive their full-term renewed copyrights (Irving Berlin comes to mind—he lived to 101 and began writing as a young man), it happened more often than you might think prior to 1992, when the U.S. Copyright Act was amended to prevent works from being thrust into the public domain for failure to file a renewal application. Prior to 1972, many songs fell into the U.S. public domain prematurely due to a failure to file for renewal of the U.S. copyright during the 28th year, and in those cases songwriters may well have outlived their U.S. copyright.

U.S. songwriters do not have to worry about outliving their copyrights for works composed after 1978, because the copyright term is no longer determined by a set number of years from registration or publication (except works made for hire, which are accorded a set number of years from creation or publication), but rather, is based on the life of the author plus 70 years. However, if you are recording a song that is in the public domain in the United States, you may still need to determine whether it is in the public domain worldwide. Because not every country follows the rule of the shorter term (Canada and the United Kingdom, for example, do not), a song that is in the public domain in the United States *may* still be protected under copyright in certain foreign countries. Irving Berlin's songs are a case in point. In 1911, Berlin had a hit with "Alexander's Ragtime Band." Copyright was renewed in 1939, and the song entered the U.S. public domain at the end of 1986. However, because Irving Berlin lived until 1989, and because Canada (a Berne country) provides a term of protection measured by the life of the author plus 50 years, and because Irving Berlin met the then-applicable requirements for protection in Berne Convention countries (by simultaneously publishing the work in a Berne Convention country) distribution of recordings embodying the Irving Berlin song "Alexander's Ragtime Band" in Canada will infringe the Irving Berlin's publisher's rights in that song under Canadian copyright law (unless a mechanical license for Canada is obtained) until 2039, even though by then the song will have been out of copyright in the United States for 53 years!

FORMALITIES

The United States has a long history of imposing technical conditions on copyright protection, such as notice, renewal, deposit and manufacturing requirements ("formalities" in international copyright parlance), and while many formalities in the U.S. Copyright Act have been eliminated or defanged in recent years, some still persist. For example, one may not sue for copyright infringement in the United States unless the infringed work has first been registered with the U.S. Copyright Office, and a registration certificate obtained. It is more advantageous for the U.S. songwriter to receive national treatment under the laws of France, for example, at least with respect to the registration requirement, than it is in the United States. A United States citizen who failed to register his or her copyright in the United States—a prerequisite to filing suit for copyright infringement in the United States—could nevertheless sue for copyright infringement in France, which has no comparable requirement.

The registration requirement is an easily met "soft" formality (because the registration can be secured at any time during the life of the copyright), compared to the harsh formalities that for many years dominated United States copyright law. Prior to 1992, if you failed to renew a pre-1978 copyrighted song during the 28th year of the copyright term, the song automatically lost U.S. copyright protection. Instead of 75 years of protection, the copyright owner enjoyed only 28 years of protection. "Rockin' Robin" by Jimmie Thomas, one of the great pop hits of the 1950s, is such a song. The U.S. copyright notice requirement was even harsher then. If copies of a song were published before 1978 without a proper copyright notice, the song was automatically injected into the U.S. public domain. Many foreign authors published works without copyright notice, not realizing that this omission would result in a permanent forfeiture of copyright protection in the United States. These are harsh penalties for hypertechnical mistakes, and the unfairness of loss of copyright for these and other technical failings under U.S. law was roundly condemned for years by the international copyright community, and impermissible under the Berne Convention. The United States was ineligible to join the Berne Convention until 1989, when it finally committed to basic revisions in U.S. copyright law to eliminate formalities as a condition of copyright protection and to provide Berne's minimum standards to Berne works. Following Berne adherence, and subsequent trade negotiations resulting in the NAFTA and TRIPS Agreements, many U.S. copyrights in foreign works have been "revived" through retroactive restoration of copyright protection in works that lost copyright protection for failure to copy with formalities. Fortunately, not long after the United States joined the Berne Convention, the U.S. Copyright Act was amended to provide that a failure to renew copyright, even by a U.S. national, would not inject the work into the public domain.

BERNE CONVENTION

The Berne Convention for the Protection of Literary and Artistic Works (referred to as the "Berne Convention" or "Berne") is the most important international copyright convention. Established in 1886, the Berne Convention is the oldest copyright convention in which reciprocal protections are granted to member countries. A number of countries are signatory to both the Berne Convention, and the Universal Copyright Convention as well as other regional or bilateral treaties. Berne is the premier copyright convention, however, by virtue of the minimum standards its members must agree to accord to works of other Berne nationals and its prohibition on formalities as barriers to protection. The other preeminent copyright convention, the Universal Copyright Convention (UCC), explicitly grants priority to Berne in relations between UCC members that are also Berne members. The United States was late to join the Berne Convention, finally joining in 1989, after many years of lobbying by members of Congress, trade groups, copyright owners and others that believed that the United States could not lead in international trade negotiations if it did not afford the minimum standards required by Berne to the works of Berne member countries.

Even though the United States did not join Berne until 1989, works by U.S. songwriters could qualify for copyright protection and national treatment in Berne Convention countries by a procedure that became known as "back door to Berne." To qualify for protection in Berne countries, a U.S. work had to be simultaneously published in a Berne country, which generally meant publication in a Berne member nation within 30 days of the original publication date in the non-Berne country. Printed sheet music copies of U.S. songs were routinely published in a Berne country within the prescribed time frame by authorization of the U.S. publisher, in order to obtain protection for the song in all Berne Convention countries. Many criticized this procedure as unfairly obtaining for U.S. works the benefits of Berne protection without providing reciprocal benefits to Berne Convention works in the United States. U.S. works were often protected in Berne countries, while foreign works were often unprotected in the United States due to the harsh operation of U.S. formalities.

If a work qualifies as a Berne Convention work, it will be protected under the national laws of all Berne countries. A Berne Convention work is defined under U.S. law as a work (1) created by at least one author who has an "habitual place of residence" in a nation adhering to the Berne Convention, (2) published works of which at least one author is a national of a Berne signatory on the date of the first publication, (3) works first published in at least one Berne country, (4) pictorial, graphic, or sculptural works incorporated in buildings or other structures located in a Berne country, and (5) audiovisual works created by at least one legal entity headquartered in a Berne country or at least one individual author who is a national of a Berne country. It is still possible for non-Berne countries to obtain protection in Berne Convention countries through a "back door to Berne" procedure, much like United States publishers followed prior to 1989.

The Berne Convention provisions are not "self-executing" in the United States (in some countries they are); that is, a foreign author cannot go into a United States court, and expect it to enforce the minimum protections required under the Berne Convention. U.S. law had to be brought into accordance (to the extent it was not already in accordance) with Berne Convention minimum standards of protection and had to remove barriers to protection, by implementing legislation. In the United States, this has been done piecemeal over the years since U.S. adherence, and many believe that U.S. law is still not in full compliance, especially with the moral rights provisions of Berne.

An interesting limitation on the Berne minimum standards obligation is that a Berne member must accord the minimum standards of protection to works from other Berne countries, but is not required to accord the minimum standards to its own authors. Although resulting from trade agreements and not directly from Berne, retroactive restoration of copyright is one area in which foreign authors are given preferential treatment under U.S. copyright law. The U.S. Copyright Act has been amended in recent years (in accordance with NAFTA and GATT Agreements) to restore copyright protection for Berne and certain other foreign works for which U.S. copyrights had lapsed or failed to vest initially due to failure to comply with U.S. formalities. However, these amendments did not restore copyright protection for U.S. works for which copyright protection had lapsed or failed to vest initially for the same reasons.

UNIVERSAL COPYRIGHT CONVENTION

Most of the larger countries of the world are signatories to the Universal Copyright Convention, in addition to the Berne Convention. In 1955, the United States ratified the UCC, becoming a founding member of this international copyright convention administered by the United Nations Educational, Scientific and Cultural Organization (UNESCO) (Berne is administered by World Intellectual Property Organization [WIPO]). UCC, which has 80 members (Berne has 77), requires member countries to accord national treatment to works from other member countries, but does not require that its members meet the rigorous minimum standards Berne requires. Berne countries that wanted to bring the United States and other countries with formalities prohibited under Berne into the world copyright community sponsored UCC originally.

The Universal Copyright Convention actually prescribes use of a copyright notice (the symbol ©, the name of the copyright owner and the year of first publication) as the condition for obtaining certain Convention benefits in UCC countries. While notice is not a prerequisite for protection, any formalities that any UCC member nation may impose upon its nationals, such as deposit, registration or first publication requirements, are deemed satisfied if the foreign (UCC) work bears the prescribed copyright notice. The "free pass" on compliance with formalities does not apply to nationals of the country in which the exemption is sought. Of course, most countries today do not impose formalities as prerequisites for copyright protection, and many UCC member countries are also members of the Berne Convention, and may not impose formalities in any case, so the UCC's relevance has been greatly diminished in recent years. A number of countries, however (primarily eastern European countries), do not belong to Berne, but do belong to the Universal Copyright Convention. For that reason, and also because under U.S. copyright law, failure to provide copyright notice can provide an infringer with a potential "innocent infringement" defense (an element of which is "lack of notice"), most copyright owners continue to use copyright notices. In addition to the standard, "© 2000 by (copyright owner)," it is also common practice to include the words "All Rights Reserved," for reasons discussed below.

BUENOS AIRES CONVENTION

The Buenos Aires Convention was executed in 1910 by the United States, Argentina, Brazil, Chili, Columbia, Costa Rica, Dominican Republic, Ecuador, Guatemala, Haiti, Honduras, Nicaragua, Panama, Paraguay, Peru and Uruguay. The essential requirement for protection in all Buenos Aires member countries is compliance with copyright law in the home country, and the use of a statement that indicates the reservation of the property right. While the copyright notice required under the Universal Copyright Convention: "© (year of publication) by (copyright owner)" arguably satisfies the reservation of the property right requirement of the Buenos Aires Convention, to ensure compliance, copyright owners have adopted the practice of combining the UCC copyright notice with the words "All Rights Reserved." Some believe that the notice "all rights reserved" alone would fulfill the requirement under the Buenos Aires Convention. However, because most of the Buenos Aires Convention countries later joined the Universal Copyright Convention, which requires a full copyright notice to secure Convention benefits, the full notice is generally given. Bolivia, Honduras and Uruguay are the only Buenos Aires Convention member countries that are not signatories of the Universal Copyright Convention. The Buenos Aires Convention superseded the Mexico City Convention, a multilateral Pan American treaty to which the United States was a signatory. All of the signatories of the Mexico City Convention signed the Buenos Aires Convention except El Salvador.

GENEVA PHONOGRAM CONVENTION/ROME CONVENTION

In 1974, the United States joined the Geneva Phonogram Convention, formerly known as the Geneva Convention of October 29, 1971, for the Protection of Producers of Phonograms Against Unauthorized Duplication. This is an agreement between countries to protect sound recordings ("phonograms" in international intellectual property parlance) of member countries against bootlegging. Not every member country protects sound recordings under copyright. In many countries, sound recordings are protected under a neighboring right—a related intellectual property or unfair competition law.

Another international treaty according national treatment and protection to owners of sound recordings is the International Convention for the Protection of Performers, Producers of Phonograms and Broadcasting Organizations (1961), commonly referred to as the Rome Convention.

WORLD INTELLECTUAL PROPERTY ORGANIZATION (WIPO)

The World Intellectual Property Organization (WIPO) is an agency of the United Nations System of Organizations, with the mission of promoting the protection of intellectual property throughout the world through cooperation among the countries of the world, and for the administration of various multilateral treaties, especially the Berne Convention. WIPO is concerned not only with copyrights, but also with trademarks, industrial designs and patentable inventions.

COLLECTING PUBLISHING ROYALTIES ABROAD

Songwriters collect royalties from foreign territories for the public performance of their music and for mechanical reproduction of their songs on compact discs, tapes, and other sound devices. Public performances primarily consist of radio and television broadcasts, although Internet streaming, live performances, music-on-hold, theatrical performances, and "storecasts" account for a portion of revenues that flow to collecting societies for distribution to the publishers and writers that own copyrights in musical compositions. In the United States, music publishers and songwriters do not receive income from movie theater performances of their music contained in films, but in other countries, such theatrical performances are licensed by the local performing rights organizations.

In the United States, ASCAP, BMI and SESAC license virtually all public performances of music. Comparable performing rights organizations exist in most countries in the world, although the United States is unusual in having three competitive performing rights organizations. In most countries, a single rights organization collects all public performance royalties, and, through reciprocal arrangements with the U.S. performing rights organizations, funnels royalties to their members. Some of the major overseas performing rights collecting organizations (some, but not all of which also collect mechanical royalties) include PRS in the United Kingdom, SACEM in France, GEMA in Germany, SIAE in Italy, and JASRAC in Japan. In the United States, the Harry Fox Agency represents the majority of music publishers in collecting mechanical royalties from record companies, and it maintains reciprocal arrangements with foreign mechanical rights collecting societies. Even though reciprocal arrangements exist between collecting organizations for the collection of public performance royalties and mechanical royalties, it is often prudent to have a publisher with foreign affiliates, or subpublishers, to oversee the collection of foreign royalties.

ALL TOGETHER NOW: HARMONIZE

"Harmonization" is a term better understood by musicians than most. In the international copyright arena, it refers to the global harmonization of national copyright and related rights laws. The goal is to ensure that similar protections and enforcement mechanisms exist globally for copyrighted works. For example, the European Union issued a Directive that required all EU member countries to provide a term of copyright protection for most copyrighted works, measured by the life of the author plus 70 years. Previously, some EU countries protected copyrights for the life of the author plus 50 years, while others provided protection for the life of the author plus 70 years, which resulted in disharmony between the EU countries' national copyright laws, and potentially inhibited the free movement of goods within the European Union. The Commission has issued a number of Directives to its member countries, requiring harmonization of domestic copyright laws. While stopping short of requiring a European

Union-wide uniform copyright code, certain substantive norms like "life plus 70" have been required, since the Commission concluded that uniformity of law is necessary to advance the goal of free movement of goods within the European Union.

Global harmonization drove the U.S.'s enactment of the Sonny Bono Copyright Term Extension Act of 1998, which extended copyright protection under U.S. copyright law by 20 years, from life plus 50 to life plus 70. Because of the economic benefits to U.S. copyright owners, due in large part to the operation of the rule of the shorter term, many argued that the United States needed to extend the terms of copyright protection in order to increase the value of U.S. copyrights, by securing protection in foreign countries that would continue to protect U.S. works for the life of the author plus 70 years, unless the copyrights had expired in the United States. The U.S. Term Extension Act harmonized U.S. law with European Union law, which had already directed a Union-wide copyright term of life plus 70 years.

Similarly, the U.S. Digital Millennium Copyright Act (DMCA) was passed in 1998 to implement provisions of the WIPO Copyright Treaty and the Performances and Phonograms Treaty. Its intent is to harmonize copyright laws in the international arena by raising minimum standards of protection for copyrighted works, including Internet commerce protection and new digital-era protections for sound recordings. Passage of the DMCA enabled the United States to ratify the WIPO treaties. The United States, which was already substantially in compliance with treaty standards, needed to enhance protection in two areas to come into full compliance, by enacting "anticircumvention" provisions (to prevent electronic theft of digital works), and prohibitions against alteration of copyright management information. Under the WIPO treaties, signatory countries must provide "adequate legal protection and effective legal remedies" against the circumvention of technological measures, such as encryption technology, used to restrict unauthorized or unlawful copying. Among other things, the DMCA prohibits the sale of "black boxes" used to circumvent anticopying technology. Both of the new WIPO treaties require signatory countries to protect the integrity of copyright management information. This includes "digital watermarking" information that identifies the work, the author of the work, and the owner of any right in the work as well as any information about the terms and conditions of its use, and any numbers or codes representing such information, when any of this information is digitally "attached" to a copy of the work or appears in connection with the communication of the work to the public. Congress added a new chapter (Chapter 12) to the U.S. Copyright Act, providing civil remedies and criminal penalties for violations of either the anticircumvention provision or the alteration of copyright management information provision.

The member nations of the World Trade Organization (WTO) adopted the TRIPS Agreement, the acronym that identifies the 1995 Trade-Related Aspects of Intellectual Property Agreement. TRIPS imposes new substantive minimum requirements, both on subject matter and nature of the rights protected, as well as specific provisions relating to enforcement of copyright laws. The TRIPS Accord requires all WTO members to pass and enforce copyright, patent and trademark laws, and to meet minimum standards for protection. The TRIPS Agreement adopts the WTO dispute settlement procedures, and the United States initiated the first TRIPS-related dispute in a case against Japan in 1996, and has since initiated 12 more cases, including a case against Ireland for failing to pass a TRIPS-consistent copyright law.

The U.S. Trade Representative has announced that one of its top priorities is to ensure full implementation of the WTO commitments on intellectual property, specifically requiring compliance by all members of the WTO with the enforcement provision of TRIPS. TRIPS goes further than Berne, in requiring that members of the WTO accord protection to more categories of works, and addressing other specific protections that enhance Berne's minimum protections. The 1996 WIPO Copyright Treaty (WCT) includes additional substantive minimum standards, including anticircumvention of encryption technology laws, which would increase harmonization of signatory countries. The Unites States has already adopted the antiencryption circumvention laws, in its Digital Millennium Copyright Act.

The Internet is driving the need for international harmonization of laws, to facilitate the global management of copyrights, and to deter infringement. File sharing technologies like Napster and Gnutella, which do not recognize national borders, emphasize the need for global harmonization of copyright and antipiracy laws to support encryption and other technology to protect copyrighted works. The answers ultimately will be found both in technology, through sophisticated copyright management systems, and encryption technology, and in the law, such as antiencryption circumvention laws. Conventions and treaties promoted by WIPO and the WTO, initiatives put forth by the International Federation of the Phonograph Industry, an international music industry association that represents about 1400 companies in 70 countries, and alliances between domestic collecting societies and their counterparts in other countries, are paving the way for a global technology-based system of rights management with enforcement mechanisms and laws to back them up. Major record companies formed the Secure Digital Music Initiative (SDMI) in part to develop an alternative to MP3. Unfortunately, so far the major record companies have been reactive rather than leading in the development of secure digital distribution technologies.

The international treaties, conventions, EU Commission Directives, and trade agreements are leading the way to global harmonization of copyright and related right laws, by establishing international norms of protection and enforcement. While variations in the national laws of countries will persist, and there may never be an international copyright per se, the expectation that a work protected in one country will be similarly protected in another, is becoming increasingly important as the significance of national borders declines in the digital era.

Music Publishing

PERFORMING RIGHTS ORGANIZATIONS: AN OVERVIEW

MUSIC PUBLISHING

ANALYSIS OF A SINGLE-SONG AGREEMENT

ANALYSIS OF AN EXCLUSIVE TERM SONGWRITER AGREEMENT

MUSIC LICENSING FOR TELEVISION AND FILM: A PERSPECTIVE FOR SONGWRITERS

POP MUSIC FOR SOUNDTRACKS

Performing Rights Organizations: An Overview

BY MARK HALLORAN

If you write songs that are commercially recorded, you must join a performing rights organization to collect money for the public performance of your songs. Which organization you join is one of the most important business decisions you will make in your career, so a basic understanding of them is crucial.

This chapter provides an overview of the three U.S. performing rights organizations—the American Society of Composers, Authors and Publishers (ASCAP), Broadcast Music Incorporated (BMI) and SESAC. The vast majority of U.S. copyrighted songs are in the repertory of either ASCAP (with a total of over 4,000,000 songs) or BMI (with more than 4,500,000 songs and compositions). We will discuss performing rights, the issue of nondramatic versus dramatic public performance rights, how television and blanket licenses work, the agreements you enter, collaboration, how money is generated and divided, and grievance procedures.

COPYRIGHT LAW UNDERPINNING

To understand exactly how performing rights organization work, you must understand one fundamental tenet of copyright law: a copyright owner in a musical work (song) has the exclusive right to perform the work publicly. The concept "performance" includes live performances and the rendering of previous performances that are fixed in records, videotape or film. When a radio station broadcasts a song, that song is being publicly performed, even though the recording artist is not performing live. Thus, the radio station must be licensed by the copyright owner to play the song. Radio stations normally obtain public performance licenses from ASCAP, BMI or SESAC for a fee. The same is true for songs in television programs. When a television program is broadcast, the songs in the program are being publicly performed. The network or local station must be licensed to publicly perform those songs.

Radio and TV are not the only kinds of public performance. When you are dancing to "We Are Family" by Sister Sledge in a nightclub, the playing of that song and recording by the disc jockey is a public performance. But at this point, you should consider an absolutely crucial distinction. What performance does the performing rights organization license? The performance of the musical composition in the record is licensed, not the performance of the sound recording. (A sound recording is a series of sounds. Its copyright is separate from the copyright in the song.) If the disc jockey is playing "We Are Family," then the song "We Are Family," not Sister Sledge's recording, is licensed. In the United States, there is no public performance right in a sound recording that applies to radio, television and nightclubs. To perform a song without violating copyright law, the nightclub must have a license to publicly perform this song. That is where ASCAP, BMI and SESAC step in. They negotiate licenses (permissions) with radio and TV stations, nightclubs, cabarets, discos and the like, that enable them to perform publicly the musical compositions contained in the performing rights organizations' catalogs.

The essence of the agreements between performing rights organizations and nightclubs is simple: the performing rights organizations grant the right to the nightclubs to use the songs (perform them publicly), and in return the performing rights organizations are paid fees by nightclubs. These fees are ultimately divided among the songwriters and publishers that create and publish the songs. The company that publishes "We Are Family" and the song's writers must authorize ASCAP, BMI or SESAC to license the public performance. Sister Sledge, who performs the song, and their label, which owns the recording, do not license the public performance of the song. They are not the copyright holders of "We Are Family," but merely the performer of the song and owner of the sound recording respectively. As such, they do not collect public performance royalties in the United States. In certain foreign territories, performing rights organizations also license public performances of sound recordings, but ASCAP, BMI and SESAC do not. However, this may change soon, as Congress is considering creating a more general public performance right in sound recordings.

There is an exception to this "blanket" license procedure. As a result of an antitrust case brought on behalf of theater owners, ASCAP, BMI and SESAC do not license the public performance of musical works in U.S. motion picture theaters. However, certain foreign performing rights organizations do so in their respective territories.

DRAMATIC VERSUS NONDRAMATIC RIGHTS

ASCAP, BMI and SESAC do not license dramatic performance rights. Dramatic performing rights ("grand rights") must be distinguished from nondramatic performance rights ("small rights"). The Copyright Act grants the exclusive right to perform publicly a dramatic work to the copyright owner. Dramatic works include, among other things, plays (both musicals and dramas), and dramatic scripts for radio, television, ballets and operas. A musical composition (a song), in and of itself, is a nondramatic work.

Drawing the line between a dramatic and nondramatic performance is sometimes difficult, if not impossible. The standard ASCAP, BMI and SESAC contracts state they license only nondramatic performances of the compositions they administer. Thus, radio and television licensees must be careful to make sure their blanket license covers their use of a song from a play or opera. The industry practice is that radio stations play unlimited numbers of instrumentals from cast albums, or will play a sequence of up to two vocals and an instrumental from the cast album. Some record companies and publishers, however, avoid this licensing problem by obtaining clearance from the copyright holder for unrestricted radio use of songs from cast albums, and notify broadcasters of such.

Dramatic performances are usually licensed directly from the writers of the music, lyrics, and book of the play, or from their agents. Writers usually reserve dramatic rights in their contracts with publishers. A sample illustration: if a theater company wants to stage *Phantom of the Opera*, they must seek permission directly from the writers of the play to perform the play and the accompanying music. On the other hand, if a radio wants to play only the song "Music of the Night" from the *Phantom of the Opera* cast album, this is not a dramatic performance, and ASCAP, BMI and SESAC license this sort of performance.

WHAT PERFORMING RIGHTS SOCIETIES DO NOT DO

Performing rights societies do not fulfill the traditional music publisher function of issuing licenses for records (mechanical license), the synchronization of music works in audiovisual words (such as films and television programs), or authorizing the printing and sale of sheet music. They also do not register songs for copyright, which only the United States Copyright Office can do. They do not license rights for sound recordings, traditionally done by record labels. And, as discussed above, they do not license dramatic performance rights.

ASCAP

In 1914, Victor Herbert and a handful of other composers organized ASCAP because performances of copyrighted music for profit were so numerous and widespread, and most performances so fleeting, that as a practical matter it was impossible for individual copyright owners to negotiate with and license the music users, and to detect unauthorized public performances of their songs. ASCAP was organized to serve as a clearinghouse for copyright owners and users and to solve those problems. Today ASCAP is a membership society that represents over 100,000 composers, lyricists and publishers. ASCAP collected more than $560,000,000 in 1999, and distributed over $435,000,000 to its members. ASCAP represents such songwriters as Irving Berlin, Garth Brooks, Bruce Springsteen, Stevie Wonder and Madonna.

BMI

BMI is a nonprofit corporation, organized in 1939, whose stock is owned by members of the broadcasting industry. BMI represents more than 250,000 publishing companies, songwriters and composers, and operates in much the same manner as ASCAP. In fiscal year 2000, BMI collected more than $500,000,000 and distributed over $414,000,000 to its affiliates. BMI represents such songwriters as The Beach Boys, Elton John, The Eagles, Babyface, Moby, The Offspring, Eminem and Sheryl Crow.

SESAC

SESAC, formed in 1930, is a privately held corporation. SESAC has approximately 5000 writer/publisher affiliates. Although traditionally known for its strength in country, gospel and band music, it is now moving into jazz, new age and pop, as evidenced by its signings of Bob Dylan and Neil Diamond. SESAC differs from ASCAP and BMI in that it is much smaller, and consequently its service is efficient and personalized. Some of SESAC's services include catalog consultation and collaboration recommendations.

TELEVISION AND RADIO LICENSING

The bulk of money paid to the performing rights organizations comes from radio and television broadcasters.

In the 1980s and early 1990s, broadcast blanket licenses came under fire by non-network television stations in both the courts and in Congress. ASCAP and BMI now often negotiate for a "per program" use fee in lieu of blanket licenses.

ASCAP, BMI and SESAC negotiate blanket licenses that cover all the works in their catalogs. Thus, television and radio stations do not have to clear the music before it is broadcast—stations can be confident the song being played is somewhere in the performing rights organizations catalog. The granting of blanket licenses makes sense when you consider the vast number of songs in the performing rights organizations catalogs. If a broadcaster or nightclub individually negotiated with the copyright holder each time a song was played, chaos could result. Blanket licenses also benefit writers and publishers, as they do not have the means to enforce their exclusive right to public performance of their songs. The performing rights organizations will sue broadcasters, clubs and others that publicly perform songs without a license. Enforcing the copyright laws is one of their most important functions.

After a performing rights organization issues its blanket license, the license holder may use any of the works of any of the members of that organization as often as desired during the license term. The performing rights organizations use sampling techniques to figure out to whom the money should go, and compute the division of income based on the frequency and the kind of public performance of songs. The computation and payment of royalties is discussed more fully below.

Through its use of BDS (Broadcast Data Systems) Airplay Recognition Services, SESAC charges for actual airplay.

CONTRACTS WITH SONGWRITERS AND PUBLISHERS

Assuming you qualify for membership in ASCAP, BMI or SESAC you will be asked to enter a contract with one of them. Basically, if you have a song that is published, recorded or publicly performed, you can join. In so doing, you give that organization the right to license the public performance of songs that you write in return for their promise to pay you royalties for the reported performances.

Publishers can also join ASCAP, BMI or SESAC. Their contracts are much the same as for writers.

MEMBERSHIP

As performing rights organizations pay writers and publishers separately, both must join. Writers can only belong to one performing rights organization at a time. Even when writers are affiliated with publishing companies, they should join performing rights organizations so that they can directly receive any royalties that are due.

Publishers always have separate ASCAP, BMI and SESAC-affiliated legal entities (e.g., A Tunes [ASCAP], B Tunes [BMI] and C Tunes [SESAC]). Each organization has name clearance procedures to avoid name duplication or the confusion of similar names.

If you are an ASCAP writer, and a publisher administers your song, it will be handled by the entity of the publisher that is affiliated with ASCAP.

ASCAP dues are $10 for writers; $50 for publishers. BMI has no dues, but charges a one-time publisher administration fee of $100. There is no fee to affiliate with SESAC for writers or publishers.

COLLABORATION

If an ASCAP writer collaborates with a BMI or SESAC writer, the song is licensed concurrently by both organizations. Thus, you will notice on some record albums some songs have more than one organization listed.

COLLECTIONS

ASCAP, BMI and SESAC also collect money from affiliated foreign performing rights organizations. However, most income comes from the United States. For example, in 1999, ASCAP's domestic receipts were $422,989,000 and foreign receipts $137,049,000. ASCAP, BMI and SESAC all charge a service fee for such collections. Many U.S. publishers, however, have subpublishers or agents overseas that collect and remit monies to American publishers directly.

REGISTRATION OF COMPOSITIONS

It is essential to collecting royalties that you or your publisher registers your composition. Prior to choosing which performing rights organization to join, you should register your songs with the U.S. Copyright Office in order to establish authorship and ownership. If music is embodied in a television program, a music cue sheet should be filed for every song.

BMI's registration (clearance) form must be completed for each song. BMI also requires cue sheets for television music.

SESAC provides index forms for the purpose of registering all musical works.

PAYING FOR PERFORMANCES

With minor exceptions, it is impractical for ASCAP, BMI and SESAC to monitor and pay for performances in bars or nightclubs. There are no significant royalties paid for nontelevision/nonradio performances. Royalties for radio and television performances come from licensing fees from radio and television. The fees collected from bars and nightclubs are allocated to the same funding pool that pays songwriters and publishers for radio and television performances.

SESAC accepts performance information from its affiliates. Payments are made for performances in bars, nightclubs, etc., upon verification.

Radio

ASCAP samples some 60,000 hours of AM and FM radio per year in order to produce a model for the music broadcast on radio. It samples larger stations more heavily. Weighted multipliers are then applied to calculate radio royalties.

BMI annually samples some 500,000 hours of selected AM and FM radio programming to develop their model. The information comes in the form of detailed logs.

SESAC's Radio Payment System is based on the premise that the charts in national music trade publications such as *Billboard, Gavin, CMJ New Music Report* and *Radio & Records* are representative of radio airplay across the United States. The Radio Payment System, one part of SESAC's royalty distribution system, uses this data to compensate affiliates whose works are, or have been, active on radio. Under the Radio Payment System, radio performances are recognized in prechart payments (prior to a song's appearance on a national chart), chart payments (based on the highest chart position a song reaches in the *Billboard, Radio & Records, Gavin* or *CMJ New Music Report* singles or tracks charts used in the SESAC system) and post chart payments (paid for three years [12 quarters] beginning in the quarter after the last chart payment is earned on songs that appear in the top 20 positions in *Gavin, Billboard* or *Radio & Records* singles or tracks charts).

In SESAC's Radio Payment System, a song begins earning royalties when it is released on a commercial phonorecord (record, cassette, CD, etc.). These prechart payments acknowledge performances of the recorded song even before it appears on national charts. When a record appears on any one of the charts used in the system, a chart payment is paid. Chart payments are determined by the position of a song or album on the particular musical format charts. Most songs that reach a top twenty or higher position on a singles (or tracks) chart are paid postchart payments. In subsequent years, works receive royalties based on then current performance information.

The independent statisticians that develop the radio broadcast models do not warn either the performing rights organizations or the stations as to which stations and periods will be surveyed. Although it surveys substantially fewer hours than BMI, ASCAP uses actual "off-the-air" audiotapes to avoid any potential alterations (as could occur with a log). BMI prefers to survey performances using lists (logs) furnished by the stations that are sampled. They sample more than eight times as many hours as ASCAP to provide for inclusion and identification of many more compositions (particularly nonhits). There is no consensus as to whether the ASCAP or BMI sampling system is more accurate.

The number of surveyed performances of the compositions, not the chart position, determines the amount of performance royalties paid. These royalties fluctuate depending on the music category (e.g., pop, country, rhythm and blues, religious, gospel, symphonic), and also whether the composition "crosses over" to other music charts or categories.

SESAC's payment fee depends on whether a song is a prechart, chart or postchart performance activity. For prechart songs, SESAC uses a new technology created by Broadcast Data Systems (a sister company of *The Hollywood Reporter*) to track actual SESAC songs that are played on any radio or TV outlet. SESAC charges licensing fees that are based specifically on airplay, and pays their songwriter and publisher affiliates a specified royalty for exactly what is used. SESAC pays a slightly higher fee for prechart songs when they appear on popularity charts in national music trade publications, and a slightly higher fee for songs and albums that appear in the top 20 positions.

Network Television

To track network television performances, ASCAP, BMI and SESAC receive cue sheets submitted by the networks' program producers, which detail the seconds of music used in network programs and the types of use. All three organizations also tape network shows to spot check information on the cue sheets.

Local Television

ASCAP uses cue sheets, a sample of regional TV Guides, audiotapes and inquiry letters to local television stations to sample 30,000 hours of local television. As with radio, this sampling is then multiplied, using statistical models, to calculate local television royalties. BMI and SESAC use similar techniques. They compile cue sheets and a complete computerized account of regional TV Guides and program listings from local television stations.

TELEVISION MUSIC

There are three main categories of television music—theme, background and feature performances. Performing rights organizations pay different rates for each. They factor in the number of stations that air the performance, the type of station (e.g., broadcast, local, cable and public television), and the duration of the performance. Payments are also made for music used for promotional purposes or for jingles.

Theme music appears at the opening or closing of a television program and during segments within programs. Background music is played to enhance the program, but is not intended as the focus of the program. There is typically about 10 (although some animated programs often contain up to 20) minutes of background music in a 30-minute program. A feature performance is music that is the visual focus of the program. For example, a composition sung on camera is considered a feature performance. Rates fluctuate depending on many factors, including whether the show is network or syndicated, time of day, and program type (e.g., series, soaps, quiz shows, movies).

PAYMENT OF ROYALTIES

The amount of royalties paid varies between ASCAP, BMI and SESAC due to many factors, the most significant of which are differences in rates and survey methods. Generally, each organization divides and pays the revenues derived from licenses and fees 50% to publisher and 50% to writer. ASCAP and BMI assign varying credit values to publishers, factoring in the size and dollar value of their catalogs, but do not do so for writers.

ASCAP

ASCAP's method of paying royalties is to "follow the dollar" (e.g., television licensing fees are paid out only as television royalties). ASCAP calculates royalties on a quarterly basis. Songs that have generated high amounts of feature performances over time (e.g., 20,000 feature performances over a five-year survey period) are called "qualifying works" and are assigned higher credit values than performance royalties for background music.

BMI

BMI pays quarterly, seven to eight months after the end of the calendar quarter in which the performance occurs. Actual rates paid are typically larger than the minimums prescribed due to quarterly rate bonuses. Royalties are paid simultaneously to writer and publisher in equal lump sums. In the absence of a publisher, payment of the full amount of royalties may be made to the writer, or by agreement between the writer and publisher, payment may be split unequally, with the writer receiving the larger share (but not vice versa).

BMI recognizes frequently performed works by awarding bonuses to both writers and publishers for songs that reach a high number of performances. Bonuses can range from 1.5 times the standard rate, to almost 17 times the standard rate.

Neither ASCAP nor BMI pay writer royalties to anyone other than the writer, unless such royalties have been assigned by the writer to legitimate creditors as collateral.

SESAC

Distributions of domestic performance royalties are made to SESAC writer and publisher affiliates four times per year. Royalty distributions are made 90 days after the close of each quarter and are based on a quarterly review and analysis of each affiliate's catalog and its performance activity.

ADVANCES

Until the early 1980s, both ASCAP and BMI routinely paid advances (nonrefundable prepayments of estimated future royalties) to writers and publishers in an effort to stabilize their incomes and entice major musical stars to join their respective organizations. However, due to legal challenges to syndicated television blanket licenses and the resulting concern about future royalties, advances were discontinued and both organizations remain wary of them.

To replace advances, both ASCAP and BMI allow assignments of royalties as collateral against bank loans to composers and publishers. BMI and ASCAP also accept assignment of writer royalties against advances made to the writer by the writer's publisher. As the documentation for such assignments is complex, assignments are usually only cost-effective for composers and publishers with substantial projected royalties.

SESAC has begun to offer advances as part of their campaign to encourage ASCAP and BMI affiliates to switch, and to entice promising unaffiliated writers and publishers.

FOREIGN COLLECTION

Foreign performing rights organizations (generally, only one performing rights organization exists in the majority of countries) monitor foreign performances of compositions in the ASCAP/BMI/SESAC domestic repertoires, and pay royalties for such performances to the U.S. writer and publisher through them. The lag in payment of foreign royalties can be as long as five years.

One constant problem is that a U.S. writer's or publisher's foreign performing rights royalties may be diluted by the payment of royalties by the foreign performing rights organization to translators of popular American songs. Monies that are collected from U.S. songs, which are not distributed to ASCAP, BMI and SESAC, are generally forfeited to the foreign organization's general fund (the infamous so-called black box) for disbursement to the members of the foreign society. To avoid the black box and accelerate payments, most publishers prefer to have their foreign royalties collected "at the source" by their foreign publishers (i.e., subpublishers). Writer royalties, however, still flow from the foreign performing rights organizations to the domestic ones.

GRIEVANCE PROCEDURES

If you have a dispute with ASCAP or BMI (for example, you do not agree with your royalty statement), you have recourse through their grievance procedures. The ASCAP grievance procedure is set out in their articles of association. ASCAP provides these articles to you when you join. BMI grievances are submitted to the American Arbitration Association in New York City. SESAC has no formally established grievance procedure.

Music Publishing

BY NEVILLE L. JOHNSON

Professional songwriters must know the dynamics and economics of song exploitation. This chapter explores the types of income that are generated in the music publishing industry and the kinds of deals that are commonly struck between publishers and songwriters. The attributes of a good publisher are summarized, suggestions for obtaining a publisher are made, and a typical music publishing agreement is examined.

Music publishing has been the major source of revenue for songwriters since the turn of this century, when vaudeville was the primary vehicle for exploiting songs. Music publishers of that era worked to persuade entertainers to publicly perform musical compositions to stimulate the sale of printed editions and player piano rolls. Over the years, the technology for merchandising music has expanded with inventions such as the phonograph record, radio, motion pictures, television, videotape and compact discs. Now, digital transmission looms large on the retail horizon, and is well placed to be the dominant way by which music will hereafter be distributed. Songwriters and publishers have benefited from each of those new sources of income. As the complexity and size of the music publishing industry increases, so does the amount of money that can be earned within it. Today, one hit song can make someone a millionaire.

Music publishing is a beautiful way to make money because the record company ordinarily does the marketing and promotion of the song—the hardest part of selling music. The costs of music publishing are dwarfed by the massive manufacturing and promotion costs of selling music to the public. This is why publishing catalogs are so valuable and currently sell for 8 to 20 times their average annual income (calculated on an average, weighted basis of the preceding few years).

TYPES OF INCOME

There are four general categories of revenue in the music publishing industry: public performance, mechanical rights, print music and synchronization.

Performance Income

The copyright laws in the United States and similar laws in virtually every other country of the world require that compensation be paid to copyright owners for the public performance of their music. Performing rights organizations exist because it is impractical for copyright owners to license the right to publicly perform their compositions to every music user separately. And it is impractical for music users to keep track of copyright owners and negotiate individual licenses to authorize the performance of each copyrighted work.

Therefore, music users throughout the world are licensed by, and make payments to, performing rights organizations. After deducting their costs of administration, these organizations distribute revenue to copyright owners and their publishers.

The United States has three performing rights organizations. ASCAP (American Society of Composers, Authors and Publishers), BMI (Broadcast Music Incorporated) and SESAC (formerly Society of European Stage Authors and Composers). These organizations perform the difficult task of collecting public performance income and distributing it in proportion to the success of each composition they license.

These organizations also license public performance rights to sister performing rights organizations that exist in other territories of the world.

The performing rights organizations divide performance income so that 50% is paid directly to the composer (writer's share) and 50% is paid to the publisher (publisher's share).

You will need to join a performing rights organization when you get your first recording or placement in a film, commercial, TV program or video. It is the publisher's job to register your compositions with your society. See the chapter, Performing Rights Organizations: An Overview, for more information.

Mechanical Income

Mechanical income is earned from the manufacture and sale of sound recordings. The current rate, payable for each recording of a composition that is distributed, is the greater of 7.55¢ for songs of five minutes or less or 1.45¢ per each minute or fraction thereof. The rates are set by the Copyright Royalty Tribunal and are periodically increased; future rates are as follows: January 1, 2002 to December 31, 2003, 8¢ for five minutes or less, 1.55¢ per minute for each song over five minutes; January 1, 2004 to December 31, 2005, 8.5¢ for five minutes or less, 1.65¢ per minute for songs over five minutes; January 1, 2006 to December 31, 2007 9.1¢ for songs under five minutes, 1.75¢ per song for songs over five minutes. Thus, for a recording containing 10 compositions of five minutes or less, 75.5¢ is paid in mechanical income to the publisher(s) of the compositions. If 100,000 albums are sold, $75,500 is paid to the publisher(s) of the compositions on that album. In a typical publishing deal the songwriter as a writer will receive half this amount from the publisher, and more if the songwriter is also a copublisher.

In the United States, mechanical income is paid to the publisher of a composition by the record company that manufactures recordings of the composition pursuant to a contract between them called a mechanical license. Usually the record company is required to account to the publisher on a quarterly basis.

In most foreign countries, mechanical rights income is computed differently than in the United States. Instead of a flat rate per song, the royalty is computed on a basis that is usually 6% to 8% of the selling price of the recordings (usually referred to as "published price to dealers"). Mechanical income is allocated evenly among the compositions on the recording. This income is collected and distributed by mechanical rights societies, which exist in most countries of the world.

The entity closest to a mechanical rights society, in the United States, is the Harry Fox Agency, Inc. *(www.nmpa.org/hfa.html)*, headquartered in New York City. Although many American publishers issue their own mechanical licenses, most prefer to use this company, which, for a 4.5% fee, issues mechanical licenses to American record companies, and conducts audits of such companies to insure that proper payments are made. Harry Fox will also issue synchronization licenses, and collect on imported sound recordings.

Print Income

Printed music can contribute substantial earnings to a songwriter. Today the industry is concentrated in a few companies that manufacture and distribute printed music across the United States. A publisher who does not print and manufacture its own edition, but licenses such rights to another company can be paid the greater of (i) 80¢ or more per single edition sold; or (ii) 20% of the wholesale selling price, but the writer usually receives only 8¢ to 12¢ per single edition (and more if he or she is a copublisher). See discussion in the chapter, Analysis of a Single-Song Agreement. Electronic sheet music is now available; songwriters are usually paid on the same basis as above, with the major publishers paying low-ball royalties, however this business is as yet almost nonexistent. This form of distribution will grow in importance in the years to come, but print music will still be important. The low royalties are unfair, as the costs of manufacturing and distribution are so much less. Expect these royalties to change for the better for composers as time goes by. For general folios, songwriters are generally paid 12.5% of the wholesale selling price of the edition (though some contracts pay on the retail selling price). Education and compilation editions usually bear a royalty of 10% to 12.5% of the retail selling price.

Synchronization Income

Synchronization income is the money paid by motion picture and television production companies and advertising agencies for the right to use compositions in motion pictures or in dramatic presentations on television. The "synch right" for a composition to be contained in a major motion picture can vary from nothing to $250,000 and even more and the attendant exposure can stimulate the generation of additional revenue from those areas discussed above. Television commercials can be particularly lucrative for a songwriter, and fees of $250,000 for the synchronization rights for the same are not uncommon.

Foreign Income

The foregoing sources of income occur throughout the world. Domestic publishers enter into foreign licensing or subpublishing agreements with music publishers that operate outside the United States. (Canada is often treated as a the 51st state, and U.S. publishers usually obtain Canadian rights when they obtain U.S. rights.) Shrewd and successful commercial songwriters often retain foreign rights and make their own subpublishing deals, which can provide substantial income.

MUSIC PUBLISHING AGREEMENTS

There are three types of contracts pertaining to songwriters: Songwriter agreements, copublishing agreements, and administration agreements.

Songwriter Agreements

These transactions come in two species—single-song agreements and long-term agreements. (See the chapters, Analysis of a Single-Song Agreement and Analysis of an

Exclusive Term Songwriter Agreement.) Under these agreements, the income is generally split as follows:

- Mechanical Income. Publisher collects all mechanical income and pays 50% to composer.

- Performance Income. Publisher receives and retains all of publisher's share of performance income. Composer is paid directly by the performing rights organization and retains all such writer's share of performance income.

- Print Income. Publisher collects all revenue and pays writer 8¢ to 12¢ per piano-vocal sheet music, and 50% of the publisher's receipts on folios and other multiple-composition editions where licensed to a third party.

- Synchronization Income. Publisher collects income and splits fifty-fifty with composer.

- Foreign Income. Net receipts (that amount received by or credited to publisher from subpublisher) are split fifty-fifty with composer. Most deals are now "at source" or modified receipts, meaning that the foreign share is computed as being received in the country where the revenue is earned, i.e., without additional subpublishing or other administrative charges being added.

In a single-song deal, the publisher owns the copyright in the composition for the term of its copyright, subject to the possibility of its reversion to its composer 35 years after its publication (its first commercial distribution) or 40 years after its assignment (transfer), whichever is earlier. Some long-term songwriter's agreements provide that compositions created pursuant to such agreements are works for hire for the publisher and, hence, incapable of being recaptured by the composer; however the trend over the last five years, and the majority of deals nowadays, provide that the songs will revert to the writer after a period of time, somewhere in the range of seven years. If the songwriter is not also a recording artist, then it will be difficult to negotiate reversions. Normally such agreements last for one year, with two to four one-year options being held by the publisher. The publisher owns all compositions created by the songwriter during the term. Under most such agreements, the writer is paid an advance on signing and with each option pickup, or a weekly salary (in the year 2001, $20,000 to $30,000 per year is the average for a fledgling writer, who receives a monthly advance against royalties). These agreements are common in Nashville, but there are very few long-term songwriter agreements these days for creators that do not also have record deals with major companies. On the other hand, those that get a deal with a major record company can virtually count on obtaining a copublishing agreement and a nice advance. Advances vary but can go as high as several hundred thousand dollars per album. Currently, there are approximately 1,000 long-term songwriter or copublishing deals in America.

Single-song agreements are entered into with or without advances paid to the songwriter: there is no common industry standard.

Under both types of agreement, the publisher administers the compositions subject to them. That is, the publisher issues all documents and contracts affecting such compositions and collects all income, other than the writer's share of performance income, earned by the compositions.

Copublishing Agreements

Copublishing agreements differ in two material respects from the standard agreements described above. Under copublishing agreements, as in standard agreements, the publisher administers the compositions subject to such agreements. However, the songwriter not only receives the writer's share of publishing income, or roughly 50% of the gross revenues (except print revenues) of the composition, but also shares in that portion of what traditionally was the publisher's share of music publishing income. Thus, under such agreements, the songwriter is ordinarily paid 75% of the mechanical income, print income, and synchronization income derived from the composition and, in addition to the writer's share of performance income, receives 50% of the publisher's share of performance income. Usually, the publisher and songwriter own copyrights to the compositions jointly.

Copublishing agreements can encompass one song, a number of stated songs, or all compositions written over a period of years, as in a long-term songwriter's agreement.

Administration Agreements

The most advantageous arrangement for a songwriter is an administration agreement. Under this type of agreement, the administrative activities of a songwriter's company are conducted by another publisher, which issues mechanical licenses, registers compositions with performing rights organizations, and collects its income throughout the world. The administrator collects all income but remits at least as much as a copublisher's share, and often more, to the songwriter's administered company (10% to 15% of the gross revenues is the percentage normally retained by an administrator).

Such agreements extend for three to five years, at the close of which all administrative rights to the compositions revert to the administered company. In practice, such agreements are difficult to obtain for songwriters that have no independent means of exploiting compositions that would be subject to such an arrangement. For singer-songwriters that have recording deals, or songwriters that can get their songs "covered" (recorded by others), such transactions are often the most beneficial and these are done frequently. The major music publishers do not do administration deals except for superstar writers. However, there are administrators in Los Angeles, Nashville and New York that will; the most successful is Bug Music, with offices in all three cities.

Points of Negotiation

Royalties and advances are always negotiable. A songwriter should always attempt to obtain a reversion of any composition subject to a single-song, long-term publishing or copublishing agreement when any such composition has not been commercially exploited within a specified time period. A composer should allow translations of, or the addition of new lyrics to, any composition only with his or her prior written consent (or at the very least be notified of the same), since in some countries a translator or lyricist may register and receive income from a translation that is never performed, sold or even recorded due to the nationalistic policies and regulations of various performing rights societies. The translator and subpublisher may receive compensation from performances of the original version and/or share in "black box" or general unattributed income, which can be sizeable. (Italy is one notable example where this can occur.) As to new lyrics, a writer should know the reasons for having such written; the writer would want the opportunity to write such lyrics in any language in which he or she is fluent. Some writers are touchy about the use in commercials of their materials and would want to approve alterations that might devalue the work. A clause permitting translations, as long as there is no diminution income by the writer should be acceptable to most writers. But be careful, if the song is written "words and music" by a songwriter, and the contribution is really separate, one for music, and one for the lyrics, then the song should be registered this way as the composer of the music will not suffer if there are translations, while the lyricist may.

Points in publishing contracts vary in importance among publishing companies. Similarly, songwriters differ on the priorities of the numerous issues involved in a songwriting agreement. Songwriters should have advisors, such as attorneys, personal managers, and business managers, to counsel them on the best methods of navigating the intricacies of music publishing.

SELF-PUBLISHING

Some composers are capable of creating and administering their catalogs. The music publishing industry is not so difficult that its mechanics would confound an attentive student. It is difficult, however, to obtain the commercial exploitation of compositions.

SONGWRITER RESOURCES

Association of Independent Music Publishers (AIMP)
(www.aimp.org)
P.O. Box 1561
Burbank, CA 91507-1561
(818) 842-6257

120 East 56th Street
New York, NY 10022
(212) 758-6157

California Copyright Conference
(www.theccc.org)
P.O. Box 1291
Burbank, CA 91507-1291
(818) 848-6783

Nashville Songwriters Association International
(www.nashvillesongwriters.com)
1701 West End Avenue, Third Floor
Nashville, TN 37203
(800) 321-6008 or (615) 256-3354

Songwriters Guild of America (SGA)
(www.songwriters.org)
6430 Sunset Boulevard
Suite 705
Hollywood, CA 90028
(323) 462-1108

1222 16th Avenue South
Suite 25
Nashville, TN 37212
(615) 329-1782

1560 Broadway
Suite 1306
New York, NY 10036
(212) 768-7902

SongwriterUniverse
(www.songwriteruniverse.com)
11684 Ventura Boulevard
Suite 975
Studio City, CA 91604

Tonos
(www.tonas.com)
Internet only

For composers interested in and capable of properly administering and promoting the products of their artistry, self-publishing can be a viable alternative to the traditional arrangements with publishers, but in practice, few writers are successful going it alone.

When a record is released on an independent label, financed by the artist, self-publishing makes sense. Universal copyrights are valuable assets—do not transfer or lessen your rights to them without a good reason.

FINDING A GOOD PUBLISHER

Music publishers play an important role in today's music industry. First, they have the best success at securing covers. Moreover, a songwriter usually needs a go-between, critic, cheerleader and business manager. Good music publishers are enthusiastic and knowledgeable about their artists and their music. They have competent royalty departments and reputations for honesty; pay for, or advance money for demos; have aggressive professional managers that work to get songs to record producers and their artists; and are responsive to the needs, suggestions, and questions of their writers.

Songwriters, with their advisors, should work out a strategy to find a good publisher and to enter an advantageous agreement with such. Some personal managers are capable of finding reputable publishers and subsequently obtaining satisfactory agreements. The songwriter's music attorney can often open doors to publishing companies. Representatives of ASCAP and BMI can be helpful, as can the recommendations of other songwriters. The Songwriters Guild of America, which has offices in New York, Nashville and Los Angeles, may also be helpful: they are on the side of authors. There are two publisher organizations in Los Angeles that have monthly meetings, and those interested in publishing and networking are advised to join or attend meetings of the California Copyright Conference and the Association of Independent Publishers (which also holds monthly meetings in New York).

Because music publishing agreements can be extremely technical, a music attorney should always be consulted to review any agreement a composer is requested to sign. Most importantly, composers should investigate carefully before choosing their advisors and business partners.

MECHANICAL LICENSE AGREEMENT

Date: ______________________
Composition Title: ____________
Composer(s): _________________
Gentlepersons: _______________
We own or control the mechanical recording rights in the copyrighted musical composition referred to above (hereinafter referred to as the "Composition"). You have advised us that you wish to use the Composition pursuant to the terms of the Compulsory License provisions of the United States Copyright Act (Title 17) relating to the making and distribution of phonorecords. We accede to such use, upon conditions specified below.

1. You shall pay royalties and shall render detailed accounting statements quarterly, within forty-five (45) days after each March 31, June 30, September 30, and December 31 for the calendar quarter year just concluded, whether or not royalties are due and payable for such period, for phonorecords made and distributed.

2. You shall pay us at the following rate for each part embodying the Composition manufactured by you, distributed and not returned (except for promotional copies distributed without charge to radio and television stations):
________ for a "single" recording;
________ for a "CD" or "cassette" recording.

(NOTE: This is a tricky area. Do not get locked into a specific rate. You want to be paid the mechanical rate in effect as set by the Copyright Royalty Tribunal at the time of download or sale [and if you cannot negotiate that, then of manufacture] of the composition. Rates will always go up, and when they do, you should share in the increase. Many artists today are still locked in at the 2¢ rate that was in effect for many years.)

3. This license is limited solely to the recorded performance of the Composition on the phonorecord, which is identified as follows:

Record #: __________________
Artist: _____________________
Label: _____________________

This license shall not supersede or in any way affect any prior agreements now in effect with respect to recordings of the Composition.

4. In the event that you fail to account to us and pay royalties as herein provided, we may give you written notice that, unless the default is remedied within thirty (30) days from the date of such notice, this compulsory license will be automatically terminated. Such termination shall render either the making or the distribution, or both, of all phonorecords for which royalties have not been paid, actionable as acts of infringement under, and fully subject to the remedies provided by the Copyright Act.

5. You need not serve or file the notice of intention to obtain a compulsory license required by the Copyright Act.

6. This license is specifically limited to the use of the Composition, and the sale of the recording within the United States of America, unless we grant you written permission to the contrary.

7. On the label affixed to each part manufactured by you, you will include the title of the Composition, our name as Publisher, the name of the performing rights society with which we are affiliated (________________), and the last names of the composer and lyricist.

8. You will not use or authorize the use of the title of the Composition in any manner whatsoever on the label, cover, sleeve, jacket, or box in which the recording is sold, except in a list of musical compositions contained thereon and then only in print of size, type and prominence no greater than that used for the other musical compositions contained thereon.

Very truly yours,

By: ________________________________

(RECORD COMPANY)

We acknowledge the receipt of a copy hereof and the accuracy of the terms contained herein:

By: ________________________________

(PUBLISHER)

Analysis of a Single-Song Agreement

BY NEVILLE L. JOHNSON

Single-song agreements are widely used. Such agreements allow publishers to pick and choose songs that they think they can get covered (recorded). I have negotiated several single-song agreements where the songs went to number one on the pop charts, so it makes sense to pay close attention to what you are signing.

There are no standard forms for single-song agreements. There is no written agreement that cannot be modified before it is executed (signed)—be wary of printed forms, and be sure to understand what you are signing. The agreement below is representative, and while it is not slanted in favor of the songwriter, it is not a total rip-off.

SINGLE-SONG AGREEMENT

AGREEMENT effective ________________ day of __________________ 200__, by and between ______________________________ hereinafter referred to as "PUBLISHER," and ______________________________ hereinafter (collectively) referred to as "WRITER."

1. ASSIGNMENT OF WORK

Writer hereby sells, assigns and delivers to Publisher, its successors and assigns, the original musical composition written and composed by Writer (hereinafter referred to as the "Composition" now entitled ________________) including the title, words and music thereof, and all worldwide rights therein, and all copyrights and the rights to secure copyrights and any extensions and renewals of copyrights therein and in any arrangements and adaptations thereof, and any and all other rights that Writer now has or to which he may be entitled, whether now known or hereafter to become known.

The composition should revert to the songwriter at a stated time if the publisher cannot get the song covered. One to two years is fair. Maybe a reversion can be obtained if there is limited success, or because that is the current trend. A typical reversion clause would provide that the composition would automatically, or upon notice by the writer, revert to the writer unless it was recorded and commercially released in the United States (or another major territory such as Japan, France, England, Australia or Germany), and placed in a major motion picture or television show. I have seen clauses that required that the song be on a top-100 single or album chart. As an artist's representative, I would hold out for release on a major label (or one with major distribution), or synchronization on a major movie or television show, on being on a single or album that was on a Billboard chart, or chart of the major music publication in the country of release.

2. USE OF COMPOSITION
Publisher shall have the free and unrestricted right to use the Composition in any way that Publisher may desire, and Writer hereby consents to such changes, adaptations, versions, dramatizations, transpositions, translations, foreign lyric substitutions, parody lyrics for commercial purposes, editing and arrangements of the Composition as Publisher deems desirable. In the event that the Composition is an instrumental composition, then Writer hereby irrevocably grants to Publisher the sole and exclusive right and privilege to cause lyrics to be written for the Composition by a lyricist or lyricists designated by Publisher, and in such event, "no less than" one-half (1/2) of the royalties provided for herein shall be payable to Writer.

Advocates for songwriters attempt to limit this type of clause as much as possible. First, writers generally resist changes made to their music without their consent. Moreover, the songwriter may suffer a substantial decrease in his or her share of the revenue if another writer is added at the unilateral discretion of the publisher. Translations are a special problem, as songwriters frequently lose substantial portions of revenue to translators that write versions that are not successful commercially. Translations should not be registered with any foreign performing or mechanical rights society until a commercial recording of the translation has been released. All major changes and additions should be made with the consent of the songwriter.

3. WARRANTIES AND REPRESENTATIONS
Writer hereby warrants and represents that the Composition is an original work, that neither the Composition nor any part thereof infringes upon the title, literacy or musical property of copyright or in any other work nor the statutory, common law or other rights (including rights of privacy) of any person, firm or corporation, that he is the sole writer and composer and the sole owner of the Composition and of all the rights therein, that he has not sold, assigned, transferred, hypothecated or mortgaged any right, title or interest in or to the Composition or any part thereof or any of the rights herein conveyed, that he has not made or entered into any contract with any other person, firm or corporation affecting the Composition or any right, title or interest therein or in copyright thereof, that no person, firm or corporation other than Writer has or has had claims or has claimed any right, title or interest in or to the Composition or any part thereof, or any use thereof or any copyright therein, that the composition has never been published, that where no copyright registration information has been given in paragraph 1 of this Agreement, the Composition has never been registered for copyright, and that the Writer has full right, power and authority to make this present instrument of sale and transfer.

This is typical boilerplate. Of course, the song must be noninfringing and not the property of someone else—this is the heart of the agreement. Virtually all publishing agreements contain language of the above nature. In any event, if the song is infringing or has been previously sold to a third party, the composer is liable.

4. ROYALTIES

Publisher shall pay or cause to be paid to Writer the following sums with respect to the Composition:

(a) Seven (7) cents per copy on all regular piano-vocal sheet music sold, paid for and not returned in the United States and Canada.

Songwriters have long received less than a fair share of print music income. Many publishing companies now split this revenue equally with the songwriter, rather than using a penny rate when they license print music to one of the major print publishers. A songwriter should receive a minimum of 50¢ per single edition when paid directly by a stand-alone print publisher, and the payment should increase with inflation, based on the Consumer Price Index.

There are six major print music companies in the United States: Warner Publications, Hal Leonard, Music Sales, Cherry Lane, Mel Bay, and Alfred. (The latter two are limited to education sales.) As these companies are manufacturers and distributors, it is very difficult for them to agree to split profits, and usually only a penny rate can be negotiated if the deal is directly with them. (The writer could seek a floor of 50¢ to be paid to him or her from a publisher who licenses to a third print outfit on the theory that the job of a publisher is in part to publish print music, and the writer should not suffer if the publisher is incapable or unable to print.). The publisher who licenses to one of the major print outfits usually makes 20% of the suggested Retail Selling Price (RSP) for pop single sheets. The RSP in 2001 is $3.95. Print music is generally sold at the wholesale price of 45% to 50% of the RSP.

Finally, in the case of "educational" markets, the royalty may be reduced to as little as 5% of the retail selling price if the choral arranger is a "big name."

(b) Ten (10) percent of the net wholesale selling price for each copy of all other editions sold, paid for and not returned in the United States and Canada.

"Net wholesale selling price" is ambiguous. What are the deductions from gross (which means all amounts received) to arrive at net? These deductions should be specified.

Some contracts, unlike this one, provide that the songwriter will be paid on the suggested retail selling price of the edition; a writer should always attempt to be paid on this higher basis. The royalty commonly paid is 10% to 12.5% of any such selling price. Again, 50% of what the publisher receives is what the songwriter should ask from a publisher who licenses others the right to print music.

(c) If the Composition is included in any song book, folio or similar publication issued by Publisher or its affiliates in the United States or Canada, a proportionate share of the royalty set forth in paragraph (b) above, which the number "one" bears to the total number of copyrighted musical compositions or arrangements of works on which royalties are payable included in such publications. If pursuant to a license granted by Publisher to an unaffiliated licensee, the Composition is included in any song book, folio or similar publication in the United States or Canada, the proportionate share of fifty percent (50%) of the net sums actually received by Publisher from said licensee, which the number "one" bears to the total number of Publisher's Compositions included in any such publication.

This is fair as the split is equal; 10% to 12.5% of the retail selling price is the going rate from the major publishers, but writers should strive for more as the net profit to the publisher is greater than a fifty-fifty split.

(d) Fifty percent (50%) of any and all sums actually received (less any costs for collection) by Publisher from mechanical rights, electrical transcription and reproducing rights, motion picture and television synchronization rights and all other rights therein (except as provided for in subparagraph (e) hereof), in the United States and Canada.

It should be specified that the songwriter be paid 50% of any advances paid to the publisher with respect to the composition. Costs of collection, such as Harry Fox Agency fees, should be charged against publisher's share. It is the publisher's job to administer. Try to limit the foreign collection or subpublishing charges. Anything more than 25% charged by a subpublisher is gouging. Then, of the 75% that comes back to North America, the publisher takes his cut. Try to get a 25% charge overall, no matter where paid, a so-called at source guarantee.

(e) Writer shall have no claim whatsoever against Publisher for any royalties received by Publisher from any performing rights society or other similar organization which makes payment directly (or indirectly other than through Publisher) to writers, authors and composers.

The writer is paid performance income directly by ASCAP or BMI, not through the publisher; however, if this were a copublishing deal, the writer would also be paid one-half of the publisher's share of revenue.

(f) Fifty percent (50%) of any and all sums, after deduction of foreign taxes, actually received in the United States (less any costs for collection) by Publisher from sales and uses directly related to the Composition in countries outside of the United States and Canada (other than public performance royalties as hereinabove set forth in paragraph (e). This provision shall not apply to copies of printed music shipped from the United States to such countries, to which the rates set forth in subparagraphs (a), (b), and (c) above shall apply.

No subpublisher (licensee of original publisher) should be permitted to take a percentage greater than 25% to collect the income, or 50% of the income "at source" (i.e., where the revenue is earned) if he secures a cover record. The shrewd songwriter will limit any subpublishing fee to no more than 15% of the income collected at source. This is an important provision and can involve substantial income for the writer. Also, the writer should be paid when monies are credited to the subpublisher, not just received.

(g) No royalties are to be paid for professional copies, copies disposed of as new issues, or copies distributed for advertising purposes. No royalties are payable on consigned copies unless paid for, and not until such time as an accounting therefor can properly be made.
(h) Except as herein expressly provided, no other compensation, royalties or monies shall be paid to Writer.

This is a superfluous statement and should be deleted and replaced by a 50% catch-all provision. See Evanne L. Levin's commentary below.

Evanne L. Levin from the chapter, Analysis of an Exclusive Term Songwriter Agreement. Provision should be made for advances to be paid to the writer under any term songwriter agreement. The publisher is requiring the writer to write exclusively for it and in exchange is paying the writer only the royalties noted above, while retaining complete ownership of the songs and keeping 100% of the publisher's share of income. Nor is there any guarantee that the publisher will successfully exploit any of the writer's material, in which case the writer will see no income.

Advances are typically paid (1) in one lump sum on execution of the agreement and at the beginning of each succeeding year of the term, and/or (2) in regular installments over the term, like a weekly or semimonthly paycheck. For the first year, $16,000 to $24,000 is not an unusual amount for a large publishing company to pay; small, independent publishers typically pay less but contend that more time will be devoted to promoting their staff writers since they have fewer of them.

The amount of the advance typically escalates 10% to 20% for each succeeding year of the term, and may be boosted by additional advances triggered by a song's commercial success. This is commonly done by tying increases to Billboard chart positions achieved or sales levels reached by previous albums. All advances are recoupable from both the writer's share and publisher's share of royalties otherwise payable to the writer (ASCAP/BMI royalties excluded).

A publisher who pays an advance to a writer will require the delivery of a specified minimum number of compositions written by the writer. Fifteen to 20 "Wholly Owned Compositions" is typical, with songs cowritten receiving partial credit. For example, if the writer writes a song with two other writers, the publisher will give the writer credit for one-third of a wholly owned composition toward the minimum delivery requirement. If the writer fails to deliver the minimum number of songs required during any contract year, the publisher will have the right to extend the term without having to increase the advances beyond the agreed amount until a sufficient number of songs are delivered. The writer should object to any provision giving the publisher the right to suspend advances in addition to extending the term.

(i) Notwithstanding anything to the contrary herein contained in this Agreement, Publisher shall have the right to deduct ten percent (10%) of all sums received in the United States from all sources throughout the world as administration fees, before computing the compensation payable to Writer hereunder.

This would reduce the writer's share by 5% of gross revenues. There is no justification for such a split—the publisher's job is to administer the composition, and he or she is well paid for it without this so-called administration fee.

5. ACCOUNTING

Royalty statements shall be rendered to Writer quarterly within forty-five (45) days following the close of each such quarterly period. Each statement shall be accompanied by a remittance of such amount as may be shown thereon to be due and payable. All royalty statements rendered by Publisher to Writer shall be binding upon Writer and not subject to any objection by Writer for any reason unless specific objection is made, in writing, stating the basis thereof, to Publisher within one (1) year from the date rendered. Writer shall have a reasonable right to audit those portions of the books and records of Publisher pertaining to the Composition.

Statements are rendered quarterly, which is nice, but the time should be stated more clearly (for example, within 45 days after each calendar quarter). Most agreements provide for semiannual accounting. The writer should have at least two and preferably three years to audit and object. The writer should, whenever possible, attempt to obtain the right to collect his or her share of income directly from any revenue generating source. Doing so could reduce delays in payment by six months to two years.

6. ASSIGNMENT OF COPYRIGHT
Writer hereby expressly grants and conveys to Publisher the copyright in the Composition, together with renewals and extensions thereof, and the right to secure any and all rights therein that Writer may at any time be entitled to. Writer agrees to sign any and all other papers which may be required to effectuate this Agreement.

The first sentence is redundant: the songwriter assigned the copyright in paragraph 1.

7. TRANSFER OF AGREEMENT
Writer shall not transfer nor assign this Agreement nor any interest therein nor any sums that may be or become due hereunder without the written consent of Publisher, and no purported assignment or transfer in violation of this restriction shall be valid to pass any interest to the assignee or transferee.

Prohibiting the assignment of income is unjustifiable and unlawful in those states that discourage agreements that prohibit assignment of monies; further, there is no good reason for doing so. Arguably, this could prevent a writer from getting an advance from BMI or ASCAP by assigning future performance royalties until recoupment.

8. ACTIONS AND INDEMNITIES
Writer hereby authorizes Publisher at its absolute discretion and at Writer's sole expense to employ attorneys and to institute or defend any action or proceeding and to take any other proper steps to protect the right, title and interest of Publisher in and to the Composition and every portion thereof acquired from Writer, pursuant to the terms hereof and in that connection to settle, compromise or in any other manner dispose of any matter, claim, action or proceeding and to satisfy any judgment that may be rendered and all of the expense so incurred and other sums so paid by Publisher. Writer hereby agrees to pay to Publisher on demand, further authorizing Publisher, whenever in its opinion its right, title or interest to any of Writer's compositions are questioned or there is a breach of any of the covenants, warranties or representations contained in this contract or in any other similar contract heretofore or hereafter entered into between Publisher and Writer, to withhold any and all royalties that may be or become due to Writer pursuant to all such contracts until such questions shall have been settled or such breach repaired, and to apply such royalties to the repayment of all sums due to Publisher with respect thereto.

This is a very tricky area. Too much control over litigation resides in the publisher. The publisher should be required to protect the copyright and to prevent and stop infringements, and should bear all costs of doing so. That is a risk of doing business.

When sued by third parties, the writer should have the right to have his or her own attorney and to consent to all settlements. Monies should not continue to be withheld unless a lawsuit is brought within six months after such monies are first withheld; any monies withheld should bear interest.

9. COLLABORATION
The term "Writer" shall be understood to include all the authors and composers of the Composition. If there be more than one, the covenants herein contained shall be deemed to be both joint and several on the part of all the authors and composers, and the royalties hereinabove specified to be paid to Writer shall, unless a different division of royalty be specified in paragraphs 2 and/or 14 hereof, be due to all the authors and composers collectively to be paid by Publisher in equal shares to each. This Agreement may be executed by the authors and composers in several counterparts.

If a lyricist and composer have written the song, their respective contributions should be delineated. The lyricist should not suffer if the music is infringing and vice versa with respect to the composer if the lyrics infringe. (I have represented writers where this has happened. The lyricist should not be liable for damages or costs if the music infringes.) Further, it is the lyricist, not the composer, who may suffer a loss in income from translations, which the composer may not wish to share. (See discussion in paragraph 2 above.) In the absence of a written agreement to the contrary, all creators are equal owners, irrespective of the amount of the contribution. If these roles are delineated, the composer of the music will not share lyric reprint royalties, and the lyricist will not share royalties on instrumental versions, unless the parties otherwise agree.

10. USE OF NAME
Writer hereby grants to Publisher the perpetual right to use and publish and to permit others to use and publish Writer's name (including any professional name heretofore or hereafter adopted by Writer), likeness and biographical material, or any reproduction or simulation thereof and the title of the Composition in connection with the printing, sale, advertising, distribution and exploitation of music, folios, recordings, performances, player rolls and otherwise concerning the Composition, and for any other purpose related to the business of Publisher, its associates, affiliates and subsidiaries, or to refrain therefrom.

The portion of this clause "any other purpose related to the business of Publisher, its associates, affiliates and subsidiaries," is too general and should be deleted. The writer should approve, or at least be consulted, anytime his or her image is used.

11. ASSIGNMENT
Publisher shall have the right to assign this Agreement and any of its rights hereunder and to delegate any of its obligations hereunder, in whole or in part, to any person, firm or corporation. Without limiting the generality of the foregoing, Publisher shall have the right to enter into subpublishing, collection, print or other agreements with respect to the Composition with any person, firm or corporation for any one or more countries of the world.

Publisher should be allowed to assign only to a person or entity acquiring all or substantially all of the assets of publisher. Writer should be allowed a "right of first refusal" to purchase the song at the same price at which it is sold to any third party (if it is part of a catalog, an independent appraiser can be appointed), but few publishers will agree to this.

12. DISPUTES
This contract shall be deemed to have been made in the State of California, and its validity, construction and effect shall be governed by and construed under the laws and judicial decisions of the State of California applicable to agreements wholly performed therein.

In the event of a dispute, the prevailing party should be entitled to reasonable attorneys' fees and costs of suit. Oftentimes it costs as much to fight about the song as the amount at stake. If this provision is not in the contract, then, in most states, such fees are lost. Further, arbitration may be the most economical method of dispute resolution—it is generally less expensive and faster than the court system. The parties might want to require mediation, which is nonbinding, as a prerequisite to filing any action. See discussion in the chapter, Analysis of a Personal Management Agreement.

13. ENTIRE AGREEMENT
This Agreement contains the entire understanding between us, and all of its terms, conditions and covenants shall be binding upon and shall inure to the benefit of the respective parties and their heirs, successors and assigns. No modification or waiver hereunder shall be valid unless the same is in writing and is signed by the parties hereto.

14. ROYALTY DIVISIONS
Royalties payable to Writer hereunder shall be divided among the parties below in the proportions following if otherwise than provided for in paragraph 9 herein.

WRITER	PERCENTAGE
______________________	______________________
______________________	______________________
______________________	______________________

IN WITNESS WHEREOF, the parties hereto have executed this Agreement as of the day and year first above written.

AGREED TO AND ACCEPTED:

______________________	______________________
(WRITER)	(PUBLISHER)
______________________	______________________
ADDRESS	ADDRESS
______________________	______________________
FEDERAL I.D./SS#	FEDERAL I.D./SS#

Analysis of an Exclusive Term Songwriter Agreement

BY EVANNE L. LEVIN

The agreement that follows is an example of an exclusive term songwriter agreement entered into between a songwriter (Writer) and a music publisher (Publisher). It provides that 100% of the ownership (Copyright) in the compositions written during a stated period of time will belong to the publisher. In many cases, an agreement of this type, either alone, or with a Copublishing Agreement (discussed later), is used to acquire the musical works of a writer who is also a recording or performing artist.

Although songwriters are required to relinquish part or all ownership in the musical compositions covered by this type of agreement, they seek term agreements for two basic reasons. First, the annual advance and maybe a weekly salary provides a financial foundation that enables the songwriter to dedicate more time and energy to writing and, with the assistance of the publisher's professional staff, develop the skills shared by successful songwriters. Second, the publisher will introduce the writer's material to a broad network of performers and record producers, increasing the likelihood of the songs being recorded. Negotiations for a term agreement typically take place only after a writer has had songs recorded by recording artists or concurrently with negotiating an exclusive recording agreement with a writer who will be recording his/her own material.

Like the single-song agreement analyzed earlier, there is no standard term agreement. Even a term agreement that is a particular publisher's standardized form is subject to modification by your legal representative. The term agreement is distinguished from the single-song agreement by the addition of provisions that may include—advances payable to the songwriter; a period of time the songwriter is employed to write and deliver original songs; the writer's exclusivity to the publisher; a guaranteed annual minimum compensation option; and the scope of the writer's earnings to be withheld for claims brought by others against the publisher. Many of the other provisions are essentially the same as those in the chapter, Analysis of a Single-Song Agreement.

At the heart of the negotiation is the publisher's interest in acquiring the maximum rights and control in the maximum number of songs for the least amount of money, and the writer's interest in relinquishing the minimum of rights and control in fewer compositions for the maximum consideration.

Given the complexity of and variations in this type of agreement, it is recommended that a writer not sign a term agreement without first seeking the advice of an attorney familiar with the subject matter.

EXCLUSIVE TERM SONGWRITER AGREEMENT

AGREEMENT effective ________________ day of ________________ 20___ , by and between ________________________ hereinafter referred to as "PUBLISHER" and ________________________ hereinafter (collectively) referred to as "WRITER."

WITNESSETH: in consideration of the mutual covenants and undertakings herein set forth, the parties do hereby agree as follows:

1. SERVICES

Publisher hereby engages Writer to render his or her services as a songwriter and composer and otherwise as may be hereinafter set forth. Writer hereby accepts such engagement and agrees to render such services exclusively for Publisher during the term hereof, upon the terms and conditions set forth herein.

Although the writer is not the publisher's employee, for the term of the agreement the writer is considered like an exclusive employee of the publisher, and as such, cannot write for anyone else.

2. TERM

The term of this Agreement shall commence with the date hereof and shall continue in force for a period coterminus with the term of that certain Exclusive Recording Artist Agreement between Writer and Publisher, entered into concurrently with this Agreement, as same is renewed, extended, amended or substituted.

Performers that record their own material often enter into term songwriter agreements with their record label's affiliated publishing company. In these instances, the writer should limit the term of the songwriter agreement to the length of the term of the record deal. Once the recording agreement is over the writer will want any new material to be available to negotiate a stronger agreement with the next record company, and by that time may be in a better position to keep some or all of the copyright in the new songs and a portion of the publisher's share of income. In instances where the songwriter agreement is not tied to a record deal, the term is usually three years with an initial term of one year and two one-year options, exercisable by the publisher. The songwriter may want to try to obtain some measure of performance by the publisher, such as obtaining a certain number of cover recordings, especially if little or no advances are paid, as a condition to the publisher's exercise of its option to extend the term. As a practical matter, the greater the advances, the less likely an option to extend the term will be exercised unless the publisher has been successful in exploiting the material.

On the other hand, a publisher will, as a condition of any sizable advance, require inclusion of two provisions:

1) Delivery during each term of a minimum number of 100% of copyright, totally original compositions; and

2) A minimum number of commercial releases in the United States

The number of songs to be delivered, as well as the number of covers, and in which territories, is an important area of negotiations. It is not unusual for the one-year term of an agreement to stretch into several actual years due to nonfulfillment of contractual commitments for commercial releases. For example if the commercial release requirement is three songs per year, but all three songs are cowritten, the Writer would have to obtain six commercial releases in one year before moving to the next term of the agreement.

There are pros and cons to a performer-writer entering into a songwriting agreement with their record company's publishing affiliate. Since the publishing company knows that the writer's material will be recorded and released by its affiliated record company, it is not taking a great risk that it will not earn back advances paid. Moreover, since the parent company will be earning money from two sources with each record sold (profits on the record and the publisher's share of mechanical royalties for the writer's compositions on the record), the writer should be able to negotiate a more favorable advance in exchange for the publisher's share of the compositions. The writer may also insist that in exchange for signing with the affiliated publishing company, the record company must pay a full mechanical royalty rather than the usual 75% rate on the writer's compositions included on the record. The publishing company will also benefit to the extent it has acquired a copyright in the recorded songs. Finally, the affiliated companies have a double incentive to promote the writer and material.

Other considerations may suggest that the writer's best interests would be served by entering into a term songwriter agreement elsewhere. The record company's publishing arm may not be offering the best terms, or may not be the best publisher for that writer's material. Are the recording contract and term songwriter contract cross-collateralized in any way, so that advances or other costs incurred by one company under one contract can be recovered from the writer's income under the other contract? How do the different publishing companies measure up in various territories? The writer may be one whose material has tremendous foreign income potential in certain major markets where a different publisher would do a better job for the writer. The writer may wish to refrain from entering into any exclusive term songwriter agreement until the record is released, to be in a position to negotiate a better deal with competing suitors (if the record catches on).

Many times, however, the writer has cash flow problems and is anxious to receive the publisher's advance, and cannot or will not adopt the riskier, but potentially more profitable, wait and see what happens posture.

3. GRANT OF RIGHTS

(a) Writer hereby irrevocably and absolutely assigns, transfers, sets over and grants to Publisher, its successors and assigns each and every and all rights and interests of every kind, nature and description in and to the results and proceeds of Writer's services hereunder, including but not limited to the titles, words and music of any and all original musical compositions in any and all forms and original arrangements of musical compositions in any and all forms, and all rights and interests existing under all agreements and licenses relating thereto, together with all worldwide copyrights (and any renewals or extensions thereof), which musical works have been written, composed, created or conceived, in whole or in part, by Writer alone or in collaboration with another or others, and which may hereafter, during the term hereof, be written, composed, created or conceived by Writer, in whole or in part, alone or in collaboration with another or others, and which are now owned or controlled and which may, during their term hereof, be acquired, owned or controlled, directly or indirectly, by Writer, alone or with others, or as the employer or transferee, directly or indirectly, of the writers or composers thereof, including the title, words and music of each such composition, and all worldwide copyrights (and renewals and extensions thereof), all of which Writer does hereby represent, are and shall at all times be Publisher's sole and exclusive property as the sole owner thereof, free from any adverse claims or rights therein by any other person, firm or corporation.

Note that the writer is assigning 100% of the compositions to the publisher even if cowritten or owned with others. The writer should be required to give the publisher only the writer's share, since the cowriter(s) or joint owner(s) will want the right to decide what to do with their share, and may even have their own term songwriter agreement with another publisher which contains an identical provision. Unless the other writers give you permission to give your publisher their share of the copyright, you may be in breach of your agreement with your publisher if you cannot grant 100% of the copyright in songs you cowrite. The prudent way to handle this common dilemma is to limit the publisher's ownership in the material to your share. It would also be acceptable to require you to use "reasonable efforts" to obtain the cowriter's copyright share. (For more information regarding cowritten compositions, see the chapter, Collaborator/Songwriter Agreements.)

Requiring the writer to also give the publisher ownership of all songs written before the term is unfair, unless the publisher is paying additional money for these. Postterm reversion clauses are becoming more acceptable. These provisions may involve one or both of the following:

1) A postterm reversion of all unrecorded songs, at a term of one to five years following the term, provided the Publisher has recouped all outstanding advances to the Writer; and

2) A postterm reassignment of administration rights to a portion of each composition, five to seven years following expiration of the term, again only if the writer is fully recouped. This latter provision is more likely to be an issue where there is a copublishing agreement, i.e. where the publisher and writer jointly own the copyright and divide the 50% publisher's share.

A similar reversion should also apply to songs written during the term if the advances are low. Advances refers to both money received by the writer at the beginning of each year of the contract and money paid out on a regular basis like a paycheck.

A concept having far-reaching effects on writers' future rights in their compositions is embedded in this provision. It is most significant that this provision, while assigning the writer's copyright in the compositions for the minimum copyright term, does not include specific language describing the writer as creating the compositions "within the scope of Publisher's employment of Writer's personal services" whereby the writer would be deemed the publisher's so-called employee for hire and the publisher would be "deemed the author of the Compositions initially created during the Term." When this language is used, the compositions are deemed works made for hire under U.S. copyright laws and the publisher is considered the writer and original copyright owner of the compositions. This would preclude the writer from having any right to reclaim the copyright in these songs after 35 years, which writers can do if they have written the material prior to the term of the Exclusive Term Songwriter Agreement, or the language of the agreement provides for the writer to assign copyrights to the publisher without saying more about the publisher being considered the author from the outset or including the works-made-for-hire language. Even where employee/writer-for-hire language has been used, writers have succeeded in challenging the status of "author" claimed by their publishers by proving that the publisher was not in a position to actually control the development of the songs to be written. The control element is one factor considered by courts in characterizing whether a composition was written (1) independent of the publisher, or (2) under the direction of the publisher. The publisher might need to demonstrate that it was involved in the creation of the song by having critiqued the material and having instructed the writer to make changes, as well as having given the writer direction about the compositions it expected to be written. The opposite of this would be a writer delivering completed songs written without input from the publisher that were done on the writer's own time at a location other than the publisher's offices.

If the publisher agrees to allow the writer to keep a share of the copyright, or publisher's share of income (roughly 50¢ on each dollar generated from exploiting the composition) it is generally handled by the writer first assigning the entire copyright to the publisher and the publisher then assigning back to the writer a part of the copyright, or publisher's share of income if the publisher wants to maintain sole ownership and control of the copyright, but is willing to share part of the 50% income that comes to the copyright owner. This can be accomplished by adding a provision to the end of this agreement assigning back to the writer a percentage of the copyright and/or providing for payment of a percentage of the publisher's share of income to the writer. A separate agreement called a "Copublishing Agreement" often accompanies the Term Songwriter Agreement and spells out the writer's interest in the songs as a publisher, as distinguished from a writer. This represents an additional source of income from the songs but does not provide any additional control over if or how the copyrights will be used.

(b) Writer acknowledges that, included within the rights and interests hereinabove referred to, but without limiting the generality of the foregoing, is Writer's irrevocable grant to Publisher, its successors, licensees, sublicensees and assigns, of the sole and exclusive right, license, privilege and authority throughout the entire world with respect to the said original musical compositions and original arrangements of compositions in the public domain, whether now in existence or hereafter created during the term hereof, as follows:

This is a more detailed version of paragraph 2 of the sample single-song agreement already commented on. The publisher should have to give the writer the first opportunity to make changes in the material.

(i) To perform said musical compositions publicly for profit by means of public and private performance, radio broadcasting, television or any and all other means, whether now known or which may hereafter come into existence;
(ii) To substitute a new title or titles for said compositions and to make any arrangement, adaptation, translation, dramatization and transposition of said compositions, in whole or in part, and in connection with any other musical, literary or dramatic material as Publisher may deem expedient or desirable;

The writer should seek to limit the changes that can be made without reasonable prior consent, at least title and lyric changes in English. Writer can also ask to be given the first opportunity to make the changes desired by the publisher.

(iii) To secure copyright registration and protection of said compositions in Publisher's name or otherwise as Publisher may desire, at Publisher's own cost and expense and at Publisher's election, including any and all renewals and extensions of copyright under any present or future laws throughout the world, and to have and to hold said copyrights, renewals, extensions and all rights of whatsoever nature thereunder existing, for and during the full term of all said copyrights and all renewals and extensions thereof;

Writers should attempt to require the publisher to secure valid copyright protection for the songs throughout the world wherever such protection is recognized. Although formal registration with the U.S. Copyright Office is no longer mandatory to claim ownership in a work, it establishes proof of ownership and is required in order to maintain a claim against another for infringement of the work. The $20 registration fee should not be a problem for the publisher. Since the United States recently joined the Berne Convention, registration in this country will be recognized by all other member countries. The specific requirements for establishing and maintaining a valid copyright are beyond the scope of this chapter but are covered in the chapter, Copyrights: The Law and You.

(iv) To make or cause to be made, master records, transcriptions, sound tracks, pressings, and any other mechanical, electrical or other reproductions of said compositions, in whole or in part, in such form or manner and as frequently as Publisher's sole and uncontrolled discretion shall determine, including the right to synchronize the same with sound motion pictures and the right to manufacture, advertise, license or sell such reproductions for any and all purposes, including, but not limited to, private performances and public performances, by broadcasting, television, sound motion pictures, wired radio, audio devices, and any and all other means or devices whether now known or hereafter conceived or developed;

Writers can protect the integrity of their music by requiring prior consent to its use in X-rated films or those taking an overt political, religious or moral stand. Writers may also seek to require their consent for the use of their music in commercials since the product or service advertised may be one that the writer feels is inappropriate and may diminish the value of the copyright by being associated with it.

(v) To print, publish and sell sheet music orchestration, arrangements and other editions of the said compositions in all forms, including the right to include any or all of said compositions in song folios or lyric magazines with or without music, and the right to license others to include any or all of said compositions in song folios or lyric magazines with or without music; and

The mandatory printing of sheet music or a folio can sometimes be tied to a song reaching a certain level on the Billboard sales charts, although this is not typically a significant source of income and is not equally suited to all types of music.

(vi) Any and all other rights of every and any nature now or hereafter existing under and by virtue of any common law rights and any copyrights (and renewals and extensions thereof) in any and all of such compositions.

Again, prior consent for the use of the song for merchandising purposes might be desired by the writer to prevent identification of the song with some ridiculous product or service. The publisher will want to limit such consent since it has a financial investment in the writer and will claim expertise as compared to the writer in determining the best use of the songs. A compromise can be reached by listing the types of goods or services that would reasonably require the writer's consent. These typically include alcoholic beverages, personal care products, firearms and tobacco products. In addition, writers may try to exclude what are called "grand" rights (the use of the musical material in combination with a dramatic rendition, such as a drama, play or opera).

(c) Writer grants to Publisher, without any compensation other than as specified herein, the perpetual right to use and publish and to permit another to use and publish Writer's name (including any professional name heretofore or hereafter adopted by Writer), likeness, voice and sound effects and biographical material, or any reproduction or simulation thereof and titles of all compositions hereunder in connection with the printing, sale, advertising, distribution and exploitation of music, folios, recordings, performances, player rolls and otherwise concerning any of the compositions hereunder, and for any other purpose related to the compositions hereunder, and for any other purpose related to the business of Publisher, its affiliated and related companies, or to refrain therefrom. This right shall be exclusive during the term hereof and nonexclusive thereafter. Writer will not authorize or permit the use of his name, likeness, biographical material concerning Writer, or the identification of Writer, or any reproduction or simulation thereof, for or in connection with any musical composition or works, in any manner or for any purpose, other than by or for Publisher. Writer further grants to Publisher the right to refer to Writer as "Publisher's Exclusive Songwriter and Composer" or other similar appropriate appellation.

The clause "any other purpose related to the business of Publisher, its associates, affiliates and subsidiaries," is too broad and should be deleted. The writer should be able to negotiate for reasonable approval of his pictures and biographical material. All uses of the writer's name and likeness, which are reasonably related to the compositions, have already been covered. In addition, the prohibition against writers allowing their names or information about them to be used in connection with any composition not covered by this agreement is overreaching and unfair since the agreement may not cover preexisting material or new material not accepted by the publisher. The designation "Publisher's Exclusive Songwriter and Composer" is merely descriptive of the writer's status and is standard in exclusive term agreements.

4. EXCLUSIVITY

From the date hereof and during the term of this Agreement, Writer will not write or compose, or furnish or dispose of, any musical compositions, titles, lyrics or music, or any rights or interests therein whatsoever, nor participate in any manner with regard to the same for any person, firm or corporation other than Publisher, nor permit the use of their name or likeness as the writer or cowriter of any musical composition by any person, firm or corporation other than Publisher.

This exclusivity provision should be qualified to state the writer retains ownership material written before the term of the agreement. In addition, the material written during the term should be evaluated by the publisher and either accepted or rejected as commercially viable within a reasonable period of time after delivery—30 to 60 days is fair. Rejected songs should be given back to the writer since the publisher does not believe in them and therefore will not promote them.

5. WARRANTIES AND REPRESENTATIONS
Writer hereby warrants and represents to Publisher that:

(a) Writer has the full right, power and authority to enter into and perform this Agreement and to grant to and vest in Publisher all the rights herein set forth, free and clear of any and all claims, rights and obligations whatsoever.

(b) All the results and proceeds of the services of Writer hereunder, including all of the titles, lyrics, music and musical compositions, and each and every part thereof, delivered and to be delivered by Writer hereunder are and shall be new and original and capable of copyright protection throughout the entire world.

(c) No part thereof shall be an imitation or copy of, or shall infringe any other original material.

(d) Writer has not and will not sell, assign, lease, license or in any other way dispose of or encumber the rights herein granted to Publisher.

This is essentially the same as the boilerplate language of paragraph 3 of the single-song agreement.

(e) Writer warrants that each composition contains no unlicensed "samples" of other copyrighted material, or if so, that all such samples have been previously licensed from the owner of the sampled material.

The writer should try to limit the warranties to "the best of Writer's knowledge."

6. ATTORNEY IN FACT
Writer does hereby irrevocably constitute, authorize, empower and appoint Publisher, or any of its officers, Writer's true and lawful attorney (with full power of substitution and delegation) in Writer's name, and in Writer's place and stead, or in Publisher's name, to take and do such action, and to make, sign, execute, acknowledge and deliver any and all instruments or documents which Publisher, from time to time, may deem desirable or necessary to vest in Publisher, its successors, assigns and licensees, any of the rights or interests granted by Writer hereunder, including but not limited to such documents required to secure to Publisher the renewals and extensions of copyrights throughout the world of musical compositions written or composed by Writer and owner by Publisher, and also such documents necessary to assign to Publisher, its successors and assigns, such renewal copyrights, and all rights therein for the terms of such renewals and extensions for the use and benefit of Publisher, its successors and assigns.

This common boilerplate provision gives the publisher the authority to act on behalf of the writer to secure and protect the rights it has obtained from the writer. The power of attorney should be exercisable only if the writer fails to sign the requested documents within a reasonable period of time. Ten (10) business days is typical.

7. ADVANCES; ANNUAL GUARANTEES

Conditioned upon, and in consideration of, the full and faithful performance by Writer of all of the terms and provisions hereof, Publisher shall pay to Writer the following annual amounts, in equal monthly installments, all of which shall be recoupable by Publisher from any and all royalties payable to Writer under this or any other agreement between Writer and Publisher:

(a) (amount) ($____) during the initial term hereof.
(b) (amount) ($____) during the first renewal term hereof.
(c) (amount) ($____) during the second renewal term hereof.

The range of yearly advances for songwriter agreements of this type, where the songwriter is not already a recording artist, is anywhere from zero to $15,000 the first year.

A more experienced writer, depending on the level of prior success, should start at anywhere from $25,000 to $100,000, and would probably be able to insist on retaining part of the copyright in the songs by entering into a separate copublishing agreement. A new writer's advances in option years would likely increase EITHER a flat amount ($2,500 each year for years two and three), with a possible bonus of at least $5,000 for the first song each year that hits the top 20 on Billboard's record sale charts, OR an amount equal to 75% of the actual earnings in the prior year of the songs covered by the agreement, subject to some minimums and maximums, as follows:

YEAR	*MINIMUM*	*MAXIMUM*
(a) first renewal term	*$12,500*	*$25,000*
(b) second renewal term	*$15,000*	*$30,000*

If the writer is also a recording artist, there will probably be no set advances as a songwriter. Instead, advances will be contingent on delivery and release in the United States by the record company of recordings of the writer's performance of the material, and will cover a wide range of amounts, with $25,000 to $75,000 fairly typical for an unknown group's first album.

8. ROYALTIES

Provided that Writer shall faithfully and completely perform the terms, covenants and conditions of this Agreement, Publisher hereby agrees to pay Writer for the services to be rendered by Writer under this Agreement and for the rights acquired and to be acquired hereunder, the following compensation based on the musical compositions which are the subject hereof.

(a) Eight ($.08) cents per copy for each and every regular piano copy and for each and every dance orchestration sold by Publisher and paid for, after deduction of each and every return, in the United States.

This rate is far too low; 10¢ per single edition is reasonable, with increases tied to the Consumer Price Index. In the alternative, and more beneficial to the songwriter, many publishers now split their receipts from single editions with the songwriter.

(b) Ten (10%) percent of the wholesale selling price upon each and every printed copy of each and every other arrangement and edition thereof printed, published and sold by Publisher and paid for, after deduction of each and every return, in the United States, except that in the event that such composition shall be used or caused to be used, in whole or in part, in conjunction with one or more other musical compositions in a folio or album, Writer shall be entitled to receive that proportion of said ten (10%) percent which the subject musical composition shall bear to the total number of musical compositions contained in such folio or album.

The writer should try for 50% of what the publisher receives, but in any event at least 15% of the wholesale selling price, or its retail equivalent. Proration for use in folios with material by other writers should be limited to copyrighted, royalty-bearing compositions. An additional 5% of wholesale to 5% of retail should be paid for use of the writer's name and likeness in a personality folio.

(c) Fifty (50%) percent of any and all net sums actually received (less any costs for collection) by Publisher from mechanical rights, electrical transcription and reproduction rights, motion picture synchronization and television rights and all other rights (excepting public performing rights) therein, including the use thereof in song lyric folios, magazines or any other editions whatsoever sold by licensees of Publisher in the United States.

While the equal split stated is fair, the agreement should also provide that the writer receive 50% of any nonreturnable and earned advances the publisher receives with respect to the composition(s). Also, since the publisher is the administrator of the compositions, collection costs should be charged against the publisher's share rather than the writer's share, if possible. This comment applies wherever collection costs are referred to in the agreement. The writer should see to it that he or she is paid on monies credited to the publisher wherever the agreement refers to the writer receiving a share of monies received by the publisher.

(d) Writer shall receive his public performance royalties throughout the world directly from his own affiliated performing rights society and shall have no claim whatsoever against Publisher for any royalties received by Publisher from any performing rights society which make payment directly (or indirectly other than through Publisher) to writers, authors and composers.

This is correct. The writer's performing rights society (usually ASCAP or BMI, but occasionally SESAC) pays the writer's share of public performance income directly to the writer.

(e) Fifty (50%) percent of any and all net sums, after deduction of foreign taxes, actually received (less any costs for collection) by Publisher from sales and uses directly related to subject musical compositions in countries outside of the United States (other than public performance royalties as hereinabove mentioned in paragraph 8(d).

Income generated through subpublishers (licensees of original publisher) or foreign affiliates of the publisher may far exceed United States income; it is important to establish ceilings that a subpublisher or affiliate of Publisher can charge. The collection fee charged by a subpublisher for obtaining a cover record (local version) of the writer's composition is usually greater than the fee charged for mechanical license and other income generated from the original recording in the territory involved. The fee should not exceed 30% to 40% (depending on the territory), of what the publisher would otherwise receive before paying the writer for income attributable to the cover recording, and 20% to 25% for original recording income. The split between the publisher and subpublisher (i.e., before the writer's share is computed) is often stated in songwriter agreements as "80/20," "75/25," etc., representing the publisher and subpublisher's shares of gross income from its origin.

(f) Publisher shall not be required to pay any royalties on professional or complimentary copies of any copies or mechanical derivatives which are distributed gratuitously to performing artists, orchestra leaders, disc jockeys or for advertising or exploitation purposes. Furthermore, no royalties shall be payable to Writer on consigned copies unless paid for, and not until such time as an accounting therefor can be properly made.

(g) Royalties as specified hereinabove shall be payable solely to Writer in instances where Writer is the sole author of the entire composition, including the words and music thereof. If this Agreement with Publisher is made and executed by more than one person in the capacity of Writer, the royalties as hereinabove specified shall be payable solely to the particular Writer or Writers who are the authors of the entire composition, including words and music thereof, and such royalties shall be divided equally among the particular Writers of such composition unless another division is agreed upon in writing between the Writers. However, in the event that one or more other songwriters are authors along with Writer on any composition, then the foregoing royalties shall be divided equally between Writer and the other songwriters of such composition unless another division of royalties is agreed upon in writing between the parties concerned.

(h) Except as herein expressly provided, no other royalties or moneys shall be paid to Writer.

Provision should be made for advances to be paid to the writer under any term songwriter agreement. The publisher is requiring the writer to write exclusively for it and in exchange is paying the writer only the royalties noted above, while retaining complete ownership of the songs and keeping 100% of the publisher's share of income. Nor is there any guarantee that the publisher will successfully exploit any of the writer's material, in which case the writer will see no income.

Advances are typically paid (1) in one lump sum on execution of the agreement and at the beginning of each succeeding year of the term, and/or (2) in regular installments over the term, like a weekly or semimonthly paycheck. (For the first year, $16,000 to $24,000 is not an unusual amount for a large publishing company to pay; small, independent publishers typically pay less but contend that more time will be devoted to promoting their staff writers since they have fewer of them).

The amount of the advance typically escalates 10% to 20% for each succeeding year of the term, and may be boosted by additional advances triggered by a song's commercial success. This is commonly done by tying increases to Billboard chart positions achieved or sales levels reached by previous albums. All advances are recoupable from both the writer's share and publisher's share of royalties otherwise payable to the writer (ASCAP/BMI royalties excluded).

A publisher who pays an advance to a writer will require the delivery of specified minimum number of compositions written by the writer. Fifteen to 20 "Wholly Owned Compositions" is typical, with songs cowritten receiving partial credit. For example, if the writer writes a song with two other writers, the publisher will give the writer credit for one-third of a wholly owned composition toward the minimum delivery requirement. If the writer fails to deliver the minimum number of songs required during any contract year, the publisher will have the right to extend the term without having to increase the advances beyond the agreed amount until a sufficient number of songs are delivered. The writer should object to any provision giving the publisher the right to suspend advances in addition to extending the term.

In any event (h) is meaningless and should be deleted, since the rest of paragraph 8 provides for payment to the writer for all types of uses.

9. ACCOUNTING

Publisher will compute the royalties earned by Writer pursuant to this Agreement within ninety (90) days after the first day of January and the first day of July of each year for the preceding six (6) month period, and will remit to Writer the net amount of such royalties, if any, after deducting any and all unrecouped advances and chargeable costs under this Agreement, together with the detailed royalty statement, within such ninety (90) days. All royalty statements rendered by Publisher to Writer shall be binding upon Writer and not subject to any objection by Writer for any reason unless specific objection is made, in writing, stating the basis thereof, to Publisher within one (1) year from the date rendered. Writer shall have the right, upon the giving of at least thirty (30) days written notice to Publisher, to inspect the books and records of Publisher, insofar as the same concerns Writer, at the expense of Writer, at reasonable times during normal business hours, for the purpose of verifying the accuracy of any royalty statement rendered to Writer hereunder.

Mechanical income should be paid on a quarterly basis since record companies usually account for mechanical income quarterly. Forty-five to 60 days after the close of an accounting period should be enough time for statements to be rendered. The writer should have at least two years from the time rendered to object to a statement.

10. COLLABORATIONS

Whenever Writer shall collaborate with any other person in the creation of any musical composition, any such musical composition shall be subject to the terms and conditions of this Agreement and Writer warrants and represents that prior to the collaboration with any other person, such other person shall be advised prior to the collaboration of this exclusive agreement and that all such compositions must be published by Publisher in accordance with the terms and provisions hereunder. In the event of such collaboration with any other person, Writer shall notify Publisher of the extent that such other person may have in any such musical composition and Writer shall cause such other person to execute a separate songwriter's agreement with respect thereto, which agreement shall set forth the division of the songwriter's share of income between Writer and such other person, and Publisher shall make payment accordingly. If Publisher so desires, Publisher may request Writer to execute a separate agreement in Publisher's customary form with respect to each musical composition hereunder. Upon such request, Writer will promptly execute such agreement. Publisher shall have the right, pursuant to the terms and conditions hereof, to execute such agreement on behalf of Writer hereunder. Such agreement shall supplement and not supersede this Agreement. In the event of any conflict between the provisions of such agreement and this Agreement, the provisions of this Agreement shall govern.

This language is not consistent with the reality that writers do collaborate without regard to existing exclusive writer agreements, and is detrimental to the natural collaborate creative process. A better approach would be to require that the publisher be entitled to its own writer's entire ownership share of the song, and perhaps also the ownership share of any cowriter not similarly signed to a publisher. Moreover, it should state, "Writer shall use best efforts to cause such other person to execute a separate songwriter's agreement" with respect to cowritten compositions. Finally, writers should never authorize others to sign agreements in their name, except possibly to the extent necessary to allow the publisher to secure and protect the copyright share obtained from them, as discussed in paragraph 6 above. (For more information about collaborations, see the chapter, Collaborator/Songwriter Agreements.)

11. DEMOS
Writer will deliver a manuscript copy of each musical composition hereunder immediately upon the completion or acquisition of such musical composition. Publisher shall advance reasonable costs for the production of demonstration records and one-half (1/2) of such costs shall be deemed an advance which shall be deducted from royalties payable to Writer by Publisher under this Agreement. All recordings and reproductions made at demonstration recording sessions hereunder shall become the sole and exclusive property of Publisher, free of any claims whatsoever by Writer or any person deriving any rights from Writer.

It is unfair, but traditional, for publishers to recover one-half the demo costs from the writer's royalties. The writer should try to get this deleted, especially if they are not also receiving part of the publisher's share of income. The writer should be able to keep copies of demos of songs that are rejected by the publisher and can offer to reimburse publisher the unrecouped share of demo costs if they are successful in exploiting the song on their own.

12. INJUNCTION
Writer acknowledges that the services rendered hereunder are of a special, unique, unusual, extraordinary and intellectual character which gives them a peculiar value, the loss of which cannot be reasonably or adequately compensated in damages in an action at law, and that a breach by Writer of any of the provisions of this Agreement will cause Publisher great and irreparable injury and damage. Writer expressly agrees that Publisher shall be entitled to remedies of injunction and other equitable relief to prevent a breach of this Agreement or any provision hereof, which relief shall be in addition to any other remedies, for damages or otherwise, which may be available to Publisher.

This standard provision allows the publisher to get a court order preventing the writer from writing for any other publisher if the writer becomes dissatisfied and wants to terminate the deal with the current publisher and write for someone else. It is doubtful, however, that a court would issue an injunction just because this clause is in the contract.

This provision should only allow the publisher to seek an injunction from the court so that the publisher would be required to prove that a money judgment would not be sufficient. In addition, this kind of relief should be available only if the writer's action or failure goes to the essence of the agreement, such as failing to deliver the songs required, or refusing to turn over the demos to the publisher.

It is also important to know that, for contracts governed by California law, the publisher cannot obtain an injunction against the writer unless it has agreed to pay certain annual minimums. The amounts for a three-year agreement are $6,000; $9,000; and $12,000, for years one through three, respectively. As all other advances, these are fully recoupable against writer's royalties.

13. REVERSION

If Publisher fails to secure a cover recording of the Compositions within the term of this Agreement, Writer may, during the fifteen (15) days following the expiration of said term, demand the return of the Compositions in writing and if Publisher receives such notice within said period, Publisher agrees to reassign the compositions and all Publisher's rights therein to Writer and to execute any documents necessary to effect such reconveyance. Notwithstanding the foregoing, Publisher shall not be obliged to reassign the Compositions to Writer until such time as Writer shall repay to Publisher any advances or unrecouped demonstration recording costs chargeable to Writer.

The maximum period of time possible should be negotiated for the writer to come up with the money to reacquire the compositions—two years is probably the most the publisher will allow. The writer should additionally have the right to recapture even those compositions that are covered but are not commercially released on a major label. Even better, but less likely to obtain unless the writer has a measure of bargaining power, is requiring that the recording be by a major artist and/or achieve a certain chart position. Top 50 is a reasonable target to request. In addition, the publisher may require at least a year following the term for exploitation of those songs delivered during the last year or two of the term so as to have at least two or three years to record them. A new writer may have to settle for reversion after four or five years after the term, but this still offers an opportunity to breathe new life into compositions that would otherwise languish in the publisher's archives and be lost to the world. Be sure that the reversion is at the writer's option if repayment of advances is tied to reversion; there is no point in being required to buy back those compositions that are not winners even in the writer's eyes. Finally, only unrecouped advances should be repaid.

14. ACTIONS; INDEMNITY

(a) Publisher may take such action as it deems necessary, either in Writer's name or in its own name, against any person to protect all rights and interest acquired by Publisher hereunder. Writer will at Publisher's request, cooperate fully with Publisher in any controversy which may arise or litigation which may be brought concerning Publisher's rights and interests obtained hereunder. Publisher shall have the right, in its absolute discretion, to employ attorneys and to institute or defend any action or proceeding and to take any other proper steps to protect the rights, title and interest of Publisher in and to each musical composition hereunder and every portion thereof and in that connection, to settle, compromise or in any other manner dispose of any matter, claim, action or proceeding and to satisfy any judgment that may be rendered, in any manner as Publisher in its sole discretion may determine. Any legal action brought by Publisher against any alleged infringer of any musical composition hereunder shall be initiated and prosecuted by Publisher, and if there is any recovery made by Publisher as a result thereof, after the deduction of the expense of litigation, including but not limited to attorneys' fees and court costs, a sum equal to fifty (50%) percent of such net proceeds shall be paid to Writer.

(b) If a claim is presented against Publisher in respect to any musical composition hereunder, and because thereof Publisher is jeopardized, Publisher shall have the right thereafter, until said claim has been finally adjudicated or settled, to withhold any and all royalties or other sums that may be or become due with respect to such compositions pending the final adjudication or settlement of such claim. Publisher, in addition, may withhold from any and all royalties or other sums that may be due and payable to Writer hereunder, an amount that Publisher deems sufficient to reimburse Publisher for any contemplated damages, including court costs and attorneys' fees and costs resulting therefrom. Upon the final adjudication or settlement of each and every claim hereunder, all moneys withheld shall then be disbursed in accordance with the final adjudication or settlement of said claim.

This version is more fair to the writer in several respects than the indemnity provision appearing in the single-song agreement in the previous chapter. It clarifies that the writer shares in any recovery obtained against infringers, limits the amount of money withheld from the writer to a sum related to the anticipated cost of the claim and continues payment to the writer for income from compositions not involved in the claim. Since many claims are made by third parties and are not pursued, the agreement should also provide that any monies withheld from the writer by the publisher when a claim is made against the publisher bear interest and be released to the writer if no formal lawsuit is filed within six months after the monies are first withheld. The writer should also have the right to be represented by his or her own attorney and to consent to at least those settlements in excess of a few thousand dollars. In addition, since the publisher has acquired the copyright and controls the compositions, the publisher should have not only the right but also the obligation to protect the copyrights by taking action against infringers, and bearing all costs of defending or instituting claims.

15. NOTICES

Any written notice, statement, payment or matter required or desired to be given to Publisher or Writer pursuant to this Agreement shall be given by addressing the same to the addresses of the respective parties referred to herein, or to such other address as either party shall designate in writing, and such notice shall be deemed to have been given on the date when same shall be deposited, so addressed, postage prepaid, in the United States mail, or on the date when delivered, so addressed, toll prepaid, to a telegraph or cable company.

Be sure that the contract includes complete addresses for both parties. A copy of notices given by the publisher should also be sent to the writer's attorney so she or he can answer any questions that might arise from the notice. Notices exercising an option or claiming that a breach has occurred should be by certified mail with a return receipt.

16. ENTIRE AGREEMENT
This Agreement supersedes any and all prior negotiations, understandings and agreements between the parties hereto with respect to the subject matter hereof. Each of the parties acknowledges and agrees that neither party has made any representations or promises in connection with this Agreement or the subject matter hereof not contained herein.

17. MISCELLANEOUS
This Agreement may not be canceled, altered, modified, amended or waived, in whole or in part, in any way, except by an instrument in writing signed by both Publisher and Writer. The waiver by Publisher of any breach of this Agreement in any one or more instances, shall in no way be construed as a waiver of any subsequent breach (whether or not of a similar nature) of this Agreement by Writer. If any part of this Agreement shall be held to be void, invalid or unenforceable, it shall not affect the validity of the balance of this Agreement. This Agreement shall be governed by and construed under the law of the State of New York applicable to agreements executed in and to wholly performed therein.

These boilerplate provisions are like paragraphs 12 and 13 of the single-song agreement. If the writer and/or attorney reside in California, it would be better for California law to apply since it is more familiar and may be more favorable to the artist inasmuch as this state's legislature and courts have adopted a role somewhat more protective of artists than have other states.

18. BREACH; NOTICE
No breach of this Agreement on the part of Publisher shall be deemed material, unless Writer shall have given Publisher notice of such breach and Publisher shall fail to discontinue the practice complained of (if a practice of Publisher is the basis of the claim of breach) or otherwise cure such breach, within sixty (60) days after receipt of such notice, if such breach is reasonably capable of being fully cured within such sixty (60) day period, or, if such breach is not reasonably capable of being fully cured within such sixty (60) day period, if Publisher commences to cure such breach within such sixty (60) day period and proceeds with reasonable diligence to complete the curing of such breach.

The writer should be given the same opportunity to cure breaches.

19. ASSIGNMENT
This Agreement may not be assigned by Writer. Subject to the foregoing, this Agreement shall inure to the benefit of and be binding upon each of the parties hereto and their respective successors, assigns, heirs, executors, administrators and legal and personal representatives.

Publisher should be allowed to assign only to a person or entity acquiring all or substantially all of the assets of Publisher. Writer should be allowed to purchase the song at the same price at which it is sold to any third party (if it is part of a catalog, an independent appraiser can be appointed), but few publishers will agree to this.

IN WITNESS WHEREOF, the parties hereto have executed this Agreement as of the day and year first above written.

AGREED TO AND ACCEPTED:

______________________	______________________
(WRITER)	(PUBLISHER)
______________________	______________________
NAME AND TITLE (AN AUTHORIZED SIGNATORY)	NAME AND TITLE (AN AUTHORIZED SIGNATORY)
______________________	______________________
FEDERAL I.D./SS#:	FEDERAL I.D./SS#:

Special thanks to Cheryl Hodgson, Esq. for contributing revisions and updates to this chapter for the third edition of The Musician's Business and Legal Guide.

Music Licensing for Television and Film: A Perspective for Songwriters

BY RONALD H. GERTZ

Television and film productions are important and accessible vehicles that can generate exposure for a writer's works and develop into immediate and long-term sources of revenue. This chapter will discuss how music is licensed by television and film producers.

Songwriters want to receive the greatest amount of income possible from the exploitation of their creations. One of the major sources is from the performance of works in feature films and in network, syndicated, cable and pay television programs. A significant portion of ASCAP, BMI and SESAC revenues are collected from television broadcasters and the royalties received from public performances of music in television and film soundtracks can far exceed the up-front money paid to composers for services in creating original songs or musical scores.

FOR THE SONGWRITER WHO IS JUST STARTING OUT

If you are a songwriter or performer starting out in the business, you will be happy to know that there are television and film producers that actively look for new material for their projects in order to capture the latest sounds and styles. Some producers are looking for hot new talent, while others just want inexpensive music. The use of a song in a television or film program, whatever the reason, means exposure; the chance to be seen, heard and paid.

LICENSING THE RIGHTS

In general terms, copyright owners can usually prevent anyone who has not secured a license from using their songs. Under the copyright law, the owner is given the specific right to publish the composition, to reproduce and distribute copies of it; to perform the composition in public; to "display" the musical work as in a printed lyric sheet; and to make derivative works, such as different arrangements of the composition. Use of any of these rights requires the grant of a written license from the copyright owner to the user.

The producer who wishes to use *preexisting* music in a program must secure a license to do so from the owner of the song. (If the copyright owner has formed a publishing company or has signed a contract with an outside publishing company, then the publisher will negotiate and grant these licenses.) Such documents will usually require certain warranties and representations (guarantees) about the ownership of the material, because the producer must be sure to license the rights from the true owner of the song. This is not always a simple process because several writers can collaborate in creating a single song, and a copyright can be divided into separate parts with each part owned either individually or by several parties. The way a song is owned can cause complications because of the number of parties that can own it. If a song has been cowritten by several writers, each writer may legally own an undivided pro rata share of the copyright and each of the writers may have assigned all or a portion of their rights to various parties (or publishers) in different territories of the world. For more information on collaboration agreements, see the chapter, Collaborator/Songwriter Agreements.

These issues can make the licensing process a very lengthy one, and can work against both new and established songwriters because music decisions are made very quickly in the television and film business. Songwriters are well-advised to make sure that a producer who wants the right to use the writer's song in a production can get the rights quickly and easily. All things being equal, the producer will usually license the song that is easiest and cheapest to use.

Since producers are ultimately liable if rights are not secured properly, they must be sure to deal with the true owner or publisher of the composition and make sure that the publisher has the legal right to grant the license, and that all rights are "cleared." The clearance process involves determining whether the copyright owner of the song will allow the producer to use the song in the way the producer intends, and negotiating the fee that the producer will have to pay for the right to use the song.

This music clearance process is important because producers, program distributors, and broadcasters can be held liable for infringing copyrights if the music they use or broadcast has not been properly cleared. Producers have contractual obligations to a number of parties, including those that have paid for the program to be produced, and the companies that insure the program in the event its exhibition violates the rights of any third party. These contractual obligations require that the program be delivered for broadcast or other exhibition with all rights secured and be free of any restrictions that could limit the exploitation of the program.

THE PERFORMING RIGHTS ORGANIZATIONS

In the copyright law, one of the exclusive rights granted to the owner of a composition is the right to perform that composition publicly, subject to certain exceptions. In this context, "perform" is a term of art that means the singing, dancing to, playing, or broadcasting of a song. Broadcasters traditionally secure licenses, which allow them to broadcast programs containing music, from the performance rights organizations that represent songwriters and publishers: The American Society of Composers, Authors and Publishers (ASCAP), Broadcast Music, Inc. (BMI), and SESAC. It must be noted that there are differences in the working processes of each of these organizations, and a composer seeking affiliation with one of them should consult knowledgeable industry sources to help in making a choice. For a more complete discussion on these organizations, see the chapter, Performing Rights Organizations: An Overview.

The performing rights organizations make their entire catalogs of compositions available to broadcasters upon the payment of a fee, which gives them the right to perform all of the songs in the organization's catalog without having to contact each publisher directly. After deducting the costs of administration, those fees are divided between the writers and publishers based upon the number of performances logged by the performing rights organization.

SYNCHRONIZATION RIGHTS

Another major source of royalties for the songwriter comes from licensing the right to reproduce music in films. The right to reproduce (like the right to perform) is another exclusive right that the copyright law grants to the owner of the copyright in a song. A mechanical license, which refers to the right to mechanically reproduce music in the form of audio records and tapes, for distribution to the public, is an example of one type of reproduction. In the television and film business, music is reproduced when it is recorded on the soundtrack of a production. The industry has come to refer to the right to do this as a synchronization right, because the music is being reproduced on the soundtrack in synchronization with the pictures. Unlike performance royalties, which the performing rights organizations traditionally collect from broadcasters on a blanket basis, synchronization rights are a matter of individual negotiation for each composition used. Rights are secured by producers or their representatives directly from publishers or their agents. In addition, there are organizations such as The Harry Fox Agency, Inc., which represent publishers in the negotiation and collection of synchronization fees. Synchronization licenses are required in most situations where the composition is reproduced on film or videotape.

PER PROGRAM LICENSING

Another important performance rights issue is the "per program" license. The performing rights societies and the broadcasting and cable television industries have been negotiating and litigating new rate structures for free television and pay, cable and subscription television broadcasters. ASCAP and BMI are required to offer broadcasters per program licenses in which local television broadcasters pay a society only for those programs which contain music from that society. A large number of television stations have opted for the per program license and are securing performing rights for certain music directly from the copyright owners instead of through the performing rights societies. The net effect for certain music owners is a splitting of the revenue stream from performance rights. Thus, a composer can get paid through ASCAP or BMI for performances on television stations that utilize the blanket license and get additional monies directly from those television stations that utilize the per program license and negotiate directly with the copyright owner.

USE OF A SONG ON A TELEVISION PROGRAM

We are now going to follow what happens when a song is actually used on a television program. Assume that Fred Composer, Wilma Words and Lydia Lyric have cowritten a song called "Sing It High," which a young crooner would like to warble on the finals of the television series *You Too Can Hit It Big*. Fred wrote the music while Wilma and Lydia wrote the words. An agreement was worked out through their attorneys, which provided that they would divide all performance income equally, but because Fred owned the studio they produced the demo in, he would receive 50% of the publisher's share of income and Wilma and Lydia would each receive 25%. It was also agreed that they would each separately administer their own shares. Synchronization rights for Fred Composer Music Publishing are administered by The Harry Fox Agency, Wilma

Words Music is administered by the law firm of Abdulla and Steinmetz, and the affairs of Lydia Lyric's publishing company Aidyl Time Music are handled by her manager. All of the above (for the sake of simplicity) are affiliated with BMI.

Let us first consider the public performance rights issues. The producer will make sure that "Sing it High," Fred, Wilma, Lydia and their respective publishing companies are registered and affiliated with a performing rights organization. If registered, the rights to publicly perform "Sing It High" will be covered under the terms of the blanket licenses secured by the broadcasters. A blanket license allows a broadcaster to broadcast any and all songs in the catalog of the performing rights organization.

The producer must also acquire a synchronization license from each of the publishers because each publisher controls its own share of the rights. The territories, term and media of distribution rights are a matter of negotiation between the parties, reflecting the producer's needs. However, synchronization licenses may run for a period of years, may cover the world or only the territories in which the producer feels the program can be distributed. If a producer feels that the program will have a long life in syndication he may try to secure these rights for worldwide distribution of the program, in perpetuity (forever) and may wish to include rights for free television, pay and cable television or any form of broadcast media. A five-year worldwide television synchronization license allows the program on which a song is used to be broadcast an unlimited number of times throughout the world over a five-year period (assuming that the stations which broadcast the program are duly licensed by a performing rights organization).

The amount of money paid for the synchronization license depends upon the way the song is used. For example, a use with a singer on camera (visual vocal) or with a musician playing an instrument on camera (visual instrumental), may be more expensive than music that is used for background purposes only. Prices are also determined by the length of the song and whether the program is produced for network television, for syndication, or otherwise. Since a network program telecast in prime time may have a higher budget than a syndicated program, fees may be negotiated accordingly. ASCAP, BMI and SESAC also pay more money for performances in prime time, on the theory that more people are watching the programs.

Synchronization fees for television uses are traditionally modest, since publishers are usually willing to give producers a break on the price to have the song performed on television, thus generating performance revenue. Remember that public performance fees are paid by the broadcasters and have no affect on the production budget. However, synchronization fee payments are the responsibility of the producer and directly affect the producer's bottom line profit. Therefore, producers fight hard to limit expenditures for synchronization licenses, knowing that the songwriter and publisher stand to make a considerable amount of money and receive exposure from the television performances.

Since Fred Composer Music Publishing is represented by The Harry Fox Agency, the producer would negotiate with The Harry Fox Agency for a license covering Fred's 50% interest. The producer would also have to negotiate a deal with Wilma's law firm and with Lydia's manager for their respective interests. It is imperative that the producer be able to contact all of the representatives and negotiate acceptable license fees prior to taping the program.

USE OF A COMPOSITION IN A FEATURE FILM

Now suppose that "Sing it High" is proposed for use in a feature film. Many of the same rules apply with respect to clearing the use of the composition. However, the fees for use of music on theatrical films can be dramatically higher than those for television programs. This is for several reasons. A complete package of rights and media are involved and these rights are always secured for the duration of the copyright in the composition. Also, theatrical films are usually produced on a much higher budget than television programs. As a result, the producer requires a broad license with the right to exploit the film in all media in order to recoup at least the cost of the film.

First, the producer must secure a U.S. theatrical performing rights license. When a film with music on its soundtrack is exhibited in a movie theater, a public performance occurs for which the composers and their publishers are entitled to receive performing royalties. However, motion picture exhibitions in the United States do not generate royalties for the performing rights organizations. It is a violation of U.S. antitrust laws for ASCAP, BMI and SESAC to charge theater owners a license fee for the right to publicly perform the music included in the films. As a result, the film producer must go directly to the publishers to negotiate fees for these rights.

The process is completely different outside the United States, where U.S. antitrust laws do not apply. Theater owners in many foreign countries are required to pay a percentage of box office receipts to the local performing rights organizations. Some portion of these monies eventually filter back to the composer and publisher through their domestic performing rights organizations by virtue of those societies' agreements with the foreign performing rights organizations. These foreign performance royalties are a major source of publishing revenue, and can mean thousands of dollars to the songwriter and publisher.

The producer must also secure worldwide synchronization rights. As in television, these rights are obtained by dealing with the publishers, and are obtained for duration of copyright in the composition. As a practical matter, both the worldwide synchronization rights and the U.S. theatrical performing rights are negotiated as a package deal in one license agreement.

The film producer will also secure the so-called broad rights, which include the right to exhibit a program in essentially all possible media, including free television, cable, subscription, pay television, closed circuit television, and in film and video trailers and advertisements for the promotion of the film.

Producers also secure home video (videocassettes and discs) rights. The actual structure of home video rights negotiations may take several forms and an adequate discussion of such would go far beyond the scope of this chapter. However, most feature film producers have been adamant about securing a buyout of home video rights for a one-time flat-fee payment. For the most part they have been successful in securing buyouts and will generally not use a song that requires any form of continuing royalty. With television programs, or programs made specifically for the home video market, which use a substantial amount of music, it is possible that some kind of per unit royalty can be negotiated.

No producer will allow "Sing It High" to be used in a feature film without receiving nonexclusive rights to the music in all possible media of distribution of the film, with no restrictions or limitations. This is because a motion picture studio might not distribute a film if the right to do so could be enjoined (prohibited by court order) by a music publisher because all rights were not secured. The film companies have too much money at stake to allow a song to restrict their right to distribute.

In some situations the producer may require a holdback regarding future licensing of a song. For example, if "Sing It High" is expected to be a prominent song in the film, the producer may want to restrict other producers from using it for any purpose for a certain period of time to avoid competition. This may increase the cost of the license because the publisher will have to turn down other license requests during the holdback period. Holdbacks occur typically where a song is written specifically for a film, or is to be used in television commercials.

CONCLUSION

This brief explanation of television and film music licensing does not include all of the possible variations and nuances. The licensing process can become complicated in the extreme. While producers are very serious about all of the legal ramifications mentioned here, they still have important creative needs. Their need for good music is an opportunity for both new and experienced songwriters to generate revenue and obtain the exposure that may lead to other successes.

DIGITAL SOUND RECORDINGS: RECENT LEGISLATION

- As a result of The Digital Performance Right in Sound Recordings Act (DPRSRA) and the Digital Millennium Copyright Act (DMCA), copyright owners of sound recordings have an exclusive right (with specified limitations) to perform sound recordings publicly by means of digital audio transmissions (e.g., subscription audio transmission services, webcasting, etc.) with certain types of transmissions subject to statutory licensing.

- The legislation authorizes copyright owners of sound recordings and any entities performing such recordings to negotiate and agree upon the terms and rates of royalty payments and the division of fees among owners, and to designate common agents to negotiate, agree to, pay or receive such payments.

- The legislation directs the Librarian of Congress to publish notice of the initiation of voluntary negotiation proceedings for purposes of determining reasonable terms and rates of royalty payments for activities involving transmissions subject to statutory licensing and requires such terms and rates to distinguish among the different types of digital transmission services then in operation. It requires the Librarian, in the absence of negotiated license agreements, to convene a copyright arbitration royalty panel to be binding on such owners and entities, and it directs the Librarian to establish requirements by which such owners may receive notice of the use of their sound recordings and under which records of use shall be kept by entities performing such recordings.

- It also directs persons wishing to perform a sound recording publicly by means of such transmissions to do so without infringing exclusive rights by complying with notice requirements of the Register of Copyrights and paying royalty fees.

- It sets forth a formula for the allocation of proceeds from the licensing of such transmissions to recording artists.

- It sets forth authorities of copyright owners with respect to licensing to affiliates.

- The DPRSRA includes, within the scope of a compulsory license to make and distribute phonorecords of nondramatic musical works, the right of the phonorecord maker to distribute or authorize distribution of the sound recording by means of digital transmission, which constitutes a digital phonorecord delivery and grants copyright owners of such works the right to receive royalty payments at the rate prescribed when the digital transmission constitutes such a delivery. It makes such transmission actionable by the owner as an act of infringement if a compulsory license has not been issued. The act sets forth provisions regarding negotiation of rates of royalty payments for digital phonorecord deliveries that are reasonably expected to result from subscription transmissions.

HOME VIDEO SYNCHRONIZATION LICENSE

In consideration of the fee(s) set forth below, Licensor hereby grants to Producer the nonexclusive right, license, privilege and authority to reproduce or fix the Composition listed below in synchronization or timed-relation with the below noted Production and to make and distribute Videogram copies of the Production for the Home Video Market, subject to the terms and conditions listed below.

PRODUCTION: ______________________________
PRODUCER: ______________________________
COMPOSITION: ______________________________
COMPOSER(S): ______________________________
PUBLISHER(S): ______________________________
ADMINISTRATIVE SHARE: ______________________________
USE: ______________________________
TIMING: ______________________________

License Media: Manufacture of Videogram copies of the Production for the purpose of distribution in the Home Video Market. The "Home Video Market" shall refer to the sale, lease, license, use, rental or other distribution of Videograms to the public primarily for home use. "Videogram," shall mean videotape cassettes, videodiscs or any similar devices of a noninteractive nature which are presently in general commercial use and which are intended primarily for use in the Home Video Market.

LICENSE ROYALTY: ______________________________
ADVANCE: ______________________________
EXHIBITION TERRITORY: ______________________________
LICENSE TERM: ______________________________
COMMENCING: ______________________________
ACCOUNTING PERIOD: ______________________________

TERMS AND CONDITIONS:
1. Upon the expiration of this license, all rights herein granted shall cease and terminate and the right to make or authorize any further use or distribution of any recordings made hereunder shall also cease and terminate.

2. This license does not include the right to alter the fundamental character of the Composition, to use the title or subtitle of the Composition as the title of the Production, to use the story of the Composition, or to make any other use of the Composition not expressly authorized hereunder. Subject to the foregoing, Producer may make arrangements, orchestrations and adaptations of the Composition for its recording purposes.

3. For the purpose of this agreement, "Home Video Market" shall refer to the sale, lease, license, use, rental or other distribution of Videograms to the public primarily for home use. "Videogram" shall mean videotape cassettes, videodiscs or any similar devices, on which the Production may be duplicated for use in the Home Video Market.

4. Subject to the recoupment of any advance, and only with respect to Videogram units finally sold and not returned after the first commercial sale of a Videogram pursuant to this license, Producer shall account to Licensee within sixty (60) days after the close of the Accounting Period in any such Accounting Period in which Videogram copies are sold.

5. In the event that Producer fails to account and pay royalties as herein provided, if royalties have been earned, Licensor shall have the right to give written notice to Producer that unless the default is remedied within thirty (30) days from the date of the notice, this license shall terminate.

6. After reasonable written notice to Producer, for the purpose of verifying the accuracy of statements rendered, an authorized representative of Licensor may examine Producer's books and records pertaining to the sales of Videograms during normal business hours at the place where Producer maintains said books and records, however, no more than once per calendar year. Statements rendered shall become binding unless written objection is received by Producer within two (2) years after the rendering of such statement.

7. Licensor warrants only that it has the legal right to grant this license and that this license is given and accepted without other warranty or recourse. If said warranty shall be breached in whole or in part, Licensor shall either repay to Producer the consideration paid hereunder or hold Producer harmless to the extent of the consideration paid for this license.

8. This license shall run to Producer, its successors and assigns, provided that Producer remain liable for the performance of all the terms and conditions of this license on its part to be performed and provided further, that any disposition of the Production shall be subject to all the terms herein.

9. At the end of the License Term, Producer shall have the right to sell off its inventory of Videogram copies for an additional period of one year subject to the continuing obligation to pay royalties therefor.

10. This license is being entered into on an experimental and nonprejudicial basis and shall not be binding upon or prejudicial to any position taken by Licensor or Producer for any period subsequent to the term of this license.

11. Producer may exercise the option(s) listed in this agreement, if any, for the stated License Media, Territory, Term and Fee, by providing written notice to Licensor within the Option Period accompanied by payment of the specified fee and execution of any appropriate license agreement.

ADDITIONAL TERMS AND CONDITIONS:

1. This license grants permission to use the Composition for in-context trailers and promos for the Production.

2. This license further grants permission to reprint the lyrics of the Composition for the purpose of an insert to be included in each videocassette copy.

3. Nothing contained in this license shall be deemed to authorize the creation of a recording which deliberately imitates the featured and commercially exploited vocal performance of the Composition by any particular recording artist.

4. Paragraph 9 under TERMS AND CONDITIONS hereof is hereby amended to include the following:
"Producer shall not duplicate excessive quantities in anticipation of the sell-off period."

5. Paragraph 3 under TERMS AND CONDITIONS hereof is hereby deleted and replaced with the following:
Manufacture of Videogram copies of the Production for the purpose of distribution in the Home Video Market. The "Home Video Market" shall refer to the sale, lease, license, use, rental or other distribution of Videograms to the public primarily for home use. "Videogram" shall mean videotape cassettes, videodiscs or any similar devices of a noninteractive nature which are presently in general commercial use and which are intended primarily for use in the Home Video Market.

6. If, during the term hereof, you pay to another music publisher a fee in excess of the fee set out herein for the synchronization of a composition in the production, you shall pay to Licensor a corresponding amount equal to the difference between the fee set out herein and the fee paid to said other music publisher.

7. Options for additional rights:
License Media: Free television distribution and exhibition.
License Fee:____________________________
Exhibition Territory: World
License Term: ____________________________
Option Term: ____________________________

License Media: All forms of television distribution and exhibition including free, pay, cable and subscription television.
License Fee: ____________________________
Exhibition Territory: World
License Term: ____________________________
Option Term: To be exercised within twenty-four (24) months from date of first broadcast and exhibition.

AGREED AND ACCEPTED:

____________________	____________________
(PRODUCER)	(LICENSOR)
____________________	____________________
ADDRESS	ADDRESS
____________________	
LICENSE DATE	

MOVIE MASTER USE RECORDING LICENSE

1. The sound recording ("Master") of the musical composition covered by this license: ______________ performed by ______________________________

2. The motion picture ("Motion Picture") covered by this license is tentatively entitled: "_________________________ "

3. The "territory" covered hereby is: ______________________________

4. The type and number of uses of the Master to be recorded are:
____

5. IN CONSIDERATION of the sum of ____________ Dollars ($__________) receipt of which is hereby acknowledged, __________________ (hereinafter referred to as "Licensor") hereby grants to _____________________ (hereinafter referred to as "Producer"), its successors and assigns the following rights:

(a) the nonexclusive, limited right, license, privilege, and authority to record in any manner, medium, form or language, in each country of the territory the aforesaid type and use of the composition in synchronism or in timed-relation with the motion picture, but not otherwise, and to make copies of such recordings in the form of negatives and prints necessary for theatrical exhibition or broadcast on television as hereinafter provided for, and to import said recordings and/or copies thereof into any country throughout the territory all in accordance with the terms, conditions and limitations hereinafter set forth;

(b) the nonexclusive, limited right and license to publicly perform for profit or nonprofit and authorize others so to perform the composition in the exhibition of the motion picture to audiences in motion picture theaters and other places of public entertainment where motion pictures are customarily exhibited throughout the world including the right to televise the motion picture into such theaters and other such public places;

(c) the nonexclusive, limited right and license to publicly perform and authorize others so to perform in all form and media of distribution and exhibition of the Production for so-called Nonbroadcast (Nontheatrical) exhibition (including, without limitation, educational, institutional organizations, in-flight or in-transit distribution, corporate locations and U.S. military bases).

6. Licensee also grants to Producer the nonexclusive, limited right to reproduce the recording, as recorded in the motion picture in audiovisual devices, whether now known or hereafter devised, including, but not limited to, videocassettes and videodiscs, manufactured primarily for distribution for the purpose of "home use" ("Videograms") and to distribute them by sale or otherwise in each and every country of the territory for any and all purposes now or hereafter known, without Producer having to make any additional payments therefor.

7. The recording and performing rights hereinabove granted include such rights for air, screen, television and audiovisual trailers, promotions and advertisements for the promotion or exploitation of the motion picture in all media now known or hereafter devised.

8. The recording and performing rights hereinabove granted shall endure for the worldwide period of all copyrights in and to the composition and any and all renewals or extensions thereof without Producer having to pay any additional consideration therefor.

9. Licensee represents and warrants that it owns or controls the Master licensed hereunder and that it has the legal right to grant this license and that Producer shall not be required to pay any additional monies, except as provided in his license, with respect to the rights granted herein. Licensee shall indemnify, defend and hold harmless Producer, its successors, assigns and licenses from and against any and all loss, damages, liabilities, actions, suits or other claims arising out of any breach, in whole or in part, of the foregoing representations and warranties, and for reasonable attorneys' fees and costs incurred in connection therewith; provided, however, that such Licensee's total liability shall not exceed the consideration paid hereunder.

10. Licensee reserves all rights not expressly granted to Producer hereunder. All rights granted hereunder are granted on a nonexclusive basis.

11. This license is binding upon and shall inure to the benefit of the respective successors and/or assigns of the parties hereto.

12. This license shall be governed by and subject to the laws of the State of California applicable to agreements made and to be wholly performed within such State.

13. In the event of any breach of an provision of this agreement by Producer, Licensee's sole remedy will be an action at law for damages, if any, and in no event will Licensee be entitled to or seek to enjoin restrain, interfere with or inhibit the distribution, exhibition or exploitation of the motion picture. In no event shall Producer have less rights hereunder than a member of the public would have in the absence of this agreement.

14. No failure by Producer to perform any of its obligations hereunder shall constitute a breach hereof, unless Licensee gives Producer written notice of such nonperformance and Producer fails to cure such alleged nonperformance within sixty (60) days of its receipt of such notice.

15. All notices hereunder required to be given to the parties hereto and all payments to be made hereunder shall be sent to the parties at their addresses mentioned herein or to such other addresses as each party respectively may hereafter designate by notice in writing to the other.

IN WITNESS WHEREOF, the parties have caused the foregoing to be executed as of ____________ on ____________.

______________________________	______________________________
(LICENSOR)	(PRODUCER)
______________________________	______________________________
ADDRESS	ADDRESS

MOVIE SYNCHRONIZATION AND PERFORMING RIGHTS LICENSE

1. The musical composition (hereafter referred to as "composition") covered by this license is: "____________________"

2. The motion picture covered by this license is: "________________"

3. The type, maximum duration and number of uses of the composition to be recorded are: ____

4. Administrative share: ____

5. The territory covered hereby is:

____

6. IN CONSIDERATION of the sum of _____________ Dollars ($__________) receipt of which is hereby acknowledged, ____________________ ("Publisher") hereby grants to __________________ ("Producer"), its successors and assigns the following rights:

(a) the nonexclusive, limited right, license, privilege, and authority to record in any manner, medium, form or language, in each country of the territory the aforesaid type and use of the composition in synchronism or in timed-relation with the motion picture, but not otherwise, and to make copies of such recordings in the form of negatives and prints necessary for theatrical exhibition or broadcast on television as hereinafter provided for, and to import said recordings and/or copies thereof into any country throughout the territory all in accordance with the terms, conditions and limitations hereinafter set forth;

(b) the nonexclusive, limited right and license to publicly perform for profit or nonprofit and authorize others so to perform the composition in the exhibition of the motion picture to audiences in motion picture theaters and other places of public entertainment where motion pictures are customarily exhibited throughout the world including the right to televise the motion picture into such theaters and other such public places;

(c) the nonexclusive, limited right and license to publicly perform and authorize others so to perform in all form and media of distribution and exhibition of the Production for so-called Nonbroadcast (Nontheatrical) exhibition (including, without limitation, educational, institutional organizations, in-flight or in-transit distribution, corporate locations and U.S. military bases).

7. The exhibition of the motion picture in the United States by means of television (other than as described in subparagraph 6(b) herein above) including by means of "pay television," "subscription television," "CATV" and "closed circuit" into homes television, is subject to the following:

(a) The motion picture may be exhibited by means of television by network, nonnetwork, local or syndicated broadcasts, "pay television," "subscription television," and "closed circuit" provided that such television stations have valid performance licenses therefor from the American Society of Composers, Authors and Publishers (ASCAP) or Broadcast Music, Inc. (BMI), from Publisher, or from

a person, firm or corporation having the legal right to issue such license.
(b) It is agreed that public performance of the motion picture in such portion of the territory as is outside of the United States, will be in accordance with their customary practices and the payment of their customary fees.

8. Publisher also grants to Producer the nonexclusive, limited right to reproduce the composition, as recorded in the motion picture in audiovisual devices, whether now known or hereafter devised, including, but not limited to, videocassettes and videodiscs, manufactured primarily for distribution for the purpose of "home use" ("Videograms") and to distribute them by sale or otherwise in each and every country of the territory for any and all purposes now or hereafter known, without Producer having to make any additional payments therefor.

9. This license does not authorize or permit any use of the composition not expressly set forth herein and does not include the right to alter the fundamental character of the music of the composition, to use the title or subtitle of the composition as the title of any motion picture, to use the story of the composition, or to make any other use of the composition not expressly authorized hereunder.

10. The recording and performing rights hereinabove granted include such rights for air, screen, television and audiovisual trailers, promotions and advertisements for the promotion or exploitation of the motion picture in all media now known or hereafter devised.

11. The recording and performing rights hereinabove granted shall endure for the worldwide period of all copyrights in and to the composition and any and all renewals or extension thereof without Producer having to pay any additional consideration therefor.

12. Publisher represents and warrants that it owns or controls the aforesaid extent of interest of the composition licensed in the aforesaid Territory hereunder and that it has the legal right to grant this license and that Producer shall not be required to pay any additional monies, except as provided in this license, with respect to the rights granted herein. Publisher shall indemnify, defend and hold harmless Producer, its successors, assigns and licenses from and against any and all loss, damages, liabilities, actions, suits or other claims arising out of any breach, in whole or in part, of the foregoing representations and warranties, and for reasonable attorneys' fees and costs incurred in connection therewith; provided, however, that such Publisher's total liability shall not exceed the consideration paid hereunder.

13. Publisher reserves all rights not expressly granted to Producer hereunder. All rights granted hereunder are granted on a nonexclusive basis.

14. This license is binding upon and shall inure to the benefit of the respective successors and/or assigns of the parties hereto.

15. This license shall be governed by and subject to the laws of the State of California applicable to agreements made and to be wholly performed with such State.

16. In the event of any breach of any provision of this agreement by Producer, Publisher's sole remedy will be an action at law for damages, if any, and in no event will Publisher be entitled to or seek to enjoin restrain, interfere with or inhibit the distribution, exhibition or exploitation of the motion picture. In no event shall Producer have less rights hereunder than a member of the public would have in the absence of this agreement.

17. No failure by Producer to perform of any of its obligations hereunder shall constitute a breach hereof, unless Publisher gives Producer written notice of such nonperformance and Producer fails to cure such alleged nonperformance within sixty (60) days of its receipt of such notice.

18. All notices hereunder required to be given to the parties hereto and all payments to be made hereunder shall be sent to the parties at their addresses mentioned herein or to such other addresses as each party respectively may hereafter designate by notice in writing to the other.

IN WITNESS WHEREOF, the parties have caused the foregoing to be executed as of ____________ on ____________.

ON BEHALF OF ______________________________

______________________________	______________________________
(PUBLISHER)	(PRODUCER)
______________________________	______________________________
ADDRESS	ADDRESS

TELEVISION MASTER RECORDING LICENSE

In consideration of the below listed License Fee, receipt of which is hereby acknowledged, Licensor grants to Producer the nonexclusive and irrevocable right, license, privilege and authority to record, rerecord, perform, dub, edit and synchronize the Recording listed below into and with the soundtrack of the Production for distribution, exhibition and exploitation in the License Media and for the advertising and promotion thereof, subject to the terms and conditions listed below.

Production: ______________________________

Producer: ______________________________

Recording: ______________________________

Artist: ______________________________

Record Label: ______________________________

Use: ______________________________

Timing: ______________________________

License Fee: ______________________________

License Territory: ______________________________

License Term: ______________________________

Commencing: ______________________________

License Media: ______________________________

TERMS AND CONDITIONS:

1. RESERVATION OF RIGHTS

Upon the expiration of this license, all rights herein granted shall cease and terminate and the right to make or authorize any further use or distribution of the Recording shall also cease and terminate. Nothing contained herein shall obligate Producer to actually use the Recording in or in connection with the soundtrack of the Production. Licensor reserves exclusively to itself, its successors, licensees and assigns, all rights and uses in and to the Recording, except the limited uses expressly licensed hereunder. By way of illustration, and not in limitation thereof, the following rights are specifically reserved by Licensor for its own use and may not be exercised by Producer, unless otherwise provided for herein:

(a) All rights of reproduction or use of the Recording on phonograph records, tapes and other types of sound only reproduction, in all media, whether now or hereafter known or in existence. Without limiting the generality of the foregoing, Producer shall not have the right to include or authorize the use of the Recording, or any portion thereof, in any phonograph record of the soundtrack of the Program.

(b) The right to use the Recording in other motion pictures or television programs including uses similar to that authorized hereunder.

(c) The right to edit, alter, or otherwise modify the Recording in any way except with respect to duration.

(d) The right to reproduce the Recording by means of video Records (including, but not limited to, videocassettes, videotapes, and any other audiovisual devices intended primarily for "home use"), unless specifically provided for herein.

(e) The right to advertise, sticker and/or otherwise market and/or identify Records embodying the Recording as being contained in the Program.

2. CLEARANCE
Producer shall be responsible for obtaining appropriate synchronization licenses from the copyright proprietor(s) of the musical composition(s) embodied in the Recording and shall obtain all requisite consents and permissions, if any, including, without limitation, those of labor organizations, and agrees that it will pay all required reuse payments, fees and royalties, if any, required to be paid for such consents and permissions, under applicable collective bargaining agreements, or otherwise, in connection with Producer's use of the Recording. Licensor shall be responsible for the payment to all parties whose performances are embodied in the Recording including, but not limited to, the artist(s) and producer(s), under its various contractual agreements with such parties, out of License Fees paid hereunder, and shall hold Producer harmless from any claims therefor.

3. DUPLICATION FEES
Producer shall promptly pay, upon Licensor's request therefor, Licensor's actual duplication costs for master tape copies of the Recording, if any, furnished to Producer by Licensor.

4. CUE SHEET
Producer shall promptly provide Licensor with a complete and accurate music cue sheet for the Program, receipt of which is hereby acknowledged.

5. NAME AND LIKENESS
Producer shall have the right to use Artist's name and approved likeness and biography in connection with the exploitation and promotion of the Production. Upon request, Licensor will provide Producer with a reasonable number of approved photographs and an approved biography.

6. REPRESENTATIONS, WARRANTIES AND INDEMNIFICATION OF LICENSOR
Licensor warrants only that it has the full right, power and authority to grant the license specified herein. Licensor shall indemnify and hold Producer harmless from any and all claims, liabilities, losses, damages or expenses (including, but not limited to, reasonable attorneys' fees and legal expenses) actually incurred by Producer by reason of Licensor's breach of said warranty, but Licensor's aggregate liability to Producer shall be limited to the amount of the consideration actually paid by Producer to Licensor hereunder.

7. REPRESENTATIONS, WARRANTIES AND INDEMNIFICATION OF PRODUCER
Producer warrants that it has the full right, power and authority to enter into this agreement and to fully perform its obligations hereunder. Producer shall indemnify and hold Licensor harmless from any and all claims, liabilities, losses, damages and expenses (including, but not limited to, reasonable attorneys' fees and legal expenses) arising out of any breach of Producer's warranties, representations or covenants under this agreement, or in any way resulting from or connected with Producer's use of the Recording in a manner not authorized hereunder.

8. NOTICES
All notices hereunder required to be given to Producer (including notification of a change in ownership or administrative control) shall be sent to Producer at the address included herein. All notices, payments and/or royalties hereunder required to be made

to Licensor shall be sent to Licensor at the address included herein or to such other address as Licensor may hereafter designate by notice in writing to Producer.

9. ASSIGNMENT
This license shall run to Producer, its successors and assigns, provided that Producer remain liable for the performance of all the terms and conditions of this license on its part to be performed and provided further, that any disposition of the Program shall be subject to all the terms hereof.

10. OPTIONS
Producer may exercise the option(s) listed in this agreement, if any, for the stated License Media, Territory, Term and Fee, by providing written notice to Licensor within the Option Period accompanied by payment of the specified fee.

AGREED AND ACCEPTED:

______________________	______________________
(PRODUCER)	(LICENSOR)
______________________	______________________
ADDRESS	ADDRESS
______________________	
LICENSE DATE	

TELEVISION SYNCHRONIZATION LICENSE

In consideration of the below listed License Fee, receipt of which is hereby acknowledged, Licensor grants to Producer the nonexclusive and irrevocable right, license, privilege and authority to record, reproduce or fix the Composition listed below in synchronization or timed-relation with the Production for distribution in the License Media, and for the advertising and promotion thereof, subject to the terms and conditions listed below.

Production: ______________________________

Producer: ______________________________

Composition: ______________________________

Composer(s): ______________________________

Publisher(s): ______________________________

Administrative Share: ______________________________

Use: ______________________________

Timing: ______________________________

License Fee: ______________________________

Exhibition Territory: ______________________________

License Term: ______________________________

Commencing: Upon execution of this license or first airdate, whichever is earlier

License Media: Free television distribution and exhibition.

TERMS AND CONDITIONS:

1. EXPIRATION OF RIGHTS

Upon the expiration of this license, all rights herein granted shall cease and terminate and the right to make or authorize any further use or distribution of any recordings made hereunder shall also cease and terminate.

2. PERFORMANCE RIGHTS

Performance of the Composition in the exhibition of the Production is subject to the condition that each television station or other entity over which the Composition is so performed shall have a performance license issued by Licensor or from a person, firm, corporation, society, association or other entity having the legal right to issue such a performance license and it is understood that the public performance of the Production outside the United States is and shall be subject to clearance by performing rights societies in accordance with their customary practices and the payment of their customary fees.

3. RIGHTS NOT INCLUDED

This license does not include the right to alter the fundamental character of the Composition, to use the title or subtitle of the Composition as the title of the Production, to use the story of the Composition, or to make any other use of the Composition not expressly authorized hereunder. Notwithstanding the foregoing, Producer may make arrangements, orchestrations and adaptations of the Composition for its recording purposes hereunder.

(a) The Production shall be for use solely as authorized hereunder, and may not be televised into theaters or other places where admission is charged. No sound records produced pursuant to this license are to be manufactured, sold and/or used separately or independently of the Production.

(b) Use of the Composition on videocassettes, videodiscs and/or any new technological methods of reproduction that are introduced into the entertainment industry for the purpose of sale and/or rental to the public for home use is specifically excluded from this license unless otherwise provided for herein.

4. WARRANTIES

Licensor warrants only that it has the legal right to grant this license and that this license is given and accepted without other warranty or recourse. If said warranty shall be breached in whole or in part, Licensor shall either repay to Producer the consideration paid hereunder or hold Producer harmless to the extent of the consideration paid for this license.

5. NOTICES

All notices hereunder required to be given to Producer (including notification of a change in ownership or administrative control) shall be sent to Producer at the address included herein. All notices, payments and/or royalties hereunder required to be made to Licensor shall be sent to Licensor at its current address or to such other address as Licensor may hereafter designate by notice in writing to Producer.

6. ASSIGNMENT

This license shall run to Producer, its successors and assigns, provided that Producer remain liable for the performance of all the terms and conditions of this license on its part to be performed and provided further, that any disposition of the Production shall be subject to all the terms herein.

7. EXERCISE OF OPTIONS

Producer may exercise the option(s) listed in this agreement, if any, for the stated License Media, Territory, Term and Fee, by providing written notice to Licensor within the Option Period accompanied by payment of the specified fee.

ADDITIONAL TERMS AND CONDITIONS:

1. If, during the term hereof, you pay to the copublisher a fee in excess of the fee set out herein for the synchronization of the Composition in the Production, you shall pay to Licensor a corresponding amount equal to the difference between the fee set out herein and the fee paid to said copublisher, on a pro rata basis.

2. OPTIONS FOR ADDITIONAL RIGHTS

License Media: All forms of television distribution and exhibition including, without limitation, free, pay, cable and subscription television.

License Fee: (Negotiated on Most Favored Nations basis with copublishers of the composition.)

Exhibition Territory: ____________________

License Term: ____________________

Option Term: ____________________

License Media: Manufacture and distribution of videogram copies of the production for the purpose of sale and/or rental to the public primarily for home use.
License Fee: One-time, flat-fee buyout.
Exhibition Territory: ______________________
License Term: ______________________
Option Term: ______________________

AGREED AND ACCEPTED:

______________________	______________________
(PRODUCER)	(LICENSOR)
______________________	______________________
ADDRESS	ADDRESS
______________________	
LICENSE DATE	

Pop Music for Soundtracks

BY MARK HALLORAN AND THOMAS A. WHITE

In recent years, successful pop/rock songwriters and recording artists have moved, seemingly en masse, into motion picture soundtrack songwriting and performing. Some, such as Madonna, have had star acting careers, and some actors, such as Jennifer Lopez, have used acting careers as the platform for a music career. However, these are exceptions. Typically, songwriters and recording artists are hired by film studios during or after the film is shot to write and record individual musical compositions specifically for the film. The songs are then synchronized with the picture and may be used in promotional trailers and television spots, included in a soundtrack album, and be released as singles and MTV promotional videos. This chapter examines relevant issues when nonacting writers/performers are commissioned to create individual songs for a film. The primary focus is on practices at major Hollywood studios, although we also discuss practices at the nonmajors. (When we say "major Hollywood studios," we mean 20th Century Fox, Warner Bros., Universal, Sony Pictures Entertainment [Columbia Pictures and Tri-Star], Paramount and Disney.) You should be aware that much of the music used in films is preexisting. The songs are typically licensed from music publishers for fees, which are split between the publishers and songwriters. Similarly, recordings are typically licensed from record companies for fees, which are split between the record companies and the performers. The licensing of music for film is discussed in more detail in the chapter, Music Licensing for Television and Film: A Perspective for Songwriters.

This chapter covers neither composers that write orchestral scores nor concert films. MTV has killed concert films, and rock concert films have joined the ranks of documentaries, with very limited audience appeal.

CURRENT PRACTICE IN WRITING AND RECORDING SOUNDTRACK MUSIC

When you are asked by a studio to write and record an original song for a motion picture, there are fundamental business and legal concerns. How much money will you be paid initially? How will your music publisher and record label be involved in the deal? What controls, concerning the use of the song and the recording, will you have? How much money can you expect later from the exploitation of the song and the recording? We will first look at the studio's viewpoint to better understand its motives.

The Creative Choices

The filmmaking team—the studio, the producer and the director—usually chooses the songs and performing artists and collectively they must reach a creative and business consensus. Most major studios have music departments that are headed by creative music executives that, combined with the filmmaking team, represent the studio's music interests and are available to its film producers for consultation referrals and other general music services. Absent a consensus, the amount of clout the individual members of the filmmaking team wield will determine the choice of songs and performers. When dealing with high-powered, experienced, successful film producers and directors, the studio will often defer to their creative choice, but will still insist on consultation or approval of both the musical talent and their deal. Some directors have so-called final cut of the film, which may or may not include final determination of the musical talent and music in the film.

In some instances another team member is hired, the music supervisor, who reports to the director and producer and represents their interests. Music supervisors have gained prominence as filmmakers have recognized the effect successful records have to stimulate box office sales and have seen the necessity for a bridge between filmmakers, the music community, the studios, and the soundtrack record labels. Soundtrack singles are routinely released in advance of a picture so that its opening coincides with demand created by the record label's marketing efforts and the studio's film advertising, which are coordinated to maximize public awareness of the film and its music. Music supervisors have varying degrees of involvement in the music that is commissioned or selected for films. The extent of their job is defined by how the filmmakers perceive their own abilities as music experts. Music supervisors are almost never delegated decision-making authority, but instead gather and present choices to the filmmakers.

Some music supervisors offer only creative services (e.g., suggesting possible songs and artists or producing records). Others provide primarily business or sales services (e.g., publishing administration, music clearance, soundtrack placement, music production coordination). The studio's music business affairs department, or the filmmaker's music counsel usually handles business affairs (i.e., deal making). Although film music is a diverse and specialized field, virtually anyone who has ever worked in the music business may offer their services as a music supervisor. Consequently, competence varies greatly. Because the market has an excess of prospective music supervisors, most practitioners are not engaged in such services on an exclusive, full-time basis.

The main concern of the filmmaking team is whether the choice of a song and artist will enhance the dramatic and commercial impact of their picture. They cast the songwriters and performers as they would any theatrical talent, by subjectively evaluating whether the writer's, or act's, musical contribution will enhance the look, feel, and profit of their picture.

Budgets

Major studios stick with top pop writers whose songs have sold millions of records and have had successful chart histories. On independent motion pictures, however, producers have less financing available and they use less recognized writers and artists that have not had hit records. Accordingly, they pay less money.

Exhibit 1 compares what major studios and independent producers typically spend. The bottom line is that independent producers pay less up-front money than the major studios. Major studios are frequently tied in with labels that own national branch distribution systems and they invest far greater sums than nonmajors in promoting their films and music. Back-end revenue potential is therefore usually higher at major studios.

Even studios that defer to the creative choices of filmmakers must approve the writer/performer deal because of the large investment. The studio intends to protect its multimillion-dollar investment, of which music is an important, but relatively minor, part. Average production budgets of major studios are around $50 million; exploitation budgets (principally ads) can run $25 million. Music budgets are usually 2% to 5% of the film budget.

Probably the most pervasive myth regarding songs that are written for soundtracks is that in some cases the studio makes more money from the music than from distribution of the film. Although it has been true in certain cases that an unsuccessful film has spawned a successful album, the authors are unaware of any case in which a film generated less money to a studio than did the film music. In contrast to this myth, there are some basic truths. One is that ultimately major studios view film music, except in the rarest cases (perhaps *Flashdance*), as a less than integral part of the film and more of a promotional tool and ancillary market for the film. If a teenager has $8 to spend for entertainment and has a choice between seeing a film or buying the soundtrack album, the studio would much rather the money be spent on a theater ticket. The studio can expect to receive approximately half of the $8 spent at the theater, but is lucky if it nets 30¢ to 50¢ from the sale of each CD.

The studio protects its investment by insisting that broad exploitation rights be obtained in the song and the recording. A studio's incentives for acquiring all rights to songs and recordings include (1) complete freedom of use and exploitation (including royalty-free use in other studio productions) without consultation, approval or further payment; (2) optimum duration of copyright ownership; (3) avoidance of third-party claims and controls; (4) actual profit from music revenues; (5) increased cash flow; and (6) the building of a publishing catalog as a perennial, liquid, and salable asset.

Limiting the Studio's Investment: Spec Writing Deals

Studios and filmmakers like to have the opportunity to choose songs that are not specifically commissioned and that require no guaranteed up-front payment. There is quite a lot of speculative songwriting for film soundtracks. By speculative we mean songs that are written or reworked for the film and submitted for consideration without the studio being committed to use or pay for the song. If the studio likes the song, a deal is negotiated. Some songwriters will not write spec songs since their time is valuable and they consider it an insult to their artistic integrity to be asked to write a song without a financial commitment. On the other hand, many songwriters are happy to have their song considered in this manner.

A variation of spec writing is the so-called songwriter's step or option deal. This means there will be an intermediate step after the song is written but before it is used in the film when the studio can decline to proceed further by not making further payment for the song. For example, in a step deal the studio may pay the songwriter $5,000 for a song to be written and demoed. If the studio approves the song and synchronizes it in the movie, the writer receives another $20,000.

Probably the most contentious point on step deals is whether or not the writer gets back rights to rejected songs, and under what conditions. Although the usual outcome is that the songwriter keeps the rights, studios may take the position that they will return the song provided it is subject to a lien for recovery of the amount the studio has invested. In the example above, if the studio were to reject the song and the song reverted to the songwriter, and it was subsequently exploited, the studio would receive the first $5,000. A variation of this is that the studio may retain a continuing financial participation in the publisher's share of music income, irrespective of recoupment of its investment. Alternatively, the writer may buy back the rights by reimbursing the studio for its out-of-pocket costs.

STUDIO/RECORD LABEL DEAL

The studio, as owner of the soundtrack album rights, makes the basic arrangement for the production and distribution of the soundtrack with the label. If we assume a pop soundtrack, rather than an orchestral one, the following delineate the basic issues.

Advances

Advances typically reflect record companies' perceptions of anticipated sales in the domestic territory, and can range from a nominal amount to, in extraordinary cases, $1 million or more. What makes the negotiations difficult is that soundtrack albums are usually one-shots, and the label cannot recover losses from subsequent product. Another difficulty is that typically the final music choices have not yet been made. A graduated scale may be created to remedy this, e.g., $150,000 with an additional $50,000 per platinum-certified artist and $25,000 per gold-certified artist, with a cap of $300,000.

Royalty Rate

Royalty rate negotiation is very similar to that for a normal recording contract. The range for a basic royalty is 10% to 20% of retail. The studio hopes to maintain a minimum royalty override in the 4% to 6% range; thus, in a 16% of retail deal, 10% to 12% of royalty would be available to third parties.

Product

The record company is going to want to know what they are buying. Also, the record company would prefer a pop soundtrack with a potential single rather than an orchestral soundtrack, although in many cases the two are combined.

Promotion Fund

Oftentimes the record company will look to the studio to put up a matching fund for promotion of the CD under the theory that both the studio and the record company will profit.

Singles

The releasing label will always want singles rights. The singles are used as promotional tools to sell the CDs, which is where the real money is. If singles rights are not available, the record company will probably cut its advance.

Guaranteed Release

Studios will often insist that as long as the necessary materials are delivered on time, the record company will be required to release the CD no later than the theatrical release of the film, with singles preceding it by six weeks.

Ownership

The studio will continue to own the underlying musical compositions and the sound recordings as embodied in the film. The record company will want to assert ownership over the sound recording as embodied in records. The record company will want worldwide rights. Split territory deals with major labels are almost nonexistent.

ARTIST VIEWPOINT: PREEXISTING AGREEMENTS

The following are major concerns when a studio approaches you to write and perform a soundtrack song. The threshold issue is whether you can grant the rights in the song and the recording that the studio requires.

Preexisting Term Songwriter's Agreement

If you are signed to a term songwriting deal, the publisher has the exclusive right to your songwriting services during the term and owns and administers the songs you compose or cowrite during the term, subject to paying the usually inviolate writer's share of music income. However, studios have music publishing holdings too. In these agreements, administration means the management of the copyright for purposes of collection and distribution of income. Like other music publishers, studios often insist on copyright ownership and administration of the song, and they normally retain all or part of the publisher's share of music income. Usually any conflict of rights between the songwriter's publisher and the studio is settled during initial discussions. In some cases, the studio's publishing arm and the songwriter's publisher will split the publisher's share of music income between the writer's publisher, and the studio.

In order to avoid potential publisher/studio conflict and to freely shop their songs for soundtracks, a very few established writers have negotiated a fixed number of songs per year that are excluded from their exclusive term songwriting deal. If you are not signed to a term songwriting deal, have negotiated an exclusion, or have already reached the maximum number of songs required under the term songwriting deal, you are free to work out whatever arrangements you desire with the studio.

If you do not have a lot of clout, the studio will end up owning and administering the song, and you will be entitled to approximately 50% of the income generated from the song as the writer's share, plus whatever nonrecoupable creative fee is negotiated. (Note the studio will grant itself a free synchronization license in connection with the use of the song in the film and in-home video devices, so you will receive no further synchronization income from these sources.) Studios typically insist on free synchronization licenses for product based on the initial film, such as remakes, sequels, and television programs that they produce or distribute, and even for totally unrelated properties that they produce or distribute. However, the writer retains the writer's share of public performance income.

Preexisting Recording Agreement

If you are signed to a term or multiple album recording contract, the label typically has the right to your exclusive recording services during the term for master recordings and phonograph records. Recording contracts usually define phonograph records as including "sight and sound devices," so unless you are the rare superstar artist who has a soundtrack exclusion (i.e., a provision excluding soundtrack recordings from the record deal) the label must grant a waiver of its services exclusivity for theatrical synchronization, home video, and phonograph records.

Record companies are understandably jealous of the services of their artists. Major record companies can invest $1 million or more to break in a new recording act. It is estimated that on average, minimum sales of 300,000 CD units are necessary for a major label to break even on a typical artist investment. Such costs include advances and royalties to artists, producers, and production companies; recording costs; manufacturing and distribution; marketing, including record promotion and advertising; mechanical licenses; video clip production; general overhead; legal expenses; salaries; taxes; product returns; etc.

In order to receive a return on their investments, some record companies insist on an "override" royalty (a royalty in addition to or to be deducted from the recording artist's royalty) from the studio as a condition to granting permission for the artist's soundtrack services. For example, if your deal with the studio is a basic album royalty of 10% of retail prorated, and you have two of ten cuts on a soundtrack album, the label may ask for a 1% override on your 2% of retail royalty. Your royalty will be about 20¢ per CD, and the label's royalty will be about 10¢ per CD.

Most studios, however, insist that the artist and the label work out the royalty arrangement between themselves. Some labels may require a 75% (artist)/25% (label) split of the prorated royalty for the sales of soundtrack records. The label retains its share and either credits the artist's royalty account or pays the 75% directly to the artist. For an illustration, see Exhibit 2. Also, just as major studios are music publishers, some major studios have record company divisions. Universal (Universal Records) and AOL-Time Warner (Warner Bros. Records) are the two leading examples.

In some cases, major labels insist that the entire royalty (and even part or all of the artist's up-front cash creative fee) be paid directly to them for their services exclusivity waiver, especially if the artist's royalty account is unrecouped. However, the artist more typically keeps the creative fee from the studio, which is deemed a fee for motion picture services rather than a recording advance.

RECORDING ARTIST AND STUDIO ISSUES

Assuming the artist and label make their arrangement, the next step is to sort out the soundtrack recording issues between the record company and its artist and the studio. These issues follow.

Marketing Fund

This is a guaranteed fund to be spent by the studio (and perhaps a matching amount by the label) to promote the soundtrack album and singles, the aggregate of which can be $100,000 to $500,000.

Video Ownership

Regardless of the investment issue, both studios and labels compete for music video ownership. The studio wants to control the exploitation of the video, especially in conjunction with marketing the film, although promotion of the video is often a joint effort by the label and studio. Because of uncertainty about the impact of commercial exploitation under union agreements, studios rarely give record companies rights, other than for promotional use, if the video contains film clips and they try to limit the promotional use to the period when the film is in active distribution.

Singles Rights

The principal issue centers on prohibition of release of the recording as a single by any label other than the artist's label. Since the label distributing the soundtrack CD wants to use singles as a selling tool for the CD, retention of singles rights by the artist's nondistributing label can diminish the attractiveness of the CD to the distributing label. Additionally, the studio is anxious to use the single to promote the theatrical release of the film. This noncompetition restriction allows the artist and the label to reap full benefit by ensuring that a potential single used in a film is included on, and stimulates the sale of, the artist's own album, rather than a soundtrack album containing other artist's recordings that yields a prorated royalty to each.

THE ARTIST/STUDIO DEAL: MAJOR POINTS

The following is a list of the major deal issues that will be discussed between artist's counsel and the studio that commissions a song and record. Exhibit 1 provides a comparison on typical deals for major studios and independents.

Cash Creative Fee

Compensation for writing and recording can be structured either as a cash creative fee, not including recording costs, or an all-inclusive recording fund that includes writing, performing, producing and recording costs. Writing fees per song range from a nominal amount for an unknown to $30,000 for a superstar's work. Recording fees are in the range of $10,000 per track for major performers.

If the deal is structured as a recording fund, the studio will pay a flat sum for delivery of the song and master, with the artist being responsible for all recording costs, keeping any balance as the creative fee. The all-in fee per song for a top writer/performer ranges from $50,000 to $100,000, and for a midlevel writer/performer from $25,000 to $50,000. New acts may receive $7,500 to $15,000. The all-in structure is an inducement for the artist to limit recording costs, and also caps the studio's investment. However, the studio has no contractual assurance the money is being allocated judiciously. Problems sometimes arise when the studio is dissatisfied with the song or recording and asks the artist to rework it. Recording fund deals are particularly attractive to acts that own recording studios and computer-based music technology, since they can keep recording costs down.

Song Royalties

The writer's share of royalties for songwriting services is negotiated the same as with a nonfilm song agreement, i.e., the writer basically receives 50% of the income, except for sheet music, which typically generates 8¢ to 12¢ per piano copy and 10% to 12.5% of wholesale for nonpiano copies. The writer may seek to guarantee a full statutory mechanical rate for the soundtrack CD or single (currently 7.55¢ per song). Most studios resist guaranteeing a full mechanical rate since the label will seek to limit the mechanical rate for CDs to 10 times 75% of statutory, which comes to 56.6¢ per CD, and for singles to 75% of statutory for each side.

If you have a lot of clout or are signed exclusively to a publisher, you may be able to structure a copublishing agreement in which song ownership and administration may be shared. This allows the artist to participate in a percentage of the publisher's share of music income. Independent producers typically pay less up-front money and do not have affiliated music publishing arms, and they are more likely than major studios to agree to grant a participation in the publisher's share. Assuming a fifty-fifty participation arrangement, the artist will receive approximately 75% of the total music income (the full writer's share and half of the publisher's share).

The split of copyright known as copublishing is considerably less common than financial participation in the publisher's share of income. In participation deals, the participant has little or no control over the use or exploitation of the copyright. Major writers/performers receive a participation in the publisher's share of income that ranges up to 50%.

Also, the publisher's share of income that is subject to participation is reducible if the studio or its music publishing arm charges an administration fee on income, if collected. For example, if there were a 15% administration fee, the publisher's net share would be reduced to about 42.5% of the total income derived from the song.

In extraordinary cases, superstars that both write and perform have been able to keep both copyright ownership (and administration) and all the publisher's share of music publishing income, subject always to a free synchronization license to the studio for use of the song in the film and home video devices.

Major writers/artists are much more likely to share in publishing revenue than writers that do not perform their own material, since successful artists are perceived to add great promotional value to the song and the film. However, to the extent the artist participates in the publisher's share of income, the up-front cash fee may decline correspondingly, because the studio is forgoing all or a portion of the publisher's share of income from which they hope to recover their investment and make some profit. However, for superstars, studios have a hard time reducing the cash creative fee, even if the publisher's share is relinquished or split.

Record Royalties

Record royalties, like music royalties, are negotiated much in the same manner as a normal recording agreement. However, there are a few points that are particularly important in soundtrack agreements.

Studios usually insist that the artist royalty be all-in, i.e., inclusive of all others that might be entitled to royalties with respect to the artist's recording, such as the record producer and the artist's label.

The royalty is usually subject to two forms of proration. First, it will be prorated for length, either by playing time or more typically by number of cuts. For example, if you have two out of the 10 cuts on the CD, and receive a prorated 10% of retail royalty, your basic royalty will be .2 x 10%, or 2%. Second, the royalty is prorated by the number of artists on the cut. For example, if on the cuts the act performs together with a second recording act, the act's royalty will be cut in half (.5 x .2 x 10% or 1%).

CD Override

Heavyweight artists ask for a CD override, e.g., an additional 2% on the entire CD, regardless of proration. This may be fair when the soundtrack CD consists of filler that does not sell CDs or promote the film.

Royalty Allocation

Studios try to keep the aggregate artist royalties in check so they retain an appropriate net portion of the overall royalty from the soundtrack CD. For example, if the studio gets 16% of retail from the record company, they may allocate 10% to 12% to all royalty participants, retaining 4% to 6% for themselves. One way the studios try to contain royalties is to give the same royalty deal to every artist, e.g., 10% to 12% prorated.

Singles

The artists that anticipate release of their master as an A-side single may try to insulate themselves from royalty reduction for the B-side of the single to assure a full single record royalty. Singles royalties are not as heavily negotiated as CD royalties.

Recoupment

Smart artist representatives insist that the only recording costs the studio or label can recoup from the artist royalty account before royalties are paid are those paid solely in connection with the soundtrack CD, as opposed to the picture, since the studio pays recording costs whether or not there is a soundtrack CD. These nonpicture recording costs are called "soundtrack conversion costs" and usually include guild new use fees, and occasionally remixing. This point can have a major financial impact on the artist royalty. If not limited to nonpicture costs, the artist royalty account could be charged with film-related recording costs. For example, if the act's royalty is 10% of retail prorated on a cut, and they have one cut of 10, the royalty per CD sold would be .1 x 10%, or 1% of retail (about 10¢ per CD). If the label sells 100,000 CD units, the artist's royalty account would be credited with $10,000. To the extent the studio recoups soundtrack conversion costs, they are deducted from the royalty. Recoupment of recording creative fees from the artist's royalty account is negotiable. New acts often have their creative fee recouped from their royalties; established acts face this less often.

Song and Master Ownership

The studio's attitude is "we own what we pay for." The studio will insist on acquiring the song and master recording copyrights as works made for hire. As discussed above, superstars may occasionally succeed in sharing ownership and administration of the song and/or master recording. Artists' ownership of master recordings may be allowed in rare cases when a superstar's recording services are furnished by their own production companies, e.g., Paul McCartney's MPL Communications, Ltd. or David Bowie's Main Man Productions, Inc.

Use of Master on Artist's Label

An act may succeed in getting a license from the studio for use of the master recording on the acts' own records. The master might then be released both on the soundtrack CD and on the artist's CD. As a condition to granting the license, the studio may ask for an override royalty from the artist's label on CDs embodying the master. In any event, the studio will insist that any release of such master by the artist's label not compete with the studio's soundtrack CD by conditioning the licensing grant on a holdback from release. This mostly applies from four to twelve months after release of the soundtrack CD, so that the record-buying public associates the soundtrack song and master with the film and is motivated to buy the soundtrack CD. Studios are finding it more difficult, at least with major acts, to negotiate a holdback on the release of the master on the artist's home label.

Approval of Record Producer

Many established acts produce themselves or insist on using a record producer they approve. Studios rarely try to interfere with the artist's producer selection or the artist/producer creative relationship, especially if the deal is the typical recording fund deal, which makes the artist responsible for the producer's compensation. However, if the studio pays the producer's cash advance or royalty separately, they insist on approving the producer deal.

Credits

As long as the song is used in the film, most studios will agree to give an "end title" screen credit in the form of "[Song Title], written by [Artist], performed by [Artist]." Sometimes credit in the form of, "courtesy of [Label]" is accorded the artist's record company. Only rarely does an artist receive main title credit (where the writer, director, producer, and other major creative elements get credit).

Paid ad credits that promote the film, e.g., credits in newspapers, magazines, and the like, are usually not granted to writers/performers by major studios, except for main title songs, or when the prestige of the soundtrack artist is considered a significant marketing benefit. Independent producers tend to grant paid ad credits to writers/performers more frequently than major studios.

Record jacket credit is a different matter. Studios rarely refuse to give the recording act credit on the jackets of soundtrack CDs since this is a selling tool. Sometimes, if there are multiple recording artists, all the acts get credit in alphabetical order. In contrast to the normal competition among actors, directors, and producers for large and prominent credit, the act and label may try to keep the credit small so the soundtrack CD does not look like it is the act's own CD, which might compete with and thereby diminish sales of the act's own records. This makes sense because the act receives the entire royalty on their own CDs (subject to recoupment of recording costs by the label) and, if they write, they receive the mechanical royalties on the entire CD (always the writer's share and sometimes a portion of the publisher's share).

Additional Artist/Studio Deal Points

One issue to consider is that the studio will also insist on a provision whereby they are not obligated to use the song or the recording (whether in the film, soundtrack CD, or as a single), although they may have to pay whether or not they use the song. From the studio perspective, the filmmaking team must be allowed the freedom to add and subtract songs and recordings during the editing process. In some instances the artist will be paid whether or not their work is actually used. If the artist is not paid, usually the song and recording revert to the artist.

Also, since music videos are an important selling tool, studios normally insist that the act provide music video services, usually at no additional cost or at minimum union scale. MTV prefers concept videos to film-clip-only videos.

Finally, songwriters and soundtrack performers that do not perform onscreen are never granted a participation in the nonmusic receipts of a film. These participations are usually divided between the actors, director, producers and the studio. However, music artists have a distinct advantage as to the payment of royalties—they do not have to wait until the studio earns back its investment before songwriter royalties are paid. The same is true for artist royalties from the soundtrack CD. Usually only relatively minimal nonpicture soundtrack conversion costs are recouped before the artist is paid for record sales.

INCOME

We shall assume you make a deal at Paramount, you are a writer/performer/ producer who writes a title song and records a title song master. You are paid $25,000 for the song and $25,000 to record. You retain the writer's share but Paramount retains the publisher's share. You receive a 12% retail U.S. record royalty, prorated, on CDs, and 9% on singles. Your master is three minutes long. The picture is a blockbuster; your single sells 1,000,000 copies in the United States, 750,000 foreign, and hits number one on Billboard's Hot 100 Pop Chart. The soundtrack CD, on which you have one of the 10 cuts, sells 500,000 copies in the United States and 375,000 copies overseas. Exhibit 3 gives you an idea of what your earnings might be.

CONCLUSION

The writing and recording of songs for films involves complex financial and business arrangements with studios, record labels and music publishers. The advantages to both new and established songwriters and recording acts in participating in soundtracks are numerous. The song and its recording may be exposed to millions of people, it may be included in the soundtrack album, and, in the best case, be released as a single and MTV video. The down side is that the artist has very little, if any, input as to how the song is used in the film. You may write and record a beautiful four-minute ballad that is blared from a radio for only a few seconds, but that is the risk you take.

The most important advice to a new writer or recording act, however, is to not play prima donna if approached by a studio to work on a soundtrack. Only major acts have this luxury. Your goal should be to get the song considered and accepted. Nonestablished writers/performers should not expect the same sort of terms that Paul McCartney gets. Do not blow the deal. Once you get your foot in the door and make a positive contribution to a soundtrack, you will have taken a substantial step in your writing and performing careers.

EXHIBIT 1
TYPICAL MUSIC ACQUISITION PRACTICES FOR EACH COMMISSIONED SONG

	MAJOR STUDIOS	INDEPENDENT PRODUCERS
Songwriter's fee	up to $25,000	zero to $10,000
Participation in publisher's share of income	zero to 50%	zero to 100%
Writer/Artist recognition level	Major label (recently signed) to superstar	Unsigned to recognized label artists
Artist's fee (off-camera)	Not less than $10,000	Zero to $15,000
Recording budget	$15,000 to $50,000	$500 to $10,000
Copyright proprietor (occasionally writer)	Major studio	Independent Producer
Artist's & producer's soundtrack royalty (subject to proration)	12% to 14% (foreign reduced)	6% to 12% (foreign reduced)
Copyright administrator	Major studio	Outside publisher
Music producer's fee (if negotiated separately)	$4,000 to $10,000	None (usually artist or supervisor produced)

EXHIBIT 2
ARTIST'S ROYALTY STATEMENT

Sales for original soundtrack of *Century City Blues* cat. no. 14899

Statement Date:	September 30, 200_
Country of Sale:	United States
Period of Sales:	Second-Half 200_
Release Date:	April 5, 200_
Distributing Label:	Megabite Records, Inc.
Film Company	Behemoth Studios, Inc.

PRORATA PER UNIT

Configuration	Pkg. Deduct	SRLP	Royalty	Share	Royalty	Sales	Earnings
CD singles	25%	4.98	8%	4 on 4	.29880	2,500	$747
CD album	25%	15.98	10%	2 on 10	.23970	1,000,000	$239,700
				Gross Earnings This Period			$240,447
				Less Soundtrack Conversion			($6,000)
				Total Payable This Period			**$234,447**

$175,835.25 remittance to artist (75%) enclosed
$58,611.75 remittance to artist's label (25%)

EXHIBIT 3
ROUGH INCOME SUMMARY

The following rough income summary is designed to alert you to sources of income rather than to provide exact figures (although we have done our best to be accurate).

A. WRITER

1. Writing Fee (nonrecoupable)	$25,000
2. Song Synchronization License For Film	0
3. Performance Income (worldwide)	
(a) From Film In Theaters	
(i) United States	0
(ii) Foreign	$20,000
(b) Radio Performances	$100,000
(c) Home Video	0
(d) Pay TV	*
(e) Free TV	
(i) U.S. Network TV (two runs)	$3,000
(ii) U.S. Syndicated TV (two runs 150 stations)	$600
(iii) Foreign	$5,000
4. Sheet Music (40,000 copies @ 10¢/copy)	$4,000
5. Mechanicals	
(a) United States (75% of statutory)	
(i) Single (A-side only) (1,000,000 x 2.831¢)	$28,310
(ii) CD (500,000 x 2.831¢)	$14,155
(b) Foreign	
(i) Single (750,000 x 3¢)	$22,500
(ii) CD (375,000 x 3¢)	$11,250
Total	**$233,815**

B. RECORDING ARTIST

1. Recording Fee (nonrecoupable)	$25,000
2. Master License For Film	0
3. United States Record Sales	
(a) Singles (A-side only) (1,000,000 x 7.65¢)	$76,500
(b) CDs (500,000 x 9.8802¢)	$49,401
4. Foreign Record Sales	
(a) Singles (750,000 x 6.37493¢)	$47,812
(b) CDs (375,000 copies x 7.26¢)	$27,225
Less Soundtrack Conversion Costs	($3,000)
Total	**$222,938**

* *(Figures presently unavailable.)*

Performing and Marketing

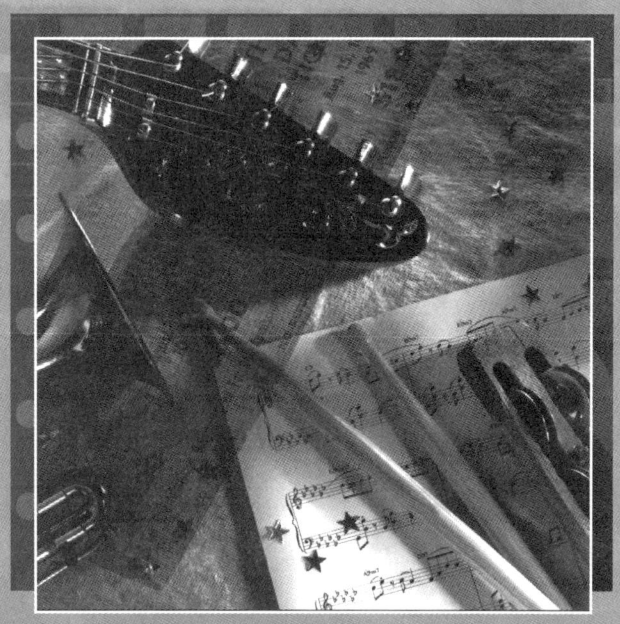

- CLUB CONTRACTS
- THE INTERNET AND MUSIC
- GETTING STARTED AS AN INTERNET ARTIST
- MUSIC UNIONS

Club Contracts

BY EDWARD (NED) R. HEARN

Many bands get their start playing in clubs. There are several types, for example, draw clubs, clubs with walk-in trades and lounge act clubs. A club or hotel room that has been booked by a private party for a special occasion, such as a wedding, anniversary, or industrial convention, etc., is called a "casual."

The draw clubs book name acts to attract an audience. They could be national recording acts or local acts that have followings. Sometimes these clubs hire opening acts to reinforce the lead act's draw and help ensure a full house.

The walk-in trade club depends on a regular crowd that frequents the club. It normally hires club bands that play Top 40 and maybe some original material. Lounge act clubs focus on groups that do highly polished performances of popular music (copy music). They are prevalent in major cities' hotels, casinos, and in resort areas.

As some clubs are signatories of agreements with the American Federation of Musicians (AFM), you must find out if you need to be a member of the AFM before a club can book you.

Sometimes bands or managers book their acts into clubs for showcase purposes to show the group's talents to industry people that have promised to attend. Showcases are also used to generate enthusiasm for a group. For example, members of a Midwest group that has a huge regional following book themselves into a Los Angeles club for almost no pay to showcase for record companies, publishers or even prospective managers. Or a record company may fill (paper) a club when a new record is released, to generate enthusiasm for the particular group being pushed by the record company, or the club may be filled by a group's personal manager or talent agency to influence record companies into developing an interest in the group.

APPROACHING THE CLUB

You should study the various kinds of clubs where you could perform and decide which best suit your act. Make presentations to clubs that most fit your style of music. It is important that you understand the reputation of the club and the makeup of the audience that is likely to enjoy your performance.

Club owners want bands that are professional and pleasing to their audiences. They want to know that the artists will work as promised, show up on time, and make money for their clubs.

The more clubs you perform in and the more reliable a track record you develop, the easier the bookings should become, particularly if you show a consistent (and growing) draw.

Most club owners also expect you to have publicity materials that they can use to help promote the performance.

Some clubs have implemented a "pay-to-play" policy, by which you, as the performing artist, guarantee that a certain number of patrons (e.g., 50) will come to the club and pay to see you for some predetermined aggregate amount (e.g., $500), which the club owner will split with you (e.g., fifty-fifty). In that example, if less than 50 friends show up and pay a total of $300, the club owner will keep the first $250 and you get the balance. If less than $250 is generated, you have to pay the club owner the difference; hence "pay to play." This approach has raised much protest and indignation by local bands and their supporters. In an area where there are many clubs in which to choose to play, boycotting a pay-to-play club may have an effective influence. In locations where the clubs are fewer in number, that tactic may not prove to be an effective remedy. You need venues in which to perform to develop your craft and your following, and to get record industry attention, in which event you may have to be forced to play the game and pay.

CLUB CONTRACTS

When dealing with clubs, you should understand that even a casual agreement to show up and play for free, to see what happens, is a contract. This section focuses on the various points you should review with the club owner in order to arrive at a performing contract. These same points are relevant for standard AFM contracts that are used when bands are booked into clubs that are affiliated with the AFM.

Remember that the contractual relationship with a club is only as good as the relationship between the club owner and the group. You should determine whether the owners of a club are people with whom you really wish to deal. Counterbalancing that, if they are not people with whom you wish to deal, but playing their club is an important milestone in the development of your band and its credibility to the music industry, then that point has to be given consideration.

The contract with a club should be written. With an oral contract, in the event of a dispute, it is difficult to prove what terms the club owner and the band agreed to. When the contract is written the agreed-to points are documented. Rather than treating the written contract as an awesome legal document, consider it a checklist of important points that should

A CHECKLIST OF THE IMPORTANT ITEMS IN A CLUB CONTRACT

- Identity of the performer and club owner.
- Dates and times of the performance.
- Number of sets to be performed and the length of those sets.
- Duration of the breaks between the sets.
- Special arrangements that need to be made in terms of equipment, stage settings, space for performance, and lighting.
- Refreshments (the house policy on drinks and food).
- Setup time and the time for sound checking.
- Whether any recording or broadcasting is to take place, and who controls the product of that effort.
- The advertising image of the group to be displayed by the club.
- What happens if the gig does not take place?
- What is your compensation?

be covered by the club owner and the group. Look at the contract as a way of clarifying the relationship between the club and you by bringing to light all of the issues that are important to both parties. This way, everyone will focus on those issues at the very beginning, hopefully eliminating any later surprises. Contract discussions are an indication of your professionalism to a club owner.

Compensation

Your compensation could come in a number of forms. It could be from door receipts, in which case you should determine, with the club owner, the number of tickets to be sold, the prices of those tickets, and the number of freebies for the owner and the performers. With that information, you will have some idea how much to expect based on the percentage of the door receipts you have agreed to accept. Your compensation could be a flat sum, in which case the door receipts are not a problem. Reach an agreement on the form of compensation (i.e., cash or cashier's check). The norm is cash, but insist on at least a cashier's check. Part of the money should be paid, if not at the beginning, then at least part way through the performance with the balance due, if any, immediately at the conclusion of the performance.

Sound and Lights

An audience's perception of how good a performance is often depends on the quality of sound and lights. Make sure that the club has equipment that is adequate for your needs and that the club owner understands what those needs are.

If you (or the club) wish to supplement the club's system with your own (or rented) equipment, work out the additional expense as part of your contract and arrange for a load-in time. If you are using an acoustic piano, your contract should state that it be tuned prior to performance. A simple performance contract is printed at the end of this chapter. Even if you do not use the contract, it is a good checklist that can be used during negotiations with the club owner.

If the club has a resident sound engineer whose job is setting up and operating the house sound reinforcement system, establish a harmonious relationship by providing a plot plan of how the stage looks when your equipment is set up. Communicate your priorities regarding sound and provide the sound person with a set list. Ask whether your sound person can sit with the club sound engineer and provide direction about the mix.

AFM UNION CONTRACTS

Certain clubs have signed collective bargaining agreements with the AFM that establish the scale and working conditions that the club must pay and provide union musicians that perform at that club, based on the amount of time they play and the number of sets they perform. Union contracts are most prevalent with hotels, pit orchestras, house bands, and major clubs in large cities.

The musician members of the AFM also sign a contract with the AFM that requires its members to deal only with clubs that meet the AFM contract requirements. AFM musicians should not play in nonunion clubs for less than union scales, since to do so is a violation of the contract.

It is not uncommon for clubs that have signed with the AFM to file, with the union local, what is known as a "dummy contract" between the performer and the club by which the club commits to pay at AFM scale, but the musician and the club owner agree (verbally) that the musician will perform at a lower price. This is done so that the AFM will not bother the club or the musician and the musician can get the work. The net effect is, the musician gets the short end.

Another common problem is that union clubs are barred by the AFM contract from hiring nonunion musicians. There is a provision in the AFM booking contract that says, "All employees covered by this agreement must be members in good standing of the Federation." Musicians that are engaged by the club and are not members of the union must become members of the union no later than the 30th day following the beginning of their employment or the effective date of the agreement, whichever of the two is later. Consequently, if you are not a union member when you start performing with a union club, you may find yourself in a situation where you must become a member of the union if you are going to continue to play in the club over a period of time—depending on the extent to which the AFM or the particular club enforce this provision.

Many of the points raised in the following checklist can be made a part of the AFM contract with the club.

Many smaller clubs do not sign contracts with the union and have no obligation to pay union scale. Union musicians, however, often perform in nonunion clubs on the q.t. or they file a dummy contract so the AFM can get its cut. If you are a union member and, on performing in a nonunion club, elect to file a dummy contract with the AFM, it means you or the club owner will need to submit a payment to the union for its fees on the performance. Since the club owner is not union, it is highly unlikely that the club will make that payment, which leaves it up to you to pay it from your fees, or build that cost into your fees to the club for performing. Most union members in that situation, especially outside of the major cities, just try to "fly below radar" and not pay, and hope it does not become an issue. The majority of times it does not, but there are occasional exceptions when it does and that may result in having to pay a fine to the relevant union chapter.

When a club has no contract with the AFM the only leverage union musicians have is to refuse to perform in that club unless union scale is paid. The economic realities of the business, however, are such that musicians frequently have no bargaining power to force clubs to pay union scale. Generally, musicians are glad to get any kind of work regardless of pay scale.

WHO SIGNS THE CONTRACT?

As a practical matter, one of the members of the group should be given authority to sign on behalf of all of the members of the group. Performing groups are, for all practical purposes, partnerships (unless its members have incorporated the business or formed an LLC) and one partner has the power to bind the other partners. Sometimes, a manager will be authorized to sign contracts on behalf of a group, although managers are better advised not to sign performance contracts if the state in which the band or manager is based requires talent agents to be licensed, as is the case in California. (See the chapter, Talent Agencies.) The extent of that authority depends on the agreements reached between the manager and the group and is another point to be considered carefully.

TAXES

Remember your tax obligations on your compensation. Generally, club owners will treat you as an independent contractor and you will be responsible for your own

OTHER POINTS THAT SHOULD BE CONSIDERED IN YOUR RELATIONSHIP WITH A CLUB THAT USES THE AFM CONTRACT

- The wage should be at least union minimum scale. Consider the costs that have to be paid from that wage, such as sound system, special instruments, and lighting.
- The customary union procedure is to pay half of the agreed-to wages in advance of the engagement and the remaining amount prior to the performance on the evening of the engagement. The AFM may demand that the entire amount be paid in advance or that a bond be posted.
- The union contract gives the club owner complete control, supervision, and direction over the musicians, including the manner, means, and details of the performance. This is more often than not a matter of bargaining power and the more popular the group, the less power the owner has over the group. As a practical matter, most club owners prefer not to be involved in decisions about a group's performance or the kind of materials to be performed. Presumably, if you have properly identified your style, the club owner has decided that you are the kind of act desired, and is expecting that kind of performance.
- Any disputes between the club owner and the musician under a union contract are, usually, resolved by an AFM arbitration proceeding and the results can be enforced by a court.
- If the performance is to be recorded or broadcast, the contract requires AFM approval. The AFM may demand additional compensation for the musicians in that event. At the same time, the club owner may insist on additional compensation for use of the club if the performance is to be recorded by a record company or broadcast over a radio station. These are points that should be negotiated in advance.

federal income tax and social security payment as well as any state, unemployment, or workman's compensation insurance that must be paid. The IRS may impose the responsibility on the club owner for withholding if it determines that there was an employer/employee relationship, but you should take responsibility for setting aside a portion of your payment so that you can pay the IRS when the time comes.

WHEN THE CLUB DOES NOT PAY YOU

If the club owner owes you money and the owner refuses to pay, you have recourse to the courts (and to your AFM local if it is a union club). Going to court, however, can be an expensive proposition, and is not one to be pursued lightly. California law provides that if the claim is no more than $5000 or if you are willing to limit your claim to that amount, you can bring your own action in the small claims court in the county where you reside or where the club is located. Generally, you will have to file the small claims action in the jurisdiction where the club is located, which can be an aggregation of time and further expense if you do not live in the same area. While you can try to file in your local court, if the club has no presence in that area, e.g., it does not advertise in the area or promote events with other promoters located in your area, it will be difficult to get jurisdiction over the club's owner. The owner could move to dismiss the case or move to transfer the case to a court in the club's jurisdiction, or even, if you get a default judgment, challenge its enforceability for lack of jurisdiction. Less than reputable club owners can rely on this distant location situation as a way to avoid the obligation to pay you. The small claims court procedure requires you to go to the county clerk for your local court system and pay a small fee for filing, stamping, and serving the complaint. The sheriff then serves the complaint on the defendant, which sets forth a date, time, and place for a hearing. The defendant can file a counterclaim within 48 hours of the hearing, but it has to be verified, or sworn to. (Your complaint does not have to be sworn to.) At the appointed date, time, and place, both parties must appear at the court and explain their stories to the judge. The judge can then order the club to pay you. If the judge does rule in your favor, the club owner can appeal to a higher level court. If you lose, you cannot appeal, and that is the end of the case. Similar small claims procedures are in effect in most states.

CONCLUSION

Making arrangements for performing in clubs deserves special consideration and planning. You should keep in mind that your ability to get gigs will be enhanced by getting your business act together.

PERFORMANCE AGREEMENT

Agreement made as of ____________, 20____, between the parties identified below. In consideration for the following covenants, conditions, and promises, the Purchaser agrees to hire the Artist to perform an engagement and the Artist agrees to provide such performance services, under the following terms and conditions:

1. Artist ____

2. Purchaser ____

3. Place of engagement

____
NAME
____
STREET ADDRESS
____
CITY, STATE, ZIP
____
TELEPHONE

4. The dates, time, duration of show, and sound check time are as follows:

Dates ______________________________ Time ________________ AM/PM
Number of Sets _______________ Duration of Each Set ________________
Sound Check Time ____

5. The consideration to be paid shall be

(a) Guaranteed Fee of $__________________________
(b) Percentage __________________ (gross/net of door)
(c) Workshop Fee of $ ___________________________
(d) Meals/Lodging ______________________________
(e) Transportation ______________________________
(i) Air ___________________________________
(ii) Ground _______________________________
(f) Materials ______________________________
(g) Total __________________________________
(h) Advance Payment of $ _______ due on _______(Date)
(i) Balance of Payment of $ _______ due on _______(Date)

6. Further consideration to Artist by Purchaser is provided in the Rider of Additional Terms attached to this Agreement.

7. Sound and/or lighting equipment to be provided by Purchaser shall be as described in the separate Sound Reinforcement and Lighting Agreement.

8. This Agreement and the attached Riders and Sound Reinforcement and Lighting Agreement, which by this reference are incorporated into and made a part of this Agreement, constitute the entire agreement between the parties and supersedes all prior and contemporaneous agreements, understandings, negotiations, and discussions,

whether oral or written. There are no warranties, representations, and/or agreements among the parties in connection with the subject matter of this Agreement, except as specifically set forth and referenced in this Agreement and the attached Riders. This Agreement shall be governed by [insert your State's name] law; is binding and valid only when signed by the parties below; and may be modified only in a writing signed by the parties. If Artist has not received the deposit in the amount and at the time specified in subsection 5(h), then Artist thereafter at anytime shall have the option to terminate this Agreement.

9. The persons signing this Agreement on behalf of Artist and Purchaser each have the authority to bind their respective principals.

10. If you have any questions, please contact our home office at ________________

AGREED TO AND ACCEPTED

PURCHASER	ARTIST
BY DATE	BY DATE
NAME AND TITLE (AN AUTHORIZED SIGNATORY)	NAME AND TITLE (AN AUTHORIZED SIGNATORY)
FEDERAL I.D./SS#	FEDERAL I.D./SS#

PERFORMANCE AGREEMENT RIDER *

1. BILLING
Artist shall receive one hundred percent (100%) sole exclusive billing in any and all advertising and publicity when appearing as the sole act. When Artist is accompanied by other musicians, Artist shall receive prominent billing, and shall close the show at each performance during the engagement unless specifically provided otherwise. When headlining, Artist shall have the right of approval of any and all other acts in the show, their set times, and set lengths.

2. PAYMENT
All payments provided hereunder shall be made by Money Order, Cash, Cashier's, Certified, or School Check, made out to ______________ unless otherwise specified.

When a percentage figure is made a part of this Agreement, the Purchaser agrees to have on hand at the end of the engagement the ticket manifest and all unsold tickets for verification by Artist or Artist's representative.

(a) If the Artist is paid according to a percentage of the gross admissions, the following applies:

(i) Purchaser must have all tickets printed by a bonded printer.
(ii) All tickets must be consecutively numbered.
(iii) Each set of tickets for a given price, and, if more than one performance is

* *(Riders to performance agreements specify additional requirements and working conditions that are essential and necessary for a quality performance. They can be extremely elaborate.)*

contemplated, each set of tickets for each performance must be printed on a ticket stock of contrasting color.

(iv) A bonded printer's manifest showing number, color and price of all tickets printed for the performance must be available for inspection by Artist's representative on afternoon of concert.

(v) All gross admission receipts shall be computed on the actual full admission price provided on each ticket, and, in the absence of prior written agreement by Artist, no tickets shall be offered or sold at a discount or a premium.

(vi) A representative of the Artist shall have the right to be present in the box office prior to and during the performance and intermission periods and such representative shall be given full access to all box office sales and shall otherwise be permitted to reasonably satisfy himself as to the gross receipts (and expenditures if required) at each performance hereunder.

(b) Purchaser warrants that tickets for the engagement will be scaled in the following prices:

____________________ TICKETS AT ____________________ DOLLARS.

____________________ TICKETS AT ____________________ DOLLARS.

____________________ TICKETS AT ____________________ DOLLARS.

If the scale of prices shall be varied in any respect, the percentage compensation payable to Artist shall be based upon whichever of the following is more favorable to Artist: the scale of prices as set forth above, or the actual scale of prices in effect for the engagement.

(c) In the event that compensation payable to Artist hereunder is measured in whole or in part by a percentage of receipts, Artist shall have the right to set a limit on the number of free admissions authorized by Purchaser.

3. WITHHOLDING

If Purchaser is required by state or local law to make any withholding or deduction from the Artist fee specified in the attached contract, the Purchaser shall furnish to Artist a copy of the pertinent law governing said deduction when returning the Agreement to Artist or Artist's agent.

4. LIMITATIONS ON RECORDING

No performance during the engagement shall be recorded, copied, reproduced, transmitted, or disseminated in or from the premises in any manner or by any means now known or later developed, including audio and video, without the prior written permission of Artist.

5. PUBLICITY PHOTOGRAPHS

Only photographs sent to the Purchaser by Artist or Artist's representative shall be used in publicizing the engagement.

6. DRESSING ROOM

Purchaser shall provide one (1) clean, lockable dressing room. Purchaser agrees to be solely responsible for the security of all items in the dressing room area, and shall keep unauthorized people from entering said area.

7. ARTIST'S PROPERTY

Purchaser shall be responsible for any theft or damage to the equipment of Artist that may occur during the time that the equipment is located on Purchaser's premises.

8. SECURITY

Purchaser will make a diligent effort during the performance to maintain a quiet listening audience. Audience shall be seated prior to the performance. Purchaser is responsible for the conduct of its audience and shall provide adequate supervision of minors attending the performance. Any damage resulting from activities of the audience shall be the responsibility of Purchaser.

9. COMPLIMENTARY TICKETS

Purchaser agrees to make (__________) complimentary tickets available to Artist or Artist's representative, the unused portion of which may be placed on sale the day of performance with the permission of Artist or Artist's representative.

10. BACKSTAGE ACCESS

Purchaser shall provide (______) backstage passes for Artist on Artist's arrival at venue.

11. MERCHANDISING

Artist shall have the option to sell albums, videos, books, and/or merchandising material at the performance and shall retain the proceeds of such sales.

(a) Artist has sole right to merchandise any and all products pertaining to Artist at no expense to the Artist, excluding normal hall and vending fees agreed upon in advance by Artist in writing. Purchaser will not, nor will Purchaser allow, any other party to sell or distribute merchandise bearing name, likeness, or logo of Artist, before, during, or after concert date.

(b) Purchaser will provide at its expense, (_____) persons to sell Artist's products.

(c) Purchaser will provide the following equipment for merchandising:

(i) One (1) cash box with fifty dollars ($50.00) starting change (ones and fives).

(ii) Six-foot (6') table (to hold records and other Artist products).

(iii) Two (2) chairs (for the persons selling the products).

(d) Merchandise shall be displayed in a prominent area of the foyer or lounge leading from the facility entrance to the performance area.

(e) Person who is to vend Artist's products shall be available from time of stage call to receive product and set up merchandise area. Artist or Artist's representative will conduct and set up merchandise area with Purchaser's designated sellers. Artist or Artist's representative will conduct inventory of merchandise prior to start of sale.

(f) After close of show (all audience will have left the facility) the vendor will close the merchandising booth and return all unsold product and receipts from sale to Artist or Artist's representative for final accounting.

(g) Purchaser is responsible for all product and monies from sales as signed for by the Purchaser's merchandising representative. Fifty dollars ($50.00) starting change is to be deducted from total receipts.

12. GROUND TRANSPORTATION

Unless otherwise indicated, Purchaser, at its expense, shall provide ground transportation to and from place of engagement, airport, and hotel. Artist requires large station wagon or van. Please send directions to concert site from the airport, or, if mode of travel is arranged other than by automobile, please send directions (and time tables) from airport, train station (etc.) to hotel, then from hotel to concert site. Copies of highlighted street maps are very much appreciated.

13. FOOD
Food and beverages appropriate for time of day for (____________) people shall be provided by Purchaser.

14. LODGING
If Purchaser is to provide lodging, it shall be at a hotel of Holiday Inn quality or better, four (4) quiet, nonsmoking rooms, in the vicinity of the venue, away from highway noise, with king-size beds in each room.

15. OUTDOOR VENUE
In the event the engagement is outdoors, there must be a covering over the stage area that will protect the Artist and equipment from the elements.

16. SEATING
House lights should be dimmed starting ten (10) minutes before the start of the concert to facilitate audience being seated on time.

17. BACKGROUND MUSIC
No background music, taped or otherwise, is to be played before the start of or after the concert without the approval of the Artist, unless the music is from Artist's albums.

18. STAGE
Stage must be accessible to performers in a manner other than through the audience. Stage and curtains must be in clean, good condition. Whenever possible, stage should be no further than fifteen feet (15') from the audience.

19. PROMOTION
Purchaser agrees to promote the scheduled performance(s) on television, radio, newspapers, and other print media, and will use its best efforts to obtain calendar listings, feature articles, interviews of the Artist, reviews of the performance and Artist's records in local major and alternative newspapers, radio, and television programs. Purchaser shall be responsible for all matters pertaining to the promotion and production of the scheduled engagement, including but not limited to venue rentals, security, and advertising.

20. CLIPPINGS
As a special request, Artist asks that Purchaser please forward clippings, reviews, advertising, and posters to Artist at ____________________. If there are any questions or suggestions, please direct them to ____________________.

21. FORCE MAJEURE
This agreement of Artist is subject to the unavailability of Artist because of sickness, accidents, riots, strikes, acts of God, or other conditions beyond Artist's control.

22. CANCELLATION
In the event Purchaser cancels the performance for any reason less than five (5) weeks

before the date of such performance, Purchaser will pay Artist, as liquidated damages, one-half (1/2) of the guaranteed fee agreed to be paid for such performance in subsection 5(a). In the event Purchaser cancels the performance for any reason less than two (2) weeks before the date of such performance, Purchaser will pay Artist, as liquidated damages, the full guaranteed fee agreed to be paid for such performance, unless Artist subsequently agrees in writing to waive all or any part of that payment.

23. ATTORNEYS' FEES

In the event of any dispute arising under this Agreement that results in litigation or arbitration, the prevailing party shall be paid its reasonable attorneys' fees and costs by the losing party.

24. INSURANCE

Purchaser agrees to obtain any and all necessary personal injury and property damage liability insurance with respect to the activities of Artist on the premises of Purchaser or at such other location where Purchaser directs Artist to perform. Purchaser agrees to indemnify and hold Artist harmless from any and all claims, liabilities, damages, and expenses for injury, damages, or death to any person, persons, or property, including attorneys' fees, demands, suits, or costs of whatever nature, arising from any action, activity, or omission of Purchaser or third parties, except for claims arising from Artist's willful misconduct or gross negligence. At least ten (10) days prior to the date of performance, Purchaser shall provide to Artist a copy of Purchaser's policy of insurance indicating coverage in the sum of at least ________ dollars for personal injury and property damage, naming Artist as an additional insured for the date of the performance.

SOUND REINFORCEMENT RIDER

This Rider for Sound Reinforcement Services is entered into as of ________, 20__, between the parties identified below.

1. NAME OF PURCHASER ______________________________

____
PURCHASER ADDRESS

____
CITY/STATE/ZIP

____
TELEPHONE

2. NAME OF ARTIST ______________________________

3. PLACE OF ENGAGEMENT ______________________________

4. DATE OF EVENT ______________________________

5. NUMBER OF SETS AND DURATION ______________________________

6. TYPE OF EVENT ______________________________

7. MAXIMUM AUDIENCE EXPECTED ______________________________

8. LOAD-IN
Hall is available for load-in and set up at (time) ____________ (date) ________
(a) Purchaser agrees to provide a safe and proper 20-foot "A" type ladder (with wheels), at time of load-in and until all of Artist's equipment has been removed from venue.
(b) Purchaser agrees to provide (_______) number of drum risers at a height of (_______) above the stage floor.
(c) Ladder and drum risers are to be in place at time of load-in.

9. SOUND CHECK
Hall is available for sound check at (time) ______________ (date) ___________
(a) Artist requires a (_________) hour sound check and technical setup period. Purchaser shall not allow the audience to enter the place of performance until such time as sound check and technical setup has been completed. Artist shall complete the setup and sound check (_____________) hour(s) prior to the time of performance, provided that Purchaser makes the place of performance available for said setup at least (_____________) hours prior to time of performance.

10. SOUND SYSTEM
Purchaser agrees to provide a complete sound system consisting of:
(______) Number of amplifiers at (______) kilowatts of power
(______) Number of main house speakers
(______) Number of monitor speakers
A main mixing board with (______) number of input channels
A monitor mixing board with (______) number of input channels
(______) Number of microphones and stands
Other special equipment ____________________

Any alterations or deviations from the above items involving extra cost of equipment or labor, or substitutions of equipment, are subject to written agreement.

11. PERSONNEL
Purchaser agrees to provide the following personnel to operate the equipment:

____

____

12. POWER
Purchaser agrees to provide at least ______ amps single phase and ____ volts of power.

13. SPEAKER SPACE
Purchaser agrees to provide adequate space for placement of loudspeakers. The space needed for the speakers will be __________ feet by _________ feet. This area must be capable of supporting the weight (_______ lbs.) of the speakers safely.

14. MIXING PLATFORM
Purchaser agrees to provide a safe platform or space in the audience within 50 to 100 feet of the stage in order to set up mixers to mix the sound for the show. Platform or area should be ________ feet by _______ feet.

15. SECURITY
Purchaser agrees to hire adequate security for stage area and accepts full liability for any stolen articles and/or destruction of Artist's equipment.

SAMPLE OF SPECIFICATIONS FOR SOUND REQUIREMENTS (SOUND REINFORCEMENT RIDER, CLAUSE 10).

(a) Purchaser shall provide a minimum of ten (10) high-quality monitor speakers. These monitor speakers shall be capable of providing at least 120 dB of clear, undistorted sound between 100 and 10,000 cycles per second (plus or minus 4 dB) at a distance of ten (10) feet. The monitor speakers shall be placed as follows:

- 3–stage center
- 1–down stage left
- 1–up stage right
- 2–monitors behind drummer
- 1–monitor behind keyboards
- 2–side fill monitors

(b) There shall be a minimum of ten (10) boom stands, six (6) short stands, two (2) gooseneck-type attachments, and ten (10) regular stands for the microphones.

(c) If the performance area of the engagement is outdoors or semioutdoors, all microphones shall be covered with filter windscreens.

(d) Purchaser further agrees to provide a six (6) station intercom hookup between the following—

- stage right or left
- both spot lights
- sound console
- monitor mixer console
- dimmer board
- house lights and curtain

All intercoms are to be headphone type with microphone and two earpieces.

The Internet and Music

BY NEVILLE L. JOHNSON

Three percent of the gross national product, commerce, is comprised of the entertainment industry; about one percent of our economy is devoted to music. Music is irrevocably intertwined with the cultures of every country. It is how a people define, analyze, motivate, remember, educate, entertain, humor themselves, and to what they dance. Music is one way in which we celebrate being human. The importance of music to a culture is far in excess of its economic importance. No matter one's station in life, chances are anyone—from a child to the President—can tell you many of the hit songs of the day and yesteryear. We must have music to survive. There will always be a need for new music, and people will always want to hear the old songs too.

"Nobody knows anything," is the famous statement about the movie business in the classic *Adventures in the Screen Trade,* by screenwriter William Goldman. The same can be said for the music business and the Internet as we roar into the new millennium. This is the consensus of the professionals in the music business at the many new technology-meets-music conferences I have attended over the past few years. There are many business models proposed and attempted, but only a few companies are making a profit. Still, the importance of the Internet as a method for distribution and promotion of music is undeniable. It is the future and it provides wonderful and fantastic possibilities for up-and-coming musicians. What is happening to the music business today is as important as the industry changing from a "singles" to an LP business in the 1950s.

The initial years of delivery of music via the Internet were chaotic. MP3.com and Napster challenged traditional norms of the music business and were met by the collective force of the major record companies in court, where the new Internet companies suffered stinging defeats. But they proved a major point; the traditional methods of distributing music are at the end of the road. The future of music is in digital delivery. Napster had over 50 million users until a Federal appellate court in February 2001, enjoined it from permitting infringing conduct. However, BMG has taken a stake in Napster, and it is moving towards a "pay" model that should establish legitimacy in the eyes of the traditional music industry. To this writer, users have been learning the wrong lesson, namely that people should expect music for free. The ease of obtaining free music has caused some consumers to disregard traditional notions of copyright ownership and protection. However, it is inevitable that sound recordings will be primarily distributed electronically.

The major record companies have been slow to react to the Internet. They have been late to the game for reasons of music piracy and because it has been difficult to make money from the delivery of music over the net. This has been due in part because broadband high-speed lines have just begun to reach the public at reasonable prices. Previously, the availability of high-speed lines was limited and their cost was prohibitively high. Broadband is just around the corner for all of us. The first to have widespread access to broadband were university students and they popularized the swapping of music without payment, via Napster, Gnutella and similar "file-sharing" arrangements. The argument against this is, if musicians and record companies do not get compensated for their labors, less music will be made and promoted. Payment and sales systems have yet to be perfected, but the majors are now selling downloadable music.

Music piracy has been the other major stumbling block for the major record companies. The majors would like to "watermark," put identifying digital tags on music as it is delivered, and to encrypt music so that it cannot be copied or downloaded to others. No system yet invented accomplishes both, and some argue there is no encryption that cannot be broken.

Some argue that the future of music is in "streaming," i.e., the delivery of music that is not downloaded. (One innovative site is Radiomoi.com, an interactive site that streams over 100 channels in all genres of music.) There is a good argument for this: what is the need for storage if you can have a virtual jukebox—you can choose any song you want, anytime you want it? Automobiles today have the capability of accepting this kind of digital radio. You will be able soon to drive from Maine to San Diego and listen to the same station all the way. It is just a matter of a few years until reasonably priced devices will enable anyone to stream music to hand-held equipment.

What this means is a radical sea change in the cost of production, delivery, and in some cases the promotion of the product—the most difficult aspects of, the barriers to, the music industry. The industry has always been old-fashioned; retailers do not pay for the records they receive until they are sold, and all record companies permit return rights. Records are sold essentially on consignment. Today, it costs about $1 to manufacture a CD, then it has to be warehoused and shipped across the United States and the rest of the world. It then sits in a record store, only to be returned if it does not sell. Over the last two decades, the major record companies have controlled the shipping and distribution of music. Independent records make up about 20% of the business, and small record companies always, and usually justifiably, complain about payment problems from independent distributors, many of which have gone bankrupt. These costs of manufacturing, delivery, and collection will no longer be necessary with the Internet. The middleman—the distributor—will be eliminated, at least to some extent. However, there will still be costs involved to digitize, store, and transmit music via the Internet. You can sell music online, and collect via a charge card for an instantaneous transaction. Also, it is now possible to manufacture CDs when and as needed for those that do not wish to download but want to receive their music by mail order—delivery on demand/just-in-time manufacturing! Some companies are already doing it.

What will happen to traditional record stores, the so-called brick and mortar? I believe that CDs will be gradually phased out, and the traditional store will become a virtual retailer, where you will get CDs pressed on demand. Music will continue to thrive and grow as a business as long as the producers of it get paid.

As for the majors, I expect that they will continue to dominate the industry because they have the skill and money needed to promote music. The majors control radio, still the way most music is promoted. But, as radio changes and becomes more Internet driven, more interactive, the majors' hold should diminish. In any event, given that broadband is now here—videos can be streamed on demand, artists can be interviewed, concert footage can be shown—an exciting and golden road lies before us. Brian Wilson's great live double CD, sold only via his Internet site, is doing well and getting great reviews. He keeps all the profit. Emusic.com was the first Internet company to sell music via downloads, and it also offers a streaming subscription, but it is nowhere near profitability, though it has acquired substantial catalogs of independent artists and record companies.

The name of the game in any business is the marketing of product and the majors will not easily let go of their dominance. The Internet companies that have sprung up typically offer a free listing on their Web site, plus 50% of sales, no great windfall for artists that need to make themselves known. It costs millions to break a new artist such as Britney Spears. Some video budgets hit $500,000 plus. Print ads must be bought in trade and consumer magazines. Music critics must be serviced, acts must travel and promote their product live, and to the press, radio and television. This methodology may change. But now, the possibility exists for greater control and profits for emerging acts and those that would otherwise be only marginally profitable for the majors, but have a substantial consumer base of fans.

We are at the advent of a new destiny for the music industry. It will be exciting to watch it develop, fortunes will be made, and old ways will change. One must stay on top of current methods and models and maximize their potential. Do not give away your Internet rights without considering what that may mean to your ability to control your art and bottom line. It will become easier and easier to market music on the Net as time goes by.

Getting Started as an Internet Artist

BY PETER SPELLMAN

The Internet is the fastest-growing communications network on the planet and the most effective at delivering multimedia content globally. In essence, the Internet collapses distance. From my desktop computer in Boston I can connect with a guitarist in Zaire, a promoter in Australia and a fan in Poland simultaneously. These developments bring tools to musicians that allow them extended reach on a playing field that grows increasingly more level and accessible. On the Internet, you can appear side-by-side with multimillion-dollar companies 24 hours a day, seven days a week, accessible by millions of people.

A HOME OF YOUR OWN: DO-IT-YOURSELF WEB PAGE DESIGN

The first thing you need is a Web site. Construction costs range from free to more than $1000 per year depending on the information included, complexity of design, and how long it takes you to learn to use an HTML (hypertext markup language) software editor such as "Page Spinner" (free) or Claris "Home," Adobe "Page Mill," Microsoft "FrontPage," etc.

There are plenty of Web designers for hire, but if you are a band on a shoestring budget, you will have to find an economical solution. Try to tap into the talents of your fans. See if there is someone who would like to help you create your band's site in exchange for a lifetime free pass to your shows and copies of your CDs. Look into art schools that have new media design or computer graphics programs. Students in these programs are often looking for opportunities to enhance their portfolios.

To design your own Web pages, you will need the following:

- A computer and a modem. Minimally, a Pentium II or PowerMac with at least a 28.8 Kbps (kilobytes per second) modem. Anything less powerful can make cruising the Web and downloading data feel like creeping in rush-hour traffic. The newer cable modems and DSLs (digital subscriber lines) are *very* fast so consider these more expensive options too.

- An HTML editor. A top-notch HTML editor software program will help you to give personality to the text of your Web page. HTML enables you to create links, fill-in forms and clickable images—all elements of a great Web page.

- A Web browser. Almost any browser will do—Netscape's, Microsoft's—even the ones built into the commercial online services, such as AOL or CompuServe. The only requirement is that the browser includes an option that allows you to view files stored on your computer's hard drive before you add them to your Web pages.

- Graphics software. Your Web page has to have attractive graphics to keep visitors. You either have to create them yourself or find a good clip art program. You need a graphic converter program, such as HiJaak Pro, to convert images into the GIF and JPEG formats that Web browsers use.

- A PPP or SLIP connection and server space. A point-to-point protocol (PPP) or serial line Internet protocol (SLIP) is your connection to the Internet's World Wide Web. You can obtain a SLIP or PPP connection through an Internet service provider, such as Earthlink, Netcom or AOL. This is the most expensive part of setting up your Web page, so shop around. These services can also provide server space for your home page. They thus become the "host" to you, the "client." Search out and critique potential hosts by using *www.budgetweb.com*. See below for more about site hosting.

- Domain name. Obtain your own domain name, such as MyCoolBand.com. It costs as little as $15 per year. Pick a domain name that your fans will be able to remember easily. Use the look-up feature at *www.internic.net* to verify that nobody else has taken your domain name.

- Find a host for your site. You can have your site hosted for free on a service like GeoCities *(http://geocities.yahoo.com/home)* or Excite's "Freetailer" *(http://freetailer.excite.com)*. Or you can pick a hosting company and pay them to host your domain. Fees range from $10 per month to $500 per month, and it is not always the case that higher-priced hosts are better. You just have to do a lot of homework to figure out which are good. Ask around.

One good way to find inexpensive providers is to use *www.budgetweb.com*. It provides all sorts of criteria to narrow your search. Features you definitely want are RealAudio and MP3 streaming (more on these later). Visit each of the suggested hosts and verify their price. Pay careful attention to the different packages they offer, since some of the low-end packages will not have all of the features you need. Find out if they have any music clients, then check out their Web sites and verify that their music servers are fast enough. Contact their clients, and see how satisfied they are.

There is a lot of help available to amateur Web page designers. A number of excellent shareware and freeware programs can be seen at *http://download.cnet.com*. You can learn a lot by seeing what other Webmasters are doing on their pages. Get involved in newsgroups and mailing lists, and utilize the resources mentioned in Hotwired's "Webmonkey" site *(http://hotwired.lycos.com/webmonkey)* to help you keep abreast of the developments in HTML authoring.

Essentially, there are two ways to deliver music on the Web. The first is to make your song into a downloadable file. There are four mail file types: WAV, AIFF, AU, and MPEG3 (a.k.a. as MP3). The sound quality for all file types is decent, but MP3 is practically CD quality. To convert your music to one of these files, use Cool Edit *(www.syntrillium.com)* or Sound Forge XP *(www.sonicfoundry.com)*. The downside of this method is the user has to wait to download the file, which takes a while.

You can stream your audio by using software like RealAudio, QuickTime3, LiquidAudio, or Netshow to avoid making the user wait. The sound quality will suffer slightly but the music starts to play immediately. Having *both* a streaming and a download option is the smartest approach.

Once you have finished designing your Web pages, you must transfer the files you created to your host's Web server. This means that your host opens an account on its file server for you. Then you use the Internet FTP (file transfer protocol) function to upload your Web-page files to the Internet provider's computer.

You can put your Web pages on other servers as well. The benefits of going with additional commercial music site providers are many: you get a built-in music-loving audience, Web design expertise (helpful for revisions), in-house familiarity with the online music market, and relatively inexpensive disk storage space for your data and sounds. You can compare prices for Web hosting at a site like *www.word.net/support/compare.htm.*

DESIGN TIPS FOR CREATING A GREAT WEB SITE

Get organized. Start visualizing your Web site before you ever turn on the computer. Think about what you want to put on your home page, what you want the visitor to get out of it, how the information will be presented, and how you want everything to look. Some Web experts recommend creating a storyboard or flowchart—small sketches of each page in outline form—before you start writing. I like to use a journey metaphor when designing. Take your visitor on a journey through your story.

Look at other Web sites. There is no sense in reinventing the wheel. Decide on which ones you like the best. What features make the site easy for you to use? What content appeals to you? What designs do you like? Select the best elements of your favorite sites and incorporate those features into your site. Be sure to bookmark (mark them in your Internet browser by using a command usually found under the "Bookmarks" or "Favorites" menu) so you have a reference. Put them in a separate bookmark folder.

Give people a reason to visit by providing content that is of value. For example, if you are an avid blues lover and want to create a Web page on that subject, tell visitors where the best blues clubs are in your area and provide directions. Pull people in with useful information.

Keep it simple. Your home page sets the tone to your Web site. The design should be bold and understandable at a glance. Avoid unnecessary details and overly complicated layouts.

Use imaginative layouts and attractive typography to give your Web pages a unique and memorable look. Make sure graphical content has practical value. Avoid pointless window dressing. Many users set their browsers to ignore graphics to save time; all they see is text. It is essential that any important messages and links in your graphics be duplicated in textual form. Test-drive your page in text-only mode to make sure it works. Create a text-only version for visitors that prefer this option.

Observe limitations. Many people have technologically challenged hardware. The World Wide Web becomes the World Wide Wait when huge graphics files are downloaded. Keep graphics to no more than 50K per graphic and your site will be a delight to visit.

Make it easy to navigate. The home page's primary role is to act as a navigational tool, which points people to the information stored on your Web site or elsewhere. Make this function as effortlessly as possible. Do not bury information in your page hierarchy. It is tedious to click through many links.

Include the essentials. Your home page should have a header that identifies your Web site clearly and unmistakably, an email address for communicating and reporting problems, copyright information as it applies to online content, and contact information, such as mailing address and phone number.

Make it fun. According to IntelliQuest, 56% of users return to entertaining sites, 54% like attention grabbing sites, 53% want extremely useful content, 45% want information tailored to their needs, 39% like imaginative sites, and 36% return to highly interactive sites.

Title your home page well. Use a headline that will attract viewers to your Web site. Many search engines use the title as the main way of selecting sites to show to requesters. The first paragraph of text after your title is also important, so be sure it contains keywords about the contents of your site. You should add proper titles to the rest of your pages as well. Follow the above principles for all your pages.

Go to Dr. HTML *(www2.imagiware.com/RxHTML)* a testing service that will test a single URL (Uniform Resource Locator—the address of a Web page) for free, and report to you on spelling, form structure, link verification, and other aspects of your Web page. Your entire site can be checked for a fee. That will cost about $25 per 50 pages, which is a good deal.

Keep it fresh. Users get bored if your Web site never changes. Encourage return visits by giving people something new on a regular basis. Include your Web site in your ongoing publicity program, so that new information (such as press releases) appears concurrently on your Web pages.

Remember that your visitors are coming in with different browsers, computers, platforms and modem speeds. You cannot please everyone, but you have only a few seconds to make your impression. Professional design, fast-loading pages and interesting content can mean the difference between a visitor that stays and one that clicks away.

ELEMENTS OF A SUCCESSFUL NET MARKETING PLAN

Okay, your Web site is ready and you understand how the various facets of the Net work. Now what? You have a rich choice of options for mounting a global presence on the Internet. You can—

- Get listed in all the free search engines and directories
- Communicate with your fans and collaborators
- Display an electronic press kit
- Share music downloads
- Sell and license music
- Have your music broadcast over Internet radio
- Webcast your shows via a virtual nightclub
- Build creative alliances
- Sign a deal with an online record label
- Build an informed music career with the Net's rich DIY library of music career guidance

But before launching into your Internet promotion options, let us lay some important groundwork. The Internet is not just a new medium, it is a new *kind* of medium, destined to surpass even television as a marketing tool. The net has the ability to reach targeted audiences quickly and efficiently, provide two-way interaction, and process sales transactions immediately, automatically.

With a Web site, your prospects are self-selecting. If you promote your site, and people are interested in what you are offering, they will come to you. Unlike a broadcast commercial or print ad, an Internet promotion can be tailored to the individual. A sophisticated Web site can actually generate a custom presentation on the spot based on the visitor's interests. This is called dynamic programming.

Remember that all marketing truths in the bricks-and-mortar world also apply on the Net. The core of your Internet marketing plan is understanding your customers. Get this right and you can carve out a successful business on the Web. Be careless in defining your customers, and you will doom your online marketing, no matter how much money you throw at it.

You should be able to answer the following questions clearly and concisely: What is your target audience? What is its age, media preferences and lifestyle? What is the size of your market? What are some subjects your audience would find interesting? It is also crucial to know what you are selling. Know your product and service inside and out. Break it down to its constituent parts. What style of music are you involved in? What differentiates your music, songs, performance, and talent from others?

When you have this critical knowledge, you can determine the ideal outlets for your marketing efforts on the Net.

The Net is a soft-sell medium. Unlike traditional media (TV, radio, magazines, etc.) that push information at us, the Internet pulls us in through the dimension of interactivity. While traditional media is unidirectional, the Net is bidirectional and, therefore, revolutionary. You can now communicate immediately with your fans and clients worldwide for pennies, without leaving your room.

However, since there are millions of Web sites, you must have an effective site that pulls people in with extra values and useful free stuff.

For example, if you are a rock band from Boston, instead of just promoting yourself and your CD, you could have interesting, hard-to-find information about Boston at your site (maybe a list of your favorite live music clubs and reasons why), or some Boston music trivia. Remember, people will check you out from all over the world and some inside information about Boston's music scene will be much appreciated by out-of-towners, as well as locals. You can also add value by sharing site space with an independent art gallery or artist collective. Photographers, painters, and graphic artists might appreciate the chance to enhance your site with their work.

Mobilize and encourage your friends and fans to be active on your behalf. Ask them to talk about your band in chat rooms and newsgroups, and on mailing lists and bulletin boards. Provide incentives to your active fans—free passes, CDs and T-shirts can go a long way towards building future support.

The Net also helps small and large music businesses run and promote their companies more effectively. Record labels, retailers, manufacturers and talent agencies use the Net to increase their customer bases and market their brands. The Web offers a powerful forum to dispense product and service information, raise awareness, and generate brand loyalty in a global and local environment. All kinds of music companies are learning that online marketing offers some significant advantages over traditional promotion dynamics:

- You are not limited by the expense of printing and postage, which makes online selling extremely economical.

- You can change your content quickly, easily, and at virtually no cost.

- An online catalog is easily searchable. All shoppers have to do is type in a keyword or two to get the information they want.

- Technology allows you to offer audio and video streaming with product demonstrations for deeper marketing.

- You can provide your customers with an essentially infinite amount of product information.

- The cost per exposure/per month is extremely reasonable compared to display ads and catalog mailings.

The Net is a great medium for providing customer service, dispensing company information and soliciting employees and interns. Any business with a mail-order component is especially well positioned for online success. If it will sell in a mail-order catalog, it will usually work online, if you target your market intelligently.

Get Listed in All the Free Search Engines and Directories

Search engines are large databases where most Web surfers go to when they want to research a new topic. This is the primary way that most people will find out about your site. Registration is usually free, but be sure to read the fine print!

Web search engines take anywhere from a few minutes to four weeks to list your site's home page, and up to six additional weeks to list the rest of your pages. In the preceding section on designing your Web site, I listed some design elements you can use to increase your rank in these search engine listings (such as titles, links, keywords at the beginning of your site, and the frequency of changes at your site).

Meta-tags are another tool you can use to obtain higher result rankings. Meta-tags are HTML commands that contain your keywords and thus help search engines categorize your Web site so that prospects can find your pages. Make sure you understand them and know their limitations, since they are the primary source that search engines read when indexing your Web site. Go to *www.promotionworld.com/tutorial/206.html* for a complete online tutorial of how meta-tags work.

Since search engines can list hundreds of thousands of pages in response to one query, it is important to do everything possible to increase your ranking (few people will look beyond the first 20 or so results listed in any Web search).

Submit your Web site to subject-specific search engines and directories. Check CNET's Search.Com *(www.search.com)*, which is actually a search engine of search engines, to discover industry-specific search

SEARCH ENGINES WHERE YOUR SITE SHOULD BE LISTED

- AltaVista *(www.altavista.com)*
- All the Web *(www.alltheweb.com)*
- Google *(www.google.com)*
- Hotbot *(http://hotbot.lycos.com)*
- NorthernLight *(www.northernlight.com)*
- Lycos *(www.lycos.com)*

engines and directories. The BigHub.com *(http://thebighub.net)* is another such search engine. Finally, search on "directories" and "indices" in the major search engines. Two examples of music-specific search engines and directories would be Music Industry Search Engine *(www.bandboard.net/html/music_search_engines.html)* and Sites & Sound Links *(http://myweb.servtech.com/~koberlan)*.

If your Web site serves the residents in a specific geographical area, you should register your site with a search engine that meets the needs of that area. For example, bands in Atlanta can submit their Web address to the Atlanta Web Ring *(http://blindslim.upyour.com/webring)*. This strategy can bring new fans and customers that are planning to vacation in your area, start a new business, or are searching for specialty items from your locale, to your site.

Search engine registration is an art in itself. For more information on designing your Web page for search engines, use the Search Engine Watch Web site *(www.searchenginewatch.com)*.

Communicating Via Email with Teammates and Fans

Email is the most universal application on the Internet. It is the first online tool people use. Studies show that almost twice as many people have access to email than to the Web. Email tools include forums, bulletin boards, chat rooms, newsgroups and mailing lists.

Consider these examples of email use in the music business:

- Artists and managers regularly use the Internet to announce new releases and tour itineraries. When a gig is added or canceled at the last minute, the email makes it possible to get the word out quickly.
- DJs post play lists to share with each other and record companies, get ideas for shows from each other, and discover artists and recordings they would not otherwise know about.
- Songwriters are collaborating via email by exchanging MIDI sound files.
- Musicians regularly put out barter calls for gear (e.g., an amp for a sequencer).

SPREAD YOUR NEWS

The Internet is a powerful dispenser of news and information. Electronic press releases often show up on electronic news networks that have large audiences. Try sending your news releases electronically to—

- Collegiate Presswire *(www.cpwire.com)*
- Eworldwire *(www.eworldwire.com)*
- News Bureau *(www.newsbureau.com)*
- Internet Wire *(www1.internetwire.com/iwire/home)*
- NetPOST *(www.netpost.com)*
- News Target *(www.newstarget.com)*
- Xpress Press *(www.xpresspress.com)*
- URL Wire *(www.urlwire.com)*

Every time a fan emails you, respond promptly. Be concise and polite. Offer (always ask for permission) to place their email addresses on a subscription list from your site only. Create a master list of your subscribers and periodically send messages about new music, shows, tours, and events that are posted on your site. Never sell or trade your email lists.

Displaying Your Electronic Press Kits

Press kit materials can be digitized for display on the Web. These can include your logo, photo gallery, CD artwork, bios, gig schedules, and industry and media reviews. Artists can broadcast sample sound clips of their songs, provide a guest book where visitors can sign in, and promote an email gateway to encourage communication.

Once your electronic press kit is designed, you will need a server to store it on so it can be seen. Most IPPs (Internet Presence Providers) have a server where you can upload your home page. Some IPPs can act as showcases for your work. For example, Indiespace *(www.indiespace.com)*, founded by independent musician and entrepreneur Jeannie Novak in January 1994, provides Web design, site hosting, online marketing, secure e-commerce, and career support services for independent musicians, artists, filmmakers, authors and performers.

Some cybershowcases model themselves after stores or malls: you bring the ready-made site; they supply the space. Others choose a magazine format. Still others seek to create the atmosphere of a club or other venue. But, do not just look at music or art-specific sites. The Internet enables cross-pollinations between different businesses and industries. Consider "lifestyle" Web sites your music relates to. If you play surf music, consider a surfing site. If you are a reggae act, try a Caribbean cruise line site. A world music act can link up with multicultural social organizations. The possibilities are endless.

The most important thing to look for in a host site is traffic. Fortunately, with the Internet you can know exactly how many times your page is seen. These viewings are called "hits" and a Web site's traffic is measured by how many hits it gets in a given day or week. But this can be deceiving. Some equate hits with people (unique visits) whereas in actuality a hit is a click, which is the action of clicking on an image or link on a Web page. Since most people average seven clicks per visit, the overall hits should be divided by at least this number to obtain a realistic measure of unique site traffic.

Some hosts provide fairly comprehensive online logs of site traffic so you can get a sense of visitor behavior at your site—how many visitors stop by, what countries they come from, which pages they go to most, how much time they spend there, etc.

When choosing a host site look for extra values—contests, promotional opportunities, cyberpublicity, order fulfillment, statistical reporting, helpful information, special programs—anything that will raise the profile of your site in that particular cyberspace.

Many other Web hosts offer free pages. Take advantage of all of them and spread your music around. Here are several more:

- Yahoo! Geocities *(http://us.geocities.yahoo.com/v/info.html)* includes 15 MB of disk space, access to Yahoo!PageBuilder (easy-to-use HTML editor), pre-designed templates, easy-to-install add-ons (e.g., feedback forms, streaming media, guest book, etc.), and you can update your page at any time.

- ArtistForum.com *(www.artistforum.com)* where for a $15 one-time setup fee (per title), you can sell your CD and they set you up with a free Web page. Each time your CD is sold, you collect the selling price minus $1 (administrative fee). You upload your own tracks, images, news and bio information.

- Net Colony *(www.netcolony.com)* offers free 100 MB of Web space, an easy-to-use homepage creator, your own messageboard, fast servers, and more.

SHARING DOWNLOADS AND SELLING CDS

The Net allows you to put your music in front of millions and millions of people easily and cheaply. This is done in three ways: song downloads, streaming audio, and selling physical CDs and tapes.

Downloads

A standard 28.8K modem can download a three-minute song in 12 minutes. A high-speed Net connection will do it in seconds.

MP3

MP3 is the common name for MPEG-1 (Motion Pictures Expert Group) Audio Layer 3, a form of sound compression approximately 12 times smaller than a CD file. It is a fast compression program; MP3 files can be sent and downloaded at a rate of 128Kbps.

MP3's use is not restricted to the Web. Anyone can make MP3 files from a CD through the use of software programs called rippers, which grab songs as WAV files (the default format for digital audio on Windows PCs) and encoders, which convert the tracks to MP3 format—or by using all-in-one MP3 players.

These characteristics, along with MP3's near CD-quality sound and free availability, have made the standard very popular.

Because MP3 files are small, they can easily be transferred across the Internet. MP3 files can also be downloaded repeatedly since the technology provides no encryption or security mechanism for copyright protection. Musicians are using this technology to distribute their songs from their Web sites to their listeners.

MP3 has several competitors including—

- Microsoft Windows Media *(www.microsoft.com/windows/windowsmedia/EN/default.asp)*
- Advanced Audio Coding *(www.aac-audio.com)*
- Lucent's Perceptual Audio Coder *(www.lucent.com)*

Getting Paid

All of this is very exciting for musicians, but they still need to generate revenue to sustain their careers. The Coalition for the Future of Music *(www.futureofmusic.com)* is in the vanguard of discovering ways for musicians to get paid in the online music environment. One idea they propose is an electronic tip jar where fans voluntarily make payments to musicians whose music they enjoy. Services like PayPal *(www.paypal.com)* and TipJar *(www.tipjar.com)* allow you to securely send money to any email user in the United States. After signing up, you simply enter the recipient's email address and a dollar amount. The money is charged to your credit card or bank account, and sent to the recipient.

MP3.com is another site that provides musicians with income based on the Web traffic they generate. Its "Payback for Playback" program awards nice monthly checks to bands and artists that have had a high number of song downloads. These payments have ranged from $2 to $12,000! EMusic.com and ARTISTdirect.com are among the other sites that have launched programs that include fifty-fifty profit sharing and giving artists a portion of ad revenue.

Streaming Audio

Streaming audio formats, such as those used by RealNetworks, Microsoft's NetShow and Macromedia's Shockwave, employ encoding techniques and players that allow the listener to play audio and video signals while they are simultaneously downloaded. Using a process called "buffering," the player downloads a small portion of the sound into the memory of the listener's computer before it begins playback. As the audio plays, the player continues to put some of the file in memory. If the file has been correctly encoded for the size of the listener's connection, and network traffic does not interrupt the stream, the listener experiences a smooth, broadcast quality transmission. Most streaming audio files do not require that special software be loaded on the host Web server. Specialized server software is required to serve archived audio to more than one listener at a time, or to stream real-time events.

There are two main types of streaming audio:

- On-demand: stored files
- Live: broadcasts of events as they happen

There are also closely related types of audio such as pseudostreaming audio (Apple QuickTime, Microsoft ActiveMovie), MIDI-streaming, and applications that combine audio and video.

For information about streaming audio, visit How to Set up Streaming Audio Files Without Using a Real Server (*www.extension.missouri.edu/webteam/tips/streamingaudio.html*).

PLACES TO UPLOAD MP3s

- AMP3.com (*www.amp3.com*)—Pays royalties to the artists.
- AudioSurge (*www.audiosurge.com*)—A free Web promotion resource for artists and musicians, free legal MP3s for download.
- The Global Muse (*www.theglobalmuse.com*)—Free promotion of independent artists' MP3s. Free MP3s.
- Mudhut.co.uk (*www.mudhut.co.uk*)—Virtual music community and MP3 e-tailer.
- Reckless Radio (*www.geocities.com/reckless_radio*)—A free MP3 site dedicated to providing bands and artists with an easy-to-use forum that allows their music to be heard by audiences they would not otherwise reach.
- Vitaminic (*www.vitaminic.com*)—MP3 community available in six languages. Promotes music on an international basis.

Selling CDs

Although the Web has changed the playing field of the music business, the game still revolves around selling CDs. Digital music formats like MP3, RealAudio, and other Web audio formats, are very much a part of the scene, but their place is mainly in the free samples department.

Online record stores have various distinct advantages over their traditional counterparts; since virtual shelf space is nearly unlimited, they do not have to restrict their stock to best-selling mainstream releases. Traditional record retailers have always lived by the 80/20 rule: 80% of your sales come from 20% of your stock: namely, new releases. On the Net, however, this rule does not hold. At this point, new releases account for only a small percentage of online sales.

Now you can make high-quality recordings with a moderate amount of equipment and market them to a worldwide audience cheaply and easily. Record some tracks on your computer, mix them down and burn a CD. Get an e-commerce-enabled Web site, and you are ready to sell your recordings to fans from Alaska to Zanzibar.

There are two ways to distribute your music on the Web—either through your own Web site, or through one of many existing music sites.

Online store setup ranges from fairly easy and inexpensive to very complicated with some hefty expenses. You can design a simple order form, which buyers print, fill out and mail in with their check or money order. Or, you can set up a secure ordering system that has a transaction processing system to accept credit card payments. The online form sends data to software, which authorizes the transaction and transmits the data to the bank. Some of these systems provide real-time authorization, while some just clear the transactions in a batch at the end of the day. Theoretically, a mail-order business does not need real-time authorization because if someone's credit card is refused, you do not ship their order. Some payment processing software systems require a certain amount of manual processing of orders, while systems like Authorize.net *(www.authorizenet.com)* automate the entire process for you.

Most musicians, however, will want to sidestep the e-commerce learning curve and piggyback on someone else's credit card setup. Yahoo and Amazon both offer deals by which a small merchant (you) can easily set up an online store, without having your own merchant account. You do not have to distribute your music on your own site at all. There are many sites that will do it for you.

If you already have national distribution, chances are your distributor is linked into online retail outlets. The main one-stop for distributors is Valley Media in California. It supplies all the big online retailers.

If you do not have national distribution, link with online retailers that specialize in niche music and indie labels.

ONLINE RETAIL OUTLETS

- Amazon.com *(www.amazon.com/advantage)*
- A&R Online *(www.aandronline.com)*
- CD Alley *(www.cdalley.com)*
- CD Baby *(www.cdbaby.com)*
- CD-Kiosk *(www.cd-kiosk.com)*
- GEMM *(www.gemm.com)*
- Guitar Music 9 *(www.guitar9.com/guitarmusic9)*
- IDN: Independent Distribution Network *(www.idnmusic.com)*
- The Orchard *(www.theorchard.com)*

For many other online record stores, go to CD Stores Online *(www.geocities.com/RodeoDrive/5860/index.html)*

LICENSING MUSIC

While most media attention has been on the consumer side of online music revolution, the professional, business-to-business (B2B) side has been quietly thriving. The B2B focus is on licensing music.

LicenseMusic *(www.licensemusic.com)* is an online music hub that licenses and downloads professional-quality digital music specifically for audiovisual production industries worldwide. It is one of several companies that are positioned as online music providers. Others include RedDotNet *(www.digitalon-demand.com)*, Beatnik *(www.beatnik.com)*, and The Music Bakery *(www.musicbakery.com)*.

These companies offer access to huge libraries of high-quality music to any professional that works in the creative industries anywhere, for a fraction of the cost and without any of the headaches, distribution hurdles, or budget uncertainties of hard-copy CDs. LicenseMusic even has an "Unsigned Artist Program" where it will make your music available for film, television and advertising. Visit *www.licensemusic.com* for details or send email to *unsigned@licensemusic.com*.

VIRTUAL NIGHTCLUBS

Cable modems and high-speed access are allowing more and more people to view Internet programming. Entire networks are now solely dedicated to digital entertainment. These companies produce original shows made specifically to be streamed over the Net.

Bands can set up in local venues and deliver their music to people over the Internet by using streaming audio. Concerts can be broadcast live, in real time, and be available for on-demand playback within 12 to 24 hours.

Webcasts can generate additional revenue streams through advertising. One of the first commercially successful music performance netcasts was the Tibetan Freedom concert in 1997. It had nearly 90,000 unique listeners, more than doubling the previous year's 35,000 listeners. This netcast generated more visitors online than attended the concert itself. As a result, producer SonicNet secured Levi Strauss as a $175,000 sponsor for its subsequent Supercast series.

Videoconferencing via the Net is now used by musicians in different locations to perform together live and transmit that performance to audiences at venues around the world.

GUIDE TO MUSIC VIDEO NETCASTERS

- 52media.com *(www.middlefingertech.com/52media/52.asp)*—Offers showcases, streaming audio and video, and webcasts for unsigned acts.
- CampusVibe.com *(www.campusvibe.com)*—Offers streaming media and video game-like experience by putting content and cameras in the hands of college students.
- IMNTV.com *(www.imntv.com)*—Promises national exposure for independent videos.
- Launch.com *(www.launch.com)*—The Net's most formidable music video alternative, direct competitor of MTV.
- MTV.com *(www.mtv.com)*—Offers snippets of videos formerly or currently in its broadcast playlist.
- MusicVideoParty.com *(www.musicvideoparty.com)*—Weekly broadcast focuses on independent video and live reviews.
- NetthisTV.com *(www.netthistv.com)*—Films live acoustic music performances in its Los Angeles studios.
- RollingStone.com *(www.rollingstone.com)*—Offers full-length videos from major artists.
- Sputnik7.com *(www.sputnik7.com)*—Provides online digital network streaming video stations, audio stations, videos on demand, and digital downloads.

As Internet technologies advance, video viewing will become a much richer experience. See the Guide to Music Video Netcasters on the previous page for possible outlets for your videos.

INTERNET RADIO

A quick search around the Internet yields thousands of radio streams, which range from online versions of popular offline broadcasts to commercial-free broadcasts that emanate from someone's kitchen. Thanks to very low or nonexistent setup costs, Net radio gives anyone with a record collection the opportunity to share it. You can listen to everything from high school football games in rural Texas to news broadcasts from the Indian subcontinent.

Anyone who has a computer can be a radio broadcaster with Net technology. Local stations are now transformed into global broadcasting powerhouses. The potential number of Web stations is exponentially greater than that of conventional radio.

You need Real Player, a technology developed by the Real Networks Corp. that enables audio signals to be streamed over the Internet, to listen to Web radio. Real Player is available free at *www.realplayer.com.*

Web radio has grown to more than 2000 stations. There are two kinds of Web radio, one is ordinary radio that is heard over the Net; the other is Internet-only radio. Since the former only broadcast online what they play on the air, getting airplay on them can be tough. But many of the Internet-only stations are small and less strictly formatted, and are more open to playing new music.

Many Net-only radio stations were founded on the idea of countering the trend toward less broadcast diversity. Web technology allows stations to offer niche programs. Some are homespun pirate stations or stations devoted to only one music style. Minneapolis-based NetRadio *(www.netradio.com)* delivers 120 audio channels including "Classic Crooners," "Lounge," "Alternative Country," "Quiet Classics," "Starstreams," "Smooth Urban Hits," "Groovin' 70s," etc. Programs run approximately one hour and change monthly. Information about featured artists can be found on the site, and they have an online CD store.

Streaming radio stations are all over the Internet. An excellent place to find mainstream options is at Yahoo! Radio *(http://radio.broadcast.com)*, and genre-specific choices at Spinner.com *(www.spinner.com)* and SonicNet *(www.radio.sonicnet.com)*

You need some specialized know-how and the right software to stream your own radio from your Web site. The main players in the streaming audio market are Real Audio *(www.realaudio.com)*, Shockwave *(www.macromedia.com/shockwave)* and Xing *(www.xingtech.com)*. Visit their sites to learn how you can put this technology to work for you.

Another program, Shoutcast *(www.shoutcast.com)*, is an MP3-based software technology from Nullsoft that allows anyone to easily start a radio station that will deliver music via streaming Internet audio—for free.

You can also send your CDs, tapes and MP3 files to many Internet broadcasters. Below is a list of Net-only stations that are open to receiving new music:

- Cyberville Radio *(www.cix.co.uk/~cyberville)*
- Hard Radio *(www.hardradio.com)*
- Premiere Radio *(www.premrad.com)*
- NetRadio *(www.netradio.com)*

- Radio Sonicnet *(www.radio.sonicnet.com)*
- TuneTo.com *(www.tuneto.com)*
- Underground Railroad Line *(www.hiphopmusic.com)*
- Virtual Radio *(www.virtualradio.com)*

For a continually updated list of Internet-only radio stations, go to the Internet Radio Index *(www.i-probe.com/i-probe/ip_radio_4.html)*.

Joint Ventures with Online Partners

A joint venture is when two or more businesses come together to work on a project for a set period of time. Online joint ventures can increase your sales and profits, save time and money, get valuable referrals, and increase your market visibility. There is strength in numbers and the Net is the great enabler of these creative partnerships.

Online joint ventures manifest in myriad ways. Here are seven possibilities to help get your creative juices flowing:

1. The simplest joint venture is the exchange of text links or banners (graphical advertisements) with other related Web sites.

2. Share a Web site with another business that has the same target market. You both market and advertise the same Web site, which means more traffic. For example, a jazz guitarist can share a Web site with a T-shirt company that specializes in jazzy designs.

3. Combine your products and services with another business into one big package. You could split the profits. For example, a band can team up with a catering company to offer a package of services for corporate party and event planners.

4. Offer a product or service as a free bonus with another business's product or service. For example, a new age artist could provide their CD to be used as a premium, to a company that sells aromatherapy products. In exchange, the artist could ask for a small portion of the profits and some advertising space on the company's Web site. Make sure, however, that you have the right kinds of controls in place to maximize results from your freebies.

5. Offer to insert a promotional ad for another business into your Web site. Pick a business that has an affinity to your style of music. If you are a country band, you can advertise a country music magazine or radio show. Ask them to do the same for your business.

6. Host a webcast show with another band. Include each other's promotional material on the Web site. Or partner with an ISP or multimedia start-up.

7. If you publish a band newsletter, consider trading some ad space with another non-competing company newsletter. Be sure the ally has some relationship to your music.

Joint ventures amplify your promotional efforts. You will discover many ideas to maximize your marketing with a little brainstorming.

Deals With Online Record Labels

There are scores of online (virtual) record labels. Some sell only physical CDs. Some only downloads, and a few sell only custom discs. Others offer various combinations of these three. These labels may also serve as distributors and retailers.

Online music labels often make big promises to new artists—wide exposure, an increased share of revenues and the freedom to create music without fear of meeting sales quotas. But do the pluses of recording for an online label make up for the minuses? Sites such as MP3.com seem to promote themselves more than the emerging artists whose music they offer.

Online labels turn away few artists, as opposed to the major labels that turn away just about everyone. But the big four recording companies are well-oiled publicity machines that manufacture as many lucrative hype opportunities as they do CDs. Ultimately, online music distributors will have to offer more than higher royalties to keep talented artists from bailing when traditional labels come calling.

Indiscriminate signings by online labels often lead to lower quality music. "There's a lot of crappy music on the Net [and] on our site," said Michael Robertson, of MP3.com, "but somebody has to make the choice. Should it be a record label or a consumer?" Robertson said he is signing up 100 bands a day to his D.A.M. online record label *(www.mp3.com/newartist/dam.html)*, which promotes physical CDs with free MP3 files and splits sales fifty-fifty with the artists. Online record label EMusic *(www.emusic.com)* signed artists Frank Black and They Might Be Giants to sell their downloadable tracks for 99¢ each or $8.99 an album in the MP3 format. Musicblitz *(www.musicblitz.com)* complements the traditional recording industry by enabling artists to record new music on a project-by-project basis. The company pays (after advances have been recouped) the artists, songwriters and producers a royalty each time the music funded by Musicblitz is downloaded.

Some feel that the digital record companies bear too close a resemblance to major labels. They sometimes demand exclusive multiyear deals, even though the technology is moving too fast for long-term commitments. Many artists are also concerned about the "cash-out" strategy a number of these companies may employ. Some companies create media buzz for themselves, splash the market with initial public offerings, and then sell out to megacorporations.

If you want to sign with an online record label, hire a music attorney to look over the contract just as you would if a traditional label offered you a deal. Be sure to ask the companies and your advisors the following questions as you assess options:

- How well-known is the label? Have you seen its name in the news? Are people talking about it?
- How will people find your music at the label's Web site? Look for smart navigational tools on the label's Web site so people can find you easily.
- What software is needed to access the site? Avoid sites that demand that the user download proprietary software in order to access its music holdings
- When will you be paid?
- What is the royalty rate? Do not accept anything below 50% of gross sales.

- How quickly can you terminate the contract, and does the label retain any rights over your music? This should require no more than a letter of termination. Never sign with a label that wants ownership of your masters.

- Does the label offer any extra values like affiliate programs, contests, etc. to drive more traffic to its site and more money into your pocket?

- Does the label require exclusive rights to anything? Most Net labels are nonexclusive and those that are exclusive must show good reason to be (for example, they are plugged into traditional radio and retail, have strong media presence, etc.).

- Is the site design consistent with your band's image?

- Does the label allow you to have your own Web site and domain name in addition to your page at their site?

ONLINE MUSIC DISTRIBUTION CONTRACTS

When artists make recordings available through online music distributors (OMDs), they are entering into contractual relationships.

The following should be considered when you enter into such a relationship:

- Avoid transferring ownership of recordings or songs contained on recordings.
- Avoid exclusive contracts that prevent you from distributing recordings through other sources.
- Keep the duration of the contract short, so you can end the relationship if it is not working out.
- You should receive at least 50% of the price of any CDs sold through the OMD.
- Although most OMDs do not pay any royalties on free downloads, some allocate a small portion of their advertising revenues among the artists whose recordings have been downloaded.
- Avoid OMDs that charge you for anything (Web page design, etc.).
- Make sure that you own or have permission to use all material you supply to the OMD (recordings, songs, artwork, etc.).
- Have realistic expectations. Do not expect to make much money. View OMDs primarily as a promotional tool.

David Moser, a Nashville-based entertainment attorney, and professor in Belmont University's Music Business program, contributed the above list. He is the author of a book on copyright law entitled *Music Copyright for the Millennium.*

- What does it cost you? A lot of labels have setup costs, but many sites are totally free.

- Have similar acts, already with the label, had much success with it?

Some other online record labels:

- AMP3.com *(www.amp3.com)*
- Amplified.com *(www.amplified.com)*
- EMusic.com *(www.emusic.com)*
- Epitonic *(www.epitonic.com)*
- J-Bird Records *(www.jbirdrecords.com)*
- Liquid Music Network *(www.liquidaudio.com/music/lmn)*
- Musicblitz *(www.musicblitz.com)*
- Musicmaker.com *(www.musicmaker.com)*

MUSIC CAREER GUIDANCE

The Web is rapidly becoming the preferred route for information publishing of all kinds. It is easy to use, brilliantly colorful, and anybody can contribute to it. There is dazzling variety, exponential growth, and the capacity for making connections around the globe.

Artists that have creative, financial, or political aversions to dealing with the music industry, or simply cannot attract music industry interest, use the Internet as a direct, uncompromised alternative to dealing with the major music companies. All they need are the right informational resources to put their dreams into action.

Music resources are abundant online. For example, a band can book its own tour by using a mapping site, such as MapQuest *(www.mapquest.com)* to plot the route, and then go to Ultimate Band List *(http://ubl.artistdirect.com)* and pull up promoters, radio stations, press contacts, and retail outlets by city, around the country, and around the world.

Knowing how to find information online is an acquired skill. It is helpful to begin searching with a human-constructed directory like *www.yahoo.com* or *www.about.com*. These services have already organized thousands of Web sites under topical headings. You can go to Yahoo > Entertainment > Music and locate thousands of music sites organized by category (Artists, Education, Industry Resources, Trivia, etc.). At About.com you will find the "Musician's Exchange," a rich repository of DIY information organized and edited by experts.

None of these sites are comprehensive so you will also need search engines to help you find information. These can be tricky and frustrating. Here are some techniques that produce better results:

Be specific: Do not type "drums;" type at least three words in your search, such as "1965 Gretsch jazz drum set."

Use "and" or "not." Adding "and" links two terms and focuses a search. Typing "not" narrows a search by excluding pages containing the second term. Some engines assume you mean "or" if you do not use a conjunction between words. "Or" expands the search and delivers sites that contain any of the words you have typed.

Use quotes. Most engines interpret quotes as "search only for sites with all words exactly as typed." So if you type, music business resources (without quotes) you will get results for every page in that search engine that has the word "music," "business," or "resources" on it. You will drown in results. The correct way to enter it is "music business resources."

Use directories. Directory search engines clump thousands of pages together under different categories, from "Old TV Shows" to "Wireless Communications." Use directories when you are looking for information on a general subject, such as "acoustic guitars," rather than for a specific site, like the Hillar's Classical Guitar page. Some directories such as Magellan *(www.mckinley.com)* offer site reviews. The most popular directory is Yahoo! *(www.yahoo.com)*, where sites are categorized into logical subsections.

Use indexes. When you need specific information on some obscure topic—and you want to blanket the entire Net—a search engine index is the best tool to use. Indexing engines use software programs called robots or spiders that comb the Web. They analyze millions of Internet pages and rank them according to the number of times a particular word appears. The biggest search engine is Digital's AltaVista *(www.altavista.com)*. But AltaVista's presentation leaves a lot to be desired. It is tricky to use properly and provides only poorly explained rules.

Do metasearches. These piggyback on other search engines. When you type a query, the software goes to several other engines and submits it to each, which provides more (and hopefully improved) results. Alltheweb.com *(www.alltheweb.com)* and Search.com *(www.search.com)* are examples of metasearch engines. Metacrawler *(www.metacrawler.com)* is one of the best. It submits your query to nine of the top search engines.

Use specialized search tools. Combing the entire Web does not necessarily turn up what you want. You may have to use a specialized directory that covers all the sites that relate to your particular topic. There are hundreds of such specialized directories. Find them by going to Search.com *(www.search.com)* and The BigHub.com *(http://thebighub.net)*.

EXPAND YOUR ONLINE PRESENCE

Join Banner and Link Exchanges

These services are typically free. The banner exchanges usually give banner impressions in return for impressions you produce for them. The ratios for the number of impressions you get for the number of impressions you generate vary from service to service.

To find out more about how these work, visit the following sites:

- Bpath *(www.bpath.com)*
- Exchange It! *(www.exchange-it.com)*
- Indie Link Exchange *(www.bigmeteor.com/ile)*

You can also exchange links with other sites without joining a service—link to some of the top sites in your category and ask them to link to you.

Join Web Rings

Web Rings allow you to join groups of Web sites that serve similar interests, trade visitors, and drive new traffic to your site. They allow visitors that are already interested in your site's subject matter to find your site easily.

To find out more go to—

- Indie Ring *(www.indiering.com)*
- Yahoo's list of Web Rings *(www.yahoo.com/Computers_and_Internet/Internet/World_Wide_Web/Searching_the_Web/Indices_to_Web_Documents/Rings)*

Start a Newsletter

A newsletter on your site is a great way to encourage repeat visitors. Have your fans enter their email addresses to subscribe. Make sure your newsletter contains useful information and updates.

Eventually your email list may grow too large for you to handle on your own. At this point, you may have it managed and maintained by any of several free services. Topica *(www.topica.com)* and Yahoo! Groups *(http://groups.yahoo.com)* are two examples.

USEFUL SITES

Music News and Internet Development

- Digital Mogul *(www.digitalmogul.com)*
- Digital Music Weekly *(www.digitalmusicweekly.com)*
- Fez Guys: Internet Audio Enlightenment *(www.fezguys.com)*
- Music Dish *(www.musicdish.com)*
- The Virtual Chronicle of the Digital Music Revolution *(www.virtualrecordings.com/mp3.htm)*
- Webnoize *(www.webnoize.com)*

Internet Stats and Surveys

- Cyber Dialogue *(www.cyberdialogue.com)*
- CyberAtlas *(www.cyberatlas.internet.com)*
- LivingInternet.com *(www.livinginternet.com)*
- Nua Internet Surveys *(www.nua.ie/surveys)*

Web Site Development Tools

- Annabella's HTML Help Guide *(www.geocities.com/~annabella/html.html)*
  Basic step-by-step tutorials.
- Great Web site Design Tips *(www.unplug.com/great)*
  Ideas for effective and quick Web site design.
- Network Solutions *(www.networksolutions.com)*
  The primary place to search and register domain names.
- WebDeveloper.com *(www.webdeveloper.com)*
  The one-stop shop for advice and tools for building better Web sites.
- Web Diner Inc. *(www.webdiner.com)*
  Tips and tutorials for beginners and intermediate Web page builders.
- Webmonkey: The Web Developer's Resource *(www.hotwired.lycos.com/webmonkey/index.html)*
  Intermediate-level resource for Web designers.

Web Site Maintenance Resources

- Internet Service Providers—Where to find ISPs *(http://the list.internet.com)*
- Web Host Providers—*(www.webhostlist.com)*
- Domain Name Registration—Network Solutions *(www.networksolutions.com)*

CONTINUED ON NEXT PAGE

CONTINUED FROM PREVIOUS PAGE

Online Business Development

- Idea Site for Business *(www.ideasiteforbusiness.com)*
- Ecommerce-Guide.com *(http://ecommerce.internet.com)*

Internet Promotion and Marketing

- ClickZ *(www.clickz.com)*
- eMarketing Digest *(www.webbers.com/emark)*
- Internet Marketing Center *(www.marketingtips.com)*
- VirtualPROMOTE *(www.virtualpromote.com)*
- Web Marketing Info Center *(www.wilsonweb.com/webmarket)*

Internet Radio

- NetRadio.com *(www.netradio.com)*
- radio-locator *(www.radio-locator.com)*
- Rolling Stone Radio *(www.rollingstone.com/radio)*
- Spinner.com *(www.spinner.com)*
- Yahoo! Radio *(http://radio.broadcast.com)*

Online Resources for Musicians

- Indie Centre *(www.indiecentre.com)*

  A well-organized site designed for musicians that want to release their own records and retain control of their own careers.
- Indie-Music.com *(www.indie-music.com)*

  Databases for radio, music press, venues, and much more. "Education" section is particularly illuminating.
- Musician's Assistance Site *(www.musicianassist.com)*

  A smorgasbord of online resources for developing artists.
- Music Business Solutions *(www.mbsolutions.com)*

  Site of author Peter Spellman, speaks to the career needs of music lovers that have entrepreneurial interests.
- Musician Online Services *(www.musicianservices.com)*

  Helpful guides for creating and promoting your online presence.
- Outer Sound *(www.outersound.com)*

  An online community established to promote music. Provides information, research tools, news, educational resources, and communication capabilities to help meet music and business needs.
- Ultimate Band List *(http://ubl.artistdirect.com)*

  One of the best databases of indie promo information on the Web.

Music Unions

BY JAMES A. SEDIVY AND GREGORY T. VICTOROFF

Unions have greater negotiating strength than individuals. A labor union is a group of people that have joined together to demand better pay and working conditions. A music union is a labor union whose membership is comprised of musicians. This chapter discusses many of the rules and benefits of the two major U.S. music unions, the American Federation of Musicians of the United States and Canada, AFL-CIO, CLC (AFM) and the American Federation of Television and Radio Artists, AFL-CIO (AFTRA). The American Guild of Musical Artists (AGMA) represents vocalists in the fields of opera, classical music and ballet. The Screen Actors Guild (SAG) represents vocalists that sing in theatrical motion pictures. These unions will not be reviewed in this chapter, although their addresses and phone numbers are included in the resource directory at the back of this book.

AFM

The AFM is one of the largest unions of performing artists, with over 250 Locals and more than 150,000 members.

AFM members are instrumentalists, leaders, contractors, orchestrators, copyists, music librarians, arrangers and proofreaders. They work in all mediums of music including, live performance, television, movies, etc.

AFTRA

AFTRA members are singers, sound effects artists, actors, announcers and narrators that work in radio, television and phonograph recording.

LOCALS

The AFM and AFTRA are comprised of local unions and governing organizations known as the International Executive Board (AFM) and the National Board (AFTRA). They grant charters to "locals" in certain geographic areas, like Los Angeles, Detroit or Nashville. AFTRA locals are usually referred to by the name of the community, whereas AFM locals are given numbers. Each local is basically autonomous and independent from other locals and the International Board or National Board, so some pay rates, such as live performance rates, and benefits vary from local to local.

SIGNATORY COMPANIES

Music employers, such as record companies and television and movie producers, negotiate contracts (agreements) with the AFM, AFTRA and SAG at two- to five-year intervals. A music employer who signs an agreement promises to hire only union members and provide at least the minimum pay and working conditions set forth in the agreement. The employer signing the agreement is called a signatory company. If you are a union member and are employed by a nonsignatory company, such as a small record label or nonunion bar or restaurant, you may be violating union rules and receiving less than union approved pay or scale. In so doing, you undermine the bargaining strength of the union and its members. Union locals can tell you whether or not your employer is a signatory company.

MEMBERSHIP BENEFITS

No union can promise professional success, especially in the highly competitive music industry, which is subject to ever changing tastes and trends. Nevertheless, union membership does offer certain opportunities for career advancement and some very real benefits. The most important of which is your eligibility for employment by signatory companies.

The benefits you get by joining a union depend on the strength of the particular union and local. For example, AFM Local 47 in Los Angeles provides job referrals for professional bands and musicians; death benefit group insurance; legal counsel and representation in grievance and arbitration proceedings; credit union membership; notary public service and business discounts; scholarship and awards programs; listings and information on agents, managers, record companies, casual leaders, nightclubs, studio contractors and community orchestras; club memberships, social activities and monthly membership meetings; a disabled musicians' fund; subscription to Local 47's monthly newspaper and International Musician, the AFM newspaper; a 24-hour telephone assistance line; contract preparation and consultation in areas concerning your musical career; free help wanted and audition notices; rehearsal space; and low-cost instrument insurance. If a person fails to pay you for your services, the union will attempt to collect your money without any cost to you. Also, through the Booking Agent Agreement, commissions charged by booking agents are limited to 15% to 20%. AFM Signatory Booking Agents that have negotiated an AFM Personal Management Agreement are allowed an additional commission of 5%.

RECORDING CONTRACTS

Another good reason to join a music union is a common provision in recording contracts between musicians and record companies that are signatories to AFM or AFTRA Agreements:

Artist represents that during the term of this recording agreement, Artist is and will remain or will promptly become and remain a member in good standing of any applicable guild and/or union to the extent that Company may legally require such membership. All applicable provisions of the collective bargaining Agreement to which Company is a party shall be deemed a part of this Agreement and shall be incorporated herein by reference.

This provision obligates a signatory record company to pay you at least minimum union pay or scale for recording sessions (as well as providing other benefits), after you become a union member.

AGREEMENTS

The following sections discuss most of the major AFM and AFTRA agreements that control phonograph recordings, movies, television, commercials and live performance. In calculating your minimum scale be sure to refer to the correct and current agreement. Also, the different payments for recording, production, sideline musicians, contractors, leaders, instrumentalists and vocalists are found in each agreement. Although these scales change periodically, many of the "terms of art" have the same meaning from one agreement to another. When an agreement expires and is not extended, the expired terms and conditions are usually followed until a new agreement can be negotiated and signed.

Much of the current information can be found online at *www.afm.org* and *www.aftra.org*.

Funds

In addition to pay scales, some union agreements also require employers to pay money to various funds. Depending on the particular fund, the money is used for pension, welfare and retirement benefits, payments to recording members, to members that perform in videos, and to members that perform free live concerts in parks, veterans' hospitals, schools and other public places.

Terms of Art

As with all professions, union musicians share certain terms of art: ordinary words that have special meanings, which derive from the various union agreements discussed in this chapter. Common terms of art used throughout the AFM Agreements follow:

Contractor

A contractor's duties are to locate and hire musicians for particular jobs. The contractor will prepare the contracts and make sure that they are filed with the union. A contractor need not be a musician, but must attend the engagement. Contractors may also be responsible for rehearsals.

Leader

When a musical group is hired one of the members is designated as the leader. The leader is responsible for the group and is the person who deals directly with the employer. The leader must file the contracts with the union and collect payment from the employer. If the leader fails to collect payment and fails to report the uncollected payment to the union, the leader is personally liable to the other union members for the uncollected amount.

Arranging

This is the art of preparing and adjusting an already written composition for presentation in other than its original form. This includes reharmonization, paraphrasing and/or development of a composition to fully present its melodic, harmonic and rhythmic structure.

Orchestrating

The orchestrator is the person who writes the musical score (a written musical composition that indicates the part to be performed by each voice and instrument) of an arrangement without changing or adding to the melodies, countermelodies, harmonies and rhythms.

AFM SCALE: RECORDINGS

One of the fundamental things a union does is establish minimum pay rates for its members. Remember that these rates are minimum and you are free to negotiate higher pay. Called "scales," "rates," "union fees," or "minimums," they all mean money paid to you (the member), at a variable minimum rate established in the applicable agreement. For the sake of consistency, throughout this article, these minimum payments will be called scales. Examples of the various scales appearing throughout this article are current only as of this writing and are included for illustrative purposes only and should not be relied upon. Always consult your local for current scale.

The AFM Phonograph Record Labor Agreement sets scale for instrumentalists, leaders, contractors, arrangers, orchestrators and copyists working in the phonograph recording industry. Vocalists are paid according to scales set by AFTRA. If you sing and play an instrument, you should join both unions.

Session Scales

For instrumentalists, leaders and contractors the AFM sets basic scale and overtime scale for regular sessions (three hours) and special sessions (one and one-half hours). You can also get premium scale for work done during specified holidays, at odd hours (between midnight and 8:00 a.m.), and after 1:00 p.m. on Saturdays and Sundays. The rates are different for symphonic and nonsymphonic work. As of this writing, the basic regular session scale is $302.85. Leaders and contractors get double scale.

Low-Budget Recordings

For full-length phonograph albums, but not including soundtrack or cast albums, with a recording cost budget of $90,000 or less, (not including producer or artist advances or travel expenses, rework and mastering costs) the minimum scale is $176.08.

Doubling, Cartage and Electronic Instruments

Additional payments may be paid if you play more than one instrument during a session. This is called doubling. If you play an electronic device to simulate sounds of instruments in addition to the normal sound of the instrument to which the electronic device is attached or applied, such use is treated as a double. For the first double you get an additional 20% of the applicable session scale, and 15% more for each additional double.

If you play multiple instruments within certain groups, such as the various components (bass drum, snare drum, cymbals, etc.) of a drummer's standard outfit, it is not considered doubling. These exceptions are specified in the AFM agreement.

You are also entitled to compensation for cartage (hauling) if an employer requires you to bring a heavy instrument to a session. If you bring a large or heavy piece of equipment, such as a harp, you are entitled to an additional $30. If you bring a string bass, tuba, drum set or amplifier you are entitled to an additional $12.

Orchestrators, etc.

Arrangers', orchestrators' and copyists' scales are set according to a detailed pay schedule based on the extent of the work done, per page or per line, or sometimes hourly.

For example, page rates for orchestrators depend on what they do: For transcribing a melody from voice, instrument or mechanical device, including chords, symbols and lyrics (one staff) an orchestrator gets $39.39 for the first page (up to 32 bars) and $28.14 for each additional page. Arrangers usually negotiate their own rates, which are to be no less than orchestrators' rates. Copyists get paid at least $20.30 per hour, or per page, according to certain detailed criteria set forth in the agreement.

Dubbing

The AFM discourages dubbing (using recordings not originally released in phonograph records [such as a film soundtrack] in a phonograph recording or using a recording made at an earlier time in a present recording). These rules relate to recordings that contain performances by persons covered by any AFM Phonograph Record Labor Agreement since January 1954. Dubbing is allowed where the record company notifies the union and pays the current scale to the artist who made the original recording that is being used.

Royalty Artists

When it comes to overdubbing, tracking, sweetening or playing multiple parts there are special provisions for "royalty artists." The AFM considers you a royalty artist if you record pursuant to a recording contract, which pays you royalties of at least 3% of the suggested retail price of records sold or, you are a member of a self-contained group of two or more, performing together in fields other than phonograph records under a group name (like a band or orchestra that performs live) and the group is under a recording agreement, which provides for a royalty payment of at least 3% of the suggested retail price of records sold. As a royalty artist, you receive the basic session rate per song for the first session at which you perform in respect to each song. This applies whether or not you play multiple parts, double, overdub or sweeten.

Sampling

Under certain circumstances, the AFM collects fees for its member musicians when a record company uses a sample of a preexisting recording in a new recording. When a portion of a recording containing the performance of an AFM member, who is a "nonroyalty artist" (i.e., a musician who plays on the recording but does not receive record royalties), not a self-contained royalty group or symphonic musician, is sampled under the following AFM definition, the company owning the recording that is being sampled makes a one-time lump sum payment of $400 for the first sample (regardless of how many times it is used in the new recording) and a one-time lump sum payment of $250 for each additional sample from the same recording, plus 2% of the gross revenue received by the company in excess of $25,000, less the lump sum payments that have already been made. These payments are made to the Phonograph Record Manufacturers' Special Payments Fund, and then distributed to the musician members. The AFM's definition of sampling is "a recording encoded into a digital sampler, computer, digital hard drive storage unit or other device for subsequent playback on a digital synthesizer or other playback device for use in another song (but not a remix or reedit of the new song)." Note that the definition includes not only samples embodied in traditional tapes and CDs, but also includes samples embodied on synthesizers, samplers, and other "playback devices."

Personal Services Contract

The AFM bylaws do not allow you to enter into any personal service contract (such as a recording contract) for any period of more than five years without the approval of the AFM. This is true even in states such as California, where the maximum length of a personal service contract is allowed, by law, to be longer.

Recoupable Payments

Most recording agreements allow record companies to recoup recording costs from artists' royalties. A record company may seek to include all payments made to the AFM as recoupable recording costs. However, payments made by the record company under the Phonographic Record Trust Agreement and Phonograph Record Manufacturers Special Fund Agreement, which are based on record sales, are not properly recoupable as recording costs.

Music Performance Trust Fund

The Phonographic Record Trust Agreement requires signatory record companies to pay the trustee of the agreement .20475% of the suggested retail price of records and tapes (to a maximum suggested retail price of $8.98) for each sold (or in the case of compact discs, a maximum retail price of $10.98). This money is used for the presentation of free live concerts in parks, veterans' hospitals, schools and other public places. During the fiscal year ending April 30, 2000, the Music Performance Trust Fund paid union musicians over $12 million to perform these concerts, making the AFM the largest employer of musicians in the world.

Phonographic Record Manufacturers Special Payments Fund Agreement (February 1999) (PRMSP Fund)

This agreement requires record companies to pay a small percentage of the price of each record sold (just under 6¢ for a top-priced CD) to the PRMSP Fund. The money in this fund is automatically paid annually, to members, in amounts determined by the number of union recording sessions each has played during the year. For example, during a recent fiscal year the Special Payments Fund distributed more than $9 million among approximately 26,000 recording musicians.

Video Promo Supplement

The Phonograph Record Labor Agreement also provides that musicians that appear in music videos be compensated when the video incorporates a recording produced by a signatory record company.

Musicians other than royalty artists that perform on camera are paid $215.87 per day.

If the record company receives money from the licensing, sale, or leasing of the video, the company pays the AFM 1% of revenues received after the company has recouped $75,000. This is distributed among all the musicians involved in producing the recording used in the video.

If the record company sells the video as a videodisc or videocassette in the consumer market, it must pay $500 to the AFM after the company has received $5,000 in revenues from sales. The $500 is considered an advance against the 1% payment revenue required after $75,000 is recouped.

AFM SCALE: MOVIES

The AFM Theatrical Motion Picture Agreement defines and sets different scales for recording, production and sideline musician members.

Recording Scale

If you play on the recording of a movie soundtrack, you are entitled to receive recording scale. The scale depends on the number of musicians employed, with the highest rate being for a group of 23 musicians or less. There are separate rates for single sessions (three hours or less) and double sessions (six hours or less) with overtime rates as well. You are also entitled to additional pay if you are asked to double. If there are 23 or fewer musicians employed, you get $265.09 for a single session and $530.18 for a double session.

Production Scale

Musicians are paid production scale when they perform at rehearsals for a movie. These musicians do not record on the soundtrack or appear on camera and are paid either single session or double session scale. Scales are quoted in the agreement for longer rehearsal periods of 30 or 40 hours per week. For a single session, $139.83; for a double session, $251.73. For a 30-hour week $1118.68; for a 40-hour week, $1342.42.

Sideline Scale

Sideline musicians appear on camera but do not record. The basic scale is $163.89 for up to eight hours. You are also paid extra for time spent in costume fittings, interviews, wardrobe and makeup and overtime in excess of eight hours.

Orchestrators, etc.

Scale for orchestrators, copyists, proofreaders and music librarians, per page, hourly and weekly, are set forth in the Theatrical Motion Picture Agreement. An orchestrator who writes a score page of not more than 13 lines is paid $23.91 per page.

Music Sound Consultant

If you are not a conductor, leader or contractor and are assigned by a producer to advise on the sound quality of the music being recorded you are entitled to $49.48 per hour.

Overscale Employees

By individual negotiations between you and a producer, it can be agreed that any payment you receive, which is in excess of the minimum scale, be applied to any of the minimum payments, premiums, allowance, doubling, penalties, overtime or other minimum requirements of the agreement.

Theatrical Motion Picture Special Payments Fund

This agreement requires a signatory movie producer to make residual payments to the AFM on behalf of musicians that perform on the film soundtrack. The producer must pay 1% to 1.66% of the accountable receipts from the exhibition of the motion picture on free television and supplemental markets (i.e., videocassettes, pay-type CATV, pay television) to the Theatrical Motion Picture Special Payments Fund. The administrator of the fund then pays members a percentage of these receipts based on a detailed formula set forth in the agreement.

AFM SCALE: TELEVISION

The AFM Television Videotape Agreement sets scale for network and syndicated television, both live and taped.

Types of Programs

In this agreement, the AFM sets rates according to the type and length of the television program. Signatory producers of 30-, 60- or 90-minute television programs, classified as variety programs, strip variety programs, nonprime-time children's variety shows, and other types, pay different rates to AFM members.

Recording Scale

You are entitled to recording scale if you actually play on the recording of the television program soundtrack. Scale is set according to the length of the program and session. For a 90-minute variety program, not a strip show (i.e., not a daily program like *The Tonight Show)*, such as a "Bob Hope Special," the scale is $545.75.

Production Scale

If you play for rehearsals only and do not record on the program's soundtrack and do not appear on camera, you are entitled to production scale. The hourly rate, for a minimum session of two hours is $63.60.

Orchestrators, etc.

Orchestrators and copyists are entitled to the per page or hourly scale set forth in the agreement. An orchestrator who writes a score page of not more than 10 lines is paid $24.38 per page.

Reuse Fees

The AFM Television Videotape Agreement also requires employers to pay reuse fees for reruns of programs. If a program is rerun in the United States or Canada, the instrumentalists, leader, contractor and music sound consultant receive 75% of the original scale payment for the second and third run; 50% for the fourth, fifth and sixth runs; 10% for the seventh run and 5% for each additional run. There are separate schedules covering payments for foreign broadcasts.

AFM SCALE: MOVIES MADE FOR TELEVISION

The AFM Television Film Labor Agreement sets rates for movies made for TV, situation comedies and dramatic series (e.g., *NYPD Blue)*. These programs are shot on film or tape and are broadcast on free commercial television first. As with the Basic Theatrical Motion Picture and Television Videotape Agreements, the TV Film Labor Agreement has separate wage scales for recording, production and sideline musicians, orchestrators, copyists and music librarians.

Recording Scale

If you play on the soundtrack recording of a program covered by this agreement, you are entitled to recording scale. For a single session of three hours, scale is $229.49. For a double session, $458.98.

Production Scale

If you play at rehearsals but are not recorded and do not appear on camera, you are entitled to receive nonrecording production scale. Scale for a single session (up to three hours) is $139.83. A double session (up to six hours) is $251.73.

Sideline Scale

If you appear on camera, but are not recorded, you are a sideline musician and are entitled to $163.89 for a session of up to eight hours.

Orchestrators, etc.

If you render services as an orchestrator, arranger, copyist, music librarian or proofreader on a TV movie, situation comedy or dramatic series you are entitled to minimum rates set forth in the agreement. An orchestrator who writes a score page of not more than 13 lines is paid $23.92 per page.

Television Film Producers Special Payments Fund

Residuals of 1% of producers' accountable receipts from the distributors of TV movies in supplemental markets (i.e., cassettes, pay-type Community Antenna Television System (CATV) and pay television) are paid by producers to the Motion Picture and Television Producers Special Payments Fund, which is distributed according to the formula set forth in the fund agreement.

BASIC CABLE TELEVISION AGREEMENT

This agreement covers exhibition of programs, other than by means of Standard television, pay television or CATV where no program charge is made other than the general cable charge. It provides rates for recording and production musicians, orchestrators, arrangers, copyists and music librarians, which are calculated in the same manner as the Television Film Agreement. For example, a one-hour variety program, other than a strip program, for a session of up to eight hours, the recording scale is $392.15.

AFM NONSTANDARD TELEVISION (PAY TELEVISION) AGREEMENT

This agreement covers pay or subscription TV, pay cable TV and closed circuit TV. It provides rates for recording and production musicians, orchestrators, arrangers, copyists and music librarians, which are calculated in the same manner as the Television and Videotape Agreement. For example, for a one-hour variety program, other than a strip program, for an eight-hour session, including four hours of rehearsal on the same day, the minimum recording scale is $441.35.

AFM NATIONAL PUBLIC TELEVISION AGREEMENT

This agreement sets minimum rates for the services of instrumentalists, leaders, contractors (varying as to the length of the program) and arrangers, orchestrators, copyists and librarians. An instrumentalist performing in one one-hour program is entitled to $153.23.

Supplemental Market Fees

All of the various television agreements call for supplemental market fees (i.e., cassettes, pay-type CATV, pay television and in-flight [commercial airlines, trains, ships and buses] exhibitions) and reuse fees.

Reuse payments must be made by signatory producers, to the AFM, for subsequent broadcast cycles. If a producer elects to pay the instrumentalist under the higher of two wage scales, the program may be exhibited for a longer initial release period. Following the initial release, the producer must pay reuse fees to the AFM, on behalf of the musicians. The exact amounts are calculated according to a formula set forth in the agreements.

AFM SCALE: COMMERCIALS

The AFM Television and Radio Commercial Announcements Agreement sets scales, which are usually paid by the signatory advertising agency making the commercial.

Session Scale

The Commercials Agreement calls for a minimum session for instrumentalists, leaders and contractors of one hour, during which three different commercial announcements may be recorded, the total length of which may not exceed three minutes. The maximum rate varies as to the number of musicians at the session. For example, for the minimum session, for one musician, you are entitled to $200, and if there are two to four musicians, $100. If, in addition to the normal sound of an instrument, an electronic device is used to simulate other instrumental sounds, such use shall be construed as a double, for which an additional 30% of the basic scale is paid for the first double and additional 15% of the base scale is paid for each additional double.

Reuse Fees

The initial scale payment allows the commercial's producer to broadcast the commercial by television or radio, but not both, during a period of 13 weeks from the date of first broadcast. Thereafter, you should be paid reuse fees for each additional 13-week cycle. The reuse fee for an instrumentalist who does not double, playing in a combo of two or more musicians, for a national broadcast, is $75.

Orchestrators, etc.

You are entitled to specific scale payments set forth in the agreement if you render services as an arranger, orchestrator, copyist or music librarian. An orchestrator who writes a score page of not more than 10 lines is paid $17.33 per page.

AFM SCALE: LIVE PERFORMANCE

The AFM represents instrumentalists and vocalists when they perform live concerts. The individual locals set minimum wage scales and working conditions for nightclubs, hotels and other venues where live music is performed.

Booking Agents Agreement

The AFM Booking Agents Agreement sets limits on the commissions agents may charge members for securing live performance engagements. Approved agent commissions range from 15% to 20% depending on the duration of the employment secured by the agent, provided your net pay, after deducting the agent's commission, is never below scale.

Union Form Contracts

Members are required to use union approved form contracts for their live performances. One advantage of using the union form contracts is the union contract provision requiring the concert promoter or venue owner to pay you interest and attorneys' fees in addition to other damages if you are not paid for your services or the contract is otherwise violated. In California, if you bring an action against a promoter for a breach of the contract and you lose, you will have to pay the promoter's attorneys' fees.

Recording or Broadcasting Prohibited

You are entitled to additional payments if your live performance is recorded (either on audio or video or both), or transmitted on television or radio. For this reason, no live performances may be recorded, reproduced or transmitted without making prior arrangements with the AFM.

Casuals

Casual engagements are one- or two-night performances. The locals negotiate minimum scale for rehearsals and various types of shows including, dance only; dance with an incidental act; show and dance; cocktail hour, tea dance, fashion shows; show with accompanying act; casual concert where admission is charged; and park concerts.

The scale is based on the number of musicians and length of show and includes payment by the employer to the union pension and welfare funds.

Continuous/Extended Engagements

The locals negotiate scale for musicians that are hired for extended live performances. There are separate scales for hotel nightclubs, freestanding nightclubs, and beer and wine establishments. Within each of these scale structures the pay is based upon the number of days per week you perform, the length of each performance and the number of musicians.

Arbitration

The union form contract provides that if any dispute or claim arises out of the engagement covered by the contract, the parties shall submit the matter to either the local's trial board or to an arbitrator who is picked by the parties. In a California lawsuit between Bill Graham, a concert promoter, and Leon Russell, a performer, the court ruled that union arbitration provisions must provide the parties with an opportunity to obtain an unbiased and neutral arbitrator.

AFM: NEW TECHNOLOGIES

The AFM has addressed the services of its members in new technology formats is several ways. As a side letter to the Phonograph Record Labor Agreement, the AFM and Signatory Companies have agreed to negotiate any disputes relating to payments that are due to musicians with respect to recordings that are digitally distributed (e.g. downloading) via online computer services, the Internet, satellite or otherwise.

The AFM also requires that companies enter into a special agreement when its members provide services in the production of CD-ROMs, DVDs, theme and menu music on Web sites, online services, interactive cable stations, virtual reality rides, live performances on the Internet, commercials on the Internet and use on enhanced CDs and CD-Plus.

AFM MEMBERSHIP

If you play a musical instrument of any kind or are a vocalist or render musical services for pay, you are classified as a professional musician and you are eligible for membership in the AFM. You may apply for membership in any local in the area where you live.

Initiation Fees

You must pay initiation fees to both the AFM local and to the International Federation. Each local sets its own initiation fee and the International Federation's fee varies according to the amount of the local's fee. You pay the total initiation fees to the local.

Indoctrination

When you apply for AFM membership you must participate in an indoctrination procedure administered by the local. This will introduce you to the rules and benefits of the AFM. The local also holds an examination meeting in which the applicant will be asked for further information about his or her musical education and proficiency. No auditions are required.

Dues-Periodic

You are required to pay annual or semiannual dues to the local and the Federation. For Local 47 the rates are $162 per year or $84 semiannually. These payments include AFM dues. The dues for Local 47 include death benefit group insurance.

Work Dues

You must pay work dues based on your total earnings for all musical services performed. Upon joining the AFM, you must authorize all employers to deduct from your pay the work dues owed, and to remit that amount to your local.

Work dues for Local 47 are 3% of scale wages for live performances. If services are rendered for any of the various recording sessions (i.e., phonorecord, television, motion picture) the work dues are 4% of scale wages.

If the musician is a traveling member (member of another local), the work dues are paid to the AFM, not to the local where the work took place.

Health and Welfare Funds

Locals use Health and Welfare Funds to provide health insurance benefits for members. To be eligible for these benefits, a total of $400 must be contributed to the Fund by your employers every six months.

Employers Pension and Welfare Fund, Strike Fund

Members can also participate in a Employers Pension and Welfare Fund. The AFM also maintains a strike fund for its members, should it be necessary for the union to call a strike.

Fines, Defaulters List

Members are not allowed to render services for an employer on the AFM's Defaulters List. It is also improper for members to record or perform for a company that is not a signatory to the AFM Agreement. The union feels that musicians that play for defaulters condone unfair practices and undermine the bargaining power of the union and its members. Also, an AFM member is not permitted to render musical services outside of

Canada or the United States, or their territories or possessions, without the approval of the union.

AFTRA SCALE: RECORDINGS

AFTRA Code of Fair Practice for Sound Recordings sets the following scales for the recording industry.

Hourly and Side Scale

Scale under this agreement is determined per hour or per side, whichever is greater. A side is defined as one song or a bona fide medley on a single record not exceeding three and one-half minutes, and for each 60-second portion thereof over three and one-half minutes playing time, an additional 50% of the applicable per side unit is paid. For soloists and duos, the minimum scale is $157.25 per person per hour or side, whichever is greater.

Solo and Group Scale

The individual scale is the same for soloists and duos but is lower for groups of three or more singers. If, however, as a singer in a group of three or more vocalists, you step out and sing 16 or more cumulative bars on a particular side, you are paid at the soloist and duo scale. There are separate scales for vocalists that make classical recordings or original cast show albums.

Dubbing

Under AFTRA rules dubbing is allowed when the record company notifies AFTRA and pays scale to the artists that were involved in making the original recording. The company must also obtain the written consent of any star, featured or overscale artist.

Royalty Artists

The minimum rates mandated by AFTRA are payable even if you are a royalty artist. AFTRA considers you a royalty artist if your recording contract pays you record royalties. As a royalty artist you are not entitled to more than three times the minimum scale per side.

AFTRA SCALE: TELEVISION

AFTRA National Code of Fair Practice for Network Television Broadcasting Agreement sets rates for AFTRA members' services in the television industry.

Solo or Group Scale

The AFTRA Code sets different wage rates for soloists, duos and chorus singers. (An example is in the following paragraph.)

Program Scale

The scale increases for programs with a longer running time. Another variable affecting scale is whether the program is a single performance or multiple performances during a calendar week. The specific scale varies for work that is done on camera, or off camera, and whether or not the program is a dramatic prime time program. For instance, if you sing on camera, in a group of three to eight singers, in a 30- to 60-minute prime-time dramatic program, you are entitled to a program fee of $556 per person for a minimum session of three hours.

Replay Fees

For the first and second network replay, you are paid 75% of the applicable minimum program fee plus 20% of the rehearsal and doubling fees for programs originally telecast after November 16, 1976. For all other replays you are paid 75% of the applicable basic minimum program fee for the first and second replay; 50% for the third, fourth and fifth replays, 10% for the sixth replay and 5% for each replay thereafter.

Supplemental Market Fees

Supplemental market fees must be paid by the producer of a program when the program is exhibited on pay television, basic cable or in-flight. The producer pays 2% of the distributor's gross receipts in the supplemental markets. This 2% is paid for the benefit of all performers, except walk-ons and extras. If the program is a network prime time dramatic program produced after July 1, 1983, the producer pays 3.6% of the distributor's gross receipts, rather than 2%. You will receive your portion of these payments directly from the producer or the producer will deposit the fees with AFTRA for distribution to you.

AFTRA SCALE: TELEVISION COMMERCIALS

Signatories to the AFTRA 1997 Television Recorded Commercials Agreement pay the following fees for commercials:

Session Scale

Session scale is based on an eight-hour day. Scale varies for soloists and duos and groups of different sizes when you work on camera. If you work off camera, the minimum session scale is for two hours. For a solo or duo, the off-camera scale for a single two-hour session is currently $359.95.

Use Scale

Scale for use of program commercials is divided into classes, according to the number of cities in which it is telecast, (class C is one to five cities, class B is six to 20 cities, class A is over 20 cities.) New York, Chicago and Los Angeles each count as 11 cities.

Principals, Group Rates

Use payments for each class have separate scales for principal performers and group performers and within each of those scales are different rates for on-camera and off-camera performances, each time the commercial is used. For example, if you are an off-camera solo vocalist, your session fee may include payment for the first class A use. For the second class A use, you get an additional $96. For the third through the 13th uses you receive $76.35 each, thereafter you are entitled to $34.65 for each additional use.

AFTRA SCALE: RADIO COMMERCIALS

Signatories to the 1997 AFTRA Radio Recorded Commercials Agreement pay for sessions of 90 minutes in duration. Reuse fees under this agreement are affected by many variables, including special scale for wild spots, dealer commercials, network program commercials, regional and network program commercials, single market commercials and foreign uses. Scales are determined according to complex formulas set forth in the agreement.

AFTRA MEMBERSHIP

You are eligible for AFTRA membership if you have performed or intend to perform as a singer in the fields of radio, television or phonograph recording. AFTRA does not regulate the musical services of its members outside the United States.

Initiation Fees

AFTRA imposes a uniform initiation fee of $1,000, however, this need not be paid when you first work. You have 30 days from your first engagement before the initiation fee and dues are payable.

Dues

Dues are payable semiannually. Each member pays base dues of $58 every six months plus additional amounts based on the performer's gross earnings under AFTRA's jurisdiction for the previous year.

Other AFTRA Benefits

Benefits of the AFTRA Health Fund are available if you have $7,500 in earnings within AFTRA's jurisdiction, during four or fewer consecutive calendar quarters. This fund includes life insurance, accidental death insurance and medical insurance.

The AFTRA Pension Fund provides benefits determined by the number of years you are active with AFTRA and your earnings during those years.

A credit union is also available to AFTRA members.

Discipline

As an AFTRA member, if you violate union rules, you may be disciplined by means of fine, suspension or expulsion from the union.

AFTRA: NEW TECHNOLOGIES

In keeping pace with ever changing technology, AFTRA has recently negotiated an agreement relating to services rendered in the production of interactive programs, the 1999-2000 AFTRA Interactive Media Agreement.

CONCLUSION

For a union to be successful, its members must respect its rules. By reporting unfair practices and conscientiously participating in union activities and elections you help protect other union members and, to an extent, you exercise a degree of control over how the union represents you and protects your interests. The complex array of union scales and payments for royalties, reuses and supplemental markets, were not guaranteed to musicians by employers out of friendship. Unions organized and fought for these payments. As long as enthusiastic and ethical professionals are involved in unions, they will help to ensure fair treatment for all musicians.

Managers and Agents

WHAT A MANAGER DOES

ANALYSIS OF A PERSONAL MANAGEMENT AGREEMENT

TALENT AGENCIES

BUSINESS MANAGERS

What a Manager Does

BY ALFRED SCHLESINGER

Let us say you are an artist who says to a prospective manager, "OK, I'm a talent, this is what I look like, here is what I do. Are you interested?" And the manager says "Yes!"

First, your manager will probably say to you, "Look, all of our energies have to go toward getting a record contract. Anything else we do is avoiding the main issue. You are not going to make it, you are not going to become a star, you will not make good money and nothing monumental will happen to you as a musical performer without a record. Let's get a record contract!"

This is still true in the era of the Internet, inasmuch as you have to look upon Internet sites as retail stores. It is quite simple to have your own Web site, as well as a number of links. But in order to have someone choose your record and have it move off the Internet "shelf," as opposed to the many thousands of others offered on the Internet, the demand for your record must be created by extensive promotion and marketing. That is where the record company machinery is needed.

WHAT TO LOOK FOR IN A MANAGER

The manager, whether an individual or a company, must have honesty and integrity, knowledge and capability. If any one of these attributes is missing, the manager will not be effective.

Your manager represents, advises and works for you. This person or organization handles all of your day-to-day business while you create, and for that receives a percentage of your earnings. If you make money, your manager makes money. If not, your manager will have spent an awful lot of time and effort for nothing.

When considering managers, check out their reputations. People have reputations because they have earned them. Nobody can be liked by everybody, but if a person is spoken of as being genuine and honest, you can assume this is probably true.

However, a good reputation means nothing unless there is a trust and good feeling between artist and manager. I do not see how anyone can have a personal manager they dislike.

The manager's enthusiasm and belief in you are essential for a successful relationship. A manager cannot and should not represent you if he or she does not understand your motives, priorities, beliefs, way of life, and what is important to you.

The personality of the manager must be considered. Some managers can break down doors (literally and figuratively), scream, holler, demand and be very effective. Some artists like that, others might want someone more laid back. The object is to enable the artist to write, rehearse and perform; to create with a free and clear mind. The idea is not, however, to remove artists from business entirely, but rather to free them from the nitty-gritty work-a-day affairs. Artists should know what is going on with their careers and be familiar with the agent, record company personnel, business manager, attorney, public relations people, and whoever else has a hand in their success or failure. Managing an artist is a difficult, time consuming job; artists choosing to do it for themselves will have great difficulty finding time to create music and run their business.

THE MANAGER'S ROLE

A manager provides knowledge, judgment and objectivity in the following key areas:

Record Companies

It is a manager's job to know the record companies and the people at those companies. It is up to the manager to know the strengths and weaknesses of each company and whether a company is right for his or her artist. Some companies do extremely well in one genre of music and are unsuccessful in others. Since distribution is of primary importance, the manager will normally look for a deal with a major record company (one that has its own distribution branches), an affiliate of a major, or an independent record company distributed by a major. (Another option is to sign with an independent record company that is distributed by a successful national distributor).

The record companies usually want to hear a tape of the artist performing three or four songs, as well as see the artist perform live before they will consider signing that artist. It is up to the manager to make sure that the demo tape shows the artist's direction and makes a statement about the artist's music. The manager also has to make sure that the artist's live performance will grab an audience. Since touring is the best promotion for an artist's album, and there is a definite correlation between touring and record sales, the record company will normally not sign an artist unless the live performance will greatly help record sales.

Once the record deal has been made, the manager will often play an important role in the selection of the producer. The manager will also be heavily involved in the artwork that is going to be part of the package. Artwork is critical to the artist, as it portrays the image of the artist in an "image" business. The album artwork is also used in advertising, as poster art and on all types of merchandise, such as T-shirts and jackets. Prior to the release of an album, and until the album has run its course, the manager will be in constant contact with the promotion and marketing departments of the record company and the distribution branches to make certain his or her artist is being properly promoted and marketed.

Scheduling

It is important for a manager to help schedule an artist's life by structuring recording and performing contracts appropriately. Some performers want to schedule 16 months of activity into a year. There is no way that can be done. A manager has to help the artist plan ahead, sometimes a year or more at a time. Time should be set aside for creative activity, vacation, recording and for touring. To help do that, the manager has to be very sensitive to the artist's habits and needs. For example, if the artist is a songwriter, the manager must realize that songs take a certain amount of time to produce. It is difficult for some artists to write songs while recording, while on the road, or on vacation. It is important to set aside enough time out of the year for this kind of creativity.

Recording Habits

A manager must understand the artist's recording habits and should know how long a recording is likely to take. Some artists can spend two days at a recording studio and come out with 10 tracks for a flawless, marvelous album. Others will take up to 18 months in the studio. One of the most devastating things that can happen to a recording artist is having a manager obtain a very heavy commitment from a record company to release a certain number of albums in a short period of time when the artist cannot handle that many albums or that kind of pressure. That contract can wind up lasting for most of the recording artist's professional life.

For example, you could be committed to deliver one album a year for seven years. If it takes 18 months to deliver each album, you could actually be under contract to that record company for more than 10 years.

Objectivity

One reason artists need help in all these areas is that they often lack objectivity. The manager provides objectivity.

Most people in the business are reasonably sensitive. They will never tell an artist, "I hated your last album, it stunk." A record company executive may sugarcoat remarks to an artist, but will level with the manager. Then it is the job of the manager to get the story across to the artist.

The artist who deals directly with this sort of feedback from a record company is making a serious error. Show business is an image business. A great deal of time, effort and money is spent to create the artist's image. It can be very damaging to an artist to do battle. The artist should always be the hero. The manager should always be the scapegoat. If, as sometimes happens, bad feeling is created, the artist should never suffer by it.

THE RECORDING TEAM

The manager's role in the successful negotiation of a recording contract is only the beginning. With the signing of the contract, the manager becomes the captain of an incredibly varied team of people, both inside and outside of the record company. Managers work with these people on behalf of artists.

Record Company

The most important of all the relationships an artist maintains (after his or her personal manager) is with the record company. It can be the artist's best friend or worst enemy. If the record company is not with the artist all the way, the artist's career is definitely going to suffer delays and setbacks.

A manager has to have a lot of insight concerning the people within the record company. It is important to keep them friendly and committed to furthering the artist's career.

If the president of the record company is behind a record, that album has a much greater chance of "happening." A manager must have access to the top people and be able to gain their support.

Artist Relations

The artist relations person, a creative, very important member of the team, takes the artist's part and stands up for the artist in the company (even though that person is employed by the company). The artist relations person introduces the artist and manager to other employees in the record company, and acts as a general communications liaison and information resource.

Promotion Representative

The national promotion representative does all the long-distance calling to the key top-40 radio markets and has a feel for what is happening in the field. Remember, airplay is absolutely essential for success.

Sales and Marketing

The head of sales and marketing helps choose the sales tools that supplement live performances and airplay. These tools range from store displays and merchandising accessories to ads in Sunday supplements, co-op deals with leading record dealers, radio time, etc.

Relationships should be maintained with local sales and promotion representatives that can help get that important extra push.

At the appropriate time, the manager will want to work with the person in charge of international sales and promotion to help set up foreign tours and release records in other countries.

RECORD RELEASES

Normally, an album is released within 90 to 120 days after delivery of the master recordings, plus all of the information (such as writers, publishers and length of each recording), album credits (such as name of producer(s), engineer(s), musicians, vocalists, studios where the album was recorded and mixed) and personal "thanks" (such as to a manager, attorney, accountant, family members, friends and inspirational third parties). Neither the manager nor the record company will want an album of a new artist released after September, since it normally takes several months for an album to build, both at radio and retail. Once Thanksgiving arrives, the building process usually comes to a halt, and any momentum gained can be blunted during the Christmas season, when radio adds fewer records to its playlist and retailers want to concentrate their efforts on the hits of major artists. The airwaves and retailers' shelves are crowded with Christmas music. Traditionally, the "heavy" albums are released when kids are going back to school and at the beginning of the year. But except for the months of October through December, an album can be released any time of the year.

Some managers will want their artist's album to be released at the same time the record company releases albums by a number of their major artists, hoping to be carried along with the tide. Most managers, however, look for that small window when their artist's album will be the only one to be released for a period of time, so the record company can concentrate their promotional and marketing efforts on it.

With respect to "singles" or album "tracks," managers' opinions differ. Some managers will urge the record company to release the first single of their new artist a number of weeks before the album, in order for the public to become somewhat familiar with the artist and also because the single may chart, either on radio playlists or on the *Billboard* or *Radio and Records (R&R)* charts. Other managers feel that it is a waste to have a single being played on radio without the listener being able to buy the album, so they will want a single released concurrent with the album. Still others feel that it is difficult for the manager or record company to determine which is the best single, so they allow radio program directors and disc jockeys to determine what the single will be by their decisions as to what to program.

TOURING

Touring by an artist is the record company's best way to promote that artist's album. The public may buy your first album based on the music alone, but after that they want to see your face, learn about you, and equate what they hear on the album with a live human being. Your manager should know what you can handle as far as touring is concerned and find a balance between sufficient touring and your other obligations. (It should be noted that a successful artist will tour overseas, and many artists earn more by playing dates in foreign countries, and have much longer careers overseas than in the United States.)

Managers differ on appropriate times to tour. Some managers want their artists to tour extensively, even without a record deal, feeling that the artist will be building a base of fans, as well as perfecting their live performance. Other managers will want an artist to begin touring immediately after the release of an album, to support that album. Still other managers will not be anxious to have their artist tour unless and until an album is either on the Billboard charts or showing some sales strength in some markets. If the manager wants the record company to help defray the cost of touring with so-called tour support (making up the deficit between what it costs to have an artist on tour and the small nightly fees that are normally commanded on a first tour), an album usually has to show signs of being a winner.

At the appropriate time, the manager will meet with the record company and the agent to help put a tour together. The record company can provide the manager with sales figures showing the markets in which the album is performing the best. The manager will work with the agent in putting a tour together that encompasses those markets. (On a first tour, the agent will include spots for the artist as an opening act for major record sellers, some small theaters, colleges and clubs.)

MANAGEMENT ORGANIZATIONS

There are one-person firms and small and large organizations. A one-person organization has its limitations because a manager cannot always be supported by one talent and probably will manage other clients. But a good manager will not take on more clients than can be served effectively.

Some management companies consist of more than one person with others working for them. Selecting a large company like this can be a mistake for a young performer. An artist might think, "John/Jane Doe who runs this organization is the heaviest manager in the business and I'm going to get Doe's personal attention." Usually this does not happen. They get the services of someone who works for the firm instead of those of the top person. This is not necessarily bad if the right relationship is established with this person, and the muscle of a large organization is behind the artist.

But if you sign a contract thinking that Ms. A will be representing you, only to find after six months or so that you are dealing with Mr. B, you should be able to terminate the contract.

Again, it depends on feelings. Many performers enter the offices of a large organization and immediately turn and walk out. They do not feel comfortable and do not want to get involved with a machine, no matter how well oiled.

MANAGEMENT CONTRACTS

If something is important to you, get it in the contract. If a manager will not put a provision in writing, then the manager probably has no intention of living up to it.

Term of Contract

Management contracts vary in term from one to five years. What is important here is for the artist to decide what goals should be reached and in what time frame. Some contracts state that if the artist does not have a recording contract in one year, he or she can terminate; another might require two network variety performances in the first year. If the manager agrees, those terms should be put into the contract.

The artist should understand that a manager needs a fair length of time to help an artist towards success. It sometimes takes two years or more before an artist starts to make any real money. It would be unfair for a hardworking, honest and reasonably effective manager to be terminated at the end of a year after laying the groundwork and not be around to collect the rewards. Artists must be realistic about the time in which they can expect to reach their goals.

Unfortunately, there are rarely outs in contracts for someone who no longer loves their manager. Personal relationships are so important, yet quite hard to define on paper. It is very difficult to frame a contract that states, "Notwithstanding the fact that we have a five-year contract, if at any time during that contract I don't like you, I can terminate."

Power of Attorney

In standard management contracts, managers are given a blanket power of attorney, meaning that they can sign and approve anything regarding the artist's career without the consent or knowledge of the artist. Certainly, artists should work to limit that power if they are available to sign; or at least specify the circumstances under which the manager has that power, e.g., not being able to sign for engagements longer than a certain period of time or for a certain amount of money. At the very least, artists can have clauses requiring consultation and approval, if only verbal, before the manager signs anything on their behalf.

Normally, a manager makes day-to-day decisions, but leaves major ones open for discussion and consultation. But artist and manager should develop a modus operandi, and an understanding of what can be done without consultation.

Percentages and Expenses

Manager percentages usually fall between 15% and 20%, although there are exceptions. For instance, a manager who invests large sums of money in an artist, at a risk, might receive 25%.

In standard contracts, the manager is not specifically obligated to advance or lend money, but many artists expect it. If a manager does advance money, the artist must repay it.

Sometimes a manager is excluded from receiving percentage commissions on publishing, songwriting or monies from ASCAP, BMI or recording, etc. My feeling is that managers promote all their artists' causes and, if you limit their income, you may find it detrimental in the long run.

Costs incurred on behalf of the artist by the manager (other than normal overhead) should be paid by the artist. These include travel, phone calls, publicity photographs, etc.

Many artists include clauses in their management contracts limiting the circumstances and amounts that a manager can spend without their consent.

CONCLUSION

The results of a manager's efforts are not realized in days or weeks, they accumulate over a period of years.

The manager's job is multifaceted: administrator, friend, salesperson, employer, negotiator, advisor. In any one day the manager may need to effectively communicate with a record company president, bartender, road manager, lead guitarist's girlfriend, lawyer, journalist, disc jockey, record producer, food caterer, etc.

Finding a competent, knowledgeable manager at the beginning of an artist's career, when he or she is most needed, is extremely difficult. Many professional managers are reluctant to sign a band until it has achieved some success in the marketplace, such as a large draw in a major city or a contract with an independent record label. Therefore many new bands must manage themselves, sharing the tasks, until they can attract a professional manager.

All bands should enter into a written agreement among themselves when they get together as a band. Among the many elements contained in such an agreement is a provision that normally appoints a band member to act as a leader of, and spokesperson for, the band. That spokesperson is basically a quasi-manager who arranges for the band to do whatever is necessary to get a record deal, including making a tape to submit to record companies and making sure the band gives dynamite live performances. Certain other matters a band must consider are whether to attempt to obtain a publishing deal, a merchandise agreement, endorsements and the like. It can take quite a while before a band can hook up with the right manager, as it is often as difficult to obtain a good manager as it is to obtain a record deal.

Analysis of a Personal Management Agreement

BY NEVILLE L. JOHNSON

It is often necessary, albeit difficult, for musicians to find good personal managers. Personal managers are the supervisors and coordinators of the business and career activities of professional entertainers, the liaison with those that do business with artists. Depending on the needs of their clients, personal managers must, at times, motivate, direct, market, make demands and advise. Managers are involved in such issues as which employment to seek and accept, their artists' public mystiques and images, and the marketing and promotion of their artists' careers. In most instances, communications with agents, attorneys, business managers, publicists, record companies and music publishers are routed through personal managers.

Many artists are unwilling, or unable to devote the time necessary to supervise and coordinate the many services required from those that build and maintain their careers. Virtually all successful recording artists have personal managers, as do some record producers.

Some personal managers invest money, in addition to time, into the acts they represent. Their profession is risky and often costly.

Fledgling or unsigned acts have difficulty obtaining qualified personal managers because those that are desirable are busy with successful acts and do not have the time or interest to focus on a developing talent. Being a personal manager is often a thankless job, sometimes lucrative, and always difficult.

Personal managers are, in effect, employees of the acts they represent, and operate in a fiduciary capacity to the artist. Thus, the artist is always boss—but has usually engaged the manager because of his or

MUSIC MANAGERS FORUM (MMF) - U.S.

The MMF was formed to further the interests of managers and their artists in the music industry, which includes the areas of live performance, recording and music publishing.

The MMF provides a forum for the discussion of issues and problems that face music industry managers.

Music Managers Forum
(www.mmf-us.org)
P.O. Box 444
Village Station
New York, NY 10014-0444
(212) 213-8787
(212) 213-9797 (fax)

MANAGERS AT PERIL

Although the personal manager is the chief executive responsible for the promotion and marketing of the artist, procuring of labor for a musician can be a difficult and treacherous area for all personal managers that operate in California. (The other state where procurement of labor may be a problem is New York.) California's Labor Code, in a section called the Talent Agencies Act, regulates the offer, promise, procurement or attempted procurement of employment for entertainers. There has been much controversy about this law over the years. Except with respect to the procurement of recording agreements, and acting directly under the supervision of a licensed agent, a personal managers are not allowed to so act without a state license giving them permission to operate as a talent agency. Most personal managers have refused to obtain such licenses because of various state rules and union regulations. For example, anyone with a talent agency license must operate in an office, not a residence.

The AFM, AFTRA and SAG allow union members to terminate agency agreements if work is not secured within a specified period of time. Many managers cannot operate within these strictures. There have been attempts over the last 20 years to produce a workable arrangement that is satisfactory to all parties but the matter has yet to be resolved and it is unlikely that it ever will. A personal manager may not solicit a live engagement or any other engagement (except a record deal) for an entertainer unless he or she possesses a talent agency license. Most talent agencies and established personal managers are not interested in musical acts that do not have record agreements with major labels. Thus, personal managers that represent talent in that position are effectively required to seek such employment, or at least deal with offers that come in, but may violate state law if they do so. Even if the manager takes no commission, his conduct is unlawful. The Talent Agencies Act has been used by many musicians over the years as a legal maneuver to terminate management agreements. Personal managers are allowed to solicit recording agreements, but without the opportunity to solicit live engagements to secure showcases and "build" the act, they are hamstrung.

Be forewarned! We have seen many cases where managers were unceremoniously fired once a deal was obtained and a "heavy" manager was willing to come on board. Do not count on loyalty if you are a manager. Very few managers have found it to exist. For example, we represented the former manager of The Deftones, who alleged in a lawsuit that he was unceremoniously dumped though he had fought for them when they were playing to empty clubs and got Maverick Records to sign them, because Guy O'Seary, the A&R executive who signed them, wanted another manager for them. The manager could not collect because the group successfully argued that notwithstanding the hard work, he had violated the Talent Agencies Act by obtaining live engagements for them when no talent agent would consider booking them, even though he took no commission. (*Park v. Deftones* [1999] 71 CA 4th 1465.) New York allows a manager to book if he does so incidentally, as just a small part of his services. Any manager who has an act that can maintain a claim under the Talent Agencies Act in California is vulnerable. Beware if you are an out-of-state manager and seek employment for your acts in the Golden State. Remember the other moral of the case of The Deftones: loyalty in the entertainment business is hard to find. Managers must "watch their backs" at all times.

her superior knowledge of, and capabilities in, the business arena. A fiduciary is one in whom a special trust is placed and who, consequently, owes special duties to the client. Like attorneys and accountants, personal managers must subordinate their own interests to those of their clients. The client's best interests always come first: There must at all times be complete disclosure of all material information and no side-dealing of any nature, and no secret profits.

Personal managers are the eyes and ears of their clients and must disclose completely all business dealings involving them. They must never obtain an unfair economic advantage with respect to their clients; exercise no undue influence over their affairs; and always operate with the highest standards of good faith and fair dealing. Personal managers must always use their best efforts to see that their clients have independent advice when necessary, as in, for example, a conflict of interest situation where a manager seeks to be an employer or partner with a client and thus may be biased when giving advice.

The personal manager relationship is the business equivalent of a marriage. It must be entered into with sobriety, intelligence and forethought. Successful artists understand, appreciate and supervise the myriad duties of their personal managers, and understand and fulfill their own obligations in those relationships.

PERSONAL MANAGEMENT AGREEMENT

1. TERM

Manager is hereby engaged as Artist's exclusive personal manager and advisor. The agreement shall continue for three (3) years (hereinafter the "initial term") from the date thereof, and shall be renewed for one (l) year periods (hereinafter "renewal period(s)") automatically unless either party shall give written notice of termination to the other not later than thirty (30) days prior to the expiration of the initial term or the then current renewal period, as applicable, subject to the terms and conditions hereof.

Most personal management agreements have a three-year term, although some can last up to five years, at the manager's discretion. Artists sometimes insert provisions that provide for a minimum of earnings that the artist must earn during the period before any option period may be exercised. Most personal management agreements with newer acts provide that if a recording agreement is not secured within a period of up to 18 months, after commencement of the term, then either party may terminate the management agreement. What "secured" means should be specified. If the personal manager is in negotiation with a record company, but a recording agreement has not actually been signed, the agreement should not be terminated if the material terms of an agreement have been negotiated and agreed upon. Additionally, the Artist could be prohibited from signing to such label for an additional two years after the end of the term of the personal management agreement, or would otherwise have to pay a management commission.

2. SERVICES

(a) Manager agrees during the term thereof, to advise, counsel and assist Artist in connection with all matters relating to Artist's career in all branches of the entertainment industry, including, without limitation, the following:

(i) in the selection of literary, artistic and musical material;

(ii) with respect to matters pertaining to publicity, promotion, public relations and advertising;

(iii) with respect to the adoption of proper formats for the presentation of Artist's artistic talents and in determination of the proper style, mood, setting, business and characterization in keeping with Artist's talents;

(iv) in the selection of artistic talent to assist, accompany or embellish Artist's artistic presentation, with regard to general practices in the entertainment industries;

(v) with respect to such matters as Manager may have knowledge concerning compensation and privileges extended for similar artistic values;

(vi) with respect to agreements, documents and contracts for Artist's services, talents, and/or artistic, literary and musical materials, or otherwise;

(vii) with respect to the selection, supervision and coordination of those persons, firms and corporations that may counsel, advise, procure employment, or otherwise render services to or on behalf of Artist, such as accountants, attorneys, business managers, publicists and talent agents; and

(b) Manager shall be required only to render reasonable services, which are called for by this Agreement as and when reasonably requested by Artist. Manager shall not be required to travel or meet with Artist at any particular place or places, except in Manager's sole discretion and following arrangements for cost and expenses of such travel, such arrangements to be mutually agreed upon by Artist and Manager.

The foregoing details what managers do. Travel requirements should be negotiated on a case-by-case basis. An artist might resist paying for travel and long-distance phone charges when the manager chooses to live in a location remote from the residence of the artist. Travel should be necessary and the cost reasonable. An artist may also require an allocation of costs if the manager, when traveling, does other business unrelated to the artist.

As far as "advising and counseling," although it is a vague job description, this is as far as most agreements go. Further, it is difficult to articulate the efforts that may be required.

Some artists find it frustrating that the manager's obligations are so vaguely defined. There is no reason why an artist cannot require the manager to specify in further detail the services required. For example, artists could require their managers not to represent more than three other acts, and require their manager to meet with them biweekly, or monthly, to create or present strategies and goals for the artist. An artist should require that all material information about his or her business be provided as soon as it is obtained or learned.

There should be a specific provision where the manager acknowledges that a fiduciary relationship (one of special trust) exists. An artist should never agree that no such relationship exists.

What are the obligations of the manager after the term of the agreement? One of our cases involves a manager who claims to own music publishing rights of the artist. We had to sue him to get him to turn over all documents relating to the same. Thus, artists should try and insert a provision that requires the manager to keep the artist informed at all times of all activities of the manager, and of all rights in which the manager claims an interest, and certainly upon request of the artist, or the artist's representative.

3. AUTHORITY OF MANAGER

Manager is hereby appointed Artist's exclusive, true and lawful attorney-in-fact, to do any or all of the following, for or on behalf of Artist, during the term of this Agreement:

(a) approve and authorize any and all publicity and advertising, subject to Artist's previous approval;

Artists will want to have written approval; managers will want a reasonable time for approval, such as 72 hours after delivery to Artist.

(b) approve and authorize the use of Artist's name, photograph, likeness, voice, sound effects, caricatures, and literary, artistic and musical materials for the purpose of advertising any and all products and services, subject to Artist's previous approval;

(c) execute in Artist's name, American Federation of Musicians contracts for Artist's personal appearances as a live entertainer, subject to Artist's previous consent to the material terms thereof; and

(d) without in any way limiting the foregoing, generally do, execute and perform any other act, deed, matter or thing whatsoever, that ought to be done on behalf of the Artist by a personal manager.

The key words "subject to Artist's written approval" should be inserted at the end of subparagraph 3(d), though managers would balk at the "written" aspect as being too restricting and impractical, but in this age of faxes and emails, there is no reason why the artist should not approve and supervise the manager in all aspects. The manager must be allowed to "have his head" and not be micro-managed, be made to feel inferior, or an employee to be bossed around. It is a team effort and trust is an integral aspect of the relationship and each must be allowed to perform his or her job without too much interference. An artist will usually want to delete any clause that gives the manager the right to execute agreements on behalf of the artist. The intelligent artist always supervises and understands his contractual relations. Too much control—and the possibility of abuse—reside in any manager that has unchecked freedom to bind the artist. Managers should only be appointed to execute AFM agreements as noted in subparagraph 3(c) and only when the artist is reasonably not available to do so, which will be rare, given the existence of courier services and fax machines.

4. COMMISSIONS

(a) Since the nature and extent of the success or failure of Artist's career cannot be predetermined, it is the desire of the parties hereto that Manager's compensation shall be determined in such a manner as will permit Manager to accept the risk of failure as well as the benefit of Artist's success. Therefore, as compensation for Manager's services, Artist shall pay Manager, throughout the full term hereof, as when received by Artist, the following percentages of Artist's gross earnings (hereinafter referred to as the "Commission"):

(i) Fifteen percent (15%) of Artist's gross earnings received in connection with Artist providing their services as a recording artist for the recording of master recordings to be manufactured and marketed as phonograph records and tapes during the term hereof. Manager shall receive said Commission in perpetuity on the sale of those master recordings recorded during the term hereof. In no event shall the term "gross earnings" be deemed to include payments to third parties (which are not owned or controlled substantially or entirely by Artist), in connection with the recordings of master recordings prior to or during the term hereof;

Managers in the music business usually take a 15% or 20% commission of an artist's earnings.

(ii) Fifteen percent (15%) of the Artist's gross earnings from live performances;

The artist should seek to, and generally does, limit the manager's compensation on live engagements to the artist's "net" derived from such engagements: i.e., after the deductions of travel, lights, and other out-of-pocket payments that an artist makes to third parties, including agents and musicians.

(iii) Fifteen percent (15%) of the Artist's gross earnings derived from any and all of Artist's activities in connection with music publishing, or the licensing or assignment of any compositions composed by Artist alone or in collaboration with others (it being understood that no commissions shall be taken with respect to any compositions that are the subject of any separate music publishing agreement between Artist and Manager).

Some managers seek to administer the compositions of their artists and/or take a higher percentage from music publishing royalties. Although nothing is inherently wrong with such practices, the personal manager will be subjected to extra scrutiny as to the fairness of the agreements if the artist has no independent advice or unless the circumstances otherwise dictate that the arrangement is fair. See discussion after paragraph 12.

(b) The term "gross earnings" as used herein shall mean and include any and all gross monies or other consideration which Artist may receive, acquire, become entitled to, or which may be payable to Artist, or on Artist's behalf, directly or indirectly (without any exclusion or deduction) as a result of Artist's activities in the music industry, whether as a performer, writer, singer, musician, composer, publisher, or artist.

Note that virtually all aspects of entertainment are covered. Artists can and do limit the authority of a manager and his or her compensation in certain areas. This must be decided on a case-by-case basis. For example, if an artist has a thriving jingle or soundtrack business, or is an established actor, then the artist may desire to exclude these areas from the manager's commission. Further, the manager will want to ensure that "other consideration" includes stock, and any other inducements that may be offered to the artist. If the Artist is offered the opportunity to participate in deals, then the manager should have a pro-rata right to likewise participate.

(c) Manager shall be entitled to receive his full commission as provided herein in perpetuity on Artist's gross earnings derived from any agreements entered into during the term of this agreement, notwithstanding the prior termination of this agreement for any reason. Artist also agrees to pay Manager the commission following the term hereof upon and with respect to all of Artist's gross earnings received after the expiration of the term hereof but derived from any and all employments, engagements, contracts, agreements and activities, negotiated, entered into, commenced or performed during the term hereof relating to any of the foregoing, and upon any and all extensions, renewals and substitutions thereof and therefore, and upon any resumptions of such employments, engagements, contracts, agreements and activities which may have been discontinued during the term hereof and resumed within one (l) year thereafter;

This is a tricky area. In the music business, many personal managers are limited to a commission derived from activities performed during the term of the agreement, and not with respect to activities performed after the personal management agreement but pursuant to agreements that were entered into during the term of the management agreement. For example, should the manager get a commission on records recorded after the management term pursuant to a record deal entered into during the term? There are two views. The manager will argue that if he or she is responsible for building up the career of the artist, the fruits of the manager's labor should be enjoyed for as long as that "contractual tree" bears fruit and it would not be fair to build up an artist's career over a five-album period, so that the artist was about to "break" on a major scale, only to be excised from the deal on the next album when the artist achieves major success. The artist will attempt to limit the compensation to only employment activity by the artist rendered to third parties during the term of the management agreement. Artists will argue that they will be forced to pay two commissions: one to the previous manager and one to a new manager, which would be unduly onerous. Moreover, what if the failure to achieve success theretofore was in some part the manager's fault? Possible compromises are a reduced percentage for the manager, an "override" that extends for a limited period, or that the parties will negotiate a fee or override at the end of the term, and if they cannot agree, a third party can decide a fair buyout.

There was major litigation and a trial in 1994 over the relationship between the personal manager of blues-great Willie Dixon and his estate. The personal manager helped Dixon obtain reversions of various copyrights and was paid up to a third of the revenue stream earned from various compositions, all written before the commencement of the personal management agreement. Such work is generally outside the traditional artist-manager relationship, but if the contract is not specific enough, the personal manager might be entitled to share in such revenues.

Some managers are so "heavy," they operate without written agreements. We foresee trouble, and recommend against any oral agreements. As Samuel Goldwyn, the movie producer, supposedly said, "A verbal contract isn't worth the paper it's written on." It is tough to establish and prove an oral contract in a court of law.

"Negotiated" could use more definition, and most times the parties will agree that this include that the material (basic) terms have been agreed upon and the final contract is executed within 90 days after the expiration of the term of the management agreement.

(d) Manager is hereby authorized to receive, on Artist's behalf, all "gross monies and other considerations" and to deposit all such funds into a separate trust account in a bank or savings and loan association. Manager shall have the right to withdraw from such account all expenses and commissions to which Manager is entitled hereunder and shall remit the balance to Artist or as Artist shall direct. Notwithstanding the foregoing, Artist may, at any time, require all "gross monies or other considerations" to be paid to a third party, provided that such party shall irrevocably be directed in writing to pay Manager all expenses and commissions due hereunder.

This is a subject near and dear to both parties. The manager wants to be assured of getting paid; the artist needs to be sure of a fair count. In the early days of a career, when there is little to be made, most managers collect and disburse revenue. Any artist who becomes successful should have an accountant or business manager to supervise the financial activities of the artist. The artist must have the absolute right to audit the books of the manager at reasonable intervals.

It is also a good idea to have the manager acknowledge there is a fiduciary relationship to the artist, particularly with respect to the financial aspects of the relationship. (The penalties are much stronger for one who violates a fiduciary relationship, as opposed to a mere contractual relationship. If a fiduciary breaches a relationship, punitive or exemplary damages may be claimed—they may not in an ordinary breach of contract situation. Most managers, however, will balk at such a provision, even though that is the true nature of the agreement.)

(e) The term "gross monies or other considerations" as used herein shall include, without limitation, salaries, earnings, fees, royalties, gifts, bonuses, share of profit and other participations, shares of stock, partnership interests, percentages music related income, earned or received directly or indirectly by Artist or Artist's heirs, executors, administrators or assigns, or by any other person, firm or corporation on Artist's behalf. Should Artist be required to make any payment for such interest, Manager will pay Manager's percentage share of such payment, unless Manager elects not to acquire Manager's percentage thereof.

Sometimes artists are offered deals that, for example, would include a stock purchase at a reduced price in return for services. The manager may want to—and should have the right to—get in on the deal.

5. LOANS AND ADVANCES

Manager will make loans or advances to Artist or for Artist's account and incur some expenses on Artist's behalf for the furtherance of Artist's career in amounts to be determined solely by Manager in Manager's best, good faith business judgment. Artist hereby authorizes Manager to recoup and retain the amount of any such loans, advances and/or expenses, including, without limitation, transportation and living expenses while traveling, promotion and publicity expenses, and all other reasonable and necessary expenses, from any sums Manager may receive on behalf of Artist. Artist shall reimburse Manager for any expenses incurred by Manager on behalf of Artist, including, without limitation, long-distance calls, travel expenses, messenger services, and postage and delivery costs. Notwithstanding the foregoing, no travel expenses and no single expense in excess of fifty dollars ($50.00) shall be incurred by Manager without the prior approval of Artist. Manager shall provide Artist with monthly statements of all expenses incurred hereunder and Manager shall be reimbursed by Artist within fourteen (14) days of receipt by Artist of any such statement. Notwithstanding the foregoing, any loans, advances or payment of expenses by Manager hereunder shall not be recoupable by Manager hereunder until Artist has earned revenue in the entertainment industry and there is sufficient such revenue to so recoup, repay and compensate Manager without causing Artist hardship or leaving insufficient funds for Artist to pursue his career.

This is another area of controversy. The artist must be careful to see that the manager is not sending them to the poorhouse. A cap on expenses, such as $50 per transaction as previously mentioned is the best type of insurance. It does cost money to promote and further the career of an artist, however, so it makes sense that managers should be reimbursed for their out-of-pocket expenses occurred on behalf of an artist. Most publicists, attorneys, accountants and business managers charge and obtain reimbursement for out-of-pocket expenses.

6. NONEXCLUSIVITY

Manager's services hereunder are not exclusive. Manager shall at all times be free to perform the same or similar services for others, as well as to engage in any and all other business activities.

The artist may wish to insert a clause that guarantees that the manager will have sufficient time to devote to the career of the artist or a "key-person" clause that guarantees that the manager, not some employee, will be primarily rendering day-to-day services to and on behalf of the artist may be inserted instead.

7. ARTIST'S CAREER
Artist agrees at all times to pursue Artist's career in a manner consistent with Artist's values, goals, philosophy and disposition and to do all things necessary and desirable to promote such career and earnings therefrom. Artist shall at all times utilize proper theatrical and other employment agencies to obtain engagements and employment for Artist. Artist shall consult with Manager regarding all offers of employment inquiries concerning Artist's services. Artist shall not, without Manager's prior written approval, engage any other person, firm or corporation to render any services of the kind required of Manager hereunder or which Manager is permitted to perform hereunder.

The manager/artist relationship is built on trust and mutual agreement. All major decisions should be mutually agreed upon, especially concerning those who will work closely with the manager and artist.

8. ADVERTISING
During the term hereof, Manager shall have the exclusive right to advertise and publicize Manager as Artist's personal manager and representative with respect to the music industry.

Managers have businesses too, which may benefit from promotion. Artists will want to approve any advertising or publicity in which their names are used.

9. AGENT
Artist understands that Manager is not licensed as a "talent agency" and that this agreement shall remain, in full force and effect subject to any applicable regulations established by the Labor Commissioner of California, and Artist agrees to modify this agreement to the extent necessary to comply with any such laws.

See the sidebar, Managers at Peril regarding this subject.

10. ENTIRE AGREEMENT
This constitutes the entire agreement between Artist and Manager relating to the subject matter hereof. This agreement shall be subject to and construed in accordance with the laws of the State of California applicable to agreements entered into and fully performed therein. A waiver by either party hereto or a breach of any provision herein shall not be deemed a waiver of any subsequent breach, nor a permanent modification of such provision. Each party acknowledges that no statement, promise or inducement has been made to such party, except as expressly provided for herein. This agreement may not be changed or modified, or any covenant or provision hereof waived, except by an agreement in writing, signed by the party against whom enforcement of the change, modification or waiver is sought. As used in this agreement, the word "Artist" shall include any corporation owned (partially or wholly) or controlled (directly or indirectly) by Artist and Artist agrees to cause any such corporation to enter into an agreement with Manager of the same terms and conditions contained herein.

11. LEGALITY
Nothing contained in this agreement shall be construed to require the commission of any act contrary to law. Whenever there is any conflict between any provision of this

agreement and any material law, contrary to which the parties have no legal right to contract, the latter shall prevail, but in such event the provisions of this agreement affected shall be curtailed and restricted only to the extent necessary to bring them within such legal requirements, and only during the time such conflict exists.

12. CONFLICTING INTERESTS

From time to time during the term of this agreement, acting alone or in association with others, Manager may package an entertainment program in which the Artist is employed as an artist, or Manager may act as the entrepreneur or promoter of an entertainment program in which Artist is employed by Manager or Manager may employ Artist in connection with the production of phonograph records, or as a songwriter, composer or arranger. Such activity on Manager's part shall not be deemed to be a breach of this agreement or of Manager's obligations and duties to Artist. However, Manager shall not be entitled to the commission in connection with any gross earnings derived by Artist from any employment or agreement whereunder Artist is employed by Manager, or by the firm, person or corporation represented by Manager as the package agent for the entertainment program in which Artist is so employed; and Manager shall not be entitled to the commission in connection with any gross earnings derived by Artist from the sale, license or grant of any literary rights to Manager or any person, firm or corporation owned or controlled by Manager. Nothing in this agreement shall be construed to excuse Artist from the payment of the commission upon gross earnings derived by Artist from Artist's employment or sale, license or grant of rights in connections with any entertainment program, phonograph record, or other matter, merely because Manager is also employed in connections therewith as a producer, director, conductor or in some other management or supervisory capacity, but not as Artist's employer, grantee or licensee.

Many managers also act as producers or packagers of television shows and live concerts or operate production companies, record companies or music publishing companies. For this reason, a manager might be in a partnership with a client, or the employer of a client. There is nothing inherently wrong with this, but because the manager may have control in excess of that ordinarily granted to them in the management agreement, or greater compensations than ordinarily would be paid in his or her capacity as manager, it is incumbent upon the manager to insure that the artist is provided for fairly. First, the manager should not obtain "double commissions"; that is, a fee and percentage as a producer or employer, in addition to a management commission from the artist from the same activity for which the manager is compensated as an employer or partner. Second, an independent third party should negotiate the artist's participation. Sometimes, the artist and manager will have the same attorney. In this kind of situation, artists should hire their own attorneys. It is generally wise for artists to have their own attorneys that do not also represent their managers.

It is foolish for managers to try and act as employers and managers, as inherent conflicts of interest are created. Managers that sign artists to their own production companies and music publishing companies will have a hard time arguing that as artists' managers they fought hard for the artists against the managers' own interests. Clint Black was in a very expensive and unpleasant litigation in the mid-1990s over this very issue; the case ultimately settled.

In the last few years, we have been embroiled in several lawsuits concerning managers that claim to represent a "group" and take positions adverse to a particular member of that group, including even terminating a musician or partner/member. From an artist's perspective, this is very troubling—any artist should demand that any personal manager and any lawyer for the group not be allowed to take sides should such problems develop.

13. SCOPE
This agreement shall not be construed to create a partnership between the parties. Each party is acting hereunder as an independent contractor. Manager may appoint or engage any other persons, firms or corporations, throughout the world, in Manager's discretion, to perform any of the services which Manager has agreed to perform hereunder except that Manager may delegate all of his duties only with Artist's written consent. Manager's services hereunder are not exclusive to Artist and Manager shall at all times be free to perform the same or similar services for others as well as to engage in any and all other business activities. Manager shall only be required to render reasonable services that are provided for herein as and when reasonably requested by Artist. Manager shall not be deemed to be in breach of this agreement unless and until Artist shall first have given Manager written notice describing the exact service that Artist requires on Manager's part and then only if Manager is in fact required to render such services hereunder, and if Manager shall thereafter have failed for a period of thirty (30) consecutive days to commence the rendition of the particular service required.

An independent contractor may also be a type of employee. As noted above, the personal manager effectively works for the artist (and hopefully, is effective).

14. ASSIGNMENT
Manager shall have the right to assign this agreement to any and all of Manager's rights hereunder, or delegate any and all of Manager's duties to any individual, firm or corporation with the written approval of Artist, and this agreement shall inure to the benefit of Manager's successors and assigns, provided that Manager shall always be primarily responsible for rendering of managerial services, and may not delegate all of his duties without Artist's written consent. This agreement is personal to Artist, and Artist shall not assign this agreement or any portion thereof, and any such purported assignment shall be void.

The artist will want the manager to be always personally responsible and liable, notwithstanding any assignment or delegation of any rights and duties, and as noted previously, this responsibility can and should be provided.

15. NOTICES
All notices to be given to any of the parties hereto shall be addressed to the respective party at the applicable address as follows:

("Artist") ____________________ and ____________________ ("Manager")

All notices shall be in writing and shall be served by mail or telegraph, all charges prepaid. The date of mailing or of deposit in a telegraphy office, whichever shall be first, shall be deemed the date such notice is effective.

16. ARTIST'S WARRANTIES

Artist is over the age of eighteen, free to enter into this agreement, and has not heretofore made and will not hereafter enter into or accept any engagement, commitment or agreement with any person, firm or corporation which will, can or may interfere with the full and faithful performance by Artist of the covenants, terms and conditions of this agreement to be performed by Artist or interfere with Manager's full enjoyment of Manager's rights and privileges hereunder. Artist warrants that Artist has, as of the date hereof, no commitment, engagement or agreement requiring Artist to render services or preventing Artist from rendering services (including, but not limited to, restrictions on specific musical compositions) or respecting the disposition of any rights which Artist has or may hereafter acquire in any musical composition or creation, and acknowledges that Artist's talents and abilities are exceptional, extraordinary and unique, the loss of which cannot be compensated for by money.

17. ARBITRATION

In the event of any dispute under or relating to the terms of this agreement or any breach thereof, it is agreed that the same shall be submitted to arbitration by the American Arbitration Association in Los Angeles, California in accordance with the rules promulgated by said association and judgment upon any award rendered by be entered in any court having jurisdiction thereof. Any arbitration shall be held in Los Angeles County, California. In the event of arbitration arising from or out of this agreement or the relationship of the parties created hereby, the trier thereof may award to any party any reasonable attorneys' fees and other costs incurred in connection therewith. Any litigation by Manager or Artist arising from or out of this agreement shall be brought in Los Angeles, County, California.

An alternative is the "Rent-a-Judge" program, a type of arbitration, which provides that controversies be heard by retired judges. Litigation via the courts is expensive and time consuming. A typical case in the Superior Court of California may take two to three years and cost hundreds of thousands of dollars. Arbitration or Rent a Judge is private, swift, and less expensive than our court trial system, but many people do not like these programs because they believe that the best form of justice is that meted out in the court system, and there is no right to appeal an arbitration. It is a good idea to specify what "discovery"—information and documents—can be obtained prior to the arbitration. Notwithstanding any arbitration clause, the Labor Commissioner will have exclusive jurisdiction over any dispute where the Talent Agencies Act is alleged to have been violated.

IN WITNESS WHEREOF, the parties hereto have signed this agreement as of the date hereinabove set forth.

____________________	____________________
("ARTIST")	("MANAGER")

Talent Agencies

BY STEVEN H. GARDNER AND BRAD GELFOND

Talent agents are highly specialized employment procurers. As agents (persons authorized by others to act for them), they are restricted in their relationship with their clients by law and by provisions in various trade union collective bargaining agreements. Leaving the day-to-day rigors of career planning to the personal manager, the talent agent's main task is to obtain and negotiate contracts of employment, including bookings, for their clients. California and New York are the major centers of the entertainment industry, so this discussion focuses on them. The first part of the chapter explores the legal reins that define the role of the talent agent, while the second portion discusses the considerations in choosing an agent.

THE LEGAL REINS

Every state has a system for the licensing and regulating of talent/employment agencies. Some license talent agencies under general employment agency laws while others have statutes tailored to the entertainment field. For instance, when the California legislature began its regulation of employment agencies in 1913, the first distinction between "general agencies" and "theatrical employment agencies" was made. Until 1967, there were four categories of talent agents licensed by California: employment agent, theatrical employment agent, motion picture employment agent and artist's manager.

California's Talent Agencies Act (first passed in 1978) attempts to provide the talent agent with the exclusive right to procure, offer, promise, or attempt to procure employment for an artist. In addition, talent agents (like personal managers) may counsel or direct artists in the development of their professional careers.

In affording this exclusive status, California has set up a variety of agent licensing regulations, including requirements for the filing of detailed applications, posting of a $10,000 bond, logging of fingerprint cards, and, most importantly, acquiring the Labor Commissioner's prior approval of all form contracts between agents and their clients. This prior approval must appear on the contract itself—look for it. Moreover, agents must post, in their offices, a schedule of fees, and a description of what to do if a dispute arises. In any event, if a problem occurs between an agent and client that cannot be worked out informally (or through an alternative dispute resolution forum as provided in the contract as discussed below), the office of the Labor Commissioner should be the artist's next stop.

However, under California Labor Code §1700.45, the contract between the artist and the talent agent may contain a provision that refers disputes to a system of arbitration other than one conducted by the Labor Commissioner. California has numerous alternative dispute resolution forums staffed by skilled attorneys, retired judges and trained mediators. While sometimes expensive, they often prove to be more effective than the arbitrations conducted by the Labor Commissioner. Under the statute, notice of such arbitration must be given to the Labor Commissioner, and the Labor Commissioner (or his/her representative) has the right to attend the arbitration proceedings. Arbitration is a dispute-resolution forum outside the court system, but it may end up as a court judgment and preclude further court action. Many states, including California, are experiencing a clogged judicial system that severely delays the decision-making process (sometimes up to five years). Arbitration avoids such delays by limiting prehearing discovery, quickly setting hearings, and making binding decisions. Also, rules of evidence, which are guidelines to the court system as to what may and may not be said in court, are generally not applicable to arbitrations, unless agreed to by all sides. Therefore, while informal in structure, arbitration has a formal result.

FEES AND COMMISSIONS

Talent agents located in the state of New York are governed by New York's general business law. Classified as "theatrical employment agencies," the agents are subject to a statutory fee ceiling, which does not have a California counterpart. In New York, for any single theatrical engagement (including employment as an actor, performer, or entertainer), the agent may take no more than 10% of the gross compensation payable to the client, except that for engagements in the orchestral, operatic or concert field, the agent's commission may go as high as 20%.

California sets no maximum on fees that agents may charge for services. Fee ceilings are imposed, however, by the various entertainment guilds (i.e., AFM, AFTRA) in the form of constitutions and bylaws. Agents are "franchised" (recognized) by these guilds and agree to abide by the rules set forth by the guilds. Artist members of the craft guilds are required to utilize only franchised agents, or face disciplinary action in the form of suspension or fines.

The union franchise stringently regulates at least two major areas: the term (length) of the agent's employment agreement with the client, and the maximum compensation payable to the agent. The franchise is essentially an agreement between the agent and the guild that commits the agent to abide by particular regulations as to the representation of their members.

For example, the American Federation of Musicians (AFM) franchise rules allow variable lengths of contract terms dependent upon the services rendered by an agent. A booking agent (one who primarily arranges such personal appearances as clubs, tours, Las Vegas shows) is restricted to a term of three or five years, while a general agent (one who represents a client for film, television, recording, personal appearance, commercials, writing, etc.) can sign a client for up to seven years. Regardless of the franchise or the services rendered, this is the longest period allowable for a personal service contract in California. However, the artist may always renew the contract after the seven years are up, if the artist so desires. (It is at this point that the artist's negotiation opportunity may be at its height.)

Fees are also governed by guild franchises. Although the norm is a 10% maximum on general services, increased fees can be obtained by the agent. For instance, the AFM uses a variable fee scale related to the length of the booked engagement. These scales escalate from 10% up to 20% for a one-day engagement, but in no event can the commission reduce the artist's net income below that specified as scale by the particular guild. These fee specifications represent the amount of money available to the artist, and other representatives (personal and business managers) may be entitled to other chunks of the gross compensation earned on a performance date. Agents should not charge commissions on BMI or ASCAP performance income received by an artist.

The incentive to become a licensed talent agent is the almost monopolistic status bestowed upon them to procure employment for artists in the entertainment field. California, however, has carved out a niche for unlicensed persons in the area of recording agreements. California Labor Code §1700.4 provides that the activities of producing, offering or promising to procure recording contracts for an artist does not, of itself, require licensing under the act. This was an experiment in the law to allow traditionally unlicensed personal managers, that normally perform the duties involved in the procurement of recording contracts, to operate free from the fear of retribution by the Labor Commissioner.

New York law permits a personal manager whose business "only incidentally involves the seeking of employment" to remain unlicensed. For the unlicensed individual in California who acts in the procurement of employment, one of the severest sanctions is the power of the Labor Commissioner to order the return of all commissions obtained while the representative was unlicensed. This result was first and most dramatically presented by the Jefferson Airplane case of *Buchwald v. Katz* where the personal manager was ordered by the Labor Commissioner to return $40,000 in commissions that he had received while managing the group, and he was also denied reimbursement for all moneys advanced by him to the group. A new trial was ordered in this particular case, however, and certain portions of the management agreement were upheld while other publishing agreements (i.e., music publishing agreements where the manager is in effect the publisher) were voided. It is now clear in California that even if a person "occasionally" procures employment for an artist, a talent agency license is required *(Waisbren v. Peppercorn)*. These cases are important in two respects: first, they ratify the powerful role of the Labor Commissioner in settling controversies in the talent agent arena; and second they begin to provide guidelines to define "unlicensed procurement activity" in California. As more of these cases are decided and reported, the line between the sanctioned activities of licensed agents and unlicensed managers will become less hazy.

In 1999, former child actress (and now Assemblyperson) Sheila Kuehl (Zelda in Dobie Gillis) sponsored the "Advance Fee Talent Services Act," which now prohibits, in California, any advance payment required to be paid to an unlicensed firm by an artist prior to the artist obtaining actual employment and receiving actual earnings from such employment. This Act was an attempt to prohibit the operation of talent service type businesses which "registered" artists for a fee, and typically added "up-front" charges for photos, demo tapes, career counseling, and "aptitude/market testing" without some governmental oversight. Now, firms offering such services must first qualify with the state as Advance Fee Talent Services in a manner similar to that of Talent Agents. Written contracts are required, and the artist is afforded a right to cancel within 10 business days of entry into such an agreement. If an Advance Fee Talent Service does not perform as it has agreed, refunds requested by the artist are due to be paid within 48 hours, or the Service may be liable for an additional penalty. An

Advance Fee Talent Service is not necessarily a licensed talent agent. In order to attempt to procure employment for the artist, the Advance Fee Talent Service must also be licensed as a talent agent. This law is a powerful weapon against predators that lure young artists with promises of "connections," "introductions," and "success" packages in exchange for up-front hard-earned dollars.

SEEKING PERSONAL APPEARANCE TALENT AGENCY REPRESENTATION

An agent is a valuable member of the artist's career team, and it is worthwhile to spend some time examining the elements involved in the agency selection process. As you begin seeking personal appearance representation by a talent agency, you will discover that there are many of them, all seemingly providing the same services. A closer look will reveal that each agency has its own areas of expertise and services it can offer an artist. Because the selection can be a difficult decision, the following should be considered.

Research Information About Agencies

The best way to do research on talent agencies is to obtain copies of the client lists of the various companies. There is a publication called *Pollstar,* (800) 344-7383 or, in California, (559) 271-7900, fax (559) 271-7979, Web site *www.pollstar.com*, that publishes a listing of every agency, their client lists and the various agents that work for the companies. It is highly advisable to get a copy of the most recent edition and to spend some time reviewing it. Pay attention to the number of clients the various agencies have. Note the agencies that have clients in your genre of music, the number of agents there, etc. You might also ask your musician friends who represents them, and how to get in contact with their agency.

Compatibility

First and foremost, it is important to be represented by people that are excited about the kind of music or art you perform. Agents that are passionate about their clients and their art are always more formidable representatives than those that are not. Even the best agency is useless unless the artist finds agents there he or she can communicate with and trust.

Many people have compared selecting an agent to selecting a spouse. It is important that you have a good feeling about the person who is about to become your agent. You must be able to communicate artistic ideas and business strategy with this person. Since your agent represents you in business deals, make sure it is someone you trust to act in your best interest, even when you are absent. Also, be sure that your agent will project an attitude and demeanor that you want to be associated with.

If you find a particular person whom you like, and you sign with their agency, make sure that this person becomes your "responsible agent." The responsible agent is the artist's conduit to the agency. It is through this agent (or team of agents in some cases) that the artist will communicate with the entire agency. The responsible agent's ability to motivate the other agents determines in large part whether the agency will succeed on behalf of the artist. You should be certain that your responsible agent is not spread so thin by overwhelming client responsibilities so as to be unable to pay attention to your needs. Sign with someone who has time to devote to you and with whom you expect to spend many years. While it is important to insure you have the best responsible agent possible, it is also important to consider your relationship with all the agents. When you sign with an agency, you are not just signing with one agent, but with the entire agency. You should evaluate the company from the top executives to the newest agent. An agency should encourage personnel stability, as it is important to insure continuity in your personal appearance career. Even the largest agencies with the most impressive client lists can become ineffectual if their personnel change too dramatically.

Developing Acts

Check an agency's client list, it can yield valuable information. A new artist should be compatible with at least some of the artists on the agency's list. For example, it might be a mistake to be a country artist in an agency dominated by heavy metal clients. But there are exceptions to this rule, especially if an agency is making concerted forays into new areas.

It is also important to examine what successes the agency has had. If you were a new act, just about to begin your personal appearance career, it would not be wise to sign with an agency that only booked arena headliners. It is important for an agent to know the proper places for you to play while you develop your personal appearance career. There are some clubs that are better for metal acts, others better for alternative acts, etc. If you play ethnic music, there are some venues where your performance will be more successful. Your agent must know this information.

Maximizing the Relationship

The best way to establish the relationship with your agent is to spend time together. You both need to learn what makes each of you tick. Your manager, if you have one, should be involved here, too. Have your agent come see you perform as often as possible.

It is to your advantage to give your new agent as much information about yourself as possible. Provide a history of the shows and tours you have done, along with copies of all your recordings. You might want to give your agent a copy of the demos for your next album, or an advance copy of the album. After the album comes out, it is a good idea to supply the following tools that are available from your record company: Radio Tracking sheets, which list the radio stations playing your record; BDS (Broadcast Data Systems) information, which lists the number of times each station plays your record and when; and SoundScan information, which lists the number of albums sold in each of the major markets in the country. It is also helpful to provide foreign sales information if your record is released internationally. Press clippings and video (MTV, VH-1, regional, etc.) airplay are also valuable information to an agent. The more information you provide, the better you will be represented.

In addition, make sure that your agent knows your show requirements, both technical and otherwise. Special staging and technical information will help your agent make sure your needs are taken care of when you perform. If you have specific show, advertising, or dressing room requirements, make sure your agent knows what they are before making any deals on your behalf. Let your agent know as much as possible in advance to make sure there are no misunderstandings.

Packaging

Packaging generally refers to the practice of placing a support act(s) on a headliner's tour. This can happen in clubs, theaters, arenas, and stadiums. In the past, agents wielded tremendous influence in placing opening acts on key tours. While agents still maintain some control over packaging, today the headliner makes the final decision on the selection of supporting acts. However, agents have great input on this decision along with the inside track on upcoming support slots. But, it is foolish for a developing band to sign with an agency because they are interested in doing a tour with one of the agency's headliners as these things are never guaranteed.You should listen to the prospective agent's ideas on how he or she feels you would be best packaged, and with which acts. Check also to see what success the agency has had packaging their clients with other agencies, as both support and headliners.

Venue Deals

If you are a headline act, you should check to see if the agency has experience making building (venue) deals. Agents are involved in negotiating venue expenses like rent, ticket commissions, and merchandising deals for their clients. Favorable deals can yield you additional tour revenue.

Clout

Clout is a product of the special relationship between agencies and major music business "players." Large agencies make repeated deals with buyers, enabling buyers many opportunities to make money. This creates a solid business relationship. An agent who delivers several money-making concerts to a talent buyer has more leverage to command maximum guarantees, more favorable deals, and to create career opportunities for the agent's developing acts. Concert promoters attempt to protect their relationships with the major agencies. They often worry that the agency will do business with a different promoter, and they will not get the opportunity to play some of the agency's acts. By playing an agency's developing acts, promoters hope to be benefited in two ways. First, if they help develop an act by playing it in its early stages, they will develop a relationship with it and be given the opportunity to play the act in the future. Second, they hope to develop good will with the agency by helping in the development process. It is possible for small agencies to develop relationships like those mentioned above with promoters, but it usually is not to the same degree as with large agencies.

Small Agencies

Small agencies do, however, have their advantages. In a small agency, the artist/agent ratio tends to be lower (although there are exceptions at large agencies). This allows each agent the opportunity to spend more time booking and working for each client. The workload of agents in a small agency allows them to initiate special projects, and to spend as much time as is needed for any given client.

Coverage

Coverage refers to the number of buyers that any given agent will be responsible for servicing. In an agency, the "buyer pie" (concert promoters, club owners, college buyers, etc.) is divided among all the agents. In a large agency, each agent will have fewer buyers to deal with and can become more specialized. Typically, the buyers are divided up geographically and by type (rock buyers, middle-of-the-road buyers, country buyers, etc.) and by size of venue (concert, club, college). Large agencies do more business, so they tend to have a thorough awareness of the concert business and of individual markets.

Specialized vs. Full-Service Agencies

There are certain differences between agencies that an artist should consider. These relate to the scope of representation that the agencies offer. A specialized agency offers representation in one area; personal appearance representation is one example. Full-service agencies offer a broad range of services, representing television, film, and commercial actors, producers, directors, writers, editors, and other "below-the-line" personnel, as well as personal appearance clients (musicians, bands, singers). Full-service agencies offer representation to their clients in whichever areas they choose. This is especially useful for musicians that want to explore acting or film scoring.

Data Management

Another consideration is the ability of an agency to manage data and efficiently communicate that data to its clients and their representatives. Innovative agencies have turned to computer technology to help them assimilate data. This technology has created the opportunity for thorough and efficient interoffice data sharing as well as new methods for providing information to clients.

CONCLUSION

It is important to consider as many variables as possible when making your agency decision. You should research prospective agencies with some current clients and their managers and with talent buyers, record company executives and attorneys. You should find out how the agency you are considering is regarded by the rest of the music business. Ask for a copy of the agency's client list. The best recommendation for an agency is a history of long associations with successful clients. Good luck.

PROVISIONS THAT SHOULD BE CONSIDERED WITH ALL AGENCY AGREEMENTS

Agent will represent no more than two clients: The agent may make the representation that he will handle you and one other client, exclusively. The trade-off is that the agent gets a larger cut, subject, of course, to your getting at least scale.

Other provisions, which can be negotiated in connection with this agreement and other agency contracts include the following:

1. The simultaneous ending of all agreements with the agency when any one (i.e., a group member who signed the agreements) is terminated or any agreement expires. This is important to a group.
2. The exclusion of commissions for performances already set, or in the areas of recording agreements, music publishing, literary fields, etc.
3. No double commissions on employment arising under different agreements, or when agent receives a commission from a buyer of talent, (i.e., packaging).
4. No commissions on residuals or repeats of TV programs or films.
5. Specific maximum commissions as to all agency contracts.
6. Commission computation on net receipts rather than gross receipts.
7. Agreements are terminated if agent has not procured employment resulting in offers exceeding a specific dollar amount in a certain amount of time.

AFM EXCLUSIVE AGENT-MUSICIAN AGREEMENT FOR USE IN THE STATE OF CALIFORNIA ONLY*

Name of Agent: ______________________________________
Legal Name of Musician: ______________________________
Address of Agent: ___________________________________
Professional Name of Musician: _______________________
Name of Musician's Group or Orchestra: ________________
AFM Booking Agent Number: ___________________________
Musician's AFM Locals: ______________________________
This Agreement Begins on ____________ 20___ and Ends on ___________ 20___.

1. SCOPE OF AGREEMENT

Musician hereby employs Agent and Agent hereby accepts employment as Musician's exclusive artist manager throughout the world with respect to musician's services, appearances and endeavors as a musician. As used in this Agreement "Musician" refers to the undersigned musician and to musicians performing with any orchestra or group that Musician leads or conducts and whom Musician shall make subject to the terms of this agreement; "AFM" refers to the American Federation of Musicians of the United States and Canada. Also, as used in this agreement, the word "Agent" shall refer to "Artists' Manager" as that term is defined in Section 1700.4 of the Labor Code of the State of California.

Note that this is an exclusive agreement. The musician may not enter into other agreements covering the specific area of concern (music); however, it would not prohibit the musician from hiring an agent for commercials, broadcasting, etc.

2. DUTIES OF AGENT

(a) Agent agrees to use reasonable efforts in the performance of the following duties: assist Musician in obtaining offers of, and negotiating, engagements for Musician; advise, aid, counsel and guide Musician with respect to Musician's professional career; promote and publicize Musician's name and talents; carry on business correspondence on Musician's behalf relating to Musician's professional career; cooperate with duly constituted and authorized representatives of Musician in the performance of such duties.

(b) Agent will maintain office, staff and facilities reasonably adequate for the rendition of such services.

(c) Agent will not accept any engagements for Musician without Musician's prior approval, which shall not be unreasonably withheld.

(d) Agent shall fully comply with all applicable laws, rules and regulations of governmental authorities and secure such licenses as may be required for the rendition of services hereunder.

These are renditions of the classic duties of the talent agent. Reasonable efforts (rather than the stricter "best efforts" found in some contracts), however, are required of the agent. Note also that although the contract provides that the duties of the agent are to

(This can be a three-year or five-year agreement in California.)

"advise, aid, counsel and guide Musician" with respect to his professional career, this is an area usually left to the personal manager.

3. RIGHTS OF AGENT

(a) Agent may render similar services to others and may engage in other businesses and ventures, subject, however, to the limitations imposed by paragraph 8 below.

Note the nonexclusivity of the agent to your professional career—the agent can take on as many clients as he or she can handle (but see below).

(b) Musician will promptly refer to Agent all communications, written or oral, received by or on behalf of Musician relating to the services and appearances by Musician.

(c) Without Agent's written consent, Musician will not engage any other person, firm or corporation to perform the services to be performed by Agent hereunder nor will Musician perform or appear professionally or offer so to do except through Agent.

(b) and (c) Everything concerning music employment must go through the agent—to accept a freelance job may be in breach of the agreement (and your agent will get his or her commission anyway). It is in the artist's best interests to refer job queries to the agent because the agent can often negotiate more favorable terms. However, stay on top of the negotiations in the event the agent is unable to close the deal.

(d) Agent may publicize the fact that Agent is the exclusive agent for Musician.

(e) Agent shall have the right to use or to permit others to use Musician's name and likeness in advertising or publicity relating to Musician's services and appearances but without cost or expense to Musician unless Musician shall otherwise specifically agree in writing.

You may find an awful picture of yourself in a brochure or on a poster. Negotiate for the right to approve all publicity releases whenever possible.

(f) In the event of Musician's breach of this agreement, Agent's sole right and remedy for such breach shall be the receipt from Musician of the commissions specified in this agreement, but only if, as, and when, Musician receives monies or other consideration on which such commissions are payable hereunder.

If you violate the contract, the agency may not enjoin (i.e., get a court order to stop) your performance—the agency is limited to the remedy of damages determined by the amount of commissions due it.

4. COMPENSATION OF AGENT

(a) In consideration of the services to be rendered by Agent hereunder, Musician agrees to pay to Agent commissions equal to the percentages set forth below of the gross monies received by Musician, directly or indirectly, for each engagement on which commissions are payable hereunder:

(i) Ten percent (10%)
(ii) In no event, however, shall the payment of any such commissions result in the retention by Musician for any engagement of net monies or other consideration in an amount less than the applicable minimum scale of the AFM or of any local thereof having jurisdiction over such engagement.
(iii) In no event shall the payment of any such commissions result in the receipt by Agent for any engagement of commissions, fees or other consideration, directly or indirectly, from any person or persons, including the Musician, which in aggregate exceed the commissions provided for in this agreement. Any commission, fee, or other consideration received by Agent from any source other than Musician, directly or indirectly, on account of, as a result of, or in connection with supplying the services of Musician shall be reported to Musician and the amount thereof shall be deducted from the commissions payable by the Musician hereunder.

The commission percentages are fairly clear, (ii) makes sure that you will always earn at least scale. This, however, does not take into consideration amounts that you may be obligated to pay to personal managers, business managers and the like. The AFM has little control over these.

(b) Commissions shall become due and payable to Agent immediately following the receipt thereof by Musician or by anyone else on Musician's behalf.

Normally, the check will be sent to the agency prior to the engagement, after which monies (less commission) will be paid to you.

(c) No commissions shall be payable on any engagement if Musician is not paid for such engagement irrespective of the reasons for such nonpayment to Musician, including but not limited to nonpayment by reason of the fault of Musician. This shall not preclude the awarding of damages by the International Executive Board to an agent to compensate him for actual expenses incurred as the direct result of the cancellation of an engagement when said cancellation was the fault of the member.

If you are not paid, your agent is not paid. But note, if you are the cause of the cancellation, you may be liable for the actual expenses (i.e., air fare or booking expenses) incurred by the agent that result from the cancellation.

(d) Agent's commissions shall be payable on all monies or other considerations received by Musician pursuant to contracts for engagements negotiated or entered into during the term of this agreement; if specifically agreed to by Musician by initialing the margin hereof, to contracts for engagements in existence at the commencement of the term hereof (excluding, however, any engagements as to which Musician is under prior obligation to pay commissions to another agent); and to any modifications, extensions and renewals thereof or substitutions therefor regardless of when Musician shall receive such monies or other considerations. However, to be entitled to continue to receive commissions on the aforementioned contracts after the termination of this agreement, agent shall remain obligated to serve Musician and to perform obligations with respect to said employment contracts or to extensions or renewals of said contracts or to any employment requiring musician's services on which such commissions are based.

The agent is entitled to commissions on engagements negotiated during the term of this agreement, even if the monies are actually received at a later time. You can exclude commissions to the agent on current engagements by not initialing the margin.

(e) As used in this paragraph and elsewhere in this agreement, the term "gross earnings" shall mean the gross amounts received by Musician for each engagement less costs and expenses incurred in collecting amounts due for any engagement, including costs of arbitration, litigation and attorneys' fees.
(f) If specifically agreed to by Musician by initialing the margin hereof, the following shall apply:
(i) Musician shall advance to Agent against Agent's final commissions an amount not exceeding the following percentages of the gross amounts received for each engagement, 15% on engagements of three (3) days or less; 10% on all other engagements.
(ii) If Musician shall so request and shall simultaneously furnish Agent with the data relating to deductions, the Agent within forty-five (45) days following the end of each twelve (12) month period during the term of this agreement and within forty-five (45) days following the termination of this Agreement, shall account to and furnish Musician with a detailed statement itemizing the gross amounts received for all engagements during the period to which such accounting relates, the monies or other considerations upon which Agent's commissions are based, and the amount of Agent's commissions resulting from such computations. Upon request, a copy of such statement shall be furnished promptly to the Office of the President of the AFM.
(iii) Any balances owed by or to the parties shall be paid as follows: by the Agent at the time of rendering such statement; by the Musician within thirty (30) days after receipt of such statement.

If you initial this clause, you agree to pay to your agent monies against commissions to be earned. (i) This is usually not to your advantage. The trade-off, however, is the detailed itemization of account that you can demand of the agent (ii).

5. DURATION AND TERMINATION OF AGREEMENT
(a) The term of this agreement shall be as stated in the opening heading hereof, subject to termination as provided in paragraphs 5(b), 6 and 10 below.
(b) In addition to termination pursuant to other provisions of this agreement, this agreement may be terminated by either party, by notice as provided below, if Musician
(i) is unemployed for four (4) consecutive weeks at any time during the term hereof; or
(ii) does not obtain employment for at least twenty (20) cumulative weeks of engagements to be performed during each of the first and second six (6) month periods during the term hereof; or
(iii) does not obtain employment for at least forty (40) cumulative weeks of engagements to be performed during each subsequent year of the term hereof.

(c) Notice of such termination shall be given by certified mail addressed to the addressee at their last known address and a copy thereof shall be sent to the AFM. Such termination shall be effective as of the date of mailing of such notice. Such notice shall be mailed no later than two (2) weeks following the occurrence of any event described in (i) above; two (2) weeks following a period in excess of thirteen (13) of the cumulative weeks of unemployment specified in (ii) above; and two (2) weeks following a period in excess of twenty-six (26) of the cumulative weeks of unemployment specified in (iii) above. Failure to give notice as aforesaid shall constitute a waiver of the right to terminate based upon the happening of such prior events.
(d) Musician's disability resulting in failure to perform engagements and Musician's unreasonable refusal to accept and perform engagements shall not be themselves either deprive Agent of its right to or give Musician the right to terminate (as provided in (b) above).
(e) As used in this agreement, a "week" shall commence on Sunday and terminate on Saturday. A "week of engagements" shall mean any one of the following:
(i) a week during which Musician is to perform on at least four (4) days; or
(ii) a week during which Musician's gross earnings equals or exceeds the lowest such gross earnings obtained by Musician for performances rendered during any one of the immediately preceding six (6) weeks; or
(iii) a week during which Musician is to perform engagements on commercial television or radio or in concert for compensation equal at least to three (3) times the minimum scales of the AFM or of any local thereof having jurisdiction applicable to such engagements.

Although the agreement is for three years, you can call it quits if any of the circumstances contained in this clause occur. You must give timely notice, however, and strictly follow the method outlined in (c). Note the various definitions of "week." Odds are you signed with the particular agency because of a personal relationship or reputation of a particular person with whom you expect to work. You may also want to negotiate a term that if that particular agent leaves the agency, you can terminate all your agreements with the agency. This so-called key-person clause insures that you will not be passed around from agent to agent within the agency.

6. AGENT'S MAINTENANCE OF AFM BOOKING AGENT AGREEMENT
Agent represents that Agent is presently a party to an AFM Booking Agent Agreement, which is in full force and effect. If such AFM Booking Agent Agreement shall terminate, the rights of the parties hereunder shall be governed by the terms and conditions of said Booking Agent Agreement relating to the effect of termination of such agreements, which are incorporated herein by reference.

7. NO OTHER AGREEMENTS
This is the only and the complete agreement between the parties relating to all or any part of the subject matter covered by this agreement. There is no other agreement, arrangement or participation between the parties, nor do the parties stand in any relationship to each other that is not created by this agreement, whereby the terms and conditions of this agreement are avoided or evaded, directly or indirectly, such as, by way of example but not limitation, contracts, arrangements, relationships or participations relating to publicity services, business management, music publishing, or instruction.

Any oral representations of the agent to "puff" the contract may not be binding due to this warranty. "Puffing" is representing more than what is written in the contract. Typical representations such as "Don't worry, we never enforce that provision" should be disregarded. Specifically, certain relationships are directly prohibited by way of example.

8. INCORPORATION OF AFM CONSTITUTION, BY-LAWS, ETC.
There are incorporated into and made part of this agreement, as though fully set forth herein, the present and future provisions of the Constitution, By-laws, Rules, Regulations and Resolutions of the AFM and those of its locals, which do not conflict therewith. The parties acknowledge their responsibility to be fully acquainted, now and for the duration of this agreement, with the contents thereof.

The AFM constitution, bylaws, rules, regulations, and resolutions run numerous pages. They are, however, controlling as to the terms of this document.

9. SUBMISSION AND DETERMINATION OF DISPUTES

(a) Every claim, dispute, controversy or difference arising out of, dealing with, relating to, or affecting the interpretation or application of this agreement, or the violation or breach, or the threatened violation or breach thereof shall be submitted, heard and determined by the International Executive Board of the AFM in accordance with the rules of such Board (regardless of the termination or purported termination of this agreement or of the Agent's AFM Booking Agent Agreement), and such determination shall be conclusive, final and binding on the parties.

(b) This provision is inserted herein by AFM, a bona fide labor union, in connection with the regulation of the relations of its members to Musician's agents and managers. Under this agreement, Agent undertakes to endeavor to secure employment for the Musician. Reasonable written notice shall be given to the Labor Commissioner of the State of California of the time and place of any arbitration hearing hereunder. The said Labor Commissioner or his authorized representative has the right to attend all arbitration hearings. The provisions of this agreement relating to said Labor Commissioner shall not be applicable to cases not falling under the provisions of Section 1700.45 of the Labor Code of the State of California. Nothing in this agreement nor in the AFM Constitution, Bylaws, Rules, Regulations, and Resolutions shall be construed so as to abridge or limit any rights, powers or duties of said Labor Commissioner.

You may not get to court immediately when a dispute occurs. A grievance procedure is outlined and adhered to, and you and the agent are bound to abide by it. Legal representation is not prohibited, and if you think you need it, get legal counsel early in the dispute.

10. NO ASSIGNMENT OF THIS AGREEMENT
This agreement shall be personal to the parties and shall not be transferable or assignable by operation of law or otherwise without the prior consent of the Musician and of the AFM. The obligations imposed by this agreement shall be binding upon the parties. The Musician may terminate this agreement at any time within ninety (90) days after the transfer of a controlling interest in the Agent.

You cannot assign (i.e., transfer) this agreement to your piano player, and the agent cannot pawn you off to "Skylab Booking Agency." Also, if the controlling interest (and this can be less than 51%) in the agency is transferred, you can get out of this contract.

11. NEGOTIATION FOR RENEWAL
Neither party shall enter into negotiations for or agree to the renewal or extension of this agreement prior to the beginning of the final year of the term hereof.

12. APPROVAL BY AFM
This agreement shall not become effective unless, within thirty (30) days following its execution, an executed copy thereof is filed with and is thereafter approved in writing by the AFM.

IN WITNESS WHEREOF,

The parties hereto have executed this agreement the _____ day of __________ 20___.

AGENT	MUSICIAN
BY	RESIDENCE ADDRESS
NAME AND TITLE	CITY/STATE/ZIP

STANDARD AFTRA EXCLUSIVE AGENCY CONTRACT UNDER RULE 12-B

THIS AGREEMENT, made and entered at ____________________ by and between ____, hereinafter called the "AGENT" and ____________________________________, hereinafter called the "ARTIST."

1. SCOPE OF AGREEMENT
The Artist employs the Agent as his sole and exclusive Agent in the transcription, radio broadcasting and television industries (hereinafter referred to as the "broadcasting industries") within the scope of the regulations (Rule 12-B) of the American Federation of Television and Radio Artists (hereinafter called AFTRA), and agrees not to employ any other person or persons to act for him in like capacity during the term hereof, and the Agent accepts such employment. This contract is limited to the broadcasting industries and to contracts of the Artist as an artist in such fields and any reference hereinafter to contracts or employment whereby the Artist renders his services, refers to contracts or employment in the broadcasting industries, except as otherwise provided herein.

This clause limits the scope of the representation to broadcasting engagements within the purview of the guild.

2. MEMBERSHIP
The Artist agrees that prior to any engagement or employment in the broadcasting industries, he will become a member of AFTRA in good standing and remain such a member for the duration of such engagement or employment. The Artist warrants that he has the right to make this contract and that he is not under any other agency contract in the broadcasting fields. The Agent warrants that he is and will remain a duly franchised agent of AFTRA for the duration of this contract. This paragraph is for the benefit of AFTRA and AFTRA members as well as for the benefit of the parties to this agreement.

You must maintain your membership in good standing in AFTRA.

3. TERM
The term of this contract shall be for a period of __________________ commencing on the __________ day of ______________, 20__.
NOTE—The term may not be in excess of three years.

4. AGENT COMPENSATION

(a) The Artist agrees to pay to the Agent a sum equal to _______ percent (not more than 10%) of all moneys or other consideration received by the Artist, directly or indirectly, under contracts of employment entered into during the term specified herein as provided in the Regulations. Commissions shall be payable when as such moneys or other consideration are received by the Artist or by anyone else for or on the Artist's behalf.

(b) Any moneys or other consideration received by the Artist or by anyone for or on his behalf, in connection with any termination of any contract of the Artist on which the Agent would otherwise be entitled to receive commission, or in connection with the settlement of any such contract, or any litigation arising out of such contract, shall also be moneys in connection with which the Agent is entitled to the aforesaid commissions; provided, however, that in such event the Artist shall be entitled to deduct arbitration fees, attorneys' fees, expenses and court costs before computing the amount upon which the Agent is entitled to his commissions.

(c) Such commissions shall be payable by the Artist to the Agent, as aforesaid, during the term of this contract and thereafter only where specifically provided herein.

(d) The agent shall be entitled to the aforesaid commissions after the expiration of the term specified herein, for so long a period thereafter as the Artist continues to receive moneys or other consideration under or upon employment contracts entered into by the Artist during the term specified herein, including moneys or other consideration received by the Artist under the extended term of such employment contracts, resulting from the exercise of an option or options given an employer under such employment contracts, extending the term of such employment contracts, whether such options be exercised prior to or after the expiration of the terms specified herein.

(e) If after the expiration of the term of this agreement and during the period the Agent is entitled to commissions, a contract of employment of the Artist be terminated before the expiration thereof, as said contract may have been extended by the exercise of options therein contained, by joint action of the Artist and employer, or by the action of either of them, other than on account of an Act of God, illness or the like and the Artist enters into a new contract of employment with said employer within a period of sixty (60) days, such new contract shall be deemed to be in substitution of the contract terminated as aforesaid. In computing the said sixty (60) day period, each day between June 15th and September 15th shall be counted as three-fifths (3/5) of a day only. No contract entered into after said sixty (60) day period shall be deemed to be in substitution of the contract terminated as aforesaid. Contracts of substitution have the same effect as contracts for which they were substituted; provided however, that any increase or additional salary, bonus or other compensation payable to the Artist (either under such contract of substitution or otherwise) over and above the amounts payable under the contract of employment entered into prior to the expiration of the term of this agreement shall be deemed an adjustment and unless the Agent shall have a valid Agency contract in effect at the time of such adjustment the Agent shall not be entitled to any commissions on any such adjustment. In no event may a contract of substitution with an employer entered into after the expiration of the term of this agreement, extend the period of time during which the Agent is entitled to commission beyond the period that the Agent would have been entitled to commission had no substitution taken place except to the extent, if necessary, for the Agent to receive the same total amount of commission he would have received had no such substitution taken place; provided, however, that in no event shall the Agent receive more than the above percentages as commissions on the Artist's adjusted compensation under the contract of substitution. A change in form of an employer for the purpose of evading this provision, or a change in the corporate form of an employer resulting from reorganization or like, shall not exclude the application of these provisions.

(f) So long as the Agent receives commissions from the Artist, the Agent shall be obligated to service the Artist and perform the obligations of this contract with respect to the services of the Artist on which such commissions are based, subject to AFTRA's Regulations Governing Agents.

(g) The Agent has no right to receive money unless the Artist receives the same, or unless the same is received for or on his behalf, and then only proportionate in the above percentages when and as received. Money paid pursuant to legal process to the Artist's creditors, or by virtue of assignment or direction of the Artist, and deductions from the Artist's compensation made pursuant to law in the nature of a collection or tax at the source, such as Social Security or Old Age Pension taxes, or income taxes withheld at the source, shall be treated as compensation received for or on the Artist's behalf.

Both the length of this contract and the commission payable under it are negotiable up to the maximums specified. The agreement can be for as little as a day or up to three years. An artist in a strong bargaining position could possibly negotiate less than the maximum 10% commission, but this will be rare.

5. EMPLOYMENT OFFERS

Should the Agent, during the term or terms specified herein negotiate a contract of employment for the Artist and secure for the Artist bona fide offer of employment, which offer is communicated by the Agent to the Artist in reasonable detail and writing, which offer the Artist declines, and if, after the expiration of the term of this agreement and within ninety (90) days after the date upon which the Agent gives such written information to the Artist, the Artist accepts said offer of employment on substantially the same terms, then the Artist shall be required to pay commissions to the Agent upon such contract of employment. If an Agent previously employed under a prior agency contract is entitled to collect commissions under the foregoing circumstances, the Agent with whom the present contract is executed waives his commission to the extent that the prior agent is entitled to collect the same.

6. DURATION AND TERMINATION

(a) If during any period of ninety-one (91) days immediately preceding the giving of the notice of termination hereinafter mentioned in this paragraph, the Artist fails to be employed and receive, or be entitled to receive, compensation for fifteen (15) days' employment, whether such employment is from fields under AFTRA's jurisdiction or any other branch of the entertainment industry in which the Agent may be authorized by written contract to represent the Artist, then either the Artist or the Agent may terminate the employment of the Agent hereunder by written notice to the other party. (1) For purposes of computing fifteen (15) days' employment required hereunder, each separate original radio broadcast, whether live or recorded, and each transcribed program, shall be considered a day's employment, but a rebroadcast, whether recorded or live, or an off-the-line recording, or a prior recording or time spent in rehearsal for any employment in the radio broadcasting or transcription industry, shall not be considered such employment. (2) During the months of June, July and August, each day's employment in the radio broadcasting industry, shall, for purposes of computing fifteen (15) days' employment under this subparagraph "(a)" and for no other purpose, be deemed one and one-half (1 1/2) days' employment. (3) For the purposes of computing the fifteen (15) days' employment required hereunder, each separate television broadcast (including rehearsal time) shall be considered two and one-half (2 1/2) days' employment. However, any days spent in rehearsal over three days inclusive of the day of the telecast, and any days of exclusivity over three days inclusive of the day of telecast, will automatically extend the ninety-one (91) day period by such coverage. (4) During the months of June, July and August, each day's employment in the television broadcasting field shall, for the purpose of computing fifteen (15) days' employment under this subparagraph "(a)" and for no other purpose, be deemed three and three-quarters (3 3/4) days' employment. (5) Each master phonograph record recorded by the Artist shall be one (1) day's employment.

(b) The ninety-one (91) day period, which is the basis of termination, shall be suspended during any period of time which the artist has declared himself to be unavailable or has so notified the agent in writing or has confirmed in writing a written communication from the agent to such effect. The said ninety-one (91) day period, which is the basis of termination, shall also be suspended (1) during the period of time in which the artist is unable to respond to a call for his services by reason of physical or mental incapacity or (2) for such days as the artist may be employed in a field in which the artist is not represented by the agent.

(c) In the event that the Agent has given the Artist notice in writing of a bona fide offer of employment as an Artist in the entertainment industry and at or near the Artist's usual places of employment at a salary and from an employer commensurate with the Artist's prestige (and there is in fact such an offer), which notice sets forth the terms of the proposed employment in detail and the Artist refuses or negligently fails to accept such proffered employment, then the period of guaranteed employment specified in said offer, and the compensation which would have been received thereunder shall be deemed as time worked or compensation received by the Artist in computing the money earned or time worked with reference to the right of the Artist to terminate under the provisions of this paragraph.

(d) No termination under paragraph 6 shall deprive the Agent of the right to receive commissions or compensation on moneys earned or received by the Artist prior to the date of termination, or earned or received by the Artist after the date of termination and during the term or terms specified herein, or commission or compensation to which the Agent is entitled pursuant to paragraphs 4(e) and 5 hereof.

(e) The Artist may not exercise the right of termination if at the time Artist attempts to do so, either:

(i) the Artist is actually working under written contract or contracts, which guarantee the Artist employment in the broadcasting industries for at least one program each week for a period of not less than thirteen (13) consecutive weeks. For the purposes of this subparagraph a "program" shall be either (1) a regional network program of one-half (1/2) hour length or more; (2) a national network program of one-quarter (1/4) hour length or more; or (3) a program or programs the aggregate weekly compensation for which equals or exceeds the Artist's customary compensation for either (1) or (2), or

(ii) the Artist is under such written contract, as described in the preceding subparagraph (i) or in subparagraph (v) below, and such contract begins

within forty-five (45) days after the time the Artist attempts to exercise the right of termination, or
(iii) where the Artist attempts to exercise the right of termination during the months of August or September, and the Artist is under such written contract as described in the preceding subparagraph (i) or in subparagraph (v) below and such contract begins not later than the following October 15th, or
(iv) if during any period of ninety-one (91) days immediately preceding the giving of notice of termination herein referred to, the Artist has received, or has been entitled to receive, compensation in an amount equal to not less than thirteen (13) times his past customary compensation for a national network program of one-half ($^1/_2$) hour's length, whether such employment or compensation is from the broadcasting industries or any other branch of the entertainment industry in which the agent may be authorized by written contract to represent the Artist.
(v) The Artist is actually working under written contract or contracts which guarantee the Artist either (a) employment in the television broadcasting field for at least one (1) program every other week in a cycle of thirteen (13) consecutive weeks where the program is telecast on an alternative week basis, or (b) employment for at least eight (8) programs in a cycle of thirty-nine (39) consecutive weeks, where the program is telecast on a monthly basis or once every four (4) weeks.

In the cases referred to in subparagraphs (i), (ii), (iii) and (v) above, the ninety-one (91) day period begins upon the termination of the contract referred to in such subparagraphs; and for the purpose of such subparagraphs any local program, which, under any applicable AFTRA collective bargaining agreement, is the equivalent of a regional or national network program, shall be considered a regional or national network program as the case may be.

(f) Where the Artist is under a contract or contracts for the rendition of his services in the entertainment industry in any field in which the agent is authorized to act for the artist, during the succeeding period of one hundred and eighty-two (182) days after the expiration of the ninety-one (91) day period in question, at a guaranteed compensation for such services of twenty-five thousand ($25,000) dollars or more, or where the Artist is under a contract or contracts for the rendition of his services during said 182 day period in the radio phonograph recording and/or television fields at a guaranteed compensation for such services of twenty thousand dollars ($20,000) or more, then the artist may not exercise the right of termination.
(g) Periods of layoff or leave of absence under a term contract shall not be deemed to be periods of unemployment hereunder, unless under said contract the Artist has the right during such period to do other work in the radio or television field or in any other branch of the entertainment industry in which the Agent may be authorized by written contract to represent the Artist. A "term contract" as used herein means a contract under which the Artist is guaranteed employment in the broadcasting industries for at least one program each week for a period of not less than thirteen (13) consecutive weeks, and also includes any "term contract" as defined in the Regulations of the Screen Actors Guild, Inc. in respect to the motion picture industry, under which the Artist is working. Also, a "term contract" as used herein relating to the television field means a

contract under which the Artist is guaranteed employment in the television field as set forth in subparagraph (e)(v) above.

(h) Where the Artist has a contract of employment in the broadcasting industries and either the said contract of employment, or any engagement or engagements thereunder, are canceled by the employer pursuant to any provision of said contract which does not violate any rule or regulation of AFTRA, the Artist shall be deemed to have been employed and to have received compensation for the purposes of paragraph 6(a) for any such canceled broadcasts, with the following limitation—where a contract providing for more than one program has been so canceled, the Artist shall not be deemed to have been employed or to have received compensation under such contract, with respect to more than one such program on and after the effective date of cancellation of such contract.

(i) For the purposes of this paragraph 6, where the Artist does not perform a broadcast for which he has been employed but nevertheless is compensated therefor, the same shall be considered employment hereunder.

(j) If at any time during the original or extended term of this contract, broadcasting over a majority of both the radio stations as well as a majority of the television broadcasting stations shall be suspended, the ninety-one (91) days period mentioned in this paragraph 6 shall be extended for the period of such suspension.

Generally, the artist must be ready, willing and able to accept employment of at least 15 days duration, every 90 days. The exact provisions and exceptions pertaining hereto are complicated, but the guild will help you sort out the time requirements if you are really interested in terminating the contract.

7. AGENT REPRESENTATION

The Agent may represent other persons. The Agent shall not be required to devote his entire time and attention to the business of the Artist. The Agent may make known the fact that he is the sole and exclusive representative of the Artist in the broadcasting industries. In the event of a termination of this contract, even by the fault of the Artist, the Agent has no rights or remedies under the preceding sentence.

8. ARTIST'S AGENCY REPRESENTATIVES

The Agent agrees that the following persons, and the following persons only, namely (HERE INSERT NO MORE THAN FOUR NAMES) shall personally supervise the Artist's business during the term of this contract. One of such persons shall be available at all reasonable times for consultation with the Artist at the city or cities named herein. The Agent, upon request of the Artist, shall assign any one of such persons who may be available (and at least one of them always shall be available upon reasonable notice from the Artist), to engage in efforts or handle any negotiations for the Artist at such city or its environs and such person shall do so. Employees of the Agent who have signed the AFTRA covenant and who are not named herein may handle agency matters for the Artist or may aid any of the named persons in handling agency matters for the Artist.

9. AGENCY CONTINUITY

In order to provide continuity of management, the name or names of not more than four (4) persons connected with the Agent must be written in the following space, and this contract is not valid unless this is done:

(HERE INSERT NOT MORE THAN FOUR NAMES)
In the event three (3) or four (4) persons are so named, at least two (2) of such persons must remain active in the Agency throughout the term of this contract. In the event only one (1) or two (2) persons are so named, at least one (1) such person must remain active in the Agency throughout the term of this contract. If the required number of persons does not remain active with the Agency, the Artist may terminate this contract in accordance with Section XXIII of AFTRA's Regulations Governing Agents.

> *This clause insures continuity of representation within the agency, which many of the other agency agreements do not provide for. (The persons named in clause 8, Artist's Agency Representatives, do not have to be the same as those named in clause 9. Also see key-person discussion under AFM Agreement paragraph 5.)*

10. USE OF ARTIST'S NAME
The Artist hereby grants to the Agent the right to use the name, portraits and pictures of the Artist to advertise and publicize the Artist in connection with Agent's representation of the Artist hereunder.

> *Any portraits and pictures used by the agency should be approved in writing by the artist.*

11. AGENT WARRANTIES
The Agent agrees:

(a) To make no deductions whatsoever from any applicable minimums established by AFTRA under any collective bargaining agreement.
(b) At the request of the Artist, to counsel and advise him in matters which concern the professional interests of the Artist in the broadcasting industries.
(c) The Agent will be truthful in his statements to the Artist.
(d) The Agent will not make any binding engagement or other commitment on behalf of the Artist, without the approval of the Artist, and without first informing the Artist of the terms and conditions (including compensation) of such engagement.
(e) The Agent's relationship to the Artist shall be that of a fiduciary. The Agent, when instructed in writing by the Artist not to give out information with reference to the Artist's affairs, will not disclose such information.
(f) That the Agent is equipped, and will continue to be equipped, to represent the interests of the Artist ably and diligently in the broadcasting industry throughout the term of this contract, and that he will so represent the Artist.
(g) To use all reasonable efforts to assist the Artist in procuring employment for the services of the Artist in the broadcasting industries.
(h) The Agent agrees that the Agent will maintain an office and telephone open during all reasonable business hours (emergencies such as sudden illness or death excepted) within the city of __________ or its environs, throughout the term of this agreement, and that some representative of the Agent will be present at such office during such business hours. This contract is void unless the blank in the paragraph is filled in with the name of a city at which the Agent does maintain an office for the radio broadcasting and television agency business.
(i) At the written request of the Artist, given to the Agent not oftener than once every four (4) weeks, the Agent shall give the Artist information in writing, stating what efforts the Agent has rendered on behalf of the Artist within a

reasonable time preceding the date of such request.

(j) The Agent will not charge or collect any commissions on compensation received by the Artist for services rendered by the Artist in a package show in which the Agent is interested, where prohibited by Section VIII of AFTRA's Regulations.

12. SUBMISSION AND DETERMINATION OF DISPUTES

This contract is subject to AFTRA's Regulations Governing Agents (Rule 12-B). Any controversy under this contract, or under any contract executed in renewal or extension hereof or in substitution herefor or alleged to have been so executed, or as to the existence, execution or validity hereof or thereof, or the right of either party to avoid this or any such contract or alleged contract on any grounds, or the construction, performance, nonperformance, operation, breach, continuance or termination of this or any such contract, shall be submitted to arbitration in accordance with the arbitration provisions in the regulations regardless of whether either party has terminated or purported to terminate this or any such contract or alleged contract. Under this contract, the Agent undertakes to endeavor to secure employment for the Artist.

(FOR CALIFORNIA ONLY)

This provision is inserted in this contract pursuant to a rule of AFTRA, a bona fide labor union, which Rule regulates the relations of its members to agencies or artists managers. Reasonable written notice shall be given to the Labor Commissioner of the State of California of the time and place of any arbitration hearing hereunder. The Labor Commissioner of the State of California, or his authorized representative, has the right to attend all arbitration hearings. The clauses relating to the Labor Commissioner of the State of California shall not be applicable to cases not falling under the provisions of Section 1647.5 and/or Section 1700.45 of the Labor Code of the State of California.

Nothing in this contract nor in AFTRA's Regulations Governing Agents (Rule 12-B) shall be construed so as to abridge or limit any rights, powers or duties of the Labor Commissioner of the State of California.

Whether or not the agent is the actor's agent at the time this agency contract is executed, it is understood that in executing this contract each party has independent access to the regulations and has relied and will rely exclusively upon his own knowledge thereof.

IN WITNESS WHEREOF, the parties hereto have executed this agreement the _____ day of ___________, 20___.

______________________________	______________________________
AGENT	ARTIST
______________________________	______________________________
ADDRESS	ADDRESS
______________________________	______________________________
CITY/STATE/ZIP	CITY/STATE/ZIP

GENERAL SERVICES AGREEMENT

1. SCOPE OF AGREEMENT

I hereby employ you as my sole and exclusive representative, talent agency and agent in the entertainment, literary and related fields throughout the world for a period of ________ years from the date hereof. You accept said employment and agree to counsel and advise me, during normal business hours at your office, in the advancement of my professional career and to use reasonable efforts to negotiate employment and other contracts providing for the rendition of my services in those branches of the entertainment, literary, music, and related fields throughout the world, in which I am now or hereafter shall be willing and qualified to render services, including without any limitation, motion pictures, television and radio, publishing, audio and video recordings, personal appearances, concerts, theater, merchandising, testimonials and commercial tie-ins, whether or not using my name, voice or likeness.

This is a general services agreement that goes beyond areas traditionally covered by union contracts. It authorizes representation in all areas of the entertainment industry, but you can exclude areas where you feel the agent may not be particularly helpful or needed (i.e., music publishing, where you may already have another established relationship). It is also exclusive (i.e., you cannot have general services representation by more than one agency).

2. WARRANTIES

I have the right to enter into this agreement. I have not entered into and will not hereafter enter into any agreement that will conflict with the terms and provisions hereof. I agree that you may have interests of any kind either in your own or in the activities of others as well as the right to render your services for others during the term hereof either in the capacity in which you are employed by me hereunder or otherwise, whether similar to or competitive with the interests and activities for which you are employed to represent me hereunder, including without limitation, on behalf of the owners of package programs or other productions in which my services are used. Such representation shall not constitute a violation of your fiduciary or other obligations hereunder. With respect to the rendition of my services outside of the continental United States, you shall have the right to designate without my consent any one or more persons, firms or corporations to carry out or do any or all acts or things hereunder otherwise to be performed by you. No breach of this agreement by you or failure to perform the terms hereof shall be deemed a material breach of this agreement unless within thirty (30) days after I learn of such breach I serve written notice upon you of such breach and you do not remedy such breach within fifteen (15) days, exclusive of Saturdays, Sundays and holidays, after receipt by you of such written notice; provided, however, that the provisions of this sentence shall not be applicable to the provisions of Paragraph 6 of this agreement.

Packaging is allowed by the agent, as is the representation of other (possibly competing) clients. Ask for a list of the agent's other clients. Note the warranty that you are free to enter into this agreement (meaning that you have not signed with another agent for representation in the same areas).

3. COMPENSATION

I agree to pay you 10%, as and when received by me or by any person, firm or corporation on my behalf, directly or indirectly, or by any person, firm or corporation owned or controlled by me, directly or indirectly, or in which I now have or hereafter during the term hereof acquire any right, title, or interest, directly or indirectly, or by my successors and assigns, of the gross compensation paid or payable to me or for my account, during or after the term hereof, pursuant to or as a result of or in connection with (a) any employment or contract now in existence or negotiated or entered into during the term hereof (or within six months after the term hereof, if any such employment or contract is on terms similar or reasonably comparable to any offer made to me during the term hereof and is with the same offeror thereof or any person, firm or corporation directly or indirectly connected with such offeror) whether procured by you, me or any third party; and (b) all modifications, extensions, renewals, replacements, supplements or substitutes for such employment or contract or pertaining thereto whether procured by you, me or any third party; however, it is expressly understood that to be entitled to continue to receive the payment of compensation on the aforementioned contracts during or after the termination of this agreement you shall remain obligated to serve and to perform obligations with respect to said employment contracts and to extensions or renewals of said contracts and to any employment requiring my services on which such compensation is based. Commissions on considerations other than money shall be payable, at your election, either in money based on the fair market value of such other considerations, or in pro rata share in kind of such other considerations.

The commission should be limited to engagements procured by the agent. The commission amount can vary, depending upon a maximum established in union-regulated areas or that negotiated by the client. At the time of signing a series of agreements, the artist may want to negotiate an "across the board commission," applicable to all areas of representation—AFM, AFTRA, general services, etc. Also, commissions may be figured either on gross receipts (all amounts paid to or on behalf of the artist) or net receipts (gross receipts less the deduction of certain expenses, such as travel, weekly guarantees to artist, or such artificial amount as 10% on monies earned after the first $50,000). And, if the agent receives a "packaging fee" from the buyer for your services coupled with that of other agency clients, no additional commission on your earnings should be allowed—no "double-dipping!" Finally, try to restrict commissions on renewed contracts after termination to those renewals actually negotiated by the agent before termination of the agent.

4. OTHER ARTIST BUSINESSES

If any firm, corporation, partnership, joint venture or other form of business entity now or hereafter owned or controlled by me in which I now or hereafter have any right, title or interest has or hereafter during the term hereof acquires directly or indirectly any right to my services in the entertainment, literary, music and related fields, then said firm, corporation, etc., shall be deemed to have engaged you as its sole and exclusive agent and shall confirm such engagement by executing an agency agreement in the same form as this agreement or your then standard form pertaining to such activity. Regardless of whether such business entity executes any such agreement with you, such agency agreement shall be deemed executed and shall be of full force and effect, and I shall remain primarily liable, jointly and severally, with such third party, to pay commission to you as provided in paragraph 3 above, based upon the gross compensation paid and/or payable to such third party, directly or indirectly, for furnishing my services, as fully and effectively as if such gross compensation were paid and/or payable to me. For the purposes of Paragraph 3 above, the term "gross compensation" shall be deemed to include such gross compensation paid and/or payable to such third party. If such third party does not, for whatever reason, execute such agreement with you, you shall nevertheless remain my exclusive agent to represent me in connection with my services on the terms and conditions as herein contained and I shall remain liable to pay commissions to you as provided in this contract and in the preceding sentence hereof.

> *This clause attempts to cover the situation where artists form other business entities, usually for tax purposes, which "loan-out" the services of the artist. Due to the legal fiction that separates the identities of a corporation from that of its shareholders, this paragraph insures that not only the artist but also his loan-out corporation is firmly bound to the representation agreement.*

5. COMPENSATION DEFINITION

As used herein, "gross compensation" means all monies, properties, considerations and other things of value of every kind and character whatsoever including but not limited to salaries, earnings, fees, royalties, rents, bonuses, gifts, proceeds, rerun fees and stock (without deductions of any kind) and shall likewise include, without limitations, any gross compensation paid and/or payable to me or for my account on a so-called pay-or-play basis, as a guarantee or otherwise in lieu of the rendition of my services; "services" shall include any and all of my services in any capacity whatsoever, whether as an employee, independent contractor or otherwise; "employment" and "contract" shall include any and all employment or contracts (including contracts to refrain from services or activities) of every kind whatsoever whether written or oral, in any way pertaining to services, materials or interests in any branch of the entertainment, literary, music and related fields.

6. DURATION AND TERMINATION

If I do not obtain a bona fide offer of employment from a responsible employer during a period in excess of four (4) consecutive months, during all of which time I have been ready, willing, able and available to accept employment, either party hereto shall have the right to terminate this contract by notice in writing to that effect sent to the other party by registered mail, provided no such bona fide offer has been obtained subsequent to the expiration of said four (4) month period and before the giving of said notice. The exercise of my right to terminate under this paragraph shall not affect your rights under Paragraph 3 hereof with respect to employment or contracts in existence or negotiated for prior to the effective date of such termination.

> *This is your "out"—if no bona fide offer of employment is received by you during at least four consecutive months during the term of the contract, you can fire the agency and they can cancel you. You may also negotiate here for a minimal annual sum to be booked by the agent in order to keep the agreement in force—i.e., if the agent fails to procure employment earning you at least "$X" per year, or 10% over the previous year's earnings, you have the option of terminating all the agency's agreements with you.*

7. ASSIGNMENT OF REPRESENTATION
You shall have the right to assign this agreement or any part thereof to any persons, firms or corporations ("companies") now or hereafter controlling, controlled by or under common control with you, any companies resulting from a merger or consolidation with you, any companies succeeding to a substantial part of your assets, or any parent, affiliated or subsidiary companies.

> *This clause allows the agency to assign your representation to another affiliated company. This should be looked at carefully, especially when you are signing because of the lure of one particular agent. The artist should include a "key-person" clause specifying that if a particular agent leaves the agency, the artist can follow the agent. (See "key-person" clause discussion under AFM Agreement paragraph 5.)*

8. DISPUTES
Controversies arising between us under the provisions of the California Labor Code relating to Talent Agencies and under the rules and regulations for the enforcement thereof, shall be referred to the Labor Commissioner of the State of California, as provided in Section 1700.44 of said Code.

> *The Labor Code permits controversies to be submitted to either the Labor Commissioner or arbitration. This clause opts for the Labor Commissioner.*

9. SIGNEES
In the event this agreement is signed by more than one person, firm, corporation, or other entity, it shall apply to the undersigned jointly and severally, and to the activities, interests and contracts of each of the undersigned individually. If any one of the undersigned is a corporation or other entity, the pronouns "I," "me" or "my" as used in this agreement shall refer to the undersigned corporation or other entity, and the undersigned corporation or other entity agrees that it will be bound by the provisions hereof in the same manner and to the same extent as it would, had its name been inserted in the place of the pronouns.

10. ORAL PROMISES AND EXTENSIONS OF TERM
This instrument constitutes the entire agreement between us and no statement, promises or inducements made by any party hereto, which is not contained herein, shall be binding or valid and this contract may not be enlarged, modified or altered except in writing, signed by both parties hereto. The term of this agreement stated in Paragraph 1 hereof shall be automatically extended for one (1) year, unless I shall give you written notice to the contrary no later than thirty (30) days prior to the end of such term. The termination of any other agency agreement between us for any reason shall not affect this agreement in any respect.

> *This is an all-inclusive clause disavowing any oral promises made. Moreover, all changes in the agreement must be made in writing. Note the automatic extension for one year of the term of the contract unless the artist gives notice 30 days before the term ends.*

Very truly yours,

____

AGREED TO AND ACCEPTED:

AGENT	ARTIST
BY	BY
NAME AND TITLE	NAME AND TITLE
(AN AUTHORIZED SIGNATORY)	(AN AUTHORIZED SIGNATORY)
FEDERAL I.D./SS#	FEDERAL I.D./SS#

Business Managers

BY MARGARET ROBLEY

Business managers oversee the financial aspects of their clients' lives. They take an active role in the collection of income, prepare budgets and monitor expenditures, actively participate in their clients' investment decisions, oversee insurance coverage, initiate and participate in estate planning, and constantly monitor the tax consequences of all transactions. While accounting is universal for all businesses, business management, as described herein, is unique to the entertainment industry.

There are no credential, licensing or educational requirements to become a business manager. However, in order to offer investment advice, the business manager must be licensed as an investment advisor. Since the problems business managers deal with are very complex, most are certified public accountants (CPAs), attorneys, or business people with varied financial backgrounds.

SELECTING A BUSINESS MANAGER

Artists usually do not engage business managers until after they have had some success in the music industry, such as a gold album. Until that time, accountants can be hired on an hourly basis to prepare tax returns and advise them on tax and business matters.

Once you have decided that a business manager is needed, you should interview several firms before making a decision and meet everyone that will be working on your account.

When searching for a business manager, the artist should ask colleagues and advisors for referrals and check out the firm (i.e., professional references, etc.) before setting up an appointment. It is very important for the business manager to have experience in dealing with music clients and the expertise to handle any specific problems or situations that the artist has. Artists should consider interviewing small local companies and international accounting firms, which have worldwide networks of services available, before deciding which is best for their specific needs. Whether you choose a large firm or small one, you should feel comfortable and have a good rapport with your individual business manager. It is very important that the artist be able to communicate openly and easily with the business management team. Normally, an engagement letters is the only contract between the artist and the business manager, so a good personal relationship is very important, and it is imperative that both feel free to sever the relationship at any time.

The business manager is generally the last member added to the management team, and the artist should consult with the other members of the team (i.e., personal manager, talent agent, and attorney) before engaging one, as it is crucial that they all work together cohesively.

DUTIES OF THE BUSINESS MANAGER

Business managers perform many functions in overseeing the financial affairs of their clients. A synopsis of some of these functions follows.

Bookkeeping and Collection of Income

In a business management firm, the bookkeepers and account managers (under the supervision of managers and partners) are responsible for reviewing invoices, verifying their validity, and processing them for payment; preparing payroll checks for clients' employees; preparing incoming checks for deposit; and monitoring bank accounts to make sure there are sufficient funds to cover checks and clients' withdrawals from ATM machines. Any excess funds that will be needed in the near future are transferred to short-term investments to earn interest.

Many artists have one or more contracts (i.e., recording, merchandising, publishing, various foreign subpublishing, etc.) that the business managers are responsible for monitoring to ensure that all contractual amounts are received. They must have monitoring systems that keep track of the various types of income due and the projected due dates. All receipts are verified to ensure that all income is received in a timely manner. If moneys are not received when due, business managers pursue collecting the delinquent amounts. They also monitors sales and advances to make sure that income is properly reported and paid and determine if record royalties are being escalated properly and whether any cross-collateralization is contractually allowed.

When artists control their own publishing, the process of monitoring income becomes more difficult, as there may be many subpublishing deals and synchronization licenses for which to account. Business managers will maintain continuous income schedules to monitor the publishing and subpublishing royalties earned and will keep in close contact with the music publishing administrators to make sure that moneys are received for all synchronization and mechanical licenses granted.

Financial Reporting

Most business management firms use computerized systems for bookkeeping that generate statements showing all cash receipts and disbursements, cash balances, and financial statements reflecting monthly and cumulative year-to-date income and expense figures. These monthly financial statements are reviewed by the accountants that use them to prepare tax projections, budgets, annual meeting packages, and special reports requested by clients.

Based on projected income and conversations with their clients, business managers prepare budgets that reflect projected expenditures. Budgets include capital items (which may be a large portion of client spending) and their clients' personal discretionary spending—an area that is hard to control due to the ease of using credit cards. Business managers prepare budgets for personal expenditures, but it is their clients that make the decision either to stay within the budget and maintain long-term financial security, or not. Periodically, budget-to-actual comparisons are prepared to show clients any discrepancies.

Tax Services and Estate Planning

Tax planning for clients is a constant process for business managers. This entails determining which type of entity (i.e., sole proprietorship, partnership, corporation, S-corporation, limited liability company) is best; whether a pension plan or medical reimbursement plan is desirable; whether to buy or lease an automobile; which investment strategies to pursue; etc.

Business managers are responsible for tax compliance and prepares payroll tax, sales tax, gift tax, city or local tax, and income tax returns for filing with the appropriate authorities. They represent clients in examinations by tax agencies, including the Internal Revenue Service. Since the establishment of the Entertainment Task Force by the IRS, there have been more examinations of entertainers' tax returns than there was in the past.

Business managers interact with attorneys and other advisors in preparing estate and retirement plans for clients. They compile information on assets and liabilities and assemble information on future goals with an emphasis on financial security of their clients and their clients' beneficiaries. Once the life insurance trusts, living trusts, wills, and other estate planning vehicles are in place, the business manager assists his client in obtaining life insurance, which will pay any projected estate taxes.

Touring Services

Before clients agree to U.S. or foreign tours, their business managers work with the personal managers to project income and expenses for the tour. Touring can be an effective method of promoting artists' current recordings. Even though tour support is recoupable by record companies, tours may generate sufficient album sales to pay any excess costs and still be profitable to some artists. Business managers monitor income and expenditures, ensure that adequate insurance (including nonappearance insurance, if applicable) is in place, ensure compliance with multistate taxing authorities, prepare budgets, negotiate to minimize tax withholding in various states and overseas, review all third party contracts, obtain social security clearances for applicable foreign countries, monitor budget-to-actual income and expense and resolve discrepancies, and prepare tax returns for all necessary jurisdictions.

The business management staff reviews tour settlements, and, when necessary, a staff member or partner may accompany their clients to assist in box office settlements with promoters and venues.

Insurance, Investments and Asset Administration

Adequate insurance coverage is a must to protect clients' long-range security. Business managers are responsible for ensuring that their clients have sufficient insurance coverage for employees, businesses, autos, real estate, and to protect assets in case of lawsuits, and cover medical bills and furnish income in case of disability.

Due to the Federal Deposit Insurance Corporation regulations and the low interest rates offered, a minimum amount of money should be kept in bank accounts. All excess cash should be invested.

Artists and business managers should develop investment policies that are comfortable for the artists. A conservative approach, which preserves capital and avoids risk, could be investing in U.S. Treasury securities and insured municipal bonds. A slightly more aggressive profile would be investment in blue chip stocks; if a client wants more growth potential with higher risk, investment can be made in more volatile securities.

Depending on the age of a client, any funds in an Individual Retirement Account (IRA) or pension plan may be invested for growth rather than income. The growth funds are best for clients that still have several years before they reach retirement age.

Business managers advise and assist their clients in the acquisition, sale, and improvement of residences or other real estate. This assistance includes working with loan brokers and direct lenders to acquire financing or refinancing of mortgages that take advantage of the most favorable plans and rates. Business managers also deal with the purchases and sales of other assets (such as automobiles) and are instrumental in obtaining asset appraisals to ensure that adequate insurance coverage is in place.

Royalty Examination

Some business management firms have separate royalty examination or audit departments that perform examinations of U.S. record and publishing companies and their foreign distributors to determine if there have been underpayments of royalty income. These examinations may be conducted for individual artists, writers, and licensors of rights. The royalty examination department may also perform examinations on merchandisers and other licensees and on the distribution records of television shows and motion pictures for profit participation clients. Due diligence/rights valuations can also be performed for clients interested in purchasing a copyright or other investment. In firms where business management and royalty examination/audit departments fall under the same roof, clients have the advantage of constant monitoring of royalties, which can result in substantially more income.

Music Publishing Administration

Some business managers have the capability to copyright, license and administer songwriter clients' musical compositions. Music publishing administration consists of analyzing domestic, foreign, and performing rights societies royalty statements and issuing royalty statements to other writers and publishers; issuing synchronization licenses, issuing mechanical licenses, and issuing print/reprint licenses. Some business management firms also assist in structuring and administering foreign subpublishing deals throughout the world and can perform computations to establish catalog valuation.

Most artist/songwriters will need to secure the services of a music publishing administrator due to the complexity of the agreements, the substantial amount of time necessary to administer the various licenses, and the potential for royalties to slip through the cracks. It is very important that music publishing administrators work very closely with business managers to ensure that the artists/songwriters receive all of the royalties due them.

THE BUSINESS MANAGER AS PART OF THE MANAGEMENT TEAM

Artists have talents and skills that must be marketed to make them successful. It is the responsibility of management teams to do that marketing.

Since business managers account for their clients' money once it has been earned, they are an important part of management teams, which consist of the personal manager (controller of the artist's life, including their recording contract, touring activities, public relations profile, and their entire career plan), the talent agent (whose primary job is to work with promoters to book and promote live performances, or to negotiate roles on television shows or in movies), and the attorney (who is involved in structuring deals and shaping the artist's career in addition to providing routine legal advice).

These four parties work together to help further their clients' careers and maintain their financial stability. Management teams make recommendations, but it is the clients that have the final say in all aspects of their lives and careers.

Each advisor has a role; by working together, yet separately, they maintain a cohesive whole. Although their total fees may range from 25% to 30% of gross income, the financial stability provided may be worth the cost.

For most creative artists, taking care of business is not the most effective use of their time. For that reason, it is important they choose business managers that have specialized knowledge of taxes, royalties, investments, and touring to handle these technical and complex matters.

In the business management firm, the bookkeepers and account managers function as their clients' bookkeeping and accounting departments. The accountants act as assistant controllers, the supervisors or managers act as treasurers or controllers, and the partner acts as the vice president or chief financial officer of their clients' businesses. Personal managers act as general managers or chief operating officers; and the clients act as presidents or CEOs and are the final decision makers.

Since the careers of most artists are of limited life, they must put their yearly income in perspective and spend accordingly. When artists are successful and money is pouring in, overspending is not noticed. When income drops, however, this overspending can lead to bankruptcy. Artists need to control spending and operate in an efficient manner so they can generate more after tax dollars and have brighter futures. Musicians' strengths lie in their musical talents, and it is the function of capable business managers to ensure that artists are prepared for the likelihood of lean years.

BUSINESS MANAGEMENT FEES

Accounting and professional fees are traditionally billed on an hourly basis. In the business management field, however, the general billing rule is a percentage fee (usually 5%) of the client's gross income. In some cases, a maximum and minimum is placed on the total yearly fee. Some business managers charge a monthly retainer fee instead of percentage billing.

GENERAL FINANCIAL ADVICE

Artists must consider how recording and publishing contracts are structured.

Recording budgets or recording funds are set forth in their recording contracts to provide funds to cover all production costs with any balance going to the artists. Since artists ultimately pay all of the costs for recordings, it is very important that these costs be minimized as much as possible. These costs must be recouped by the record companies before artists receive any royalties. Even if an artist's attorney has negotiated a fantastic royalty rate, the initial royalties must cover the recoupment of recording costs, free goods, packaging, a hold back for reserves, tour support, video costs, and recoupable promotion costs. Thus, there are often no royalty payments until substantial sales take place. Artists may also receive publishing advances, which must be recouped before any publishing royalties are payable to them. Often, much of the recording budgets and publishing advances are spent on ordinary living expenses and the meager royalties may be quite shocking.

Artists should prepare budgets (with their business managers) and make every effort to stay within their guidelines. Whenever income is received, the amount that will be necessary to pay income taxes should be segregated so that it won't be available for personal expenses. Artists should not overextend finances when purchasing real estate, autos, equipment, and other assets. If possible, they should pay cash so there will be no payments due if money gets tight. Adequate insurance coverage should be maintained (including life and medical) to protect against lawsuits and catastrophes. Artists should establish retirement plans in which investments of after tax dollars will accumulate. Additionally, estate planning should be a priority in order to minimize the effect of estate taxes.

Cost-cutting measures implemented now will result in more money in the future. To live comfortably later, it is necessary for artists to conserve money in the peak years.

CONCLUSION

By overseeing all financial aspects of their clients' lives, business managers strive to maximize earnings, plan for the future, and preserve and expand asset bases. Although it is difficult for some artists to entrust their business and personal finances to someone else, no matter how highly regarded, it is necessary to do so in order to focus on furthering their careers. Once this happens, artists can build for the future secure in the knowledge that their finances are being handled properly.

Because of the trust that is placed in them by their clients, business managers must have integrity and be able to make sound decisions. Since most business management clients are not experienced business people, business managers must be able to explain transactions, situations, and laws in language that their clients' can understand. Business managers will deal closely with their clients' personal managers, attorneys, agents, and personal assistants; however, their loyalty is to their clients, and they must, therefore, protect their clients in all matters.

Recording

PRACTICAL ASPECTS OF SECURING MAJOR LABEL AGREEMENTS

ANALYSIS OF A RECORDING CONTRACT

HOW TO READ AND EVALUATE ARTIST ROYALTY STATEMENTS

ROYALTY STATEMENTS: AUDITS AND LAWSUITS

ANALYSIS OF A RECORD PRODUCER AGREEMENT

RECORDING AND DISTRIBUTION CONTRACTS WITH INDEPENDENT LABELS

CONTRACTS AND RELATIONSHIPS BETWEEN INDEPENDENT AND MAJOR LABELS

Practical Aspects of Securing Major Label Agreements

BY NEVILLE L. JOHNSON

Talent alone will not guarantee a record deal, and seeking one can be discouraging and fruitless. There are only a few hundred deals available each year and many of them go to artists that are moving from one label to another. Still, there are deals to be had, and if you are a good musician, success may be just around the corner.

TODAY'S REALITY: CREATE YOUR OWN BUZZ

Generally, acts are signed only after being released on their own or on a small independent label. Since the advent of SoundScan, which, via bar coding, measures nearly 75% of the sales of recorded music in the United States, record companies can realize immediately when a local act is hot, or when a regional breakout is occurring.

The Internet, though still in its nascent stages, is becoming the number one way by which a band can get noticed and get others interested. Making music is easy compared to the difficulty in getting the right entity to market and sell it.

You must create the excitement for your music. Get connected via chat groups. Start your own Internet site. Get yourself noticed on MP3.com, garageband.com and any other site that features new music and unsigned bands. As this goes to press, Farmclub.com is a "contest" site where groups can get on television and obtain a major record agreement; it may be worth a try. Figure out what will attract people to your site, your gigs, and your music. Remember, Madonna started from nowhere, just like everybody else.

THE MUSIC PACKAGE

The music package consists of the artist, the act, a demonstration sound recording (usually a CD), and materials such as lyric sheets, pictures, reviews, biographical information, letters and invitations.

A demonstration sound recording (demo) is necessary for most acts that have not had a record deal prior to the time of the presentation. A demo must contain music that is unique, creative and commercial. The majors want music that will sell in large quantities. These days, it is rock and roll, pop, AAA (Adult Album Alternative), country, R&B, rap/hip-hop, Americana (singer-songwriters, roots music), jazz and classical, with the latter two categories being particularly difficult to break into because their market share is so limited. Most companies want million sellers, and A&R (Artists and Repertoire) executives that do not deliver acts that provide meaningful sales and airplay do not have jobs for long. One function of A&R executives is talent acquisition, but most are primarily busy with, and responsible for, the talent that is already signed to their label, so it is tough to get their attention.

The artist should keep in mind that the ultimate sale will be to the public, not to a record company. Music executives evaluate music, in large part, on the basis of its sales potential. Record companies are not philanthropic organizations: they are in business to make money, and can only do so with records that have commercial appeal.

A demo should have the following characteristics.

Good Performance

Artists must prove they are ready to cut tapes of master quality. Many acts record demos in home studios that are equipped to simulate the sound quality of commercial 16- and 24-track studios.

Best Songs First

Record company personnel that listen to demos are very busy and listen to many in a day's work. Do not provide too many selections, and put your best songs first. Four is enough. However, if you submit a self-produced and released album, it may get attention.

Container Information

The name of each selection and the order of performance should be clearly written or typed on the demo box. Make it easy for listeners to name the songs they like. Include the person to contact about the demo (personal manager, attorney, band leader). List the name, address, phone and fax numbers, and email of the contact person for the demo on the package, not just on the accompanying materials.

The other components of the physical package, listed below, can significantly enhance the listener's evaluation, and should accompany the demo.

Lyric Sheets

Lyric sheets help to involve the listener in the music.

Photographs/Videotape

The record company should know about the artist's look and image. A professional and attractive appearance is a valuable asset in today's music industry. Record companies are interested in an artist's visual impact due to MTV, The Box (and similar channels) and videotape markets, and the growing interrelationship between motion pictures, television and records. Some acts have been signed on the strength of a videotape of their live performance sent in lieu of, or in addition to, a demo. If your act has significant visual appeal, a videotape demo should be considered.

Biographical Information

A succinct, factual statement of the artist's credentials and background helps to distinguish the artist from others. The bio is analogous to a resume: it informs the reader of the qualifications of the applicant.

Reviews and Itinerary

Favorable reviews tell the reader that the artist has stage experience and is enjoyable to hear. If the artist can excite an audience, and has a following, the record company will want to know about it because live performance is an important method of promoting records. If a number of impressive gigs have been played, or if the artist is regularly working, an itinerary should be enclosed to communicate that the talent is stage wise and has a source of income.

By paying attention to details, an aura of professionalism can be projected to the record company by the artist, the music, and the people that advise and work with him or her. A clever, enticing package will merit special attention by its recipient.

THE HUMAN PACKAGE

Most successful artists are members of a team. A critical issue in a record company's decision whether to sign an act is who will carry the ball after a record is released. If an act has inexperienced, incompetent, or no personnel to support and direct it, the record company's job of selling records will be difficult. An artist will substantially improve the chance of securing a recording agreement if he or she is part of a functioning, well-organized business machine that can work with the record company towards the common goal of generating income. The most important aspect of any person working with you is whether he or she is credible, has a track record, and is respected.

The Personal Manager

The personal manager is the most important member of the human package. If the would-be recording artist is able to arrive at a record company arm-in-arm with a highly regarded manager, the record company will be more easily swayed to invest its monies. Record company executives feel secure when a professional is coordinating an artist's career, recording duties, public performances, songwriting and other professional activities on a day-to-day basis.

The artist must be extremely selective in choosing a personal manager. Some managers are persona non grata because of their pushy and demanding demeanor, unsavory reputation or incompetence. Most established personal managers are not interested in unsigned acts, but they do have their antennas up and can be wooed with the right approach.

Talent Agent

The human package can include a talent agent who is successfully booking the artist in live engagements. The artist who has a talent agent offers the record company an added inducement for making a deal, because it will be able to rely upon a skilled professional to book the artist into live engagements before, during, and after the release of the artist's album. This will promote record sales.

Attorney

Attorneys can be important members of the human package because of their contacts at record companies, and elsewhere in the industry, through the clients they represent. It is predominantly lawyers, managers, music publishers, and record producers that shop record deals to the major labels, but the majority of music lawyers do not ordinarily shop deals. An artist should have the guidance of a professional to assist with legal needs and to help select the other members of the human package. Sound advice: get a lawyer and someone else who has influence with record companies to work for you.

Business Manager

A business manager who has a strong relationship with executives at a label can also function as part of the human package.

Record Producer/Production Company

A record producer or production company (an entity that finances and shops record deals) is another route to a deal. One caveat must be stated with regard to an artist who is already signed to a production deal, or firmly allied with a record producer. The record company may be unimpressed with your producer's talent or track record. This consideration may be a deal-breaker if the artist cannot or refuses to work with another producer. If the artist is required contractually to work with the producer/production company, it removes any flexibility for the artist and the potential label.

An artist who is signed to a production company will generally make less money than if signed directly to a label because the producer and the production company will both takes shares of the revenue. Often, the artist gets 50% of less than the total revenue from the deal. Without a production company, the artist would only have to pay the producer and would retain approximately 75% of the revenues.

Anybody with Influence

The music business is very insular. Other musicians or even those outside the music industry that have personal relationships with an A&R person may be willing to go to bat for you. Network, network, and network some more. The word will get out. Garth Brooks made it in part because an executive at a performing rights society believed in him, and ultimately became his manager. Attend seminars and music industry lectures. There are various professional organizations where one can meet and learn from professionals. The Association of Independent Music Publishers and the California Copyright Conference are two such groups. I recommend that everyone join NARAS (The National Academy of Recording Arts and Sciences), which puts on the Grammy show each year. It has local chapters in many cities and there you can meet others with similar interest and find out who are the important and talented musicians and executives in your area.

WRITE A HIT SONG

Write a hit song for or with another artist—there is no faster entree into the world of the major labels.

TOTAL PACKAGE

There are two ways of presenting the total package to a record company. The first is to have a representative of the record company see the artist perform live; the second is to present or send a demo to the record company. An artist will usually have to do both in order to clinch a deal. What you want to present are credits and credibility. Write a hit song and the doors are wide open. If the critics love your show, it may be all that is needed.

Showcases and Live Performances

Record companies want to sign artists that perform well on stage. Performing live, by "showcase" (an act performed primarily for representatives of record companies) or other engagement, can be an effective way of attracting the attention and interest of a record company. If an artist's performance is a knockout, it will enhance the prospects of a record deal or a future demo at the company's expense.

It is not easy to induce record executives that are involved with talent acquisition to attend a gig or showcase. If the artist is performing in, say, Phoenix, Arizona, the chances of getting a record company person to attend are poor. New York City, Los Angeles, and Nashville are the main cities where record companies are located, and it is still very tough to get executives to turn out for shows there. Virtually all country acts are signed in Nashville.

Invitations to attend a showcase or gig should be in writing. A follow-up telephone call the day before or on the day of the performance is the best reminder. Be certain that the names of all you have invited are on the guest list so they get in for free.

Demos

The most effective way of presenting a demo is through a personal meeting with the individual to whom it is to be given. If this cannot be arranged, a concise, clearly typed letter that states the purpose for which the demo is sent, whether the songs are original, and who the members of the human package are, should accompany the demo.

Because of the problems with live engagements and showcases (such as getting record company executives to attend), the artist who is in search of a deal should provide the record company with both a demo and an invitation to a subsequent showcase or gig.

Occasionally, a record company will request other material or that the artist return with subsequently written material. Some companies will pay for recording sessions to make additional demos.

SHOPPING THE PACKAGE

When the total package is ready to be shopped, it must be decided who will perform this function and who will be approached. If an individual who is unknown to the record company sends an invitation to a showcase, it will probably be ignored. If a demo is sent solo to a record company—through the mail with a letter of introduction by the artist—the probable response of the record company will be to reject it and return it to the sender as unwanted unsolicited material. If the record company accepts the demo, in most cases it will be referred to a listener in the A&R department. This person listens to thousands of demos a year, and most demos get less than two minutes. The listener is a filter for the rest of the A&R department with a mandate to say, "No."

Where possible, the artist should bypass individuals on the lower rungs of the record company and attempt to get the package presented to the president of the company, the chairman of the board, or the head of the A&R department, persons that have the authority to commit the record company to signing an artist. The product should "flow downhill." Many companies work on a committee basis, and most signings occur via the A&R department. Other members of the A&R hierarchy and employees in other departments of the company, such as promotion or marketing, may be approached also. The higher up the person approached is, the better the chances are of serious consideration by the head of the A&R department or other executives involved with talent acquisition. Many acts have been signed as a result of recommendations from local or regional promotion people that noticed them in cities other than New York or Los Angeles.

There is, generally, but one avenue of reaching someone at the record company who wields substantial influence or is in a decision-making position to sign an artist-personal contact. Invitations to showcases or gigs will be favorably answered and demos will get serious consideration only if they are sent or referred by someone who is recognized and respected by the persons receiving such invitations and demos. This does not mean that the person sending such invitation or demo need be famous within the music industry; he or she simply needs to be credible. The adage that it is not what you know, but who you know, definitely applies to the music business.

A number of personal managers, producers, lawyers, artist, writers and publishers can, because of their success and power, induce the president or chairman of the board of a record company to listen to a demo. Each member of the human package should be called upon to present the package to those at the record company with whom they are acquainted. Because personal contacts are so important in the industry, the artist should attempt to get to know as many people in the music business as possible. The young promotion man at a record company today may be the head of the A&R department tomorrow. An artist who is friendly with a promoted person may have both a friend and a business acquaintance that will be helpful in advancing the artist's career.

A number of music attorneys are well connected throughout the industry. Many of these attorneys will "run a demo," doing so for anywhere from a flat fee ($250 to $5,000 or more!) to a percentage (of the initial advance or the entire deal and all music publishing revenues earned from compositions on sound recordings subject to the record deal), to a percentage of the artist's earnings derived from the record deal, should one be secured. One must be cynical about the success ratio of attorney-shopped acts, but it has happened on rare occasion. Also, deals do not happen overnight; there is usually a wooing process. It takes time for the parties to get to know and respect each other.

The human package must show the same level of professionalism as the music package. Any person that presents the total package must have a good relationship with, and be enthusiastic about, the artist; know and understand the music; be aware of the long-term career goals of the artist; and most importantly, be able to communicate with, and be credible to, the record company that is approached. The artist and his or her marketing team must be aggressive, but never rude, when approaching those that have influence or signing ability. One must be relentless, patient, cunning and charming, and distinguish one's product from others, to make sure it is heard. The best method of seducing a record company is the team approach: a strong manager, attorney, publisher, producer, and agent all working for a talented artist will eventually succeed.

Email is now the rage, we cannot live without it, but we do not want to get spammed. I have been approached via email by many acts to see if there is interest on my part to shop them, and occasionally I have been intrigued. Few labels will consider seriously such approaches, but others, such as managers and lawyers may be more open, but do not expect results unless there is something extraordinary going on with the act that demands attention. Web sites are a way to market yourself. The better your Web site, the better your chances of getting signed.

CHOOSING A RECORD COMPANY

Record companies all press, distribute, and promote records, but there the similarity ends. The artist must carefully investigate the business structure, the standing in the industry, and the marketing philosophy of any record company pursued. An artist needs a company that is committed to the artist and has the organization to support that commitment.

Most artists want a company that is, or is part of, a strong and successful worldwide enterprise. This does not mean however, that an artist need pursue only the big companies. Look for a capable company that has the organization and financial wherewithal to exploit records successfully throughout the world. At this time, the record industry is dominated by the following major distributors: BMG (BMG, RCA, Arista, Zomba); EMD (Capitol, EMI, Virgin); Sony (Sony, Columbia, Epic); Universal (Universal, Geffen, Polygram, A&M, Island, Motown, Interscope); and WMG (Warner Brothers, Elektra/Asylum, Atlantic). These companies control 90% of the music industry. (As this chapter is written, EMI is seeking to merge with BMG.) Know which personnel at which companies support the music you make. Approach companies that specialize in your genre.

READ THE TRADES

Billboard is the industry magazine that charts the events of the music business on a week-to-week basis. Artists that want to obtain record deals in today's competitive music business should read it to become aware of the trends and developments in the industry and to keep track of key executives. *Music Connection*, based in Los Angeles, is an excellent source of information for artists. Twice a year, it publishes a list of all A&R executives, major publishers, managers and attorneys. *Hits* and *Radio and Records* are bibles for radio programmers and promotion men and provide useful information as to what is being played and where.

THE FUTURE

The times are definitely changing, and technology is evening out the playing field. The impediments to entry into the marketplace are the cost of manufacture and the vagaries of independent distribution, where the name of the game often is slow pay or no pay. The digital transmission of sound recordings is here now. The record companies of the future will become primarily marketing and financing entities, and the record stores of the future will be "downloaders," as opposed to purveyors of preexisting stamped pieces of plastic. This augurs well for musicians. Artists can release their material and sell it mail order via the Internet. As distribution channels open up (the majors control the flow now), it will become easier and much cheaper to distribute your product. Keep up with the developments in technology and use them to your benefit. This is not to say that it will not be tough, expensive and perilous it is to put out your own music, but this may be the only choice you have. At least with the Net, the music is available to the masses; getting the attention of the public is another matter.

CONCLUSION

The individuals that evaluate music at record companies are asked to make extremely difficult decisions. They must determine what music will be commercially viable. No amount of hype can sell a demo or a performance that does not have it "in the grooves," yet no reliable definition of this phrase has ever been articulated.

Moreover, an artist should seek a record deal only if he or she is ready, dedicated, and willing to spend years in the studio and on the road. The effort necessary to launch a career is enormous, the rewards far from guaranteed.

However, with enthusiasm, hard work and perseverance, a talented artist can achieve the goal of a record deal. Sure, rejection is commonplace, but there is only one person who really matters—the executive who says, "Yes." That executive wants to find you as much as you want to find him or her. Keep at it!

Have a backup plan. There are labels overseas that may be interested in your music. Attend MIDEM, the annual music business convention in Cannes, France, where music publishers and record executives congregate at the end of each January. I know of at least 30 U.S. acts that have foreign deals and whose records are imported into the United States. There are other conventions where one can network and make contacts. The biggest and best is South by Southwest *(www.sxsw.com)*, which is held every March in Austin, Texas, but there are conventions in many other cities that should be considered.

The Internet is the best thing that has happened to the music business. You can get noticed, sell records via mail order or via downloads, promote yourself, stream your video, and generally make a splash. You can hang onto your copyrights. It can be done. Ani DiFranco has done so—she owns her masters and puts them out on her own label, Righteous Babe, in Buffalo, New York. But that is a difficult path. Most acts need marketing and distribution muscle behind them. Radio is still the dominant way by which music is promoted, and the majors control radio because they pay the independent promoters that get songs on commercial radio. There are virtually no independent acts played on major radio. It costs millions of dollars to break a new act. That kind of money went into Christine Aguilara, Britney Spears, The Backstreet Boys, and most other popular acts. On the other hand, DIY (do-it-yourself) is what most have to do until interest is generated.

Be patient. It may take years to nurture the relationship that gets you signed. Frustration is simply a part of the process; it should not be a stumbling block.

Enthusiasm and hard work are the main ingredients of achieving financial and artistic success. Musicians that make it to the top are energetic, indefatigable, and will not take no for an answer. They are respectful of others at all times, willing to listen and learn, and understand that it takes persistence.

Analysis of a Recording Contract

BY LAWRENCE J. BLAKE, ESQ. AND DANIEL K. STUART, ESQ.

Entering into a recording contract is one of the most important steps in any recording artist's career. While a record deal does not guarantee success, it moves the artist from the sidelines onto the playing field. A record deal can generate enough immediate cash to allow an artist to quit his or her day job and focus exclusively on music. The release of a successful record can lead to substantial royalties, valuable exposure on radio, television, nightclubs and the Internet, and significant income from performing at live concerts. If the artist also writes or cowrites his or her own material, record sales and public performances of their compositions can generate publishing royalties, which can sometimes exceed record royalties. When an artist achieves success, the amount of record and publishing royalties that will ultimately be obtained is largely determined by the language of the artist's recording agreement, which makes this the most important document an artist will sign.

Recording agreements come in many variations. The major labels generally provide agreements that are somewhat standardized and straightforward, but some smaller labels have been known to include all sorts of strange and bizarre clauses to their benefit. For example, a recent agreement drafted by a small independent label provided for an initial contract period and four option periods, and during each such period the artist was to deliver one album. This is absolutely normal and customary. However, elsewhere in the agreement the label had inserted language that gave it the option to require the recording artist to deliver not one, but two albums per contract period with no additional advances for artist or for recording costs. This clause changed the five-album deal, with an already modest recording budget per album, to a ten-album deal, so the budgets for each album were cut in half! In another recent agreement, a record company very carefully laid out all of the methods for calculating the royalties payable to the artist, but inserted a provision that provided that if the artist's aggregate royalty rate payable on cassettes (which typically retailed for $10.98) was less than the aggregate royalty rate payable to the artist in respect of the sale of CDs (which retailed for $16.98), the "penny rate" (the actual dollars-and-cents payable per unit after factoring in all adjustments and deductions) for cassettes would be applied and substituted for the royalty rate otherwise payable on CDs. Based on the retail prices of cassettes and CDs at the time and the terms of the royalty provisions of the agreement, the artist believed he was to receive a royalty of about 80¢ per cassette and $1.20 per CD. Had this "trick" language not been uncovered, the artist would have actually received 80¢ on the sale of cassettes and CDs alike, slashing his CD royalty by one-third! These true-life examples are illustrated here to simply draw your attention to the importance of having an experienced representative comb through your agreement line by line, and word by word, to uncover all of the factors that can affect the bottom line.

The agreement reproduced and discussed here is a composite of several agreements and is representative of what a major label might present to a debut artist who had some bargaining power at the beginning of negotiations. Typically, before a label provides an artist with such an agreement, certain basic deal points such as the length of the deal, advances and royalties, will have already been agreed to in a brief deal memo. The points in a deal memo should be aggressively negotiated by the artist's representatives.

While this chapter discusses several issues and areas where the artist should seek to change and improve the agreement, this agreement is not unusually one-sided. No one should ever expect any record company to present an agreement that an artist should feel good about signing without negotiating substantial changes. The artist and his or her advisers are responsible for negotiating the agreement to their satisfaction. The degree to which a record company will improve its first draft depends in large measure on how badly it wants to sign the artist and other factors, including potential competition from other labels. An unknown artist will obviously have less leverage than a well-known or platinum selling artist. However, there are many points most record companies will likely concede, even to an unknown artist, if the issues are timely and properly raised. The artist's representative should ask for all concessions the record company could reasonably agree to, and perhaps even a few more. The artist should not fear being branded as "difficult" simply because he or she thoroughly negotiates the recording contract. If anything, a thorough negotiation sends a message to the record company that the artist is taking the contract seriously and is handling it in a professional manner. However, the artist and the artist's representatives must be careful not to overnegotiate the contract and risk losing what might otherwise be a fair and successful deal.

Recording contract negotiations can involve heated bargaining over many different points and these contracts have grown more and more complex over the years, due to the advent of music videos and the Internet. Therefore, it is a practical necessity for the artist to engage an attorney who has experience negotiating recording agreements. The attorney and the artist's manager generally handle the actual head-to-head negotiations with the record company so that the artist is insulated from any personal friction with record company personnel. The artist should, however, carefully monitor progress and insist on being consulted on key issues and being kept advised of the resolution of all significant points.

When aspiring recording artists dream of getting a recording contract, they usually envision a deal with a major record label, such as WEA (Warner Bros., Elektra and Atlantic), Sony (Columbia and Epic), UMG (Universal, Polygram, MCA, Island/Def Jam, and Motown), BMG (RCA and Arista), or EMD (Capitol and Virgin). Quite often, however, the first deal offered to an artist is from an independent label or production company. Accordingly, before analyzing a typical major label deal, let us briefly review some of the issues arising in deals with independent labels and production companies.

A recording contract with an independent record label is typically shorter and simpler. But, despite their smaller size, the term of these contracts will often outlast the average recording artist's career, so it is essential that the artist have experienced legal representation.

Production companies work to assemble a "package" for a record company, which typically consists of an artist, recorded musical material, and a producer. Some well-established production companies have ongoing deals with record companies to provide a specified number of packages per year. These production companies sometimes have the right to control all of the creative elements of making the album and will simply deliver a completed master tape to the record company, which is then obligated to release and promote the album. Other production companies search for deals with record companies and use artists' demos to help secure such deals. These companies may offer either a package, which includes their rights to an artist and producer or a finished master recording ready for release and distribution.

Whether the production company already has a deal or is still looking for one, it will usually try to put the artist under contract as part of its effort to assemble a package for the record company. The form of the recording agreement presented to the artist will be very similar to the one offered by the record label, but the artist will be under contract to the production company, not the label. The production company, in turn, will furnish the artist's services to the label under a separate agreement, generally known as a "production contract" or "production deal."

The production company is an intermediary that stands between the artist and the record company. The goal of the production company is to collect more money from the record company than it pays to the artist. Whether the production company deserves the share it keeps depends entirely on the value of the services it provides. Some of the factors an artist should consider are whether the production company is likely to secure a deal that the artist could not land on his or her own, or if the track record of the production company increases the chances that the artist's record will ultimately be successful. Entering a fair contract with a strong production company can result in a genuine "win-win" for the artist and the company. On the other hand, if an artist signs an exclusive recording contract with a production company that is unable to land a deal, the artist can become trapped—while the artist's recordings grow stale on the company's shelves, the artist remains bound to the production company and cannot record for any other company. Under these circumstances, a career can be delayed for years.

The artist's strategy, when negotiating with a production company, must be different from when negotiating with a record label. The main point to remember is that the production company is only useful if it can actually get the artist a deal and even then, its usefulness is determined by the value of the deal it makes. It is crucial to learn whether the production company has a prearranged deal with a record company and the nature of that deal. If a deal is in place, the artist should ask for a copy of it. The production company may want to white out certain financial provisions, but since the artist's contract must follow the form of the production company's contract with the major label, and since the major label is going to provide the funds the production company will use to pay to the artist, it is not unfair or unreasonable for the artist to insist on knowing what the production company is keeping as its profit-margin. Indeed, if the production company is unwilling to disclose the terms of its agreement with the major label to the artist, the artist should seriously reconsider doing business with that company.

A production company that does not already have a deal with a recording label may try to justify a one-sided recording contract by arguing that because they cannot predict what the terms of its deal with the record company will be, they cannot make concessions to the artist that they are not certain the record company will accept. However, such one-sided agreements, which are designed to protect only the production company, can be extremely unfair to the artist and the consequences of such agreements may burden the artist for a long time. Fortunately, there are ways an agreement can be drafted that fairly balance the interests of the artist and the production company. The agreement between the artist and production company should provide that the artist is free to walk away from the deal and all of the obligations to the production company unless there is a deal with a major label by a certain date and the deal must either meet certain criteria or, if it fails to meet such criteria, be reviewed and approved by the artist. If a production company tries to sign an artist and is unwilling to commit to such an arrangement that balances its interests with those of the artist, the artist should consider walking away.

Most recording agreements deal only with the artist's services as a performer on records. When an artist composes songs, the rights to the artist's songs should be addressed in a separate publishing agreement, if at all. It used to be a common practice of record companies to demand that performers grant publishing rights to a publishing company that was affiliated with the record company. The major record labels have generally discontinued this practice, although some production companies will still seek to obtain publishing rights. Artists should avoid granting publishing rights as part of a recording agreement, as those rights have enormous potential value and they can be parlayed into lucrative publishing deals if the artist's compositions become popular.

Now let us turn our attention to the major label's first draft of a recording agreement.

EXCLUSIVE ARTIST'S RECORDING AGREEMENT

AGREEMENT made and entered into as of this ____ day of __________________ , ______ by and between LABEL RECORDS, INC., Conglomerate Plaza, New York, New York ("Label") and ________________________________ ("Artist") whose address is: ____.

1. TERM

1.01. (a) The term of this agreement and the initial Contract Period will begin on the date first written above.

(b) Each Contract Period of the term will end, unless extended as provided herein, five (5) months after Label's United States retail street date for the last Master Recording Delivered by you in fulfillment of your Recording Commitment for that Contract Period under paragraph 3.01 below. Notwithstanding the foregoing, but subject to the other provisions of this Agreement, no Contract Period will end prior to the date ten (10) months after the date of commencement of such Period.

The term of a recording agreement means the period of time during which the artist is under contract exclusively to the record company. During the term, the artist cannot record for any other company without the record company's approval. The company's rights to sell the artist's records and its obligations to account and pay royalties to the artist are perpetual and therefore extend beyond the term. The term of this recording agreement is not measured by years but instead is defined as five months after the retail street date for the last recordings delivered during the contract period. Because the artist cannot control the date on which the record company releases his or her album, the artist should try to have the term measured from the date of delivery as opposed to the retail street date. Record companies prefer to measure the term from the retail street date so they can have an opportunity to evaluate the commercial performance of the artist's album before having to decide whether to exercise their option to extend the term for another album. A compromise that many record companies will often agree to is to define the term as the delivery date plus a longer period of months, generally nine to twelve, excluding a certain period of weeks surrounding the year end holidays (i.e., November 15 through January 15 is a common period excluded for such purposes.)

Note that the capitalization of the word "Delivery" in the agreement is not a typographical error. Whenever you see a capitalized word in the middle of a sentence, that word has a special meaning that is defined in the agreement. In this agreement, such definitions are set forth in section 14. In contracts where the expiration of the term is measured from delivery, it is essential that the artist know how delivery is defined and takes all necessary steps to ensure that the conditions of delivery under the contract are satisfied and, whenever possible, have the record company acknowledge the date delivery occurs in writing. Record companies have been known to take the position that "Delivery" under the recording agreement has not occurred, even months after the recordings in question were actually released as a commercial album.

Nearly every record company now defines the term of its recording agreements by the delivery of albums and not by the passage of time. Under California law, personal service contracts cannot be enforced for a term longer than seven years so, arguably, a recording artist cannot be prevented from recording for another company after his current contract has been in effect for seven years. However, this same California law gives the record companies the right to recover damages in cases where the artist fails to complete his or her recording commitments under the agreement by the time the seven years have expired. This provision has never been conclusively interpreted in the courts. Although lawsuits have been filed that involve certain high-profile artists (Metallica, Don Henley) neither artists nor record companies are particularly anxious to set a precedent in this regard, and the cases have settled.

1.02. You grant Label five (5) separate, consecutive and irrevocable options to extend the term for additional Contract Periods ("Option Periods") on the same terms and conditions, except as otherwise expressly provided in this Agreement. Each of those options shall be exercised by Label, if at all, by notice to you not later than the expiration date of the Contract Period, which is then in effect (the "current Contract Period"). Each Option Period for which Label exercises its option will begin immediately after the end of the then-current Contract Period (or, if Label so advises you in its exercise notice, such Contract Period will begin on the date of such exercise notice).

In most new artist recording contracts, the minimum recording commitment for the initial contract period is one album, but the record company typically retains the right to extend the agreement to include additional albums. The right to extend a contract on this basis is typically called an option, and the additional contract periods under this agreement are often referred to as option periods. The number of options in a recording agreement is often the subject for serious negotiations, as the record company will want to obtain as many as possible and the artist will want to grant as few as possible. A major label will rarely accept fewer than five options and will sometimes insist on as many as seven. Independent labels, however, generally require one to three options and sometimes will enter into contracts for one album with no options (so-called one-off deals). Generally, when a new artist signs with an independent label, he or she wants to use the independent label to generate buzz and build an audience base so the artist can later sign with a major label for big bucks. The best way to achieve this goal is through an agreement with a small number of options or with a clause that gives the artist the right to buy out of the contract.

1.03. Notwithstanding anything to the contrary contained herein, in the event that Label does not, prior to the expiration date of the current Contract Period, exercise it's option for an Option Period, the term of the current Contract Period shall, subject to the following provisions hereof, continue, unless Label notifies you to the contrary. However, you shall at any time after the expiration date of the current Contract Period, have the right to send Label written notice (hereinafter "Termination Request") of your desire that the current Contract Period and the term of this Agreement shall terminate unless Label shall, within ten (10) days after its receipt of such Termination Request (hereinafter "10-day Period"), exercise the Option Period. If Label does not, prior to the end of such 10-day Period, exercise its option for the applicable Option Period, the current Contract Period and the term of this Agreement shall expire as of the eleventh (11th) day after receipt of your Termination Request. If Label shall, prior to the expiration of the current Contract Period (or such 10-day Period, as applicable) exercise the Option Period, then the Option Period shall commence and the current Contract Period shall expire, both upon the later of (i) the expiration date of the then current Contract Period, or (ii) the date of Label's such notice to you exercising the Option Period.

This clause places the burden on the artist to seek termination of the agreement if the record company fails to exercise its option prior to the expiration of the current term. A record company that has invested significant sums in an artist's career does not want to risk losing the artist if it loses track of its deadline to exercise its option. At the same time, an artist does not want to be bound indefinitely because he or she has failed to take the initiative to notify the company that the term has expired. If the artist has enough clout during negotiations, the record company will often accept the responsibility of exercising its option before the expiration of the current term. If the record company makes this concession, then if the company fails to exercise its option on time, the contract will automatically terminate. If the record company does not make this concession, the result will often be similar to the language set forth above, which requires the artist to notify the company of its failure to exercise its option and then provides the company with a fixed period of time to exercise its option to avoid the termination of the agreement.

2. SERVICES

2.01. During the term of this Agreement you will render services as a performing artist for the purpose of making Master Recordings for Label, you will cause those Recordings to be produced and you will Deliver the Recordings to Label, as provided in this Agreement.

This clause clarifies that this deal only pertains to artist's exclusive services as a recording artist and does not pertain to artist's services as a songwriter.

2.02. (a) Your obligations will include furnishing the services of the producers of those Master Recordings and you will be solely responsible for engaging and paying them. (Producers of Master Recordings hereunder are referred to herein as "Producers.")

(b) If Label, instead, engages Producers for any of those Master Recordings, or if the Producers of any such Recordings are regularly employed on Label's staff or render their services under contract with Label, your royalty account and the production budget for the recording project concerned will be charged with a Recording Cost item in the amount of the fee concerned and/or advance payable to such Producer(s) pursuant to their agreement with Label and your royalty on Phonograph Records made from those Recordings under Articles 9 and 10 will be reduced by the amount of the royalty payable to such Producer(s) pursuant to their agreement with Label. This subparagraph (b) will not apply unless you have consented to the engagement of the Producer concerned, or the assignment of the staff or contract Producer concerned, to the recording project.

(c) Label will accept letters of direction irrevocably authorizing Label to pay and account to the Producers of Master Recordings Delivered in satisfaction of your Recording Commitment on your behalf, in the form of Exhibit B attached to this Agreement, subject to the following:

(1) The total Producing Royalty (as defined in Exhibit B) pursuant to such letters of direction shall not, without Label's prior written consent, exceed three percent (3%) per Album.

(2) The total Producing Royalty pursuant to such letters of direction will be deducted from all monies payable or becoming payable to you under this Agreement; and

(3) The total advances to such Producers will in no way increase Label's obligations to you under Article 6.

This section defines the artist's obligations under the agreement and specifically obligates the artist to engage his or her own producers while it retains the label's rights to engage the producer directly and pay the producer from sums otherwise payable to artist. If the artist wishes to maximize control over who produces, as most artists do, the artist should seek to remove the language that limits the producer royalty to 3% and permits the label to engage the producers directly. Financially, this contract is structured as an all-in deal, i.e., the payments agreed to be made by the record company are inclusive of all payments due to the record producer and any other third parties that may be entitled to be paid money in connection with the recording of the masters or the sale of records. Normally, producers are paid a fee for their services in producing the masters, which is usually treated as a fully recoupable advance against their royalties. Their fee is normally paid half upon commencement of their services and half upon completion of the album. This is paid out of the recording fund and is one element of the recording costs of the album. Most commonly, producers are paid a royalty rate of approximately 3% of the royalty base price, assuming it is computed on a retail basis, as is the case in this contract. Generally, producers' royalties are paid retroactively to the first record sold after recoupment of the recording costs of the album at the net artist's rate. This means that if the record is not successful enough to recoup its recording costs, the producer will not be paid any royalties in addition to the fee paid to him, but if it is, the producer will be paid royalties on all records sold. The net artist's rate means the all-in rate payable to the artist, which would be the rate set forth in this agreement, less the producer's rate, e.g., 13% less 3% equals 10%. If the record is successful enough that the recording costs have been recouped at the net artist's rate, then the producer will be credited with royalties on all records sold, not merely those sold after recoupment. Of course, those royalties will be reduced by the producer's fee since it is really an advance of royalties. Ultimately, if the record is successful, the producer does not bear any of the recording costs, but rather all such recording costs are borne by payment out of the artist's net royalties.

3. RECORDING COMMITMENT

3.01. During the initial Contract Period, you will Deliver two Commitment Albums required to be Delivered during such Contract Period. You will deliver the first such Commitment Album within the first six (6) months and you will Deliver the second Commitment Album (subject to Label's rights to terminate the term pursuant to clause 3.04 hereof) required to be Delivered during such Contract Period to Label not earlier than ten (10) months and not later than thirteen (13) months after the earlier of the date when you Delivered the first Commitment Album or the date on which the first Commitment Album was required to have been Delivered hereunder. During each Option Period, you will perform for the recording of Master Recordings sufficient to constitute one Album, cause those Master Recordings to be produced and Deliver them to Label (the "Option Recording Commitment"). The Initial Recording Commitment and the Option Recording Commitment are sometimes collectively referred to herein as the "Recording Commitment." Each Album required to be recorded and Delivered by you hereunder is herein sometimes referred to as a "Commitment Album."

3.02. You will fulfill the Recording Commitment for each Option Period within the first six (6) months of the Contract Period.

These clauses set forth the timetable for artist's delivery of the album required during each contract period and are generally quite negotiable. The record company wants to have a steady flow of product. The artist, however, sometimes needs additional time to create new material and therefore needs to be protected from the record company having the right to terminate the agreement abruptly if the delivery schedule is not met. Generally, the artist is given a longer cure period in the case of the failure to timely deliver recordings than with respect to other breaches of the recording contract. Most initial recording agreements provide for only one album to be delivered during the initial period but, if the artist has enough clout, record companies may agree to commit to two albums during the initial term, which is the case in this agreement. The record company's commitment to a second album is not absolute, however, as pursuant to clause 3.04 below, the company does have the right to opt out in the event the first album is a commercial failure.

3.03. Each Commitment Album (or other group of Master Recordings) Delivered to Label will consist entirely of Master Recordings made in the course of the same Album (or other) recording project, unless Label consents otherwise. Label may withhold that consent in its unrestricted discretion.

This language is designed to prevent an artist from using songs he or she recorded in years past to satisfy current recording commitments. Some artists record new material throughout their careers and then cobble together songs with similar themes and flavors to comprise a particular album. Because it is in the artist's best interests to retain as much flexibility as possible, the artist's representatives should try to have this language omitted or modified to permit any songs recorded during the term, which have not been previously rejected by the label, to be included in any commitment album. If the label refuses to grant that concession, it may agree to modify the consent language to provide that its consent to use such recordings shall not unreasonably be withheld.

3.04. In the event that the first Commitment Album sells less than two hundred thousand (200,000) copies in the United States (as measured by Soundscan) in the first nine (9) months after the initial release of the same in the United States ("the Opt-Out Date") then Label shall have the right, at any time within ninety (90) days after the Opt-Out Date, to terminate the term of this Agreement by written notice to you, in which case all parties will be deemed to have fulfilled all of their obligations under this Agreement save for those obligations which are expressed to survive the termination of the term (e.g., warranties, rerecording restrictions and royalty payment, accounting and audit rights). In no event shall Label be obliged to pay any recording Costs or other Advances in connection with the second Album of the Recording Commitment prior to the last day that it may terminate the term of this agreement pursuant to this clause 3.04.

In recording agreements that provide for two albums to be delivered during the initial period, record labels will typically try to include an opt-out clause like the one set forth above. These clauses allow the label to bail out on a second album if the first album flops. The artist's representatives should try to have such opt-out clauses excluded if at all possible. If the label insists on an opt-out clause, then it is important that the timing of the opt-out rights and the delivery requirements of the second album be coordinated so that the artist is never placed in a situation where he or she is under the gun to record the second album while there is still a risk of the label exercising its opt-out rights. For example, in this first draft agreement, the label's opt-out rights do not expire until 15 months (e.g., 12 months plus 90 days) after the commercial release of the artist's first album. However, the artist is required under paragraph 3.01 to deliver the second album within 10 to 13 months after the delivery date (or actual delivery, if earlier) of the first album. These terms create a potential conflict, as the artist is required to record a second album during a period in which the label may retain the right to opt-out of its obligations regarding the second album. Another issue to consider is the fact that Soundscan, a company that collects sales data from most major record store chains and many independent record stores, does not always accurately reflect 100% of records sold. Accordingly, the artist should try to have the sales figures in an opt-out clause based on the record company's actual sales data or Soundscan data, whichever is greater. This is particularly important in certain genres of music (e.g., hip-hop) in which many sales are generated by independent stores that do not participate in Soundscan's database. Soundscan may underreport sales in such genres by as much as 20%.

4. RECORDING PROCEDURE

4.01. You will follow the procedure set forth below in connection with Master Recordings made hereunder:

(a) Except as expressly noted otherwise in this Agreement, prior to the commencement of recording in each instance, you and Label shall mutually approve each of the following; provided, however, in the event you and Label shall not be able to reach an agreement, Label's decision shall be final:

(1) Selection of Producer.

The most important creative approval to both the company and the artist is generally the right to approve the producer of the individual masters. The label's position that it should be able to dictate to the artist who the producer should be in the event they fail to reach a mutual agreement is not an unusual position for a company to take. However, the selection of a producer is such a key creative decision in the recording process that the artist should try to have the agreement modified to require a mutual approval of the producer. One example of compromise language would be to provide that the artist shall have the right to select the producers of his or her material, provided that producer agrees to render services in exchange for fees consistent with the artist's recording budget, and further subject to the record company's approval, which shall not be unreasonably withheld. Such an approach still effectively requires mutual agreement, but does not allow the record company to be unreasonable in its decision not to approve any given producer. Perhaps the most important creative element to the company is its right to approve the producer of the masters. In certain types of music, e.g., R&B, the producer is often the person who writes much of the material and shapes the overall sound of the recordings and certain producers have reputations that can help drive airplay and record sales. In certain other types of music, e.g., rock and alternative rock, the producer may not be involved with songwriting at all, but may simply be responsible for shaping and capturing the sound of the artist. Most commonly, recording contracts provide that the producer will be mutually designated by the artist and the record company. In practice, the artist or the artist's manager will select the producer or producers and the record company will be consulted, but will generally defer to the artist's choice unless it has had a negative experience with a particular producer.

(2) Selection of material, including the number of Compositions to be recorded provided that, in the event that you and Label cannot agree, Label shall have the right to choose two Controlled Compositions from demos delivered by you. You will advise Label of the content of each medley before it is recorded. Unless you are solely an instrumentalist, no Master Recording made hereunder shall embody solely an instrumental Performance. Label will have the right to disapprove and reject any material which in Label's reasonable, good faith opinion, is patently offensive, constitutes an obscenity, violates any law, infringes or violates the rights of any Person, or which might subject Label to liability or unfavorable regulatory action. You shall not record a Multiple Record Set without Label' s consent, which may be withheld for any reason.

The foregoing is normal and customary language that typically would not be subject to negotiation. However, in the event that the artist performs music that might be considered offensive or obscene and is concerned that the record label might require the artist to tone down the creative content, the artist can seek to have language added to this clause whereby the record company would acknowledge that, for the purposes of determining what material is offensive or obscene and therefore subject to disapproval and rejection by the label, the master recordings embodied in the demonstration tape presented to the label shall hereby be deemed not to be offensive or obscene.

It is less common today for a record company to insist on the right to designate the songs to record. However, until the artist has established a track record, it is unlikely that the artist will be given the right to decide which songs to record without the record company having a right of approval. As a practical matter, however, there are very few disputes between record companies and artists as to the songs to be recorded.

(3) Selection of dates of recording and studios where recording is to take place, including the cost of recording at such studios. You shall not begin recording any Commitment Album within five (5) months after the Delivery of the prior Commitment Album. Label may disapprove a studio if it is not a first-class recording studio, if its use would be inconsistent with any of Label's union agreements, if Label anticipates that its use would cause labor or other difficulties, or if Label anticipates that its use would require expenditures inconsistent with the approved recording budget, and not any other reason. Other than in respect of the demos to be recorded in the initial Contract Period, the scheduling and booking of all studio time will be done by Label, in accordance with your requests and the approved recording budget.

In the event that the artist has a particular studio in mind, such as a home studio or another favorite spot, the record company should be asked to acknowledge in this paragraph that such studio is approved by the record company. Generally, the record company will approve any recording studio the artist or the artist's producer wishes to use, so long as it has satisfactory recording equipment and the studio's rates fit within the recording budget.

(4) A proposed budget (which you will submit to Label sufficiently in advance of the planned commencement of recording to give Label a

reasonable time to review and approve or disapprove it at least fourteen [14] days before the planned commencement of recording). A recording budget (inclusive of Producer advances and/or fees) for any Commitment Album that does not exceed eighty percent (80%) of the amount of the (applicable minimum [in the case of the second Option Album onwards]) Recording Fund prescribed in paragraph 6.02 will not be disapproved by reason of its overall amount.

The insistence upon the submission and approval of written recording budgets prior to the commencement of each recording session is designed to give the company an opportunity to control the recording costs and prevent cost overruns. As a practical matter, however, written recording budgets are not always submitted and recording budgets are often exceeded. It is important for the artist to remember that it is in the artist's interest to keep recording costs down, since they are recoupable dollar-for-dollar from the royalties earned by the artist under the contract. Accordingly, a successful artist ultimately pays 100% of the recording costs.

The artist should be well rehearsed before going into the studio and have a definite plan for what is to be accomplished at each session.

(b) You shall notify the appropriate Local of the American Federation of Musicians in advance of each recording session.

(c) In connection with the requirements of the U.S. Immigration Law, you shall not engage or permit the engagement of any Person to perform services with respect to any Master Recording unless and until you have caused such Person to properly complete an INS Form I-9, you have executed, completed and signed the employer verification section thereof, you have attached copies of documents verifying employment eligibility, and you have delivered same to Label with respect to each such Person within seventy-two (72) hours after the applicable Person first renders services with respect to Master Recordings hereunder. You will comply with any revised or alternative employment verification procedure of which Label advises you in the future.

The laws of the United States require that each musician or other performer on phonograph records be either a United States citizen or otherwise permitted to work in the United States. The violation of these laws can result in criminal penalties and fines. The record company passes these obligations on to the recording artist who is in a position to control who is hired and to require documentation of their eligibility to be employed. It is therefore a serious matter for the artist to obtain the completed Form I-9 in respect of each individual who renders services on the project, whether as a musician, vocalist, producer, engineer, or otherwise. Artists may, in turn, pass these obligations onto their producers by making them responsible for obtaining the completed I-9 forms as a condition of their receiving producers' fees.

(d) As and when required by Label, you shall allow Label's representatives to attend any or all recording sessions hereunder at Label's expense. (Those expenses will not be recoupable as Recording Costs.)

(e) You shall timely supply Label with all of the information it needs in order to make payments due in connection with such Recordings; to comply with any other obligations Label may have in connection with the making of such

Master Recordings; and to prepare to release Phonograph Records derived from such Master Recordings. Without limiting the generality of the preceding sentence:

(1) You shall furnish Label with all information it requires to comply with its obligations under its union agreements, including, without limitation, the following:

(i) If a session is held to record new tracks intended to be mixed with existing tracks (and if such information is requested by the American Federation of Musicians), the dates and places of the prior sessions at which such existing tracks were made, and the AFM Phonograph Recording Contract (Form "B") number(s) covering such sessions;

(ii) Each change of title of any Composition listed in an AFM Phonograph Recording Contract (Form "B"); and

(iii) A listing of all the musical selections contained in Recordings Delivered to Label hereunder; and

(2) You will deliver to Label all AFM or AFTRA session reports, tax withholding forms, and other documentation required by Label within seventy-two (72) hours after each recording session hereunder so that Label may timely make all required union payments to the session musicians and other employees concerned, if any.

All of the major record companies are signatories to the AFM Phonograph Record Labor Agreement and their related trust fund agreements. These collective bargaining agreements require the signatory record companies to pay musicians at the specified minimum scale rates and to make specified pension, health and welfare payments. In this agreement, since the artist is being given control of the recording fund, the artist is delegated the obligation to comply with the union's requirements. However, although artists may be members of the AFM, they are not likely to become signatories to the AFM Phonograph Record Labor Agreement and therefore licensed employers for purposes of conducting recording sessions. Therefore, where this type of clause is used, it is largely ignored by artists. An alternative is for the sessions to be conducted under the record company's license, in which event the record company will generally insist on controlling the payment of the recording costs and will want to limit the amount of the fund that is paid out to the artist prior to delivery of the completed record. As mentioned above, many of these administrative obligations can be passed by the artist to the producer under the agreements with the producer.

(f) You shall deliver to Label fully mixed, edited, and unequalized and equalized Master Recordings (including but not limited to a final two-track equalized tape copy), which are technically and *commercially* satisfactory to Label for the production, manufacture and sale of Phonograph Records in accordance with paragraph 14.09, all original and duplicate Master Recordings of the material recorded, together with all necessary licenses and permissions, including, without limitation, those relating to all samples, if any, interpolated in the Master Recordings, and all materials reasonably required to be furnished by you to Label for use in the packaging and marketing of the Records, including, without limitation, complete and accurate label copy and liner note information. Each Master Recording will be clearly marked to identify you as the recording artist, and to show the title(s) of the Composition(s) and recording date(s).

The most troublesome stipulation in this clause is that the masters be commercially satisfactory in the company's opinion and that, if they are not, the artist must rerecord a song or songs until they are commercially satisfactory to the company. There is no objective standard to determine whether a recording is commercially satisfactory or not. This essentially becomes a question of the company's subjective opinion versus the artist's and producer's subjective opinions. Generally, the artist's representatives will fight for a "technically satisfactory" standard, which means that the recordings have been recorded in a professional manner, and does not address the artistic quality or commercial sales potential of the music. Some record companies use the term, satisfactory, rather than commercially satisfactory. This eliminates the apparent offensiveness of suggesting that the artist's intent should be making records that will sell well, as distinguished from records that are artistically meritorious, but it does not avoid the fundamental problem that the results of the artist's creative efforts are subject to the company's approval.

There is simply no way to eliminate contractually the possibility that the record company will not be excited about the record the artist delivers. What can be resolved are the parties' respective rights and obligations if this should occur. In this contract, the artist must rerecord whatever the company asks to be rerecorded, and there is no additional money required to be provided by the record company to pay for such additional recording sessions. Generally, however, the record company will be prepared to pay the additional cost of rerecording certain songs or, more commonly, will request the artist to record an additional song or songs approved by the company until the artist has delivered a record that the record company believes it can successfully market. Often, in a new artist's deal there will not be sufficient money left in the artist's recording fund to cover much additional recording, so the company will be forced to pay for whatever additional recording it may require. This tends to discourage record companies from exercising this right too frequently. However, major record companies have been known to shelve records by established artists, which the record company felt were not up to the caliber of that artist's prior recordings. In summary, the relative bargaining power of the artist will determine how this clause is ultimately resolved, but contractual language can only go so far and if the record company is not satisfied with the record delivered by the artist, it will take the parties' mutual cooperation to work out a satisfactory solution.

(g) You shall comply with Label's policies with respect to samples, and you hereby warrant and represent that all information supplied by you to Label in that regard is and shall be complete and correct. As of the date hereof, Label's policies with respect to all samples embodied in any Master Recording (including remixes of Master Recordings, regardless of whether such remixes will be commercially released) are as follows:

(1) Prior to Label's authorization of premastering (e.g., equalization and the making of reference dubs or the equivalent thereof in the applicable configurations) for a particular set of Master Recordings hereunder, you shall deliver the following to Label for the applicable set of Master Recordings:

(i) A detailed list of any and all samples embodied in each Master Recording;

(ii) A written clearance or license for the perpetual, nonrestrictive use of each such sample interpolated in each Master Recording in any and all media from the copyright holder(s) of the Master Recording and the Composition sampled; and

(iii) Any and all necessary information pertaining to credit copy required by the copyright holder(s) of each sample interpolated in each Master Recording.

(2) No Master Recording will be scheduled for release and no Master Recording shall be deemed to be Delivered to Label hereunder (and no Advances due on Delivery, if any, will be paid) until such written sample clearances (including credit copy, if any) have been obtained and approved by Label.

(3) If any such sample clearance provides for an advance, a flat-fee "roll-over" payment and/or a royalty payment for Net Sales of the applicable Master Recording and your record royalty account hereunder is in an unrecouped position at the time such royalties are due, then, notwithstanding anything to the contrary contained herein, you shall be solely responsible for making, and shall make, such payment(s) to the applicable Person promptly upon receipt from Label of such Person's accounting statement thereof. If Label makes any such payment(s), such payment(s) will constitute an Advance and will be recoupable from all monies becoming payable by Label to you under this Agreement.

Record companies generally take a very aggressive stance against samples in their first draft of recording agreements. However, if the artist is in a genre where the effective use of samples can help drive record sales, the record company may be persuaded to take a more moderate approach to samples. Some labels will agree to accept the responsibility for negotiating with the owners and publishers of sampled material and to pay all so-called clearance costs as additional recoupable recording costs. This is yet another example of certain obligations of the artist that can be effectively passed on to the producers of masters embodying sampled material. When the producer must thoroughly identify all sampled material and the respective interest holders of such material, and the contract requires that the producer shall not receive a full fee until any samples embodied on the masters produced are cleared, the artist is, at least partially, insulated from some of the liabilities incurred when samples are used during recording prior to said samples being cleared.

4.02. No Composition previously recorded by you will be recorded under this Agreement. No "live" Recording, solely instrumental Recording (unless you are solely an instrumentalist), Joint Recording, or Recording not made in full compliance with this Agreement will apply in fulfillment of your Recording Commitment, nor will Label be required to make any payments in connection with any such Recording except any royalties which may become due under this Agreement if the Recording is released by Label. No Recordings shall be made by unauthorized dubbing or sampling.

Generally, live albums are not allowed to be delivered in satisfaction of the recording commitment, since they generally do not sell as well as studio albums, although there are notable exceptions (e.g., MTV's "Unplugged" albums). However, after an artist has achieved enough success to create market demand for a live album, the right to deliver one may be negotiated. Often, however, that album will be in addition to, and will not count toward, the number of albums required to be delivered under the deal.

4.03. Nothing in this Agreement shall obligate Label to continue or permit the continuation of any recording session or project, even if previously approved hereunder, if Label reasonably anticipates that the Recording Costs will exceed those specified in the approved budget or that the Recordings being produced will not be technically and commercially satisfactory to Label for the production, manufacture and sale of Phonograph Records.

This is a fairly standard clause that gives the record company some measure of protection in the event that an artist is spending money at a pace that exceeds his or her budget.

4.04. You will not be required to perform together with any other royalty artist without your consent, which may be withheld for any reason.

5. RECOUPABLE AND REIMBURSABLE COSTS

5.01. Label will pay all union scale payments required to be made to you in connection with Recordings made hereunder, all costs of instrumental, vocal and other personnel specifically approved by Label for the recording of such Master Recordings, and all other amounts required to be paid by Label pursuant to any applicable law or any collective bargaining agreement between Label and any union representing Persons who render services in connection with such Master Recordings. If Label incurs any penalties for late payments caused by your delay in submitting union contract forms, invoices or other similar forms, you will promptly reimburse Label for same upon demand, and without limiting Label's other rights and remedies, Label may deduct an amount equal to all such penalties from all monies otherwise becoming payable by Label to you under this Agreement. Notwithstanding the foregoing, you agree that the Advances hereunder include the prepayment of session union scale to you as provided in the applicable union codes, and you agree to complete any documentation required by the applicable union to implement this sentence. (Union contracts will be filed and supplied to Label and pension benefits will be paid on your behalf by Label which payments shall be an Advance.)

Again, the administrative responsibility set forth in this paragraph can be passed along from the artist to the producer so that in the event any late charges are incurred by the producer's failure to collect and submit the union contract forms, invoices and so forth, the penalties can be deducted from the producer's fee and the artist will remain unscathed.

5.02. (a) All Recording Costs will constitute Advances. Any Recording Costs in excess of the budget initially established under section 4.01(a)(4) or other amount approved in writing by Label, and all Special Packaging Costs, will be your sole responsibility and will be paid by you promptly (or reimbursed by you if paid by Label). Those amounts will also be recoupable from all monies becoming payable by Label to you under this Agreement or "any other agreement" (as such phrase is defined in subparagraph 14.01(a)) to the extent to which they have not actually been paid or reimbursed as provided in the preceding sentence. Subject to subparagraph 14.01(b) below, all costs incurred by Label in connection with the production or acquisition of rights in Covered Videos, and fifty percent (50%) of all direct expenses paid or incurred by Label in connection with independent promotion of Recordings of your Performances (i.e., promotion by Persons other than regular employees of Label), will constitute Advances.

The important elements of this clause are the establishment of how video production costs and independent promotion costs are recouped. Many record companies will agree to designate 50% of video production costs as nonrecoupable. Sometimes, such a fifty-fifty arrangement is subject to a maximum budget, over which the company will deem 100% of video production costs recoupable. An artist should always attempt to limit the recoupability of video costs to 50%. Of greater importance is the establishment of the video production budget itself, which ideally should have specific limits that cannot be exceeded without the artist's consent. Some labels will even agree that if the label decides to spend in excess of a certain amount, such amount will not be recoupable. In the era of the multimillion-dollar video, it truly is unreasonable to expect recording artists to recoup 100% of video production costs at their royalty rate. In this agreement, the relevant clauses are actually set forth in the "definitions" section of the agreement, specifically in subparagraph 14.01(b), which provides that one-half of video production costs up to $100,000 are recoupable from record royalties, 100% of such costs are recoupable from video royalties, and in the event video production costs exceed $100,000, all such excess costs are recoupable from record royalties.

Independent promotion is the practice whereby individuals outside the company obtain radio airplay of the company's singles. The practice has been much criticized and has been the subject of investigations into payola, the crime of paying to obtain the broadcast of records. However, independent promotion remains a key ingredient to the success of a hit single. When record companies spend money for independent promotion, it is usually either 100% or 50% recoupable, depending on the contract. When a major record company hires independent promotion people, it is in addition to the promotional efforts of the company's in-house promotion department. However, if the artist is contracting with a small company that does not have its own promotion staff, it is difficult to justify 100% recoupability of independent promotion, since one of the primary functions of a record company is to market and promote the records and therefore some portion of the promotion expense ought to be nonrecoupable.

(b) The amounts applicable to any Joint Recording, which are payable by you or chargeable against your royalties under this paragraph 5.02, will be computed by apportionment as provided in paragraph 10.01.

Joint recordings are essentially duets between the artist subject to the recording agreement and outside artists. Royalties for such recordings are typically divided between the artist and the duet partner on a pro rata basis.

(c) Payments to the AFM Special Payments Fund and the Music Performance Trust Fund based upon Record sales (so-called per-record royalties) will not be recoupable from your royalties or reimbursable by you. With respect to the preparation of a lacquer, copper, or equivalent master from a fully mixed, edited, and equalized master tape, an amount equal to the normal engineering charges which would reasonably be incurred in connection with the production of such a master on a real time basis at Label's studios (or other studios designated by Label) will be excluded in the calculation of Recording Costs, but all costs in excess of those normal engineering charges will be included in that calculation.

This clause provides that payments to certain funds and the preparation of manufacturing masters are not recoupable expenses. While some companies will try to recover some or all of these costs from artists, the norm among major labels is to absorb these costs as part of their cost of doing business.

6. ADDITIONAL ADVANCES

6.01. All monies paid by Label to you during the term of this Agreement, except royalties paid pursuant to Articles 9, 10 and 12, will constitute Advances. Each payment (except such royalties) made by Label during the term to anyone else on your behalf will also constitute an Advance if it is made with your knowledge, if it is required by law, or if it is made by Label to satisfy an obligation incurred by you in connection with the subject matter of this Agreement.

6.02. (a) In connection with the Commitment in the initial Contract Period and each Commitment Album, Label will pay you an Advance in the amount by which the applicable sum indicated below ("Recording Fund") exceeds the Recording Costs (including anticipated costs not yet paid or billed) for such Commitment Album:

In nearly all record deals with major record companies today, the company's financial commitment to the artist is made by way of an all-inclusive recording fund. This replaces the older approach of an allocated recording budget for each album and agreement to pay a separate, specified cash advance to the artist for each album. In the recording fund, the budget for recording costs and the artist's advance are combined, which achieves the company's objective of having a fixed production cost for the album. It also gives the artist an incentive to minimize the recording costs, since the unspent portion of the recording fund is paid to the artist as a cash advance. However, the downside for the artist is that if the entire recording fund is spent on recording costs, there will be no cash advance to cover the artist's expenses during the period of time from the delivery of the album until royalties have begun to be earned, which, even with a successful album, may take many months from the commercial release of the album. Even worse, if the recording costs exceed the recording fund, the artist may be required to repay the excess to the company or, in any event, the company will have the right to deduct the excess from other monies, which may include mechanical royalties and future advances as well as artist royalties that become payable to the artist.

Fundamentally, the entire amount of the recording fund is recoupable from royalties payable to the artist. This is one of the most basic principles of recording contracts and it is rarely varied in any significant way. Accordingly, before the artist receives any royalties from the sale of an album, the company repays to itself the entire cost of recording the album, as well as any cash advances it paid to the artist. This recoupment is not achieved by deducting the recording costs off the top, out of the company's gross receipts, as would be the case if the company and the artist split net profits, but is instead accomplished by deducting those recording costs and advances solely from the artist's royalties. Because the company's profit margin per unit will typically be much higher than the artist's royalty per unit, the company will often enjoy a profit long before the artist receives any royalties. The higher the artist's royalty rate, the more quickly recording costs will be recouped.

(1) The amount of the Recording Fund for the first Commitment Album shall be two hundred seventy thousand dollars $270,000. The amount of the Recording Fund for each Commitment Album (other than the First Album) Delivered hereunder will be two-thirds (2/3) of whichever of the following amounts is less (subject to section 6.02(a)(2) below):

(i) the net amount of the royalties credited to your account on Net Sales Through Normal Retail Channels in the United States of the Commitment Album released most recently before the Delivery of the Commitment Album concerned (the "Prior Album"), as determined by Label from its most recent monthly trial balance accounting statement as of the date twelve (12) months after the initial United States release of the Prior Album, after deduction of reasonable (as determined by reference to Soundscan sales reports) reserves for returns and credits; or

(ii) the average of the amounts of such royalties on the two (2) Prior Albums.

These clauses that define how recording funds are to be calculated for second and subsequent albums are fairly standard. The two major variables at issue are (1) the fraction that is applied to the earned royalties to determine the fund and (2) the number of months of sales that are applied to the formula. Two-thirds is a fairly standard fraction, but if the artist has enough clout, the record company can sometimes be persuaded to use three-fourths or more. With respect to the applicable sales period, some labels will seek to apply as few as six months of sales, but the artist should always try to have 12 full months of sales included in that formula. Additionally, the artist should try to have the formula include so-called pipeline royalties (e.g., royalties earned by the label but not yet credited to the label's account). Finally, the use of Soundscan data in determining recording funds is not preferred because, for reasons described previously, Soundscan often underreports actual sales. The provision that "reasonable reserves for overturns and credits" should be deducted from the 12-months sales figure is normal and generally appropriate, but the artist should try to secure a cap on such reserves of 15% to 20% in order to protect itself from the record company deducting an unreasonable amount of reserves from its sales figures. In some cases, Soundscan data is used as a compromise figure since the underreporting of actual sales by Soundscan can sometimes approximate the actual sales less reasonable reserves. Accordingly, if a record company agrees to base its calculation of recording funds on Soundscan data and not otherwise ask for a reduction for reserves, it will sometimes be in the best interests of the artist. Bear in mind, however, that Soundscan is a private company, its methods of determining sales change frequently, and there is some risk in tying recording funds to Soundscan's sales data. If, for example, Soundscan's methodology were to change in a manner that might artificially underreport sales, it could cost the artist and other artists with similar clauses in their deals substantial amounts of money.

(2) No such Recording Fund will be more than the applicable maximum or less than the applicable minimum amount prescribed below:

(i) the second Commitment Album Delivered in the initial Contract Period:

Minimum	**Maximum**
$250,000	$500,000

(ii) Commitment Album Delivered in the first Option Period:

Minimum	**Maximum**
$275,000	$550,000

(iii) Commitment Album Delivered in the second Option Period:

Minimum	**Maximum**
$300,000	$600,000

(iv) Commitment Album Delivered in the third Option Period:

Minimum	**Maximum**
$325,000	$650,000

(v) Commitment Album Delivered in the fourth Option Period:

Minimum	**Maximum**
$350,000	$700,000

(vi) Commitment Album Delivered in the fifth Option Period:

Minimum	**Maximum**
$400,000	$800,000

The foregoing is the most common structure for allocating recording funds. As discussed above, the fund for the first album is a fixed amount, and the fund for all subsequent albums is determined by multiplying a fraction by the gross amount of royalties earned by the artist from the sales of the prior album or albums. Under this "mini-max" structure, the fund always has a minimum, which generally escalates modestly from album to album, and a maximum, which is generally twice the minimum.

(b) Each such Advance will be reduced by the amount of any reasonably anticipated costs of mastering, remastering, remixing and/or "sweetening"; any such anticipated costs that are deducted but not incurred will be remitted promptly to you. If any Commitment Album is not Delivered within ninety (90) days after the end of the time prescribed in Article 3 (the "Determination Date"), the Recording Fund for that Album will be reduced by five percent (5%) for each thirty (30) day period (or fraction thereof) occurring subsequent to the Determination Date and prior to the Delivery of such Album; provided, however, that in no event shall the Recording Fund for said Album be reduced to an amount less than the actual and approved Recording Costs for said Album.

This clause imposes a fairly significant penalty on artists for late delivery of albums. An artist should try to have such penalty clauses eliminated or significantly modified to avoid the unfair result of losing tens of thousands of dollars for late delivery. Some record companies will remove the penalty clause entirely upon request. Others will reduce the penalty to a one time fixed amount. In genres where entire albums are produced by a single producer with little oversight from the record company, such penalty clauses are arguably appropriate incentives for punctual delivery. However, in genres where the A&R department of the record company takes a very active role in choosing songs and multiple producers, such penalty clauses are often genuinely unfair. In the hip-hop and R&B genres, for example, a single album might feature the work of 10 or more producers and an equal number of side artists, all of which are coordinated by hands-on A&R executives. In certain circumstances, albums can be delayed through no fault of the artist and the artist should not be required to forfeit monies for such delays.

(c) (1) Following the execution of this Agreement and the commencement of its term Label will pay you the sum of Forty Thousand dollars ($40,000) ("the Initial Sum"). In addition, Label shall pay you Three Thousand dollars ($3,000) per month for a period of six (6) months commencing on the first day of the month four (4) months after the date of commencement of this Agreement.

Record companies often seek to spread out payment of an artist's initial advance for several reasons: they continue to earn interest on the unpaid portion of the advance; a payment schedule gives them leverage over an artist who may not be rendering services on time or within budget; and many new recording artists have little experience managing large sums of money, and if the advance is paid in one lump sum, the artist may spend it quickly and then need the label to provide additional funds during the recording of the album. However, if an artist is financially responsible or has a business manager, it is generally in his or her best interests to get the money up front.

(2) The Advance for each subsequent Commitment Album will be made by payment to you of:

(i) fifteen percent (15%) of the minimum Recording Fund for the Album in question, following the commencement of recording of the Album concerned; and

(ii) the balance, if any, of the Advance, within thirty (30) days after the Delivery to Label of the Commitment Album concerned.

The portion of any recording fund that is paid to the artist upon either the execution of the agreement or the exercise of the applicable option generally ranges from 10% to 33%. For very well-known artists and artists that have a proven ability to deliver albums at or below budget, that percentage can increase to as much as 50%.

6.03. (a) A "qualifying Recompilation Album," in this paragraph 6.03, means a Recompilation Album consisting of: (1) Master Recordings made under this Agreement and previously released in different Album combinations; and (2) new Master Recordings made hereunder of at least two (2) new Compositions, made expressly for initial release in that Recompilation Album and not applicable in reduction of your Recording Commitment. You shall Deliver the two (2) new Master Recordings made under this Agreement to Label within sixty (60) days after Label's request therefor.

(b) Promptly after Label's release of a qualifying Recompilation Album on Top-Line Records for Sales Through Normal Retail Channels in the United States during the term hereof, Label will pay you an Advance in the amount by which seventy thousand dollars ($70,000) exceeds the Recording Costs for the new Recordings referred to in section (2) of subparagraph 6.03(a). (No other Advance will be payable in connection with those Recordings.) Each such Advance will be reduced as provided in subparagraph 6.02(b). If your royalty account is in an unrecouped position (i.e., if the aggregate of the Advances and other recoupable items charged to that account at the time of payment of that Advance exceeds the aggregate of the royalties credited to that account at the end of the last semiannual royalty accounting period), the Advance payable under the first sentence of this subparagraph will be reduced by the amount of the unrecouped balance; provided, however, in any event, Label shall pay Recording Costs in connection with each new Master Recording in an amount not in excess of a recording budget approved in accordance with the provisions of section 4.01(a)(4).

This clause establishes the rules and advances applicable to greatest hits or other compilation albums that bear recordings of the artist. Most of these terms are normal and customary; however, record companies will sometimes agree that, even if the artist is in an unrecouped position at the time a recompilation album is released, the artist will receive at least one-half of the recompilation album advance. An artist who is in a deeply unrecouped position will have very little incentive to support a recompilation project when there is no hope of receiving a reasonable amount of money upon its release.

6.04. (a) Label guarantees to pay annual compensation ("Annual Payments") to each of the "Applicable Members" (as hereinafter defined) during each of the first seven (7) "Fiscal Years" (as hereinafter defined) of such amounts as are set forth in sections (1), (2) and (3) below. Each of the Applicable Members hereby agrees to accept all such Annual Payments. As used in this paragraph, "Fiscal Year" shall mean each consecutive twelve (12) month period during which this Agreement is in effect, commencing with the date of commencement of the term of this Agreement. At least thirty (30) days before the end of each Fiscal Year, you shall notify Label in writing if each Applicable Member has not received compensation equal to the Annual Payment for such Fiscal Year and the amount of the deficiency, and Label will pay you the amount of the deficiency.

(1) Nine Thousand Dollars ($9,000) for the first Fiscal Year of this Agreement;

(2) Twelve Thousand Dollars ($12,000) for the second Fiscal Year of this Agreement; and

(3) Fifteen Thousand Dollars ($15,000) for each of the third through seventh Fiscal Years of this Agreement.

(b) You hereby warrant and represent that all payments made to you under this Agreement during each Fiscal Year will be distributed equally among those members in whose names such payment is made (and for such purpose, any payment in the name of "New Group" shall be apportioned equally among all members of you; each such apportioned share of a payment is referred to as the "Appropriate Share"). Each member of you hereby acknowledges that each Appropriate Share to which he is entitled pursuant to the foregoing shall be deemed received by him for purposes of California Civil Code Section 3423.

(c) If in any Fiscal Year the aggregate amount of the compensation (other than Mechanical Royalties) paid to the Applicable Members or allocated to the Applicable Members as an Appropriate Share under this Agreement exceeds the Annual Payments due to the Applicable Members, such excess compensation shall apply to reduce the Annual Payments due to the Applicable Members for any subsequent Fiscal Years.

(d) Each Annual Payment shall be due on or before the last business day of the Fiscal Year to which it applies; provided that if this Agreement expires or terminates prior to the end of a particular Fiscal Year, the applicable Annual Payment to each Applicable Member shall be reduced proportionately, or shall be such greater amount, if any, as is required pursuant to California Civil Code Section 3423. Any failure by Label to make an Annual Payment will not constitute a material breach of this Agreement.

(e) Label shall have the right to pay any Applicable Member or any other member of you at any time any additional amounts, which may be required to be paid as a condition to Label's petitioning for an injunction pursuant to Section 526 of the California Code of Civil Procedure and Section 3423 (5th) of the California Civil Code ("Additional Payments"). Each member of you hereby agrees to accept any and all such Additional Payments. The Appropriate Share of all compensation (other than Mechanical Royalties) paid to you hereunder which is not applied to the Annual Payments theretofore due the Applicable Members will be credited toward satisfying the obligation to make Additional Payments as a prerequisite to seeking injunctive relief hereunder. If Label actually makes any Additional Payments and thereafter elects not to seek such injunction, such Additional Payments shall constitute Advances hereunder.

(f) Each Annual Payment and Additional Payment, if any, will constitute an Advance and will be applied in reduction of any and all monies (other than Mechanical Royalties) due or becoming due you under this Agreement. Notwithstanding anything to the contrary contained herein, whenever in this Agreement Label has the right to deduct excess expenditures (including, without limitation, excess Recording Costs, Mechanical Royalties and Special Packaging Costs) from any and all monies otherwise due or becoming due you under this Agreement, Label's such right shall not extend to deducting such excess expenditures from any Annual Payments or Additional Payments.

(g) As used in this Agreement "Applicable Members" shall mean the persons comprising ____________ (name of band) from time to time being parties to this Agreement.

For many years California Civil Code §3423 provided that in order for a company to obtain an injunction preventing an artist from breaching a contract for unique personal services, the company was required to have guaranteed payment to the individual of at least $6,000 per year. In 1993, it was amended without any legislative debate to $50,000 per year. The record companies learned of this to their horror and mounted a lobbying effort that resulted in the law being amended as of January 1, 1994 to require minimum annual payments to start at $9,000 and escalate as outlined in this paragraph. The statute is quite a bit more complicated than it used to be and has yet to be interpreted in a judicial decision. Since the minimum payment applies to each member of a group, the company may be put to a difficult choice as to whether it should guarantee the minimum compensation to all members of a group that is newly signed to a label and therefore has no track record of sales, or perhaps only to the key member or members, or whether it should forego entirely the possibility of injunctive relief. In this regard it is important for the artist to realize that even if the company is not entitled to injunctive relief to prevent the artist from recording for a new label in breach of the artist's recording contract, the company would be entitled to recover damages, which could be greater than the entire amount of royalties the artist may be paid by the new record company.

7. RIGHTS IN RECORDINGS

7.01. All Master Recordings made or furnished to Label (including the Prior Recordings as hereafter defined) by you under this Agreement or during its term from the Inception of Recording, and all matrices and Phonograph Records manufactured from them, together with the Performances embodied on them, all Covered Videos, and all artwork created for use in connection with the Phonograph Records hereunder ("Artwork") as well as all Web Site Material and ECD Material shall be the sole property of Label, free from any claims by you or any other Person; and Label shall have the exclusive right to copyright those Master Recordings, Covered Videos, Artwork, Web Site Material and ECD Material in its name as the author and owner of them and to secure any and all renewals and extensions of such copyright throughout the world. In connection therewith you hereby acknowledge that each Master Recording made or furnished to Label by you under this Agreement or during its term, from the Inception of Recording, each Covered Video made hereunder, all Artwork, Web Site Material and ECD Material are *works made for hire* for Label in that (a) it is prepared within the scope of Label's employment of you hereunder and/or (b) it constitutes a work specifically ordered by Label for use as a contribution to a collective work. To the extent, if any, that you may be deemed an "author" of any such Master Recordings, Covered Videos, Artwork, Web Site Material or ECD Material you hereby grant to Label a power of attorney, irrevocable and coupled with an interest, for you and in your name, to apply for and obtain, and on obtaining same, to assign to Label all such copyrights and renewals and extensions thereof. You will execute and deliver to Label such instruments of transfer and other documents regarding the rights of Label in the Master Recordings, Covered Videos, Artwork, Web Site Material and ECD Material subject to this Agreement as Label may reasonably request to carry out the purposes of this Agreement, and Label may sign such documents in your name and make appropriate disposition of them. Label will give you ten (10) days notice before signing any document in your name. Label may dispense with that waiting period when necessary, in Label's judgment, to protect or enforce its rights, but Label will notify you in each instance when it has done so. Label will not be required to notify you before signing applications for copyright and/or short form assignments of rights granted in this Agreement for recordation in the Copyright Office. All Artwork, Web Site Material and ECD Material shall contain all such, trademarks, trade names, information, logos and other items, as Label customarily includes on such Artwork or Web Site Material and ECD Material including, without limitation, so-called watermarks, metadata, and hyperlinks to Artist Domain Names and other URLs.

This is fairly standard language that grants to the record company all rights to records, videos and artwork, which are created under the recording agreement. In some cases, when an artist has enough clout, he or she may carve out and retain certain rights to artwork developed for use as album art or promotional art, but it is unusual for a debut artist to have enough clout to secure those rights. Note that this paragraph also refers to material developed for use on the Internet and in any form of enhanced CDs (ECDs). Again, typically a record company would retain ownership in anything that it developed for use in its authorized Web sites promoting the artist. However, as the Internet is creating all manner of opportunities for artists to develop additional strings of revenue that are not covered by the recording agreement (e.g., merchandise, etc.), the artist may wish to negotiate terms that will allow certain artwork and development costs to be shared with the label. Thereafter, both will retain the nonexclusive right to use such materials in their own Web sites. For example, the exclusive rights to a logo that the artist wants to use on his or her own merchandise and fan Web site should not be transferred to the record company.

Whether the recordings made by a recording artist under a typical recording contract such as this are truly "works made for hire" within the meaning of the United States Copyright Act is not entirely clear. Accordingly, it is important to the company that there be a clause that provides that even if the recordings are not works made for hire, nevertheless, all the rights therein are transferred and assigned to the record company by this agreement. One difference between works made for hire and sound recordings that are not works made for hire is that the term of copyright protection for works made for hire is 75 years from their first publication, whereas the term of copyright for recordings that are not works made for hire is the life of the author plus 50 years. More importantly, the record company's rights as owner of a work made for hire would not be subject to termination at any time, whereas the present copyright act gives a right of termination to authors of works that are not works made for hire, which right is exercisable 35 years after the grant of rights was made.

7.02. Without limiting the generality of the foregoing, Label and any Person authorized by Label shall have the unlimited, exclusive rights, throughout the world: (a) to manufacture and or distribute Phonograph Records in any form and by any method now or hereafter known, derived from the Master Recordings and Covered Videos made or Delivered under this Agreement or during its term; (b) to sell, lease, rent, transmit, import, export, transfer or otherwise deal in or dispose of the same under any trademarks, trade names and labels, or to refrain from such manufacture, sale and dealing; (c) to reproduce, adapt, and otherwise use those Master Recordings, Covered Videos, Web Site Material and ECD Material in any medium and in any manner, including but not limited to use in audiovisual works; and (d) to publicly perform such Master Recordings, Web Site Material and ECD Material and Covered Videos and to permit the public performance thereof.

This is a typical grant of rights clause in a recording contract. In nearly every recording contract, the record company owns the copyright in the recordings made under that agreement (i.e., the sound recording copyright, designated by the symbol ℗, as distinguished from the copyright in the underlying song, which is an entirely different matter). Only in the cases of a handful of superstars, e.g., Bruce Springsteen, is the artist able to maintain ownership of the master recordings or to obtain a reversion of ownership at some point in the future. However, this is not something that should be of great concern to the typical artist, since the record company's obligations to pay royalties will continue throughout the term of copyright.

In this contract, the company's ownership purportedly extends not only to the masters that are recorded for the company with the company's money, but to any other masters made during the term. This is intended to give the company ownership of alternate takes and extra songs that did not make the album (outtakes), but, if strictly interpreted, also encompasses other recordings made outside the record company's purview, e.g., live concert recordings or recordings made for television or radio programs. Obviously, if a third party such as a television or radio broadcaster were to undertake the production of certain live recordings, e.g., the BBC's recordings of the Beatles' early radio performances or MTV's recordings of the "Unplugged" series, there would be a conflict of rights that would need to be worked out before the recordings are released on records.

7.03. You hereby irrevocably authorize, empower, and appoint Label your true and lawful attorney (a) to initiate and compromise any valid claim or action against infringers of Label's rights with respect to Covered Videos, Master Recordings and Artwork made under this Agreement or otherwise furnished to Label by you; and (b) to execute in the your name any and all documents and/or instruments necessary or desirable to accomplish the foregoing. Label will give you ten (10) days notice before signing any such document in your name. The power of attorney granted under this paragraph 7.03 is coupled with an interest and is irrevocable.

7.04. Label will have the right to conduct a trademark search with respect to the name "________________" and to register such trademark in your name with each applicable trademark authority. You will execute and deliver to Label those documents regarding such name as Label may reasonably request to carry out any trademark search and registration. Notwithstanding the foregoing, Label may sign those documents in your name and make appropriate disposition of them. Label will give you ten (10) days notice before signing any such document in your name. All costs paid or incurred by Label in connection with any trademark search or registration under this Agreement will constitute Advances.

The foregoing two paragraphs essentially give the record company the right to negotiate with any party who exploits the artist's recordings, videos and artwork made under the agreement and further requires the artist to cooperate with the label in connection with registering the artist's trademark. These clauses are normal and standard, however, the artist should try to negotiate terms that would provide the artist with the right to consent to any compromise or settlement of any claim against any party who exploited the artist's performances. The artist may rightfully be entitled to some measure of compensation as a result of such compromises and settlement and the record company should not be allowed to enter into such compromises without paying the artist his or her due.

8. MARKETING

8.01. (a) Label and its Licensees shall have the perpetual and exclusive rights during the term of this Agreement (and the nonexclusive rights thereafter) throughout the world and may grant to others the rights:

(1) to use the names, portraits, pictures and likenesses of you and Producer(s) and all other Persons performing services in connection with Master Recordings and Covered Videos made under this Agreement (including, without limitation, all past, present or future legal, professional, group, and other assumed or fictitious names used by you or them), and biographical material concerning you or them, as news or information, for the purposes of trade, or for advertising purposes, in any manner and in any medium in connection with the marketing and exploitation of Phonograph Records and Covered Videos hereunder, including on Web Sites (including Artist Web Sites) and Label's institutional advertising (i.e., advertising designed to create goodwill and prestige and not for the purpose of selling any specific product or service); and

(2) to reproduce your names, portraits, pictures and likenesses (including, without limitation, all past, present or future legal, professional, group, and other assumed or fictitious names used by you) (collectively "artist's Name and Likeness") on promotional merchandise (i.e., merchandise not intended for resale to consumers) of any kind, without payment of additional compensation to you or any other Person, in connection with the marketing and exploitation of Phonograph Records and Covered Videos hereunder, Label's institutional advertising and your career; and
(3) to create, host and/or maintain any Web Sites which incorporate Artist's name, likeness or any Master Recordings and Covered Videos or Artwork.

Here the label seeks a very broad grant of rights, which should be whittled down a bit before the agreement is finalized. Ideally, the label's right to use the artist's professional names should be limited to names used during the term of this agreement that pertain to the artist's career as a recording artist. If, after the termination or expiration of this agreement, the artist chooses to change his or her name or to join a group or change his or her group's name, the label should not have the right to use such names without the artist's consent. With respect to promotional merchandise, the language should be clear that this is merchandise intended solely to be given away to promote the artist's recordings and the artist ought to have reasonable approval rights with respect to such promotional merchandising campaigns. Depending on the popularity of the artist, a free flow of promotional merchandise from the record company might have a negative impact on the artist's ability to sell merchandise that fans might otherwise readily purchase.

(b) During the term of this Agreement, you shall not authorize any Person other than Label to use the Artist's Name and Likeness in connection with the advertising or sale of:
(1) Phonograph Records; or
(2) Blank recording tape or tape recording equipment, other than professional tape or equipment not intended for resale to consumers.
(c) Save as otherwise set forth herein during the term of this Agreement neither Artist nor any Person deriving rights from Artist will use, authorize any person other than Label and its Licensees to create, host and/or maintain any Web Sites which incorporate Artist's name, likeness, or any Master Recordings, Covered Videos or Artwork.

The language that pertains to the company's rights to host or maintain Web sites should be narrowed considerably. The label ought only be able to host and maintain Web sites that are directly involved with the promotion and sale of artist's master recordings or covered videos. Such rights should be nonexclusive vis-à-vis the artist who ought to be able to retain the right to use authorized artwork and, perhaps, even authorized audio and audiovisual clips on his or her own Web site. If the record company is allowed to have the exclusive right to host and maintain Web sites that incorporate the artist's name, then the artist would not be able to host and maintain a fan site or any other site to sell nonrecord merchandise. As the Internet has become more important in the recording industry, many record companies have sought broad rights in the context of recording agreements that cross the line into rights that ought to be reserved for merchandising agreements. Record companies need to be reminded often that recording agreements are not merchandising agreements and all rights that would normally and customarily be reserved by an artist's merchandising company must be removed from recording agreements.

8.02. (a) You will cooperate with Label, as it reasonably requests, in making photographs and preparing other materials for use in promoting and publicizing you, the Recordings and Covered Videos made under this Agreement, at Label's expense and subject to your prior professional commitments.
(b) Label will make available to you for your approval, at its offices, any pictures of you or biographical material about you that it proposes to use for packaging, advertising or publicity in the United States during the term of this Agreement. Label will not use any such material which you disapprove in writing, provided you furnish substitute material, satisfactory to Label in its sole discretion, in time for Label's use within its production and release schedules. If you object to any previously approved likeness (other than any likeness embodied in Covered Videos or on the packaging for any Record hereunder) or biographical material and provide Label with replacements therefor which are approved by Label, Label shall not make any new use of those likenesses and biographical material to which you have objected. No inadvertent failure to comply with this paragraph will constitute a breach of this Agreement, and you will not be entitled to injunctive relief to restrain the continuing use of any material used in contravention of this paragraph. Notwithstanding the foregoing, upon receipt by Label of notice from you specifying its failure to comply with the provisions of this subparagraph 8.02(b), Label will use its reasonable efforts to prospectively cure such failure, it being understood that Label shall have no obligation to recall any material used in contravention of this subparagraph 8.02(b).

Since the artist has agreed to cooperate with the label in connection with creating photographs and other materials, it really ought to be incumbent upon the label to make sure that such photography sessions and so forth take place early enough in the album preparation (the album setup cycle) so that the artist has ample time to review and approve and, if necessary, reject and redo photographs. Record companies will often agree to furnish, as opposed to make available, artwork for the artist's review and commit to a specific time frame during which the artist may choose to accept or reject the proposed artwork. The artist may also request that language be added to this paragraph that will put the burden on the label to ensure that all photography sessions take place early enough so that in the event that the artist rejects the photography from the first session, there is sufficient time to schedule a second session so the artist can choose from another set of photographs. This is less likely to happen for a debut artist than it is for an artist who already has had some success or significant buzz in the industry.

8.03. During the term of this Agreement, in respect of Records, other than Audiovisual Records, manufactured for sale in the United States, Label will not, without your consent and notwithstanding anything in Article 9:
(a) initially release any Commitment Album under any Record label other than a label then used by Label for Recordings of Performances by Label's best selling artists in your genre then under exclusive term contract to Label;
(b) release "live" recordings originally recorded in the form of "cybercasts" or

"streaming audio" except in connection with Artist Web Sites "live" Records and Electronic Transmissions other than "digital downloads;
(c) Sell Album format Records derived from any Master Recording made or furnished under this Agreement as "cut-outs" within eighteen (18) months, as Midprice Records within twelve (12) months, and as Budget Records within eighteen (18) months, after the initial release of the Master Recording concerned on Phonograph Records in the United States. Sales as "cut-out," Midprice or at Budget during the relevant restriction period shall not be a breach of this agreement provided that royalty in respect of such sale is accounted at the full applicable rate and shall count towards any escalation or fund calculation where the sale would have counted had it been at "full" price at the relevant time; or
(d) edit otherwise than for radio or technical (configuration) purposes any Master Recording Delivered by you.

This clause sets forth commonly granted marketing restrictions. Normally, these are not contained in a first-draft recording contract for a new artist. However, since these are relatively minor concessions, this company has granted them in advance in order to show that it is artist oriented and to reduce the need for negotiation. There are a whole host of marketing restrictions that are commonly requested, the most prevalent of which are restrictions on coupling the artist's recordings with recordings by other artists, and restrictions on synchronizing the artist's masters in motion pictures, television programs, or commercials without the artist's consent.

Note that the agreement distinguishes between digital downloads of music and cybercasts or "streaming audio" broadcasts of artist's music. The artist and the artist's representatives should realize that so-called streaming audio and audiovisual programming can be captured by computer savvy consumers and stored on their hard drives just as if the performance in question was posted on a Web site for digital download. While the percentage of Internet consumers with such technology and expertise is still relatively small, there is a possibility that over time it will become easier and easier for consumers to capture streamed Internet content, which will make the distinction between Internet webcasts and digital downloads relatively meaningless. Therefore, wherever this language comes up in a recording agreement, the artist should clarify that consent rights apply to any use of his or her audio or audiovisual performances on the Internet that can be captured and stored by the consumer.

8.04. Label will not use Master Recordings made under this Agreement on "Premium Records" without your consent and notwithstanding anything in Article 9. (A "Premium Record" is a Record produced for use in promoting the sale of merchandise other than Phonograph Records.)

8.05. Label will not release "outtakes" of Phonograph Records without your consent.("Outtakes" are preliminary, unfinished, or alternate versions of Master Recordings made under this Agreement.)

This paragraph is actually very important as record labels will not hesitate to release unfinished or, in some cases, downright poor recordings of a popular artist after he or she has left the label for greener pastures. Here, I would amplify the consent language to read "... without your consent, which shall be determined in your sole discretion." An artist should not give a label any wiggle room in this regard.

8.06. (a) Provided you have fulfilled all of your material obligations under this Agreement, Label will release each Commitment Album Delivered hereunder in the United States within five (5) months after your Delivery to Label of such Album. If Label fails to do so your sole remedy shall be the right to notify Label, within three (3) months after the end of the five (5) month period concerned, that you intend to terminate the term of this Agreement unless Label releases such Album within three (3) months after Label's receipt of your notice (the "Cure Period"). If Label fails to release such Album before the end of the Cure Period, you may terminate the term of this Agreement by giving Label notice within sixty (60) days after the end of the Cure Period. On receipt by Label of your termination notice the term of this Agreement will end and all parties will be deemed to have fulfilled all of their obligations under it except those obligations which survive the end of the term (e.g., warranties, rerecording restrictions, audit rights and obligation to account and pay royalties). If you fail to give Label either of those notices within the period specified, your right to terminate will lapse.

This is a very typical release commitment for a new artist. It is limited to albums only; it does not provide a guaranteed release of any singles. The rationale for this is that the company has all the necessary incentive to release singles and will release them when it believes it is going to be helpful to promote the artist. Additionally, it is difficult to craft a remedy for the failure to release a single that would be fair and appropriate. On the other hand, if the company fails to release any album of the artist's recording commitment in the United States, and fails to cure that after written notice, the customary remedy is that the artist has the right to terminate the contract.

One of the important keys to this language is the use of the word, Delivered (again, note the capital "D"). An inexperienced artist may make the mistake of believing that delivery has occurred when he or she has simply delivered the master recordings to the label. This is often not the case. As you will see in paragraph 14.09 of this agreement, delivery requires a full complement of documentation that must be in place before the "Delivery" clock starts running. An artist should try to persuade the company to reduce the time frame for the release commitment.

(b) (1)Provided you have fulfilled all of your material obligations under this Agreement, Label will release each Commitment Album Delivered hereunder which has been listed among the first fifty (50) Albums in the principal weekly chart of best-selling Albums in the United States published in *Billboard Magazine* (i.e., currently "The *Billboard* 200") in the following territories ("Release Territories") within five (5) months after the initial commercial release of such Album in the United States (the "Foreign Release Date"):

(i) Canada
(ii) United Kingdom
(iii) France
(iv) Germany
(v) Japan

This section (1) will not apply in any Release Territory for which you have not fully complied with your obligations to grant or obtain licenses for the use of the Compositions concerned (Controlled or otherwise) in accordance with Article 12, or if you have failed to furnish Label with any other authorization or documentation required for release there without additional expense or liability.

Depending on the company involved and the artist's potential for international appeal, you may expect to see terms in an agreement whereby the company will commit to release the artist's album in certain foreign territories. Here the label has agreed to release an album in certain territories, but only if the album achieves top 50 status in the United States. The remedy for company's failure to do so is generally limited to allowing the artist to negotiate with third party licensees to release the record outside of the United States. In such event, the licensee generally pays the advances and royalties to the label, which will then apply half (50%) to the artist's account and keep the other half (50%) for itself. Here, by limiting the release territories to five countries, and making such release contingent on the success of the album in the U.S., the artist is not able to license the recordings to companies outside of that list without the label's consent.

(2) If Label fails to comply with section 8.06(b)(1) in any Release Territory, your sole remedy shall be to notify Label, within sixty (60) days after the Foreign Release Date concerned, that you intend to invoke this section 8.06(b)(2) if Label does not release such Album in that Release Territory within the Cure Period. If Label fails to do so you will have the right ("Outside License Option") to require Label to enter into an agreement with a licensee designated by you and approved by Label, who is actually engaged in the business of manufacturing and distributing Phonograph Records in that Release Territory, authorizing the licensee to manufacture and distribute Records derived from the Recordings comprised in that Album in that Release Territory. You may exercise your Outside License Option by giving Label notice within sixty (60) days after the end of the Cure Period. If you fail to give Label either of those notices within the period specified, your rights under this subparagraph will lapse. Fifty percent (50%) of all revenues actually received by or credited to Label under such licenses will be credited to your royalty account under this Agreement, in lieu of any royalties under Articles 9 or 10 on Records sold under those licenses. Each such license agreement will provide for such compensation for the license as you negotiate with the licensee, and will contain such other provisions as Label shall require, including, but not limited to, the following:

(i) The licensee will be required to obtain and deliver to Label, in advance: (A) all consents by other Persons which Label may require (including but not limited to consents by recording artists); and (B) all agreements by other Persons which Label may require to look to the licensee, and not to Label, for the fulfillment of any obligations arising in connection with the manufacture or distribution of Records under the license (including such agreements by unions and funds established under union agreements). The licensee will also become a first party to the AFM Phonograph Record Manufacturers' Special Payments Fund Agreement, or any successor agreement then in effect. The license will not become effective until the licensee has complied with all of the provisions of this subsection (i).

(ii) The licensee will make all payments required in connection with the manufacture, sale or distribution in that Release Territory of Phonograph Records made from those Master Recordings after the effective date of the license, including, without limitation, any royalties and other payments to other performing artists, Producers, owners of copyrights in Compositions, the Music Performance Trust Fund and Special Payments Fund, and any other unions and union funds. The licensee will comply with the applicable rules and regulations of the American Federation of Musicians and any other union having jurisdiction and any other applicable laws, rules and regulations covering any use of the Recordings by the licensee or any Person deriving rights from the licensee, in the manufacture and sale of Phonograph Records or otherwise.

(iii) No warranty of merchantability or fitness for a particular purpose or any other warranty or representation, express or implied, will be made by Label in connection with the Recordings, the license, or otherwise. You and the licensee will indemnify and hold harmless Label and its Licensees against all claims, damages, liabilities, costs, and expenses, including reasonable counsel fees, arising out of any use of the Recordings or exercise of such rights by the licensee or any Person deriving rights from the licensee.

(iv) Label will instruct its Licensees in that Release Territory not to manufacture Records derived from those Master Recordings for sale there, except as permitted under subsection 8.06(b)(2)(viii) below. If the licensee notifies Label of such manufacture, Label will instruct the Label Licensee concerned to discontinue it, but neither Label nor the Label Licensee shall have any liability by reason of such manufacture occurring before Label's receipt of such notice, and Label shall have no liability by reason of such manufacture at any time.

(v) Each Record made under the license will bear a sound recording copyright notice identical to the notice used by Label for its initial United States release of the Recording concerned, or such other notice, as Label shall require. Otherwise, those Records will not be identified directly or indirectly with Label.

(vi) Label shall have the right to examine the books and records of the licensee and all others authorized by the licensee to manufacture or distribute Records under the license, for the purpose of verifying the accuracy of the accountings rendered to Label by the licensee.

(vii) The licensee will not have the right to authorize any other Person to exercise any rights without Label's prior written consent.

(viii) Label and its Licensees will have the continuing right at all times to manufacture and sell Recompilation Albums which may contain those Master Recordings in that Release Territory.

(c) The running of the five (5) month and three (3) month periods referred to in subparagraphs 8.06(a) and 8.06(b) will be suspended (and the expiration date of each of those periods will be postponed) for the period of any suspension of the running of the term of this Agreement under paragraph 15.03. If any such five (5) month and/or three (3) month period would otherwise expire on a date between November 1 and the next January 16, its running will be suspended for the duration of the period between November 1 and January 16 and its expiration date will be postponed by the same amount of time. A Commitment Album will be deemed released, for the purposes of this paragraph 8.06, when Label has announced its availability for sale in the territory concerned.

This paragraph dovetails into the artist's release commitment set forth in 8.06(a) above. Essentially this clause freezes the clock from November 1st through January 16th. This language is contained in almost every recording agreement, although sometimes the freeze period can be tightened (e.g., from November 15th to January 10th). Note that if a 2 1/2-month freeze period is imposed, the artist may be precluded from terminating an agreement for company's failure to release his or her album until 10 1/2 months after delivery, and that is assuming that the artist promptly notifies the company of its failure to release the record exactly five months after the delivery date.

8.07. In the event that you and Label agree you shall have the right to produce and deliver to Label the "Album Artwork" (as herein defined) to be used in connection with such Album in accordance with the provisions of this paragraph. As used herein, the term "Album Artwork" means all artwork, photography or other graphics and related materials for the packaging of the applicable Album.

(a) You shall not commence production of such Album Artwork until Label has approved in writing the concept for the proposed Album Artwork and the individuals (e.g., photographers, designers and illustrators) whom you intend to engage to produce such Album Artwork and Label has assigned a budget for the artwork costs.

(b) You will produce the Album Artwork in accordance with the concept and budget approved by Label and will deliver "camera ready" artwork to Label, together with all licenses and consents required in connection with it, not later than seventy-five (75) days before the scheduled release date of the Album. If any of that material has not been delivered to Label within that time, Label will have the right to prepare such Album Artwork, and Label shall not be obligated to make any payments to you or any other Person to whom you have incurred any obligation in connection with any artwork produced for the Album concerned. Label shall use reasonable efforts to consult with you regarding Label's concept for such Album Artwork prior to preparing same, however, Label's decisions with respect thereto shall be final.

(c) You will deliver to Label, together with the Album Artwork, an itemized statement of your actual costs in connection with it. After Label's acceptance of the Album Artwork, Label will pay, or reimburse you for, those costs not in excess of the approved budget. If Label, in its sole discretion, shall elect to pay or reimburse you for costs in excess of the approved budget, such excess shall constitute Special Packaging Costs and also shall be recoupable from all monies becoming due to you under this Agreement.

(d) All Album Artwork shall be subject to Label's reasonable approval. Label shall also have the right to reject any Album Artwork which in Label's reasonable, good faith opinion, is patently offensive, constitutes an obscenity, violates any law, infringes or violates the rights of any Person, or which might subject Label to liability or unfavorable regulatory action. Label will consult with you prior to rejecting any Album Artwork by reason of this subparagraph 8.07(d) and will further consult with you in connection with the preparation of any new Album Artwork; however, Label's decisions with respect thereto shall be final.

(e) Upon your delivery of Album Artwork, Label shall determine the costs for the manufacturing of the packaging therefrom. If the costs for the manufacturing of the packaging would require Label to incur Special Packaging Costs, Label will advise you prior to manufacturing packaging from such Album Artwork and give you the opportunity to redesign such Album Artwork within five (5) days thereafter. If you do not redesign the applicable Album Artwork to come within Label standard packaging costs (i.e., so that Label would not be required to incur Special Packaging Costs) within such five (5) day period, Label shall have the right, at its election, to:

(1) create different Album Artwork if it is not reasonably possible for Label to redesign such Album Artwork to come within Label's standard packaging costs (in which event you shall, upon Label's request, promptly repay to Label all amounts paid or incurred by Label in connection with the Album Artwork prepared by you, and all such amounts not repaid by you will constitute Advances and may be recouped from all monies otherwise becoming due you hereunder);

(2) redesign the Album Artwork as provided by you to come within such standard packaging costs; or

(3) use the Album Artwork provided by you. If Label uses the Album Artwork as provided by you, all Special Packaging Costs will be reimbursed by you on Label's request, and all such Special Packaging Costs not reimbursed will constitute Advances and may be recouped by Label from all monies becoming due to you hereunder.

(f) All matters relating to Label's trademarks, legal obligations, notices or disclosures deemed advisable by Label's attorneys or other requirements will be determined in Label's sole discretion.

(g) You will act as an independent contractor in all arrangements you make with others in connection with the production of the Album Artwork; you will not purport to make any such arrangements as Label's agent or otherwise on behalf of Label.

(h) Any premium charges that are incurred by Label to meet the release schedule of the Album concerned because of late delivery of the Album Artwork or costs incurred by Label to correct or otherwise modify the Album Artwork will be reimbursed by you on Label's request, and all such costs not reimbursed will constitute Advances and may be recouped by Label from any and all monies becoming due to you hereunder.

8.07.1. (a) In the event that you do not deliver to Label Album Artwork in accordance with paragraph 8.07 above (or Label elects that you shall not produce and deliver to Label the Album Artwork pursuant to paragraph 8.07 above) then in preparation for the initial release in the United States during the term hereof of each Commitment Album and any Recompilation Album, Label will consult with you regarding the Album Artwork. You shall have the right, exercisable, if at all, within five (5) business days after such Album Artwork has been submitted to you for review and comment, to disapprove such Album Artwork. Unless otherwise provided in this paragraph 8.07.1, Label will make such changes in the Album Artwork as you reasonably request.

(b) Label will not be required to make any changes which would delay the release of the applicable Album beyond the scheduled date or which would require Label to incur any Special Packaging Costs. Any premium charges incurred to meet the release schedule because of delays in approvals by you will constitute Advances and may be recouped by Label from any and all becoming due to you hereunder. Upon completion of the Album Artwork, Label will determine and advise you if the costs for the manufacturing of the packaging would require Label to incur Special Packaging Costs. If, within five (5) days thereafter, you notify Label of your objection to such Special Packaging Costs in connection with such Album Artwork, and Label nevertheless uses such Album Artwork, Label shall not recoup Special Packaging Costs hereunder. No failure to so advise you will be deemed a breach hereof, provided that if Label fails to so advise you, Label will not recoup any such Special Packaging Costs.

(c) Label will not be required to make any change which in Label's reasonable, good faith opinion is patently offensive, constitutes an obscenity, violates any law, infringes or violates the rights of any Person, or which might subject Label to liability or unfavorable regulatory action. All matters relating to Label's trademarks, legal obligations, notices or disclosures deemed advisable by Label's attorneys or other requirements will be determined in Label's sole discretion.

Generally, the company's in-house department prepares album cover artwork for the artist's approval. However, in some instances the artist will be given a budget to hire outside artists to create the album artwork, in which event the company will insist on the right to approve it, at least to ensure that it is not offensive or objectionable, and to ensure that the costs of manufacturing album covers, CD booklets, etc., will not be excessive. If they are, the company will usually insist that the artist pay these costs out of pocket.

8.08. Label will either (a) produce or cause to be produced at least one (1) Covered Video for each of Commitment Album released during each Option Period hereof, provided that you have fully complied with your material obligations to Label hereunder; or, on a Commitment Album by Commitment Album basis, at Label's election, (b) produce a television advertisement for the Commitment Album concerned released hereunder and purchase television advertising time to show the same on television in the United States.

With respect to any initial television advertisement produced for a Commitment Album for broadcast in the United States Label shall agree with you the principle theme and content of the advertisement provided that a principle theme of the key Artwork for the Commitment Album and a sound bed of Singles to be taken from the Commitment Album shall be deemed approved in any event.

With respect to all Covered Videos, the following shall be applicable:

(a) With respect to Covered Videos made in connection with the initial release of a Commitment Album, the selection(s) to be embodied in each Covered

Video shall be mutually designated by you and Label, provided that you shall be deemed to have approved any selection that has been or will be embodied on a Single.

(b) Each Covered Video shall be shot on a date or dates and at a location or locations to be mutually designated by you and Label, subject to your reasonable prior professional commitments.

(c) The producer and director of each Covered Video, and the concept or script for each Covered Video, shall be approved by both you and Label. Label shall engage the producer, director and other production personnel for each Covered Video, and shall be responsible for and shall pay the production costs of each Covered Video in an amount not in excess of a budget to be established in advance by Label and you (the "Production Budget"). In the event that you and Label cannot agree on the Production Budget Label's say shall be final. You shall be responsible for and shall pay the production costs for each Covered Video that are in excess of the Production Budget. In the event that Label shall pay any production costs for which you are responsible pursuant to the foregoing sentence (which Label is in no way obligated to do), you shall promptly reimburse Label upon Label's request, and all such costs not reimbursed will constitute Advances and may be recouped by Label from any monies otherwise payable by Label to you hereunder. Your compensation for performing in such Covered Videos (as opposed to your compensation with respect to the exploitation of such Videos which is provided elsewhere in this Agreement) shall be limited to any minimum amounts required to be paid for such Performances pursuant to any collective bargaining agreements pertaining thereto; provided, however, that you hereby waive any right to receive such compensation to the extent such right may be waived.

Video production costs are a hotly negotiated item as runaway expenses can cause an artist to be deprived of royalties even on a top-selling album. A typical arrangement is for the record company to recoup 50% of the video production costs from the artist's royalties. In many deals, the record company will agree that 50% of the costs shall be recouped but only up to a certain amount, above which all costs will be recouped against the artist. This agreement is unusual in that it appears that the company is willing to accept full responsibility for production costs within the production budget. However, this agreement provides that the label has final say so on what the production budget ought to be. As this is a first draft, the artist would typically fight for greater control over the budget, and the record company may agree to establish a minimum budget and, perhaps, a maximum budget that could not be exceeded without the artist's separate consent. While videos are an extremely valuable marketing tool, in recent years the consolidation of many of the major video broadcasters has made it increasingly difficult for new bands to secure airplay for their videos. Accordingly, many expensive videos have never been seen and the artists are typically on the hook for at least a portion of the video production costs. Accordingly, artists may want to consider having the option to instruct the company <u>not</u> to produce a video in the event that the artist believes it is unlikely that the video will be broadcast on major video outlets.

(d) As set forth in paragraph 12.02 below, you shall issue (or shall cause the music publishing company[ies] having the right to do so to issue) (1) worldwide, perpetual synchronization licenses, and (2) perpetual licenses for public performance in the United States (to the extent that ASCAP and BMI are unable to issue same), to Label at no cost for the use of all Controlled Compositions in any such Covered Videos effective as of the commencement of production of the applicable Covered Video (and your execution of this Agreement shall constitute the issuance of such licenses by any music publishing company[ies] which is owned or controlled by you or by any Person owned or controlled by you). In the event that you shall fail to cause any such music publishing company[ies] to issue any such license to Label, or if Label shall be required to pay any fee to such music publishing company[ies] in order to obtain such license, then Label shall have the right to deduct the amount of such license fee from all monies becoming due to you under this Agreement. Notwithstanding the foregoing, although the synchronization license is perpetual and remains in effect, if the costs incurred with respect to any such Covered Video is entirely recouped, then after such recoupment, and only with respect to prospective commercial uses of such Covered Video, at your written request prior to such prospective commercial uses of such Covered Video, Label and you shall negotiate in good faith with respect to compensation consistent with the then-current Label standards, to be paid by Label for such a synchronization license for the Controlled Compositions used in such Covered Video.

(e) Each Covered Video shall be deemed an item of "Materials" covered by your warranties, representations and indemnification obligations under Article 13. Label will have the right to reject any Covered Video or any element contained in a Covered Video which in Label's reasonable, good faith opinion is patently offensive, constitutes an obscenity, violates any law, infringes or violates the rights of any Person, or which might subject Label to liability or unfavorable regulatory action.

The foregoing clauses are generally standard and provide for the artist to grant synch licenses for the use of their compositions in videos, and clarify the record company's rights to reject objectionable content in videos.

8.09. (a) Label and any licensee of Label each has the perpetual and exclusive right, and may grant to others the right, without any liability to any Person, to create, maintain and host Web Sites relating to the Artist (each an "Artist Web Site") and to register and use the name "______________" and all variations thereof which embody the Artist's name or use a name similar to Artist's name as Uniform Resource Locators ("URLs"), addresses and/or domain names (each an "Artist Domain Name") in connection with such Artist Web Sites. As used in the preceding sentence "______________" shall mean each and every so-called second level domain name now in existence or hereafter implemented including without limitation, .com, .net, .org together with territorial identifiers, e.g., .UK. All such Artist Domain Names, and all rights thereto or derived therefrom shall be Label's property throughout the Territory and in perpetuity.

Because of the potential to generate additional streams of revenue from the sale of merchandise, an artist should fight to limit the record company's right to use his or her domain name. In some cases, it may be beneficial for the artist, prior to entering into negotiations with the record company, to enter into a deal with the merchandising company with high Internet exposure so that certain of the rights that would inevitably be sought by the record company will simply be unavailable to transact. Record companies are digging their heels in on this issue and the artist may have to make painful concessions if he or she does not have the clout to walk away from the deal. However, the rights to a domain name should not be given up without the artist's representative presenting a most persuasive case on the subject.

(b) Label will have the right to designate any Artist Web Site as the "official" Artist Web Site, and neither you, nor any Person deriving any rights from you shall designate any other Artist Web Site as the "official" Artist Web Site.

The designation of official Web site is an important one as the consumers in the Internet marketplace are sophisticated enough to distinguish between official and unofficial Web sites. Record companies will strongly insist on this language in most deals unless the artist has already established an official Web site that is generating a sufficient number of hits and revenue. Again, the best argument against the designation of such Web site as an official Web site is the position that the record company is not obtaining an interest in the artist's merchandising rights and therefore should not be taking rights that would diminish the artist's value in the merchandising marketplace.

(c) Notwithstanding the foregoing, but without limiting Label's right during and after the term to create, maintain and host Artist Web Sites in connection with your services hereunder, at any time after the later of the end of the term or nine (9) months after the date of the initial United States release of the last Album of the Recording Commitment for the last Contract Period, Label shall assign to you (on a quit-claim basis) all of its right, title and interest in and to the Artist Domain Names within thirty (30) days of Label's receipt of written notice from you requesting such assignment.

(d) Notwithstanding the foregoing, you shall have the right to register one (1) mutually approved Artist Domain Name in your or your designee's name and to create, host and maintain one Artist Web Site located at such Artist Domain Name, provided, however, that neither you nor any Person deriving any rights from you shall, use, authorize, or endorse such Artist Web Site as the "official" Artist Web Site, and provided further that Label shall have the right to require you to include on such Artist Web Site so-called hyperlinks to Artist Domain Names and other URLs in Label's sole discretion.

Assuming that the artist loses the battle with the label over the designation of the official artist Web site, this is fairly standard language. However, the artist should seek to make hyperlinks between the artist's personal Web site and the label's official Web site mutual so that fans visiting the label's site can click over to the artist's personal site.

8.10. (a) With respect to Artist Web Sites, Web Site Material and ECD Material, all artwork and other creative elements produced in connection therewith, including, without limitation, production personnel, shall be mutually approved by you and Label, provided, however, that any Artwork or other materials furnished or approved by you for any other purpose hereunder shall be deemed approved by you for use in connection with such Artist Web Sites, Web Site Material and ECD Material and provided further that Label shall have the right to include on Artist Web Sites and within ECD Material so-called hyperlinks to Artist Domain Names and other URLs in Label's sole discretion.

The right to place hyperlinks on the artist's official Web page to other URLs is a potentially valuable one and should not be given away lightly. For example, if the artist is known for wearing Reebok attire, he or she may wish to negotiate a sponsorship deal with Reebok pertaining to his or her personal Web site. However, if the record company has the right to post hyperlinks on its official site it may negotiate its own deal with Reebok, which could cost the artist a potentially lucrative hyperlink agreement fee. In theory, the purpose of the label's official Web site should be limited to promoting the artist's recordings and should not be used as a vehicle to generate additional revenue for the company without the artist's consent and participation in the proceeds.

(b) Label is and will be the sole owner of all worldwide rights in and to all ECD Material and Web Site Material created hereunder and to each Artist Web Site, all individual elements thereof (excluding underlying software architecture), and the selection and arrangement of such elements, including the worldwide copyrights therein and thereto, throughout the Territory and in perpetuity.

(c) You will issue (or cause the music publishing companies having the right to do so to issue) (1) worldwide, perpetual synchronization licenses, and (2) worldwide, perpetual licenses for public performance to Label at no cost for the use of all Compositions in Web Site Material and ECD Material effective as of the commencement of production of the applicable Web Site Material or ECD Material (and your execution of this agreement constitutes the issuance of such licenses by you and any music publishing company that is owned or controlled by you, or any Person owned or controlled by you). In the event that you fail to cause any such music publishing company to issue any such license to Label, or if Label is required to pay any fee to such music publishing company in order to obtain any such license, Label will have the right to deduct the amount of such license fee from any and all royalties otherwise payable to you hereunder.

(d) Label will have the right to use and allow others to use Web Site Material and ECD Material for advertising and promotional purposes (a use for which Label receives no monetary consideration from licensees other than an incidental fee being a reasonable amount for reimbursement of its administrative, duplication and shipping costs) and for commercial purposes (being a use which is not an advertising or promotional use as defined in this subparagraph).

This clause gives the label the right to exploit the artist's Web site for commercial purposes. The label should not have such rights without the artist's consent and participation in the revenue.

(e) You will be available, at Label request, for online chats hosted on Artist Web Sites.

(f) You will supply Label, at Label's request, with Web Site Material for possible inclusion on Artist Web Sites, including, without limitation, transcripts of all published interviews of Artist, transcripts of all articles relating to Artist, photographs, and other similar materials.

(g) Each Artist Web Site, Web Site Material and ECD Material will be deemed a Material as provided herein. Label will have the rights in and to each Artist Web Site, Web Site Material and ECD Material as are otherwise applicable hereto with respect to Masters made hereunder, including, without limitation, the right to use and publish, and to permit others to use and publish, your name and likeness in each Artist Web Site, Web Site Material and ECD Material and for advertising and purposes of trade in connection therewith.

(h) Label is under no obligation whatsoever to create, host or maintain Artist Web Sites or ECD Material hereunder.

If the label is successful in securing from the artist the right to use the artist's name as a URL address and the exclusive right to designate such URL as the artist's official Web site, then the label should be obliged to create, host and maintain such Web sites. If the label does not wish to be so obliged, then it should provide that in the event that the label does not create, host and maintain such Web sites that it shall transfer all of the rights to do the same to artist. In no circumstances during this Internet era should the artist be in a position where he or she would have no official Web site and be contractually barred from creating one.

9. ROYALTIES

9.01. Label will pay you a royalty computed at the applicable percentage, indicated below, of the applicable Royalty Base Price in respect of Net Sales Through Normal Retail Channels of Phonograph Records consisting entirely of Master Recordings recorded under this Agreement during the respective Contract Periods specified below and sold by Label or its Licensees ("NRC Net Sales"). The royalties payable pursuant to the provisions of paragraphs 9.01, 9.02, 9.03, 9.04, and 9.05 and the provisions of Article 10 shall apply to all Phonograph Records except Audiovisual Records. The royalties payable pursuant to the provisions of paragraph 9.07 shall apply solely to Audiovisual Records.

(a) On Albums sold for distribution in the United States:

(1) (i) Master Recordings made during the initial Contract Period in connection with the Commitment Album: 13%

(ii) The royalty rate pursuant to subsection 9.01(a)(1)(i) will apply to the first 250,000 units of NRC Net Sales in the United States ("USNRC Net Sales") of the first Commitment Album. The royalty rate will be:

(A) 13.5% on USNRC Net Sales of any such Album in excess of 250,000 units and not in excess of 500,000 units, and

(B) 14% on USNRC Net Sales of any such Album in excess of 500,000 units.

(2) (i) Master Recordings made during the initial Contract Period in connection with the Second Commitment Album: 14%

(ii) The royalty rate pursuant to subsection 9.01(a)(2)(i) will apply to the first 500,000 units of USNRC Net Sales of the second Commitment Album. The royalty rate will be:

(A) 14.5% on USNRC Net Sales of any such Album in excess of 500,000 units and not in excess of 1,000,000 units, and

(B) 15% on USNRC Net Sales of any such Album in excess of 1,000,000 units.

(3) (i) Master Recordings made during the first Option Period: 14.5%.
(ii) The royalty rate pursuant to subsection 9.01(a)(3)(i) will apply to the first 500,000 units of USNRC Net Sales of each Album consisting of Master Recordings made during the first Option Period. The royalty rate will be:
(A) 15% on USNRC Net Sales of any such Album in excess of 500,000 units and not in excess of 1,000,000 units, and
(B) 15.5% on USNRC Net Sales of any such Album in excess of 1,000,000 units.

(4) (i) Master Recordings made during the second and third Option Periods: 15%.
(ii) The royalty rate pursuant to subsection 9.01(a)(4)(i) will apply to the first 500,000 units of USNRC Net Sales of each Album consisting of Master Recordings made during the second and third Option Periods. The royalty rate will be:
(A) 15.5% on USNRC Net Sales of any such Album in excess of 500,000 units and not in excess of 1,000,000 units, and
(B) 16% on USNRC Net Sales of any such Album in excess of 1,000,000 units.

(5) (i) Master Recordings made during the fourth Option Period: 15.5%.
(ii) The royalty rate pursuant to subsection 9.01(a)(3)(i) will apply to the first 500,000 units of USNRC Net Sales of the Album consisting of Master Recordings made during the fourth Option Period. The royalty rate will be:
(A) 16% on USNRC Net Sales of any such Album in excess of 500,000 units and not in excess of 1,000,000 units, and
(B) 16.5% on USNRC Net Sales of any such Album in excess of 1,000,000 units.

(6) (i) Master Recordings made during the fifth Option Period: 16%.
(ii) The royalty rate pursuant to subsection 9.01(a)(3)(i) will apply to the first 500,000 units of USNRC Net Sales of the Album consisting of Master Recordings made during the fifth Option Period. The royalty rate will be:
(A) 16.5% on USNRC Net Sales of such Album in excess of 500,000 units and not in excess of 1,000,000 units, and
(B) 17% on USNRC Net Sales of such Album in excess of 1,000,000 units.

The above stated royalty rates are fairly high for a new artist recording agreement, although they could be somewhat lower or higher. Sometimes the base royalty rate stays the same for all albums under a deal and only escalates based on sales of the particular album. Sales escalations are normally given, on a prospective basis, at gold (for sales of more than 500,000 copies) and platinum (for sales of over 1,000,000 copies). The base or basic royalty rate in all record negotiations is the rate for sales of albums through normal retail channels in the United States at a top-line price. Likewise, escalations are generally limited to those same sales. That basic rate, without regard to escalations based on sales, is the rate upon which virtually all other royalties set forth in this contract are based. In nearly all contracts, the rate for sales of singles is substantially less than the rate on albums, since the profit that may be derived by the company from singles is much lower, and companies tend to regard singles primarily as promotional tools.

One interesting feature of these royalty terms is that with respect to the first album, escalations are triggered at 250,000 and 500,000 units. This would likely have been the result of a prenegotiation of the royalty terms as it is not standard for a first draft long-form agreement. Note the use of the phrase, Royalty Base Price, in the royalty provisions. Most recording agreements will base royalties on multiplying the royalty rate by the suggested retail list price or some variation thereof. Here, the royalty base price is defined in paragraph 14.25 as the suggested retail list price less certain taxes and the applicable "container charge," which we will rediscuss later. Some labels will define royalty base price as some variation of the wholesale price (e.g., the wholesale price multiplied by 130% is common). Sony Music typically defines its royalty base price as 50% of retail, which results in the very odd system of doubling royalty rates, and therefore paying twice the royalty rates on one-half of the retail price. To thoroughly analyze any artist's royalty provisions, it is important to digest all of the factors that will affect the calculation of the artist's "penny rate" for records sold under the agreement. More on that later.

(7) As used herein, the "Base U.S. Album Royalty Rate" for a particular Album Delivered hereunder (and each Master Recording embodied therein) shall mean a royalty rate equal to the royalty rate for the first USNRC Net Sale of such Album on a configuration-by-configuration basis.

(8) The only Net Sales to be considered for the purposes of escalating the royalty rates pursuant to sections 9.01(a)(1), 9.01(a)(2), 9.01(a)(3), 9.01(a)(4), 9.01(a)(5) and 9.01(a)(6) above shall be USNRC Net Sales. Without limiting the foregoing, Net Sales subject to the remainder of Articles 9 and 10 hereof (other than those USNRC Net Sales referred to in subparagraph 9.03(b) below) shall not be considered for the purposes of such escalations. None of the foregoing escalations shall result in an increase in any royalty rates contained herein other than for USNRC Net Sales under sections 9.01(a)(1), 9.01(a)(2), 9.01(a)(3), 9.01(a)(4), 9.01(a)(5) and 9.01(a)(6) above and subparagraph 9.03(b) below, even though other royalty rates may be based on the royalty rates set forth in those paragraphs.

(b) On Albums sold for distribution outside the United States:

(1) On Albums Delivered hereunder and sold for distribution in Canada: 85% of the Base U.S. Album Royalty Rate;

(2) On Albums Delivered hereunder and sold for distribution in the United Kingdom, Japan, Australia, Germany, Spain, Italy, Holland and France: 75% of the Base U.S. Album Royalty Rate; and

(3) On Albums Delivered hereunder and sold for distribution in the rest of the world: 60% of the Base U.S. Album Royalty Rate.

(c) On Singles, Twelve-Inch Singles and Extended Play Records sold for distribution in the United States: 11%. As used herein, the Base U.S. Single Royalty Rate shall mean 11%.

(d) On Singles, Twelve-Inch Singles and Extended Play Records sold for distribution outside the United States:

(1) On Singles, Twelve-Inch Singles and Extended Play Records sold for distribution in Canada: 85% of the Base U.S. Single Royalty Rate;

(2) On Singles, Twelve-Inch Singles and Extended Play Records sold for distribution in the United Kingdom, Germany, France, Japan Eire, Spain, Italy, Holland and Australia; 75% of the Base U.S. Single Royalty Rate; and
(3) On Singles, Twelve-Inch Singles and Extended Play Records sold for distribution in the rest of the world: 60% of the Base U.S. Single Royalty Rate.
(e) If any Label Licensee accounts to Label on the basis of less than one hundred percent (100%) of Net Sales, Label will account to you for the Records concerned on the same basis, but not on less than ninety percent (90%) of Net Sales.

The royalty rates in these subclauses are fairly typical reductions that reflect the fact that the company receives less income and arguably has a lesser profit margin on sales of singles and on sales in foreign territories than on U.S. sales. The countries to which the higher rates are applicable are generally those in which U.S. originated product sells well.

9.01.1. Notwithstanding anything to the contrary contained in this Agreement, with respect to Records sold in Brazil, India, Kenya, Zambia, Zimbabwe, Nigeria and any other territory in which governmental or other authorities place limits on the royalty rates permissible for remittances to the United States in respect of Records sold in such territory(ies), the royalty payable hereunder shall equal the lesser of: (a) the applicable royalty payable under subparagraph 9.01(b) or (d); or (b) the effective royalty rate permitted by such governmental or other authority for remittances to the United States less a royalty equivalent to three percent (3%) of the retail list price and such monies as Label or its Licensees shall be required to pay to all applicable union funds in respect of said sales.

This typical clause is quite technical and does not generally have much economic impact and, therefore, is not highly negotiated.

9.02. (a) The royalty rate on any Record described in this sentence will be one-half (1/2) of the royalty rate that would apply if the Record concerned were sold Through Normal Retail Channels: (1) any catalog Phonograph Record sold by the special products operations of Label or its Licensees ("SPOs") to educational institutions or libraries, or to other SPO clients for their promotion or sales incentive purposes (but not for sale to the general public Through Normal Retail Channels); (2) any noncatalog Phonograph Record created on a custom basis for SPO clients; and (3) any Phonograph Records sold by Label in the United States through direct mail or phone order or other mail order distribution method.

This provision provides for the record company to pay one-half of the otherwise applicable royalty rate on sales of records to schools, libraries and by mail order or phone order. This is not a highly negotiated item, but the artist should make sure that the agreement clarifies that records sold through popular Internet sites such as Amazon.com are not considered to be mail-order items and are therefore not subject to this type of reduction.

(b) In respect of any Master Recording: (1) leased by Label or its Licensees to others for their distribution of Phonograph Records in the United States; (2) embodied on Phonograph Records sold by Label's Licensees in the United

States through a direct mail or mail order distribution method (including, without limitation, through so-called record clubs); or (3) embodied on Phonograph Records sold by Label's Licensees in the United States through retail stores in connection with special radio or television advertisements (sometimes referred to as "key-outlet marketing"), Label will pay you fifty percent (50%) of Label's "Net Receipts" with respect to such exploitation. (Net Receipts, in the preceding sentence, means Label's gross receipts as computed after deduction of all AFM, union and other applicable third-party payments actually made or incurred. If another artist, a Producer, or any other Person is entitled to royalties on sales of such Records, that payment will be divided among you in the same ratio as that among your respective basic royalty percentage rates. No royalties shall be payable with respect to Records given away as "bonus" or "free" Records as a result of joining a record club or purchasing a number of Records from a record club or in connection with any introductory, incentive or other offer made by a record club; provided, however, for the purposes hereof, the number of such nonroyalty Records shall not exceed fifty percent (50%) of the total number of Records distributed through such means.

The payment of a 50% royalty rate on record club sales is one of the fixtures of the business, which even superstars must generally accept. It is important to pay special attention to the definition of net receipts and to make sure that, as provided in this agreement, the percentage of overall record club records that can be deemed free, and therefore yield no royalties, is capped at 50%.

(c) If Label sells or licenses third parties to sell Records via telephone, satellite, cable or other direct transmission including by way of Electronic Transmission to the consumer over wire or through the air, the royalty rate will be the otherwise applicable royalty rate prescribed in paragraph 9.01 but, for purposes of calculating royalties payable in connection with such sales, the retail list price of such Records shall be deemed to be eighty-five percent (85%) of the actual sales price for sales in the United States and, with respect to sales outside of the United States, the actual sales price received by Label of such records, less any referral fees, commissions or similar fees payable to any person who, through their Web Site, electronic mail or other means, refers or directs to Label a purchaser of an Electronic Transmission or otherwise facilitates Label's sale to such consumer, less the applicable Container Charge; provided, however, with respect to Records sold by Label's Licensees, in no event shall your royalty exceed one-half (1/2) of Label's net receipts after deduction from Label's gross receipts of union and all other applicable third party payments actually made or incurred by Label.

As this chapter is being written, BMG and Napster are putting together a method to sell music via digital download on what may become a pay-per-download or subscription basis. Meanwhile, other labels are working toward developing their own method of selling music via electronic transmission. No one really knows yet how the sale of music via electronic transmission will evolve and the record companies are doing what they can to hedge their bets and protect their interests. With respect to this paragraph, note that the label is not only paying a reduced royalty on U.S. sales, but is also deducting all referral and commission fees and costs before applying the royalty rate and is also applying the container charge to the sale of digitally downloaded music. Historically, record companies have imposed container charges to offset the costs of manufacturing album jackets, cassette cases and CD jewel cases. The decision of most record companies to apply container charges to music that is sold via digital download has caused some controversy as, arguably, there are no manufacturing costs when a consumer simply downloads an MP3 file to his personal hard drive. The record companies' counter argument is that the container charge is necessary to offset the cost of establishing and maintaining its computer mainframes, digitizing all of the music and updating its databases. However, at this stage of the game, there is no standard that is universally accepted and, accordingly, the artist and his or her representative ought to negotiate these terms aggressively to see how far back they can push the record companies from the positions they are trying to stake out.

9.03. (a) The royalty rate on any Budget Record, any Premium Record or any "picture disc" (i.e., a disc phonorecord with artwork reproduced on the surface of the Record itself) or any Record sold for distribution through military exchange channels will be one-half (1/2) of the applicable royalty rate prescribed in paragraph 9.01. The royalty rate on any Midprice Record will be two-thirds (2/3) of the applicable royalty rate prescribed in paragraph 9.01. (The preceding two sentences will not apply to a Budget Record sold within twelve (12) months, or to a Midprice Record sold within nine (9) months, after the initial release of the Master Recordings concerned on Phonograph Records in the United States.) The royalty on any Premium Record or Record sold for distribution through military exchange channels will be computed on the basis of the actual sales price (or Post Exchange list price where applicable) less all taxes and Container Charges. The royalty rate on any Record which is not an Album, a Single, a Twelve-Inch Single, or an Extended Play Record will be one half (1/2) of the applicable Album royalty rate prescribed in paragraph 9.01.

It is typical for record companies to pay reduced royalties on budget records and midpriced records (the definitions of which are set forth in the definition section of this agreement, which we will get to later). The key to negotiating this paragraph is to try to secure as long a holdback period as possible. This agreement provides that royalties will not be reduced for budget and midpriced records until 12 months or nine months, respectively, after the initial release of the record in question. These are decent holdback periods, although record companies may be persuaded to extend them to as long as 18 months for budget records and 12 months for midpriced records, in many cases.

(b) (1) The royalty on any compact disc Record will be a royalty computed at one hundred percent (100%) of the rate which would otherwise apply under this Agreement.

The various major record companies have different policies with respect to the payment of royalties on compact discs. When CDs were first introduced, the manufacturing costs were very high and, of course, CD sales accounted for only a very small percentage of all record sales. Accordingly, the record companies developed policies whereby for an introductory period of three years or so, artists were paid the same number of pennies for a sale of a CD as they were paid for a sale of a record in vinyl disc form, even though the CDs had a much higher suggested retail list price. This policy was not negotiable. After the introductory period elapsed and manufacturing costs had decreased and market share had grown somewhat, each record company evolved its own policies to limit royalties on CDs. Every major record company in the United States has adopted a 25% packaging deduction for sales of compact discs. Some have reduced the royalty rate for CDs to 80% to 90% of the artist's normal rate. Others base the royalty rate on a so-called constructed retail price that is determined by utilizing the wholesale price of the record multiplied by an "uplift," generally 130%. As the overall market share of CDs has increased to where CDs now comprise the vast majority of record sales in the United States, more and more record companies appear to be eliminating the standard CD reduction and are now paying royalties on CDs on 100% of the retail price. This does not necessarily represent a windfall for the artist as the record companies simply factor this method of calculation into their analysis when they prepare recording agreements. What the artists and the record companies are ultimately concerned with is the "penny rate," which is the per-unit royalty rate actually payable to the artist after factoring in all of the various adjustments and deductions. Because removing the CD deduction has not been standardized, comparing recording agreements between different companies can often yield results where a 14-point deal at one label actually yields a higher royalty than a 15-point deal at another label where the former does not impose a CD reduction and the latter does.

(2) The royalty on any New Medium Record will be seventy percent (70%) of the rate that would otherwise apply under this Agreement. In the event during the term hereof a particular New Medium Record configuration (including, without limitation, Electronic Transmissions) comprises at least twenty percent (20%) of the total market for Records sold in the United States for a period of six (6) consecutive months as determined by the Recording Industry Association of America, then, following your written request during the term, Label agrees to renegotiate with you with respect to the percentage of the applicable royalty rate payable to you for the New Medium Record configuration concerned based on factors such as, without limitation, the individual performance of Records in that new configuration featuring the performance of Artist and the then current balance in your royalty account, but in no event shall such new percentage exceed one hundred percent (100%) of the otherwise applicable royalty rate in the country concerned for the configuration and price category concerned and the new percentage, if any, will become effective prospectively commencing on the first day of the first full accounting period immediately following the accounting period during which such agreement is reached with respect to such percentage of the applicable royalty rate. The foregoing shall not be construed to restrict in any manner Label's right to (or elect not to) manufacture, distribute, sell, license or otherwise exploit Records hereunder in the form of such New Medium Record configuration either prior to, during or after such renegotiation.

Because the technology surrounding the sale and distribution of recorded music is changing so rapidly and is so uncertain, there is a significant chance that new technologies will become available to the consumers over time and the record companies typically pay a reduced royalty on any new technology. Here, the record company is imposing a 30% reduction on new technologies. That may or may not be negotiable depending on the record company and the bargaining position of the recording artist, but 10% to 30% reductions for new technologies are very common. What is interesting in this language is that it does provide for the reduction to be renegotiated if any particular new technology comprises at least 20% of U.S. record sales during any six-month period. The artist should try to have that threshold reduced from 20% to the maximum extent possible, but be prepared to accept inflexibility from record companies, which are very concerned about the uncertainties caused by the development of new technologies.

(c) The royalty rate on a Multiple Record Set will be the otherwise applicable royalty rate multiplied by a fraction (which shall in no event be larger than one [1]), the numerator of which is the SRLP of such Multiple Record Set in the applicable configuration in the territory where the Multiple Record Set is sold and the denominator of which is Label's then-prevailing SRLP for Label's newly-released Top-line Albums in such configuration in the applicable territory multiplied by the number of Records contained in such Multiple Record Set.

The prices for multiple record sets can vary considerably. In some cases, artists have released two CD sets for the price of a single CD. This paragraph simply makes the royalties for multiple record sets calculated on a pro rata basis. For example, if a multiple record set is sold at a price 50% higher than a single CD, then the artist's royalty will be 50% higher than the royalty for a single CD.

9.04. In respect of Phonograph Records derived from Master Recordings furnished by Label or its Licensees to others for their manufacture and distribution of Records outside the United States, Label will pay you fifty percent (50%) of the net receipts derived from those transactions by Label after deduction from Label's gross receipts of all Mechanical Royalties, AFM, union and all other applicable third-party payments (which payments will be apportioned as provided in paragraph 9.02 if another artist, a Producer, or any other Person is entitled to royalties in respect of such Records), but not in excess of the amount of the royalties which would be payable to you for those Records under subparagraph 9.01(b) or (d) if they were manufactured and distributed by Label or its Licensees.

This is a standard paragraph that provides that if the label licenses any of the artist's master recordings for manufacture and sale outside of the United States, the label will pay the artist 50% of its net receipts.

9.05. If Label authorizes the use of any Master Recording made under this Agreement on a flat-fee basis, royalty rate or cent rate basis for any type of use not specifically covered elsewhere in this Article 9, (such as, but not limited to, use in a commercial or motion picture other than a Covered Video), it will credit your royalty account with an amount equal to fifty percent (50%) of its net receipts attributable directly to that use. Net receipts, in the preceding sentence, means Label's gross receipts as computed after deduction of all payments required to be made by Label to others in connection with those uses (for example, re-use payments under Label's agreements with the American Federation of Musicians). If another recording artist, a Producer, or any other Person is entitled to royalties on such uses, the amount to be credited under this paragraph will be apportioned in the same ratio as that among your respective basic royalty percentages. If any item of such receipts is attributable to Master Recordings made under this Agreement and other Master Recordings, the amount of that item includible in gross receipts under this paragraph will be computed by apportionment on the basis of the number of Master Recordings involved.

This clause applies to licenses of the masters for use in motion picture soundtracks, compilation albums released by third parties, such as soundtrack albums or tribute albums, and other uses not specifically set forth in the agreement. The fifty-fifty split is universally accepted.

9.06. In respect of any Ancillary Exploitation for which Label receives a royalty or other payment, which is directly attributable to such Ancillary Exploitation, your royalty shall be an amount equal to a percentage of Label's Net Receipts from such royalty or other payment which is the same as the percentage of the minimum Basic Rate for Albums in the country from which the license for the Ancillary Exploitation originates. Net Receipts, in the foregoing sentence, shall mean royalties or flat payments received by Label in connection with the Ancillary Exploitation less any costs or expenses that Label incurs (such as, without limitation, technical and/or production costs, mechanical royalties and other copyright payments, AF of M and other union or guild payments).

"Ancillary Exploitations," as defined in this agreement, include advertising revenue and hyperlink fees derived from the artist's Web site. Historically, record labels have always shared licensing fees and other nontraditional revenue streams with artists on a fifty-fifty net receipts basis. Here, however, the record company seeks to split revenues derived from Ancillary Exploitations in accordance with the artist's basic record royalty rate, which starts at 13%. Depending on how valuable the revenues generated by banner advertising and hyperlinks placed on popular artist's Web sites become, this type of paragraph can have a dramatic impact on an artist's bottom line. Record companies consider Ancillary Exploitations to be a significant source of potential revenue, but no universally accepted standard of revenue sharing has been developed. It is very important that such language be aggressively negotiated by the artist's representatives starting from the position that royalties payable to the label from ancillary exploitation ought to be split on a fifty-fifty net receipts basis just like all other licenses of artist's recordings. Aggressive head-to-head negotiations with major record companies on this subject matter have yielded some very interesting results. Suffice it to say that nothing regarding the subject matter of this paragraph has been carved in stone.

9.07. Label will pay you royalties as follows in connection with the following uses of Audiovisual Records (including for sales of Audiovisual Records which contain Covered Videos):

(a) (1) Label will pay you a royalty (the "Net Receipts Royalty") in the amount equal to fifty percent (50%) of Label's "Net Video Receipts" (defined below) derived from all uses of Audiovisual Records which produce revenues directly for Label other than the sales described in subparagraph 9.07(b) below.

(2) "Gross Receipts," in this subparagraph 9.07(a), means all monies actually received by Label (or credited to Label's account against advances previously received) in the United States which are specifically allocated to the exploitation of Audiovisual Records. "Net Video Receipts" means Gross Receipts, less all direct out-of pocket expenses, taxes, adjustments, and collection costs incurred by Label in connection with the exploitation of such Audiovisual Records, all payments required to be made to Persons other than you or any other "Royalty Participant" (as hereinafter defined), including, without limitation, to unions or guilds or to publishers of non-Controlled Compositions and "Independent Interests" (as hereinafter defined) in Controlled Compositions in connection with the production and/or exploitation of such Audiovisual Records and any Covered Videos embodied therein, and a distribution fee equal to twenty percent (20%) of those Gross Receipts. Any item of expenses that is actually recouped from Gross Receipts under this section will not be chargeable against royalties under paragraph 5.02. If any item of revenue or expenses is attributable to an Audiovisual Record or a Covered Video and to other audiovisual works, the amount of that item includible in Gross Receipts or deductible in computing Net Video Receipts will be determined by apportionment based on actual playing time of the Record concerned.

A fifty-fifty net receipts split for the exploitation of videos, other than the sale of videos, is ordinary and customary. Here, the record company seeks to have a distribution fee of 20% deducted from gross receipts before splitting the net. While many labels may dig in their heels and not waver on that point, it should at least be raised during negotiations. If the label simply licenses a video to a third-party company, then a distribution fee should not be factored in to the calculation of net receipts.

(3) You shall be solely responsible for and shall pay any and all monies payable to the Producers, to the producers and directors of the visual portion of the Audiovisual Records or Covered Videos, to the publishers of Controlled Compositions and to any other Persons (except publishers of non-Controlled Compositions or of Independent Interests in Controlled Compositions which are embodied in the Audiovisual Records or Covered Videos and any unions or guilds or their funds) who are entitled to a royalty or any other payment in respect of the exploitation of the Audiovisual Records (each such person being herein referred to as a "Royalty Participant"). Notwithstanding the foregoing, if Label shall pay or be required to pay any such monies directly to any Royalty Participant, then Label shall have the right to deduct same from any and all royalties payable to you hereunder.

(b) If Label or Label's Distributor or Licensee manufactures and distributes Audiovisual Records embodying one or more Covered Videos, then, Label will pay you royalties at the rates and in the manner set forth in this subparagraph 9.07(b), rather than the Net Receipts Royalty payable to you pursuant to subparagraph 9.07(a).

(1) On Net Sales of Audiovisual Records distributed in the United States: fifteen percent (15%) of the applicable Royalty Base Price for such

Audiovisual Records, and on Net Sales of Audiovisual Records distributed outside of the United States: ten percent (10%) of the applicable Royalty Base Price for such Audiovisual Records.

Careful! This clause provides for royalties for sales of audiovisual records at 15% of the "Royalty Base Price," which has a different definition with respect to audiovisual records. Do not be fooled into thinking that this is a retail-based royalty rate. In fact, under the terms of this paragraph and the applicable definition of royalty base price, the label will pay the artist a royalty of 15% of wholesale. That being said, this is a generally customary provision for new artists.

(2) The royalty rate payable to you on any Audiovisual Record containing a Covered Video and other audiovisual works will be determined by apportionment based on actual playing time on the Record concerned.

This clause can help you or hurt you, depending on the duration of your audiovisual record compared to those of other artists embodied on the record. If an artist feels that there is a great likelihood that the running time of his or her video will be much shorter than the running time of videos of other artists, the artist should try to have the royalty rate determined by dividing the number of his or her videos on the record by the total number of videos embodied on the record.

(3) The provisions of paragraphs 10.03 and 10.04 shall be applicable to sales of Audiovisual Records under this subparagraph 9.07(b); provided, however, that Label shall not distribute "Standard Free Goods" (as hereinafter defined), but Label shall have the right to distribute "Special Free Goods" (as hereinafter defined) with respect to Audiovisual Records hereunder.

(4) The royalties payable in accordance with this subparagraph 9.07(b) shall be inclusive of all royalties that may be payable to all Persons (other than unions or guilds and their funds), including, without limitation Royalty Participants and the publishers of both Controlled Compositions and non-Controlled Compositions or Independent Interests. If Label makes any payments to any Person with respect to any such Audiovisual Record, then Label shall have the right to deduct such payments from royalties otherwise payable to you with respect to Audiovisual Records.

This subparagraph requires the artist to pay publishing royalties to the publishers of compositions embodied in videos out of the video royalties payable by the label to the artist. The artist should insist that the label pay such royalties independently of the artist's own video royalties. With respect to audio-only records, the record company pays the publishers separately and should do the same with respect to audiovisual records.

10. MISCELLANEOUS ROYALTY PROVISIONS

Notwithstanding anything to the contrary contained in Article 9:

10.01. In respect of Joint Recordings, the royalty rate to be used in determining the royalties payable to you shall be computed by multiplying the royalty rate otherwise applicable thereto by a fraction, the numerator of which shall be one (1) and the denominator of which shall be the total number of royalty artists whose Performances are embodied on a Joint Recording.

If the artist performs a duet with another artist, the artist and the duet partner will each receive one-half of the royalties applicable to that song. However, in many cases, a guest artist will agree to receive a buyout and forego any eligibility for royalties. To the extent possible, the artist should try to have this language modified so that the royalty with respect to joint recordings will only be reduced to the extent that royalties become payable to the guest artist appearing on his or her record. This is particularly important in the hip-hop and the R&B genres where there can be several guest artists on any given album. As a practical matter, however, it is unlikely that most reputable record companies would reduce an artist's royalty pursuant to this paragraph unless it was also paying a prorated royalty to the guest artist in question.

10.02. The royalty rate on a Phonograph Record embodying Master Recordings made hereunder together with other Master Recordings will be computed by multiplying the royalty rate otherwise applicable by a fraction, the numerator of which is the number of Sides embodying Master Recordings made hereunder and the denominator of which is the total number of royalty-bearing Sides contained on such Record.

This is a typical proration clause, which would apply, for example, if the company released a compilation or sampler of its own artists' recordings on its own label.

10.03. Except as otherwise provided in paragraph 10.04, no royalties will be due or payable in respect of Phonograph Records:

(a) sold (for less than 50% of Label's posted wholesale price), distributed or furnished on a no-charge basis by Label or its Licensees for promotional purposes (including, without limitation, Records to disc jockeys, publishers, motion picture companies, television and radio stations, and other customary recipients of promotional Records) or to Label's or its Licensees' employees and relatives;
(b) sold, distributed or furnished on a no-charge basis to members, applicants or other participants in any "record club" or other direct mail distribution method (subject to subparagraph 9.02(b) above);
(c) sold at close-out prices or as surplus, overstock or scrap;
(d) sold as cutouts after the listing of such Records has been deleted from the catalog of Label or its Licensees;
(e) given away or shipped as "free," "no charge" or "bonus" Records (whether or not intended for resale); and
(f) sold at a discount from the Record's posted wholesale list price (but for more than 50% of such price), whether or not intended for resale.

In determining the number of Records as to which no royalties are payable pursuant to subparagraph (f) above, Label shall multiply the percentage amount of such discount by the number of Records sold at such discount. No royalties will be payable to you on Records containing Recordings of not more than two (2) Master Recordings made hereunder sold as "samplers" at a price which is fifty percent (50%) or less of the SRLP of Label's then current newly-released Top-line Records, on Records intended for free distribution as samplers to automobile or audio and/or audiovisual equipment purchasers (whether or not postage, handling, or similar charges are made), or distributed for use on transportation carriers.

This clause addresses a variety of distributions of nonroyalty bearing records. These fall into three principal categories: (1) Truly promotional records, which are given away to customary recipients, e.g., radio stations, record reviewers, etc.; (2) records sold at drastically reduced prices, i.e., cut-outs, which are records marked with a hole punched or cut in the packaging so that they cannot be returned to the record company for credit at full price; and (3) free goods, records that are given away as sales incentives or are sold at a discount to stimulate sales. If an artist has enough clout, record companies sometimes agree to split the net proceeds of records sold on a "scrap" or "close-out" basis.

10.04. Those Records distributed pursuant to subparagraphs 10.03(e) and (f) are herein referred to as "Free Goods." Label shall have the right to distribute Free Goods not in excess of its then current Distributor's standard policy ("Standard Free Goods"), which, for Albums currently is fifteen percent (15%) of the aggregate units of all Top-line Albums distributed under this Agreement. In addition, from time to time, Label or its Distributor, jointly or separately, shall have the right to conduct special sales programs of limited duration, which include the distribution of Free Goods in excess of the limitation set forth in the preceding sentence ("Special Free Goods"). If Label distributes Free Goods in excess of the foregoing limitations, Label will not be in breach hereof, but Label will pay you your normal royalty on such excess.

This clause defines the percentages of records sold that will be deemed to be nonroyalty bearing free goods. All of the major labels have this same 15% standard free goods allowance, although some labels accomplish that result differently, namely by calculating the royalty rate on 85% of records sold. This clause is generally not applicable outside the United States, although this contract does not specifically limit its applicability to the United States. Be careful, particularly with smaller labels, that the language in the agreement cannot be interpreted to apply both a 15% reduction for free goods and a 15% reduction on the definition of net sales. Some small labels will try to get away with this approach.

In addition to the so-called standard or policy free goods, there are also "special free goods," which are special sales incentive or discount programs that are offered from time to time for limited periods, generally on a seasonal basis, e.g., in the fall as an incentive to retailers to stock up on product in anticipation of the Christmas season.

Some labels will try to provide for special free goods to be made exempt from the 15% cap on free goods, or subject to a higher cap. This agreement, as drafted, has no cap on special free goods.

11. ROYALTY ACCOUNTINGS

11.01. Label will compute your royalties as of each June 30th and December 31st (or such other semiannual periods as Label may elect in its sole discretion) for the prior six (6) months, in respect of each such six-month period in which there are sales or returns of Records or any other transactions on which royalties are payable to you, or liquidations of reserves established previously. Within three (3) months following the end of each such semiannual period, Label will send you a statement covering those royalties and will pay you any royalties which are due after deducting unrecouped Advances and chargeable costs under this Agreement and such amount, if any, which Label may be required to withhold pursuant to the California Revenue and Taxation Code, the U.S. Tax Regulations or any other applicable statute, regulations, treaty or law. After the term, no royalty statements shall be required for periods during which no additional royalties accrue unless you give Label a written request therefor before the expiration of the semiannual accounting period to which the desired royalty statement relates. In computing the number of Records sold, only Records for which Label has been paid shall be deemed sold, and Label shall have the right to deduct returns and credits of any nature and to withhold reasonable reserves therefor from payments otherwise due you. For purposes herein, the "reasonableness" of such reserves shall be determined by Soundscan sales figures. Each royalty reserve against anticipated returns and credits will be liquidated not later than the end of the fourth semiannual accounting period following the accounting period during which it is established. If Label makes any overpayment to you, you will reimburse Label for it; Label also may deduct it from any payments due or becoming due to you. If Label pays you any royalties on Records that are returned later, those royalties will be considered overpayments. Label may at any time elect to utilize a different method of computing royalties so long as such method does not decrease the net monies received by or credited to you hereunder.

The frequency of accounting is typically not negotiable and while smaller companies will sometimes account on a quarterly basis, major labels typically account twice annually. The three main issues in this paragraph are (1) the timing of semiannual payments, (2) the withholding of reserves, and (3) the liquidating of such reserves. While the timing of payments is generally not negotiable, the artist should try to limit the waiting period for semiannual payments to six weeks from the end of the period as opposed to three months as provided for in the agreement.

This contract is typical in that all recordings made under this agreement are treated as part of a single, consolidated account. For example, if the artist's first album is quite successful, but the artist's second album is costly and unsuccessful, the recording costs and advances attributable to the second album will offset the royalties earned from sales of the first album, on a dollar-for-dollar basis, so that there may be no net payment due to the artist. This concept of consolidating the recoupable advances and charges and the earned royalties associated with one project with the recoupable advances and charges and the earned royalties associated with another project is known as cross-collateralization. Cross-collateralization limited to the recordings made under a single agreement is almost universally accepted. However, this agreement goes beyond that to cross-collateralize any other agreement to which the artist may be a party with the company, e.g., a prior or subsequent recording agreement. This is always a point to be negotiated. It becomes particularly contentious when the company requires cross-collateralization with mechanical royalty payments or with a publishing agreement with the company's affiliate. While it is very difficult to persuade a record company to not cross-collateralize accounts for separate albums under the agreement, the artist should negotiate aggressively to prevent the label from cross-collateralizing record royalty accounts with mechanical royalty accounts. An artist should not be penalized for composing or cocomposing his or her own recordings and a label that insists on the right to deduct unrecouped recording expenses from mechanical royalties is doing just that.

It is typical for a recording contract to allow a company to maintain reserves against anticipated returns of records. Often, there is no limit on the amount of reserves that a company can maintain, except that they will be "reasonable." Such a provision makes it very difficult for the artist to do anything if the company is maintaining levels of reserves that the artist believes to be unreasonable in view of the company's actual returns experience with respect to the artist's records. In this contract, a specific maximum limitation is established. Where such limitations are stated, they are generally in the range of 20% to 30%. In the United States, records are generally sold with a 100% privilege of return and without any limit on the time period during which the stores can return the records to the company. Accordingly, it is quite important for the company to be able to maintain a royalty reserve. Generally, the company will agree to liquidate the reserve within three or four semiannual periods, i.e., 18 months to 24 months, after it has been established. This means that the reserve will either be used up by applying returns against it, or it will be paid out in the form of royalties to the artist if it is not used up. However, in this contract the company further protects itself by providing that if it did not hold sufficient reserves, i.e., returns exceed reserves, the artist must reimburse the company.

11.02. Sales of Records for distribution outside the United States are called "foreign sales." Label will compute your royalties for any foreign sale in the same national currency in which Label's Licensee pays Label for that sale, and Label will credit those royalties to your account at the same rate of exchange at which the Licensee pays Label. For purposes of accounting to you, Label will treat any foreign sale as a sale made during the same six-month period in which Label receives its Licensee's accounting and payment for that sale. (For the purposes of this paragraph, any royalties credited by a Licensee to Label's account but charged in recoupment of a prior advance made to Label and retained by the Licensee by reason of that charge will be deemed paid to Label and received by it when it receives the Licensee's accounting reflecting the credit and charge concerned.) If any Label Licensee deducts any taxes from its payments to Label, Label may deduct a proportionate amount of those taxes from your royalties. If any law, any government ruling, or any other restriction affects the amount of the payments that a Label Licensee can remit to Label, Label may deduct from your royalties an amount proportionate to the reduction in the Licensee's remittances to Label. If Label cannot collect payment for a foreign sale in the United States in U.S. Dollars, it will not be required to account to you for that sale, except as provided in the next sentence. Label will, at your request and at your expense, deduct from the monies so blocked and deposit in a foreign depository the equivalent in local currency of the royalties which would be payable to you on the foreign sales concerned, to the extent such monies are available for that purpose, and only to the extent to which your royalty account is then in a fully recouped position. All such deposits will constitute royalty payments to you for accounting purposes.

This provision clarifies how revenues for foreign sales are applied to the accounting provisions in the agreement. This agreement provides that if the label does not receive payments for foreign sales in the United States in U.S. dollars that it is not required to pay the artist for that sale. This is fairly common language, and it is important that the language be further clarified to provide that if the label <u>does</u> receive payment but not in the United States and not in U.S. currency, that the label will nonetheless convert such payment into U.S. currency and deposit it into the artist's account. The language of this agreement takes a step in that direction but with some additional negotiating, the label would likely agree to such clarifying provisions.

11.03. Label will maintain books and records which report the sales or other exploitations of Phonograph Records and Master Recordings hereunder on which royalties are payable to you. You may, at your own expense, designate a certified public accountant (CPA) to examine those books and records, as provided in this paragraph only. Such examination: (a) may be made only for the purpose of verifying the accuracy of the statements sent to you under paragraph 11.01; (b) may be made for a particular statement only once and only within two (2) years after the date when Label sends you that statement; and (c) may be made only during Label's usual business hours, and at the place where it keeps the books and records to be examined, and upon reasonable notice to Label. (Label will be deemed conclusively to have sent you each statement on the date prescribed in paragraph 11.01 unless you notify Label otherwise, with respect to any statement, within sixty [60] days after that date.) No examination may be made of any manufacturing records or any other records that do not specifically report sales or other distributions of Phonograph Records or other transactions on which royalties are payable to you. Further, such examination shall be conditioned upon the CPA's written agreement to Label that the CPA will not voluntarily disclose any findings to any Person other than you, your attorney or other advisers.

Recording contracts typically place specified time limits upon the artist's right to audit the company's books and records. These time periods are generally shorter than those that are otherwise allowable under state law. The company justifies such limitations because of the tremendous amount of record keeping involved and the cost associated therewith. Generally, companies try to limit the audit and objection period to one year, whereas artists' representatives seek to make it as long as possible, but two years is a fairly typical compromise.

11.04. If you have any objections to a royalty statement, you will give Label specific notice of that objection and your reasons for it within two (2) years after the date that Label is deemed to have sent you that statement under paragraph 11.03. Each royalty statement will become conclusively binding on you at the end of that two-year period, and you will no longer have any right to make any other objections to it. You will not have the right to sue Label in connection with any royalty accounting, or to sue Label for royalties on Records sold or receipts derived by Label during the period a royalty accounting covers, unless you commence the suit within six (6) months after the end of that two-year period. If you commence suit on any controversy or claim concerning royalty accountings rendered to you under this Agreement, the scope of the proceeding will be limited to determination of the amount of the royalties due for the accounting periods concerned, and the court will have no authority to consider any other issues or award any relief except recovery of any royalties found owing. Your recovery of any such royalties will be the sole remedy available to you by reason of any claim related to Label's royalty accountings. Without limiting the generality of the preceding sentence, you will not have any right to seek termination of this Agreement or avoid the performance of your obligations under it by reason of any such claim. The preceding three sentences will not apply to any item in a royalty accounting if you establish that the item was fraudulently misstated.

Again, this is a typical restriction on the artist's right to sue in connection with objections to any particular royalty statement. The language, as written, limits the artist's recovery under such lawsuit to the collection of royalties unless the artist can demonstrate that the company's failure to pay was due to fraud, which is typical.

12. LICENSES FOR MUSICAL COMPOSITIONS

This section of the contract addresses in a typical way the royalties payable to the owners (music publishers) of the musical compositions recorded by the artist, known as mechanical royalties. Even if the artist does not write his or her own material, this section is nonetheless important, because its main purpose is to limit the amount of mechanical royalties the company will be required to pay to the writers that contribute to any record it releases and to hold the artist responsible for exceeding the specified limits.

These clauses typically distinguish between controlled compositions and noncontrolled compositions, although the definitions may differ somewhat from contract to contract. Generally, a company will seek to obtain a lower mechanical royalty rate and more favorable payment terms on controlled compositions than on noncontrolled compositions. The definition of a controlled composition is important. Generally, the entire composition is treated as a controlled composition even if the artist is a writer or cowriter of the composition and even if the artist has already transferred his or her publishing rights to an unrelated music publisher. Moreover, the definition, as herein, often applies to compositions written or cowritten by the producer, which has the effect of requiring the artist to obtain the same rates and terms from the producer in the artist's agreement with the producer. These points are often hotly negotiated.

12.01. (a) (1) You grant to Label and its Licensees and their designees an irrevocable license, under copyright, to reproduce each Controlled Composition on Phonograph Records of Master Recordings made under this Agreement, other than Audiovisual Records, and to distribute them in the United States and Canada.

(2) For that license, Label will pay Mechanical Royalties, on the basis of Net Sales, at the following rates:

(i) On Records sold for distribution in the United States:

(A)(aa) If the copyright law of the United States provides for a minimum compulsory rate: The rate equal to seventy-five percent (75%) of the minimum compulsory license rate applicable to the use of Compositions on phonorecords under the United States copyright law on the date of initial release of the Master Recording concerned. (The minimum statutory rate is currently seven and fifty-five hundreds cents ($.0755) per Composition.)

(bb) If the copyright law of the United States does not provide for a minimum compulsory rate: The rate equal to seventy-five percent (75%) of the minimum license rate agreed to by the major record companies and major music publishers in the United States on the date of initial release of the Master Recording concerned.

(cc) In the event that any Commitment Record shall sell in the United States USNRC Net Sales in excess of five hundred thousand (500,000) units then a rate equal to eighty-seven and one-half percent (87.5%) instead of the seventy-five percent

(75%) rate detailed above in subclauses (aa) and (bb) in respect of such sales for such Album shall apply prospectively only in respect of such sales in excess of five hundred thousand (500,000) such units.

(dd) In the event that any Commitment Record shall sell in the United States USNRC Net Sales in excess of one million (1,000,000) units then a rate equal to one hundred percent (100%) instead of the seventy-five percent (75%) and eighty-seven and one-half (87.5%) percent rates detailed above in subclauses (aa), (bb) and (cc) in respect of such sales for such Album shall apply prospectively only in respect of such sales in excess of one million (1,000,000) units.

A 75% rate is customarily required in agreements with new artists. This is based upon the minimum statutory rate, so that the company would pay the same rate for a 10-minute song as for a two-minute song. More importantly, it fixes the rate at the time the master is released by the company. The minimum statutory rate for records made and distributed as of January 1, 2000 is 7.55¢. When the current copyright act became effective on January 1, 1978 the minimum statutory rate was 2.75¢. As you can see, it has risen quite dramatically and it is anticipated that it will continue to rise in the future. However, under this provision the mechanical royalty rate on a master delivered will never increase regardless of increases in the statutory rate. One of the critical issues in determining the applicable rate is the date that controls the determination of that rate. Often, record companies will try to apply the date that a master is delivered or even the date on which the recording of a master is commenced. For the record company's purposes, the earlier the date the better. Here, as the result of a prenegotiated agreement, the record company has agreed to establish the date a master is initially released as the controlling date, which is definitely to the artist's benefit, since if such release occurs after another statutory rate increase, the artist will benefit from the increase. Also, this agreement provides for escalations in mechanical royalties so that the artist will receive 87.5% of the statutory rate for all USNRC net sales in excess of 500,000 copies and will receive 100% of the statutory rate for all such sales in excess of 1 million copies. This is unusual for an unsigned artist and is reflective of this particular artist's clout and the degree to which the terms of the agreement were prenegotiated before the record company drafted the long form.

(ii) On Records sold for distribution in Canada: The rate prescribed in subsection (i) above or the rate equal to seventy-five percent (75%) of the lowest Mechanical Royalty rate prevailing in Canada on a general basis with respect the use of Compositions on Standard Records, whichever is lower, but not less than four cents ($.04) (Canadian) in either event.

Canada has its own copyright laws, which operate independently of U.S. Copyright Law. However, the Canadian Musical Reproduction Rights Agency Limited (CMRRA), the Canadian record industry's mechanical rights organization, generally follows the U.S. trend, so that in a typical recording contract mechanical royalty rates for Canadian sales are generally the same number of Canadian pennies as U.S. pennies.

(3) The Mechanical Royalty on any Record sold through a so-called record club will be one hundred percent (100%) of the amount fixed in subsection (i) or (ii) above. The Mechanical Royalty on any Record described in subparagraph 9.03(a) will be three-fourths (3/4) of the amount fixed in subsection (i) or (ii) above without regard to escalations based on sales. If the Composition is an arranged version of a public domain work, the Mechanical Royalty on it will be one-half (1/2) of the amount fixed in subsection (i) or (ii) above, unless a different rate applies under section 12.01(a)(4) below. No Mechanical Royalties will be payable for any Records described in paragraph 10.03. Notwithstanding the preceding sentence, Label shall pay Mechanical Royalties pursuant to this subparagraph 12.01(a) with respect to Controlled Compositions embodied on Albums hereunder on fifty percent (50%) of those units of such Albums distributed in the United States as Standard Free Goods, but Label shall not be obligated to pay Mechanical Royalties on any such Albums distributed as Special Free Goods.

This clause describes on what basis mechanical royalties are reduced on records for which record royalties are reduced. Note that the label has agreed to pay mechanical royalties on 50% of free goods, which is a fairly typical give from major labels, even in debut artist deals.

(4) If ASCAP or BMI accords regular performance credit for any Controlled Composition which is an arranged version of a public domain work, the Mechanical Royalty rate on that Composition will be apportioned according to the same ratio used by ASCAP or BMI in determining the performance credit. Label will not be required to pay you at that rate unless you furnish it with satisfactory evidence of that ratio.

This paragraph pertains to royalties payable to the author of a new arrangement of a composition in the public domain.

(b) (1) The total Mechanical Royalty for all Compositions on any Album, including Controlled Compositions, will be limited to ten (10) (eleven (11) for digital format Albums) times the amount which would be payable on it under section 12.01(a)(2) if it contained only one (1) Controlled Composition. The total Mechanical Royalty will be limited to two (2) times that amount on any Single, four (4) times that amount on any Extended Play Record, and three (3) times that amount on any Twelve-Inch Single or any other Record which is not an Album, a Single, or an Extended Play Record.

This paragraph determines the maximum budget available to pay mechanical royalties to the writers and owners of the compositions on any album. By way of example, this agreement provides for an album cap of 10 songs, which are payable at 75% of the statutory rate (currently 7.55¢). This multiplies out to a budget of 56.625¢ per album. If the artist writes all of his or her own material, then the artist will simply receive 56.625¢ per album for his or her compositions. However, if the artist uses compositions that were written or cowritten by other songwriters, this budget or album cap, as it is more commonly referred to, is very important. Some writers will not agree to accept 75% of the statutory rate and will instead require the full rate. Additionally, many record companies insist that artists include 12, 15, or in some cases even more than 15 songs on their albums in order to be competitive with other artists in the marketplace. Say, for example, an artist uses outside writers for six songs on his or her album and each writer requires the full rate. In that circumstance, those writers will gobble up 45.3¢ of the budget, leaving just over 11¢ for the artist. In the R&B and hip-hop genres where sampling of compositions continues to be prevalent, the album cap can be of even greater importance. Top-flight producers in R&B and hip-hop can require 50% of the compositions they produce as part of their deal and many require payment on the full mechanical rate without reduction for the album cap. There are many cases in which a hip-hop artist, after deducting mechanical royalties payable to his producers and to the writers and owners of the sampled compositions, is left with little or nothing in the way of mechanical royalties. In some extreme cases, payments to outside writers can exceed the album cap. When this happens, the "excess mechanicals" are actually deducted from the artist's record royalties. A cap of 10 songs is the typical first offer from most record companies. Some artists can get the cap increased to 11 songs and in some cases 12 songs, if they have leverage. Caps of more than 12 songs are rare. Deals can also be structured whereby the cap climbs during the life of the contract from 10 songs to 11 and eventually to 12, while the statutory rate climbs from 75% to 87.5% and ultimately to 100%.

(2) The maximum Mechanical Royalty under this subparagraph (b) on a Multiple Record Set will be the same amount prescribed in section 12.01(b)(l), multiplied by a fraction, the numerator of which is the SRLP of such Multiple Record Set in the applicable configuration in the United States and the denominator of which is Label's then-prevailing SRLP for Label's newly-released Top-line Albums in such configuration in the United States.

(c) Label will compute Mechanical Royalties on Controlled Compositions as of each February 28th (or 29th, if applicable), May 31st, August 31st and November 30th (or such other quarter-annual periods as Label may elect in its sole discretion) for the prior three (3) months, in respect of each quarter-annual period in which there are sales or returns of Records on which Mechanical Royalties are payable to you, or liquidations of Mechanical Royalty reserves established previously. On the 15th day of the second month following the end of each such quarter-annual period, Label will send a statement covering those Mechanical Royalties, less a reasonable reserve against anticipated returns and credits, and will pay any net Mechanical Royalties which are due. Mechanical Royalty reserves maintained by Label against anticipated returns and credits will not be held for an unreasonable period of time; retention of a reserve for two (2) years after it is established will not be considered unreasonable in any case. If Label makes any overpayment of Mechanical Royalties to you or any Person, you will reimburse Label for it; Label may also recoup it from any payments due or becoming due to you hereunder. If Label pays any Mechanical Royalties on Records that are returned later, those Mechanical Royalties will be considered overpayments. If the total amount of the Mechanical Royalties which Label pays on any Record consisting of Master Recordings made under this Agreement (including Mechanical Royalties for Compositions which are not Controlled Compositions) is higher than the limit fixed for that Record under subparagraph 12.01(b), that excess amount will be considered an overpayment also. Paragraphs 11.03 and 11.04 will apply to Mechanical Royalty accountings.

This paragraph deals with the accounting schedule for the payment of mechanical royalties, which are typically paid on a quarterly basis as opposed to a semiannual basis for record royalties. As with record royalties, record companies typically retain reserves against returns when paying mechanical royalties, which they generally liquidate within two years. This language also provides for the record company to recoup any mechanical royalties paid in excess of the album cap from record royalties as discussed above.

12.02. You also grant to Label and its Licensees and their designees an irrevocable license under copyright to reproduce each Controlled Composition in Covered Videos and Audiovisual Records, to reproduce those Covered Videos and Audiovisual Records, distribute them, and perform them in any manner (including, without limitation, publicly and for profit), to manufacture and distribute Audiovisual Records and other copies of them, and to exploit them otherwise, by any method and in any form known now or in the future, throughout the world, and to authorize others to do so. Label will not be required to make any payment in connection with those uses, and that license will apply whether or not Label receives any payment in connection with any use of any Covered Video or Audiovisual Record. If any exhibition of a Covered Video or Audiovisual Record is also authorized under another license (such as a public performance license granted by ASCAP or BMI), that exhibition will be deemed authorized by that license instead of this Agreement. (In all events, Label and its Licensees will have no liability by reason of any such exhibition.)

This provision calls for a free synchronization license, which is a license to fix or synchronize the musical composition with visual images, in each video. Publishers ordinarily do not object to this, since it is generally considered a promotional use for which the publisher will reap the rewards by increased airplay of the composition, which generates public performance royalties to the publisher. However, this provision also provides that in the event the record company does receive a fee for the exploitation of the video that it is not required to pay any license fee to the artist for his or her contribution to the composition embodied in the video. Publishers should object to this clause because it does not provide royalties to songwriters even where the use of the video is commercial in nature. If anything, this clause points out the inequity in the record company's position that it should not pay any royalty to the artist for the commercial use of his compositions in videos, and this point ought to be negotiated.

12.03. (a) If any Recordings made under this Agreement contain copyrighted Compositions that are not Controlled Compositions, you will use reasonable efforts to obtain licenses covering those Compositions for Label's benefit on the same terms as those that apply to Controlled Compositions under this Article 12. In all events, you will obtain licenses covering them for the United States providing for royalties at the minimum rate applicable to the use of Compositions on phonorecords under the compulsory license provisions of the United States copyright law, and licenses for them for Canada providing for royalties at the lowest rates prevailing in Canada on a general basis with respect to the use of Compositions on Standard Records, and otherwise on terms not less favorable to

Label in any respect than those prescribed in the attached Exhibit A; and subparagraph 12.01(b) will continue to apply.

(b) You will cause the issuance of effective licenses, under copyright and otherwise, to reproduce each Controlled Composition on Phonograph Records and distribute those Records outside the United States and Canada, on terms not less favorable to Label or its Licensees than the terms prevailing on a general basis in the country concerned with respect to the use of Compositions on comparable Records.

These paragraphs require the artist to try to get outside writers and publishers to agree to grant a free license for the promotional and commercial exploitation of videos that embody their compositions and compels the artist, in any event, to obtain licenses from outside writers and publishers at the minimum rate set by statute.

12.04. You warrant and represent that the "Schedule of Publishers" appended to this Agreement is a complete list of the music publishers in which you have a direct or indirect interest. You will notify Label promptly of each additional music publisher in which you acquire any such interest and of every other change required to keep the list currently accurate.

12.05. Neither you, nor any Person deriving rights from you, will authorize the use of any Controlled Composition in a radio or television commercial or any other advertising or promotional matter, unless you first require the Person authorized to make the use concerned to agree in writing, for Label's benefit, that the use will not involve a "sound-alike" Recording resembling a Performance of that Composition by you. (A sound-alike Recording is a different Recording that imitates or simulates the Recording concerned by using a substantially similar musical arrangement or otherwise.)

Record companies typically reserve the right to license an artist's sound recordings for use in advertising and such licenses can be very lucrative for the company. Therefore, it is very important to the record company, and ostensibly to the artist, that no third-party artists rerecord the artist's popular songs and then license those recordings for use in commercials. What this clause does is prevent the artist, who composes his or her own material, from granting a license to anyone else to use those compositions in connection with sound-alike recordings.

12.06. Subject to the provisions of section 12.01(a)(3) above, if the copyright in any Controlled Compositions is owned or controlled by a Person other than you, you shall cause that Person to grant Label and its Licensees and their designees the same rights as you are required to grant to Label and its Licensees pursuant to this Article 12. Any assignment, license or other agreement made with respect to any Controlled Composition shall be subject to the terms hereof.

12.07. You also grant to Label and its Licensees and their designees an irrevocable license under copyright to print and reproduce, at their election, the title and lyrics to any Controlled Composition on Album Artwork and in connection with Covered Videos or Audiovisual Records, and the packaging therefor, throughout the world in perpetuity, without payment to you or any other Person of any monies or other consideration in connection therewith.

This clause grants to the record company the right to reproduce, in writing, the title and lyrics to compositions that the artist has written or cowritten.

13. WARRANTIES; REPRESENTATIONS; RESTRICTIONS; INDEMNITIES

In every recording contract, the artist is required to make warranties and representations. These are statements of fact upon which the record company is entitled to rely. If they should turn out to be untrue, or if a third party should claim that they are not true, the indemnification provisions of the agreement will be triggered. The warranties and representations that the artist is free to enter into the contract and is not a party to any conflicting contract are fundamental. Many agreements will contain a representation and warranty that the artist or, if the artist is a group, that each member thereof, is a United States citizen and has reached the age of majority, which in most states is 18 years old. If the artist or any member of the group is a minor when he or she enters into the agreement, the company will need to take steps to make sure that the artist cannot void the contract by reason of his or her age. For example, in California, any artist who signs an agreement when he or she is under 18 years old has the absolute right to disaffirm that contract even after performances under the contract have begun, unless the contract is approved by the court. This could prove disastrous to the company, and cause them to lose the benefit of their investment in an artist if such a contract is broken.

13.01. You warrant and represent:

(a) You have the right and power to enter into and fully perform this Agreement.

(b) Label shall not be required to make any payments of any nature for, or in connection with, the acquisition, exercise or exploitation of rights by Label pursuant to this Agreement except as specifically provided in this Agreement.

(c) You are or will become and will remain, to the extent necessary to enable the performance of this Agreement, a member in good standing of all labor unions or guilds, membership in which may be lawfully required for the performance of the your services hereunder.

This type of clause is required whenever the company is a signatory to the AFM and AFTRA agreements. All of the majors are signatories, whereas most independent record companies are not.

(d) No "Materials," as hereinafter defined, or any use thereof, will violate any law or infringe upon or violate the rights of any Person. Materials, as used in this Article, means: (1) the Master Recordings made or furnished under this Agreement, (2) all Controlled Compositions, (3) each name used by you, individually or as a group, in connection with Recordings made hereunder, and (4) all other musical, dramatic, artistic and literary materials, ideas, and other intellectual properties, furnished or selected by you or any Producer and contained in or used in connection with any Recordings made hereunder or their packaging, sale, distribution, advertising, publicizing or other exploitation, including, without limitation, all label copy and liner note information, any Artist Web Site, Web Site Material and ECD Material, provided by you.

These warranties and representations are also fundamental and are contained in all recording contracts. The basic thrust is that the artist is solely responsible for the content of the records and any other material or elements furnished by the artist that are used in the packaging or advertising thereof, e.g., album cover artwork. However, it is somewhat broadly drafted in favor of the company in that it makes the artist responsible for musical compositions even if they are not written or controlled by the artist and because it is silent as to the company's obligations with respect to materials, ideas and elements furnished or selected by the company.

(e) No Person other than Label has any right to use any existing Master Recordings of your Performances for making, promoting, or marketing Phonograph Records

This is a typical clause but in the event that the artist has recorded master recordings prior to entering into the recording agreement, the status of such recordings ought to be clarified in the agreement to avoid any misunderstandings or conflicts with the record company. For example, if an artist has licensed or sold prior recordings to a third-party company, the artist may wish to have that disclosed in the agreement so that later, in the event those old recordings are ever exploited, the record company does not question whether it has any ownership right in the prior recordings.

(f) Each and every vocalist, musician, Producer and other individual whose services you furnish in connection with the preparation of a Master Recording or Covered Video under this Agreement either will have done so as an employee within the scope of his or her employment or will have expressly agreed in a written instrument signed by him or her and by the party commissioning the services that the Recording or Covered Video, as applicable, will be considered a *work made for hire.* A copy of any and all such instruments will be furnished to Label upon the request of Label.

By declaring the work of third-party vocalists, musicians, producers and so forth to be works made for hire, the record company is protecting itself from any future claim by such third parties that the copyright in their performances should revert to them under U.S. copyright law. Under such law, certain types of works revert to the authors after a certain number of years unless they are deemed works made for hire. This is standard language and typically not negotiable.

13.02. (a) You warrant and represent that during the term of this Agreement: (1) You will not enter into any agreement which would interfere with the full and prompt performance of your material obligations hereunder; and (2) Subject to paragraphs 13.02.1 and 13.02.2 below, during the term hereof, you will not perform or render any services as a recording, performing and video artist, or a producer for the purpose of making, promoting, or marketing Master Recordings or Phonograph Records for any Person except Label.

This paragraph limits the artist's ability to record for other companies. As drafted, this is very broad because it prevents the artist from even acting as a producer outside the bounds of the recording agreement, which is an unreasonable restriction. Typically, record companies will agree to allow recording artists to act as producers so long as such activity does not interfere with their obligations under the recording agreement. Guest appearances are very common in some genres of music, and if there is a likelihood that the artist's services as a guest artist will be in some demand, this language should be tempered so that the rights to perform on outside projects will be subject to the reasonable consent of the record company.

Please note that the definition of phonograph records is very broad (see Paragraph 14.23) and includes such things as video games and software. If the artist expects to be involved in performing such services for such other industries, an exception should be negotiated in the recording agreement, if the record company will compromise on that front. As a practical matter, however, most record companies will generally permit recording artists to perform such nontraditional services subject to their review of the agreements and their right to consent thereto. If a record company feels that such work might diminish the artist's value or might interfere with the artist's services under the recording agreement, however, the record company could refuse to grant such consent.

(b) (1) A "restricted Composition," for the purposes of this subparagraph, is a Composition which shall have been recorded by you for a Master Recording made or delivered to Label under this Agreement or any other agreement with Label.

(2) You will not authorize or knowingly permit your Performance, and you shall not render any Performance, of any restricted Composition or any adaptation of a restricted Composition to be recorded for any Person except Label for the purpose of making Master Recordings or Phonograph Records, or for any other purpose (including, without limitation, radio or television commercials), at any time before the later of the following dates: (i) the date five (5) years after the date of Delivery to Label of all the Master Recordings made in the course of the same Album (or other) recording project as the Recording of the restricted Composition concerned, or (ii) the date two (2) years after the expiration or termination of the term of this Agreement or any subsequent agreement between Label and you (or any Person furnishing your recording services or the results and proceeds thereof) with respect to your recording services.

This is a typical rerecording restriction that prohibits the artist from recording or authorizing anyone else to record a composition recorded under this agreement until the later of five years after the album in question is delivered to Label or two years after the termination of the agreement. It is, of course, to the artist's benefit to reduce such periods of restriction. Some labels will reduce the five-year period to as few as two years. As a practical matter, a recording artist who composes a song cannot prevent another artist from recording a true cover version of that song (provided that the song is not significantly altered and the artist pays the full statutory mechanical royalty rate), so this clause is primarily designed to prevent artists from recording new versions of songs from their own catalog after severing ties with a record company.

13.02.1. Any member of you may perform as a background instrumentalist or vocalist ("sideman") accompanying a featured artist for the purpose of making Phonograph Records for others, provided:

(a) (1) Only one member may perform in any such engagement; and
(2) The member may not do so unless you have fulfilled all of your then-current material obligations under this Agreement, and the engagement does not interfere with the continuing prompt performance of your obligations to Label, including any professional engagement to which you are committed which is intended to aid in the promotion of Phonograph Records hereunder.

(b) (1) The member's Performance shall be only in a background capacity. The member may not render a solo, duet or "step-out" performance, and
(2) The musical style of the Recording may not be substantially similar to the characteristic musical style of Recordings made by you for Label (i.e., likely to cause confusion as to the identity of the featured performer);

(c) The member may not record any material that you have then recorded for Label;

(d) The member may not accept the sideman engagement unless the Person for whom the Recordings are being made agrees in writing, for Label's benefit, that:
(1) The name of the member performing (but not your group name) may be used in a courtesy credit to Label Records on the Album liners used for such Records, in the same position as the credits accorded to other sidemen and in type identical in size, prominence, and all other respects;
(2) Except as expressly provided in section 13.02.1(d)(1) above, neither your name (or any similar name), nor the name of the member, nor any picture, portrait or likeness of you or member of you may be used in connection with such Recordings, including, without limitation, on the front covers of Album containers, on sleeves or labels used for Singles, or in videos, advertising, publicity or any other form of promotion or exploitation, without Label's express written consent, which Label may withhold in its unrestricted discretion; and
(3) The member may not perform or appear visually in Audiovisual Records, promotional videos or any other reproductions of any kind. You will furnish Label with a copy of each such agreement promptly after its execution.

(e) Before the member accepts the sideman engagement you will notify Label of the name of the Person for whom the Recordings are being made and the record company that will have the right to distribute the Records.

These paragraphs set forth the restrictions that prohibit the artist from performing as a guest or a sideman on other artists' records. This is a very broad and strict limitation that only allows the artist to perform as a background vocalist for music of a style different than that which the artist normally records, and does not permit the artist to grant the right to use his or her name or likeness or appear in any videos in connection with his or her performance. As a practical matter, what this restriction does is cause the artist to negotiate with and obtain the record company's written consent before rendering services as a guest artist. Record companies are often very careful to protect their artists from overexposure, so their approvals should not be taken for granted.

In some cases, the record label will agree to allow the artist to make one or two side appearances per album cycle, at the artist's discretion. This is particularly true when the artist is already well known and has a history of appearing on other people's records.

13.02.2. Any member of you may serve as a record producer for the purpose of making Phonograph Records for others, provided:

(a) You have then fulfilled all of your then-current material obligations under this Agreement, and the engagement does not interfere with the continuing prompt performance of your obligations to Label;

(b) (1) The member will not produce Recordings of any material that you have then recorded for Label;

(2) The musical style of the Recording may not be substantially similar to the characteristic musical style of Recordings made by you for Label (i.e., likely to cause confusion as to the identity of the featured performer);

(c) The member will not accept the producing engagement unless the Person for whom the Recordings are being produced agrees in writing, for Label's benefit, that:

(1) The name of the member producing (but not your group name) may be used in credits on Record labels and the reverse sides of Record packages, comparable in size and prominence to the credits generally accorded to record producers, and in advertising and publicity in a manner accurately descriptive of your (the member's) producing function; and

(2) Except as expressly provided in section 13.02.2(c)(1) above, neither your name (or any similar name), nor the name of the member, nor any picture, portrait or likeness of you or the member, will be used in connection with such Recordings, including, without limitation, on the front of any Record package or in advertising, publicity or any other form of promotion or exploitation, without Label's express written consent, which Label may withhold in its unrestricted discretion.

This is analogous to the language that pertains to limiting the artist's right to perform as a guest on other artists' records. This section limits the artist's right to perform as a producer. The main problem with the language, as drafted, is the prohibition against producing recordings of a musical style similar to the style of recordings made for the label. As a practical matter, this does not make much sense. If a recording artist is known for a particular style and is also a talented producer, it is to be expected that he or she will be hired to produce songs in the same style. Accordingly, an artist who wants to reserve his or her rights to work as a producer in the music industry should negotiate to have that particular portion of this section deleted.

13.03. You warrant and represent that if you become aware of any unauthorized recording, manufacture, distribution, sale, or other activity by any third party contrary to the restrictions in this Agreement, you will notify Label of it and will cooperate with Label in any action or proceeding Label commences against such third party.

13.04. You shall not authorize or knowingly permit the distribution of Audiovisual Records embodying any musical Performance by you that is rendered during the term hereof without the prior written consent of Label.

13.05. Intentionally deleted.

13.06. Your services are unique and extraordinary, and the loss thereof cannot be adequately compensated in damages, and Label shall be entitled to seek injunctive relief to enforce the provisions of this Agreement. (The preceding sentence will not be construed to preclude you from opposing any application for such relief based upon contest of the other facts alleged by Label in support of the application.)

This is a standard clause, which states that the artist's services are unique. The purpose of this clause is to establish the company's entitlement to obtain an injunction against the artist should the artist attempt to breach the agreement by recording for another record company. However, this alone is not enough to entitle the company to obtain an injunction. The company will still be required to prove its entitlement according to the standards that have been developed in the case law. Additionally, for contracts governed by California law, which may include not only those that specifically state that California law is applicable but may also include those that the artist signed before becoming a resident of California, there are specific guarantees that must be made by the company in order to entitle it to injunctive relief.

13.07. (a) You will at all times indemnify and hold harmless Label and any of its Licensees (collectively the "Indemnitee") from and against any and all claims, damages, liabilities, costs and expenses, including legal expenses and reasonable counsel fees, arising out of any breach or alleged breach of any warranty or representation made by you in this Agreement or any other act or omission by you, provided the claim concerned has been settled (subject to the provisions of subparagraph 13.07(b) below) or has resulted in a judgment against any Indemnitee. Label will notify you of any action commenced on such a claim. You may participate in the defense of any such claim through counsel of your selection at your own expense, but Label will have the right at all times, in its sole discretion, to retain or resume control of the conduct of the defense. If any claim involving such subject matter has not been resolved, or has been resolved by a judgment or other disposition that is not adverse to any Indemnitee, you will reimburse Label for fifty percent (50%) of the expenses actually incurred by Indemnitee in connection with that claim. Pending the resolution of any such claim, Label will have the right to withhold monies which would otherwise be payable to you under this Agreement in an amount not exceeding your potential liability to Label under this paragraph; provided, however, Label will not withhold monies which otherwise would be payable to you under this Agreement if you make satisfactory bonding arrangements in accordance with subparagraph 13.07(b) below.

(b) If Label pays more than $10,000 in settlement of any such claim, you will not be obligated to reimburse Label for the excess unless you have consented to the settlement, except as provided in the next sentence. If you do not consent to any settlement proposed by Label for an amount exceeding $10,000 you will nevertheless be required to reimburse Label for the full amount paid unless you make bonding arrangements, satisfactory to Label in its reasonable discretion, to assure Label of reimbursement for all damages, liabilities, costs and expenses (including legal expenses and reasonable counsel fees) that Indemnitee may incur as a result of that claim. If no action or other proceeding for recovery on such a claim has been commenced within one (1) year after its assertion, Label will not continue to withhold monies in connection with it under this paragraph.

This is a fairly typical indemnification clause, which has been stepped up a bit from normal first-draft language, but still has some room for improvement. What an indemnification clause does is provides that if a third party files a claim that the company considers to be inconsistent with the artist's representations and warranties (e.g., a claim that a song on the artist's album infringes the copyright of a third party's composition), then the company shall have the right to pass the buck to the artist, who would then be ultimately responsible for resolving the claim. What the artist wants to do in the indemnification clause is to retain as much control over such claims as possible. Here, the record company has allowed the artist to participate in the defense of any claim through his or her own attorney, but has retained the right to retain control over the conduct of the defense. The artist will want to have the right to handle the defense. The record company will typically insist on the right to withhold payments of monies payable to the artist in an amount reasonably related to the claim unless the artist posts a bond to cover the potential judgment, which would be difficult for most artists to do. Such language is difficult to negotiate, but the artist should at least request that mechanical royalties be exempt from such withholding. The agreement as drafted further limits the indemnity to claims of $10,000 or less but does require the artist to post a bond for all amounts over $10,000, which may become subject to the claim. What the artist will want to do here is reduce the settlement threshold so that the label cannot settle a claim for more than $5,000 without the artist's consent, unless the label is willing to soak up the amount in excess of $5,000. Major labels will typically insist on making any maximum settlement amount contingent upon the artist posting a satisfactory bond. A label does not want to find itself in a position where an artist refuses to accept a reasonable settlement offer and thereby exposes the label to a large claim without the financial resources to compensate the label in the event the third party prevails on the claim. On the other hand, artists are understandably reluctant to give record companies the right to settle claims that the artist may consider to be without merit and to charge the artist for the settlement and attorneys' fees.

14. DEFINITIONS

Many definitions are straightforward, self-explanatory and not negotiable, but certain definitions can be negotiated and these can have a profound effect on the artist's bottom line.

14.01. (a) "Advance"—a prepayment of royalties. Label may recoup Advances from royalties to be paid to or on your behalf pursuant to this Agreement or any other agreement, except as provided in the last sentence of this subparagraph (a) "Any other agreement," in this paragraph, means any other agreement relating to you as a recording artist or as a Producer of Recordings of your own Performances. Advances paid under Article 6 will not be returnable to Label except as provided in Article 15 or elsewhere in this Agreement or in other circumstances in which Label is entitled to their return by reason of your failure to fulfill your obligations. Mechanical Royalties will not be chargeable in recoupment of any Advances except those that are expressly recoupable from all monies payable under this Agreement.

This is a typical definition of advances, which are those funds that are deemed to be prepayment of royalties and that must be recouped by the artist at his royalty rate prior to the artist receiving any additional royalties.

(b) (1) Fifty percent (50%) of the production and acquisition costs incurred in connection with any Covered Video will be recoupable from your royalties on sales of Records which do not reproduce visual images ("audio royalties") under subparagraph 5.02(a), and one hundred percent (100%) of such costs will be recoupable from monies otherwise payable to you from the exploitation of such Covered Videos pursuant to paragraph 9.07 above; provided, however, that any such costs incurred in respect of any Covered Video hereunder in excess of One Hundred Thousand Dollars ($100,000) shall be one hundred percent (100%) recoupable from audio royalties. If any such costs are recouped from audio royalties and additional royalties accrue under paragraph 9.07 subsequently, the latter royalties will be applied in recoupment of those costs and the amount of those audio royalties that were previously applied against those costs will be credited back to your account.

This paragraph clarifies that 50% of video production and acquisition costs incurred in connection with any one video are recoupable, except for costs in excess of $100,000, which are 100% recoupable. The artist should insist that the agreement, either here or elsewhere, provides that the record company cannot exceed the $100,000 threshold without the artist's consent unless such costs are due to the artist's own acts or omissions.

(2) All costs incurred in connection with creating the so-called enhanced or multimedia portion (including without limitation, videos, photography, graphics, technology, etc.) of an enhanced CD, CD-ROM, DVD or any other similar configuration (whether now known or hereafter created) embodying Masters hereunder (the "Enhanced Costs") including, without limitation, ECD Material will be recoupable from record royalties otherwise payable to you hereunder.

This paragraph means that the costs for developing multimedia records are recoupable advances.

(3) All costs incurred by Label in excess of Label's standard costs (currently in the amount often thousand dollars ($10,000) in connection with securing, registering and/or protecting Artist Domain Names, and creating, hosting and maintaining Artist Web Sites, including, without limitation, costs incurred in creating and/or acquiring the Web Site Material, will constitute Advances recoupable from royalties (excluding mechanical royalties) payable to you hereunder.

This paragraph is interesting in that it establishes that all expenses over $10,000 incurred in connection with artists' Web sites are recoupable advances. If such costs are to be recoupable, the artist ought to retain some level of control over how much money the label spends on the Web site and should require the artist's consent for costs over the nonrecoupable budget.

(4) Label shall be entitled to recoup from record royalties payable hereunder fifty percent (50%) of the third party costs of Label and or its Licensees in producing advertisements and buying airtime for television and radio

advertising for Phonograph Records and Covered Videos incorporating Master Recordings and Covered Videos Delivered hereunder.

This is a typical clause that provides for half of the costs incurred in connection with producing ads and buying advertising time shall be recoupable. Many agreements further provide that 50% of all so-called independent promotion costs are also recoupable.

14.02. "Album"—a sufficient number of Masters embodying Artist's Performances to comprise one (1) or more compact disc Records, or the equivalent, of not less than forty-five minutes of playing time and containing at least ten (10) different Compositions.

What if the record consists of more than 10 masters but is less than 45 minutes in playing time? Is it an album or an EP or something different? As a practical matter, if the artist was required to deliver an album and if the company accepts it and releases it, it will be treated as an album.

(b) "Single"—a vinyl-disc Record not more than seven (7") inches in diameter, or the equivalent in a nonvinyl-disc configuration, which contains Recordings of not more than two (2) Compositions.
(c) "Twelve-Inch Single"—a twelve-inch (12") vinyl-disc Record, or the equivalent in a nonvinyl-disc configuration, which contains Recordings of not more than three (3) Compositions and does not constitute an Album.

The above two definitions are somewhat archaic as very few vinyl twelve-inch singles are manufactured and virtually no seven-inch singles are currently manufactured. However, record companies are often hesitant to reinvent definitions, no matter how archaic, which have served them well in the past.

(d) "Extended Play Record"—a Record which contains Recordings of four (4) or more Compositions but does not constitute an Album.

14.03. "Ancillary Exploitations"—(a) the leasing of commercial advertising space to Persons other than Label or its licensees on an Artist Web Site; (b) the placement on an Artist Web Site of links to so-called e-commerce Web Sites owned or controlled by Persons other than Label or its licensees; and (c) the inclusion of computer software, or Web Site links in ECD Material.

14.04. (a) "Budget Record"—a Record, whether or not previously released, bearing a Suggested Retail List Price which is sixty-seven percent (67%) or less of the Suggested Retail List Price in the country concerned applicable to the Top-line Records in the same configuration (e.g., long-playing Album, two-disc long-playing Album, Twelve-Inch Single, analog tape cassette, compact disc, etc.) released by Label or its Licensees in the territory concerned.
(b) "Midprice Record"—a Record, whether or not previously released, bearing a Suggested Retail List Price in the country concerned in excess of sixty-seven percent (67%) and less than eighty-five percent (85%) of the Suggested Retail List Price applicable to the Top-line Record in the same configuration.

These are ordinary definitions of budget and midpriced records; however, many record companies will agree to limit midpriced records to records with a retail price between 67% and 80% of the suggested retail list price of top-line records.

14.05. "Composition"—a single musical composition, irrespective of length, including all spoken words and bridging passages and including a medley. Recordings of more than one (1) arrangement or version of the same Composition, reproduced on the same Record, will be considered, collectively, a recording of one (1) Composition for all purposes under this Agreement.

14.06. "Container Charges"—the applicable percentage, specified below, of the Suggested Retail List Price applicable to the Records concerned:

(a) Audiovisual Records-twenty percent (20%).

(b) Compact disc Records/New Medium Records-twenty-five percent (25%).

(c) Other Records-twelve and one-half percent (12.5%) on analog vinyl-disc Records in single-fold packaging; fifteen percent (15%) on analog vinyl-disc Records in double-fold packaging and twenty percent (20%) on analog Records in nonvinyl disc configurations. Container Charges will not be deducted for Singles packaged only in stock paper sleeves.

So-called container or packaging deductions are another fixture of computing royalties in the record business. The amounts of these deductions have much more to do with the history and customs of the industry than they do with actual cost structures. For example, the 20% packaging deduction for tape configurations became an unwavering standard and remains so even after the costs of manufacturing cassettes, originally much higher than manufacturing vinyl discs, dropped to approximately the same level. Likewise, the 25% deduction for compact discs has become the universal standard, despite the fact that manufacturing costs have dropped drastically and are significantly less than 10% of the suggested retail list price of a typical newly released compact disc. Accordingly, these packaging deductions are generally not negotiable. Some have argued that container charges ought to be adjusted to reflect the true manufacturing costs. However, record companies conduct sophisticated profit and loss analyses of their recording agreements and even if they did reduce container charges for compact discs to 10%, the result would almost certainly be a proportionate reduction in royalty rates yielding the same "penny rates" as the artist would receive with a higher royalty rate and a higher container charge.

14.07. "Contract Period" and "Period"—the initial period, or any Option Period, of the term hereof (as such Periods may be suspended or extended as provided herein).

14.08. "Controlled Composition"—a Composition wholly or partly written, owned or controlled by you, a Producer (except any Producer engaged by Label pursuant to subparagraph 2.02(b)), or any Person in which you, or a Producer (except any Producer engaged by Label pursuant to subparagraph 2.02(b)) has a direct or indirect interest.

14.09. "Delivery," when used with respect to Master Recordings—means the actual receipt and acceptance by Label of the Master Recordings concerned and all documents and other materials required to be furnished to Label in connection with them. Without limiting the generality of the preceding sentence, no Master Recordings will be deemed Delivered and accepted until Label has received all of the related documentation required under subparagraphs 4.01(c), 4.01(e) and 4.01(g) and all other materials referred to in subparagraph 4.01(f). Label will have the right to disapprove and reject any Master Recording which in Label's reasonable, good faith opinion, is patently offensive, constitutes an obscenity, violates any law, or infringes or violates the rights of any Person, or which might subject Label to liability or unfavorable regulatory action. A Master Recording will be considered technically and commercially satisfactory under this Agreement if: (a) it is technically satisfactory to Label for Label's manufacture and sale of Phonograph Records; (b) the Performance recorded in it is "first class" (as that term is understood in the record industry); (c) that Performance is at least of the quality of the demonstration recordings of your Performances submitted to Label in the case of the first Album and your previous Albums in the case of subsequent Albums; (d) your Performance in the Recording concerned is in the same style as your those demonstration recordings in the case of the first Album and your previous Albums in the case of subsequent Albums, and the musical material recorded in the Recording concerned is of the same genre as the musical material recorded in those demonstration recordings in the case of the first Album and your previous Albums in the case of subsequent Albums and embodies your vocal musical Performances; and (e) otherwise conforms with all of the other requirements set forth in this Agreement. In addition to the foregoing, an Album will be considered technically and commercially satisfactory if the proportionate number and playing time of the Compositions in it written by you is at least substantially equivalent to the proportionate number and playing time of such Compositions in each of your previous Albums.

This is another uncommon definition, since it encompasses not only physical delivery, but also the delivery of all consents, approvals, licenses, and permissions necessary for the release of the record. This is intended to give the company remedies in the event that any such consent, etc., is never delivered, as well as to defer the company's payment obligations until all such consents, etc., are delivered. This particular definition also adds the requirement that the masters be commercially satisfactory. This is rather sneaky. It would be more straightforward for the company to state that recordings must be delivered to the company and accepted by the company. This is a way of hiding the requirement of acceptance, and is why definitions must always be carefully read and negotiated.

14.10. "ECD Material"—all material acquired or created for inclusion in the enhanced or multimedia portion of an enhanced CD, CD Plus, CD ROM, DVD, or any other similar configuration, whether now known or hereafter created, (including, without limitation, Covered Videos, photography, graphics, technology, software, so-called hyperlinks to URLs, etc.).

14.11. "Electronic Transmission"—any transmission to the consumer, whether sound alone, sound coupled with an image, or sound coupled with data, in any form, analog or digital, now known or later developed (including, but not limited to, cybercasts, webcasts, streaming audio, streaming audio/video, digital downloads, direct broadcast satellite, point-to-multipoint satellite, multipoint distribution service, point-to-point distribution service, cable system, telephone system, broadcast station, and any other forms of transmission now known or hereafter devised) whether or not such transmission is made on-demand or near on-demand, whether or not a direct or indirect charge is made to receive the transmission and whether or not such transmission results in a specifically identifiable reproduction by or for any transmission recipient. All references in this Agreement to the distribution of Records, unless expressly provided otherwise, shall be understood to include the distribution of records by way of Electronic Transmission thereof.

This is a very broad definition of electronic transmission intended to encompass all forms of digital delivery to consumers of music, even through methods not currently known or contemplated.

14.12. "Inception of Recording"—the first recording of Performances or other sounds with a view to the eventual fixation of a Master Recording. Master Recordings from the Inception of Recording include, without limitation, all rehearsal recordings, outtakes, and other preliminary or alternate versions of sound recordings that are created during the production of Master Recordings made under this Agreement.

14.13. "Joint Recording"—any Master Recording embodying your Performance and any Performance by another artist with respect to which Label is obligated to pay royalties.

14.14. (a) "Licensees"—all Persons (whether or not affiliated with Label or Label's Distributor) to which Label has licensed the right of sale, distribution or exploitation of Master Recordings and/or Records made hereunder, including, without limitation, wholly or partly owned subsidiaries, affiliates, and other divisions of Label or its Distributor.
(b) "Distributor"—the record company having the exclusive right at any time to distribute Label's newly released Records through USNRC.

14.15. "Master Recording" and "Recording"—every recording of sound, whether or not coupled with a visual image, by any method and on any substance or material, whether now or hereafter known, which is used or useful in the recording, production and/or manufacture of Phonograph Records.

14.16. "Mechanical Royalties"—royalties payable to any Person for the right to reproduce and distribute copyrighted Compositions on Phonograph Records other than Audiovisual Records.

14.17. "Multiple Record Set"—an Album which contains a sufficient number of Masters embodying Artist's Performances to comprise two (2) or more compact disc Records, or the equivalent, each of not less than forty-five minutes of playing time and each containing at least ten (10) different Compositions packaged as a single unit, or which, because of the number of Master Recordings embodied thereon or the playing time thereof, bears a Suggested Retail List Price which is greater than that of the majority of Label's then-current releases in that particular configuration. For purposes of the Recording Commitment hereunder and for computing the applicable Recording Fund or Advance, a Multiple Record Set accepted by Label shall be deemed only one (1) Album.

14.18. "Net Sales"—gross sales, less returns, credits and reserves against anticipated returns and credits. Returns will be apportioned between Records sold and free goods in the same ratio in which Label's customer's account is credited.

14.19. (a) "New Medium" Records—Records (other than Audiovisual Records) in any software medium (including, without limitation, digital audio tape, digital compact cassette and MiniDisc and transmission directly into the home) in which recorded music is not in general commercial distribution in the United States as of January 1, 1999.

This definition will evolve over time and if a contract is negotiated while a particular technology is on the cusp of general consumer acceptance, the artist should try very hard to have such technology excluded from the definition of new medium.

(b) "Standard" Records, units, etc.—Records other than New Medium Records and Audiovisual Records.

14.20. "Performance" (whether audio only or audiovisual)—means singing, speaking, conducting or playing an instrument, alone or with others.

14.21. "Person"—any natural person, legal entity, or other organized group of persons or entities, or legal successors or representatives of the foregoing. (All pronouns, whether personal or impersonal, which refer to Persons include natural persons and other Persons.)

14.22. "Recompilation Album"—an Album containing Master Recordings hereunder previously released in different Album combinations, such as a "Greatest Hits" or "Best of" Album.

14.23. "Records" and "Phonograph Records"—all forms of reproductions (including, sound alone and audiovisual reproductions), now or hereafter known, manufactured or distributed primarily for home use, institutional use (e.g., library or school), jukebox use, or use in means of transportation (including, without limitation, video games and any software media or transmission of such reproductions via telephone, cable, satellite or other transmissions to consumers directly into the home (e.g., CD-ROM, CD-I and similar disc systems, interactive cable and/or telephony).

A person reading a recording contract for the first time would likely find this most surprising, but it is a long-established common practice in the record industry to treat audiovisual recordings sold for home use as records. This is fundamental to the understanding of the rights and obligations prescribed by the recording contract.

(b) "Audiovisual Record"—a Phonograph Record including sound accompanied by visual images intended primarily for home consumer or institutional (e.g., library or school) use, jukebox use or use in means of transportation, including, without limitation, videocassettes, laser discs, videodiscs or other media or devices now or hereafter known that, among other things, allow consumers to control the viewing of, or to interact with, the Audiovisual Record, including, without limitation, transmissions to consumers directly into the home that enable consumers to view such Records at any time. Audiovisual Records are not Albums, Singles, Twelve-Inch Singles, or Extended Play Records.

With the advent of enhanced CDs (compact discs playable on standard CD players that also embody video files playable through computer CD-ROM drives) and the advent of DVDs, which also have the capacity to embody visual images, it is important for artists to try to have the recording agreement provide that royalties payable on CDs that are playable in normal CD players and also contain some additional digital information, are not to be subject to royalty reductions applicable to audiovisual records. The rationale behind this is that there is virtually no difference in the manufacturing costs of a CD that bears only music and a CD that bears music and audiovisual files. An artist in good standing ought to be able to negotiate an amendment to the agreement consistent with the foregoing prior to rendering his or her consent to release an album that embodies some video or other enhanced content, even if the record company will not modify the agreement prior to its execution.

14.24. "Recording Costs"—all amounts representing direct expenses paid or incurred by Label in connection with the production of finished Master Recordings under this Agreement. Recording Costs include, without limitation, the amounts referred to in paragraph 5.01, travel, rehearsal, and equipment rental and cartage expenses, advances to Producers, transportation costs, hotel and living expenses approved by Label, studio and engineering charges in connection with Label's facilities and personnel or otherwise, all costs and expenses of obtaining rights to all samples of Master Recordings, selections and other materials embodied in Master Recordings hereunder (including, without limitation, all advances, license fees, attorneys' fees and clearinghouse fees), all costs of mastering, remastering, remixing and/or sweetening and all costs necessary to prepare Master Recordings for release on digital media. Recording Costs do not include the costs of producing metal parts, but include all studio and engineering charges or other costs incurred in preparing Master Recordings for the production of metal parts. (Metal parts include lacquer, copper, and other equivalent masters.)

This is a rather typical definition of recording costs, although it could be argued that mastering costs are manufacturing costs and therefore should be borne entirely by the company. However, such arguments are unlikely to be successful for most new artists.

14.25. "Royalty Base Price"—

(a) The Royalty Base Price for Records (other than Audiovisual Records) shall be the Suggested Retail List Price applicable to the Phonograph Records concerned, less all excise, purchase, value added or similar taxes included in the price and less the applicable Container Charge.

(b) The Royalty Base Price for Records (other than Audiovisual Records) sold through any so-called record club will be the same as that for the identical Records sold through Normal Retail Channels in the territory concerned.

(c) The Royalty Base Price for Audiovisual Records manufactured and distributed by Label or its Licensees shall be Label's or its Licensee's published wholesale price as of the commencement of the accounting period concerned, less all excise, purchase value added or similar taxes included in the price and less the applicable Container Charge.

As discussed in the paragraph pertaining to royalties for audiovisual records, record companies traditionally pay royalties on audiovisual records based on the wholesale price as opposed to the retail price. The way that is accomplished in this agreement is by placing such language in the definition section as opposed to that in the royalty provisions themselves. This is another example of why it is so important that all definitions be reviewed very carefully before you enter into a recording agreement.

14.26. "Sales Through Normal Retail Channels"—Net Sales other than as described in paragraphs 9.02, 9.03(a), 9.04, 9.05, 9.06, 9.07 10.03 and 10.04.

This is a typical definition of sales through normal retail channels. However, it is important that the artist review each paragraph referenced in a clause like this to make sure that no types of sales are excluded that ought to be deemed through normal retail channels.

14.27. "Side"—a Master Recording of a continuous Performance of a particular arrangement or version of a Composition, not less than two and one quarter (2 1/4) minutes in playing time. If any Album (or other group of Master Recordings) Delivered to Label in fulfillment of a Recording Commitment expressed as a number of Sides includes Master Recordings of more than one (1) arrangement or version of any Composition, all of those Recordings will be deemed to constitute one (1) Side.

14.28. "Special Packaging Costs"—costs incurred by Label in creating and producing Album covers, sleeves and other packaging elements, in excess of Label's then standard costs for design of artwork (including expenses for reproduction rights), engraving, separations, and then standard packaging manufacturing costs.

14.29. "Suggested Retail List Price" or "SRLP"—

(a) With respect to Records sold for distribution in the United States:

(1) Other than with respect to Audiovisual Records, compact disc Records or New Medium Records: the suggested retail list price in the United States established by Label or its Licensees during the applicable accounting period for the computation of royalties to be made hereunder, it being understood that a separate calculation of the suggested retail list price shall be made for each price-series and configuration of Records manufactured and sold by Label or its Licensees.

(2) With respect to compact disc Records and New Medium Records and sales by way of Electronic Transmission but not direct to the consumer (sales by way of Electronic Transmission direct to the consumer shall be computed as set forth in subparagraph 9.02(c)): one hundred thirty percent (130%) of Label's or its Licensee's lowest published wholesale price in the category of sale concerned.

Here is another curve ball that could be overlooked if an artist is not careful. Paragraph 14.25 defines the royalty base price for records to be the suggested retail list price less applicable taxes and the container charge. Here, the suggested retail list price for compact discs, which comprise a vast majority of units sold, as 130% of wholesale instead of 100% of retail. While the wholesale prices may vary from company to company, this clause has the effect of reducing the royalties that would be payable on CDs if they were based on a true retail price by approximately 15% to 20%. In a way, this is a hidden CD reduction. While negotiating an agreement that has any clause that ties royalties to wholesale prices, it is essential to compel the record company to reveal its then current wholesale price for top-line records so that the artist can do a thoughtful and thorough analysis of the royalty terms.

(b) With respect to Records sold for distribution outside the United States (other than Audiovisual Records, or Records sold through direct transmission which shall be computed as set forth in subparagraph 9.02(c)), Label's or its Licensees' suggested or applicable retail price in the country of manufacture or sale, as Label or its Licensee is paid; provided, however, that in any country where there is an absence of such suggested or applicable retail price, the price as may be established by Label or its Licensees in conformity with the general practice of the recording industry in such country, provided that Label or its Licensees may, but shall not be obligated to, utilize the price adopted by the local mechanical copyright collection agency for the collection of Mechanical Royalties. Notwithstanding anything to the contrary expressed or implied in the preceding sentence, it is understood and agreed that if the suggested or applicable retail price cannot be established in a particular country, the price shall be that amount equal to the published dealer price payable by the largest category of Label's or its Licensee's customers in the normal course of business with respect to such Records sold for distribution during the applicable semiannual accounting period, multiplied by one hundred twenty-six percent (126%).

This is fairly standard language with respect to royalties payable on record sales outside of the United States. The artist should not be shy about asking the record company to provide a list of then-current applicable retail prices in the primary territories where the artist anticipates selling records, as part of a thorough analysis of the deal.

(c) Label or its Licensees may at some time change the method by which it computes royalties in the United States from a retail basis to some other basis (the "New Basis"), such as, without limitation, a wholesale basis. The New Basis will replace the then-current Suggested Retail List Price and the royalty rates shall be adjusted to the appropriate royalty which would be applied to the New Basis so that the dollars and cents royalty amounts payable with respect to the Record concerned would be the same as that which was payable immediately prior to such New Basis. If a Record was not theretofore sold in a particular configuration or in a particular price-series (e.g., a Budget Record), the adjusted royalty rate for any such configuration shall be the adjusted royalty rate on Top-line Records multiplied by a fraction, the numerator of which is the royalty rate for sales in the configuration (or price-series) concerned prior to the New Basis and the denominator of which is the royalty rate for sales of Top-line Records in the applicable configuration prior to the New Basis.

(d) Royalties will be calculated separately with respect to each price series in which units of a particular Record release are sold or returned during the semiannual accounting period concerned.

14.30. "Top-line Record"—a Record released bearing the same Suggested Retail List Price as the majority (or plurality) of the Record releases in the same configuration then in initial release in Label's active catalog. (For the purposes of the preceding sentence, a Record release will not be deemed in its initial release if it bears a Suggested Retail List Price lower than that which applied to it when it was first released by Label.)

14.31. "Web Site"—a series of one (1) or more interconnected documents or files that are formatted using the Hypertext Markup Language, or any similar language, and that are intended to be accessible by Internet users.

14.32. "Web Site Material"—all material acquired or created for inclusion on an Artist Web Site (including, without limitation, Covered Videos, photography, graphics, technology, so-called hyperlinks to URLs, online chats, and electronic press kits or so-called EPKs).

15. REMEDIES

15.01. If you do not fulfill any portion of your Recording Commitment within ninety (90) days after the end of the time prescribed in Article 3, Label will have the following options:

(a) to suspend Label's obligations to make payments to you under this Agreement until you have cured the default. This subparagraph (a) will not apply to remittances of royalties under Articles 9, 10 and 12 actually becoming due to you under Articles 11 and 12 or to Annual Payments or any Additional Payments payable pursuant to paragraph 6.04. Advances will not be deemed "royalties" for the purpose of the preceding sentence;

(b) to terminate the term of this Agreement at any time, whether or not you have commenced curing the default before such termination occurs; and

(c) to require you to repay to Label the amount, not then recouped, of any Advance previously paid to you by Label and not specifically attributable under Article 6 to any Commitment Album which has actually been fully Delivered, except as expressly provided in the next sentence. You will not be required to repay any such Advance to the extent to which you furnish Label with documentation satisfactory to Label establishing that you have actually used the Advance to make payments, to parties not affiliated with you and in which you have no interest, for Recording Costs incurred in connection with the Album concerned before Label's demand for repayment. ("Recording costs," in the preceding sentence, means items that would constitute Recording Costs if paid or incurred by Label.) Label may exercise each of those options by sending you the appropriate notice. Label will not exercise its rights under subparagraph 15.01(a) if the default concerned is attributable to your death or disability. If Label terminates the term under subparagraph 15.01(b), all parties will be deemed to have fulfilled all of their obligations under this Agreement except those obligations that survive the end of the term (e.g., indemnification obligations, royalty accounting and payment obligations, rerecording restrictions and your obligations under subparagraph 15.01(c)). No exercise of an option under this paragraph will limit Label's rights to recover damages by reason of your default, its rights to exercise any other option under this paragraph, or any of its other rights.

If the artist fails to fulfill his or her responsibilities, the record company ought to be required to provide the artist with written notice to that effect and provide the artist with a reasonable cure period to remedy the situation before such draconian measures as the termination of the agreement and forced repayment of advances occur.

15.02. If Label refuses without cause to allow you to fulfill your Recording Commitment for any Contract Period and if, not later than sixty (60) days after that refusal takes place, you notify Label of your desire to fulfill such Recording Commitment, then Label shall permit you to fulfill said Recording Commitment by notice to you to such effect within sixty (60) days after Label's receipt of your notice. Should Label fail to give such notice, you shall have the option to terminate the term of this Agreement by notice given to Label within thirty (30) days after the expiration of the latter sixty-day period; on receipt by Label of such notice, the term of this Agreement shall terminate and all parties will be deemed to have fulfilled all of their obligations hereunder except those obligations which survive the end of the term (e.g., warranties, rerecording restrictions and obligation to pay royalties). In addition and also in the circumstance where Label exercises its option to terminate the term pursuant to clause 3.04. hereof, Label shall pay to you, in full settlement of its obligations to you (other than those royalty obligations) an Advance in the amount equal to:

(a) The aggregate of the minimum Recording Funds fixed in paragraph 6.02 for each Commitment Album, then remaining unrecorded, for the Contract Period during which such termination occurs, less:

(b) The average amount of the Recording Costs for the last two (2) Commitment Albums recorded hereunder. If Master Recordings sufficient to constitute at least the first and or second Commitment Album to be recorded under this Agreement have not been completed then, the amount of the Advance payable to you hereunder will be a minimum of twenty thousand dollars ($20,000) less any Advances (including any Recording Costs) already paid or committed to by Label to or on behalf in respect of the second Commitment Album. If you fail to give Label either notice within the period specified therefor, Label shall be under no obligation to you for failing to permit you to fulfill such Recording Commitment.

The first part of this section is fairly typical language that establishes a timetable and a method for the artist to terminate the agreement in the event the company refuses to fund the recording of the then-current album commitment. If possible, the artist should try to have removed that portion of the paragraph that requires notification to the label of his or her intent to fulfill such recording agreement within 60 days of that refusal. Depending on how things unfold, there might be some debate about when such refusal actually occurs. Ideally, an artist ought to be able to initiate the process of terminating the agreement at any time if the record company is refusing to fund the project. The second part of this section is the so-called pay or play provision of the agreement. This requires the record company to pay a specified sum to the artist in the event that the company is obligated to fund the recording of an album but refuses to do so. The amount of the payment is typically the amount of the minimum recording fund less the anticipated recording costs or, in other words, the amount of money that the artist would expect to pocket upon completion and delivery of the album in question.

15.03. If because of: act of God; inevitable accident; fire; lockout, strike or other labor dispute; riot or civil commotion; act of public enemy; enactment, rule, order or act of any government or governmental instrumentality (whether federal, state, local or foreign); failure of technical facilities; failure or delay of transportation facilities; illness or incapacity of any performer or Producer; or other cause of a similar or different nature not reasonably within Label's control; Label is materially hampered in the recording, manufacture, distribution or sale of Records, then, without limiting Label's rights, Label shall have the option by giving you notice to suspend the running of the then-current Contract Period for the duration of any such contingency plus such additional time as is necessary so that Label shall have no less than thirty (30) days after the cessation of such contingency in which to exercise its option, if any, to extend the term of this Agreement for the next following Option Period. If any suspension imposed under this paragraph by reason of an event affecting no Record manufacturer or distributor except Label and/or its Distributor continues for more than six (6) months, you may request Label, by notice, to terminate the suspension by notice given to you within sixty (60) days after its receipt of your notice. If Label does not do so, the term of this Agreement will terminate at the end of that sixty-day period (or at such earlier time which Label may designate by notice to you), and all parties will be deemed to have fulfilled all of their obligations under this Agreement except those obligations which survive the end of the term (such as warranties, rerecording restrictions, and obligation to pay royalties).

This is a typical force majeure clause, which absolves the company from performance of its obligations if performance is prevented by an act of God or similar occurrence. Typically, the artist's representative will seek to limit the duration of any suspension period due to a cause that only affects the particular company and will try to clarify that accounting statements will be rendered and royalty payments will continue to be made except to the extent that the company is rendered unable to do so.

16. AGREEMENTS, APPROVAL & CONSENT

16.01. As to all matters treated herein to be determined by mutual agreement, or as to which any approval or consent is required, such agreement, approval or consent will not be unreasonably withheld (except as otherwise expressly provided in this Agreement).

Most record companies seek this language to give them the flexibility to move forward on issues that require the artist's consent if, in the record company's judgment, the artist is unreasonable in withholding such consent. It is unlikely that a record company that asks for this language will agree to delete it. Accordingly, if an artist's agreement has such language, it is very important to review every area in the contract where the artist's consent is required so that it is clear to the artist's satisfaction when he or she has the genuine discretion to grant or withhold consent and when such consent shall be subject to this paragraph, which requires that such consent not be unreasonably withheld.

16.02. Except as otherwise expressly provided in this Agreement, your agreement, approval or consent, whenever required, shall be deemed to have been given unless you notify Label otherwise within five (5) business days following the date of Label's written request to you therefor.

Record companies like to have a free hand in marketing the artist's masters and records as they see fit. When they do agree to give the artist rights of approval over creative and marketing matters, they want to be sure that the artist will exercise that right of approval promptly. Accordingly, this type of clause whereby the artist's approval is deemed given if the artist does not expressly disapprove the company's proposal within a specified period of time, has been adopted by most record companies. That being said, the artist should try to increase the number of days and many companies will agree to extend this approval period to 10 business days, except in extraordinary time-sensitive circumstances.

17. NOTICES

17.01. Except as otherwise specifically provided in this Agreement, all notices under this Agreement shall be in writing and shall be given by courier or other personal delivery or by registered or certified mail at the appropriate address below or at a substitute address designated by notice by the party concerned:

ARTIST'S ADDRESS	LABEL'S ADDRESS
______________________________	______________________________
	Attention: Head of Business Affairs

Label will undertake to send a copy of each notice sent to you to your attorney at ______________________________ , but Label's failure to send any such copy will not constitute a breach of this Agreement or impair the effectiveness of the notice concerned. Notices shall be deemed given when mailed, except that a notice of change of address shall be effective only from the date of its receipt. All royalties, royalty statements and/or payments to you hereunder may also be sent to you at your address above via regular mail and shall be deemed sent on the date the applicable statement is mailed.

This is a bit of an unusual paragraph that seeks to relieve the label of its normal obligation to send a copy of each notice under this agreement to the artist's attorney. Because artists are sometimes on the road performing or otherwise out of town, it is important that the record company be required to send all notices to artist's counsel in order to trigger the various notice-driven deadlines in the agreement. Most record companies will be reasonable and agree to this, if asked.

18. INTENTIONALLY DELETED.

19. MISCELLANEOUS

19.01. You will, during the term of this Agreement, actively pursue a career as an entertainer in the live engagement field.

19.02. Label will have the right, throughout the term of this Agreement, to obtain or increase insurance on your life, at Label's sole cost and expense, in such amounts as Label determines, in Label's name and for its sole benefit or otherwise, in its discretion. You will cooperate in such physical examinations without expense to you, supply such information, sign such documents, and otherwise cooperate fully with Label, as Label may request in connection with any such insurance. You warrant and represent that, to your best knowledge, you are in good health and do not suffer from any medical condition that might interfere with the timely performance of your obligations under this Agreement. You will not be deemed in breach of this Agreement by reason of Label's inability to obtain any such insurance, unless it results from failure by you to comply with your obligations under this paragraph.

Some artists are leery about granting record companies life insurance rights, but this is a standard provision used by record companies to protect their investment in an artist's career. Often, record companies will agree to add language to such clauses that allows the artist to choose a doctor in connection with the physical examination, and specifically provides that the results of such physical examinations will remain confidential between the artist, the physician and the insurance company, and they shall not be shared with the record company. All the record company needs to know is whether the insurance company is willing or unwilling to provide the life insurance coverage. It is not the business of the record company to be privy to the results of a physical examination.

19.03. This Agreement contains the entire understanding of the parties relating to its subject matter and supersedes all prior or contemporaneous written or oral agreements, representations, understandings and/or discussions between the parties relating thereto. No change or termination of this Agreement will be binding upon Label unless it is made by an instrument signed by an officer of Label. No change of this Agreement will be binding upon you unless it is made by an instrument signed by you. A waiver by either party of any provision of this Agreement in any instance shall not be deemed to waive it for the future. All remedies, rights, undertakings, and obligations contained in this Agreement shall be cumulative and none of them shall be in limitation of any other remedy, right, undertaking or obligation of either party. The captions of the Articles in this Agreement are included for convenience only and will not affect the interpretation of any provision.

This paragraph encompasses a number of standard boilerplate provisions. Artists must realize that upon signing a recording agreement, all verbal promises between the artist and the record company are extinguished forever. Therefore, if there is any aspect of the agreement that was agreed to verbally prior to negotiations of the long-form agreement, it is important that the artist convey them to his or her representatives and that every effort be made to reflect the terms of the verbal agreements into the written agreement.

19.04. Those provisions of any applicable collective bargaining agreement between Label and any labor organization which are required, by the terms of such agreement, to be included in this Agreement shall be deemed incorporated herein.

19.05. Label may assign its rights under this Agreement in whole or in part to any subsidiary, affiliated or controlling corporation, to any Person owning or acquiring a substantial portion of the stock or assets of Label, or to any partnership or other venture in which Label participates, and such rights may be similarly assigned by any assignee. Label may also assign its rights to any of its Licensees if advisable in Label's sole discretion to implement the license granted. Without limiting the foregoing, you acknowledge and agree that this Agreement may be subject to assignment to Label's Distributor or to any joint venture partnership or corporation between Label (or any affiliate) and its Distributor, or to Label's coventurer, partner or coshareholder. You may assign this Agreement only to a corporation wholly owned and controlled by you, but no such assignment shall relieve you from any of your obligations hereunder.

19.06. Each option and election granted to Label in this Agreement including, without limitation, to suspend the running of one or more periods of time, to terminate the term, to acquire the direct and individual services of a leaving member (if a group artist is involved), or otherwise, is separate and distinct, and the exercise of any such option or election shall not operate as a waiver of any other option or election unless specifically so stated by Label in its notice of exercise of such option or election.

19.07. Neither party will be entitled to recover damages or to terminate the term of this Agreement by reason of any breach by the other party of its material obligations, unless the latter party has failed to remedy the breach within sixty (60) days following notice (except thirty (30) days with respect to payment by Label of any monies due hereunder). (The preceding sentence will not apply to your warranties hereunder, where a specific cure period is provided herein, breaches incapable of being cured, an application for injunctive relief, any termination by Label under subparagraph 15.01(b) or to any recovery to which Label may be entitled by reason of your failure to fulfill your Recording Commitment.)

These paragraphs encompass a number of standard boilerplate provisions, most important of which is the cure provision. It is important that any cure provision operate reciprocally and not merely in the company's favor.

19.08. This Agreement has been entered into in the State of California, and the validity, interpretation and legal effect of this Agreement shall be governed by the laws of the State of California applicable to contracts entered into and performed entirely within the State of California. The California courts (state and federal), only, will have jurisdiction of any controversies regarding this Agreement; any action or other proceeding that involves such a controversy will be brought in those courts, in Los Angeles County, and not elsewhere. Any process in any such action or proceeding may, among other methods, be served upon you by delivering it or mailing it, by registered or certified mail, directed to the address designated in Article 17 or such other address as you may designate pursuant to Article 17. Any such process may, among other methods, be served upon the Artist or any other person who approves, ratifies, or assents to this Agreement to induce Label to enter into it, by delivering the process or mailing it by registered or certified mail, directed to the address designated in Article 17 or such other address as the Artist or the other person concerned may designate in the manner prescribed in

Article 17. Any such delivery or mail service shall be deemed to have the same force and effect as personal service within the State of California.

This clause specifies that California law will govern the contract. Generally, a record company will choose the law of a jurisdiction other than California if there is a sufficient nexus with such other jurisdiction. For example, if the company is located in New York and California, it will often choose New York law to govern its contracts, since California law has certain provisions that are more favorable to the artist than the laws of New York.

This clause also contains an exclusive jurisdiction and venue clause, which is designed to ensure that all legal proceedings are conducted in the company's home state. Again, where the company has offices outside California, this is generally insisted on by the company in order to avoid the prospect of the artist bringing suit in California, which is generally viewed as pro artist.

19.09. In entering into this Agreement, and in providing services pursuant hereto, you have and shall have the status of independent contractors and nothing herein contained shall contemplate or constitute you as Label's agents or employees.

19.10. Monies to be paid to you under this Agreement will not be assignable by you without Label's written consent, which Label may withhold in its unrestricted discretion, subject to the next sentence. You may assign royalties to be paid to you under this Agreement, provided: (a) no more than one such assignment will be binding on Label at any time, and if Label is notified of more than one it will have the right to rely conclusively on priority of notice to it in according priority among them; (b) each such assignment will be subordinate to Label's continuing right to apply all such royalties due or becoming due in recoupment of all Advances, loans and other offsets which may be recoupable from your royalties, including, but not limited to, those made under agreements entered into by Label and you after the date of the assignment concerned; and (c) no such assignment will be effective until it has been accepted in writing by Label. Label will not unreasonably withhold acceptance of any assignment that is consistent with this paragraph.

19.11. You recognize that the sale of Records is speculative and agree that the judgment of Label with respect to matters affecting the sale, distribution and exploitation of Records hereunder shall be binding upon you. Subject to the terms of this Agreement, nothing contained in this Agreement shall obligate Label to make, sell, license or distribute Records manufactured from the Master Recordings recorded hereunder except as specified in this Agreement.

19.12. This Agreement shall not become effective until executed by all proposed parties hereto.

19.13. Any and all riders annexed hereto together with this basic document shall be taken together to constitute the Agreement between you and Label.

The foregoing paragraphs are typical boilerplate provisions that are generally not negotiable.

20. GROUP PROVISIONS

20.01. (a) As used herein, the term "Artist" includes all members of the group presently professionally known as ____________ (name of band), whether presently or hereafter bound by the terms and provisions of this Agreement. The obligations, liabilities, prohibitions and restrictions imposed upon you hereunder shall be deemed to apply individually and collectively to each of the members of the Artist, whether performing alone, with others, or as a member of the Artist, regardless of the name by which the Artist or any of its members may then be identified. A failure by any member of the Artist to satisfy the obligations of the Artist shall, at Label's election, be deemed a breach of this Agreement. In the event of any such breach, Label may, by notice to you, and without limiting Label's other rights or remedies hereunder, terminate the term of this Agreement, or alternatively, may terminate the term of this Agreement only as to the member or members of the Artist who have failed to satisfy your obligations hereunder.

(b) Notwithstanding any change in the membership of the group, Label will continue to have the right to remit all payments under this Agreement in the name of ____________ (name of band).

20.02. (a) (1) As used herein, a "Leaving Member" means (i) any member of Artist who, during the term hereof, ceases to be an actively performing member of Artist for any reason whatsoever including, without limitation, as a result of the death or physical or mental disability of such member, and (ii) if you disband or Label decides to terminate this Agreement because of there being a Leaving Member, each member of Artist. If there shall be a Leaving Member, you will notify Label promptly and, in such event, or if Label terminates the term of this Agreement with respect to fewer than all members of you as set forth herein, then, if you and Label so agree, the Leaving Member will be replaced by a new member, which replacement member shall be mutually approved by you and Label. Each such replacement member, as well as any additional new member of the Artist, will be deemed a party to this Agreement, and you will cause each new member (whether additional or replacement member) to execute and deliver to Label any and all documents as Label, in its reasonable judgment, may require to accomplish that addition or substitution. Thereafter, the Leaving Member will not render services for Performances under this Agreement, but the Leaving Member will continue to be bound by the other provisions of this Agreement, including, without limitation, subparagraph 20.02(b) below. You will not permit any Person to perform in place of the Leaving Member, or any additional new member to perform, in making Recordings under this Agreement, unless that Person has executed and delivered to Label the documents referred to in this section. Label will continue to have the right to use the name ____________ and any other professional, group, and other assumed or fictitious names used by you at any time, in connection with Recordings of the your Performances made at any time; no Leaving Member will make any use of the name ____________ or any such other name in any circumstances.

(2) Label will have the right to terminate the term of this Agreement with

respect to the remaining members of the Artist by notice given to you at any time before the expiration of ninety (90) days after Label's receipt of your notice. In the event of such termination, all of the members of the Artist will be deemed Leaving Members as of the date of such termination notice, and subparagraph 20.02(b) will apply to all or any of them, collectively or individually as Label elects.

(b) You grant to Label an option to engage the exclusive services of each Leaving Member as a recording artist ("Leaving Member Option"). Each Leaving Member Option may be exercised by Label by notice to the Leaving Member at any time before the expiration of sixty (60) days after the date of: (1) Label's receipt of your notice under section 20.02(a)(1), or (2) Label's termination notice pursuant to section 20.02(a)(2), as the case may be. If Label exercises a Leaving Member Option, the Leaving Member concerned will be deemed to have entered into a new agreement ("LM Agreement") with Label containing the same provisions as this Agreement, except as follows:

(1) The LM Agreement will apply only to that Leaving Member, and all references to "you" will be deemed to refer to the Leaving Member;

(2) The term of the LM Agreement will commence on the date of Label's exercise of such Leaving Member Option and may be extended by Label, at its election exercisable in the manner provided in paragraph 1.02 of this Agreement, for the same number of additional Periods as the number of Option Periods, if any, remaining pursuant to paragraph 1.02 at the time of Label's exercise of the Leaving Member Option (but at least four (4) such additional Periods in any event);

(3) The Recording Commitment for the first Contract Period of the term of the LM Agreement will be two (2) Sides, with an option for additional Master Recordings sufficient to constitute the balance of an Album. The Recording Commitment for each Option Period of the LM Agreement will be Master Recordings sufficient to constitute one (10) Album;

(4) Paragraph 6.02 and the second sentence of section 4.01(a)(4) will not apply; instead, Recordings will be made on an approved budget basis;

(5) The royalty percentage rates in respect of Master Recordings made during that term will be sixty-six and two-thirds percent (66⅔%) of the royalty percentage rates prescribed in paragraph 9.01; and

(6) If your royalty account under this Agreement is in an unrecouped position at the date of Label's exercise of the Leaving Member Option, the unrecouped balance in your royalty account under this Agreement ("Unrecouped Group Advance"), will constitute an Advance recoupable from the royalties payable under the LM Agreement; provided, that Label shall nevertheless have the right to recoup the entire Unrecouped Group Advance from royalties payable under this Agreement; provided, further, that the Unrecouped Group Advance shall at all times be deemed to be the last monies recouped from royalties payable under the LM Agreement. If Label recoups any of the Unrecouped Group Advance from royalties payable with respect to the applicable Leaving Member's Recordings and thereafter recoups all or any portion thereof from royalties payable with respect to Recordings embodying your Performances hereunder, then Label shall thereupon recredit the royalty account under the LM Agreement with

respect to such portion of royalties. Moreover, solely with respect to Master Recordings recorded by you hereunder prior to the commencement of the term of the LM Agreement, Label shall have the right to apply the "Prorated Royalty" (as defined below) earned by you hereunder to the recoupment of any unrecouped balances in your account under the LM Agreement. As used herein, the term "Prorated Royalty" means the royalty payable to you hereunder with respect to the Master Recordings in question multiplied by a fraction, the numerator of which is the number of Leaving Members subject to the LM Agreement and the denominator of which is the total number of members of Artist (including all Leaving Members) who participate in such royalty.

(7) If there shall be more than one (1) Leaving Member for whom Label has exercised its option as provided in this subparagraph and two (2) or more of such Leaving Members shall, with Label's consent, elect to perform together as a duo or group, then Label shall have the right to treat such Leaving Members collectively as if they were only one (1) Leaving Member for the purpose of the royalty rates, advances and other monies payable in respect of their joint recordings pursuant to this subparagraph.

An important part of any recording agreement for a group artist is the section that deals with changes in the group membership, the so-called leaving member provisions. In the typical first-draft agreement, if any member leaves the group, the company has the right to terminate the agreement. This could be disastrous and unfair to the group, particularly if the member is not a key member. Accordingly, artist's representatives should negotiate to restrict this clause to situations where a specified key member has left the group. Of course, this is a tricky subject for the artist's representative to address, since merely discussing who is key and who is not key can cause strains in relationships among group members and their representatives.

Another primary function of these provisions is to provide that the individual who leaves the group is still bound by the agreement in certain respects. For example, the leaving member is bound by the rerecording restrictions and is prohibited from using the group name in connection with their own activities thereafter. This section also provides that the remaining group members are solely responsible for making any payments due to the leaving member. Where a member has been thrown out of the group by the rest of the members, there is a likelihood of protracted litigation over the right of that leaving member to share not only in income derived by the group from the member's activities with the group, e.g., albums on which the departed member performed, but also on future income of the group. Courts have found there is goodwill in the group name, for which the remaining members must pay the departing member his or her allocable share of the value thereof at the time the departed member left the group. In the case of a superstar group, this can be an enormous sum of money. In this contract, the company is stating that this is the group's problem, not the company's. This issue, and many of the other issues touched on by this section, is best addressed in a written partnership agreement among the group members. Ideally, a written partnership agreement should exist for every group, and it should be created as soon as the group is able to afford it, preferably at the same time they make their first recording agreement. However, the various issues that relate to how the group members share in money, who makes the decisions for the group, and what happens if a member voluntarily leaves the group or if the other members want to force a member out of the group are extremely emotional and sensitive, and many groups simply do not wish to confront them legally. They prefer instead to work out informal rules. The downside of this approach is that if the group becomes successful and these issues have not been addressed in a written agreement, the consequence can be years of litigation that costs tremendous amounts of time, money, and emotional distress.

Finally, the company takes the right to approve replacement members and requires that they become a party to this agreement. In most instances, record companies do not take an active role in the process of selecting replacement members, although in certain situations, e.g., the replacement of the lead singer of a superstar act, a company will exercise this right if it has it. Also, if an original member of a superstar act leaves the group for any reason, it is common not to make the replacement an equity member of the group, but merely a paid employee of the rest of the members or their affiliated corporation, in which event that replacement member would not have all of the rights of the original members and would not be a party to the recording agreement, although the company might insist on having the member sign an inducement letter whereby the member would give the company certain rights and agree to some or all of the same restrictions placed on the equity members, e.g., rerecording restrictions.

The warranties and representations regarding the artist's ownership of the group name are quite important. If there are concerns at the time of signing the agreement that the artist's group name may infringe upon someone else's name, a resolution of the competing claims ought to be worked out quickly, or the artist should pick a new name, before the stakes escalate, which will happen if the artist has a hit record.

Perhaps the most important consequence of a member leaving the group or the group disbanding is that the company has the option to retain the services of the leaving member or, if the group disbands, of any individual member(s). However, record companies are usually not content to obtain the services of the leaving member(s) on the same terms as would have been applicable had the group stayed together. Instead, contracts often require the leaving member(s), in effect, to go back to square one, i.e., be compensated on the same basis as for the first album of the contract. Sometimes the terms are even less favorable than that. For example, in this contract, the leaving member is obligated to record demos and there is no recording fund or advance payable in connection with albums by the leaving member. Instead, the company merely allocates a recording budget. Royalty rates are reduced to two-thirds of what the group's royalty rate would have been for its next album. Moreover, in this agreement the company is allowed to cross-collateralize all or least a pro rata portion of the unrecouped balance of the group's royalty account against the leaving member's royalty account, and is allowed to use a pro rata portion of the group's account to recoup recording costs and charges under the leaving member's agreement. Accordingly, although a group breakup may be the furthest thing from the members' minds at the time they are being signed to a recording contract, it is important that they be aware of these provisions and negotiate the best possible terms.

21. PUBLISHING

21.01. If, during the term of this agreement, Artist desires to grant to a third party the exclusive right to Artist's songwriting services or the right to own or administer any interest in or to one (1) or more Controlled Compositions (whether written prior to or during the term hereof) (such rights being herein referred to as "Publishing Rights"), then prior to commencing negotiations with any such third party with respect to any such Publishing Rights, Artist shall notify Label thereof and Artist and Label shall promptly begin good faith negotiations regarding the material terms and conditions of an agreement between Artist and Label's publishing company designee relating to such Publishing Rights ("Publishing Agreement"). If, after such good faith negotiations, Artist and Label are unable to agree on the material terms of such Publishing Agreement, then Artist shall have the right to offer such Publishing Rights to third parties and to enter into a Publishing Agreement with any person with respect thereof ("Third Party Publishing Agreement"), subject, however, to the following conditions:

(a) In no event shall Artist have the right to offer such Publishing Rights to any third party prior to the date occurring sixty (60) days after the commencement of negotiations regarding the terms of a Publishing Agreement between Artist and Label; and

(b) In the event Artist shall receive a proposal for a Third Party Publishing Agreement ("Third Party Proposal"), Artist shall first:

(1) Notify Label in writing ("Your Notice") of the Third Party Proposal;

(2) Furnish Label with complete copies of all of the instruments constituting the Third Party Proposal; and

(3) Offer to enter into an agreement with Label on the same material terms as are contained in the Third Party Proposal. If Label does not accept that offer within thirty (30) days after Label's receipt of Artist's Notice ("Offer Period"), Artist may then enter into the agreement set forth in the Third Party Proposal, provided that agreement is consummated within thirty (30) days after the end of the Offer Period upon the same terms and in the same form set forth in the Third Party Proposal. If that agreement is not so consummated within the latter thirty (30) day period, the right of preemption granted to Label in this paragraph will be revived and no party other than Label will be authorized to enter into any agreement concerning the Publishing Rights unless Artist first notify Label and offer to enter into an agreement with Label as provided in this paragraph.

This is not a clause typically found in a major record label contract, but clauses of this type are often found in contracts with smaller record companies. This is essentially a compromise between having no provision regarding ownership of the artist's music publishing interests and one that automatically grants to the record company an ownership interest (usually 50%) in the artist's publishing. This is a combination right of first negotiation and right of last refusal, which is designed to give the company the right to match any offer that the artist would otherwise be willing to accept. The justification for these types of clauses is that the company is the entity primarily responsible for creating the value of the artist's songs and therefore ought to have an edge in acquiring the publishing rights. This type of clause gives the artist the freedom not to make a publishing deal if the artist so chooses and gives the artist the benefit of being able to obtain the fair market value for his or her compositions. The only downside for the artist is that it may be difficult to obtain an offer for the fair market value of the musical compositions if the third party knows that the company has a matching right. This may lead any third party to believe that it is being used as a stalking horse to raise the price, without it having a realistic prospect of getting the deal.

IN WITNESS WHEREOF, the parties hereto have executed this Agreement as of the day and year first above written.

AGREED TO AND ACCEPTED:

______________________	______________________
(ARTIST)	(LABEL RECORDS, INC.)
______________________	______________________
FEDERAL I.D./SS#:	FEDERAL I.D./SS#:

How to Read and Evaluate Artist Royalty Statements

BY JACK PHILLIPS

Suppose you are, or represent, a newly successful artist who has a hit album. In September, *Billboard* shows the album has been certified "gold," which means "... sales of 500,000 units or more." In early October the first royalty statement is received, which seems to add up to only about 100,000 album units. Is something amiss? Not necessarily.

REPORTABLE ARTIST ROYALTY UNITS

First of all, the 500,000 unit criterion includes sales plan and special program free goods that can range from 15% to 25% of the units counted for certification, although royalties by agreement are not normally paid on them. Additionally, gold album criteria include record club sales, bonus and free units (if the album has been out long enough), which may be communicated from the club to the record company for certification purposes well before the record club remits the money due on the sales. Even then, all or at least a portion of the club bonus and free units are usually royalty free by agreement. Also by agreement, artist royalties may only be payable on a percentage of net sales, say 85% or 90%. Usually these "royalty reducers" are offset by a royalty rate that is higher than a record company would pay in their absence. The typical artist contract also allows for a reserve for returns in calculating royalties, which can amount to 25% or more. Royalties will eventually be received on units held in reserve to the extent returns do not deplete

EXAMPLE OF GOLD ALBUM VS. REPORTABLE UNITS

Release Date	January 15, 200X
Certification Date	September 15, 200X
Certified Units	500,200
Record Club Distribution	(99,950)
Record Company Distribution	400,250
Standard Free Goods - 15%	(60,038)
Special Program Free Goods - 10%	(34,021)
90% Unit Base Adjustment	(30,619)
30% Reserve Adjustment	(82,672)
Units Distributed After June 30	(89,250)
Units Reported on June 30, 200X Statement	**103,650**

them. Lastly, some of the 500,000 units could be from the period between the June 30th royalty statement period end and the certification date in September.

Similar situations can occur with the reporting of royalties on foreign sales. Suppose a friend or colleague from London has mentioned what a big hit the album is there and nil royalties for the United Kingdom show on the statement. The problem is probably a matter of time lag. The English affiliate or licensee record company has a normal accounting period to accumulate, process and report the sales and royalties to the record company in the United States, which should report them on the next royalty statement.

ARTIST ROYALTY STATEMENT FORMAT

Each record company's royalty statements are different, and the statements of the individual labels of a record company may differ. Often, preceding the details is a summary of the various types of earnings, including domestic, which may or may not include Canada, domestic licensee sales such as record clubs, and foreign licensee (that may actually be affiliates) sales. The summary will give the previous statement balance and payment, if any, reserves currently held and prior reserves released, recording costs and advances deducted, charges (including session costs), video costs, producer royalty deductions, miscellaneous adjustments and an ending balance.

DOMESTIC ROYALTIES

The common thread among record companies in reporting domestic royalties is the presentation of selections, units, royalty rates and amounts. A number and title usually identify each recording. Presently, there are two primary configurations of an album, i.e., the compact disc (CD) and cassette tape (often abbreviated TC, CT, CA or MC–we will use TC for our example record company). They are also identified by the addition of a prefix or suffix letter or number, for example 2 = CD, and 4 = TC. Seven-inch 45 RPM singles may be identified by a 7 prefix. Or, a configuration code (Cfg), may be given, such as AQ for a CD album, SS for a 45-rpm single and S3 for a three-inch CD single. Generally you can tell the difference between the products by the royalty cent rate. CDs should have the highest rate to correspond with their higher prices. Forty-fives generally have the lowest rate. To confuse things, however, there can

RCX RECORD COMPANY ARTIST ROYALTY STATEMENT
EXAMPLE OF A ROYALTY STATEMENT SUMMARY

Period 07/01/0X to 12/31/0X	
Balance Forward	267,246.03
Royalty Payments	(267,246.03)
Prior Reserves Held	76,812.82
Beginning Balance	**76,812.82**
Earnings	
Domestic Sales	1,101,599.52
Military Sales	32,262.83
Licensee Sales	474,509.67
Licensee Club Sales	6,982.52
Licensee Miscellaneous	1,250.00
Total Earnings	**1,616,604.54**
Charges	
Advances	(300,000.00)
Session Charges	(348,790.18)
Miscellaneous Charges	(94,512.88)
Total Charges	**(743,303.06)**
Reserves	(392,411.31)
Balance Payable	557,702.99
Producer Deduction (Album #2)	(251,546.07)
Ending Balance Payable	**$306,156.92**

also be 12-inch vinyl singles, CD singles and cassette singles at prices in between. Ultimately, the record company may have to be consulted to identify some or all of the selections, particularly if titles are not given.

Our example record company, RCX, discloses all the elements used to calculate royalties for normal domestic sales. This information includes the catalog number, title description, configuration code, royalty percentage rate, packaging deduction percentage, suggested retail list price (SRLP), and the royalty cent rate. It also includes the quantity base (if other than 100%), quantity of royalty units, royalty amount for each configuration and the total for the catalog number. Since it would be beyond the scope of this chapter to cover all the variations between record companies, we will utilize RCX as an example for further discussion. To calculate the royalty for album #2 CD, you multiply the SRLP, $17.98 by 100% minus the packaging percentage (i.e., 100% - 25% = 75%), multiplied by the royalty percentage rate, 16%, to arrive at $2.1576. This cent rate multiplied by the quantity of units gives the royalty amount.

Simple? Not exactly, as you will see.

Prices

RCX negotiates contractually to pay royalties on a suggested retail list price basis. Other companies may use a wholesale price basis or variation thereof.

For new releases in 2000, RCX's prices (SRLPs) for full-priced normal retail channel sales were $17.98 for CDs and $11.98 for TCs. CD singles were $4.98, cassette singles $3.49 and 45s were $1.98. Most albums are currently being released primarily on prerecorded TCs and CDs. This may change if DVDs and digital downloads from the Internet continue to gain popularity. For new product configurations the contract may provide that royalties are based on the CD "penny" rate, at least for some time period. If older releases remain popular, they are usually sold at mid prices, such as $11.98 for CDs and $7.98 for TCs.

Military sales through post exchanges (PXs) and ship's stores, etc., have lower list prices, generally $15.75 for CDs and $9.95 for TCs.

Care must be taken to assure that price changes are properly reflected in the calculation of royalties. Suppose, unlike RCX that retains a "dollar" reserve for returns, a record company has held a "unit" reserve on the first album released. Two years, and two albums later, the first album is reduced to mid price. Any reserves still held on the first album relating to sales at the higher price should be reported at the higher royalty than the current midprice sales. For another illustration, assume all CDs go from $16.98 to $17.98. To the extent that there are any returns after the price increase that relate to sales at the old price they should be segregated and charged back at the old, lower royalty rate.

Packaging Deductions

Packaging allowances are customarily deducted to arrive at a royalty base price on which your royalty percentage rate is applied. Generally, they are 20% for TCs and 25% for CDs or any new album length configuration. The recording agreement may allow a 10% packaging deduction for seven-inch and 12-inch vinyl singles in four-color sleeves, 20% for cassette singles and 25% for CD singles. Many contracts even allow a 25% deduction for albums that are delivered digitally over the Internet. Actually, the packaging deduction is more like a distribution fee. Everyone knows it does not cost anywhere near as much as $4.50 ($17.98 x 25%) to "package" a CD. However, it is generally a nonnegotiable "royalty reducer" in every recording agreement.

Royalty Percentage

Typically, for the succeeding albums of an artist's commitment there are higher rates. There may also be increases of royalty percentage rates, or "escalations," for reaching plateaus of sales levels. Suppose an album was released and within the first six-month royalty statement period 600,000 units were reported. Assume an escalation of 1% was contractually required at 500,000 units. Suppose further that the sales were 80% CDs and 20% TCs. Therefore, 80,000 units of CDs and 20,000 units of TCs should receive 1% more,

CDs:	$17.98 x 75% x 1%	=	$.1349	x	80,000	=	$10,792
TCs:	$11.98 x 80% x 1%	=	$.0958	x	20,000	=	$ 1,916
					100,000		$12,708

However, some record companies claim their systems are not capable of prorating unit sales between the different configurations. One configuration is counted first and only the last one falls over the plateau and gets the entire escalation. For example,

TCs: $.0958 x 100,000 = $9,580

Since TCs have a lower base price, an underpayment of $3,128 would occur.

Artist agreements may also allow the record company royalty relief for albums sold at mid prices. Often an artist receives 75% of the normal royalty rate for albums sold at a mid price, which may be defined as selling at a price between 66.6% and 80% of the normal full price. For budget price sales, which are probably defined as selling for less than 66.6% of the normal full price, an artist generally receives 50% of the normal royalty rate.

The recording agreement may also state that approval must be obtained for the record company to lower the pricing, or that a certain amount of time must have passed since the initial full-priced release.

PX sales are often paid at a reduced royalty percentage rate, as are singles, record club and foreign sales. One needs to summarize the differing percentages from the contract and compare them to what is shown on the statement. For record companies where just a cent rate is presented, it is more difficult to check. In this case knowing the contractual royalty percentage rate and packaging percentage, one can check if the price is reasonable. For example, if the agreement specifies a 16% rate and 25% packaging for the CD version of album #1, the royalty statement simply shows a royalty cent rate of $2.0376, which divided by 16%, divided by 75% (100% less the 25% packaging allowance) equals $16.98. If, however, when the album was on the charts, *Billboard* showed a SRLP of $17.98 (shown right after the album title, label and selection number on the Top 200-album chart), that discrepancy would deserve a phone call to the record company.

Quantity

Since only net units payable are shown on the statements, not much can be done to check the quantities reported without access to the record company's internal records. Primarily, one can check reasonableness and make inquiries about an omission of product known to be out in the market. Considering all possible reasons, if quantities still appear too low, consideration should be given to a royalty examination by professionals.

FOREIGN ROYALTIES

Record companies vary widely in their presentation of foreign royalties. While some simply report the total amount due for each territory, some give a substantial amount of detail. RCX first has a summary of total royalties earned by territory and all the details of the royalty calculation for each selection sold in each territory in a "foreign detail" attachment. Generally, record companies show only a U.S. dollar equivalent base price, i.e., the local currency suggested retail list price or "constructed price" (if there is no SRLP), has already been reduced by taxes and packaging allowances and a conversion rate has been applied. The conversion rate may have been adjusted for withholding taxes in the territory. All these actions are probably permitted by the recording agreement. However, you cannot tell if they have been done correctly. For example, the constructed retail price may have been incorrectly marked up or not marked up at all. The sales or value added tax (VAT) deducted might also be incorrect. Suppose the royalty is to be calculated on a wholesale price basis defined as 50% of the territory's marked up retail price. Suppose further that the foreign VAT was calculated applying the correct percentage incorrectly to the marked up price. Since the VAT is imposed on the wholesale price, we have an over deduction. The packaging deduction may also have been calculated at the correct percentage, but on the price including tax. Further deductions may have been made which conform to the local copyright society's allowances, but which may differ from the artist's agreement.

Unfortunately, it would require prohibitively detailed statements to give all the necessary information to check all of these concerns. However, you can check for reasonableness and inquire about what looks really odd. For example, you would expect a higher rate for CDs than TCs corresponding to their higher price. Prices generally are higher in foreign territories, so you should not see a significant number of albums being sold at an equivalent U.S. price that is notably lower than on domestic sales, although sales could be in a territory that has runaway inflation. Older albums may be mid or budget priced, if allowed by the artist's contract. Nevertheless, foreign sales of the older albums that are being reported at the contractually reduced midprice rate must fit the price criterion required by contract, just like domestic sales.

One can also check that the rates specified in the recording contract are being correctly utilized in reporting. If the record company is supposed to report 75% of the normal 16% domestic rate for major foreign territories you would expect to see 12% for the United Kingdom, Germany, etc., as major is defined in the agreement. Also, if the particular artist's recordings are generally successful overseas, inquiries should be made about significant missing territories for any selections.

RECORD CLUB AND OTHER DOMESTIC LICENSEES

RCX has a summary section that gives the total of royalties earned for each licensee club's sales whether a domestic or foreign record club. Details of RCX's domestic record clubs' reporting will be found among the other foreign record clubs in the "foreign detail" attachment. Artists usually receive one-half of their normal domestic album royalty rate or one-half of the record company's receipts from the club as their share of royalties. Sometimes the recording agreement calls for the artist to receive a one-half share of the record club's reporting of excess bonus and free units distributed, i.e., units, in excess of sales, distributed to club members at no charge for joining or

RCX RECORD COMPANY ARTIST ROYALTY STATEMENT
EXAMPLE OF ROYALTY STATEMENT DOMESTIC DETAIL AND LICENSEE SUMMARY

Period 07/01/0X to 12/31/0X

OPENING BALANCE AND ADJUSTMENTS	**AMOUNT**	
Balance Forward 06/30/0X	267,246.03	
09/30/0X Payment of Royalty	(267,246.03)	
Reserve Held 06/30/0X	76,812.82	
Opening Balance and Adjustments		**76,812.82**

Domestic Earnings

Domestic Sales

	LABEL	CATALOG NO	DESCRIPTION	CFG	ROY%	PACK%	SRLP	$RATE	QUANTITY	AMOUNT	NET PAYABLE
7	RCX	10001	Single #1	SS	16.00%		1.98	$0.3168	41	12.99	
7	RCX	10001	Single #1 - Producer	SS	-4.00%		1.98	-0.0792	41	(3.25)	
2	RCX	10001	Single #1	S3	16.00%	25.00%	4.98	0.5976	463	276.69	
2	RCX	10001	Single #1 - Producer	S3	-4.00%	25.00%	4.98	-0.1494	463	(69.17)	
4	RCX	10001	Single #1	TC	16.00%	20.00%	3.49	0.4467	104	46.46	
4	RCX	10001	Single #1 - Producer	TC	-4.00%	20.00%	3.49	-0.1117	104	(11.61)	252.10
7	RCX	10002	Single #2	SS	16.00%		1.98	0.3168	3,753	1,188.95	
2	RCX	10002	Single #2	S3	16.00%	25.00%	4.98	0.5976	96,374	57,593.10	
4	RCX	10002	Single #2	TC	16.00%	20.00%	3.49	0.4467	17,921	8,005.67	66,787.72
2	RCX	20001	Album #1	AQ	12.00%	25.00%	11.98	1.0782	32,106	34,616.69	
2	RCX	20001	Album #1 - Producer	AQ	-3.00%	25.00%	11.98	-0.2696	32,106	(8,654.17)	
4	RCX	20001	Album #1	TC	12.00%	20.00%	7.98	1.0541	3,052	3,217.11	
4	RCX	20001	Album #1 - Producer	TC	-3.00%	20.00%	7.98	-0.2635	3,052	(804.20)	28,375.43
2	RCX	20002	Album #2	AQ	16.00%	25.00%	17.98	2.1576	418,324	902,575.86	
4	RCX	20002	Album #2	TC	16.00%	20.00%	11.98	1.5334	67,566	103,608.41	1,006,184.27
		Total Domestic Sales									**1,101,599.52**

Military Sales

	LABEL	CATALOG NO	DESCRIPTION	CFG	ROY%	PACK%	SRLP	$RATE	QUANTITY	AMOUNT	NET PAYABLE
2	RCX	20001	Album #1	AQ	12.00%	25.00%	9.75	0.8775	2,266	1,988.42	
2	RCX	20001	Album #1 - Producer	AQ	-3.00%	25.00%	9.75	-0.2194	2,266	(497.10)	
4	RCX	20001	Album #1	TC	12.00%	20.00%	5.95	1.0541	350	368.94	
4	RCX	20001	Album #1 - Producer	TC	-3.00%	20.00%	5.95	-0.2635	350	(92.23)	1,768.02
2	RCX	20002	Album #2	AQ	12.00%	25.00%	15.75	1.4175	20,275	28,739.81	
4	RCX	20002	Album #2	TC	12.00%	20.00%	9.75	0.9360	1,875	1,755.00	30,494.81
		Total Military Sales									**32,262.83**

CONTINUED ON NEXT PAGE

CONTINUED FROM PREVIOUS PAGE

Licensee Earnings

Licensee Sales **COUNTRY**	**REPORTING PERIOD (YEAR-QUARTER)**	**AMOUNT**	**NET PAYABLE**
Australia	0X-02	30,699.25	
Australia	0X-03	14,074.28	44,773.53
Canada	0X-02	16,425.37	
Canada	0X-03	6,782.67	23,208.04
RCX Special Products	0X-03	62.21	62.21
Others	0X-02	294,668.26	
Others	0X-03	111,797.63	406,465.89
Total Licensee Sales			**474,509.67**
Licensee Club Sales			
Australia R/C	0X-02	288.84	288.84
BMG Record Club	0X-03	1,233.66	1,233.66
BMG R/C Free Goods	0X-02	972.96	972.96
Others	0X-02	4,487.06	4,487.06
Total Licensee Club Sales			**6,982.52**
Licensee Miscellaneous			
RSP Sync3125 Commercial		1,250.00	
Total Licensee Miscellaneous			**1,250.00**
Charges			
Session - 999999		(648,790.18)	
11/05/0X Transfer of video costs		(94,512.88)	
Total Charges			**743,303.06**
Adjustments and Reserves			
Royalty Reserve			392,411.31
Total Adjustments and Reserves			**392,411.31**
Ending Balance Payable			**557,702.99**

purchasing a certain number selections. The clubs, at the end of a three-year or more contract period, usually report the excess units to the record companies. Some record companies will share this income only if an audit is performed.

If there is a provision for a percentage of record club receipts in the artist agreement, it might allow club royalties to be paid on less than 100% of net sales. Often clubs pay on a reduced unit basis, for example, 85%.

A special product licensing arrangement may also have occurred on which the record company is reporting a reduced royalty. These may be compilation albums, which usually have an intense media advertising campaign and a short life. Normally

RCX RECORD COMPANY ARTIST ROYALTY STATEMENT
EXAMPLE OF ROYALTY STATEMENT ARTIST COST DETAIL

Period 07/01/0X to 12/31/0X

TRAN CODE	SESSION NO	INVOICE CONTRACT	INV/CON DATE	LEDGER NO	DESCRIPTION	NONRECOVERABLE	RECOVERABLE
SC	999999	26096	11/13/0X	5220-00	Sunset Sound		(1,400.00)
SC	999999	26097	11/14/0X	5220-00	Sunset Sound		(1,400.00)
SC	999999	26098	11/15/0X	5220-00	Sunset Sound		(1,400.00)
					Others		(36,400.00)
					Studio Time		**(40,600.00)**
SC	999999	C/R088	11/15/0X	5224-00	Mr. Producer		(100,000.00)
					Producer Fee/Advance		**(100,000.00)**
SC	999999	A7505	11/15/0X	5226-00	Mr. Engineer		(4,500.00)
					Others		(31,115.00)
					Engineers Fees		**(35,615.00)**
SC	999999	1344	11/15/0X	5227-00	Limousine connection		(80.73)
SC	999999	60299	11/15/0X	5227-00	Hotel Sofitel		(1,276.06)
					Others		(22,943.55)
					Travel and Living Expense		**(24,300.34)**
					Miscellaneous Other		**(148,274.84)**
SC	999999	C/R087	07/15/0X	5267-00	The Artist		(300,000.00)
					Recording Advance		**(300,000.00)**
Artist Total							**(648,790.18)**

the royalties are prorated among the tracks included based on their share of the total number of tracks. Our example record company has its affiliate, RCX Special Products, administer and collect from licensees for these uses. If artist approval was contractually required one can check for unreported product. However, the approval may have been obtained and then the track may not have been included or the product never released. One can check the All Music Guide on the Internet *(www.allmusic.com)*, or a subscriber service, such as Muze's *PhonoLog* to see if they list any selections, which are not being reported.

LICENSEE MISCELLANEOUS

If allowed in the recording agreement, the record company may have licensed an album master for use in a commercial or motion picture or TV show for a flat fee. Generally, artist contracts require 50% of receipts for such uses to be reported as a royalty.

RCX RECORD COMPANY ARTIST ROYALTY STATEMENT
EXAMPLE OF ROYALTY STATEMENT FOREIGN DETAIL

Period 07/01/0X to 12/31/0X

CATALOG PRE	NO. TITLE	SELECTION	ARTIST ROY%	QTY%	RATE	QUANTITY	UNIT PRICE	RECEIPTS	ROYALTIES EARNED
		Australia-RCX	0X-02						
2	20001	Album #1	12.0000%	100.0000%	1.27642	32,068	10.63686		40,932.34
2	20001	Album #1 - Producer	-3.0000%	100.0000%	-0.31911	32,068	10.63686		(10,233.08)
									30,699.25
		Australia-RCX	0X-03						
2	20001	Album #1	12.0000%	100.0000%	1.24747	15,043	10.39559		18,765.70
2	20001	Album #1 - Producer	-3.0000%	100.0000%	-0.31187	15,043	10.39559		(4,691.43)
									14,074.28
		Australia R/C							
2	20001	Album #1	50.0000%					770.24	385.12
2	20001	Album #1 - Producer	-12.5000%					770.24	(96.28)
									288.84
		BMG Record Club							
2	20001	Album #1	50.0000%					3,289.76	1,644.88
2	20001	Album #1 - Producer	-12.5000%					3,289.76	(411.22)
									1,233.66
		BMG R/C Free Goods							
2	20001	Album #1	50.0000%					2,594.56	1,297.28
2	20001	Album #1 - Producer	-12.5000%					2,594.56	(324.32)
									972.96
		Canada-RCX	0X-02						
2	20001	Album #1	13.6000%	100.0000%	1.30632	10,059	9.60531		13,140.29
2	20001	Album #1 - Producer	3.4000%	100.0000%	0.32658	10,059	9.60531		3,285.07
									16,425.37
		Canada-RCX	0X-03						
2	20001	Album #1	13.6000%	100.0000%	1.33761	6,761	9.83535		9,043.56
2	20001	Album #1 - Producer	-3.4000%	100.0000%	-0.33440	6,761	9.83535		(2,260.89)
									6,782.67
2	20001	Others-RCX	0X-02						294,668.26
2	20001	Others-RCX	0X-03						111,797.63
									406,465.89
2	20001	Others-R/C	0X-01						1,122.90
2	20001	Others-R/C	0X-02						3,364.16
									4,487.06
		RCX Special Products	0X-03						
2	21401	Rock 2000 - Song Title		100.0000%	0.06500	957			**62.21**
Artist Total									**481,492.19**

PREVIOUS STATEMENT BALANCE

Surprisingly, sometimes the amount labeled "Previous Balance Forward" on your current statement does not agree with the balance on the previous statement. Perhaps an undetailed adjustment has been made, which should be queried.

Payment dates for the statement balance are contractually specified, normally within 60 or 90 days of the royalty statement period end. If late, someone should call the record company. The large record companies are generally reliable in getting their statements and payments out on time.

RESERVES

A record company can withhold the normally allowed reserve for returns and credits in two ways-in units or in dollars. In the former instance, the royalty statement may or may not show the quantities held in reserve. If not, the record company should supply this information, if requested, at least for domestic sales.

Sometimes record companies withhold a percentage of "royalties otherwise payable..." as a reserve. This will usually be shown on the royalty statement. The recording contract should limit the percentage of allowable reserves and specify a time schedule for release. With the necessary information at hand, one can readily see if the limits are being exceeded, or that the release schedule is not being adhered to.

Many contracts permit the record company to hold "reasonable" reserves in their best business judgment. If the artist is new and the record company has pushed product into the stores, expect a high reserve percentage. About all one can do is reason with the company for a reduction. Perhaps delivery of another album is imminent. Also, if there have been several releases that are cross-collateralized, i.e., negative royalties from net returns on one are offset against positive royalties otherwise payable on another, there is a good deal less justification for a high reserve percentage. High reserves on foreign royalties are a possibly objectionable area as well. Returns are not as readily accepted overseas. Normally, 5% to 10% is the maximum actually accepted. If reserves have been held in a foreign territory, the domestic record company has no reason to hold reserves on that income.

CHARGES AGAINST ROYALTIES

Session charges, other recording costs and advances are usually the largest charges on royalty statements, at least on the royalty statements immediately following a release. Combined with producer fees and advances and some miscellaneous charges, these elements usually make up the recording fund as defined in the recording agreement.

It is important to remember that record companies desire to foster artists' good will by cooperating and providing explanations and reasonable support for any significant charges they have questions about. The amount of details involved with sessions will prohibit total disclosure in the royalty statement. If any detail is given on sessions, it is likely to be invoice dates, descriptions, or just the vendor's name and amounts. About all you can do with this information is to look for familiar company and individual names.

The record company is normally contractually allowed to charge all recording costs up to the point where the recording is ready for manufacture. One may also notice miscellaneous charges for hotels and per diems, limos, gold record copies, etc. Despite the erroneous assumption that these items are being given free, it is normal for them to be charged against artist royalties.

The recording fund for an album, after the first album's release, may be based on the results of the previous album. For example, the agreement may say that the current recording fund will amount to 66.6% of the net royalties earned on the last album. Producer fees and advances, along with the recording costs and artist advances, will normally equal the current fund, i.e., the delivery advance will be adjusted to make it so.

Promotional videos, because of their high cost and modest independent earning power in the past, have developed their own customary treatment. Typically, 50% of the cost is chargeable against artist royalties from audio recordings. If you are aware of the budget and actual costs, you can check that no more than 50% is charged to the audio royalty account, unless contractually permitted.

Currently, even with commercially exploited video for home viewing, it is not unusual for the video earnings to be less than production costs. The artist agreement may or may not allow the record company to apply 100% of earnings to the 50% share of costs not charged to audio royalties. In other words, the earnings, however modest, should be shared fifty-fifty from the first dollar unless the contract allows the record company to first recoup their share. Also, one might question how the record company distributes the earnings between the videos submitted to MTV, VH1, etc. For example, record companies may receive large catalog guarantee advances periodically, with no identification of the airplay of individual videos and simply apportion a share equally to all videos submitted, which would be detrimental to an artist whose video received a great deal of airplay.

Producer Royalty Deductions

Producer royalty deductions are shown on the artist royalty statement in one of three ways: (1) the producer's royalty cent rate is deducted from the artist's and just a net rate shown; (2) the producer deduction is shown by a repetition of a line showing the unit sales, etc., but using the negative producer cent rate to calculate the amount to be deducted; or (3) the total producer royalties payable are deducted in a lump sum on the summary page. In the last case, request a copy of the producer's statement, which gives the details of the calculation. The producer may be receiving a higher percentage rate than appropriate. The producer royalty calculation may not be reflecting the same royalty reductions as the artist, as is often contractually required. Finally, the artist royalty may be reduced for the producer royalty on both a line item and lump sum basis.

There is the concern about when the producer royalty starts to be payable. The artist's agreement should be reviewed as to whether the producer royalty should commence only when the costs are recouped and whether the costs and advances should be recouped at rates inclusive or exclusive of the producer's rate, and whether the producer is then paid from record one, or just after recoupment. In addition, if the recording costs charged to the artist's account include producer advances, then the artist should not see any producer royalty deductions until the producer advance is recouped from the producer's royalties. At that point, only royalties in excess of this advance should be deducted from the artist.

Miscellaneous Adjustments

On succeeding royalty statements, adjustments may be made that correct errors made by the record company on previous statements rendered. If, for example, a rate is being corrected, the applicable quantities adjusted should agree with those on the previous statement. Analyzing the rate should reveal if the correction is appropriate.

Another adjustment, if the artist writes songs as well, may be for the deduction of "excess mechanicals." The recording agreement may provide in a "controlled composition" clause that states, for example, artist royalties may be charged for the excess of mechanical royalties the record company must pay over ten times 75% of the minimum statutory rate at time of release of the album. In other words, if you have cowritten one or more songs with individuals not in your recording group, and there are ten or more songs on the album, you are likely to be charged excess mechanicals. This is generally because the outsider will have to be paid at the full statutory rate. Multiple cowritten songs, statutory rate changes, and escalations of the maximum based on reaching sales levels can complicate this calculation. It may be best to simply request the record company to provide support for their calculation.

There may also be charges for costs of special packaging or artwork, which exceed contractually allowed amounts, and are therefore deductible from artist royalties

ROYALTY EXAMINATIONS

If all of the procedures discussed herein have been applied to the artist royalty statements, either some comfort has been gained that there are no glaring improprieties, or a royalty examination is being considered. If an examination appears warranted, and routine periodic examinations are usually warranted after several releases/royalty statements, the artist agreement should be checked concerning any limitation on the time period to object to statements rendered. Record companies put a great deal of effort into making timely and accurate royalty accountings. However, errors do occur and contracts often contain language that can be interpreted in various ways.

When we review artist royalty statements on behalf of clients, we ask ourselves the same questions and apply the same procedures heretofore described. However, we often find that the royalty statements do not supply enough information. To get satisfaction, we need to actually see the details available only at the record company.

Royalty examinations, when preceded by thorough analysis, usually have cash benefits that exceed their cost. They just make good business sense. Otherwise you may never know the record company has, for example, exceeded the contractual limit of nonroyalty bearing free goods, has not reported a share of income received from a licensee, or has not correctly applied a VAT in calculating royalties on foreign sales.

Royalty Statements: Audits and Lawsuits

BY STEVEN AMES BROWN

Perhaps the most perplexing part of a musician's career centers around royalties and control over how works are exploited.

Under typical writer and artist agreements, ownership of the copyrights in compositions and sound recordings are transferred in exchange for a right to receive contractual royalties.

The conventional wisdom is that publishers and labels own the copyrights free and clear of all claims, except for conduct that violates specific terms of the contract. While such agreements do provide for an express right of audit, it is generally limited to a short window; there is no express right to receive interest in the event of underreporting and neither audit nor attorneys' fees are reimbursed. The company is usually relieved of any obligation to actually exploit the material, and has the right to delete songs and recordings at will and without recourse.

Musicians are at a decided disadvantage when it comes to self-protection, and enforcing their rights requires constant vigilance and resourcefulness.

ROYALTY STATEMENTS

Royalty statements are for the most part vague and confusing.

The first thing to do is compare the statements with goods available to the public. Numerous Web sites exist that sell recorded music. Many of these sites list sufficient information to determine if all configurations in the market are reflected on the statements. Unofficial fan sites and some label sites often contain this information.

Wherever in the world there are sales or airplay chart activity on a title, there is likely to be a Web site that lists its local catalog number for that particular country's release. This information should be compared with the numbers on the royalty statements.

An important market now exists in "compilations," where tracks of various artists are included on a single release. Not only do labels release their own compilations, a substantial business is done in licensing between different companies. This compounds the possibility of royalties being underreported.

Comparing catalog numbers and licensing activity on royalty statements with goods available around the world can identify substantial discrepancies.

Nothing takes the place of conducting your own preliminary investigation. Even if you ultimately engage an auditor or file suit, you simply cannot accumulate too much information on your own.

Understanding the financial calculations for artist royalties is always problematic.

Historically, labels combated rising artist royalty rates by introducing corresponding deductions and reductions. Many years ago, it was assumed that 10% of records shipped were lost, broken or stolen. Therefore, many labels simply declared that only 90% of records shipped were "sold" and multiplied the artist rate against the published retail price for each of those sold units.

Armed with modern computing facilities, many labels now pay royalties on only those units they deem as sold, which by definition excludes regular "free goods" or records shipped as gratis under "special" sales plans (some of which inexplicably last for years at a time), and apply either a multitude of base prices instead of a "retail" price or reduce the royalty percentage under a variety of conditions.

To make matters worse, labels seldom reveal the details on the statements, which results in royalty rates that are nearly impossible for a musician to decipher without assistance. There is no easy means to determine whether the number of units sold was accurately reported or whether the correct rate was applied.

Writer statements are often not quite as difficult to understand. The bulk of income comes from mechanical (records, CDs, etc.) and synchronization (movies and commercials) licenses where the writer receives half the income. Verifying most income on writer statements is simpler than with recording artist statements.

Most publishers delegate their domestic licensing to The Harry Fox Agency. It is a relatively simple matter to match up income reported by Fox to what is reported on writer statements. More difficult to verify is foreign income. Even though mechanical licensing income in most major territories is collected by local collection societies, foreign subpublishers rarely include copies of those reports with their statements, although they should be available when the foreign subpublisher is owned or controlled by the domestic publisher.

AUDITS

Experienced auditors are the professionals best equipped to verify the accuracy of statements. The question of whether to conduct a formal audit is really one of cost versus expected benefit.

Statements for a title that sells millions of units should be audited, but it is a tougher decision for sales of less than 500,000 units.

At the very least, if more than a few hundred thousand units are reported, an auditor should be engaged to perform a simple "bench audit" to determine whether discrepancies on the face of the statement can be identified and other issues clarified.

Artist statements really cannot be accurately verified without a detailed review of the label's business records.

Complicating matters are provisions in most writer and artist agreements that prohibit the musician from engaging an auditor who is engaged in another audit of the company, or from compensating the auditor on a contingent fee basis (i.e., paying the auditor a percentage of what is recovered instead of hourly or guaranteed fees).

Further roadblocks are in the form of restrictions on the type of information that is available in an audit. For instance, record companies limit documents to those relating to sales and will not produce inventory or manufacturing documents.

By limiting access to auditors (e.g., to those musicians that can afford to pay up-front fees) and by restricting the information available to verify the accuracy of statements on an industry-wide basis, labels present significant obstacles to royalty verification.

SUING

The most efficient way to level the playing field in a royalty dispute is to file suit. Once a dispute is in court, the labels and publishers lose the advantage of contractual restrictions.

Should You Sue?

Many artists are understandably nervous about suing a label or publisher. After all some 90% of the music business is in the hands of only five companies and only one of them is American owned.

However, the risks of suing are more apparent than real.

Artists of all stature and levels of success have sued to enforce their rights. And if the company believes it can make money from the artist's creative talent, the existence of a dispute will not change its insistence that future product be delivered.

It is not unusual for active lawsuits to be temporarily stayed while the parties release new material; nor is it unusual for companies to settle disputes by signing new agreements.

As a general rule, the only tragedy is where an artist tolerates a company underpaying royalties or releasing material in a way that disparages the creator.

Retaining an Attorney

In very general terms entertainment attorneys either practice transactional law (deal making) or litigation (deal enforcing).

Each of these subspecialties has a different purpose and seems to require a different approach.

By the nature of their practice, transactional attorneys generally maintain the best of relations with labels and publishers. Persuading, cajoling and enticing companies to pay large advances and higher-than-average royalties seems to require a fraternal and salesperson-like approach, whereas pushing companies into doing something they don't want to do through the brute force of litigation seems to require dogged determination and an indifference to being liked.

Yet, there are music lawyers that have demonstrated effectiveness at both subspecialties. Some very aggressive attorneys are successful at making deals and some very low-key litigators obtain perfectly acceptable recoveries from recalcitrant companies.

The point is that neither a transactional nor litigation attorney should be selected based on stereotype or personality.

It is very important to have a candid talk with an attorney about his or her preferences and track record.

The artist should ask pointed questions, like how does the attorney feel about the prospect of souring his or her own relationship with the company, should that be necessary to advance your claim?

Executives at competing companies can be surprisingly good sources of information about attorneys. It could be well worth the effort to ask which music litigation attorneys produce good results for clients and have a reputation for being honest. Be sure to distinguish between the attorneys executives like and those that are effective. The most important factors are consistent success and truthfulness, not whether an executive would like to have a particular litigator as a friend or coworker.

Attorneys are generally compensated by either guaranteed or contingent compensation. Most attorneys charge an hourly fee for services. Other forms of guaranteed fees, although less frequent, are flat fees for an entire case or a reduced hourly fee plus a flat or percentage bonus based on results.

The other system of compensation is a pure contingent fee, where the attorney is paid a percentage of the winnings but nothing if the case is lost.

Each system has its merits and should be carefully evaluated.

An hourly fee can become an open-ended expense item, depending on the complexity of the action and the defendant's recalcitrance. In a protracted battle, most artists simply cannot match the resources of a major adversary.

Some attorneys will accept a reduced hourly fee with a bonus either in the form of fixed sum(s) or a percentage of the recovery. That could be a boon or bust for the artist, depending on the recovery and the amount of attorney services it takes to obtain the settlement or judgment.

Flat fees are more theory than reality. They are rarely available since the attorney would be underwriting a substantial risk with only a fixed fee at the end of the road.

A pure contingent fee eliminates all risk to the artist, but generally at a price. The attorney is paid only out of a recovery, but the percentage is rarely small and if the attorney reinstates a royalty stream or increases the royalty rate, the contingent participation lasts as long as the reinstated or increased royalty stream itself.

The precise percentage varies among attorneys and is also affected by whether the attorney or the client advances third-party expenses, such as deposition transcripts and expert witness fees.

However, a purely contingent fee means the artist bears none of the risk that the litigation will be protracted or lost. The artist can hold out against the largest and best-heeled adversary. The ultimate price paid for attorneys' fees under a contingent arrangement could equate to a very high or very low hourly rate, but the artist cannot be starved out of a claim and for that reason, the company should be advised of that fact at the earliest stage, since it effectively levels the playing field.

Whom to Sue

The choice of whom to sue is an easy one if the artist has a contract with a large company and that company handles the money.

More difficult choices are faced where the artist has an agreement with a smaller company that transferred the masters/songs to another company and agreed to be responsible for paying the artist.

For instance, "production deals" for recording artists commonly involve an artist signing with a producer who then sells the masters to another company, but continues to handle the artist's royalties.

A production company with few assets, or hard-to-find executives can be difficult to find and is a hard target when it comes to satisfying a judgment.

Most states follow the "common law," which states that a party who accepts the benefits of a contract, must also bear its burdens. Thus, if a record company accepts the benefits of the grants of rights to the masters, and the authorizations to use the name and likeness that are embodied in an artist agreement it becomes responsible for the royalties that are due under the agreement.

In practical terms that means (unless the artist signed a specific agreement waiving the right to sue third parties), the company that actually ends up with the copyrights can be directly sued for any unpaid royalties, even if the company and the producer agree otherwise between themselves. The company may have a claim against the producer for failing to pay the artist royalties, but that has no bearing on the artist's right to sue the company.

This affects how much money is due the artist. The prevailing practice for third-party income (such as from compilations and synchronization) is that an artist receives 50% of the earnings. The question is 50% of whose income? Is the artist's 50% share calculated at the level of the owner of the master or at the lower level of the royalty paid by the owner to the producer?

In cases where the artist sells the master to a producer or a company and that transferee in turn sells the master to another, the artist's share is properly calculated at the source of income received by the party that owns the master at the time the income accrued to that owner.

Moreover, a successor company is responsible for royalties that a prior owner failed to pay.

None of this works a hardship on successive purchasers of copyrights since as part of their acquisition they routinely perform what is known as "due diligence" reviews and hold reserves to cover any claims.

Theories of Recovery

Lawsuits are initiated by the filing of a "complaint" that sets out the nature and theories underlying the claim.

The most obvious complaint is a claim for breach of contract; that the defendant committed a material breach by failing to timely and accurately pay the full royalties due.

Since the general nature of the relationship between an artist/writer and a label/publisher would be one of contract, it is often assumed that the claims have to be limited to damages that flow from the breach of contract.

However, there are more theories that should be considered.

For instance, while the full and timely payment of royalties due for the manufacturing or exploitation by the defendant is considered a mere contractual duty, the reporting of income derived from the exploitation by third parties is, at least in California, held to a higher standard.

When a label handles third-party income (such as royalties for compilations or fees for synchronization) and when a publisher handles third-party income (such as mechanical or synchronization royalties from other companies), the defendant has what is called a "fiduciary duty" to timely and accurately report.

A contractual duty is merely an ordinary promise to do that which is required under the contract and the damages collectable are only lost income and interest. However, a "fiduciary" is more like a trustee; and when a trustee breaches a trust, such as by failing to timely and fully pay over "trust" funds due, not only is the lost income recoverable, but so are "exemplary damages" (an amount that is intended to punish the defendant and make an example of it to others).

If a company only faces contractual damages, it has little incentive to avoid trial and pay over what it owes. However, if there is the possibility of a runaway jury award, the company faces greater pressure to cure any underpayment.

Another remedy is to ask that the copyrights or at least the income be put into the hands of a receiver. That need not be as disruptive as it might sound. For instance, virtually all publishers use The Harry Fox Agency to handle mechanical licensing. It is a very simple matter for a court to order the Agency to pay over the writer's share to the writer's own company.

Just seeking such a remedy will get the company's attention since control over the administration and the float from holding royalty income for six months at a time are a company's financial lifeblood. A single successful artist or writer claim can result in similar attacks by others; it is a powerful incentive to a company to pay any underreported income without delay.

The ultimate remedies are "rescission" and "restitution." If successful, the artist not only ends up getting the copyrights back, but possibly the entire gross royalty received by the record company as well.

These remedies are generally reserved for instances of very serious company breaches, such as the total or near total failure to pay royalties.

The most famous case involved The Kingsmen's recording of "Louie, Louie." As with most artists, The Kingsmen signed an agreement transferring ownership of the master to a record company in exchange for the right to receive royalties. Even though the masters changed hands several times, nobody ever paid royalties to the artists. Decades later The Kingsmen sued to rescind the original agreement and asked that ownership of the master be returned to them.

The appellate court affirmed the judgment in favor of the artists and the artists were awarded ownership of the master again. Left unsettled in that case was how total the failure to pay royalties must be (how substantial must the breach be) before an artist can rescind an agreement. However, the court did hold that the statute of limitations on the right to rescind starts anew with every accounting period. Thus, the artists were able to sue for rescission because within the four years preceding their lawsuit (California has a four-year statute of limitations for disputes over written contracts) the artists had not been paid.

Interestingly enough, The Kingsmen waived their right to seek restitution (the money earned by the defendant for the four years prior to the time they gave notice that they were rescinding). There may indeed have been a good strategic reason why they waived that claim, but it does not appear to be a requirement in any state.

Elsewhere in this book are discussions of additional theories, such as a label licensing a recording for use in commercials or movies that are objectionable to the artist. Issues concerning who has the right to approve such uses should not be overlooked when drafting a lawsuit.

Discovery of Information

Under federal discovery rules and the practices of most states, all relevant information is discoverable, not merely that allowed under the agreement.

Among the most important documents are the intracompany agreements by which record companies and publishers have access to the catalogs of foreign affiliates and vice versa. These agreements provide a road map to how affiliates report sales and income information to each other. Although there is nothing inherently proprietary or confidential about these agreements, virtually no company will disclose these documents without a court order.

Modern pretrial discovery also affords an easy way to track royalties. For little more than the cost of postage, a plaintiff can send written questions to a defendant, asking such things as how many copies of a recording have been manufactured; the names and addresses of all those who have been given licenses to exploit a particular work; the amounts, dates and sources of all income pertaining to a particular title. The defendant is obligated to sign the responses under oath.

Defendants often seek confidentiality orders, to restrict the artist from discussing with others the material turned over in discovery.

Some courts, like the Los Angeles County Superior Court have express rules making such confidentiality orders difficult to obtain.

It is generally not in a plaintiff's interest to consent to a confidentiality order since it drastically curtails the artist's ability to communicate with others and swap useful information. It is precisely this sort of information pooling that companies seek to prevent.

As the information available in discovery basically revolves around the exploitation of an artist's work and since a company has no greater expectation of privacy concerning the exploitation than the royalty artist, it is hard to justify restricting a plaintiff from discussing the success of his own works.

Virtually no writer or artist agreements contain a provision that awards attorneys' fees to the prevailing party in a dispute over royalties. The conventional wisdom is that such a clause would only encourage artists to pursue claims, since if successful they would be repaid their legal fees.

Most jurisdictions have a discovery device that requires the defendant to admit or deny the truth of matters in dispute. The sanction for the failure to admit a fact generally shifts the costs of proving the matter to the party that failed to admit it was true.

In practical terms, an artist can ask a company to admit or deny that the royalty statements in dispute report lower sales than were actually made. If the company wrongly denies the fact and the artist proves there was underreporting at trial, the costs associated with proving that fact can be assessed against the company, even if the artist loses the lawsuit. The policy behind this procedure is to discourage people from unreasonably running up the costs and length of a trial by failing to eliminate issues on which there really is no dispute.

Proving the Claim

At trial or in a motion for summary judgment, the artist is responsible for proving that he has sustained damage at the hands of the defendant, i.e., that the defendant breached some legal duty it owed to the plaintiff and that as a result of the breach, the plaintiff has sustained a quantifiable loss.

The most difficult issue to prove is damages. There are rarely disputes over who signed what contract and which party is liable for any underpayment. The problem is proving the amount of underpayment.

This is particularly true in the case of modern recording artist agreements that subject royalty calculations to numerous adjustments and reductions.

Worse still, are the cases where the defendant either refuses to produce adequate documentation or simply does not have the necessary documents.

Withholding such information has turned out to be a fools paradise at best. The seminal dispute involving inadequate and otherwise missing financial information involved B. J. Thomas, Gene Pitney and The Shirelles. There the record company kept very sketchy documentation and much of what it did have, it sent to a state where it was beyond discovery through a subpoena.

Undaunted, the artists' expert witness simply created a chart with estimates of the income and then to resolve any doubts in favor of the artists and against the company (that had caused the information vacuum), he upped the estimate by 30%. The judgment in favor of the artists was affirmed on appeal.

The lesson to be learned is simple, no artist need be afraid of a company that hides documents; that only leaves the artist free to estimate the income and then up the estimate to resolve any lingering doubts.

The appellate court was quite specific in holding that when a defendant fails to maintain and produce the documents necessary to calculate damages it cannot at the same time complain that the plaintiff did not prove the underpayment with certainty. All that is required is that the plaintiff's expert demonstrate a stable basis for making the estimate. That could come from market share projections; income earned by comparable recordings, etc.

The artist could end up with a judgment that exceeds the amount of royalties that were actually due; that is the risk a company assumes when it hides financial documents.

Should You Settle?

Over 90% of all cases settle before the first witness is called at trial. Therefore, all parties should be talking about settlement from the moment the complaint is filed with the court. Only a fool refuses to discuss a reasonable resolution at every stage of the proceedings.

A litigant should always consider the risks of forcing a case to judgment, and the quality of the other side's position. If there is some merit to the other side's view, it should be taken into account when valuing the case.

Litigation is not a moral battleground; it is not a place for making statements or punishing people.

Ultimately, obtaining a satisfactory result and eliminating risk is the best outcome and if that point is reached before judgment, it is time to settle; if it cannot be reached, then and only then should the case proceed to trial.

Analysis of a Record Producer Agreement

BY LINDA A. NEWMARK

The record producer is one of the most important individuals involved in creating recordings. Certain producers are sought out by recording artists because they believe those producers can assist them in creating the sound that will help them achieve record sales at platinum or multiplatinum levels.

This chapter focuses upon the situation in which the producer is engaged to produce a master recording for use on an album by an artist who already has a recording agreement with a major record company.

PRODUCER COMPENSATION

The producer of master recordings, for an artist with a record deal, generally receives an advance that is recoupable from future royalties. Generally, the artist's recording agreement with the record company will provide that the artist receives an "all-in" royalty on net sales of the artist's records. An all-in royalty means that the artist must pay the producer out of the artist's royalty. However, in certain genres, such as country music, the recording agreement may provide for the artist to receive a net artist royalty, with no payment obligations to the producer. In most cases, the record company will agree to pay the producer directly, after receiving a "letter of direction" from the artist requesting it to do so. Thus, if the artist's all-in royalty rate is 12% of the retail selling price (after deduction of a packaging charge) on net sales of records sold through normal retail channels in the United States, and the producer's royalty rate on such sales is 3% of the retail price (with appropriate reductions), the royalty rate that the artist is really entitled to is 9% of the retail price. However, the artist and the producer must both bear in mind that they will not receive royalties from the moment the first record is shipped from the record company to the record store (or other purchaser). The record company only pays royalties on "net sales," which are some portion of the records that are sold and not returned, with no royalties payable on "free goods." (See the chapter, Analysis of a Recording Contract for an explanation of free goods.) Furthermore, the artist and the producer will not receive royalties until they have recouped recording costs and advances from the royalties earned in connection with the sales of records embodying the relevant master recordings. The artist and the producer will have to recoup different sums at different royalty rates. The concept of recoupment for record producers is discussed below in paragraph 6 of the sample Producer Agreement.

WHO CHOOSES THE PRODUCER?

Generally, when an artist receives an all-in royalty, the recording agreement will specify that the artist is responsible for engaging (i.e., entering into an agreement to engage) the producer; however, the record company usually retains the ultimate control over determining which producer will be engaged. The artist's attorney should always attempt to obtain the right for the artist to approve the producer. Nevertheless, recording agreements for new artists generally provide that the record company and the artist will mutually approve the producer and if the record company and the artist disagree, the record company's decision will prevail. As the artist becomes more successful, the record company will probably allow the artist to have more control over creative decisions, including the selection of a producer.

In some cases, a producer who is on the staff of the record company will produce the album. Many recording agreements contain provisions relating to the minimum compensation (for example, a $2,000 advance per master or $20,000 advance per album and a 3% of retail royalty) that would be payable if the record company's staff producer produces any master recordings for the artist. The artist's attorney should require that a provision be included in the recording agreement stating that a staff producer can only be engaged with the artist's consent and that the advances and royalties that are payable to the staff producer will be prorated if there are coproducers on the master recordings or if there are other master recordings on the album that are produced by someone else.

When the producer is not an employee of the record company and is not the artist, a producer agreement is prepared, either by the artist's attorney or by the record company. The producer agreement provided below was prepared by an attorney for a record company. With slight modifications, it could easily be an agreement between an artist and a producer.

Since most producer agreements favor the artist or the record company, I will review the provisions of the following agreement from the perspective of the attorney who is negotiating on behalf of the producer.

PRODUCER AGREEMENT

The subject matter of this Agreement is your services to us as the producer of ___________ (insert #) master recording(s) ("Master(s)") embodying performances by _____________ ("Artist"). You and we agree as follows:

1. The term of this Agreement ("Term") shall commence as of the date hereof and shall continue until the Master(s) are completed to our satisfaction and delivered to us or until we terminate the Term upon written notice to you. During the Term, you shall render your services as the producer of the Master(s) in cooperation with us and Artist, at times and places designated or approved in writing by us. You shall produce the Master(s), and you shall deliver the Master(s) to us or our designee promptly after the Master(s) are completed. All elements for the creation and production of the Master(s), including, without limitation, the compositions to be recorded in the Master(s) and other individuals rendering services in connection with the production of the Master(s), shall be designated or approved by us in writing. We shall pay or cause to be paid all costs to produce and record the Master(s) in an amount not to exceed a recording budget therefor, which is designated or approved by us in writing. If the costs to produce and record the Master(s) exceed the recording budget for reasons within your control or which you could have avoided, then you shall, upon our demand, pay to us the amount of those excess costs, and we may, at our election, deduct the amount of those costs from any royalties or other monies payable to you under this Agreement.

The agreement should contain a more definite completion standard than "completed to our satisfaction." The producer's attorney should attempt to obtain a "technically satisfactory" delivery standard (i.e., the masters must be of suitable sound quality from a sound engineer's perspective); however, if (as most current recording agreements provide) the artist's recording agreement contains a "technically and commercially satisfactory" delivery standard, the artist's or record company's attorney should not provide a more favorable provision to the producer than "until the completion of technically and commercially satisfactory Masters as determined by the record company."

Generally, the artist and/or record company will retain rights of approval over the elements for the creation and production of the masters. If the producer intends to use his or her own studio, a statement that the studio is approved for recording the masters should be included in the agreement to avoid any doubt about what studio will be used. The titles of the musical compositions to be recorded, if known, should be included as well.

This agreement provides that the record company will pay the recording costs. (In some instances the producer's agreement provides that the producer will receive an all-in advance, which is a lump sum that may be paid in two or three installments during the recording of the masters, which includes the money to pay the recording costs and the producer's advance.)

The producer should be certain to find out the amount available to record the masters before agreeing to take on the project. If the recording costs for the masters exceed the amount of the authorized budget, those excess costs may be charged against monies payable to the producer and; accordingly, the producer could lose part of the advance or be delayed or prevented from receiving royalties.

Many agreements provide that any excess recording costs will constitute a direct debt from the producer to the artist or record company, which must be repaid on demand. The producer's attorney should attempt to delete the record company's and artist's right to direct repayment from the producer and should limit the rights of recovery to the excess costs caused only by situations that were within the producer's control. Furthermore, those excess costs should be recoverable only from any royalties or advances payable to the producer under the specific agreement. In any event, the producer should know at the beginning of the project how much money is available to record the masters and should bear that figure in mind while working. Although the record company may pay excess recording costs, the producer should make every effort to complete the masters within the originally approved budget.

2. From the inception of the recording of the Master(s), we shall own the entire worldwide right, title and interest, including, without limitation, the copyright, in and to the Master(s), the performances embodied therein and the results and proceeds of your services hereunder, as our employee for hire for all purposes of the applicable copyright laws, free of any claims by you or any person, firm or corporation. Alternatively, you grant to us the entire worldwide right, title and interest derived from you, including, without limitation, the copyright, in and to the Master(s).

This language is very standard in producer agreements and would not be subject to negotiation by the producer's attorney. The artist and record company want the masters created by the producer to be "works made for hire" as defined in the United States Copyright Act of 1976. The benefit to the artist and record company of this is the creator of a work made for hire has no right to terminate the transfer of the work and reacquire the copyright at a later date. Nevertheless, since there is some question as to whether the masters that are created as the result of the producer's services qualify as works made for hire, the agreement also contains language stating that the producer grants all rights in the masters to the artist or record company. To protect the artist's or record company's interests better, this agreement should state that the last sentence of paragraph 2 would apply only if the masters were determined not to be works made for hire. The Recording Industry Association of America (RIAA) recently obtained an amendment to the United States Copyright Act that is intended to ensure that recording artists', record producers' and others' contributions to masters constitute works made for hire. However, this amendment to the Copyright Act has come under fire from recording artists, record producers and their representatives, and is currently the subject of much debate.

If the producer will write all or part of any of the musical compositions embodied in the masters, those musical compositions should be specifically excluded from the provisions of paragraph 2. The agreement would also contain a provision (that is often referred to as a "controlled composition clause") that requires the producer to grant a reduced rate mechanical license, giving the record company the right to reproduce the compositions on records (in all configurations) in exchange for payment to the producer/songwriter of mechanical royalties at 75% of the minimum statutory rate on a specified date (which could be the date of the commencement of recording, the date of delivery of the master to the record company or the date of initial commercial release in the United States of the master–the later the date the better for the producer because the mechanical royalty rate has tended to increase every few years and a later date may wind up occurring after an increase in the rate). The producer's attorney should attempt to revise this provision to provide for payment of mechanical royalties based on 100% of the minimum statutory rate in the United States (as of January 1, 2000 that rate is 7.55¢ for each record sold that embodies one use of a musical composition that is five minutes or less in length); however, many record companies refuse to negotiate on this issue unless the producer has some clout. This provision may also contain a requirement that the producer/songwriter issue a free "synchronization license" to the record company. A synchronization license is an agreement that grants the right to synchronize, or use a musical composition in the soundtrack of an audiovisual work (e.g., a music video or television program). The producer should only be required to grant a free synchronization license for MTV-type free promotional videos. The terms that relate to the licensing of musical compositions, written by a producer, can be very complex. Accordingly, those terms should be reviewed very carefully by the producer and his or her attorney. Also, if the producer has assigned to a music publisher rights to musical compositions that he or she writes, the producer or the producer's attorney should make certain that the controlled composition clause is provided to the producer's music publisher so that the publisher can review, comment on and approve the clause before the producer signs the producer agreement.

3. You hereby grant to us and our designees the worldwide right in perpetuity to use and to permit others to use, at no cost, your name, likeness and biographical material concerning you in connection with any and all phonograph records and other reproductions made from the Master(s), the advertising in connection therewith and institutional advertising. We shall accord you appropriate production credit on the jackets, labels or liner notes of all records embodying the Master(s), which you agree may be in substantially the following form: "Produced by ____________________." Any failure to comply with the provisions of this paragraph shall not be a breach of this Agreement. Your sole right and remedy in that event shall be to notify us of that failure, after which we shall use reasonable efforts to accord that production credit to you on records manufactured after the date we receive that notice.

The producer should have a right of approval over all photographs, likenesses and biographical material concerning him or her that are used under this paragraph. "Institutional advertising" should be limited to the record company's institutional advertising. Producer credit should be placed on all record labels and on jackets or liner notes on all records in all configurations (including compact disc and tape packaging). The producer should receive credit in all one-half page or larger trade and consumer advertisements featuring a master produced by the producer. The producer's attorney should attempt to obtain a provision relating to credit so that the producer's credit will be of similar size and placement as any other producer's credit on the album and will appear in advertising relating to the album if another producer is credited (unless the advertisement features a master that is produced by another producer). The agreement should state that the credit will be in the following form: "____________," not "may be in substantially the following form."

The failure to provide the credit should not be a material breach of the agreement provided that the record company and/or artist use their best efforts to cure the failure on records (in all configurations) manufactured after receipt of the notice of the failure from the producer and in advertisements authorized after the receipt of such notice.

4. In full consideration for your entering into and executing this Agreement and your fulfilling all of your obligations hereunder, you shall be paid ____________ Dollars ($__________), payable one-half (1/2) promptly after the later of the execution of this Agreement or the commencement of recording sessions for the Master(s) and one-half (1/2) promptly after the later of the completion and delivery to us of all Master(s) or our determination of the aggregate costs to record the Master(s). Those monies payable to you shall be an advance recoupable from royalties earned by you hereunder.

The producer's attorney may wish to delete the word "full" in the first sentence since the possibility of the producer receiving royalties under the agreement is also consideration to the producer. ("Consideration" is a legal concept that requires that in order for a contract to be binding upon the parties, one party must give or do something of value in exchange for receiving something of value from the other party.) Additionally, the word "material" should be added before the word "obligations" because the producer should still receive his or her advance even if there is some kind of failure to fulfill a minor, nonmaterial obligation under the agreement. The agreement should specify that the advance is nonreturnable once it is paid.

The amount of the advance is based upon the experience and reputation of the producer. As the status and role of the record producer has expanded over the last several years, it has become more difficult to provide generalizations about the level of advances that a producer should receive. Accordingly, any discussion of the amount of advance payments to producers needs to include a disclaimer that each situation is different and the actual advances that a producer may obtain will be influenced by a number of factors. The advance for a single master could range from a few thousand dollars to $15,000, $20,000 or more. Of course, there are always exceptions (both at the high end and the low end), including certain superstar producers who receive very significantly higher advances. The amount of the producer's advance can depend on both the producer's status and the status of the artist. The advances paid by independent labels are generally smaller than the advances paid by major labels. Also, the advances paid in connection with certain genres of music (for example, traditional jazz) can be significantly less than other genres (such as pop). As mentioned previously, this agreement presents the situation where the record company pays the recording costs and pays a separate advance to the producer.

In the all-in advance situation, the producer would receive a sum of money from which the recording costs would be paid and any remaining monies would be retained by the producer. This works best for a producer who has his or her own studio and can keep recording costs down. But, in this case, the producer may have a real need to obtain the advance monies more quickly than as set forth in this agreement. One method of payment of the all-in advance could be 50% upon the commencement of recording, 25% upon the producer's delivery of a rough mix of the master, and 25% upon delivery of the completed master. An all-in advance for producing a master for a new rock artist on a major label could be $20,000 to $25,000 (or more). A more established producer producing a master for a more established rock artist might receive an all-in advance of $40,000 or $50,000 (or more). Again, bear in mind that the actual numbers could vary widely from the numbers presented here. The amount of the recording fund available to the artist from the record company will have a strong impact on the amount of the advance available to the producer (whether the producer's advance is an all-in advance or not).

The producer's attorney should try to limit the time that the artist or the record company has to determine the aggregate costs to record the masters to no more than 30 days after delivery. I am aware of at least one situation where a record was released and on the charts for several months and the record company's attorney still claimed that the recording costs had not yet been determined, notwithstanding the fact that all recording was conducted in the artist's own studio.

5. Conditioned upon your full and faithful performance of all the terms hereof, you shall be paid a royalty on reproductions and exploitations of the Master(s) at the following rates in accordance with the following terms:

The word "material" should be inserted before the word "terms" in the first sentence of this paragraph. The producer should request to be paid directly from the record company rather than from the artist. The artist should sign a letter of direction to that effect, which would be attached to the agreement as an exhibit.

(a) (i) On sales of full-priced, top-line long-playing phonograph records embodying solely Master(s) (in the form of conventional vinyl-discs and cassette tapes), which are sold through normal retail distribution channels in the United States ("Base Rate") of ____________ percent (___%) of the suggested retail list price ("SRLP") of those Base Rate Records (or the equivalent). Your Base Rate on Base Rate Records shall be prorated, calculated, adjusted and paid on the same percentage of net sales of Base Rate Records as Artist's royalty rate on sales of Base Rate Records is prorated, calculated, adjusted and paid under the recording agreement between us and Artist ("Artist Agreement"). On sales in and outside of the United States of all records other than Base Rate Records, you shall be paid a royalty at a rate equal to the Base Rate but which is prorated, calculated, proportionately reduced, adjusted and paid on the same percentage of net sales as Artist's base royalty rate on sales of Base Rate Records is prorated, calculated, proportionately reduced, adjusted and paid under the Artist Agreement; and

A producer royalty rate generally ranges between 3% and 4% of the suggested retail list price of Base Rate Records (as defined in the producer agreement), with top producers receiving 5%. If two producers coproduce a master they might each receive a royalty at the rate of 1.5% or 2% of the retail price of records embodying the master. If the artist's royalty is computed on the basis of the wholesale price of records, rather than the retail price, then the producer's royalty would be computed based on the wholesale price of records. In that event, the producer's royalty rate would be approximately double (e.g., approximately 6% of wholesale rather than 3% of retail). Many producers receive increased royalties if the record they produce sells a certain number of units. A typical royalty rate structure is a 3% of retail royalty rate escalating to 3.5% on sales in excess of 500,000 units and escalating to 4% on sales in excess of 1,000,000 units.

The producer's royalty is generally paid on the same basis as the artist's. In the situation where the artist has a recording agreement with a production company and the production company has an agreement with the record company whereby it agrees to provide the artist's services to the record company, the producer's attorney should attempt to have the producer's royalty paid on the same basis as the production company's. Note that this agreement states that the producer's royalty is to be prorated on the same basis as the artist's royaltyóthis is not technically correct: the producer's royalty is prorated based on the number of masters produced by the producer that are on the particular record, and the artist's royalty is prorated based upon the number of masters recorded by the artist on the record. For example, if the producer produced five of 10 masters on Artist A's most recent album and the producer's basic royalty rate was 3% of the retail price of records comprised entirely of masters produced by the producer, the producer's royalty on Artist A's album would be reduced from 3% to 1.5% because the producer only produced half of the masters. The artist's royalty rate would not be reduced in this fashion since the entire album was comprised of masters embodying the artist's performance.

Many established producers obtain a special exception to one of the proration provisions in their producer agreements. This is known as "A-side protection" and it applies only to singles where the A-side is produced by one producer and the B-side is produced by another. When a producer who does not have A-side protection produces only the A-side of a single, that producer's royalty rate is cut in half. The producer with A-side protection does not receive this royalty rate reduction on singles where that producer's master appears on only the A-side, because the vast majority of people who buy a single do so because of the A-side. Since few people buy a single for the B-side, the theory is that the royalty of the producer of the A-side should not be reduced because of the B-side. In most instances, the producer of the B-side of a single would still be entitled to a prorated royalty on the B-side of the single, even if the producer of the A-side of the single has A-side protection.

(ii) On exploitations of the Master(s) for which Artist is paid a percentage of our net royalty or net flat fees under the Artist Agreement, you shall be paid a royalty equal to _____________ percent (______%) of our net flat fees or net royalties on such exploitations. On exploitations of the Master(s) embodied in audiovisual devices (such as videodiscs and videocassettes), however, you shall be paid a royalty equal to _________ percent (______%) of our net flat fees or net royalties on those exploitations;

When the artist is paid based on a percentage of the record company's net royalty or net flat fee, then the producer should be paid a percentage of the amount received by the artist computed by dividing the producer's basic royalty rate (without regard to escalations) by the artist's basic all-in royalty rate (without regard to escalations). For example, if the producer's basic royalty rate is 3% of retail and the artist's basic all-in royalty rate is 12% of retail, the producer would receive 25% of any monies that the artist received as a percentage of the record company's net royalties or net flat fees. On net receipts from the exploitation of audiovisual devices, the producer would generally receive 50% of the otherwise applicable net receipts royalty.

Thus, in the foregoing example, the producer would receive 12.5% (rather than 25%) of the monies the artist received from the record company for the exploitation of audiovisual devices. Again, if the artist is signed to a production company instead of directly to the record company, the producer's attorney should attempt to have the producer's royalty calculated based upon the royalties payable by the record company to the production company rather than on the royalties payable from the production company to the artist; however, the producer's attorney should be aware that this may be a difficult concession to obtain.

In any event, subparagraphs 5(a)(i) and 5(a)(ii) make it clear that in order to know what royalties may be payable on a particular project, the producer must know the royalty provisions of the artist's recording agreement. Accordingly, a copy of the royalty provisions relating to the applicable album and the definitions provisions of the artist's (or, if applicable, the production company's) recording agreement should be attached, as an exhibit, to the producer agreement.

(b) Your royalty rate on records and other devices embodying Master(s) and other master recording shall be the otherwise applicable royalty rate multiplied by a fraction, the numerator of which is the number of Master(s) embodied in that record or other device and the denominator of which is the total number of master recordings (including Master[s]) embodied in the record or other device;

This paragraph sets forth the appropriate proration of the producer's royalty. The words "royalty-bearing" should be inserted after the words "total number of" towards the end of the sentence.

(c) Your royalty rates hereunder shall not be increased due to increases in Artist's royalty rates under the Artist Agreement based on record sales; and

The producer does not generally share in sales escalations received by the artist; however, as discussed in subparagraph 5(a)(i), the producer or the producer's attorney can sometimes negotiate for escalations based on sales, which would be separate from the sales escalations received by the artist.

(d) Your royalties hereunder shall be reduced by the royalties payable by us for the services of any other person to produce or complete the production of the Master(s) until they are satisfactory to us.

The producer's attorney should request that the producer be accorded the first opportunity to do any mixing, remixing, editing or other material altering of the masters produced by the producer. If any other person performs these services, the producer should have the right, at the producer's sole discretion, to remove his or her name from the master. Also, if another person is engaged to perform production work on the master, the producer's royalty should not be reduced unless the producer is in material breach of the agreement. The producer's attorney should require that if a mixer is engaged to mix the masters, the artist or the record company should bear any royalties payable to the mixer. If the producer's attorney is not able to obtain this protection for his or her client, the producer should not have to bear more than one-third, or at most one-half, of the royalty payable to the mixer (but as noted above, the best situation would be for the producer to not have to bear any portion of the royalty payable to a mixer).

6. No royalties shall be credited to your account hereunder unless and until the aggregate of recording costs of the Master(s) and advances and fees payable to you for the Master(s) are recouped from royalties on reproductions and exploitations of the Master(s) at the "Net Artist Royalty Rate." The term Net Artist Royalty Rate shall mean the aggregate royalty rate payable to Artist and the producers on reproductions of the Master(s), less the aggregate royalty rate payable to the producers on reproductions and exploitations of the Master(s). After that recoupment, your royalty account shall be credited with royalties earned by your hereunder on all exploitations of the Master(s)

retroactive to the first record sold. We shall account for and pay royalties earned by you hereunder within ninety (90) days after the end of each of our then-current six-month accounting periods, currently ending on June 30 and December 31. Accountings and statements for royalties earned by you on reproductions and exploitations of the Master(s) shall be based upon our receipt in the United States of an accounting and payment or final credit for the actual reproductions and exploitations of the Master(s) in the accounting period for which a statement is rendered. We shall have no obligation to account for or pay to you any royalties unless and until we receive in the United States an accounting for and payment of or final credit for royalties on actual reproductions and other exploitations of the Master(s). All statements and accountings rendered to you shall be binding and not subject to any examination, audit or objection for any reason unless you shall notify us in writing of your specific objection thereto within one (1) year after the date the statement is rendered or was to be rendered. No action, suit or proceeding regarding any royalty statement or accounting rendered to you may be maintained by or on behalf of you unless commenced in court within one (1) year after the date the statement is rendered or was to be rendered. We may deduct from any amounts payable to you hereunder that portion hereof required to be deducted under any statute, regulation, treaty or other law, or under any union or guild agreement.

The first three sentences of this paragraph deal with recoupment of the recording costs and the producer advance and fees. The producer will not receive royalties until the recording costs incurred by the record company and the artist and all advances and fees paid to the producer in connection with the masters produced by that producer are recouped from royalties earned at the Net Artist Royalty Rate (i.e., the artist's royalty rate minus the producer's royalty rate) from sales of records embodying the masters produced by the producer. The producer's attorney should attempt to exclude any advances or fees to the artist from the recording costs for the purposes of determining recoupment by the producer. Furthermore, the advances to the producer should be excluded as well since paragraph 4 states that the advance to the producer will be recouped from royalties payable to the producer. A failure to exclude the producer advance from this provision may result in double recoupment of the producer advance and, accordingly, may delay (or prevent) the producer's receipt of royalties.

Once the appropriate costs are recouped at the Net Artist Royalty Rate, the producer's royalty account is credited with all royalties earned from the first record that was sold. These royalties will be paid to the producer after deduction of the producer's advance. This provision is favorable to the producer. The artist receives royalties "prospectively" after recoupment of all recording costs for the album at the artist's all-in rate. This means that if the appropriate costs are recouped after sales of 200,000 units, the artist will receive royalties for the 200,001st unit and future units sold, as long as the artist's royalty account remains in a recouped position; however, the artist will not receive any royalties on the first 200,000 units sold prior to recoupment.

If the producer is entitled to receive royalties "retroactively from the first record sold" and the costs chargeable against the producer's account are recouped after sales of 100,000 units, the producer's account would be credited with the producer's royalty on units one through 100,000 and these royalties would be paid to the producer after deduction of the advance previously paid to the producer. The producer would then be paid royalties on all sales in excess of 100,000 units. In some cases the producer agreement specifies that the producer is only to be paid royalties prospectively after recoupment of the recording costs. In that event, the producer's attorney should request that the producer be paid retroactively from the first record sold after recoupment of the appropriate costs at the Net Artist Royalty Rate. This is an important deal point that should not be overlooked in any producer agreement.

The producer should be paid directly from the record company. Accounting statements and any royalty payments that may be due should be sent to the producer at the same time that accounting statements are sent to the artist. If the record company fails or refuses to send accounting statements directly to the producer, the artist should be required to send such statements and any royalty payments that are due within 30 days after the artist receives them. The producer should have a minimum of two years after the date a statement is rendered (delete "or was to be rendered") to audit the artist or record company and to object to that statement, and two and one-half to three years from the date the statement was rendered in which to file a lawsuit based on that statement.

7. You warrant, represent, covenant and agree as follows:

(a) You have the right and power to enter into this agreement, to grant the rights granted by you to us hereunder and to perform all the terms hereof; and

(b) No materials, ideas or other properties furnished or designated by you and used in connection with the Master(s) will violate or infringe upon the rights of any person, firm or corporation.

This is a standard provision in producer agreements. Subparagraph 7(b) should be limited to elements "furnished" by the producer, not "designated" by the producer. The producer's attorney should require a warranty from the artist or record company be included in the agreement similar to subparagraph 7(b) stating that all elements not furnished by the producer will not violate or infringe on the rights of others.

8. You hereby indemnify, save and hold us and any person, firm or corporation deriving rights from us harmless from any and all damages, liability and costs (including legal costs and attorneys' fees) arising out of or in connection with any claim, demand or action by us or by any third party that is inconsistent with any of the warranties, representations, covenants or agreements made by you in this Agreement. You shall reimburse us, on demand, for any loss, cost, expense or damage to which the foregoing indemnity applies. Pending the disposition of any claim, demand or action to which the foregoing indemnity applies, we shall have the right to withhold payment of any monies payable to you hereunder and under any other agreement between you and us or our affiliates.

This paragraph is called an indemnity provision. If the artist or record company is sued (or sues the producer) based on any facts (or purported facts) that are inconsistent with any of the promises made by the producer in the producer agreement, the record company and/or artist could look to the producer to pay all costs incurred in connection with that lawsuit or claim.

The producer's attorney should limit the producer's indemnity of the artist and record company to claims reduced to final judgment by a court of competent jurisdiction or to settlements with the producer's consent. The word "reasonable" should be inserted before the words "attorneys' fees" in the first sentence of this paragraph. This provision should also state that monies will not be withheld in an amount exceeding the producer's probable liability under the producer agreement, would be held in an interest bearing account, and would be released if no action was taken on the claim during a one-year period. The following phrase at the end of the paragraph should be deleted: "and under any other agreement between you and us or our affiliates." The artist or record company should indemnify the producer with respect to materials not furnished by the producer to the same extent that the producer indemnifies the artist or record company pursuant to this paragraph.

9. The respective addresses of you and us for all purposes hereunder are set forth on page 1 hereof, unless and until notice of a different address is received by the party notified of that different address. All notices shall be in writing and shall either be served by certified mail return receipt requested or by telex, in each case with all charges prepaid. Notices shall be deemed effective when mailed or sent by telex, all charges prepaid, except for notices of a change of address, which shall be effective only when received by the party notified. A copy of each notice to us shall be sent to: ______________________________ (Attorney's name and address).

This is a standard provision. If the producer is represented by an attorney, the attorney should receive a copy of any notice sent to the producer so that the attorney can advise the producer whether any action needs to be taken on any notices received by the producer.

10. We may, at our election, assign this Agreement or any of our rights hereunder or delegate any of our obligations hereunder, in whole or in part, to any person, firm or corporation. You may not delegate any of your obligations hereunder.

The record company's right to assign its rights or obligations under the producer agreement should be limited to a person, firm or corporation that acquires all or substantially all of its stock or assets. If the agreement is with the artist, the artist's right to assign his or her rights under the agreement should be limited to assigning it to the record company. Any assignment by the artist or record company should not relieve them of liability for their obligations to the producer under the producer agreement.

11. During the Term and for three (3) years thereafter, you shall not produce or coproduce any recording for any person, firm or corporation oher than us embodying, in whole or in part, the musical selections recorded in the Master(s).

This provision is called a rerecording restriction. The restriction period should be reduced from three years to two.

12. You acknowledge and agree that your services hereunder are of a special, unique, intellectual and extraordinary character which gives them peculiar value, and that if you breach any term hereof, we will be caused irreparable injury which cannot adequately be compensated by money damages.

This language assists the artist and/or record company in obtaining an injunction against the producer should the producer engage in activities that violate the terms of the producer agreement. An injunction is a court order that demands that an individual or firm stop doing something. An injunction could prevent the producer from working for someone else. Since issuing an injunction is such a drastic action, a court will not issue an injunction in the situation where a person is rendering personal services unless there is a showing that the person's services are unique and that the injured party would not be made whole by the payment of money. The language contained in paragraph 12 is almost always found in the artist's recording agreement, but is not as common in a producer agreement. The producer's attorney should attempt to delete the paragraph or, at a minimum, insert the word "material" before the word "term" and substitute the word "may" for "will" and the words "may not" for the word "cannot."

13. (a) This document sets forth the entire agreement between you and us with respect to the subject matter hereof and may not be modified except by a written agreement signed by the party sought to be bound. Except as expressly provided herein to the contrary, you are performing your obligations hereunder as an independent contractor;

(b) In the event of any action, suit or proceeding arising from or based upon this Agreement brought by either party hereto against the other, the prevailing party shall be entitled to recover from the other its attorneys' fees in connection therewith in addition to the costs of that action, suit or proceeding;

(c) The validity, construction, interpretation and legal effect of this Agreement shall be governed by the laws of the State of California;

(d) Nothing contained in this Agreement or otherwise shall obligate us or any other person, firm or corporation to reproduce or exploit the Master(s) in any manner or media;

These provisions are all very standard. In subparagraph 13(b), the word "reasonable" should be inserted before the words "attorneys' fees."

(e) We may terminate the Term for any reason, with or without cause, on the date of our notice to you terminating the Term;

This subparagraph should be deleted. If the subparagraph is not deleted it should be limited to the situation in which the producer is in material breach of the producer agreement and has failed to cure that breach within 30 days after the artist or record company provides written notice to the producer of that breach. In any event, the producer should receive the advances and royalties that he or she is otherwise entitled to under the agreement.

(f) We shall not be in breach of any of our obligations under this Agreement unless and until you notify us in writing in detail of our breach or alleged breach and we fail to cure that breach or alleged breach within thirty (30) days after our receipt of that notice from you; and

This subparagraph should be made mutual (i.e., the artist or record company should have to provide notice and a 30-day cure period to the producer prior to the producer

being placed in breach of the agreement). The cure period for the artist or record company should be reduced to 15 days if the artist or record company fails to pay any monies owing to the producer.

(g) You have been represented by independent counsel or have had the unrestricted opportunity to be represented by independent counsel of your choice for purposes of advising you in connection with the negotiation and execution of this Agreement. If you have not been represented by independent legal counsel of your choice in connection with this Agreement, you acknowledge and agree that your failure to be represented by independent legal counsel in connection with this Agreement was determined solely by you.

This paragraph is a standard provision in producer agreements. Due to the complexity of the issues involved in the negotiation of a producer agreement, the producer is advised to seek an attorney's advice in the negotiation and execution of any agreement.

If the foregoing sets forth your understanding and agreement with us, please so indicate by signing in the space provided below.
Very truly yours,

AGREED TO AND ACCEPTED:

______________________________	______________________________
BY:	BY:
______________________________	______________________________
FEDERAL I.D./SS#:	FEDERAL I.D./SS#:

Recording and Distribution Contracts with Independent Labels

BY EDWARD (NED) R. HEARN

An alternative to seeking a major label recording contract or raising funds to produce your own recording is to approach independent record companies. Many independent record labels have become very successful in reaching and developing niche markets. By researching these labels, you may find one that successfully markets music that fits your style and is interested in producing, manufacturing and distributing your record. Some of these independent labels have been very successful and have become subsidiaries to major recording labels, such as GRP (Universal), Narada and Higher Octave (Virgin/EMI), Tommy Boy (Warner Bros.) and Windham Hill/Private Music (BMG), or have developed affiliations with major label branch distribution, such as Rounder Records.

SMALL LABEL ADVANTAGES

The chief advantages of releasing your album with independent record labels are similar to the reasons for signing with major labels. They generally have a distribution mechanism in place. They are organized to handle the time and costs of financing and administering the production, manufacture, marketing and distribution of records. They can better absorb the financial risks and have more leverage in collecting money from the wholesalers and retailers of records. In addition, the company may have developed a reputation in the music community for a certain style of music and can move a great volume of records in a wide geographical territory.

Bear in mind, however, that if a small label invests time and money in your career and is successful in generating a reasonable level of income for you, you should carefully weigh the benefits of signing with a major label if asked (where you probably will be one of many)—against staying with the smaller one (where you may be the star!). Far too often, the benefits of a smaller label are discovered only after an unhappy relationship with a major recording label occurs. Much depends on the style of music involved, for example, pop and rock may get more attention from a major label than music aimed at more narrow and focused audiences, such as jazz, new age, children's music, or Yiddish folk songs. Both small and large labels have demonstrated effectiveness at marketing heavy metal, dance, hip-hop and rap music.

CONTRACTS

Although contracts with independent labels can be very similar to those negotiated with major labels, smaller independent companies sometimes work out arrangements that do not mirror these standards. These companies may be willing to step away from obtuse and confusing language to create a contract in plain English that is balanced between the interests of the record company and those of the artist to more equitably share the economic benefits realized from the skills and talents of the artist and the business expertise and mechanisms of the recording company. Sadly, however, smaller labels are increasingly reflecting the contractual style and approach of the major labels, perhaps because of the investment costs and financial risks incurred in developing an artist and the desire to be secure that the contract with the artist is sufficiently strong so that a larger label will not be in a position to tempt the artist to switch labels without the smaller label participating in the benefits of that switch. Many smaller labels also insist on participating in some or all of the music publishing of the artist. That is an issue that needs to be carefully examined, and if it occurs should be the subject of a separate deal.

Here are some options not usually available to musicians signing with major labels:

Distribution Deals

In this type of deal, you deliver an agreed amount of packaged cassettes or compact discs to a record company. Some labels only distribute product, while you do the marketing and promotion; others do everything.

In a distribution only deal, the record label will either contract directly with stores or deal with networks of independent distributors or both, selling to them at wholesale prices.

If the company only distributes your record, you will receive a sum equivalent to the wholesale price, minus a fee of 20% to 30% and other direct expenses that you authorize the company to spend, but you pay for all the manufacturing costs and all associated marketing and promotion costs. A standard contractual agreement is that you will receive money only on records actually sold and paid for.

These types of deals often result after bands release recordings for a regional audience, find themselves with growing popularity, and use the added leverage to make a deal that will broaden their audiences.

Unlike major recording labels, independent labels sometimes encourage the sale of records, cassettes or compact discs at performances or to fan mailing lists. In this case, a clause can be added to the standard recording contract that will state that the musician can buy product at a low wholesale price. This inventory may be provided as an "advance" against the royalties or other fees that will be owing. This practice is actively discouraged by most major recording labels.

Pressing and Distribution (P&D) Deals

In P&D deals, you deliver a fully mixed recording master and artwork to the record label, which then assumes the responsibility of manufacturing and distributing your records, cassettes or compact discs. If the label advances the manufacturing costs, it will reimburse itself out of the sales proceeds of your recordings, plus, perhaps, some value for the use of its money, in addition to the distribution fee.

If the record label also picks up promotion, publicity and marketing, then the deal is usually structured as a royalty deal that will leave the record label with a sufficient margin to cover all of its costs and make a reasonable profit. The royalty is sometimes higher than in standard recording contracts because you have already invested the costs of recording and producing. That is not always the case, however. When negotiating this type of deal, ask that any royalty percentages be specified as net cents per unit for each configuration.

As an alternative, if marketing and promotional duties are involved, these expenses could be deducted as direct costs also, along with the distribution fee and manufacturing costs, with the balance paid to you, but more likely the deal will be structured on a royalty basis, with a royalty of anywhere from 10% to 18% of retail, plus mechanical royalties on the music.

Production Deals

In this type of deal, you sign as an artist with a production company. The company is responsible for recording your music and for obtaining distribution through independent distributors or a record company. In many cases, contracts for these deals are structured similarly to record contracts because the production company will typically make a pressing and distribution deal with a record label that also includes marketing and promotion and then contract with you for a percentage of the royalty paid to it by the record company.

For example, a production company may have a deal with a record company that pays 14% to 18% of the retail selling price on records sold, depending in part on whether the recording costs are paid by the production company or advanced by the record company. The production company might then have contracted with the artist to pay a royalty from between 6% and 10% of the retail selling price or 50% to 60% of the royalty paid to the production company by the record company.

Contracts and Relationships Between Independent Labels and Major Labels

BY BARTLEY F. DAY AND CHRISTOPHER KNAB

Record companies come in all sizes and shapes. Major labels usually focus on the most popular forms of contemporary music. Independent labels, though not always small, are typically more concerned with developing new styles of contemporary music or specializing in certain niche genres.

Over the years, various kinds of relationships and contracts between major and independent labels have evolved that play an enormous role in how the industry operates. There are now more synergies between labels than ever before. To understand why this is so, it is important to consider some recent trends in the recording industry.

First, there has been a dramatic decline of "artist development" at major labels.

Artist development refers to any and all support tactics and strategies labels use to enhance the performance and marketability of musical acts. For example, songwriting skills may need to be improved, or the onstage presence and the overall images of acts may need enhancement. Artist development deals with the slow and gradual building of strong and loyal fan bases that buy the CDs, tapes and downloadable songs labels release.

Until the late 1980s, artist development was a well-established practice at major and independent labels alike. But, by the early 1990s, Wall Street had become more aware of the rapid growth in recording sales, and major labels increasingly became subsidiaries of huge publicly traded corporate conglomerates. With that came increasing pressure on the major labels from their parent companies to perform quickly and return greater profits. Consequently, artist development, a process requiring substantial investment and a long-term view, quickly fell into disfavor. Artists whose first or second albums showed slow sales were dropped. The major labels began looking for talent whose recordings were already selling before giving them a shot at the big time. Even then, if those acts did not catch on quickly, they too were dropped.

Today, artist development is largely the domain of independent labels, and major labels increasingly depend on them for essential artist development work.

By the same token, independent labels that want their artists promoted to the mass audience, need certain things that major labels can provide. In recent years, the parent companies of many major labels have consolidated their control of the mass media (including radio, television, as well as the music publications and lifestyle publications that expose music to the public). In addition, major labels have long-established distribution systems and have gradually formed alliances with, or have bought outright, some of the key independent record distribution companies. As a result, independent labels have fewer independent distribution options, and have become more reliant on the distribution systems established by the major labels. Independent labels that wish to gain ready access to those media and distribution outlets must form some kind of alliance with a major label.

In short, the major labels and the independent labels today rely more on each other than ever before. Independent labels benefit from the strong ties to media exposure and distribution that major label affiliation provides. The major labels need independent labels, because they find and champion most new trends in popular music and do the bulk of the artist development work.

What does it take for an independent label to be able to enter into some kind of relationship with a major label? Unless the independent label has been started by an established "player" in the music business (for example, one who was previously a highly placed executive at a major label, or a well-known producer), it must first demonstrate a successful track record of artist development and significant sales.

Summarized below, are the main kinds of deals and business relationships that exist today between independent and major labels. An understanding of the various possible relationships with major labels, and the advantages and disadvantages of each, can help an independent label determine the best strategy for attaining its long-term objectives. And for those independent labels presently being courted by one or more major labels, an understanding of the ramifications of the various types of relationships can enable them to negotiate more knowledgeably and effectively.

ADVANTAGES AND DISADVANTAGES OF MAJOR LABEL AFFILIATION

There are numerous potential advantages and disadvantages of affiliating with a major label. Some of the main advantages are as follows:

- Major label affiliation may enable an independent label to increase its artists' exposure in commercial media and expand its distribution networks by increasing its access to major retail record chain stores and rack jobbers.

- It can provide an independent label with a substantial cash infusion, eliminating the need to continually focus on day-to-day survival issues and allowing more effective operation. The major label may also take on manufacturing and promotion.

- Affiliation may permit an independent label to expand and upgrade its artist roster, or enter a mainstream genre where developmental and promotional costs are much higher than for niche market music.

- Affiliation increases the likelihood of the independent actually getting paid for recordings sold.

The potential disadvantages of affiliating with a major label are as follows:

- An association with a major label makes the independent label vulnerable to events completely out of its control, such as internal corporate power struggles and firings at the major label, and corporate mergers.

- If an independent label has several independent distributors, it can likely survive a late payment or lack of cooperation from one or two of its distributors. But, if distribution is through a single major distributor, the lack of payment or cooperation can be seriously damaging.

- There can be a high degree of bureaucracy in major labels. This may impact an independent label's ability to sign an artist quickly enough when other labels are interested, or it may impact the independent label's ability to get a promising recording into distribution quickly enough to fully capitalize on a particular trend.

ISSUES TO CONSIDER

When an independent label is considering an affiliation with a major label, there are many issues to consider. Here are some specific questions that will help to focus research and analysis:

- What are the independent label's present sales volumes and what are they likely to be in the next few years (i.e., with major label affiliation versus without)?

- Will the major label effectively distribute to the mom-and-pop stores that carry the independent label?

- What are the major label's strategies for developing its online retailing and distribution capabilities, and for taking advantage of Web marketing opportunities? Are the major label's philosophies and attitudes toward the Internet compatible with the independent label's? Will the independent label's existing deals with online distributors and retailers be violated by the terms of the deal between it and the major label?

- Will the major label be responsive to regional demands and the demands of niche markets?

- What kind of reputation and support does the independent label have among its fans? Will a major label affiliation jeopardize this? Will the independent label's core fans be best served by the major label's distribution system?

- Will an affiliation with a major label create an unhealthy pressure on the independent label to sell more recordings than it can comfortably or realistically sell?

- What is the present financial status of the independent label and what is its access to additional resources without major label affiliation?

- Assuming affiliation, what will the cash infusion (if any) be used for?

- How can the independent label's existing staff—promotion, marketing and administrative—be best utilized after affiliation?

- How will the long-term business objectives of the independent label be served by affiliating with a major label?

- Do the owners of the independent label really want the responsibilities and financial burdens of operating a fully-staffed record company and overseeing the promotion and marketing of recordings? Or are they only interested in the creative process of signing artists and producing recordings?

- What is the personal style of the independent label's owner(s)? Do they place a high value on being able to operate independently? Are they willing to take input and direction from a large corporate entity?

- What is the major label's real motivation for entering into the relationship? Is it to use the independent label as an "indie front," or to take over the label's strongest artists? Or does it view the relationship as a mutually beneficial long-term strategic alliance?

- Will a relationship with a major label serve the best interests of the independent label's artists? (Often, a major label will not have the same degree of commitment to the independent label's artists.)

- What is the corporate style of the major label's management? Is there sound long-term vision?

- Is there good personal chemistry between the managers of the major label and the independent label?

TYPES OF DEALS

There are numerous types of deals between independent and major labels, the most common of which are as follows: (1) pressing and distribution (P&D) deals; (2) multi-tiered pressing and distribution deals; (3) distribution only deals; (4) fulfillment deals; (5) piggyback deals; (6) production deals; (7) joint ventures; (8) equity deals; (9) the licensing of recordings by independent labels to major labels (licensing out); (10) the licensing of recordings by independent labels from major labels (licensing in); and (11) rights buyouts.

The type of contract offered by a major label, its specific terms, and the degree of flexibility in the major label's bargaining position, are dictated by the extent to which the independent label has strong artists, a healthy and ever-improving sales record, and the confidence of the major label in the independent's key personnel. There are a number of independent labels that resisted the repeated entreaties of major labels until they achieved sufficient bargaining power to obtain acceptable terms.

Be aware that there may be several types of deals in place at any given time between a particular major label and a particular independent label. For example, an independent label might have a joint venture agreement with a major label for certain artists, and a distribution agreement for other artists. Or the independent label might have agreements with several major labels, each covering a particular artist or territory.

These multifaceted situations most often occur when an independent label has savvy and experienced management that structures its relationships with major labels in the most advantageous and strategic way.

Whenever an independent label plans to have multiple agreements in effect with various other labels at the same time, it must ensure that its obligations under one contract do not conflict with the terms of any of the other contracts. Otherwise, it will face the ongoing risk of litigation from one or more of those labels, based on claims that the independent label has breached its contractual obligations.

PRELIMINARY CONSIDERATIONS

Before entering into a contract with a major label, it must first be determined whether such arrangements are permissible under the terms of the independent label's existing recording contracts with its artists. Do the contracts limit or prohibit assignment of artists' rights to the major label? Are there clauses that entitle artists to review, or reject, any affiliation?

Even if there is no contractual limitation on the assignment of rights, the independent label should find out how its artists feel about major label affiliation. Some artists perceive it as a wonderful windfall, while others view it as an abandonment of principles. Such considerations should be addressed prior to entering into any contracts.

The independent label should also examine its existing royalty and other obligations to its artists, to determine whether the terms offered by the major label make economic sense.

Listed below are the various types of deals between major and independent labels, and the essential features of such deals.

PRESSING AND DISTRIBUTION (P&D) DEAL

In the typical P&D deal, the independent label signs recording artists to recording contracts, produces the recordings and the graphics, and delivers the master to the major label. The independent label is financially responsible for these tasks.

The major label then presses the recordings and distributes them through its distribution system. After recordings are sold, the major label deducts its pressing costs and a distribution fee from the monies it receives from its distributors and pays the balance to the independent label. The independent label is responsible for handling (and paying for) all advertising, promotion and publicity, including exposure in commercial and noncommercial media.

P&D deals used to be the most common kind of deal between independent and major labels. However, major labels often found themselves involved with numerous independents, each one selling only small numbers of recordings.

Major labels concluded that it was not worth clogging their distribution pipelines with low-selling recordings merely to receive a distribution fee. Therefore, P&D deals are now less common than they were. Today the relationship is more likely to involve a joint venture or equity deal, or the licensing of the independent label's recordings, because these types of deals are potentially more profitable for the major labels.

Even so, an independent label in strong financial condition with high sales volumes may still be able to secure a P&D deal.

Artistic Control

The independent label usually retains control over the content of songs, the design and copy of artwork, and the content of promotional and advertising materials. However, the major label may require a right to screen content for any extreme language.

Ownership of Masters

Typically, the independent label retains ownership of master recordings. However, the major label will have the right to use those masters as collateral for the financial obligations of the independent to the major label. The major label is entitled to be reimbursed its manufacturing costs from the income generated by its sales of the independent label's recordings. But sometimes those recordings do not sell in sufficient quantities to do this. In anticipation of this possibility, P&D contracts generally grant to the major label a security interest in the independent's masters, and in the recordings manufactured.

Bonds and Letters of Credit

As an additional means of assuring that it will be fully paid for its manufacturing costs, a major label often requires that the independent provide a bond or letter of credit from a financial institution.

Exclusivity

Most P&D agreements require that the independent label's recordings be distributed to retail record stores, chains, and rack jobbers only through the major label's normal distribution system (or through an ostensibly independent distributor owned by the major label).

However, P&D agreements sometimes provide for one or more of the following exceptions:

1. The independent label may be allowed to sell a limited number of recordings directly or through its own independent distributors to certain retail outlets not serviced by the major label—for example, health food stores, specialty book and record stores, nonprofit organizations, etc.

2. The independent label or the bands on the label may be allowed to sell recordings at gigs and by direct mail-order sales.

These special sales channels will be specified in the contract, and the number of recordings that the independent label will be allowed to sell may be limited. In most cases, the independent will be entitled to buy product from the major at a price determined by a formula specified in the contract. (The price is often one or a variation of the following: the actual manufacturing cost [calculated on a per recording basis], the manufacturing cost per recording plus a certain additional amount per recording, or the regular wholesale price, or some percentage of the regular wholesale price.)

Term of Agreement

Typically, a P&D deal will be for an initial term of one to three years (most often two or three), with the major label then having the unilateral right to extend the term of the agreement for an additional two to four years. (Usually, these options are exercisable on a year-to-year basis by the major label.) Quite often, a P&D agreement will provide for a total possible term (the initial period, plus extensions) of five years.

Distribution Fees and Manufacturing Costs

The most significant fees and costs deducted by the major label are as follows:

1. The manufacturing costs (i.e., for the fabrication of recordings, printing of artwork,

etc.). The manufacturing prices are often itemized in a price schedule attached to the P&D contract.

2. A distribution fee, which in most P&D contracts is defined as being a percentage of the wholesale price (usually 18% to 25%).

3. Sometimes the major label will provide the services of its in-house promotion and marketing staffs, and possibly its sales staff. If so, it will receive an additional fee (often 10%) on top of the distribution fee. The contract may also provide that the major label will be reimbursed for its out-of-pocket costs (e.g., the costs of hiring independent promotion companies to promote recordings to radio programmers), sometimes up to a certain specific dollar limit per recording. The contract should provide that the independent label will have the right to approve (or at least the right to be consulted about) the marketing and promotion strategies involved and the way in which monies will be spent.

The major label will deduct these fees and costs from the monies it receives from record buyers (chain stores, rack jobbers, etc.), and then pay the balance to the independent label. In some P&D deals, these fees and costs are subtracted from the full wholesale price, in others from a percentage (for example, 90%) of the wholesale price. (But note—the royalties paid by record labels to recording artists are, in the typical recording contract, computed as a percentage of the retail price of recordings.)

Reserves for Returns

P&D agreements often include a reserve clause that allows the major label to temporarily withhold a percentage (usually 20% to 35%) of the sums that may be otherwise owing to the independent label. This reserve is to avoid overpayments that might result from returns of unsold recordings.

The reserves are generally released to the independent label within 12 to 24 months after each reserve period, as established in the contract.

The independent label should seek the lowest possible reserve percentage. A low reserve percentage is especially warranted now because of the new SoundScan technology that allows distributors to efficiently monitor sales patterns and reduce the oversupply of recordings in the marketplace. As a result, the actual percentage of recordings being returned today is much lower than previously experienced.

In any event, vague terminology, such as "reasonable reserves," should be avoided, since it gives the major label considerable leeway about what percentage of sale proceeds can be reserved. The independent should also try to avoid provisions that require an additional letter of credit or bond against reserves.

Free Goods

The major label may wish to provide its wholesale and retail accounts with free goods. For example, a distributor might give a store 15 recordings as free goods for every 100 recordings purchased, as a sales incentive.

The independent label should seek a clause that specifies what percentage of manufactured recordings can be distributed as free goods.

Key Person Clause

The contract may include a key person clause, which gives the major label the right to terminate the agreement if one of the principals of the independent label dies, becomes incapacitated, or ceases to be actively involved.

Major labels will not normally agree to a reciprocal key person clause that allows the independent label to terminate the agreement if and when a key executive at the major label leaves. Major labels will argue that they will be fully able to perform their contractual obligations with or without the presence of a particular executive, whereas the continued presence of key personnel at the independent label is essential.

Advances

The amount of money (if any) to be advanced by the major label will depend on the leverage and negotiating ability of the independent label. The major label will be entitled to recoup any such advances from future monies owed by the major label to the independent.

MULTITIERED P&D DEAL

In addition to their own distribution companies, each major label also owns, or has substantial financial interests in, separate companies that act and look for all practical purposes like independent distribution companies. These ostensibly independent distribution companies have names that do not use any part of a major's name to avoid suggesting any connection with major labels.

The reasons why major labels own such distribution companies are simple. Every developing new sound originating from the street is initially championed by a devoted underground fan base, which tends to be anticorporate by nature, and tends to buy its recordings from mom-and-pop independent record stores and other nontraditional retailers, those that are normally serviced by independent distributors. By having companies that are active in the independent distribution world, major labels are much better able to keep their "ears to the street," keep current on new music trends, and have street credibility ("street cred") with the generally anticorporate fans of new kinds of music.

As a result, for many new groups it can be advantageous to first be marketed and distributed through the major label's independent distribution company. Then, as the group's sales increase and its fan base becomes broader, their recordings can be distributed to a more mainstream audience through the traditional major label system.

In the case of a multitiered deal, recordings will be distributed first through an independent distribution company owned by the major label, and then once sales reach a certain level, recordings will be distributed through the traditional major label system.

DISTRIBUTION ONLY DEALS, FULFILLMENT DEALS AND PIGGYBACK DEALS

There are three other types of contracts—distribution only deals, fulfillment deals and piggyback deals—which are similar to P&D deals, but are distinguishable in certain important respects.

Distribution Only Deal

The independent label manufactures recordings and delivers them to the major label, which is then responsible for distribution through its system. In almost all other respects, a distribution only contract will be identical to a P&D contract.

Fulfillment Deal

The major label manufactures the recordings and ships them to the independent label's usual independent distributors, rather than to the major label's own distribution system (as is the case with a P&D deal). The major label will collect from the independent distributors, deduct the manufacturing costs and a distribution fee, and then pay the balance to the independent label. The deal may also include the major label's collection of previous monies owed to the independent label by those independent distributors with whom the major label has an existing business relationship. Major labels generally have more leverage than independents to collect from distributors. Once sales warrant, the parties to a fulfillment deal may agree to change to the major label's own distribution system.

Piggyback Deal

Independent labels that do not have sufficient leverage to obtain a distribution deal with a major label can try to piggyback onto another independent label's existing deal.

In a piggyback deal, the independent label with the existing relationship will deduct a separate and additional distribution fee for itself, then pay the balance to the piggybacked label. For example, the major label may first deduct an 18% distribution fee from the wholesale proceeds, and pay the balance to the independent label with which it has a relationship. That independent label may deduct another 7% from the wholesale price as its own distribution fee, before paying the piggybacked label the balance of the monies. In that situation, the piggybacked label is being charged a total combined distribution fee of 25%.

Typically, the piggybacking label will depend on accountings and payments from the independent label. Therefore, before entering into this type of deal it should fully understand the exact terms of the relationship between the other independent label and the major.

PRODUCTION DEAL

Production companies ("imprints") find and sign talent and produce recordings. Many are owned by producers that have reputations for turning out commercial hits. Others are vanity labels, owned by successful recording artists that have been rewarded by their labels with production deals.

The production company signs artists to recording contracts, and agrees to pay royalties at a specified rate. The production company also signs a separate production agreement with the major label. This agreement provides for a somewhat higher royalty rate to be paid by the major label to the independent, than the royalty rate that the independent label has agreed to pay to the artist. The production company's profit is based on the difference between the rate it receives from the major label and the rate that it pays its artists.

The production company delivers master recordings to the major label, which manufactures, distributes, markets and promotes them directly or through its subsidiaries.

Often these production companies have names and logos that make them look like record companies, and their names and logos will appear on recordings next to the major labels'.

Term of Agreement

A production deal will typically have an initial term of two or three years, with the major label having options for an additional one to three (or more) years.

Signing of Artists

These contracts typically limit the total number of artists the production company may sign over the entire term of the agreement, or for each year during the term. The more established and successful the production company is, the more artists it will be entitled to sign.

The contract will specify the total number of recordings the production company is required to supply from each artist. The production company (and its artists) will be obligated to ultimately deliver that number of recordings, even if the term of the production agreement expires before that happens.

Most production agreements are "first look" agreements, which give the major label the first rights to recordings delivered by the production company, but the major label will not be obligated to commercially release any recordings delivered by the production company. For example, the major label might reject a recording or artist it considers lacking in commercial potential. Therefore, the production agreement should allow the production company the right to offer any rejected artists or masters to another label.

Royalties

A production deal provides for the major label to pay royalties to the production company, based on a percentage of the retail price. The typical range is 15% to 18%, less the same packaging and other deductions that are standard in most recording agreements. (For more information, see the chapter, Analysis of a Recording Contract.)

Advances

The major label may advance monies for administration costs and other overhead costs not necessarily attributed to any specific recording project; and it may advance the recording costs for each recording produced. It will have the right to recoup those costs before it pays any royalties. Recording budgets for each project will be specified in detail in the contract.

From a production company's perspective, recording costs should be recouped only on an artist-by-artist basis; a production company should avoid any cross-collateralization clause that allows the major label to recoup recording costs for all artists from the total amount of royalties owing for all artists. Otherwise, the monies paid by the major label to the production company may not be sufficient for it to cover its royalty obligations to those artists that are commercially successful.

Ownership of Masters

Typically, the major label, not the production company, owns the masters of any recordings released and sold.

Because the production company is not acquiring any equity interest in the masters, unlike the situation with joint venture agreements (discussed below), production deals are sometimes referred to as "the poor man's joint venture."

Some production companies, however, have been successful in negotiating for a reversion of that ownership to occur sometime after the end of the term of the agreement (typically seven to ten years).

JOINT VENTURE

Under the terms of a joint venture agreement, the major label fronts all operating costs (overhead costs, money needed to sign artists, recording, manufacturing and marketing costs). The independent label and the major label then share the net profits of the joint venture. To compute the net, the major label typically deducts a fee of 10% of the joint venture's gross income for overhead; an additional 15% to 25% for distribution; and the actual out-of-pocket costs incurred by the major label. It will also deduct and pay itself back 50% to 100% (the exact percentage depends on what the labels negotiate with each other) of the monies previously advanced for the independent label's operating costs. After the major label deducts all of these costs and fees from the joint venture's gross income, the parties divide the profits in whatever proportions their contract says, usually equally. The master recordings will be owned either by the joint venture entity or by the major label.

Scope of Agreement

Sometimes the joint venture will apply to the sale of recordings in only certain territories (e.g., North America), in which case only one of the partners will have the right to sell such recordings in other territories, outside the scope of the joint venture.

In some instances, the joint venture will be limited in scope to certain named artists, in which case the independent label will be entitled to continue operating as a stand-alone label with respect to its other artists.

The agreement may also include a clause that states that after an artist sells a specified amount of recordings on the joint venture's label, the major label will have the option to release any new recordings by that artist exclusively under the major's name.

Signing of Artists

Normally the joint venture agreement will provide that a certain number of artists will be signed each year, with the major label often having the right to make the final decision about which artists are signed.

Marketing and Promotion Issues

Depending on the independent label's bargaining power, it may be able to obtain the right to oversee all marketing and promotion decisions, and perhaps the right to spend up to a certain specified amount each year for that marketing and promotion. However, since the major label holds the purse strings, the independent will have little practical recourse if the major label later decides to spend more (or less) money than agreed, unless the independent had been able to insert favorable remedy clauses into the agreement.

Term of Agreement

The agreement will provide that the joint venture will last for a certain period of time, often three to five years (with the major label usually having the right to extend the term of the agreement for a specified number of additional years). Often, the major label can terminate the agreement early if the joint venture's losses reach a certain amount ("stop loss" termination).

There are several methods for determining how assets will be allocated between the parties once the joint venture is terminated. For example, the agreement might contain buy-sell provisions, which state that each party will have the right to buy out the other's rights, and specify which party has the first right and priority to do so. An important issue is determining which of the parties will have first dibs on the acts that are still signed to the joint venture as of the date of its termination.

From an independent label's point of view, it is crucial that the agreement contain clearly defined termination provisions. History has shown that many major labels are enthusiastic about a joint venture at its beginning, but quickly lose interest if profit expectations are not met, or there are changes in corporate management.

EQUITY DEAL

In an equity deal, the major label will either buy an independent label outright, or buy a part interest in it. The major label owns shares of stock in the independent company itself, rather than merely receiving rights to sell its recordings.

Terms of Purchase

Often, the major label's buyout rights will have been originally negotiated between the parties as part of a P&D or joint venture deal, whereby the major label receives an option to buy part or all of the independent label. Sometimes the major label will exercise its buyout rights incrementally.

When a major label purchases an independent outright, the price is heavily negotiated. Independent labels generally sell for six to ten times annual net earnings or two and one-half times annual gross revenues.

Allocation of Costs and Income

When a major label wants to buy only a partial interest in an independent label, there are other issues that will be as heavily negotiated as the price. For example, the major label may agree to pay all of the independent's operating costs, and the parties must resolve the specific terms regarding how future income will be allocated.

The Future Role of the Independent Label's Owners

Normally, the major label will want the original owners of the independent label to remain active because they had the vision to make it a success in the first place.

If the original owners of the label will continue to be involved, there must be contractual arrangements for determining how the label's operations will be shared. Also, those original owners may sign an employment agreement as part of the overall deal, typically for a two- to five-year employment term.

Certain questions arise when original owners of an independent label try to decide whether they want to remain active in the label. For example—

- How much autonomy (if any) will they have with regard to the signing of new artists?

- Who will have the direct day-to-day relationship with artists?

- How much say will they have in marketing and promotion decisions, and other operational decisions?

- Who will be making the day-to-day decisions about how money is spent?

- Will the major label commit to spend a certain amount of money each year on marketing, promotion, tour support, etc.?

- Will the original owners be primarily responsible for promotion and marketing activities on a day-to-day basis? If not, who will be?

- Do the independent label's original owners have a clear contractual right to terminate the relationship if the major label does not meet its commitments?

There are no standard answers to these questions. The terms of an equity deal should be customized to fit the specific needs of the parties involved. These issues must be considered by the independent label if it is to make a wise decision.

LICENSING OF RECORDINGS BY AN INDEPENDENT LABEL TO A MAJOR LABEL (LICENSING OUT)

The independent label may license recordings of one or more of its artists to a major label, generally in exchange for a specified royalty. The independent label might license only certain existing recordings, or agree to license certain future recordings.

Often this licensing is done on an artist-by-artist basis. For example, an independent label might license the recordings of Artist #1 to one major label, and license the recordings of Artist #2 to a different one. This can happen when a major label does not want to acquire the rights to all of the independent label's artists. It can also happen when an independent label feels that it wants to find the major label most interested in, and most committed to, each particular artist.

Term of Agreement

These agreements are normally for three to seven years (most often five years) and often are only for certain specified territories.

Royalties

The licensing royalty rate for recordings sold in the United States is typically 15% to 20% of the retail price. But from this 15% to 20%, the independent label must pay artist/producer royalties of usually 10% to 14% of the retail price, or a percentage (often 50%) of the licensing receipts.

For the licensing of recordings to be sold outside the United States, the royalty rate is generally 12% to 26% of the wholesale price, often referred to as the "Published Price to Dealers" (PPD).

RIGHTS BUYOUTS

When an artist's career is breaking faster than the independent label's financial and promotional capacities can handle, it may enter into a one-artist agreement, whereby the independent label assigns to the major all of its rights in that artist. In return, the major label pays a substantial "recoupable but nonrefundable" cash advance against future "override royalties" on some or all of the artist's recordings.

The term, override royalties, means royalties paid by the major label directly to the independent label; these royalties are separate from the artist royalties paid by the major label to the recording artist. Often the override royalty rate is 2% or 3% (but sometimes more) of the retail price of recordings sold, and the major label customarily pays such royalties at the same intervals as artist royalties (usually semiannually).

Sometimes an independent label has an artist who is the subject of a major label bidding war. In that situation, the independent label may have the bargaining power to demand that part of the cash payment from the major label will not be considered recoupable (deductible) from the future override royalties.

LICENSING OF RECORDINGS BY INDEPENDENT LABELS FROM MAJOR LABELS (LICENSING IN)

An independent label can license particular recordings from a major label. The recordings may be either new or previously released.

New Recordings

New artists are sometimes licensed to an independent label when that label has credibility and marketing strength in a specific genre of music and will help build a fan base for the artist. The major label will usually provide marketing and promotion funds to enable the independent label to effectively promote the artist's recordings. This type of deal resembles a joint venture in some respects, since the parties often agree to split the net profits after all costs have been paid.

They may agree that the major label will have the right to take back the artist once recording sales reach a certain level. When that happens, the independent label's financial participation may change—for example, from a share of profits to a royalty structure, which may be substantially less rewarding.

Previously Released Recordings

Licensing by a major label to an independent label can also occur in connection with an independent label's reissue of recordings that are no longer available to the public. This can happen when the major label feels that the market for the reissued recording is too small (under 10,000 units).

This kind of licensing is usually on a royalty basis, with a prepayment of royalties to the major label for a certain number of units, generally 5,000 to 20,000.

To avoid legal problems, it is crucial that the independent label acquiring the reissue rights be certain that the party with whom it is dealing is the true owner of the masters being licensed. That is often the label that had previously handled the product. However, the ownership of the masters may have been sold, or the rights may have reverted to the artist. In any event, ownership must be clearly determined, and the licensing agreement should contain all appropriate ownership warranties, as well as an indemnification clause. (For an explanation of indemnification clauses, see paragraph 13 of the recording contract in the chapter, Analysis of a Recording Contract.)

A LOOK AT THESE DEALS FROM THE ARTIST'S PERSPECTIVE

An artist's relationship with his or her label may be substantially impacted by changes in record company personnel, or by a new affiliation between the artist's independent label and a major label, or by the independent label's assignment of the artist's contract to another label (major or independent). Therefore, artists should address these possible changes in their recording contracts.

An artist should seek clauses that prohibit the independent label from assigning their recording contract to another label without prior written consent.

Also, a key person clause should be inserted that permits the artist to terminate the contract if certain personnel leave the label (the key personnel being those particular individuals whose presence has caused the artist to have confidence in the independent label).

THUMBNAIL SKETCHES OF THE DIFFERENT KINDS OF DEALS

What distinguishes one kind of deal from another can be very confusing. Here are thumbnail sketches of each.

- Pressing and Distribution (P&D) Deal: The name of this deal describes its basic premise. The indie label finances the recording process and delivers the final master recording to a major label distribution company, which then manufactures the recordings and distributes them to subdistributors, retailers, etc. In P&D deals, as in the case of the next three distribution-oriented deals discussed below, the independent label retains all ownership rights in the master recordings.

- Distribution Only Deal: Basically the same as the P&D deal, but here the *indie label,* not the major label distributor, manufactures the recordings. The major label's role is distribution only.

- Fulfillment Deal: Basically the same as the P&D deal. Here the recordings are not distributed through the major label's traditional distribution system, but instead through an ostensibly independent distributor that is owned by the major label. This independent distributor, acting on behalf of the indie label, ships such recordings as are ordered by indie subdistributors and indie record stores, and it also handles all billing responsibilities. In short, the independent distributor's role here is to fulfill orders from third parties for the independent label's recordings.

- Piggyback Deal: Used when an indie label does not have the clout to get its own distribution deal. In order to find distribution, the indie label must "piggyback" onto *another* indie label's already-existing distribution deal with a record distributor.

- Production Deal: The independent label is a production company financed by the major label, created solely for the purpose of producing recordings. The production company uses the major label's financing to sign artists and produce recordings, and then delivers the masters to the major label. The major label manufactures and distributes the recordings and handles the marketing and promotion activities. *The major label owns the masters.*

- Joint Venture Deal: A joining of forces by a major label and an indie label, whereby they agree to share responsibility for making recordings and their marketing and promotion. These responsibilities are divided in whatever way the two labels agree upon in their formal joint venture agreement. The major label finances the joint venture, and reimburses itself from recording sales income for the expenses that it has incurred. The net profits are then divided between the two labels. The master recordings can be owned either by the joint venture entity or by the major label.

- Equity Deal: The major label invests money in the independent label. In exchange, the major label acquires a part ownership or total ownership of the independent label, its assets and its contracts with artists.

CONTINUED ON NEXT PAGE

CONTINUED FROM PREVIOUS PAGE

- Licensing by a Major Label: Here the major label owns the masters, but licenses (i.e., leases) the masters to the independent label for a limited amount of time (usually a few years). The independent label has the rights to sell recordings made from those masters. In return, the independent label pays a royalty to the major label for each recording sold. All manufacturing, marketing and promotion costs are paid by the independent label. The major label continues to *own* the masters at all times.

- Licensing to a Major Label: The independent label owns the masters, and licenses them to the major label for a limited time. In exchange, the major label pays royalties to the independent label. The major label also pays all manufacturing, marketing and promotion costs.

- Rights Buyout: Here the independent label will have previously signed a recording contract with an artist. Then, the independent label and a major label sign an agreement, whereby the major label buys all of the rights the independent label has in the artist under the terms of its recording contract with the artist. The major label pays a cash advance and a small royalty to the indie label on sales of their recordings featuring that artist.

If such clauses are obtained and the independent label later undertakes to establish a relationship with another label, it is important that the artist review the nonassignment and key person clauses in his or her contract, and take all necessary and required procedural steps to preserve their rights.

Groups should avoid "leaving member" clauses, which give labels the rights to the future recordings of members that branch out with recordings of their own.

An artist who signs a contract with an independent label that already has a relationship with a major label, should clearly understand how that relationship works and how responsibilities are allocated between the two labels. He or she should meet with key personnel at the major label to determine whether it has a sincere commitment to promoting the artist's recordings, and determine whether the proposed relationship will be a boost or a hindrance. This evaluation process is particularly relevant when an artist has contract offers from more than one label.

CONCLUSION

A clear understanding of the possible relationships between independent and major labels will help an independent label to take the best advantage of any such opportunities that come its way. However, it is also important to remember this: Even though you may now have a basic understanding of the issues and possible ramifications of these deals, many of the everyday activities involved with working these deals are about cultivating and building personal relationships. The music business ends up being about people, and the personal relationships you develop as you go along.

In closing, let us say that your passion for your music is as important as all of the legal and business considerations we have discussed above. You must maintain your passion for your music, and at the same time grasp the business realities that ultimately protect that music for the good of all. You must consciously balance art and commerce, so that neither is sacrificed for the other.

Resources

INDUSTRY DIRECTORIES

AFIM Directory
Association For Independent Music
(www.afim.org)
147 East Main Street
P.O. Box 988
Whitesburg, KY 41858
(606) 633-0946

The Album Network's Yellow Pages of Rock
(www.musicbiz.com)
120 North Victory Boulevard
Burbank, CA 91502
(818) 955-4000

Billboard Directories
(www.billboard.com/directories)
575 Prospect Street
Lakewood, NJ 08701
(732) 363-4156
Billboard International Buyer's Guide
Billboard International Latin Music Buyer's Guide
Billboard International Talent & Touring Directory
Billboard Record Retailing Directory
International Tape/Disc Directory
Musicians Guide to Touring and Promotion
The Radio Power Book

Festivals Directory Northwest
(www.festivalsdirectory.com)
P.O. Box 7515
Bonney Lake, WA 98390
(253) 863-6617

The Music Business Registry
(www.musicregistry.com)
7510 Sunset Boulevard
Suite 1041
Los Angeles, CA 90046
(818) 769-2722
A&R Registry
Film/TV Music Guide
Music Business Attorney, Legal and Business Affairs Registry
Music Publisher Registry

The Music Yellow Pages
(www.musicyellowpages.com)
National Music & Entertainment Inc.
184 Hempstead Avenue
West Hempstead, NY 11552
(516) 489-6514

Performance Guides
(www.performancemagazine.com)
1101 University Drive
Suite 108
Fort Worth, TX 76107
(817) 338-9444
Black Book
Concert Production
Equipment Manufacturers and Production Personnel
Facilities
Talent Agencies
Talent Buyers
Talent Management
Transportation

The Recording Industry Sourcebook
(www.musicdispatch.com)
Music Dispatch
P.O. Box 13920
Milwaukee, WI 53213
(800) 637-2852

GOVERNMENT AGENCIES

Copyright Arbitration Royalty Panel (CARP)
(www.loc.gov/copyright/carp)
P.O. Box 70977
Southwest Station
Washington, DC 20024
(202) 707-8380

United States Copyright Office
Register of Copyrights
Library of Congress
(www.loc.gov/copyright)
101 Independence Avenue, S.E.
Washington, DC 20559
(202) 707-3000 (Information)
(202) 707-9100 (Forms hotline—use this number if you know which form[s] you need.)

United States Patent and Trademark Office
(www.uspto.gov)
2021 Jefferson Davis Highway
Arlington, VA 22202
(800) 786-9199 or (703) 308-4357

United States Securities and Exchange Commission (SEC)
(www.sec.gov)
450 Fifth Street, N.W.
Washington, DC 20549
(202) 942-7040

World Intellectual Property Organization (WIPO)
(www.wipo.org)
2 United Nations Plaza
Suite 2525
New York, New York 10017
United States of America
(212) 963-6813

World Trade Organization (WTO)
(www.wto.org)
Centre William Rappard
Rue de Lausanne 154
CH-1211 Geneva 21, Switzerland
+41 22 739 51 11

ORGANIZATIONS, TRADE ASSOCIATIONS AND CONFERENCES

Academy of Country Music
(www.acmcountry.com)
6255 Sunset Boulevard
Suite 923
Hollywood, CA 90028
(213) 462-2351

American Bar Association
(www.abanet.org)
750 North Lake Shore Drive
Chicago, IL 60611
(312) 988-5000

American Federation of Musicians (AFM)
(www.afm.org)
1501 Broadway
Paramount Building
Suite 600
New York, NY 10036
(212) 869-1330

AFM—Hollywood
1777 Vine Street, Suite 500
Hollywood, CA 90028
(213) 461-3441

American Federation of Television & Radio Artists (AFTRA)
(www.aftra.com)
(Offices in major music markets)
260 Madison Avenue
7th Floor
New York, NY 10016
(212) 532-0800

AFTRA—Hollywood
6922 Hollywood Boulevard
8th Floor
Hollywood, CA 90028
(213) 461-8111

American Guild of Musical Artists
(www.musicalartists.org)
1727 Broadway at 55th Street
New York, NY 10019
(212) 265-3687

American Society of Composers, Authors and Publishers (ASCAP)
(www.ascap.com)
(Offices in major music markets)
One Lincoln Plaza
New York, NY 10023
(212) 621-6000

ASCAP—Los Angeles
7920 Sunset Boulevard
Suite 300
Los Angeles, CA 90028
(323) 883-1000

ASCAP—Nashville
2 Music Square West
Nashville, TN 37203
(615) 742-5000

Arts Resolution Services
National Mediation Hotline
(800) 526-8252

Association For Independent Music (AFIM)
(www.afim.org)
147 East Main Street
P.O. Box 988
Whitesburg, KY 41858
(606) 633-0946

Association of Independent Music Publishers (AIMP)
(www.aimp.org)
P.O. Box 1561
Burbank, CA 91507-1561
(818) 842-6257

AIMP—New York
120 East 56th Street
New York, NY 10022
(212) 758-6157

Audio Engineering Society (AES)
(www.aes.org)
60 East 42nd Street
Room 2520
New York, NY 10165-2520
(212) 661-8528

Beverly Hills Bar Association
(www.bhba.org)
300 South Beverly Drive
Suite 201
Beverly Hills, CA 90212
(310) 553-6644

The Blues Foundation
(www.blues.org)
49 Union Avenue
Memphis, TN 38103
(901) 527-2583

Blues Music Association (BMA)
(www.bluesmusicassociation.com)
P.O. Box 3122
Memphis, TN 38173
(901) 572-3842

Broadcast Music Incorporated (BMI)
(www.bmi.com)
320 West 57th Street
New York, NY 10019
(212) 586-2000

BMI—Los Angeles
8730 Sunset Boulevard
3rd Floor West
Hollywood, CA 90069-2211
(310) 659-9109

BMI—Nashville
10 Music Square East
Nashville, TN 37203-4399
(615) 401-2000

California Copyright Conference
(www.theccc.org)
P.O. Box 1291
Burbank, CA 91507-1291
(818) 848-6783

California Lawyers for the Arts (CLA)
(www.calawyersforthearts.org)
Fort Mason Center
Building C, Room 255
San Francisco, CA 94123
(415) 775-7200

CLA—Santa Monica
1641 18th Street
Santa Monica, CA 90404
(310) 998-5590

CLA—Oakland
1212 Broadway Street
Suite 834
Oakland, CA 94612
(510) 444-6351

CLA—Sacramento
926 J Street
Suite 811
Sacramento, CA 95814
(916) 442-6210

Canadian Academy of Recording Arts and Sciences (CARAS)
(www.juno-awards.ca)
124 Merton Street
Suite 305
Toronto, Ontario M4S 272 Canada
(416) 485-3135

Canadian Conference of the Arts
(www.culturenet.ca/cca)
189 Laurier Avenue East
2nd Floor
Ottawa, Ontario K1N 6P1 Canada
(613) 238-2631

Canadian Country Music Association (CCMA)
(www.ccma.org)
3800 Steeles Avenue West
Suite 127
Woodbridge, Ontario L4L 4G9 Canada
(905) 850-1144

Canadian Independent Record Producers Association (CIRPA)
(www.cirpa.ca)
150 Eglinton Avenue East
Suite 403
Toronto, Ontario M4P 1E8 Canada
(416) 485-3152

Canadian Recording Industry Association (CRIA)
(www.cria.ca)
890 Yonge Street
Suite 1200
Toronto, Ontario M4W 3P4 Canada
(416) 967-7272

Chamber Music America
(www.chamber-music.org)
305 Seventh Avenue
New York, NY 10001
(212) 242-2022

Children's Entertainment Association (CEA)
(www.kidsentertainment.com)
75 Rockefeller Plaza
New York, NY 10019
(212) 275-1605

Country Music Association (CMA)
(www.countrymusic.org)
1 Music Circle South
Nashville, TN 37203
(615) 244-2840

Country Music Society of America
One Country Music Road
P.O. Box 2000
Marion, OH 43306
(800) 669-1002

Creative Music Coalition
(www.aimcmc.com)
1024 W. Willcox Avenue
Peoria, IL 61604
(309) 685-4843

Electronic Industries Alliance (EIA)
(www.eia.org)
2500 Wilson Boulevard
Arlington, VA 22201
(703) 907-7500

Fischoff Chamber Music Association
(www.fischoff.org)
P.O. Box 1303
South Bend, IN 46624-1303
(219) 237-4871

Folk Alliance
North American Folk Music and Dance Alliance
(www.folk.org)
1001 Connecticut Avenue, N.W.
Suite 501
Washington, DC 20036
(202) 835-3655

Foundation to Assist Canadian Talent on Records (FACTOR)
(www.factor.ca)
125 George Street
2nd Floor
Toronto, ON M5A 2N4 Canada
(416) 368-8678

Gospel Music Association (GMA)
(www.gospelmusic.org)
1205 Division Street
Nashville, TN 37203
(615) 242-0303

The Harry Fox Agency, Inc.
(www.nmpa.org/hfa.html)
711 3rd Avenue, 8th Floor
New York, NY 10017
(212) 370-5330

Home Recording Rights Coalition
(www.hrrc.org)
P.O. Box 14267
1145 19th Street, N.W.
Washington, DC 20044
(800) 282-8273

Intercollegiate Broadcasting System (IBS)
(www.ibsradio.org)
367 Windsor Highway
New Windsor, NY 12553-7900
(845) 565-0003

International Association of Jazz Educators (IAJE)
(www.iaje.org)
P.O. Box 724
Manhattan, KS 66505-0724
(785) 776-8744

International Bluegrass Music Association (IBMA)
(www.ibma.org)
1620 Frederica Street
Owensboro, KY 42301
(270) 684-9025

International Federation of the Phonographic Industry (IFPI)
(www.ifpi.org)
IFPI Secretariat
54 Regent Street
London, W1B 5RE England
+44 (0) 20 7878 7900

International Music Products Association (NAMM)
(www.namm.org)
5790 Armada Drive
Carlsbad, CA 92008
(760) 438-8001

International Trademark Association (INTA)
(Formerly, the U.S. Trademark Association)
(www.inta.org)
1133 Avenue of the Americas
New York, NY 10036-6710
(212) 768-9887

International Recording Media Association (IRMA)
(www.recordingmedia.org)
182 Nassau Street
Suite 204
Princeton, NJ 08542-7005
(609) 279-1700

Lawyer Referral and Information Service (LRIS)
Los Angeles County Bar Association
(www.smartlaw.org)
P.O. Box 55020
Los Angeles, CA 90055-2020
(213) 243-1525

Los Angeles Music Network (LAMN)
(www.lamn.com)
P.O. Box 8934
Universal City, CA 91618-8934
(818) 769-6095

Los Angeles Women in Music
(www.lawim.org)
P.O. Box 1817
Burbank, CA 91507-1817
(213) 243-6440

Midem
Reed Midem Organisation, Inc.
(www.midem.com)
125 Park Avenue South
24th Floor
New York, NY 10017
(212) 370-7470

Music and Entertainment Industry Educator's Association (MEIEA)
(www.meiea.org)
Loyola University - Box 83
6363 St. Charles Avenue
New Orleans, LA 70118
504) 865-3975

Music Managers Forum
(www.mmf-us.org)
P.O. Box 444
Village Station
New York, NY 10014-0444
(212) 213-8787

Nashville Entertainment Association (NEA)
(www.nea.net)
P.O. Box 121948
1105 16th Avenue South
Suite C
Nashville, TN 37212
(615) 327-4308

Nashville Songwriters Association International
(www.nashvillesongwriters.com)
1701 West End Avenue
Third Floor
Nashville, TN 37203
(800) 321-6008 or (615) 256-3354

National Academy of Recording Arts and Sciences (NARAS)
(www.grammy.com)
3402 Pico Boulevard
Santa Monica, CA 90405
(310) 392-3777

NARAS—Nashville
1904 Wedgewood Avenue
Nashville, TN 37212
(615) 327-8030

NARAS—New York
156 West 56th Street
No. 1701
New York, NY 10019
(212) 245-5440

National Association of Music Merchants (NAMM)
see International Music Products Association (NAMM)

National Association of Recording Merchandisers (NARM)
(www.narm.com)
9 Eves Drive
Suite 120
Marlton, NJ 08053
(856) 596-2221

National Federation of Community Broadcasters (NFCB)
(www.nfcb.org)
Fort Mason Center
Building D
San Francisco, CA 94123
(415) 771-1160

National Music Publishers Association (NMPA)
(www.nmpa.org)
475 Park Avenue South
29th Floor
New York, NY 10016-6901
(646) 742-1651

North by Northeast (NXNE)
(www.nxne.com)
189 Church Street
Lower Level
Toronto, Ontario M5B 1Y7 Canada
(416) 863-6963

North by Northwest Music and New Media Conference and Festival (NXNW)
(www.nxnw.com)
P.O. Box 4999
Austin, TX 78765
(512) 467-7979

Pacific Music Industry Association (PMIA)
(www.pmia.org)
404-3701 Hasting Street
Burnaby, BC V5C 2H6 Canada
(604) 873-1914

Rap Coalition
(www.rapcoalition.org)
111 East 14th Street
Suite 339
New York, NY 10007
(212) 714-1100

Recording Industry Association of America, Inc. (RIAA)
(www.riaa.org)
1330 Connecticut Avenue, N.W.
Suite 300
Washington, DC 20036
(202) 775-0101

Screen Actors Guild (SAG)
(www.sag.org)
5757 Wilshire Boulevard
Los Angeles, CA 90036
(323) 954-1600

SAG—New York
1515 Broadway
44th Floor
New York, NY 10036
(212) 944-1030

SESAC, Inc.
(www.sesac.com)
55 Music Square East
Nashville, TN 37203
(615) 320-0055

SESAC—New York
421 West 54th Street
New York, NY 10019
(212) 586-3450

SESAC—Santa Monica
501 Santa Monica Boulevard
Suite 450
Santa Monica, CA 90401-2430
(310) 393-9671

Society of Composers, Authors and Music Publishers of Canada (SOCAN)
(www.socan.ca)
41 Valleybrook Drive
Don Mills, Ontario M3B 2S6 Canada
(416) 445-8700

Society for the Preservation of Bluegrass Music of America (SPBGMA)
(www.spbgma.com)
P.O. Box 271
Kirksville, MO 63501
(660) 665-7172

Society of Professional Audio Recording Services (SPARS)
(www.spars.com)
364 Clove Drive
Memphis, TN 38117-4009
(901) 821-9111

Songwriter Universe
(www.songwriteruniverse.com)
11684 Ventura Boulevard
Suite 975
Studio City, CA 91604

The Songwriter's Guild of America (SGA)
(www.songwriters.org)
6430 Sunset Boulevard
Suite 705
Hollywood, CA 90028
(323) 462-1108

SGA—Nashville
1222 16th Avenue South
Suite 25
Nashville, TN 37212
(615) 269-7664

SGA—New York
1560 Broadway
Suite 1306
New York, NY 10036
(212) 768-7902

South by Southwest Music and Media Conference and Festival
(www.sxsw.com)
P.O. Box 4999
Austin, TX 78765
(512) 467-7979

Contributors

STEPHEN BIGGER is a graduate of Yale Law School and a partner in the New York law firm of Fross Zelnick Lehrman & Zissu. He has for many years authored the "International Notes" column in *The Trademark Reporter,* the official publication of the International Trademark Association.

LAWRENCE J. BLAKE is a partner in the Los Angeles office of the law firm of Manatt, Phelps & Phillips, LLP, which has one of the largest music industry practices in the United States. They represent a broad and diverse clientele in the music industry, including recording artists (from those about to sign their first deal to superstars), songwriters, composers, music publishers, record producers, independent record labels and some of the leading companies engaged in the distribution of music over the Internet. Mr. Blake represents clients in all of these areas of the music business. His practice consists of structuring, negotiating, drafting and reviewing the entire gamut of contracts that pertain to the music industry and related areas, such as merchandising. He also advises clients with respect to related intellectual property matters, such as copyright, trademark, rights of publicity and entertainment-related dispute resolution.

Mr. Blake has written various articles about the music business and has testified as an expert witness in connection with music industry matters. He has also taught a course for industry professionals at the UCLA Extension entitled "Understanding Contracts in the Music Industry." Mr. Blake received his law degree from Harvard Law School in 1976 and has practiced with Manatt, Phelps & Phillips, LLP since 1978.

STEVEN AMES BROWN practices both litigation and transactional entertainment law in San Francisco. He specializes in enforcing the rights of performers and authors in the areas of music, film, rights of publicity, unfair competition and royalty collection. He is a graduate of the University of Michigan with a degree in mass communication and clinical psychology. He was an undergraduate teaching fellow and earned teacher certification. He is a graduate of the University of California, Hastings College of the Law, where he was Associate Editor of *COMM/ENT, A Journal of Communications and Entertainment Law.* He was a law clerk to the California Court of Appeal, First District; U.S. District Court, Northern District of California; and the San Francisco District Attorney. He was a broadcast journalist and produced public service radio programs in Michigan. He also taught radio and television production and performance.

His client roster has included the estates of Fred Astaire, Judy Garland and Orson Welles, and actors such as Ginger Rogers, Annette Funicello, Shelley Fabares and James Darren. His roster has also included pop stars of the '50s and '60s, such as the Supremes, Mary Wells, Sam The Sham and The Pharos, Nina Simone, Barbara Lewis, The Flamingos, and the estates of Frankie Lymon and Little Eva.

BARTLEY F. DAY has been an entertainment attorney since 1977 and is now based in Portland, Oregon. Prior to law school, he was a musician and personal manager. Today, he represents numerous nationally known recording artists, record producers, independent record companies, personal managers, music publishing companies and Internet companies. Mr. Day is currently an elected member of the Board of Governors of the National Academy of Recording Arts and Sciences (The Recording Academy), Pacific Northwest Branch, and is a national chairperson of The Recording Academy's Entertainment Law Initiative. He also lectures and writes extensively on entertainment industry issues, including a monthly entertainment law column in *Two Louies,* a Pacific Northwest music industry magazine. Mr. Day can be reached at (503) 291-9300.

ROBERT M. DUDNIK is a partner in the law firm of Paul, Hastings, Janofsky & Walker, which has offices throughout the United States and in Tokyo and London. Mr. Dudnik, whose office is in Los Angeles, cochairs the firm's Entertainment Practice Group, which functions on a nationwide basis and handles both litigation and transactional matters covering all aspects of the entertainment and related industries. This includes theatrical motion pictures, television, recorded music and broadcasting. The Group's litigation practice deals with intellectual property and business related disputes of all types, and handles matters in various state and federal courts, as well as a broad range of arbitrations. Mr. Dudnik is a graduate of Cornell University and the Yale Law School, where he was a member of the Order of the Coif and graduated cum laude.

Mr. Dudnik practiced and taught law in Cleveland, Ohio from 1964 to 1969. Since moving to Los Angeles in 1969, his practice has been primarily related to the handling of entertainment litigation matters and providing prelitigation counseling to clients in all areas of the entertainment industry.

STEVEN GARDNER is a partner in the Century City (Los Angeles), California law firm of Cohon and Gardner, PC, where he practices entertainment law and litigation. He is a founding member of the Committee for the Arts, a past president of the Committee for the Arts, Beverly Hills Bar Association Barristers and Beverly Hills Bar Association Foundation and a former member of the Beverly Hills Bar Association board of governors.

BRAD GELFOND began his career at Regency Artists, a small, specialized agency. He moved with the company when it merged with a literary agency and a motion picture and television talent agency to become Triad Artists. Triad, a full-service agency, ultimately merged with the William Morris Agency after eight years and Mr. Gelfond became Vice President and West Coast Head of the Contemporary Music Department. Since leaving the agency business, Mr. Gelfond has become a personal manager and consultant. He has also taught music business courses at UCLA Extension.

Some of the artists Mr. Gelfond represented during his career are Lou Reed, Paul Simon, David Byrne, Bjork, Laurie Anderson, Kate Bush, Paul Westerberg, Rickie Lee Jones, Nanci Griffith, The Pet Shop Boys, Johnny Clegg, Dead Can Dance, Electronic, New Order, Cyndi Lauper, The Posies, Kirsty MacColl, Love & Rockets, Alison Moyet, Lush, Jellyfish, Deborah Harry, X, The Sugarcubes, Mike Oldfield, Ofra Haza, and Ladysmith Black Mambazo.

RONALD H. GERTZ is the President and Chief Executive Officer of Music Reports, Inc. (MRI). MRI represents broadcasters and other corporate users of music in the licensing and administration of music rights license payments to music copyright owners and the organizations that issue licenses and collect royalties on behalf of music composers, artists, and copyright owners in the United States (i.e., ASCAP, BMI, SESAC, HFA, SOCAN, RIAA, etc.). MRI also provides music license consulting and data processing services to the television, radio, music and online industries. MRI's music licensing subsidiary, Copyright Clearinghouse, Inc. (CCI), negotiates and executes individual licensing transactions for the right to perform, reproduce and distribute musical works (i.e., musical compositions and sound recordings). CCI works on behalf of broadcasters, television/film producers, digital transmission services, Web sites and other corporate users of music in traditional, interactive and online media.

Mr. Gertz is a copyright attorney whose legal practice began with the representation of clients in the television, publishing, and recording fields. In 1980, he formed The Clearing House, Ltd., an intellectual property licensing organization that was the predecessor to MRI. Mr. Gertz has served as an expert witness for the broadcast industry in copyright royalty proceedings in the United States and Canada, and is currently on the Board of Directors of the Intellectual Property Section of the Los Angeles County Bar Association. He has been a director of the Academy of Interactive Arts and Sciences and the National Academy of Songwriters, a member of the Interactive Multimedia Association's Intellectual Property Task Force, and he is a past president of the California Copyright Conference.

A frequent speaker at colleges, law schools and seminars throughout the world, Mr. Gertz has been widely published in such legal and entertainment industry publications as the *Los Angeles Daily Journal, Billboard Magazine,* the *Century City Bar Association Journal,* the *Beverly Hills Bar Association Journal, The Entertainment Law Journal, Entertainment Publishing and the Arts* and the *Journal of the International Association of Entertainment Lawyers.* Mr. Gertz was trained as a classical vocalist and guitarist and has performed professionally in many rock tours. He is also a member of ASCAP and The Society of Composers and Lyricists.

MARK HALLORAN, a graduate of UCLA and Hastings College of Law, is one of the founding partners of Erickson, Halloran & Small, a law firm that specializes in film, television and music law. Previously, he was a founding partner of Alexander, Halloran, Nau & Rose, and Vice President, Feature Business Affairs, at Universal Pictures. Prior to his stint at Universal, Mark was business affairs counsel at Orion Pictures. He specializes in entertainment financing, production and distribution deals.

Mark has coauthored two nationally published books on the music business, *The Musician's Guide to Copyright* (with Gunnar Erickson and Edward (Ned) R. Hearn), and the current *The Musician's Business and Legal Guide,* as well as numerous articles on entertainment business and legal issues.

He is a director of the USC/Beverly Hills Bar Association Entertainment Law Institute and has taught classes on film finance at UCLA.

EDWARD (NED) R. HEARN is in private law practice. His principal office is in San Jose, California. Mr. Hearn's practice concentrates on the entertainment, Internet and computer software industries. These include recording, production and publishing; multimedia production, licensing, distribution and marketing; copyright and trademark matters, merchandising, sponsorships, film and television scoring and soundtracks, content syndications, clearances for use of intellectual property in all forms of media, talent services negotiation and contracting, business start-ups and development, strategic alliances, content catalog sales and purchases, private financing, private mergers and acquisitions. His clients include record labels, music publishers, traditional and Internet-based media, production, technology and content distribution companies, webcasting companies, recording artists, producers, writers, managers, software designers and multimedia product and Web site developers.

He is a director of the California Lawyers for the Arts, an organization that provides legal assistance to musicians and other artists; Board President of the Northern California Songwriters Association, and coauthor of *The Musician's Guide to Copyright.* Mr. Hearn also lectures on music business and related legal issues.

CHERYL HODGSON is a member of the firm of Probstein, Weiner & Hodgson, with offices in New York and Los Angeles. She is admitted to practice in California, New York, Oregon, Tennessee, and Colorado. Ms. Hodgson has been involved in a number of significant music industry litigation matters, including successful rescission of artist recordings agreements, royalty collection issues and group name infringement actions. Her practice involves the negotiation of a wide variety of agreements within the music and entertainment industries. Ms. Hodgson specializes in the registration and protection of entertainment service marks, including domain name issues, licensing use of artist names to record companies and intragroup disputes.

She has extensive hands-on experience in the music industry, having begun her career as a theatrical agent and having been a member of the artist management team at Bill Graham Presents.

Ms. Hodgson is a member of the Board of Directors, California Copyright Conference; a member of the National Academy of Recording Arts and Sciences; Association of Independent Music Publishers; Los Angeles Copyright Society; Intellectual Property Section of California State Bar; and the Beverly Hills Bar Association.

Ms. Hodgson frequently speaks on issues relative to the music industry, at the Los Angeles Copyright Society, the ABA Entertainment and Sports Forum, Tulane University College of Law, University of Texas College of Law and the University of Colorado, Denver.

NEVILLE L. JOHNSON is an attorney with Johnson & Rishwain LLP, in West Los Angeles. He is a Phi Beta Kappa graduate of the University of California at Berkeley, where he was the music critic for *The Daily Californian.* He obtained his law degree from Southwestern University School of Law, graduating near the top of his class. Mr. Johnson has practiced as a music industry attorney since 1975, representing such clients as Yoko Ono Lennon and the estate of John Lennon, the Academy of Country Music, Bug Music, Nancy Sinatra, MUZAK Europe, David Carradine, numerous independent labels, publishers and managers. Most recently, he has been advising Internet companies on business and financing strategies. He has extensive litigation experience in music industry-related matters and is a specialist at collecting unpaid royalties, in which regard he has represented Mitch Ryder and the Detroit Wheels, the heirs of the estates of Gram Parsons and Kid Ory, and others.

Besides being an expert in entertainment law and domestic and international copyright, Mr. Johnson is nationally recognized as expert in the law of privacy and defamation. He has tried cases throughout California and in Philadelphia, Atlanta, Austin, Phoenix, Denver and New Brunswick, New Jersey. In 1998, in a precedent setting case, Mr. Johnson convinced the Supreme Court of California to unanimously uphold a $1 million verdict against ABC News, including substantial compensatory and punitive damages, because of the unlawful utilization of a hidden camera on a news magazine show. *Editor and Publisher* magazine named him, in late 2000, as one of the top six plaintiff media attorneys in the United States.

He is the author of a definitive law review article on California law applicable to personal managers and talent agencies. In 2000, Mr. Johnson published *The John Wooden Pyramid of Success,* the authorized biography of the greatest basketball coach in history, which the Los Angeles Times described as "everything that anyone could possibly want to know" about the coach (who is also a philosopher) and "worth the price." Go to Cool Titles *(www.cooltitles.com)* for more information and to obtain a copy.

In 2001, Mr. Johnson, creating as Dr. Trevor McShane, authored *First Love, Last Love,* a weepy but literate romantic novel, and coproduced the "soundtrack" (20 songs; available for separate purchase) to it. He wrote the songs, played rhythm guitar, and performed lead vocals backed by his band of crack professional musicians. His musical style has been compared to that of Mark Knopfler, Jimmy Buffett, Lou Reed and Leonard Cohen. Mr. Johnson owns Cool Records, which puts out sound recordings; visit it at *www.coolrecords.com,* where you can see Dr. McShane perform in a music video that features a cameo by David Carradine. The Web site for his law firm can be found at *www.jandrlaw.com.*

Mr. Johnson has spoken at many universities and music industry groups and during the 1990s hosted a television show where he interviewed prominent judges and lawyers on legal issues.

He wishes to gratefully acknowledge the help of print music publishing expert Ronnie Schiff, and Milt Okun and Peter Primont of Cherry Lane Music in advising him in connection with the print music aspects relating to the article on music publishing; attorney Guy Blake of Warner-Chappell Music who assisted on the music publishing article; and to especially thank Don Biederman, former Executive Vice-President and General Counsel of and presently Consultant to Warner-Chappell Music and the Director of the Entertainment and Media Law Institute and a law professor at Southwestern University School of Law, who read and commented on all the chapters.

E. SCOTT JOHNSON is a shareholder with Ober, Kaler, Grimes & Shriver, a law firm with offices in Maryland, Virginia and Washington, D.C. Mr. Johnson concentrates on copyrights, trademarks, entertainment and media industry matters. A former studio musician and record producer, Mr. Johnson has served as an advisor to the Maryland State Arts Council, is a vice president of Mid-Atlantic Arts Foundation, immediate past president of Maryland Lawyers for the Arts (1990-1998) and Young Audiences of Maryland (1994-1997). He also serves on the Boards of Directors of Washington Area Music Association, Concert Artists of Baltimore and is a member of the National Academy of Recording Arts and Sciences and American Society of Composers, Authors and Publishers

Mr. Johnson has written and lectured extensively on copyright, trademark and music industry legal matters. Since 1993, he has served as Editor-in-Chief of *Public Domain Report.* His clients include record companies, publishing companies, television and film production companies, producers, authors and recording artists.

Mr. Johnson can be reached at (800) 638-6547, esjohnson@ober.com (email), and (410) 547-0699 (fax).

CHRISTOPHER KNAB is the owner of FourFront Media and Music, a Seattle-based consultation service dedicated to helping independent musicians promote, market and sell their music. He is a former president of the Northwest Area Music Association, Station Manager of alternative radio station KCMU and cofounder and Vice President of 415/Columbia Records. He is currently on the faculty of the Audio Production program at the Art Institute of Seattle. His Web site, *www.4frontmusic.com,* posts many useful articles and resources for the independent musician. He has been involved with the business side of independent music for over 25 years.

Mr. Knab can be reached at (206) 282-6116 or by e-mail at Chris@Knab.com. The mailing address for FourFront Media and Music is 3825 34th Avenue West, Apt. 7, Seattle, Washington 98199.

EVANNE L. LEVIN graduated with honors from UCLA and Loyola Law School in her native Los Angeles. Since 1974, she has specialized in the music and entertainment law fields and she has been associated with the law firm of Mason & Sloane, where she has represented clients such as Motley Crue, Olivia Newton-John, Kenny Rogers and Sammy Hagar, and with Ervin, Cohen & Jessup as attorney to the California Jam II that attracted 250,000 concert-goers. Her in-house legal and business affairs experience includes Twentieth Century Fox, Orion Pictures, Paramount and ABC. Additionally, she has served as outside counsel to MTM, International Family Entertainment, The Family Channel, Hanna Barbera and Warner Bros. TV. She currently maintains her own practice in Los Angeles where she continues to specialize in entertainment and music matters.

Ms. Levin was a founding member and Cochair of the Beverly Hills Bar Association Committee for the Arts. She chaired its annual symposium that produced the written materials, subsequently edited, and now published as *The Musician's Business and Legal Guide* that you are currently reading. She has also served on the board of directors of the Hollywood Women's Coalition and Los Angeles Women in Music and is currently a member of the Executive Committee of the Los Angeles County Bar Association Intellectual Property and Entertainment Law Section. In addition to offering personal management, music publishing, television and general entertainment law courses at institutions including UCLA, Ms. Levin has contributed to numerous music and entertainment publications. Her civic activities include board membership on the fundraising arm of The Wellness Community, a nonprofit organization that provides free-of-charge counseling, psychological support and education to those diagnosed with cancer.

LINDA A. NEWMARK is Vice President, Acquisitions, for Universal Music Publishing Group. She obtains opportunities for Universal Music Publishing Group to acquire rights to musical compositions and music publishing catalogs, evaluates and negotiates acquisition, administration and subpublishing agreements and promotes the general business development of the company. Prior to this, Linda was Vice President, Business Affairs for PolyGram Music Publishing and handled the drafting and negotiation of songwriter and copublishing agreements, as well as other legal and business affairs matters for PolyGram.

Previously, she was a music attorney with the law firm of Cooper, Epstein & Hurewitz in Beverly Hills. Linda received her law degree from Stanford Law School. She is based in Universal Music Publishing Group's Los Angeles offices.

PETER T. PATERNO, a 1976 graduate of UCLA Law School, formerly practiced law as a partner with Manatt, Phelps, Rothenberg, Tunney & Phillips in Los Angeles, specializing in music law. He was president of Hollywood Records until 1993 when he left to return to private practice. He is now with the firm of King, Purtich, Holmes, Paterno & Berliner.

JACK PHILLIPS directs the auditing activities at the Los Angeles office of Gelfand, Rennert & Feldman, LLP. Since 1979, he has specialized in royalty and profit participation examinations on a worldwide basis. He and his group also have many years of experience in conducting financial due diligence reviews of record company and music publisher potential acquisitions and valuations of intangible assets, such as recording and music publishing catalogs and film libraries. Mr. Phillips has testified in judicial proceedings, and authored several articles and lectured on the subject of royalties.

Mr. Phillips has a graduate degree in finance and several years of prior financial auditing experience with Price Waterhouse & Co. and internal audit experience with CBS, Inc. He is a member of the American Institute of Certified Public Accountants, the New York and California State Societies of CPAs and several entertainment industry organizations. He can be reached by phone at (310) 556-6605.

MARGARET ROBLEY, E.A. is a senior manager in the business management firm of NKS Management, Inc. Margaret has a MBA from Chapman College and a MST from California State University Northridge.

ALFRED SCHLESINGER has been a music business attorney for over 30 years. Prior to becoming an attorney, he had his own record and music publishing companies. His entire practice is now, and has been, in the field of music, representing record companies, music publishing companies, recording artists, record producers, songwriters, personal managers, talent agents and disc jockeys.

In addition to his activities as an attorney, he was the personal manager of the recording and performing group Bread, from its inception in 1968 to its dissolution in 1978.

Alfred Schlesinger has written articles for the *Beverly Hills Bar Association Journal,* the National Academy of Songwriters (of which he is a founding member), the Association of International Entertainment Attorneys (of which he is a charter member) and various educational institutions throughout the United States. He has also taught courses on the music business and has been a guest lecturer and panelist for many educational institutions and music-oriented organizations. He currently teaches a yearly intensive 10-day, 80-hour music business course at Full Sail Center for the Recording Arts in Winter Park, Florida.

Mr. Schlesinger is a past president of the California Copyright Conference, a past president of the Los Angeles Chapter of the National Academy of Recording Arts and Sciences (NARAS) and past two-term national chairman of the board of said academy. He is also a past recipient of *Billboard Magazine's* award as Entertainment Attorney of the Year.

JAMES A. SEDIVY is an attorney who has worked in both Los Angeles and Las Vegas representing artists and companies in the areas of music, film, television, e-commerce, copyright and trademark. In addition to his experience with entertainment transactions, Mr. Sedivy has a background of litigating disputes arising out of entertainment industry agreements along with copyright and trademark infringement actions. He also assists in the formation and maintenance of businesses in California and Nevada. A past president of the Beverly Hills Bar Association Barristers and Cochair of the Committee for the Arts, Mr. Sedivy is currently associated with the firm of Levinson & Kaplan in Encino, California.

MADELEINE E. SELTZER, formerly a practicing attorney, is a partner in Seltzer Fontaine Beckwith, a legal search firm based in Los Angeles. She received her JD from the University of Southern California Law School in 1975. She is a volunteer mediator for Arts Arbitration and Mediation Services, a program of California Lawyers for the Arts and an advisory board member for Sojourn Services for Battered Women and Their Children.

PETER SPELLMAN is Director of Career Development at Berklee College of Music, Boston and founding director of Music Business Solutions *(www.mbsolutions.com)*, a company specializing in the information needs of music entrepreneurs. He is the author of *The Self-Promoting Musician: Strategies for Independent Music Success* (Berklee Press) and spent several years (1993-96) with an Internet startup where he consulted on Web design, online music marketing and software development. He is a popular speaker at colleges and conferences and has written for *Musician Magazine, Gig, Performing Songwriter, International Musician* and numerous other publications. Peter is also drummer for the improvisational collective, Friend Planet.

DANIEL K. STUART is an associate in the Los Angeles office of the law firm of Manatt, Phelps & Phillips, LLP. Mr. Stuart represents recording artists, producers and songwriters. The main focus of his practice is negotiating and drafting recording agreements, publishing deals, merchandising agreements, producer agreements and agreements pertaining to live concerts. As an attorney, Mr. Stuart coauthored an article about the shortcomings of the old Coogan Law for the *Beverly Hills Bar Association Law Journal* and later helped draft the current version of the Coogan Law that was passed into California law in 1999. Prior to becoming an attorney, Mr. Stuart covered the music industry as a print and broadcast journalist and wrote dozens of articles for such magazines as *Billboard*. Mr. Stuart received his law degree from Loyola Law School in Los Angeles in 1996 and has practiced with Manatt, Phelps & Phillips, LLP since 1999.

GREGORY T. VICTOROFF has been an entertainment litigation attorney since 1979, representing clients in the music, film and fine art businesses in Los Angeles. He is a frequent author and lecturer on copyright and art law. Mr. Victoroff is editor and coauthor of *The Visual Artist's Business and Legal Guide*. As an orchestral musician, he has backed such artists as Huey Lewis and the News, Santana and Bobby McFerrin.

THOMAS A. WHITE is a consultant in the record and music publishing industries. He is based in Beverly Hills, California and is the author of "The Crisis of A&R Competence and Record Industry Economics" and other analytical articles. Mr. White headed the Artist Development Department at CBS Records (Epic, Portrait and the CBS Associated Labels), West Coast and was president of the European label CBO Records Inc., and president of Harmony Gold Music Inc.

Index

About Jerome Headlands Press, Inc.

Jerome Headlands Press Inc., based in Jerome, Arizona, designs and produces business books for professionals that work in entertainment and the arts. It was founded in 1990 by Diane Rapaport with the goal to provide artists with access to business information and training to help them make a living and avoid costly mistakes.

How to Make and Sell Your Own Recording (revised fifth edition, 1999), by Diane Sward Rapaport, with a foreword by Loreena McKennitt, has been a friend and guide to more than 200,000 musicians, producers, engineers and owners of recording labels. It has helped revolutionize the recording industry by providing information about setting up independent record labels.

The Acoustic Musician's Guide to Sound Reinforcement and Live Recording (1997) by Mike Sokol, tells how to set up and operate a sound system and describes the techniques that must be learned to provide good performance experiences for musicians and audiences.

The Visual Artist's Business and Legal Guide (1994), a presentation of the Beverly Hills Bar Association Committee for the Arts, was compiled and edited by Gregory T. Victoroff, Esq. Written by prominent art lawyers, professionals and business experts, this comprehensive resource can improve artists' chances for financial success. It provides valuable legal and business information. It is scheduled for revision and reprint in 2002.

New books tentatively scheduled for publication in 2002 include *A Music Business Primer* by Diane Rapaport and *The Independent Film Producer's Legal Survival Guide* by Gunnar Erickson, Mark Halloran and Harris Tulchin, prominent Los Angeles film attorneys.

Jerome Headlands Press, Inc.
P.O. Box N
Jerome, Arizona 86331
jhpress@sedona.net